AutoCAD® 2007 for Inte
and Spa

AutoCAD® 2007 for Interior Design and Space Planning

Beverly L. Kirkpatrick

Adjunct Faculty, Eastfield College

James M. Kirkpatrick

Eastfield College

with cover art and chapter opening art from

Pei Cobb Freed & Partners, Architects, LLP

PEARSON

Prentice
Hall

Upper Saddle River, New Jersey
Columbus, Ohio

Library of Congress Cataloging-in-Publication Data

Kirkpatrick, Beverly L.
 AutoCAD 2007 for interior design and space planning / Beverly L. Kirkpatrick, James
M. Kirkpatrick.—[New ed.].
  p. cm.
"With cover art and chapter opening art from Pei Cobb Freed & Partners, Architects, LLP."
Includes index.
ISBN 0-13-222510-7
 1. Interior decoration—Computer-aided design. 2. Space
(Architecture)—Computer-aided design. 3. AutoCAD. I. Kirkpatrick, James M.
II. Kirkpatrick, Beverly L. AutoCAD for interior design and space planning using AutoCAD
2006. III. Pei Cobb Freed & Partners. IV. Title.

NK2114.K57 2007
729.0285′536—dc22

2006050650

Editor in Chief: Vernon Anthony
Acquisitions Editor: Jill Jones-Renger
Editorial Assistant: Yvette Schlarman
Production Editor: Louise N. Sette
Production Coordination: Karen Fortgang,
 bookworks

Design Coordinator: Diane Ernsberger
Art Coordinator: Jaclyn Portisch
Cover Designer: Ali Mohrman
Production Manager: Deidra Schwartz
Marketing Manager: Jimmy Stephens

This book was set in Berkeley Book by *Techbooks*. It was printed and bound by
Bind-Rite Graphics. The cover was printed by Coral Graphic Services, Inc.

Certain images and materials contained in this publication were reproduced with
permission of Autodesk, Inc. © 2006. All rights reserved.

Autodesk and AutoCAD are registered trademarks of Autodesk, Inc., in the U.S.A. and
certain other countries.

Cover art and chapter opening art used with permission of and under the copyright of
Pei Cobb Freed & Partners, Architects, LLP.

Disclaimer:

The publication is designed to provide tutorial information about AutoCAD® and/or other
Autodesk computer programs. Every effort has been made to make this publication complete and as accurate as possible. The reader is expressly cautioned to use any and all precautions necessary, and to take appropriate steps to avoid hazards, when engaging in the
activities described herein.

Neither the author nor the publisher makes any representations or warranties of any kind,
with respect to the materials set forth in this publication, express or implied, including
without limitation any warranties of fitness for a particular purpose or merchantability. Nor
shall the author or the publisher be liable for any special, consequential or exemplary dam-
ages resulting, in whole or in part, directly or indirectly, from the reader's use of, or reliance
upon, this material or subsequent revisions of this material.

Pearson Education Ltd.
Pearson Education Singapore Pte. Ltd.
Pearson Education Canada, Ltd.
Pearson Education—Japan

Pearson Education Australia Pty. Limited
Pearson Education North Asia Ltd.
Pearson Educación de Mexico, S.A. de C.V.
Pearson Education Malaysia Pte. Ltd.

10 9 8 7 6 5 4 3 2 1
ISBN: 0-13-222510-7

Preface

AutoCAD has become the industry-standard graphics program for interior design and space planning. It is used to complete the many drawings that make up a design project. Many design firms have adopted AutoCAD as their standard because

☐ it saves time;
☐ affiliated professions use it, and these firms need to be able to exchange files to work on the same drawing;
☐ their competitors are using it; and
☐ their clients expect it.

To be successful in design today, students must be proficient in the use of AutoCAD as it relates to interior design and space planning. This need for an AutoCAD textbook specific to interior design and space planning is what led us to write this text.

AutoCAD 2007 for Interior Design and Space Planning is divided into three parts:

☐ Part I: Preparing to Draw with AutoCAD (Chapters 1 and 2)
☐ Part II: Two-Dimensional AutoCAD (Chapters 3–13)
☐ Part III: Three-Dimensional AutoCAD (Chapters 14–15)

This new edition includes many features designed to help you master AutoCAD 2007:

- The prompt–response format is now clearly defined with color rules and numbered steps. This step-by-step approach is used in the beginning exercises of all chapters and then moves to an outline form in later exercises within the same chapters. This approach allows students to learn commands in a drawing situation and then apply them on their own.
- Exercises are geared to architects, interior designers, and space planners, allowing students to work with real-world situations.
- More than 500 illustrations (many printed to scale) support the text and reinforce the material.
- Illustrations in the margins help the user locate AutoCAD commands within the AutoCAD menus and toolbars.
- "Tips," "Warnings," and "Notes" boxes in the text give students additional support and information.
- Practice exercises in every chapter review the commands learned.
- Learning objectives and review questions in every chapter reinforce the learning process.
- An online Instructor's Manual (which is updated with new exercises between editions) is available to support the text.

The command prompts and margin art throughout the book have all been updated to AutoCAD 2007. The Dynamic Input, Command Line changes, Workspaces command, and changes to many basic commands such as Offset, Copy, Rotate, Hatch, Calculator, Table, and Attribute Extraction have been incorporated into relevant chapters in the book. Entertaining and useful exercises have been added, such as making a business card in the text and raster image chapter (chapter 5). Exercises have also been added to the project chapters. These exercises include projects such as drawing and furnishing a hotel room, a log cabin, and a bank.

Online Instructor Materials

To access supplementary materials online, instructors need to request an instructor access code. Go to **www.prenhall.com,** click the **Instructor Resource Center** link, and then click **Register Today** for an instructor access code. Within 48 hours after registering you will receive a confirming e-mail including an instructor access code. Once you have received your code, go to the site and log on for full instructions on downloading the materials you wish to use.

Autodesk Learning License

Through a recent agreement with the publisher of AutoCAD, Autodesk®, Prentice Hall now offers the option of purchasing *AutoCAD® 2007 for Interior Design and Space Planning* with either a 180-day or a 1-year student software license. This provides adequate time for a student to complete all the activities in this book. The software is functionally identical to the professional license, but is intended **for student personal use only.** It is not for professional use. For more information about this book and the Autodesk Learning License, contact your local Pearson Prentice Hall sales representative, or contact our National Marketing Manager, Jimmy Stephens, at 1(800)228-7854 ×3725 or at Jimmy_Stephens@prenhall.com. For the name and number of your sales rep, please contact Prentice Hall Faculty Services at 1(800)526-0485.

Most important, this text was written to help you, the reader, master the AutoCAD program, which will be a valuable tool in your professional career.

We would like to thank the reviewers: Melinda Lyon, University of Central Oklahoma; Wen Andrews, J. Sargeant Reynolds Community College; David Epperson, University of Tennessee at Chattanooga; and Stephen Huff, High Point University.

Acknowledgments

We would also like to acknowledge the following people, who contributed ideas and drawings: Mary Peyton, IALD, IES (Lighting Consultant), Roy Peyton, John Sample, Katherine Broadwell, Curran C. Redman, S. Vic Jones, W. M. Stevens, John Brooks, Bill Sorrells, Valerie Campbell, and the CAD students at Eastfield College. Finally, we would like to thank Autodesk, Inc.

B.L.K.

J.M.K.

Contents

Part III   Three-Dimensional AutoCAD   483

14   Solid Modeling of Simple Shapes   483

AutoCAD® 2007 for Interior Design and Space Planning

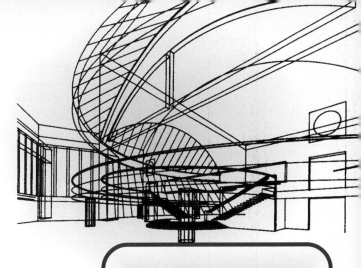

chapter

1

Introducing the AutoCAD Program

objectives

After completing this chapter, you will be able to:

Create and save a workspace.

Describe the AutoCAD screen and begin using parts of the screen.

Activate, hide, dock, float, and reshape toolbars.

Exercise 1–1: Create a Workspace and Examine the AutoCAD Screen

This book is written for interior designers and space planners who want to learn the AutoCAD program in the most effective and efficient manner—by drawing with it. AutoCAD commands are introduced in tutorial exercises. The tutorial exercises specifically cover interior design and space planning drawings. Exercise 1–1 introduces you to the AutoCAD Classic Workspace and the AutoCAD screen.

Create a Workspace

Step 1. Start the AutoCAD program.

Step 2. Select the AutoCAD Classic workspace:

Prompt	Response
The Workspaces dialog box appears (Figure 1–1):	CLICK: **AutoCAD Classic** (in the list) CLICK: **OK**
The AutoCAD Classic workspace appears.	

FIGURE 1–1
Workspaces Dialog Box

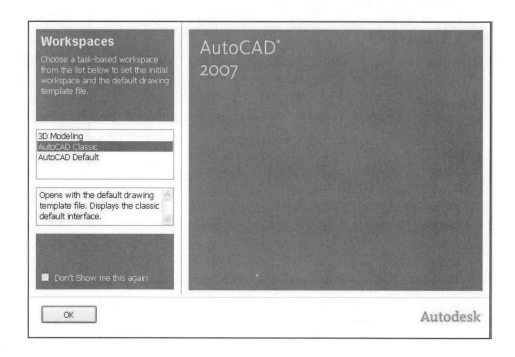

Step 3. Close any open palette, such as the Sheet Set Manager and the Tool Palettes, by clicking the X on the palette title bar.

Step 4. Use the toolbar list (Figure 1–2) to modify the Classic workspace so it looks like the AutoCAD screen in Figure 1–3:

Prompt	Response
Command:	Activate the toolbars list by holding your mouse over any tool icon and clicking the right mouse button.
The toolbars list appears (Figure 1–2):	A toolbar is active if a check appears to the left of the toolbar name in the toolbar list. Clicking on the name makes the check appear or disappear. Make the following toolbars active: Draw, Layers, Modify, Standard, and Workspaces. Be sure that no check appears to the left of any other toolbar name.

3D Navigation
CAD Standards
Camera Adjustment
Dimension
✔ Draw
Draw Order
Inquiry
Insert
✔ Layers
Layers II
Layouts
Lights
Mapping
Modeling
✔ Modify
Modify II
Object Snap
Orbit
Properties
Refedit
Reference
Render
Solid Editing
✔ Standard
Styles
Text
UCS
UCS II
View
Viewports
Visual Styles
Walk and Fly
Web
✔ Workspaces
Zoom

Lock Location ▶
Customize...

FIGURE 1–2
Toolbars List with
Five Toolbars Open

FIGURE 1–3
Modify the Classic
Workspace

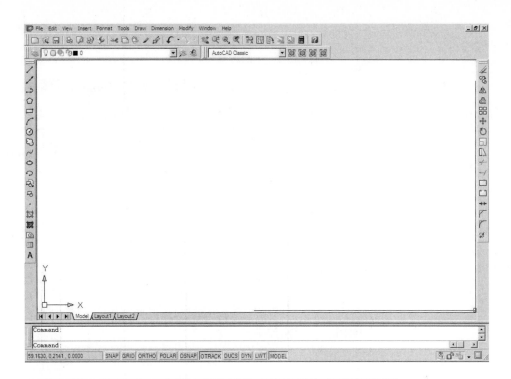

Step 5. Save your workspace:

Prompt	Response
Command:	CLICK: **Tools – Workspaces – Save Current As...**
The Save Workspace text box appears:	TYPE: **your first name in the Name: textbox** **<enter>** (in this book, **<enter>** means to press the Enter key)

Your name appears in the Workspaces toolbar list.

The AutoCAD Screen

The AutoCAD screen provides the display area for drawing and the commands used to create, modify, view, and plot drawings. You can begin by naming a new drawing, or you may immediately begin drawing without naming the drawing. When you are ready to end a drawing session, save the drawing using Save or SaveAs..., at which time you must name the drawing. AutoCAD communicates with you on various parts of the screen. You may have a slightly different appearing screen, depending on the options selected. A brief introduction to each part of the screen (Figure 1–4) follows.

Title Bar

The title bar contains the name of the program and the name of the current drawing, in this case, [Drawing1], because you have not yet named the drawing.

AutoCAD Program and Drawing Buttons

This button on the program window minimizes the AutoCAD program. The program remains active, so you can return to it if you choose. To return to it, click the AutoCAD button on the taskbar at the bottom of the screen. You can also minimize a drawing by clicking this button on the drawing window.

This button resizes the program or drawing window.

This button maximizes the size of the program or drawing window.

This button closes the AutoCAD program or drawing window.

FIGURE 1–4
The AutoCAD Screen

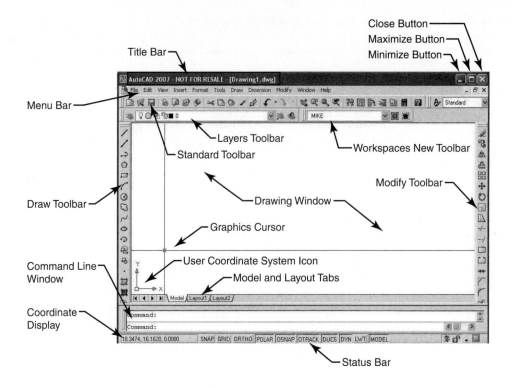

Drawing Window and Graphics Cursor

The drawing window is where your drawing is displayed. The graphics cursor (or crosshair) follows the movement of a mouse when points of a drawing are entered or a command is selected.

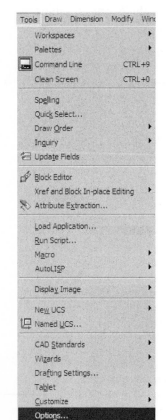

Step 6. Change the size of the graphics cursor so it appears as shown in Figure 1–4:

Prompt	Response
Command:	CLICK: **Tools – Options...**
The Options dialog box appears (Figure 1–5):	CLICK: **the Display tab**
The Display tab appears:	Move the Crosshair size slider in the lower left corner to the right to increase the size of the cursor to 100%
	CLICK: **Apply**
	CLICK: **OK**

Command Line Window

The command line window shown at the bottom of the screen (which may be moved and resized or turned off if you want) is where AutoCAD communicates with you once a command is activated. AutoCAD prompts you to enter specific information to further define a command and then responds with action on the screen or additional prompts. Always watch the command line to make sure you and AutoCAD are communicating. The Command Line Window command, which may be used to hide the command window, is located on the Tools menu on the menu bar.

FIGURE 1–5
Change Crosshair Size to
100%

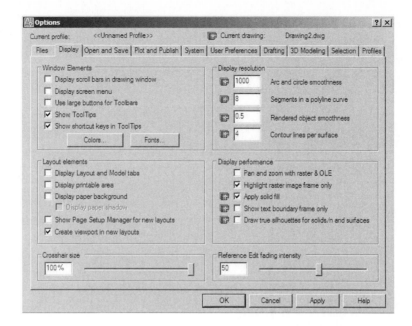

User Coordinate System Icon

The user coordinate system (UCS) icon in the lower left corner of the drawing window shows the orientation of the X, Y, and Z axes of the current coordinate system. When AutoCAD is started, you are in the world coordinate system (WCS). There are two types of model space UCS icons—2D and 3D. The 3D icon is the default and is shown in Figure 1–4.

Coordinate Display

Using an X- and Y-axis Cartesian coordinate system, the coordinate display numbers in the extreme lower left corner tell you where the cursor or crosshair on the screen is located in relation to point 0,0 (the lower left corner).

Step 7. CLICK: **on the coordinate display to turn it ON and OFF.**

Status Bar

The status bar at the bottom of the screen keeps you informed about your drawing by displaying the status of modes that affect your drawing: SNAP, GRID, ORTHO, POLAR, OSNAP, OTRACK, DUCS, DYN, LWT, and MODEL. These modes can be turned on and off by clicking on the mode name with the pick button of your mouse.

Model and Layout Tabs

The model tab is where you make your drawing. The layout tabs allow you to select different means of plotting your drawing.

Menu Bar

You can open a menu item on the menu bar by holding the pointer on the menu name and clicking it; click the menu name again to close the menu, or use the Esc key to cancel any command activated. A pull-down menu will appear for each item on the menu bar when the item is clicked (Figures 1–6 through 1–16). Pull-down menus provide access to many of the same commands that are included on the toolbars. The commands followed by an ellipsis (...) display a dialog box when clicked. Use the Esc key or click the Cancel button in the dialog box to cancel it. Those pull-down menu items with an arrow to the right have a cascading menu.

FIGURE 1–6
File Menu

When you hold your mouse steady over each pull-down menu command or cascading menu command, a text string at the bottom of the display screen (in the coordinate display and status bar area) gives a brief description of the commands. Many of the menu bar commands are used in the following chapters; however, the following brief description of the general content of the menu bar provides an introduction:

File   (Figure 1–6) This menu bar item contains the commands needed to start a new drawing, open an existing one, save drawings, print or plot a drawing, export data, and exit from AutoCAD. It also shows the most recently active drawings, which may be opened by clicking on them.

Edit   (Figure 1–7) This item contains the Undo command (allows you to undo or reverse the most recent command) and the Redo command (will redo as many undo commands as you have used). It also contains the commands related to the Windows Clipboard such as Cut, Copy, and Paste. Drawings or text from other applications (such as Word or Paintbrush) can be cut or copied onto the Windows Clipboard and then pasted from the Clipboard into an AutoCAD drawing.

View   (Figure 1–8) This menu contains commands that control the display of your drawing.

Insert   (Figure 1–9) This menu contains the commands that allow you to insert previously drawn objects into an AutoCAD drawing. These objects may be other AutoCAD drawings or pictures from other drawing programs.

Format   (Figure 1–10) This menu bar item contains commands that help you set up your drawing environment.

Tools   (Figure 1–11) This menu contains commands used to customize the drawing environment, provide information about the drawing, and perform specialized tasks such as spell check.

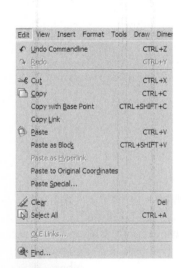

FIGURE 1–7
Edit Menu

FIGURE 1–8
View Menu

FIGURE 1–9
Insert Menu

FIGURE 1–10
Format Menu

FIGURE 1–11
Tools Menu

FIGURE 1–12
Draw Menu

FIGURE 1–13
Dimension Menu

FIGURE 1–14
Modify Menu

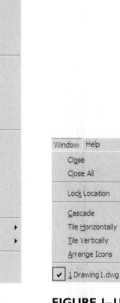

FIGURE 1–15
Window Menu

Draw (Figure 1–12) The Draw menu has all the commands used to draw objects in AutoCAD.

Dimension (Figure 1–13) This menu contains the commands used to place dimensions on drawings.

Modify (Figure 1–14) The Modify commands are used to change the position, shape, or number of objects after they have been drawn. Commands to change text are also on this menu.

Window (Figure 1–15) This menu is used to arrange multiple drawings when you are working on more than one drawing at the same time.

Help (Figure 1–16) The AutoCAD Help command provides information about how to use AutoCAD commands.

FIGURE 1–16
Help Menu

Toolbars

The AutoCAD screen shown in Figures 1–4 and 1–20 has five docked toolbars displayed: the Standard toolbar, the Workspaces toolbar, the Layers toolbar, the Modify toolbar (docked at the right side of the screen), and the Draw toolbar (docked at the left side of the screen).

Tooltips When you hold the mouse pointer steady (do not click) on each tool of the Standard toolbar, a tooltip will display the name of the command. A text string at the bottom of the display screen (in the coordinate display and status bar area) gives a brief description of the command.

Step 8. Activate the Standard toolbar's tooltips (Figure 1–17).

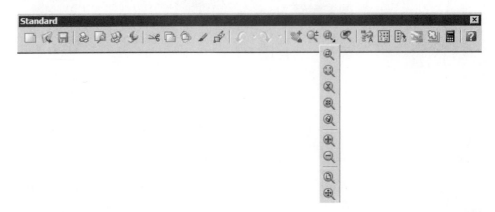

FIGURE 1–17
Standard Toolbar with Tooltips Displayed

FIGURE 1–18
Standard Toolbar Flyout

Flyouts   Tools with a small black triangle have flyouts. When you hold your mouse on the tool and press and hold the pick button, the flyout will appear, as shown in Figure 1–18. When you position the mouse on a tool in the flyout and release the pick button, the command is activated; a dialog box will appear or a command sequence will begin. The most recently activated tool icon will replace the top icon that was previously visible in the toolbar.

Step 9.   Activate the Standard toolbar's flyouts (Figure 1–18).

Undocking Toolbars   To undock a toolbar, pick on the double bars on the edge of the toolbar, hold down the pick button, and drag the toolbar away from the edge.
Floating Toolbars   A floating toolbar floats or lies on any part of the AutoCAD screen. A floating toolbar can be moved to another part of the screen and can be reshaped.
Reshaping Toolbars   A floating toolbar can be reshaped by slowly moving the mouse over the borders of the toolbar until the double-arrow pointer appears that allows you to reshape the width and height of the toolbar.

Step 10.   Float the Draw and Modify toolbars to the approximate position shown in Figure 1–19. Change the shape of the toolbars to match those shown in Figure 1–19.

Docked Toolbars   One way to dock a toolbar is to pick on the name of the toolbar and drag it to an edge. When you see an outline of the toolbar along an edge (showing you how the toolbar will look in the docking area), release the pick button on the mouse to dock the toolbar.

Step 11. Dock the Draw and Modify toolbars as shown in Figure 1–20.

FIGURE 1–19
Floating and Reshaping
Toolbars

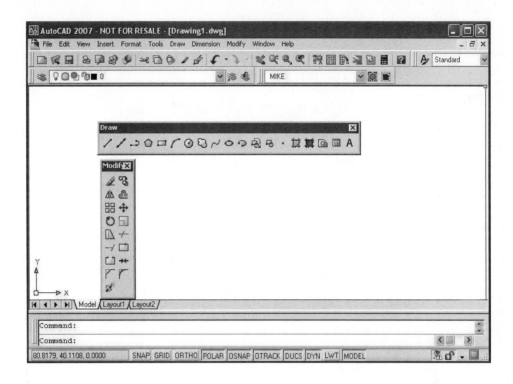

Step 12. Use the Toolbar command to dock the Modify toolbar on the right side of the drawing area (Figure 1–20):

Prompt	Response
Command:	TYPE: **-Toolbar**<enter> (be sure to include the hyphen)
Enter toolbar name or [ALL]:	TYPE: **Modify**<enter>

FIGURE 1–20
Docking the Draw and
Modify Toolbars

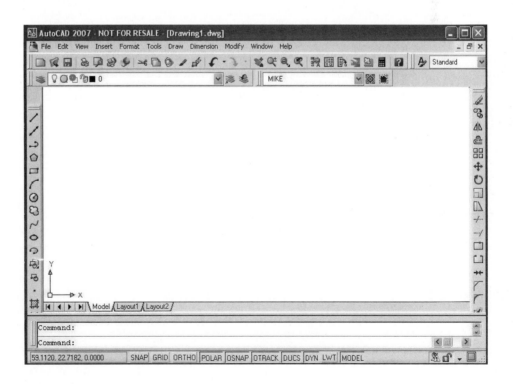

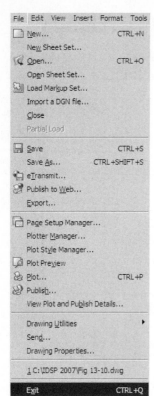

Prompt	Response
Enter an option [Show/Hide/ Left/Right/Top/Bottom/ Float]<Show>:	TYPE: **R<enter>**
Enter new position (horizontal, vertical) <0,0>:	**<enter>**
The Modify toolbar is docked on the right side of the drawing area, Figure 1–20.	

Exit AutoCAD

The Exit command takes you out of the AutoCAD program. If you have made changes to the drawing and have not saved those changes, AutoCAD will give you the message "Save changes to Drawing1.dwg?" If you have named the drawing, the drawing name will replace the word "Drawing1." This is a safety feature because the Exit command, by itself, does not update or save a drawing. For now, you will not name or save this exercise.

Step 13. Exit AutoCAD.

Prompt	Response
Command:	**Exit** (from File on the menu bar)
The AutoCAD warning appears: Save changes to Drawing1.dwg?	CLICK: **No**
If you have not drawn anything or made any settings, the message will not appear.	

1. When clicked, the commands in the pull-down menus that are followed by an ellipsis display
   a. Another pull-down menu
   b. A flyout
   c. A toolbar
   d. A tooltip
   e. A dialog box

2. Which tab of the Options dialog box contains the slider bar used to change the size of the graphics cursor?
   a. File
   b. Display
   c. Drafting
   d. Selection
   e. Profiles

3. Clicking the X in the upper right corner of the AutoCAD program window
   a. Closes the AutoCAD program
   b. Closes the Program Manager and displays the Exit Windows dialog box
   c. Enters the AutoCAD program
   d. Opens the AutoCAD screen
   e. Resizes the AutoCAD screen

4. The area of the AutoCAD screen where AutoCAD communicates with you once a command is activated is called the
   a. Styles toolbar
   b. Layout tab
   c. Status bar
   d. Command line window
   e. Drawing window

5. Which menu on the AutoCAD menu bar contains the command needed to start a new drawing?
   a. File
   b. Edit
   c. Tools
   d. Format
   e. Options

6. Which menu on the AutoCAD menu bar contains the commands related to the Windows Clipboard?
   a. File
   b. Edit
   c. Tools
   d. Format
   e. Options

7. Which menu on the AutoCAD menu bar contains commands that help you set up your drawing environment?
   a. File
   b. Edit
   c. Tools
   d. Format
   e. Options

8. Which item on the Standard toolbar takes you to the Toolbars list?
   a. Print
   b. Cut
   c. Any icon—right-click
   d. Zoom
   e. Properties

Complete.

9. List the 10 modes displayed on the status bar.

   _____

10. If you have not named a new drawing, what name does AutoCAD assign to it?

   _____

11. Describe the purpose of the command line window.

   _____

12. Describe how to open a toolbar.

   _____

13. Describe how to close a toolbar.

   _____

14. Describe how to undock a toolbar.

   _____

15. Describe how to reshape a toolbar.

   _____

16. Describe how to activate the toolbars list.

   _____

17. Describe how to activate a toolbar's tooltips and flyouts.

   Tooltips: _____

   Flyouts: _____

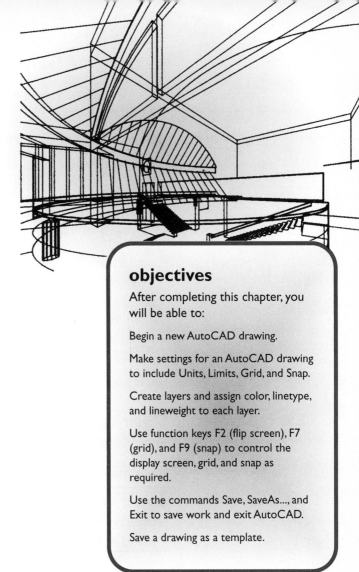

chapter

2

Preparing to Draw with AutoCAD

objectives

After completing this chapter, you will be able to:

Begin a new AutoCAD drawing.

Make settings for an AutoCAD drawing to include Units, Limits, Grid, and Snap.

Create layers and assign color, linetype, and lineweight to each layer.

Use function keys F2 (flip screen), F7 (grid), and F9 (snap) to control the display screen, grid, and snap as required.

Use the commands Save, SaveAs..., and Exit to save work and exit AutoCAD.

Save a drawing as a template.

Introduction

When a project is started, decisions are made about the number of drawings required, the appropriate sheet size, scale, and so on. This chapter describes the settings that must be made when preparing to draw with AutoCAD.

The following is a hands-on step-by-step procedure to make the settings for your first drawing exercise in Chapter 3.

Following the Exercises in This Book

Before you start the exercises in this book, it will help to have a description of how to follow them.

Drives

This book assumes that the hard drive of the computer is called drive C. It also assumes that there is a disk drive labeled A. Not all computers are configured the same; drives may be labeled differently, or you may be working on a network drive. Substitute the letter name of the drive on which you are working for the C drive used in this book. If you cannot save to a disk drive labeled A, substitute the drive you can save to.

Prompt and Response Columns

Throughout the exercises in this book, Prompt and Response columns provide step-by-step instructions for starting and completing a command. The Prompt column text repeats the AutoCAD prompt that appears in the command prompt area of the display screen. The text in the Response column shows your response to the AutoCAD prompt.

Exercise 2–1: Beginning an AutoCAD Drawing: Setting Units, Limits, Grid, and Snap; Creating Layers; Saving Your Work and Exiting AutoCAD

Beginning an AutoCAD Drawing

Step 1. If your named workspace is not active, select it by using the Workspaces command on the tools menu on the menu bar. If it is not available, repeat Exercise 1–1.

> **NOTE:** If the Startup dialog box appears, turn it off. Go to the Tools menu and choose Options.... In the Options dialog box, select the System tab. Under General Options, beside Startup:, select the Do not show a startup dialog, pick the Apply button and the OK button, and restart AutoCAD.

When you CLICK: **New...** from the File menu, AutoCAD allows you to select a template file from the Template folder. A template file has settings already established. These settings can include units, limits, grid, snap, and a border and title block. You will save the settings completed in this chapter as a template. This template will be used to start a new drawing in Chapter 3. Templates save time because the settings (such as units, limits, grid, snap and layers) are already made.

If you CLICK: **New...** and select the acad.dwt template, you are in the same drawing environment as when you simply open the AutoCAD program and begin drawing. AutoCAD uses the acad.dwt template for the drawing settings if no other template is selected.

You do not need to CLICK: **New...** from the File menu. You can stay in the drawing environment that appeared when you started AutoCAD. Before you begin to make the settings for your first drawing, you will learn how to name and save your work.

Saving the Drawing

You must understand two commands, Save and SaveAs and their uses to save your work in the desired drive and folder.

Save

When the command Save is clicked and the drawing has been named, the drawing is saved automatically to the drive and folder in which you are working, and a backup file is created with the same name but with the extension .bak. If the drawing has not been named, Save behaves like SaveAs.

SaveAs

SaveAs activates the Save Drawing As dialog box whether or not the drawing has been named and allows you to save your drawing to any drive or folder you choose.

Some additional features of the SaveAs command are as follows:

1. A drawing file can be saved and you may continue to work because with the SaveAs command the drawing editor is not exited.
2. If the default drive is used (the drive on which you are working), and the drawing has been opened from that drive, .dwg and .bak files are created when "Create backup copy with each save" is checked on the Open and Save tab on the Options dialog box.
3. If a drive other than the default is specified, only a .dwg file is created.
4. To change the name of the drawing, you may save it under a new name by typing a new name in the File Name: button.
5. If the drawing was previously saved, or if a drawing file already exists with the drawing file name you typed, AutoCAD gives you the message "drawing name.dwg already exists. Do you want to replace it?" When a drawing file is updated, the old .dwg file is replaced with the new drawing, so the answer to click is Yes. If an error has been made and you do not want to replace the file, click No.
6. A drawing may be saved to as many disks or to as many folders on the hard disk as you wish. You should save your drawing in two different places as insurance against catastrophe.
7. Any drawing can be saved as a template. A drawing template should include settings such as units, limits, grid, snap, layers, title blocks, dimension and text styles, linetypes, and lineweights. When you use the template file to start a new drawing, the settings are already made.

Step 2.   **Name and save Exercise 3–1 on the hard drive, or select the drive and folder you want to save in (Figure 2–1):**

Prompt	Response
Command:	SaveAs...
The Save Drawing As dialog box appears with the file name highlighted:	TYPE: **CH3-EX1** (Because the file name was highlighted, you were able to type in that place. If you had used any other part of the dialog box first, you would have had to pick to the left of the file name, hold down the pick button, and drag the cursor across the name or double-click the text to highlight it and then begin typing.)

FIGURE 2–1
Save Drawing As Dialog Box;
Save CH3-EX1

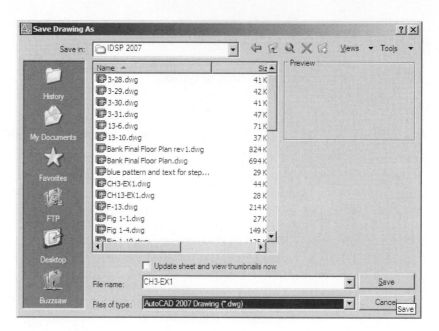

Prompt	Response
The Save Drawing As dialog box appears as shown in Figure 2–1:	**Select the drive and/or folder in which you want to save CH3-EX1.**
	CLICK: **Save**

Be sure to make note of the drive and folder where the drawing is being saved so you can retrieve it easily when you need it.

Drawing Name and File Name Extension

The drawing name can be up to 255 characters long and can have spaces. The drawing name cannot have special characters that the AutoCAD or Microsoft® Windows programs use for other purposes. The special characters that cannot be used include the less-than and greater-than symbols (<>), forward slashes and backslashes (/ \), backquotes (`), equal signs (=), vertical bars (|), asterisks (*), commas (,), question marks (?), semicolons (;), colons (:), and quotation marks ("). As you continue to learn AutoCAD, other objects will be named also, like layers. These naming conventions apply to all named objects.

AutoCAD automatically adds the file extension .dwg to the drawing name and .bak to a backup file. The symbol or icon to the left of the file name describes the type file. If you would also like to see the .dwg and .bak extensions, activate Windows Explorer and complete the following steps:

1. CLICK: **Folder Options...** on the **Tools** menu in Windows. (Earlier versions of Windows **Folder Options** will be on the **View** menu.)
2. Select the View tab. Remove the check in the check box before the setting "Hide file extensions for known file types."

If you lose a drawing file, the drawing's .bak file can be renamed as a .dwg file and used as the drawing file. Using Windows Explorer, RIGHT-CLICK: on the file name and select Rename from the menu. Simply keep the name, but change the file extension. If the .dwg file is corrupted, you may give the .bak file a new name and change the extension to .dwg. Don't forget to add the .dwg extension in either case, because the file will not open without a .dwg extension.

Now that you have named and saved a new drawing, select the units that will be used in making this drawing.

NOTE: To cancel a command, PRESS: Esc (from the keyboard).

Units

Units refers to drawing units. For example, an inch is a drawing unit. In this book architectural units, which provide feet and fractional inches, are used. The Precision: button in the Drawing Units dialog box allows you to set the smallest fraction to display when showing dimensions and other unit values on the screen. There is no reason to change any of the other settings in the Drawing Units dialog box at this time.

Step 3.   Set drawing Units... (Figure 2–2) and status bar drawing aids:

Prompt	Response
Command:	(Move the mouse across the top of the display screen on the menu bar. See the menu bar illustration in the book margin to locate the command.) **Units...** (or TYPE: **UNITS<enter>**)
The Drawing Units dialog box appears (Figure 2–2):	CLICK: **Architectural** (for Type: under Length) CLICK: **0'-0 1/16″** (for Precision: under Length) CLICK: **OK**

FIGURE 2–2
Drawing Units Dialog Box

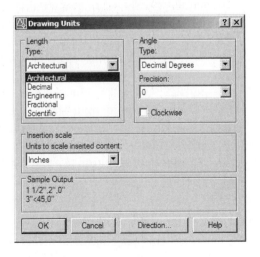

NOTE: The Precision: button has no bearing on how accurately AutoCAD draws. It allows you to set the smallest fraction to display dimensions and other values shown on the screen such as coordinates and defaults. No matter what the Precision: setting, AutoCAD draws with extreme accuracy.

Controlling Your Drawing

When you begin drawing with AutoCAD, you may click a tab or drawing aid that you do not need. If you select the Layout1 or Layout2 tabs at the bottom of your drawing window and are not sure where you are in the drawing, simply select the Model tab to return to your drawing. The Layout tabs are used for printing or plotting and will be described later.

The status bar at the bottom of the screen contains various drawing aids. The aids can be turned on and off by clicking on the name with the pick button of your mouse. The drawing aid is on when the button is in, and off when the button is out. **Three of these drawing aids that should be on are:**

SNAP   Your crosshair snaps to snap points as you move the cursor across the screen when SNAP is on.

GRID   A visible pattern of dots you see on the screen when GRID is on.

MODEL   Model space is where you create your drawing. If you click this button your drawing changes and PAPER appears on the button. Click the Model tab on the drawing to get back into model space.

Drawing aids that you will learn about as you continue through this text but **should be off** until you learn more about them are:

ORTHO   Allows you to draw only horizontally and vertically when on.

POLAR   Shows temporary alignment paths along polar angles when on.

OSNAP   This is object snap. Osnap contains command modifiers that help you draw very accurately. If you have an osnap mode on that you do not want, it can make your cursor click to points on your drawing that you do not want.

OTRACK   Shows temporary alignment paths along object snap points when on.

DUCS   Turns Dynamic UCS on and off—most useful in drawing 3D models.

DYN   Dynamic input—gives you information attached to the cursor regarding commands, coordinates, and tooltips.

LWT   You may assign varying lineweights (widths) to different parts of your drawing. When this button is on, the lineweights are displayed on the screen.

Drawing Scale

A drawing scale factor does not need to be set. While using AutoCAD to make drawings always draw full scale, using real-world feet and inches. Full-scale drawings can be printed or plotted at any scale. Plotting and printing to scale is described in Chapter 6.

FIGURE 2–3
Drawing Limits

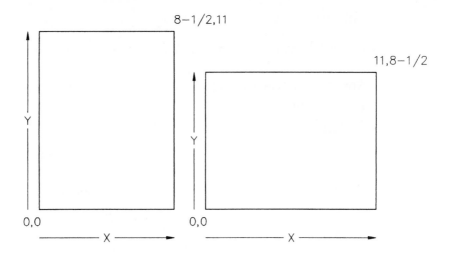

Drawing Limits and the Cartesian Coordinate System

Step 4. Set drawing limits:

Prompt	Response
Command:	**Drawing Limits** on the Format menu (or TYPE: **LIMITS**<enter>)
Specify lower left corner or [ON/OFF] <0'-0", 0'-0">:	<enter>
Specify upper right corner <1'-0", 1'-0">:	TYPE: **8-1/2,11**<enter>

Think of drawing limits as the sheet size or sheet boundaries. This sheet of paper is also called the *workplane*. The workplane is based on a Cartesian coordinate system. A Cartesian coordinate system has three axes, X, Y, and Z. Here, 8-1/2,11 was set as the drawing limits. In the Cartesian coordinate system that value is entered as 8-1/2,11 using a comma with no spaces to separate the X- and Y-axis coordinates. The X-axis coordinate of a Cartesian coordinate system is stated first (8-1/2) and measures drawing limits from left to right (horizontally). The Y-axis coordinate is second (11) and measures drawing limits from bottom to top (vertical). You will be drawing on a vertical 8-1/2″ × 11″ workplane similar to a standard sheet of typing paper. The Z axis is used in 3D.

The lower left corner, the origin point of the drawing boundaries, is 0,0 and is where the X and Y axis intersect. The upper right corner is 8-1/2,11 (Figure 2–3). These are the limits for Exercise 3–1. To turn the 8-1/2″ × 11″ area horizontally, enter the limits as 11,8-1/2. With units set to Architectural, AutoCAD defaults to inches, so the inch symbol is not required.

The coordinate display numbers in the extreme lower left corner of the AutoCAD screen tell you where the crosshair on the screen is located in relation to the 0,0 origin. The display updates as you move the cursor.

If you need to change the drawing limits, you may do so at any time by entering new limits to the "Specify upper right corner:" prompt. Changing the drawing limits will automatically show the grid pattern for the new limits.

GRIDDISPLAY

GRIDDISPLAY is a system variable that controls the display limits of the grid.

Step 5. **Set GRIDDISPLAY to zero so the grid will show the area specified by the limits:**

Prompt	Response
Command:	TYPE: **GRIDDISPLAY**<**enter**>
Enter new value for GRIDDISPLAY <10>:	TYPE: **0**<**enter**>

Grid and Snap

Step 6. **Set the Grid and Snap Spacing:**

Prompt	Response
Command:	TYPE: **GRID**<**enter**>
Specify grid spacing(X) or [ON/ OFF/Major/aDaptive/ Follow/Aspect] <0'-0 1/2">:	TYPE: **1/4**<**enter**>

You have just set ¼″ as the grid spacing. The grid is the visible pattern of dots on the display screen. With a setting of ¼″, each grid dot is spaced ¼″ vertically and horizontally. The grid is not part of the drawing, but it helps in getting a sense of the size and relationship of the drawing elements. It is never plotted.

Pressing function key F7 or Ctrl + G turns the grid on or off. The grid can also be turned on or off by selecting either option in response to the prompt "Specify grid spacing(X) or [ON/OFF/Major/aDaptive/Follow/Aspect]" or by clicking GRID at the bottom of the screen.

Prompt	Response
Command:	TYPE: **SN**<**enter**>
Specify snap spacing or [ON/ OFF/Aspect/ Style/Type] <0'-0 1/2">:	TYPE: **1/8**<**enter**>

You have set ⅛″ as the snap spacing. Snap is an invisible pattern of dots on the display screen. As you move the mouse across the screen, the crosshair will snap, or lock, to an invisible snap grid when SNAP is on. With a setting of ⅛″, each snap point is spaced ⅛″ horizontally and vertically.

Pressing function key F9 or Ctrl + B turns the snap on or off. The snap can also be turned on or off by selecting either option in response to the prompt "Specify snap spacing or [ON/OFF/Aspect/Style/Type]" or by clicking SNAP at the bottom of the screen.

It is helpful to set the snap spacing the same as the grid spacing or as a fraction of the grid spacing so the crosshair snaps to every grid point or to every grid point and in between. The snap can be set to snap several times in between the grid points.

Some drawings or parts of drawings should never be drawn with snap off. Snap is a very important tool for quickly locating or aligning elements of your drawing. You may need to turn snap off and on while drawing, but remember that a drawing entity drawn on snap is easily moved, copied, or otherwise edited.

Zoom

Step 7. View the entire drawing area:

Prompt	Response
Command:	TYPE: **Z\<enter>**
Specify corner of window, enter a scale factor (nX or nXP), or [All/ Center/Dynamic/Extents/Previous/ Scale/Window/object]\<real time>:	TYPE: **A\<enter>**

The Zoom-All command lets you view the entire drawing area. Use it after setting up or entering an existing drawing so that you are familiar with the size and shape of your limits and grid. Otherwise, you may be viewing only a small part of the drawing limits and not realize it.

Drafting Settings Dialog Box and Components of All Dialog Boxes

You can also set snap and grid by using the Drafting Settings dialog box.

To locate the Drafting Settings dialog box, RIGHT-CLICK: on SNAP or GRID in the status bar and CLICK: **Settings...**, or move the pointer across the top of the display screen and highlight "Tools" on the menu bar. When you CLICK: **Tools** a pull-down menu appears. Move your pointer to highlight Drafting Settings... and CLICK: **Drafting Settings...**. The Drafting Settings dialog box (Figure 2–4) now appears on your screen.

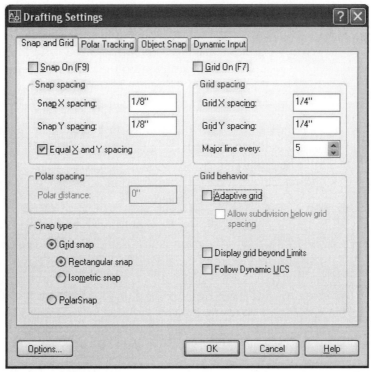

FIGURE 2–4
Drafting Settings Dialog Box

All dialog boxes have some basic components. The following is a description of the components that appear in the Drafting Settings dialog box (Figure 2–4) as well as in other dialog boxes you will use:

1. *Cursor:* Changes to an arrow.
2. *Tabs:* Click the title of the tab to select the **part** of the dialog box you want to use. The Drafting Settings dialog box has four tabs: Snap and Grid, Polar Tracking, Object Snap, and Dynamic Input.
3. *OK button:* Click this button to complete the command, leave the dialog box, and return to the drawing. If any changes have been made, they will remain as changes. Pressing <**enter**> has the same effect.
4. *Cancel button:* Click this button to cancel the command, leave the dialog box, and return to the drawing. If any changes have been made, they will be canceled and the original settings will return. Pressing the Esc key has the same effect.
5. *Input buttons:* An input button has two parts, its name and the area where changes can be made by typing new input. Click the second part of the input button Snap X spacing:, located under Snap, and experiment with the text cursor that is attached to the point of the arrow. As you move the mouse and pick a new spot, the text cursor moves also. The following editing keys can be used to edit the text in input buttons:

   Backspace key: Deletes characters to the left of the text cursor one at a time as it is pressed.
   Delete key: Deletes characters to the right of the text cursor one at a time as it is pressed.
   Left arrow: Moves the text cursor to the left without changing the existing text.
   Right arrow: Moves the text cursor to the right without changing the existing text.
   Character keys: After existing settings are deleted, new settings can be typed from the keyboard.
   Snap X spacing input button: Enter the X spacing in this input button, and the Y spacing is automatically set to the same spacing.
   Grid X spacing input button: Enter the X spacing in this input button, and the Y spacing is automatically set to the same spacing.
   Snap angle, X base, and Y base input buttons: These buttons relate to the Rotate option and are discussed in later chapters.

6. *Check buttons:* A check button has two parts, its mode name and the area that can be clicked to toggle the check mark and mode on and off. A check mark in the box indicates the mode is on.
7. *Radio buttons:* A round button within a circle. A dark circle in the selection indicates that selection is picked.

While in the Drafting Settings dialog box experiment with the different editing keys to become familiar with their functions. The dialog box is a handy tool to use in setting the snap and grid spacing, but if you are a fair typist, typing these commands from the keyboard is faster. After experimenting, be sure to return the grid spacing to 1/4 and the snap to 1/8 to have the correct settings for Exercise 3–1. Close the dialog box.

Layers

Different parts of a project can be placed on separate layers. The building shell may be on one layer, the interior walls on another, the electrical on a third layer, the furniture on a fourth layer, and so on. There is no limit to the number of layers you may use in a drawing. Each is perfectly aligned with all the others. Each layer may be viewed on the

display screen separately, one layer may be viewed in combination with one or more of the other layers, or all layers may be viewed together. Each layer may also be plotted separately or in combination with other layers, or all layers may be plotted at the same time. The layer name may be from 1 to 255 characters in length.

Step 8. Create layers using the Layer Properties Manager dialog box (Figures 2–5 and 2–6):

Prompt	Response
Command:	Layer... (or TYPE: LA<enter>)
The Layer Properties Manager dialog box appears:	CLICK: the **New Layer icon three times** (see Figure 2–5)
Layer1, Layer2, Layer3 appear in the Layer Name list (Figure 2–6):	CLICK: **the box under Color, beside Layer1**

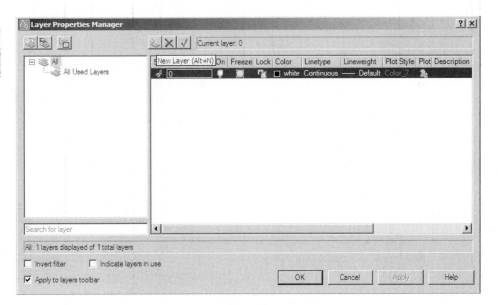

FIGURE 2–5
Layer Properties Manager
Dialog Box

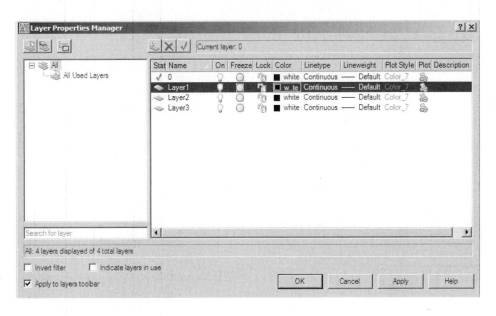

FIGURE 2–6
Layer1, Layer2, Layer3 Appear
in the Layer Name List

FIGURE 2–7
Select Color Dialog Box

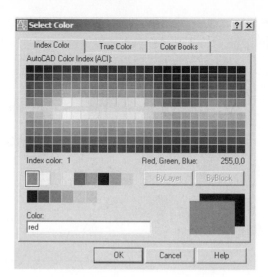

NOTE: The Standard Colors are: 1—red, 2—yellow, 3—green, 4—cyan, 5—blue, 6—magenta, and 7—white or black.

Step 9. Assign colors to layers (Figure 2–7):

Prompt	Response
The Select Color dialog box appears (Figure 2–7):	CLICK: **the color Red** (Index color: 1) CLICK: **OK**
The Layer Properties Manager dialog box appears:	CLICK: **the box under Color, beside Layer2**
The Select Color dialog box appears:	CLICK: **the color Magenta** (Index color: 6) CLICK: **OK**
The Layer Properties Manager dialog box appears:	CLICK: **the box under Color, beside Layer3**
The Select Color dialog box appears:	CLICK: **the color Cyan** CLICK: **OK**

Step 10. Assign linetypes to layers (Figures 2–8, 2–9, and 2–10):

Prompt	Response
The Layer Properties Manager dialog box appears:	CLICK: **the word Continuous under Linetype, beside Layer2**
The Select Linetype dialog box appears (Figure 2–8):	CLICK: **Load...** (to load linetypes so they can be selected)
The Load or Reload Linetypes dialog box appears (Figure 2–9):	**Move the mouse to the center of the dialog box and** CLICK: **the right mouse button** CLICK: **Select All** CLICK: **OK**

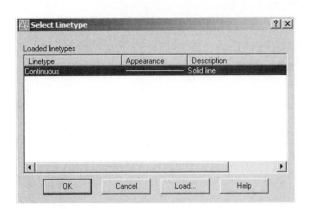

FIGURE 2–8
Select Linetype Dialog Box

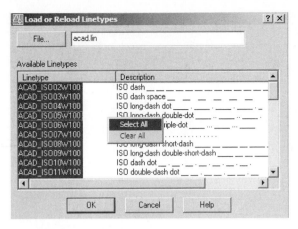

FIGURE 2–9
Load or Reload Linetypes Dialog Box

Linetypes must be loaded before they can be selected. You can load individual linetypes or you can load several by holding down the Shift key as you select. The AutoCAD library of standard linetypes provides you with three different sizes of each standard linetype other than continuous. For example, the DASHED line has the standard size called DASHED, a linetype half the standard size called DASHED2(.5x), and a linetype twice the standard size called DASHEDX2(2x).

Prompt	Response
The Select Linetype dialog box appears (Figure 2–10):	CLICK: **Dashed**
	CLICK: **OK**

Step 11. Make a layer current (Figure 2–11):

Prompt	Response
The Layer Properties Manager dialog box appears with layer names, colors, and linetypes assigned as shown in Figure 2–11:	CLICK: **Layer1** (to select it). Be sure to CLICK: on a layer name, not on one of the other properties such as lock or color.

FIGURE 2–10
Select the DASHED Linetype

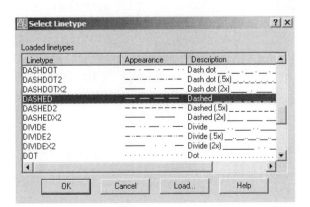

FIGURE 2–11
Layers with Colors and Linetypes Assigned and Layer1 Current

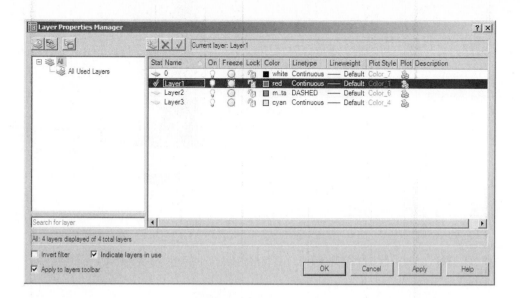

 NOTE: You can also double-click the layer name to set it current.

3D Navigation
CAD Standards
Camera Adjustment
Dimension
✓ Draw
Draw Order
Inquiry
Insert
✓ Layers
Layers II
Layouts
Lights
Mapping
Modeling
✓ Modify
Modify II
Object Snap
Orbit
Properties
Refedit
Reference
Render
Solid Editing
✓ Standard
Styles
Text
UCS
UCS II
View
Viewports
Visual Styles
Walk and Fly
Web
✓ Workspaces
Zoom

Lock Location   ▶
Customize...

FIGURE 2–12
Toolbar List with Layers Toolbar Selected

Prompt	Response
	CLICK: **Current** (the green check icon)
	CLICK: **OK**

Anything drawn from this point until another layer is set current will be on Layer1.

Step 12. If the Layers toolbar is not visible, make it visible (Figures 2–12 and 2–13):

Prompt	Response
Command:	**Place your mouse over any command icon and right-click.**
The Toolbar list appears (Figure 2–12):	CLICK: **the Layers** name (so a ✔ appears as shown in Figure 2–12)
The Layers toolbar appears docked at the top of the screen with Layer1 current:	CLICK: **the down arrow** (as shown in Figure 2–13)

FIGURE 2–13
Layer Status on the Layers Toolbar

File Edit View Insert Format Tools Draw Dimension

Layer1
0
Layer1
Layer2
Layer3

The Layer option icons on the Layers toolbar that can be changed, reading from left to right, are:

1. *On or Off:* These pertain to the visibility of layers. When a layer is turned OFF, it is still part of the drawing, but any entity drawn on that layer is not visible on the screen and cannot be plotted. For instance, the building exterior walls layer, interior walls layer, and electrical layer are turned ON and all other layers turned OFF to view, edit, or plot an electrical plan. One or more layers can be turned OFF and ON as required.

2. *Frozen or Thawed in All Viewports:* These also pertain to the visibility of layers. The difference between ON/OFF and FREEZE/THAW is a matter of how quickly the drawing regenerates on the display screen. If a layer is frozen, it is not visible and cannot be plotted, and AutoCAD spends no time regenerating it. A layer that is turned OFF is not visible and cannot be plotted, but AutoCAD does regenerate it.

3. *Frozen or Thawed in Current Viewport:* When you are working with more than one viewport, you may freeze or thaw a layer only in the current viewport. The same layer in other viewports remains unaffected.

4. *Locked or Unlocked:* When a layer is locked, it is visible, and you can draw on it. You cannot use any of the Edit commands to edit any of the drawing entities on the layer. You cannot accidentally change any entity that is already drawn.

 NOTE: With the Layers toolbar displayed, CLICK: the icon on the left showing three sheets of paper to activate the Layer Properties Manager dialog box.

To change the state of any layer pick the icon to select the alternate state. For example, Figure 2–14 shows that Layer1 was turned off by picking the lightbulb to turn it off. Experiment with changing the state of layers, then open the Layer Properties Manager dialog box to see the changed state reflected in it. Three additional layer properties that are shown in the Layer Properties Manager dialog box are:

1. *Lineweight:* A lineweight can be assigned to a layer. Lineweights are expressed in millimeters, similar to pen widths. The default lineweight initially set for all layers is .25 mm. The display of the lineweight is controlled by clicking LWT on the status bar. Lineweights are displayed in pixels on the screen; they plot with the exact width of the assigned lineweight. Lineweights can be varied, for example, to show thick lines for a floor plan and thin lines for dimensions, to emphasize something on the drawing, to show existing and new construction, or existing and new furniture.

2. *Plot Style:* Plot styles are created using a plot style table to define various properties such as color, grayscale, and lineweight. A layer's plot style overrides the

FIGURE 2–14
Turn Off Layer1

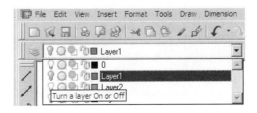

layer's color, linetype, and lineweight. Plot styles are used when you want to plot the same drawing with different settings or different drawings with the same settings.

3. *Plot:* This allows you to make visible layers nonplottable. For example, you may not want to plot a layer that shows construction lines. When a layer is nonplottable, it is displayed but not plotted.

Experiment with all parts of the Layer Properties Manager dialog box. If you create some layers that you do not need, delete them by highlighting them and picking the Delete icon. Return all layers to their original state before you exit.

Options Dialog Box, Open and Save Tab

To locate the Options dialog box, move the pointer across the top of the display screen and highlight **Tools** on the menu bar. CLICK: **Tools,** and a pull-down menu appears. Move your pointer to highlight Options... and CLICK: **Options....** The Options dialog box (Figure 2–15) appears on your screen. CLICK: the **Open and Save** tab.

Controls under the **File** Save section of the Options dialog box pertain to settings related to saving a file in AutoCAD. Controls under the File Safety Precautions section of the dialog box pertain to preventing data loss and detecting errors.

Save the Settings and Exit AutoCAD

Step 13. Save the settings and layers for Exercise 3–1:

Prompt	Response
Command:	**Save**
The drawing is saved in the drive and folder selected at the beginning of this exercise.	

FIGURE 2–15
Options Dialog Box with Open and Save Tab Selected

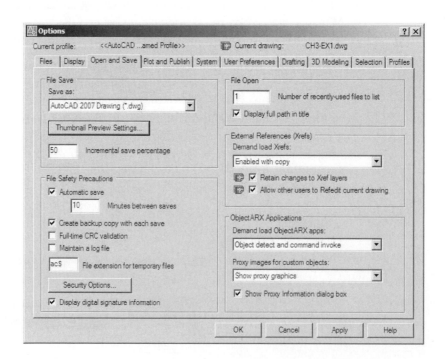

FIGURE 2–16
Save CH3-EX1 on the
Removable Disk (D:)

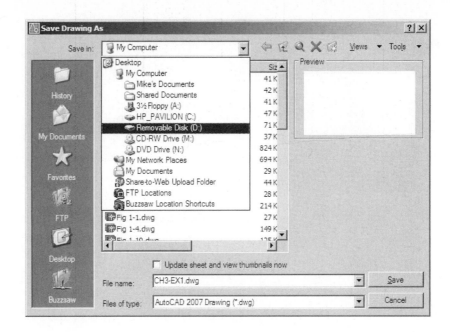

Step 14. Save the same drawing to another disk (a flash or floppy disk) (Figure 2–16):

Prompt	Response
Command:	Save As...
The Save Drawing As dialog box appears:	CLICK: **the down arrow in the Save in: button, highlight 3½ Floppy [A:] or Removable Disk (D:)**
The Save Drawing As dialog box appears as shown in Figure 2–16:	CLICK: **3½ floppy [A:] or Removable Disk (D:)** CLICK: **Save**

The light should brighten on the A: (or D:) drive, indicating that the drawing is being saved. Because the drawing was named when you saved it on the hard drive, you did not have to type the name again to save it with that name on the floppy disk. You could have chosen to give the drawing another name when you saved it on the floppy disk, in which case you would have to type the new name in the File name: input button.

Step 15. Save the drawing as a template to the template folder on the hard drive, or select the drive and folder you want to save it in (Figures 2–17 and 2–18):

Prompt	Response
Command:	SaveAs...
The Save Drawing As Dialog box appears:	CLICK: **the down arrow in the Files of type: button and move the cursor to** CLICK: **AutoCAD Drawing Template [*.dwt]** TYPE: **A-Size** (in the File name: input area so the Save Drawing As dialog box appears as shown in Figure 2–17.

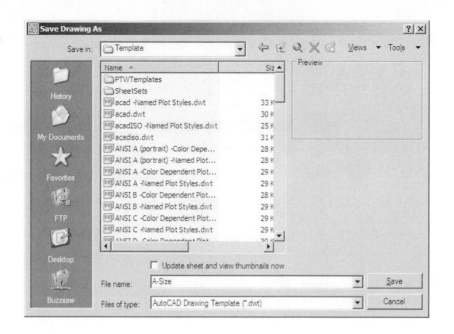

Prompt	Response
	CLICK: **the down arrow in the Save in: button, highlight the drive and folder you want to save in.**
	CLICK: **Save**
The Template Description dialog box appears (Figure 2–18):	TYPE: **Setup for 8-1/2,11 sheet** (as shown in Figure 2–18)
	CLICK: **OK**

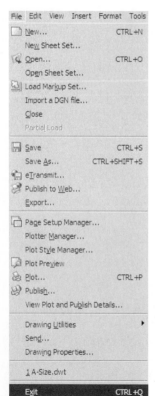

Step 16. Save the A-Size template to another disk in case something happens to the other template.

Exit (or Quit)

If you have not made any changes to the drawing since you last saved it, the Exit command takes you out of the AutoCAD program. If you have made changes to the drawing and have not saved these changes, AutoCAD will display the message "Save changes to C:\CH3-EX1.dwg?" (or whatever the drawing name is). This is a safety feature because the Exit command, by itself, *does not update or save a drawing.* You have three options: Yes, save the changes; No, do not save changes; or Cancel the Exit command.

FIGURE 2–18

Template Description Dialog Box

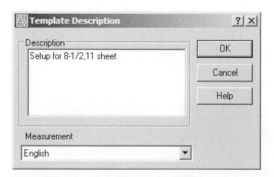

If you have just entered a drawing, have made a lot of mistakes, and just want to get rid of everything, respond with No to the Save changes questions. If you opened an existing drawing and use the Exit command without making any changes, the stored .dwg file and .bak files are preserved unchanged.

While you are making a new drawing AutoCAD is creating a .dwg (drawing) file of your drawing. There is no .bak (drawing file backup) file for a new drawing.

Each time an existing drawing file is opened for editing, the original drawing file (.dwg) becomes the drawing file backup (.bak) when "Create backup copy with each save" is checked in the Open and Save tab in the Options dialog box. The new edited version of the drawing becomes the .dwg file. Thus there is a copy of the original drawing file (.bak) and a copy of the new edited version (.dwg).

Step 17. Exit AutoCAD:

Prompt	Response
Command:	**Exit** (You may also TYPE: **QUIT** <enter> to exit, or simply close the program by clicking the **X** in the upper-right corner).

 NOTE: The File menu **Exit** and the Command line: **QUIT** are the same command.

1. Which of the following is *not* on the list of unit length types in the Drawing Units dialog box?
   - a. Scientific
   - b. Metric
   - c. Decimal
   - d. Fractional
   - e. Architectural

2. The Precision: button on the Drawing Units dialog box does which of the following?
   - a. Determines how accurately AutoCAD draws
   - b. Has a default value of 1/16″, which may not be changed
   - c. Sets decimal places for fractional units
   - d. Allows you to set the smallest fraction to display dimensions and other values shown on the screen
   - e. Sets decimal places for architectural units

3. While using AutoCAD to make drawings always draw full scale.
   - a. True
   - b. False

4. The default lower left corner of the drawing limits is 8-1/2,11.
   - a. True
   - b. False

5. The function key F7 described in this chapter does which of the following?
   - a. Provides a check list of the layers created
   - b. Turns snap ON or OFF
   - c. Flips the screen from the text display to the graphics display
   - d. Turns grid ON or OFF
   - e. Turns ortho ON or OFF

6. Units, Limits, Grid, and Snap can all be found under the Format menu.
   - a. True
   - b. False

7. Which of the following function keys is used to turn snap ON or OFF?
   - a. F1
   - b. F2
   - c. F7
   - d. F8
   - e. F9

8. How many layers may be used in a drawing?
   - a. 1
   - b. 2
   - c. 3
   - d. 16
   - e. An unlimited number

9. When a layer is OFF, it will regenerate but is not visible.
   - a. True
   - b. False

10. AutoCAD provides how many sizes of each standard linetype (except continuous)?
    - a. 1
    - b. 2
    - c. 3
    - d. 4
    - e. As many as you want

Complete.

11. Describe the effect of using the Esc key while in a command.

_____

12. What is an invisible grid to which the crosshair will lock called?

_____

13. What Windows® program do you use to change a setting to make all three-letter file name extensions visible?

_____

14. What special characters *cannot* be used in a layer and drawing name?

_____

15. What are the coordinates that represent the origin point where the X and Y axes intersect in the Cartesian coordinate system?

_____

16. Explain what .dwg and .dwt files are.

    .dwg: _____

    .dwt: _____

17. Before a linetype other than continuous may be selected or changed in the Layer Properties Manager dialog box, what must be done?

_____

18. Name the three axes of a Cartesian coordinate system and describe them.

_____

_____

_____

19. What does the Exit or Quit command do when used by itself?

_____

20. Describe how Save differs from SaveAs when the drawing has been named.

_____

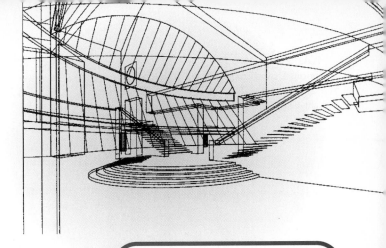

chapter

3

Drawing with AutoCAD: Basic Commands and Settings

objectives

When you have completed this chapter, you will be able to:

Correctly use the following commands and settings:

2D Solid	
Arc	Ortho
Blipmode	Pan
Circle	Redo
Donut	Redraw
Ellipse	Regen
Erase	Scale
Highlight	Select
Line	Undo
Ltscale	Zoom
Move	

Turn ORTHO mode on and off to control drawing as required.

Turn the screen coordinate display off and on.

Correctly use the following selection set options contained in many Modify commands:

All	Add
Window	Undo
Last	Fence
Previous	Window Polygon
Crossing Window	Crossing Polygon
Remove	

Use the transparent Zoom and Pan commands while another command is in progress.

Following the Exercises in This Book

Prompt and Response columns continue to provide the steps required to start and complete each new command sequence. A new Response column item used in this and following chapters describes the location of points picked on the screen. Figures are provided throughout the chapters to show the location of the points. Points are indicated in bold type in the Response column by a **D** followed by a number (for example, **D1,D2**). Look at the figure provided to locate the point on the drawing, and pick a point in the same place on your screen drawing. Another feature added to this and following chapters is that sometimes the response is described generally in the Response column (for example, **Pick the middle of the windowed view**).

Using the Mouse and Right-Click Customization

You may be using a two-button mouse, a three-button mouse, or a mouse with a small wheel between the buttons. With all three, the left button is the pick button used to select commands and specify points on the screen.

FIGURE 3–1
Options Dialog Box, with
User Preferences Tab and
Right-Click Customization...
Clicked

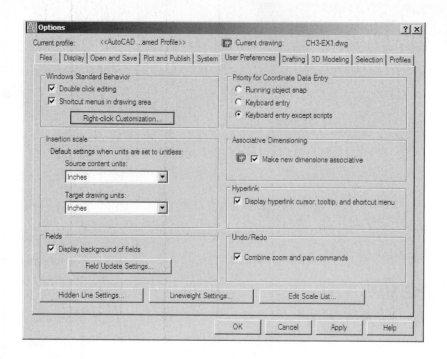

The Right-Click Customization dialog box settings control what happens when the right mouse button (shown as **<enter>** in this book) is clicked. To access the Right-Click Customization dialog box, select Options... under Tools in the menu bar. Select the User Preferences tab of the Options dialog box (Figure 3–1). CLICK: the **Right-click Customization...** button in the Windows Standard Behavior area, and the Right-Click Customization dialog box (Figure 3–2) appears.

In the Response columns of this book **<enter>** indicates that the right mouse button should be clicked. Notes in parentheses are used to clarify how **<enter>** is used; for example, **<enter>** (to return the Line command prompt). Leave the Right-Click Customization dialog box set as the default shown in Figure 3–2. As you become more familiar with AutoCAD you may decide to change this setting.

FIGURE 3–2
Right-Click Customization
Dialog Box

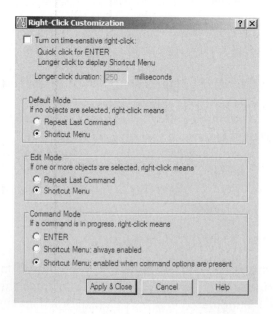

Exercise 3–1: Drawing Lines and Circles

In Chapter 2, the settings and layers were made for drawing CH3-EX1. In Exercise 3–1, that setup is used to complete your first drawing exercise. When you have completed Exercise 3–1, your drawing will look similar to the drawing in Figure 3–3.

Open an Existing Drawing

Step 1. Use your workspace to open existing drawing CH3-EX1:

Prompt	Response
Command:	CLICK: **Open...**
The Select File dialog box appears:	CLICK: **the down arrow in Look in:**
	CLICK: **the correct drive and folder**
	CLICK: **CH3-EX1**
	CLICK: **Open** (or DOUBLE-CLICK: **CH3-EX1**)
CH3-EX1 is opened.	

FIGURE 3–3
Exercise 3–1: Drawing Lines
and Circles

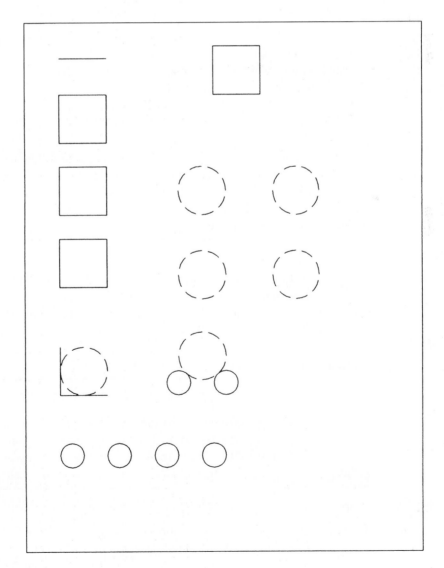

Step 2. If your drawing is on a CD or floppy disk, save the drawing to the hard drive or network drive.

Prompt	Response
Command:	Save As...
The Save Drawing As dialog box is displayed:	CLICK: **the correct drive and folder**
	CLICK: **Save**

Now you are working on the hard drive or network drive. Do not work on a disk. Always work on the hard drive or network drive.

Zoom

The Zoom-All command lets you view the entire drawing area. Use it after setting up or entering a drawing so that you are familiar with the size and shape of your limits and grid. Otherwise, you may be working on a small part of the drawing and not realize it.

Step 3. Use Zoom-All to view the entire drawing area.

Prompt	Response
Command:	**Zoom-All** (or TYPE: **Z<enter>**)
Specify corner of window, enter a scale factor (nX or nXP), or [All/ Center/Dynamic/Extents/Previous/ Scale/Window/Object]<real time>:	TYPE: **A<enter>**

Grid

The grid is visible when it is ON. Press the F7 function key to turn the grid OFF and ON, or CLICK: **GRID** at the bottom of your screen. Turn the grid OFF and ON to clean up any blips that appear on the screen while you are drawing.

Step 4. Turn the grid on.

Ortho

Press the F8 function key to turn Ortho ON and OFF, or CLICK: **ORTHO** at the bottom of your screen. Ortho mode, when ON, helps you to draw lines perfectly, horizontally and vertically. It does not allow you to draw at an angle, so turn Ortho OFF and ON as needed.

Step 5. Turn Ortho ON.

NOTE: When Ortho mode is on, drawing or editing of a drawing part is restricted to horizontal and vertical movements only. Turn Ortho ON and OFF to accommodate your drawing activity.

Snap

Function key F9 turns Snap ON and OFF, or you may CLICK: **SNAP** at the bottom of your screen. Snap helps you to draw accurately; it is desirable to draw with Snap ON most of the time. If you need to turn Snap OFF to draw or edit a drawing entity, remember to turn it back ON as soon as possible.

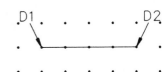

FIGURE 3–4
Draw a Horizontal Line 1″
Long, Using Grid Marks

Step 6. On your own:

1. Turn Snap ON.
2. Check the Layer Control; Layer1 should be current.
3. Make sure that POLAR, OSNAP, OTRACK, and DYN are OFF at the bottom of your screen.

Line and Erase

Use Figure 3–3 as a guide when locating the line and squares drawn using the Line command.

Drawing Lines Using the Grid Marks

Lines can be drawn by snapping to the grid marks visible on the screen.

Step 7. Draw a horizontal line 1″ long, using the grid marks (Figure 3–4):

Prompt	Response
Command:	**Line** (or TYPE: **L<enter>**)
Specify first point:	**D1** (Do not type "D1." Look at Figure 3–4 and click the point D1, approximately three grid spaces down (3/4″) and three grid spaces to the right of the upper left corner of the page.)
Specify next point or [Undo]:	**D2** (move four grid marks to the right)
Specify next point or [Undo]:	**<enter>** (to complete the command)

Step 8. Erase the line and bring it back again:

Prompt	Response
Command:	**Erase** (or TYPE: **E<enter>**)
Select objects:	**Position the small box that replaces the crosshair any place on the line and click the line.**
Select objects: 1 found	
Select objects:	**<enter<** (the line disappears)
Command:	TYPE: **U<enter>** (the line reappears)

Do not be afraid to draw with AutoCAD. If you make a mistake, you can easily erase it using the Erase command. When you are using the Erase command, a small box replaces the screen crosshair. The small box is called the *pickbox*. The Undo feature will restore everything erased by the *last* Erase command.

FIGURE 3–5

Draw a 1″ Square Using Grid
Marks

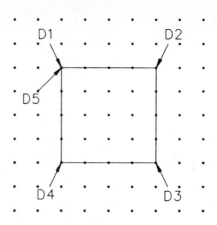

Step 9. Draw a 1″ square using the grid marks and undo the last two lines
(Figure 3–5):

Prompt	Response
Command:	**Line**
Specify first point:	**D1** (CLICK: a point 3/4″ directly below the left end of the line just drawn)
Specify next point or [Undo]:	**D2** (Figure 3–5)
Specify next point or [Undo]:	**D3**
Specify next point or [Close/Undo]:	**D4**
Specify next point or [Close/Undo]:	**D5**
Specify next point or [Close/Undo]:	TYPE: **U<enter>** (move your mouse to see that the line is undone)
Specify next point or [Close/Undo]:	TYPE: **U<enter>**
Specify next point or [Close/Undo]:	**<enter>** (to stop and return to the Command: prompt)

While in the Line command, if you decide you do not like the last line segment drawn, use the Undo command to erase it and continue on with the "Specify next point of [Close/Undo]:" prompt. Clicking more than one undo will backtrack through the line segments in the reverse order in which they were drawn.

Step 10. Complete the square (Figure 3–5):

Prompt	Response
Command:	**<enter>** (to return the Line command prompt)
Specify first point:	**<enter>** (the line is attached)
Specify next point or [Undo]:	**D4,D5**
Specify next point or [Close/Undo]:	**<enter>** (to stop)

The Line command has a very handy feature: If you respond to the prompt "Specify first point:" by pressing the Enter key or the space bar, the line will start at the end of the most recently drawn line.

The following part of this exercise describes how to draw lines using absolute coordinates, relative coordinates, and polar coordinates. It is important that you are aware of and take the time to understand the various methods, because they apply to drawing other objects also. Of course, you can always refer to this section of the book if you are faced with a situation in which you do not know the best method of drawing.

Drawing Lines Using Absolute Coordinates

Remember, 0,0 is the lower-left corner of the page, the origin point of the Cartesian coordinate system. When you use absolute coordinates to draw, the X-axis coordinate is entered first and identifies a location on the horizontal axis. The Y-axis coordinate is entered second and identifies a location on the vertical axis. The page size is 8-1/2,11. A little adding and subtracting to determine the absolute coordinates will locate the square on the page as follows.

Step 11. Draw a 1″ square using absolute coordinates (Figure 3–6):

Prompt	Response
Command:	**Line** (move the crosshair to the center of the screen)
Specify first point:	TYPE: **4,10-1/2<enter>** (the line begins)
Specify next point or [Undo]:	TYPE: **5,10-1/2<enter>**
Specify next point or [Undo]:	TYPE: **5,9-1/2<enter>**
Specify next point or [Close/Undo]:	TYPE: **4,9-1/2<enter>**
Specify next point or [Close/Undo]:	TYPE: **C<enter>**

On Your Own

1. CLICK: on the coordinate display to turn the screen coordinate display on and move your pointer to each corner of the square. Watch how the screen coordinate display shows the X,Y coordinate position of each corner. Compare those coordinates with the coordinates you just typed and entered. They are the same.

2. Hold the crosshair of the cursor (with snap on) on the lower left corner of the grid; the coordinate display reads 0′-0″,0′-0″. Move the cursor to the upper right corner of the grid; the coordinate display reads 0′-8 1/2″,0′-11″.

FIGURE 3–6
Draw a 1″ Square Using
Absolute Coordinates

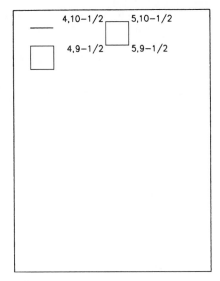

Drawing Lines Using Relative Coordinates

Relative coordinates are used after a point is entered. (Relative to what? Relative to the point just entered.) After a point has been clicked on the drawing, relative coordinates are entered by typing @, followed by the X,Y coordinates. For example, after a point is entered to start a line, typing and entering @1,0 will draw the line 1″ in the X direction, 0″ in the Y direction.

Step 12. Draw a 1″ square using relative coordinates:

Prompt	Response
Command:	**Line**
Specify first point:	**CLICK: a point on the grid 1/2″ below the lower left corner of the first square drawn**
Specify next point or [Undo]:	TYPE: **@1,0<enter>**
Specify next point or [Undo]:	TYPE: **@0,−1<enter>**
Specify next point or [Close/Undo]:	TYPE: **@−1,0<enter>**
Specify next point or [Close/Undo]:	TYPE: **C<enter>**

A minus sign (−) is used for negative line location with relative coordinates. Negative is to the left for the X axis and down for the Y axis.

Drawing Lines Using Polar Coordinates

Absolute and relative coordinates are extremely useful in some situations; however, for many design applications (for example, drawing walls) polar coordinates or direct distance entry is used. Be sure you understand how to use all types of coordinates.

Polar coordinates are also relative to the last point entered. They are typed starting with an @, followed by a distance and angle of direction. Figure 3–7 shows the polar coordinate angle directions. The angle of direction is always preceded by a < sign when polar coordinates are entered.

FIGURE 3–7
Polar Coordinate Angles

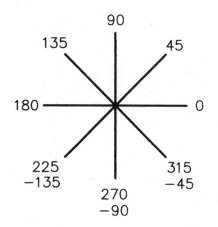

Part II: Two-Dimensional AutoCAD

Step 13. Draw a 1″ square using polar coordinates, then erase the square:

Prompt	Response
Command:	<enter> (to return the Line command prompt)
Specify first point:	CLICK: **a point on the grid 1/2″ below the** **lower left corner of the last square drawn**
Specify next point or [Undo]:	TYPE: **@1<0<enter>**
Specify next point or [Undo]:	TYPE: **@1<270<enter>**
Specify next point or [Close/Undo]:	TYPE: **@1<180<enter>**
Specify next point or [Close/Undo]:	TYPE: **C<enter>**
Command:	TYPE: **E<enter>**
Select objects:	Select the entire square **<enter>**

Drawing Lines Using Direct Distance Entry

Direct Distance Entry is a quick, accurate, and easy way to draw lines. It can also be used with any other command that asks you to specify a point. Move your mouse in the direction you want to draw, TYPE: **the distance**, and PRESS: **<enter>**.

Step 14. Draw a 1″ square using direct distance entry:

Prompt	Response
Command:	**With ORTHO ON Line** (or TYPE: **L<enter>**)
Specify first point:	CLICK: **a point on the grid in the same location** **as the beginning of the square you just erased**
Specify next point or [Undo]:	**Move your mouse to the right;** TYPE: **1<enter>**
Specify next point or [Undo]:	**Move your mouse down;** TYPE: **1<enter>**
Specify next point or [Close/Undo]:	**Move your mouse to the left;** TYPE: **1<enter>**
Specify next point or [Close/Undo]:	TYPE: **C<enter>**

Circle

In the following part of this exercise, four circles of the same size are drawn, using four different methods.

Step 15. On your own:

1. Look at Figure 3–3 to determine the approximate location of the four circles you will draw.
2. Set Layer2 current. Layer2 has a dashed linetype.
3. Turn ORTHO OFF.

Center, Radius

Step 16. Draw a circle with a 1/2″ radius (Figure 3–8):

Prompt	Response
Command:	**Circle-Center, Radius**
Specify center point for circle or [3P/2P/Ttr(tan tan radius)]:	**D1**
Specify radius of circle or [Diameter]:	TYPE: **1/2<enter>** (the circle appears)

FIGURE 3–8

Draw the Same Size Circle Using Four Different Methods

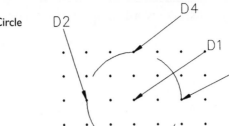

Center, Diameter

Refer to Figure 3–3 to determine the approximate location of the next circle.

Step 17. Draw a circle with a 1″ diameter (Figure 3–8):

Prompt	Response
Command:	<enter> (to return Circle command prompt)
Specify center point for circle or [3P/2P/Ttr(tan tan radius)]:	D1
Specify radius of circle or [Diameter]<0′-0 1/2″>:	TYPE: D<enter> (to specify diameter)
Specify diameter of circle <0′-1″>:	<enter> (the circle appears)

2 Points

Step 18. Draw a 1″ diameter circle by locating the two endpoints of its diameter (Figure 3–8):

Prompt	Response
Command:	**Circle-2 Points**
Specify center point for circle or [3P/2P/Ttr(tan tan radius)]: _2p	
Specify first end point of circle's diameter:	**D2** (on a grid mark)
Specify second end point of circle's diameter:	**D3** (move four grid spaces to the right)

3 Points

Step 19. Draw a 1″ diameter circle by clicking three points on its circumference (Figure 3–8):

Prompt	Response
Command:	**Circle-3 Points**
Specify center point for circle or [3P/2P/Ttr(tan tan radius)]: _3p	
Specify first point on circle:	**D2**
Specify second point on circle:	**D3** (move four grid spaces to the right)
Specify third point on circle:	**D4** (the center of the top of the circle)

FIGURE 3–9
Draw Two 1″ Lines That Form a Corner and Two 1/2″ Diameter Circles, 1″ on Center

You have just learned four different methods of drawing the same size circle. You can watch the size of the circle change on the screen by moving the pointer, and you can select the desired size by clicking the point that indicates the size.

Step 20. On your own:

1. Set Layer1 current.
2. Draw two 1″ lines that form a corner and two 1/2″ diameter circles, 1″ on center, as shown in Figure 3–9. Figure 3–3 will help you to determine the approximate location of the corner and two circles on your drawing.
3. Set Layer2 current again.

TTR

The next option of the Circle command is Tan, Tan, Radius. This stands for tangent, tangent, and radius. A tangent touches a circle at a single point.

Step 21. Draw a circle with a 1/2″ radius tangent to two lines (Figure 3–10):

Prompt	Response
Command:	**Circle-Tan, Tan, Radius**
Specify center point for circle or [3P/2P/Ttr(tan tan radius): _ttr	
Specify point on object for first tangent of circle:	**D1** (pick anyplace on the line)
Specify point on object for second tangent of circle:	**D2** (pick anyplace on the line)
Specify radius of circle<0′-0 1/4″>:	TYPE: **1/2<enter>**

Step 22. Draw a circle with a 1/2″ radius tangent to two other circles (Figure 3–10):

Prompt	Response
Command:	RIGHT-CLICK: **Repeat Tan, Tan, Radius**
Specify point on object for first tangent of circle:	**D3**

FIGURE 3–10
Draw a Circle with a 1/2″ Radius Tangent to Two Lines; Draw a Circle with a 1/2″ Radius Tangent to Two Other Circles

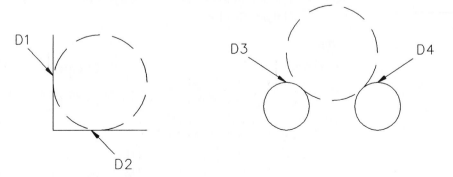

Prompt	Response
Specify point on object for second tangent of circle:	D4
Specify radius of circle<0'-0 1/2">:	<enter>

Ltscale

AutoCAD provides a variety of linetypes that you may use. For example, the dashed linetype provided by AutoCAD consists of 1/2" line segments with 1/4" spaces in between. The given line segment length (1/2") and spacing (1/4") for the dashed line-type are drawn when the global linetype scale factor is set to 1 (the default).

To make the line segment length or spacing smaller, enter a linetype scale factor smaller than 1 but larger than 0 to the Ltscale prompt. To make the line segment length and spacing larger, enter a linetype scale factor larger than 1. Look closely to see the circle's DASHED linetype scale change when the following is entered.

Step 23. **Use Ltscale to change the size of the DASHED linetype:**

Prompt	Response
Command:	TYPE: **LTSCALE<enter>**
Enter new linetype scale factor <1.0000>:	TYPE: **1/2<enter>**
Regenerating model.	

Zoom

The most commonly used Zoom commands (Realtime, Previous, Window, Dynamic, All, Extents) control how you view the drawing area on the display screen. While drawing the lines and circles for this chapter you have been able to view the entire 8-1/2" × 11" drawing limits on the screen. The Zoom-All command was used earlier to assure that view. The Zoom commands are located on the Standard toolbar and on the menu bar View menu under Zoom.

Zoom-Window

The Zoom-Window command allows you to pick two opposite corners of a rectangular window on the screen. The cursor changes to form a rubber band that shows the size of the window on the screen. The size of the window is controlled by the movement of the mouse. The part of the drawing inside the windowed area is magnified to fill the screen when the second corner of the window is clicked.

The following will use the Zoom-Window command to look more closely at the three tangent circles previously drawn.

Step 24. **Use Zoom-Window to look more closely at the three tangent circles (Figure 3–11):**

Prompt	Response
Command:	TYPE: **Z<enter>**
Specify corner of window, enter a scale factor (nX or nXP), or [All/Center/Dynamic/Extents/ Previous/Scale/Window/Object] <real time>:	**D1** (lower left corner of the window)
Specify opposite corner:	**D2** (upper right corner of the window)

FIGURE 3–11
Use Zoom-Window

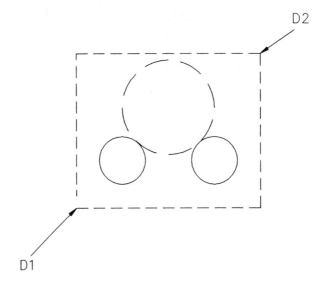

The area that was windowed is now displayed to fill the screen.

When the magnification of the circles was enlarged with the Zoom-Window command, to save time AutoCAD did not regenerate the drawing. The part of the drawing that was windowed and magnified was *redrawn* only. That is why the circles are not smooth. Small line segments called vectors make up a circle. When the entire page is displayed, fewer line segments are used to make up the smaller circles. By zooming in and not regenerating, you are able to see the small number of vectors.

Step 25. **Use REGEN to regenerate the drawing:**

Prompt	Response
Command:	TYPE: **RE<enter>**

By typing and entering REGEN, you issued a regeneration of the drawing. AutoCAD regenerated the circles with the optimal number of line segments (making the circle smoother) for the larger magnification.

Zoom-All

Now that you have a windowed area of the drawing, how do you view the entire drawing again? Zoom-All will provide a view of the entire drawing area.

Step 26. **Use Zoom-All to view the entire drawing:**

Prompt	Response
Command:	**Zoom-All** (or TYPE: **Z<enter>**)
Specify corner of window, enter a scale factor (nX or nXP), or [All/Center/Dynamic/Extents/Previous/Scale/Window/Object] <real time>:	TYPE: **A<enter>**

Zoom-Previous

Zoom-Previous is a very convenient feature. AutoCAD remembers up to 10 previous views. This is especially helpful and saves time if you are working on a complicated drawing.

Step 27. **Use Zoom-Previous to see the last view of the tangent circles again:**

Prompt	Response
Command:	\<enter\>
Specify corner of window, enter a scale factor (nX or nXP), or [All/Center/Dynamic/Extents/ Previous/Scale/Window/Object] \<real time\>:	TYPE: **P\<enter\>** (to repeat Zoom command)

Zoom-Dynamic

Another Zoom command that saves time is Zoom-Dynamic.

Step 28. **Use Zoom-Dynamic to change the display (Figure 3–12):**

Prompt	Response
Command:	\<enter\>
Specify corner of window, enter a scale factor (nX or nXP), or [All/Center/Dynamic/Extents/ Previous/Scale/Window/Object] \<real time\>:	TYPE: **D\<enter\>**

FIGURE 3–12
Use Zoom-Dynamic

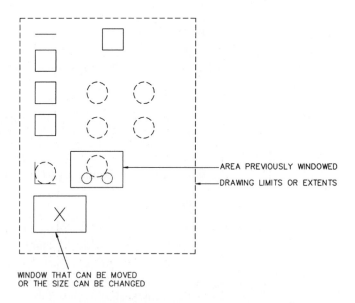

AREA PREVIOUSLY WINDOWED

DRAWING LIMITS OR EXTENTS

WINDOW THAT CAN BE MOVED OR THE SIZE CAN BE CHANGED

You now see three areas on the screen (Figure 3–12):

1. The tangent circle area previously windowed.
2. The drawing limits or the drawing extents, whichever is larger.
3. The box with the X in it is the same size as the window that you just made when you windowed the circles. This window can be moved; it follows the movement of your mouse. Experiment by moving it around the screen.

The size of the window can also be changed. Change the size of the window by pressing the pick button on the mouse. The X inside changes to an arrow when you press the left button. When the arrow is in the window, the movement of the pointer changes the size of the window. Experiment with changing the size of the window. Press the left button on the mouse to return the X to the center of the window. With the X in the center of the window, the size remains constant and you may move the window to the area of the drawing that you want to window or zoom in on next.

When you have decided which area of the drawing you want to view next and have the size of window needed, with an X in the center, place the window on the area to be enlarged. When you press the Enter button on the mouse, the area inside the window will appear enlarged on the screen.

Zoom-Extents

The Zoom-Extents command allows you to view the extents of a drawing. To understand Zoom-Extents, you need to understand the difference between drawing *limits* and drawing *extents*. The limits of a drawing are the size of the sheet set with the Limits command. The extents of a drawing include whatever graphics are actually drawn on the page. If only half the page is full, the extents will be half the page. Sometimes a drawing entity is drawn outside the limits; this, too, is considered the drawing extents. The Zoom-Extents command provides a view of all drawing entities on the page as large as possible to fill the screen. The Zoom-All command displays the entire drawing limits or extents, whichever is larger. The extents are larger than the limits when a drawing entity is drawn outside of the limits.

Step 29. **Use Zoom-Extents to view the extents of drawing CH3-EX1:**

Prompt	Response
Command:	**Zoom-Extents**

Zoom-Object

Zoom-Object allows you to select an object or objects to describe the area that will be displayed.

Step 30. **Use Zoom-Object to view a circle:**

Prompt	Response
Command:	**Zoom-Object (or TYPE: Z<enter>** **then TYPE: O<enter>)**
Select objects:	CLICK: **one of the circles**
Select objects:	**<enter>**

Real-Time Zoom

The Real-Time Zoom command is located on the Standard toolbar and on the menu bar View menu under Zoom. You may also TYPE: **RTZOOM<enter>** from the keyboard to activate this command. After activating the command, to zoom in or out, hold down

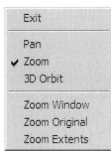

the left mouse button and move the mouse up or down to change the magnification of the drawing. PRESS: **the right mouse button** to get a shortened zoom and pan menu, as shown in the margin. CLICK: **Exit** or PRESS: **Esc** to exit the command.

 NOTE: PRESS: <enter> to the Zoom prompt to activate Real-Time Zoom.

Wheel Mouse

You can also zoom in and out by turning the wheel of a two-button mouse.

Pan

The Pan command allows you to maintain the current display magnification and see parts of the drawing that may be off the screen and not visible in the display. It allows you to move the entire drawing in any direction. Pan does not change the magnification of the view.

 TIP: The Zoom and Pan commands may also be activated by typing **Z** or **P** from the keyboard.

Real-Time Pan

The Real-Time Pan command is located on the Standard toolbar and on the menu bar View menu under Pan. You may also TYPE: **P<enter>** to activate this command. To move the view of your drawing at the same magnification, hold down the left button on your mouse and move the mouse in any direction to change the view of your drawing. PRESS: **the right mouse button** while in Real-Time Pan to get a shortened zoom and pan menu. CLICK: **Exit** or PRESS: **Esc** to exit from the command.

Wheel Mouse

If you have a wheel mouse, you can pan by pressing down on the wheel and moving the mouse.

Transparent Commands

A *transparent command* is a command that can be used while another command is in progress. It is very handy to be able to change the display while a command such as Line is in progress. To use the Zoom commands transparently, after you have entered the Line command, TYPE: **'Z<enter>**. An apostrophe (') must precede the command name. The **'Z** prompt is ">>Specify corner of window, enter a scale factor (nX or nXP), or [All/Center/Dynamic/Extents/Previous/Scale/Window/Object] <real time>." The >> preceding the command prompt indicates that the command is being used transparently.

You can also use Pan as a transparent command. While another command is in progress: TYPE: **'P<enter>**, or click it from the View menu in the menu bar.

All the Zoom commands from the View menu in the menu bar may be used transparently; you can simply click them. You can also change grid and snap settings transparently: enter an apostrophe (') before entering the command at any prompt.

Blipmode

When a point is entered on a drawing, AutoCAD generates small marker blips on the screen. Commands such as Redraw or Regen that redraw or regenerate the drawing erase the marker blips. When you TYPE: **BLIPMODE<enter>**, the Blipmode command has two responses: ON and OFF. When the Blipmode command is OFF, no marker blips are displayed. When the Blipmode command is ON, the marker blips appear.

 NOTE: Sometimes it is very helpful to have Blipmode on, because you can see where your mouse has entered a point on your drawing.

Redraw

When you pick Redraw from the View menu or TYPE: **R<enter>**, AutoCAD redraws and cleans up your drawing. Any marker blips (when a point is entered, AutoCAD generates small marker blips on the screen) on the screen disappear, and drawing entities affected by editing of other objects are redrawn. Pressing function key F7 twice turns the Grid OFF and ON and also redraws the screen.

Regen

When you click Regen from the View menu, AutoCAD regenerates the entire drawing. As you have already learned, other View commands do this, and it is seldom necessary to issue a regeneration with the Regen command.

Highlight

When you select any object such as a circle or line to erase, or move, or otherwise modify, the circle or line is highlighted. This highlighting is controlled by the HIGHLIGHT system variable. When you TYPE: **HIGHLIGHT<enter>**, the Highlight command has two responses: enter 1 to turn highlighting ON, or 0 to turn highlighting OFF. You will probably prefer to have this variable on so the items selected are confirmed by the highlighting.

Move and Editing Commands Selection Set

You may want to move some of the items on your page to improve the layout of the page. The Move command lets you do that.

Step 31. On your own:

1. Set Layer3 current.
2. Use Zoom-All to view the entire drawing.
3. Set Blipmode to ON.
4. Set Highlight to 1 (ON).
5. Draw a row of four 1/2″-diameter circles, 1″ on center, as shown in Figure 3–13.
6. Pick Move from the Modify menu (or TYPE: M<enter>).

FIGURE 3–13
Draw a Row of Four 1/2″
Diameter Circles, 1″ on
Center

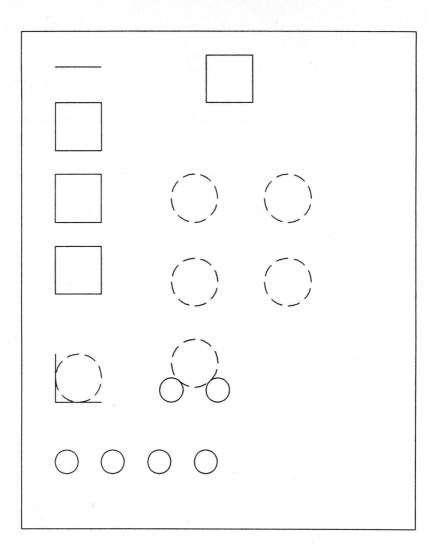

After you pick Move, the prompt in the prompt line asks you to "Select objects:." Also, a pickbox replaces the screen crosshair. The pickbox helps you to select the item or group of items to be moved by positioning the pickbox on the item. The item or group of items selected is called the *selection set*. Many of the AutoCAD Modify commands provide the same prompt, the pickbox, and also the same options used to select the object or objects to be edited. The options are Window/Last/Crossing/BOX/ALL/Fence/WPolygon/CPolygon/Group/Add/Remove/Multiple/Previous/Undo/AUto/SIngle/Subobject/Object. We will cover some of the more commonly used options used to select objects.

The Move command is used in the following part of this exercise to demonstrate various options many of the Modify commands use to select objects. Notice that when the item is selected AutoCAD confirms your selection by highlighting it.

 TIP: PRESS: function key F9 to turn Snap OFF if it interferes with clicking on an object; turn it back on as soon as the object is selected.

Step 32. Select a circle by clicking a point on the circle, and move it by clicking a point on the drawing (Figure 3–14):

FIGURE 3–14

Select a Circle by Clicking a
Point on the Circle, and
Move It by Clicking a Point
on the Drawing

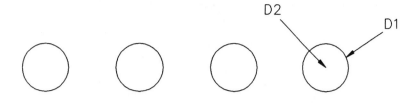

Prompt	Response
Select objects:	**D1** (any point on the circumference of the circle as shown in Figure 3–14)
Select objects: 1 found	
Select objects:	<enter> (you have completed selecting objects)
Specify base point or [Displacement] <Displacement>:	**D2** (the center of the circle—be sure SNAP is ON)
Specify second point or <use first point as displacement>:	CLICK: **a point three grid marks (3/4″) to the right** -or- **with ORTHO ON, move your mouse to the right. TYPE: 3/4<enter>**

NOTE: Keep Snap ON while moving a drawing entity. Snap from one grid point (base point or displacement) to another (second point).

Step 33. Select a circle by clicking a point on the circle, and move it by entering relative coordinates (Figure 3–15).

Prompt	Response
Command:	<enter> (to repeat Move command prompt)
Select objects:	**D1**
Select objects: 1 found	
Select objects:	<enter>
Specify base point or [Displacement] <Displacement>:	**D2** (the center of the circle)
Specify second point or <use first point as displacement>:	TYPE: @−3/4,0<enter>

You can give the second point of displacement by clicking a point on the screen or by using absolute, relative, polar coordinates, or direct distance entry.

FIGURE 3–15

Select a Circle by Clicking a
Point on the Circle, and
Move It by Entering Relative
Coordinates

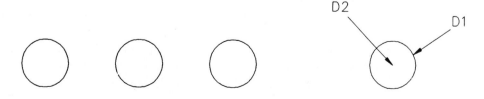

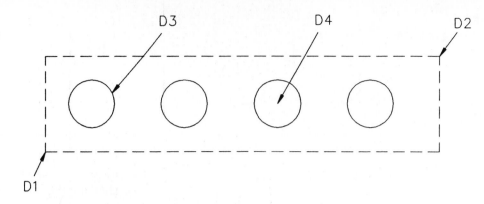

Step 34. Select items to be edited by using a window, and then remove an item from the selection set (Figure 3–16):

Prompt	Response
Command:	\<enter\>
Select objects:	**D1**
Specify opposite corner:	**D2**
4 found	
Select objects:	TYPE: **R\<enter\>** (or hold down the Shift key)
Remove objects:	**D3**
Remove objects:	\<enter\>
Specify base point or [Displacement] \<Displacement\>:	**D4** (the center of the circle)
Specify second point or \<use first point as displacement\>:	CLICK: **a point two grid marks down the Y axis**

TIP: Press F7 twice to clean up the blips (turn grid off and on). You can also turn BLIPMODE to OFF.

Window (W), Crossing Window (C), Window Polygon (WP), and Crossing Polygon (CP)

The Window and Crossing (Window) responses allow you to pick two opposite corners of a rectangular window on the screen. The crosshair of the pointer changes to form a rubber band that shows the size of the window on the screen. The size of the window is controlled by the movement of the pointer. Window Polygon and Crossing Polygon allow you to make a polygon by clicking points that are used to select objects.

With the Window response, only the parts of the drawing that are *entirely contained within the window* are selected to be edited. If the window covers only a part of a drawing entity, that entity is not selected. You may also type and enter **W** to activate the Window response, or **WP** to activate Window Polygon.

When you use the Crossing Window command, any part of the drawing that is contained within or *crossed by the crossing window* is included in the selection set. With a crossing window, a drawing entity such as a line or circle does not have to be entirely contained within the window to be selected. The colors of both the crossing window and the window is controlled by the Visual Effect Settings on the Selection tab of the Options dialog box.

Picking an empty area on the drawing and moving your mouse to the right creates a window. Picking and moving to the left creates a crossing window.

TIP: Typing W <ENTER> and C <ENTER> to activate window and crossing window is helpful when the drawing area is dense and clicking an empty area is difficult or impossible.

Step 35. On your own:

1. Experiment with the difference between Window and Crossing Window. You may also type and enter C to activate the Crossing Window response, or CP to activate Crossing Polygon.
2. Return the circles to the approximate location as shown in Figure 3–13.

All (All)

Selects all objects on thawed layers.

Fence (F)

Fence allows you to click points that draw a line that selects any objects it crosses.

Remove (R) and Add (A)

The Remove response allows you to remove a drawing part from the selection set. If you are in the Remove mode and decide to add another drawing part to the selection set, TYPE: **A<enter>** to return to the Add mode.

 TIP: To remove objects from a selection set, hold the Shift key down and click the object.

Last (L) and Previous (P)

The Last response selects the most recent drawing entity created. The Previous response selects the most recent selection set. Both are handy if you want to use several editing commands on the same drawing entity or the same selection set. You may also type and enter **L** or **P** from the keyboard while you are in a command and selecting objects.

Undo (U)

While in an editing command, if you decide you do not want something in a selection set, you may use the Undo command to remove it and continue on with the "Select objects:" prompt. Typing **Undo** backtracks through the selection sets in the reverse of the order in which they were selected. You may also type and enter **U** from the keyboard.

Select

The Select command allows you to preselect the items to be edited. Then you can use the "Previous" option in the Modify commands to refer to the selection set. TYPE: **SELECT<enter>** to the Command: prompt.

Selection Settings

To access the Selection settings, select Options... under Tools in the menu bar. Select the Selection tab of the Options dialog box. The left side of this tab shows Selection

FIGURE 3–17
Options Dialog Box
Selection Tab

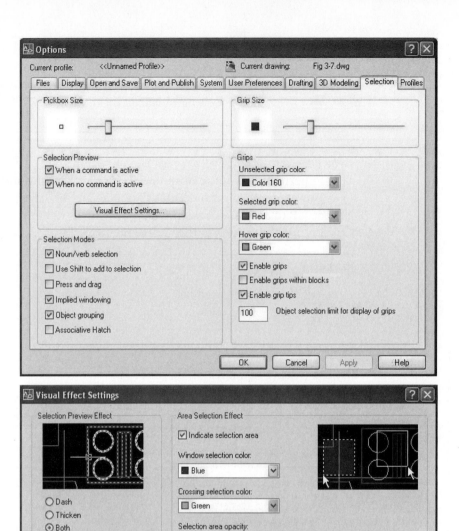

Modes, Selection Preview, and how to change the Pickbox Size. A check mark in the box indicates that the mode is on (Figure 3–17). The right side of the Selection tab shows the settings for grips, which are discussed next.

Grips

Grips are small squares that appear on an object if it is selected with no command active. You have probably done that already and had to press the Esc key to remove those annoying blue squares. Grips are, however, very useful and can speed up your use of many of the modify commands.

There is no need to change any of the default settings on this side of this tab, but a brief exercise in the use of grips is given here to introduce you to this feature of the AutoCAD program. Other uses of grips will be described later.

 TIP: If grips appear when you do not want them, PRESS: the Esc key.

Step 36. Use grips to change the size of a circle, then move, scale, and rotate several circles at the same time:

Prompt	Response
Command:	With no command active CLICK: **on one of the circles you have drawn**
Small blue squares (grips) appear at each quadrant and at the center of the circle:	CLICK: **one of the grips at one of the quadrants of the circle**
The grip changes color (becomes HOT). Specify stretch point or [Base point/Copy/Undo/eXit]:	**Move your mouse to see that the size of the circle changes, then** TYPE: **3/4<enter>**
The radius of the circle is now 3/4″	CLICK: **Undo** (or TYPE: **U<enter>**) to return the circle to its previous size
Command:	Using a window, SELECT: **all four circles at the bottom of your drawing**
Grips appear at each quadrant and at the centers of all circles:	CLICK: **the grip at the far left quadrant**
The grip changes color (becomes HOT). **STRETCH** Specify stretch point or [Base point/Copy/Undo/eXit]:	PRESS: **the space bar to advance to the MOVE grip mode in the command area**
MOVE Specify move point or [Base point/Copy/Undo/eXit]:	**Move your mouse to the right to see that the circles move with your cursor. You can now** TYPE: **the distance to move the circles or you can** CLICK: **the destination** point. For now, TYPE: **5<enter>** to move the circles 5″ to the right.
With all circles still displaying grips:	CLICK: **the grip at the far left quadrant**
The grip changes color (becomes HOT). **STRETCH** Specify stretch point or [Base point/Copy/Undo/eXit]:	PRESS: **the space bar twice to advance to the ROTATE grip mode**
ROTATE Specify rotation angle or [Base point/Copy/Undo/Reference/eXit]:	**Move your mouse so you can see that the circles are rotated. You can now** TYPE: **an angle or you can** CLICK: **a point to select the angle.** For now, TYPE: **45<enter>** to rotate the circles 45°.
Command:	CLICK: **Undo twice** (or TYPE: **U<enter>twice**) to return the circles to their original position.

There is an additional GRIP mode called MIRROR, which will be used in a later exercise.

Step 37. When you have completed Exercise 3–1, save your drawing in at least two places. Exercise 3–1 is printed in Chapter 5, "Printing and Plotting."

Exercise 3–2: Drawing Arcs, Ellipses, and Solids

When you have completed Exercise 3–2, your drawing will look similar to the drawing in Figure 3–18.

Step 1. Use your workspace to make the following settings:

1. Set drawing Units: **Architectural**
2. Set drawing Limits: **8-1/2,11″**
3. **Use SaveAs... to save the drawing on the hard drive or network drive with the name CH3-EX2.**
4. Set Grid: **1/4″**
5. Set Snap: **1/8″**

FIGURE 3–18
Exercise 4–2: Drawing Arcs, Ellipses, and Solids

6. Create the following Layers:

LAYER NAME	COLOR	LINETYPE
Arcs	Blue	Continuous
Ellipses	Green	Continuous
Solids	Red	Continuous

7. Be sure to use **Zoom-All** to view the entire drawing area.

NOTE: To change a layer name after using New Layer to create layers: Click the layer name to highlight it, click the name again, in the Name: input area, and type over the existing name. You can also name the layers by clicking New and then typing the layer names separated by commas. When you type the comma you move to the next layer.

Undo

Understanding how to use the Undo command can be very helpful while drawing with AutoCAD.

When the Undo button on the Standard toolbar is clicked, the most recent command is undone. To undo more than one command, click the small arrow next to the Undo button to display a list of commands. Click the last command in the list that you want to undo. **Use the Redo button or Redo list on the Standard toolbar to redo as many undos as you need.**

When **U** is typed from the keyboard to the Command: prompt, and the Enter key is pressed (or Undo is selected), the most recent command operation is undone. Most of the time the operation that is undone is obvious, such as when a line that you have just drawn is undone. The most recent mode settings that are not obvious, such as snap, will be undone also. Typing **REDO** and pressing <**enter**> will redo only one undo.

When **U** is typed and entered from the keyboard, no prompt line appears. If **UNDO** is typed and entered, the prompt "Enter the number of operations to undo or [Auto/Control/BEgin/End/Mark/Back] <1>:" appears.

<1>

The default is "<1>." You may enter a number for the number of operations to be undone. For instance, if 5 is entered to the prompt, five operations will be undone. If you decide you went too far, you can type and enter **REDO** or select Redo from the Standard toolbar, and all five operations will be restored.

Typing **U** from the keyboard and pressing the Enter key is the same as entering the number 1 to the Undo prompt. In that instance, **REDO** will redo only one undo, no matter how many times you typed and entered **U**. Right-click menus also have the Undo and Redo commands.

Arc

There are many methods from which to choose when you are drawing arcs. Whatever the situation, you can select a method to suit your needs. Experiment with the different methods described next and decide which ones you prefer to use. Use Figure 3–18 as a guide when locating the arcs on your drawing.

FIGURE 3–19
Draw Arcs Using the
3-Point Method

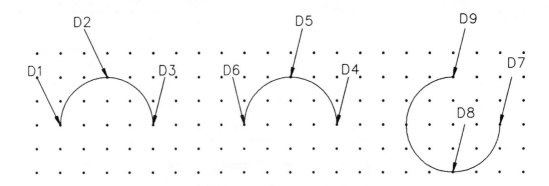

Step 2. On your own:

1. Set Layer Arcs current.
2. Set Blipmode ON.

3-Point

Using the 3-point method, you can draw an arc clockwise or counterclockwise by specifying the start point, second point, and end point of the arc.

Step 3. Draw three arcs using the 3-point method (Figure 3–19):

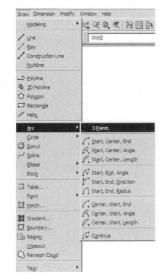

Prompt	Response
Command:	**Arc-3 Points** (or TYPE: **A<enter>**)
Specify start point of arc or [Center]:	**D1** (pick a point five grid marks down (1-1/4″) and three grid marks to the right of the upper left corner of the page)
Specify second point of arc or [Center/End]:	**D2**
Specify endpoint of arc:	**D3**
Command:	**<enter>** (repeat 3 points)
Specify start point of arc or [Center]:	**D4**
Specify second point of arc or [Center/End]:	**D5**
Specify endpoint of arc:	**D6**
Command:	**<enter>** (repeat 3 points)
Specify start point of arc or [Center]:	**D7**
Specify second point of arc or [Center/End]:	**D8**
Specify endpoint of arc:	**D9**

Start, Center, End

The Start, Center, End method allows you to draw an arc only counterclockwise, by specifying the start, center, and end. You can draw the same arc using the Center, Start, End method, which also draws counterclockwise.

Step 4. Draw two arcs using the Start, Center, End method (Figure 3–20):

Prompt	Response
Command:	**Arc-Start, Center, End**
Specify start point of arc or [Center]:	**D1** (pick a point 1-3/4″ below the right end of the first arc drawn)

FIGURE 3–20
Draw Arcs Using the Start,
Center, End Method

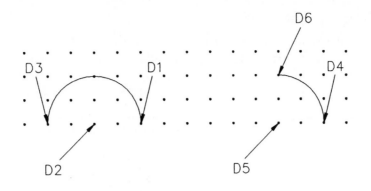

Prompt	Response
Specify second point of arc or [Center/End]:_c Specify center point of arc:	**D2**
Specify endpoint of arc or [Angle/chord Length]:	**D3**
Command:	**Arc-Start, Center, End**
Specify start point of arc or [Center]:	**D4**
Specify second point of arc or [Center/End]:_c Specify center point of arc:	**D5**
Specify endpoint of arc or [Angle/chord Length]:	**D6**

Start, Center, Angle

In the Start, Center, Angle method, A is the included angle (the angle the arc will span). A positive angle will draw the arc counterclockwise; a negative angle will draw the arc clockwise.

Step 5. Draw an arc using the Start, Center, Angle method (Figure 3–21):

Prompt	Response
Command:	**Arc-Start, Center, Angle**
Specify start point of arc or [Center]:	**D1** (2-1/4″ to the right of the last arc drawn)
Specify second point of arc or [Center/End]:_c Specify center point of arc:	**D2** (move mouse up)
Specify endpoint of arc or [Angle/chord Length]: _a Specify included angle:	TYPE: **90<enter>**

FIGURE 3–21
Draw Arcs Using the Start,
Center, Angle and Start,
Center, Length Methods

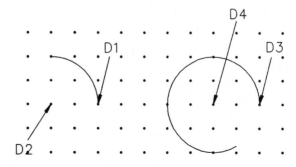

Start, Center, Length

In the Start, Center, Length method, L is the chord length. A *chord* is a straight line that connects an arc's start point and endpoint. A positive chord length can be entered to draw a minor arc (less than 180°), and a negative chord length can be entered to draw a major arc (more than 180°). Both are drawn counterclockwise. See Figure 3–21.

Step 6. Draw an arc using the Start, Center, Length method (Figure 3–21):

Prompt	Response
Command:	**Arc-Start, Center, Length**
Specify start point of arc or [Center]:	**D3**
Specify second point of arc or [Center/End]:_c Specify center point of arc:	**D4**
Specify endpoint of arc or [Angle/chord Length]: _l Specify length of chord:	TYPE: **−1/2<enter>**

Start, End, Angle

With the Start, End, Angle method, after the start point and endpoint of the arc have been picked, a positive angle draws the arc counterclockwise; a negative angle keeps the same start and endpoints but draws the reverse arc or draws clockwise.

Start, End, Radius

In the Start, End, Radius method, Radius is the arc radius. When you use this method, enter a positive radius to draw a minor arc (less than 180°), and enter a negative radius to draw a major arc (more than 180°). Both are drawn counterclockwise.

Start, End, Direction

In this method, Direction is the specified direction that the arc takes, from the start point. The direction is specified in degrees. You can also specify the direction by pointing to a single point. Major, minor, counterclockwise, and clockwise arcs can be drawn with the Start, End, Direction method.

Continue

If Continue is picked at the first prompt of any of the arc methods that start with S, the new arc starts at the endpoint of the last arc or line drawn. Pressing the Enter key has the same effect. The new arc's direction follows the direction of the last arc or line drawn.

Ellipse

Look at Figure 3–18 to determine the approximate location of the ellipses drawn with the Ellipse command.

Step 7. Set Layer Ellipses current.

Axis, End

The minor axis of an ellipse is its smaller axis, and the major axis is the larger axis.

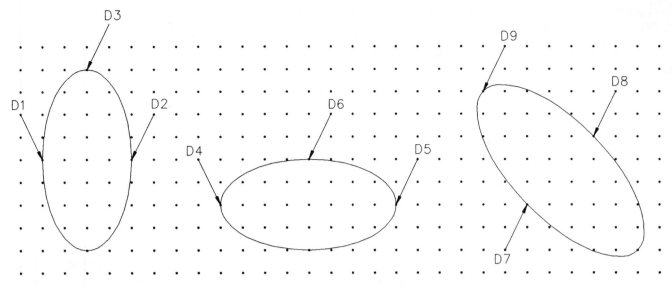

FIGURE 3–22
Draw an Ellipse by Entering Points for the Minor and Major Axes of the Ellipse, and Draw an Ellipse at an Angle

Step 8. Draw an ellipse by entering points for the minor axis of the ellipse (Figure 3–22):

Prompt	Response
Command:	Ellipse-Axis, End (or TYPE: **EL**<enter>)
Specify axis endpoint of ellipse or [Arc/Center]:	D1
Specify other endpoint of axis:	D2
Specify distance to other axis or [Rotation]:	D3

Step 9. Draw an ellipse by entering points for the major axis of the ellipse (Figure 3–22):

Prompt	Response
Command:	Ellipse-Axis, End
Specify axis endpoint of ellipse or [Arc/Center]:	D4
Specify other endpoint of axis:	D5
Specify distance to other axis or [Rotation]:	D6

Step 10. Draw an ellipse at an angle by entering points for the minor axis of the ellipse (Figure 3–22):

Prompt	Response
Command:	Ellipse-Axis, End
Specify axis endpoint of ellipse or [Arc/Center]:	D7
Specify other endpoint of axis:	D8
Specify distance to other axis or [Rotation]:	D9

FIGURE 3–23
Draw Ellipses by Specifying
the Rotation Angle

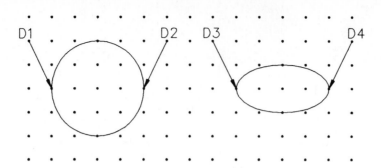

Rotation Arc

The Rotation arc option specifies an actual rotation into the third dimension, around the major axis. To visualize this, hold a coin between two fingers and rotate it.

Step 11. Draw two ellipses by entering points for the major axis and specifying the rotation angle around the major axis (Figure 3–23):

Prompt	Response
Command:	**Ellipse-Axis,End**
Specify axis endpoint of ellipse or [Arc/Center]:	**D1**
Specify other endpoint of axis:	**D2**
Specify distance to other axis or [Rotation]:	TYPE: **R<enter>** (rotation changes the minor axis to the major axis)
Specify rotation around major axis:	TYPE: **0<enter>** (a 0° ellipse is a circle)
Command:	**<enter>** (repeat Axis, End)
Specify axis endpoint of ellipse or [Arc/Center]:	**D3**
Specify other endpoint of axis:	**D4**
Specify distance to other axis or [Rotation]:	TYPE: **R<enter>**
Specify rotation around major axis:	TYPE: **60<enter>**

Center

You may also draw an ellipse by specifying the center point, the endpoint of one axis, and the length of the other axis. Type **C** and press <enter> to the prompt "Specify axis endpoint of ellipse or [Arc/Center]:" to start with the center of the ellipse. Entering the center point first is similar to the first two methods described above, and either the minor or major axis may be constructed first. As with all methods of drawing an ellipse, you can specify the points either by clicking a point on the drawing or by typing and entering coordinates.

Donut

Look at Figure 3–18 to determine the approximate location of the solid ring and solid circle drawn using the Donut command.

Step 12. Set Layer Solids current.

FIGURE 3–24
Use the Donut Command to
Draw a Solid Ring and a Solid
Circle

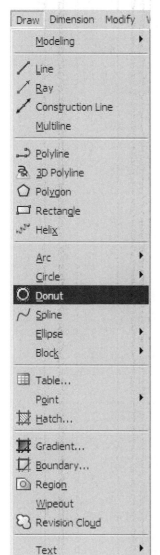

Draw Dimension Modify

- Modeling ▸
- / Line
- / Ray
- / Construction Line
- Multiline
- ⌐⌐ Polyline
- ⅗ 3D Polyline
- ⬡ Polygon
- ▭ Rectangle
- ⸜ Helix
- Arc ▸
- Circle ▸
- ○ **Donut**
- ∿ Spline
- Ellipse ▸
- Block ▸
- ▦ Table...
- Point ▸
- ▨ Hatch...
- ▨ Gradient...
- ▱ Boundary...
- ◎ Region
- Wipeout
- ☁ Revision Cloud
- Text ▸

Step 13. Use the Donut command to draw a solid ring (Figure 3–24):

Prompt	Response
Command:	**Donut** (or TYPE: **DO**<enter>)
Specify inside diameter of donut <default>:	TYPE: **1/2**<enter>
Specify outside diameter of donut <default>:	TYPE: **1**<enter>:
Specify center of donut or <exit>:	CLICK: **a point on the drawing**
Specify center of donut or <exit>:	<enter>

Step 14. Use the Donut command to draw a solid circle (Figure 3–24):

Prompt	Response
Command:	<enter> (Repeat donut)
Specify inside diameter of donut <0'-0 1/2">:	TYPE: **0**<enter> (so there is no center hole)
Specify outside diameter of donut <0'-1">:	<enter>
Specify center of donut or <exit>:	CLICK: **a point on the drawing**
Specify center of donut or <exit>:	<enter>

Donut can be used to draw solid dots of any size as well as solid rings with different inside and outside diameters.

2D Solid

With the 2D Solid command you can draw angular solid shapes by entering them as three-sided (triangle) or four-sided (square and rectangle) sections. The trick with the 2D Solid command is entering the third point; to draw a square or a rectangle, you must pick the third point diagonally opposite the second point. If four points are picked in a clockwise or counterclockwise progression, a bow-tie shape is drawn.

In the following part of this exercise, first, the 2D Solid command will be used to draw a solid rectangle and a solid triangle at the bottom of the page. Second, the Scale command will be used to reduce the rectangle and enlarge the triangle.

Step 15. Use the 2D Solid command to draw a solid rectangle (Figure 3–25):

Prompt	Response
Command:	TYPE: **SO**<enter>
Specify first point:	**D1** (Be sure Snap is ON)
Specify second point:	**D2**
Specify third point:	**D3** (notice that D3 is diagonally opposite D2)
Specify fourth point or <exit>:	**D4**
Specify third point:	<enter>

FIGURE 3–25
Use the 2D Solid Command
to Draw a Solid Rectangle
and a Solid Triangle

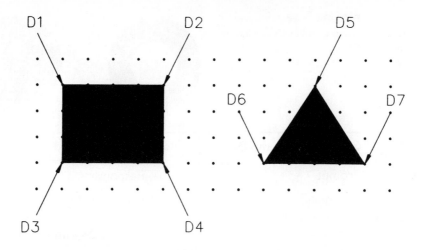

Step 16. Use the Solid command to draw a solid triangle (Figure 3–25).

Prompt	Response
Command:	<enter> (repeat Solid)
Specify first point:	**D5**
Specify second point:	**D6**
Specify third point:	**D7**
Specify fourth point or <exit>:	<enter>
Specify third point:	<enter>

When the "Third point:" prompt appears a second time, you can continue with another section of the shape or press Enter to complete a shape.

Fill ON and Fill OFF

The options FILL ON and FILL OFF affect both the Donut and the 2D Solid commands and any other "filled" areas.

Step 17. On your own:

1. TYPE: FILL<enter>, then TYPE: OFF<enter>, and then TYPE: RE<enter> to regenerate the drawing. All the shapes made with the Donut and 2D Solid commands will no longer be solid.
2. TYPE: FILL<enter>, then ON<enter> to make them solid again.
3. Regenerate the drawing.

Scale

The Scale command lets you reduce or enlarge either drawing entities or an entire drawing. The Copy option of the Scale command allows you to copy and enlarge or reduce the object at the same time.

FIGURE 3–26
Use the Scale Command to
Reduce the Solid Rectangle
and Enlarge the Solid Triangle

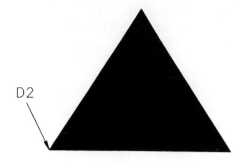

D1   D2

<Scale factor>

Step 18. Use the Scale command to reduce the solid rectangle (Figure 3–26).

Prompt	Response
Command:	**Scale** (or TYPE: **SC<enter>**)
Select objects:	**Window the rectangle** (or click the outside edge of the solid).
Select objects:	**<enter>**
Specify base point:	**D1**
Specify scale factor or [Copy/Reference]:	TYPE: **.5<enter>**

The relative scale factor of .5 was used to reduce the rectangle. A relative scale factor of 2 would have enlarged the rectangle.

Reference

Step 19. Use the Scale command to enlarge the solid triangle (Figure 3–26).

Prompt	Response
Command:	**<enter>** (Repeat SCALE)
Select objects:	**Window the triangle**
Select objects:	**<enter>**
Specify base point:	**D2**
Specify scale factor or [Copy/Reference]:	TYPE: **R<enter>**
Specify reference length <1>:	**<enter>** (to accept 1 as the default)
Specify new length:	TYPE: **2<enter>**

The Reference option allows you to type and enter a number for the Reference (current) length of a drawing entity. You can also enter the Reference (current) length by picking two points on the drawing to show AutoCAD the Reference (current) length. You can type and enter the new length by using a number, or you can enter it by picking two points on the drawing to show the new length.

Step 20. When you have completed Exercise 3–2, save your drawing in at least two places. You can plot Exercise 3–2 after completing Chapter 5, "Printing and Plotting."

FIGURE 3–27
Exercise 3–3: Drawing
Shapes I

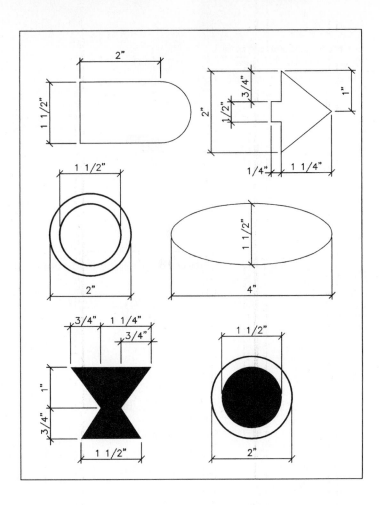

Exercise 3–3:   Drawing Shapes I

Draw, full size, the shapes shown in Figure 3–27. Use the dimensions shown. Locate the shapes approximately as shown. Use your workspace and the A-Size template created in Chapter 2, Exercise 1, or make the following settings:

1. **Use SaveAs... to save the drawing on the hard drive with the name CH3-EX3.**
2. Set drawing Units: **Architectural**
3. Set Drawing Limits: **8-1/2,11**
4. Set GRIDDISPLAY: **0**
5. Set Grid: **1/4″**
6. Set Snap: **1/8″**
7. Create the following Layers:

LAYER NAME	COLOR	LINETYPE
Single	Blue	Continuous
Solid	Red	Continuous

Exercise 3–4:   Drawing a Pattern

Draw the pattern design shown in Figure 3–28. Use an architectural scale to measure the pattern design and draw it full scale. Your drawing will be the size shown in the figure. Use your workspace and the A-Size template created in Chapter 2, Exercise 1, or make the following settings:

1. **Use SaveAs... to save the drawing on the hard drive with the name CH3-EX4.**
2. Set drawing Units: **Architectural**

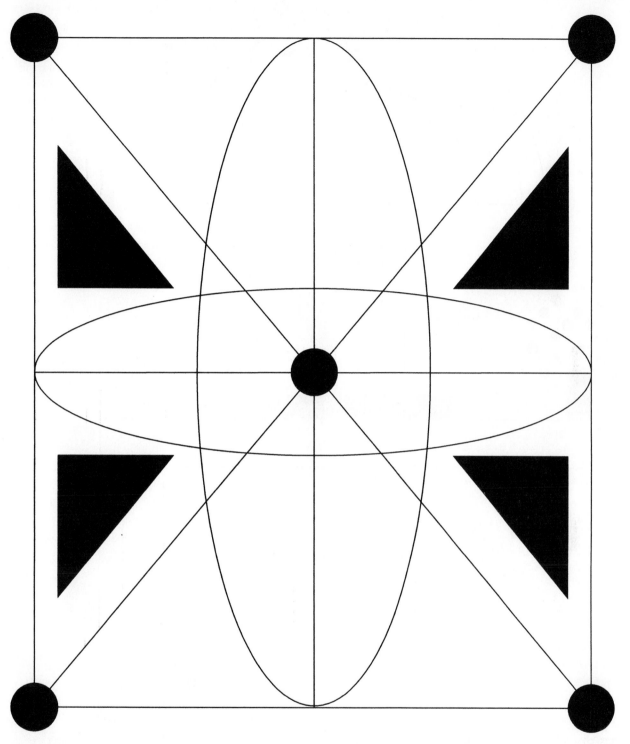

FIGURE 3–28
Exercise 3–4: Drawing a Pattern (Full Scale)

3. Set Drawing Limits: **8-1/2,11**
4. Set GRIDDISPLAY: **0**
5. Set Grid: **1/4″**
6. Set Snap: **1/8″**
7. **Create the Layers on your own.**

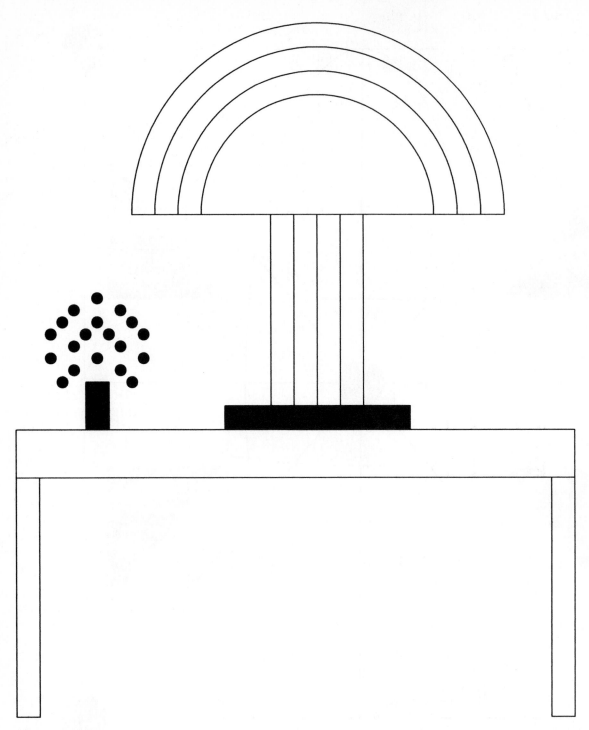

FIGURE 3–29
Exercise 3–5: Drawing Shapes II (Full Scale)

Exercise 3–5: Drawing Shapes II

Draw the shapes shown in Figure 3–29. Use an architectural scale to measure the shapes and draw them full scale. Your drawing will be the size shown in the figure. Use your workspace and the A-Size template created in Chapter 2, Exercise 1, or make the following settings:

1. **Use SaveAs... to save the drawing on the hard drive with the name CH3-EX5.**
2. Set drawing Units: **Architectural**
3. Set Drawing Limits: **8-1/2,11**

4. Set GRIDDISPLAY: **0**
5. Set Grid: **1/4″**
6. Set Snap: **1/8″**
7. **Create the Layers on your own.**

Exercise 3–6: Drawing a Door

Draw the door shape shown in Figure 3–30. Use an architectural scale to measure the figure and draw it full scale. Use your workspace and the A-size template created in Chapter 2, Exercise 1, or make the following settings:

1. **Use Save As… to save the drawing on the hard drive with the name CH3-EX6.**
2. Set drawing Units: **Arcitectural**

FIGURE 3–30
Exercise 3–6: Drawing a Door (Full Scale)

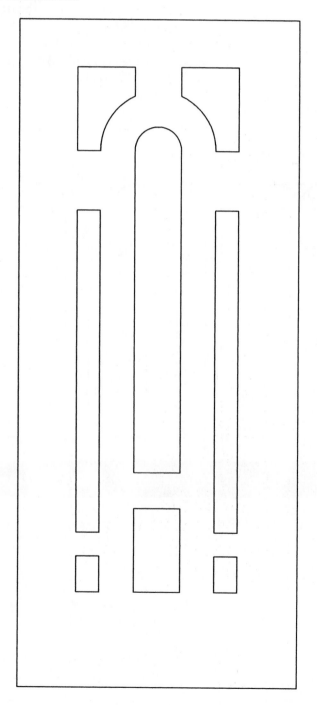

3. Set Drawing Limits: **8-1/2,11**
4. Set GRIDDISPLAY: **0**
5. Set Grid: **1/4″**
6. Set Snap: **1/8″**
7. **Create the Layers on your own.**

Exercise 3–7:   Drawing Shapes III

Draw the shape shown in Figure 3–31. Use an architectural scale to measure the figure and draw it full scale. Use your workspace and the A-Size template created in Chapter 2, Exercise 1, or make the following settings:

1. **Use SaveAs… to save the drawing on the hard drive with the name CH3-EX7.**
2. Set drawing Units: **Architectural**
3. Set Drawing Limits: **8-1/2,11**
4. Set GRIDDISPLAY: **0**
5. Set Grid **1/4″**
6. Set Snap: **1/8″**
7. **Create the Layers on your own.**

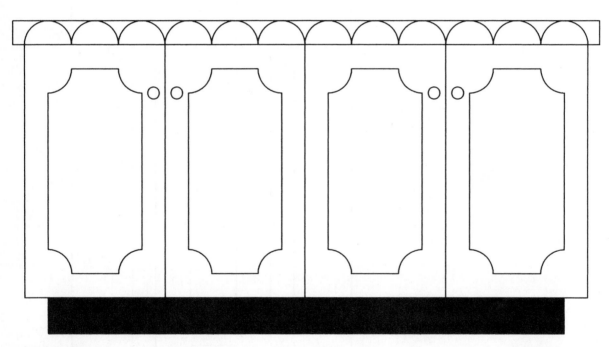

FIGURE 3–31
Exercise 3–7: Drawing Shapes III (Full Scale)

1. When an existing drawing is stored on a disk, you should open the drawing and immediately save it on the hard disk.
   a. True   b. False

2. To make the line segment length and spacing larger for a dashed linetype, enter a number higher than 1 to the Ltscale prompt "Enter new linetype scale factor <1.0000>:".
   a. True   b. False

3. Always use the Zoom-All command after setting up a new drawing.
   a. True   b. False

4. Snap may be turned OFF and ON while you are drawing.
   a. True   b. False

5. When the Copy command is used with a selection window (CLICK: left, drag right)—not a crossing window,
   a. Everything the window touches is selected.
   b. Everything entirely within the window is selected.
   c. The last item clicked is selected.
   d. The entire screen is selected.
   e. Nothing is selected.

6. When the Copy command is used with a crossing window (CLICK: right, drag left),
   a. Everything the window touches is selected.
   b. Everything entirely within the window is selected.
   c. The last item clicked is selected.
   d. The entire screen is selected.
   e. Nothing is selected.

7. Many of the Modify commands use the same variety of subcommands to select the object or objects to be edited. Which of the following options is not used to select the objects to be edited?
   a. Window   d. Crossing
   b. Remove   e. Add
   c. Circle

8. The 3-point method of drawing arcs allows you to draw arcs clockwise or counterclockwise.
   a. True   b. False

9. The Reference option of the Scale command allows you to pick two points on the drawing to show AutoCAD the current length of the drawing entity to be reduced or enlarged.
   a. True   b. False

10. Pressing the Esc key cancels a command.
    a. True   b. False

Complete.

11. Name the dialog box that has the settings that control what happens when the right mouse button is clicked.

   _____

12. Using relative coordinates to draw a 3″ square, write the information you type and enter in response to the Command: line prompt "Specify next point or [Undo]:" after the first point of the square has been clicked. Draw the square to the right and up.

   1. _____
   2. _____
   3. _____
   4. _____

13. Using absolute coordinates to draw a 3″ square, write the information that you type and enter in response to the Command: line prompt "Specify next point or [Undo]:" after the first point of the square has been clicked. The first point of the square is at coordinates 4,4. Draw the square to the right and up.

   1. _____
   2. _____
   3. _____
   4. _____

14. Using polar coordinates to draw a 3″ square, write the information that you type and enter in response to the Command: line prompt "Specify next point or [Undo]:" after the first point of the square has been clicked. Draw the square to the right and up.

   1. _____
   2. _____
   3. _____
   4. _____

15. Write the name of the command that you use to turn ON (or OFF) blips that AutoCAD makes when a point is entered on a drawing.

   _____

16. Write the name of the function key that can be pressed twice to redraw the screen.

   _____

17. Write the name of the function key that when pressed helps to draw lines perfectly, horizontally and vertically.

   _____

18. Describe what Direction means in the arc method Start, End, Direction.

_____

_____

_____

_____

19. Describe what Length means in the arc method Start, Center, Length.

_____

_____

_____

_____

20. Write the name of the small squares that appear on an object when it is selected with no command active.

_____

21. Name the Zoom command option that displays only the objects actually drawn on the page.

_____

22. Describe what is meant by a transparent command.

_____

_____

23. When using the Move command, and AutoCAD prompts for the second point of displacement, describe four methods you can use to give the second point of displacement.

_____

_____

_____

_____

24. Describe how the Reference option of the Scale command works.

_____

_____

25. What is the inside diameter size of the donut when the Donut command is used to draw a solid circle?

_____

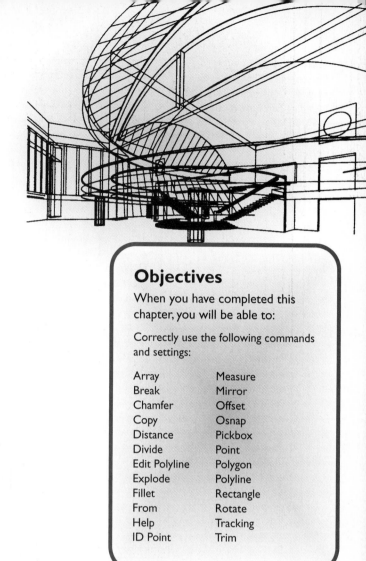

Chapter

4

Drawing with AutoCAD: Conference and Lecture Rooms

Objectives

When you have completed this chapter, you will be able to:

Correctly use the following commands and settings:

Array	Measure
Break	Mirror
Chamfer	Offset
Copy	Osnap
Distance	Pickbox
Divide	Point
Edit Polyline	Polygon
Explode	Polyline
Fillet	Rectangle
From	Rotate
Help	Tracking
ID Point	Trim

Exercise 4–1: Drawing a Rectangular Conference Room, Including Furniture

A conference room, including walls and furnishings, is drawn in Exercise 4–1. When you have completed Exercise 4–1, your drawing will look similar to Figure 4–1.

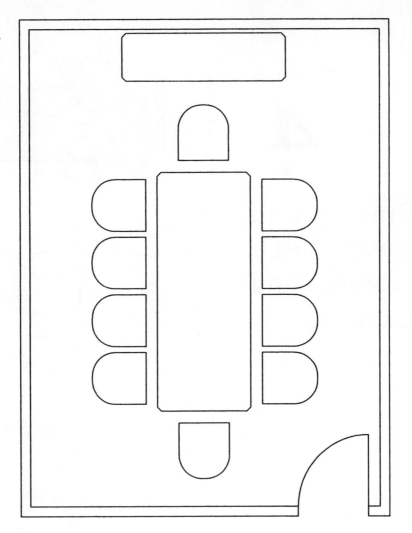

Step 1.   Use your workspace to make the following settings:

1. **Use SaveAs... to save the drawing with the name CH4-EX1.**
2. Set drawing Units: **Architectural**
3. Set Drawing Limits: **25′,35′** (Don't forget the foot mark.)
4. Set GRID DISPLAY: **0**
5. Set Grid: **12″**
6. Set Snap: **6″**
7. Create the following Layers:

LAYER NAME	COLOR	LINETYPE
Walls	White	Continuous
Furniture	Red	Continuous

8. Set **Layer Walls** current.
9. Use **Zoom-All** to view the limits of the drawing.

Polyline

We will begin by drawing the conference room walls using the Polyline command. Polylines are different from regular lines in that regardless of the number of segments that make up a polyline, AutoCAD treats a polyline drawn with one operation of the

Polyline command as a single entity. This is especially helpful when you are drawing walls, because after you draw the outline of a single room or entire building, you can offset the entire polyline to show the thickness of the walls. Any of the various line-types may be drawn with Polyline, but the CONTINUOUS linetype will be used to draw the walls of the conference room.

Step 2. Use Polyline to draw the inside lines of the conference room walls (Figure 4–2):

Prompt	Response
Command:	**Polyline** (or TYPE: **PL <enter>**)
Specify start point:	TYPE: **5′,5′ <enter>**
	(You have just entered absolute coordinates; the polyline starts 5′ to the right on the X axis and 5′ up on the Y axis.)
	Set ORTHO ON (PRESS: **F8** or CLICK: **ORTHO**)
Current line-width is 0′-0″.	
Specify next point or [Arc/Halfwidth/ Length/Undo/Width]:	**Move your mouse to the right and** TYPE: **15′ <enter>** (direct distance entry)

FIGURE 4–2
Draw the Conference Room Walls

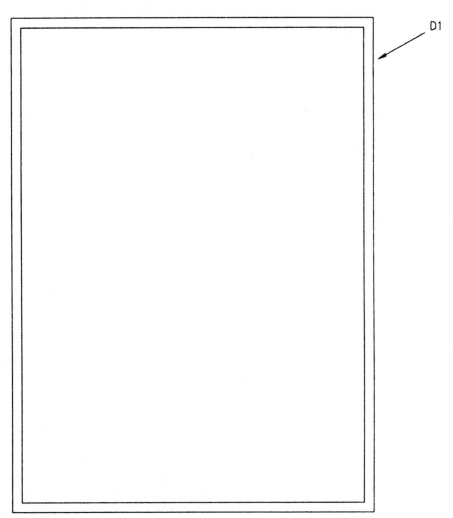

D1

Prompt	Response
Specify next point or [Arc/Close/ Halfwidth/Length/Undo/Width]:	**Move your mouse up and** TYPE: **20′ <enter>**
Specify next point or [Arc/Close/ Halfwidth/Length/Undo/Width]:	**Move your mouse to the left and** TYPE: **15′ <enter>**
Specify next point or [Arc/Close/ Halfwidth/Length/Undo/Width]:	TYPE: **C <enter>**

Undo

The Polyline Undo option is similar to the Line command: If you do not like the last polyline segment drawn, use the Undo option to erase it and continue with the "Specify next point or [Arc/Close/Halfwidth/Length/Undo/Width]:" prompt.

You can enter all the options in the Polyline prompt from the keyboard by typing (upper- or lowercase) the letters that are capitalized in each option. The remaining options in the Polyline prompt will be described later in this chapter.

Offset

Because the polyline is treated as a single entity, when you click one point on the polyline, you are able to offset the entire outline of the conference room at once. If the outline of the room had been drawn with the Line command, using Offset would offset each line segment individually, and the corners would not meet.

Step 3. Use Offset to draw the outside line (showing depth) of the conference room walls (Figure 4–2):

Prompt	Response
Command:	**Offset** (or TYPE: **O <enter>**)
Specify offset distance or [Through/ Erase/Layer] <Through>:	TYPE: **5 <enter>**
Select object to offset or [Exit/Undo] <Exit>:	CLICK: **anyplace on the polyline**
Specify point on side to offset or [Exit/Multiple/Undo] <Exit>:	**D1** (outside of the rectangle)
Select object to offset or [Exit/Undo] <Exit>:	**<enter>**

There are four options in the Offset prompt, offset distance, Through, Erase, and Layer. To complete the conference room walls, 5″ was set as the offset distance. When the option Through is used, you click the object you want to offset and then click a point on the drawing through which you want the object to be offset. Erase allows you to erase the source object, and Layer allows you to leave the object on the same layer as the source object or place it on the current layer.

Explode

Because the polyline is treated as a single entity, it must be "exploded" before individual line segments can be edited. The Explode command splits the solid polyline into separate line segments. After the polyline is exploded into separate line segments, you will be able to add the conference room door.

Step 4. Use Explode to split the two polylines that make the conference room walls:

Prompt	Response
Command:	**Explode** (or TYPE: **X <enter>**)
Select objects:	CLICK: **anyplace on the outside polyline**
Select objects:	CLICK: **anyplace on the inside polyline**
Select objects:	**<enter>**

After you use the Explode command, the walls do not look different, but each line segment is now a separate entity.

ID Point

A very useful command, ID Point allows you to locate a point on a drawing and have the position of the point displayed in coordinates. AutoCAD remembers the coordinate location of the point. A command, such as Line, can be initiated *immediately* after the ID Point command has located a point on the drawing. You can enter the start point of the Line command by using relative or polar coordinates, or you may also use direct distance entry, to specify a distance from the established ID Point location.

Step 5. On your own:

1. Use Zoom-Window to magnify the lower right corner of the conference room where the door will be located.

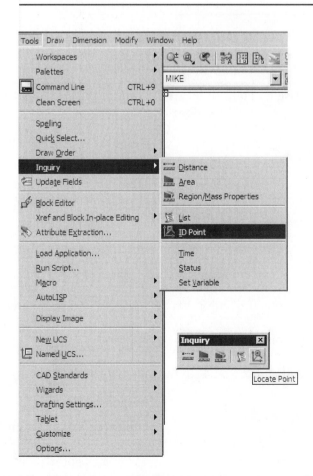

FIGURE 4–3
Draw the Door Opening and
Door; Draw a Credenza and
Conference Table

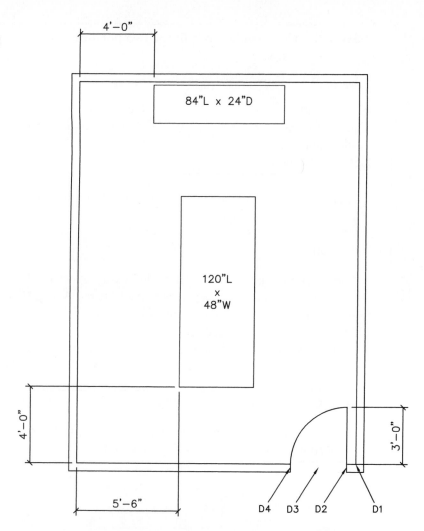

4'–0"

84"L x 24"D

120"L
x
48"W

4'–0"

3'–0"

5'–6"

D4   D3   D2   D1

Step 6. Use ID Point to locate a point on the drawing. Use Line to draw the
right side of the door opening (Figure 4–3):

Prompt	Response
Command:	**ID Point** (or TYPE: **ID** <enter>)
Specify point:	**D1** (with SNAP ON, snap to the inside lower right corner of the conference room)
Point: X = 20'-0" Y = 5'-0" Z = 0'-0"	
Command:	TYPE: **L** <enter>
Specify first point:	TYPE: **@6<180** <enter> (you have just entered polar coordinates; move your mouse so you can see where the line is attached)
Specify next point or [Undo]:	TYPE: **@5<−90** <enter> (using polar coordinates; the line goes down 5")
Specify next point or [Undo]:	<enter>

Step 7. Offset the line 3' to the left to form the door opening:

Prompt	Response
Command:	**Offset** (or TYPE: **O** <enter>)
Specify offset distance or [Through/ Erase/Layer] <0'-5">:	TYPE: **3'** <enter>

Prompt	Response
Select object to offset or [Exit/Undo]<Exit>:	D2 (the 5″ line you just drew; turn SNAP OFF if necessary)
Specify point on side to offset or [Exit/Multiple/Undo]<Exit>:	D3 (to the left)
Select object to offset or [Exit/Undo]<Exit>:	<enter>

Trim

Step 8. Use Trim to trim the horizontal wall lines between the two 5″ vertical lines that represent the door opening (Figure 4–3):

Prompt	Response
Command:	**Trim** (or TYPE: **TR** <**enter**>)
Current settings: Projection = UCS Edge = None	
Select cutting edges	
Select objects or <select all>:	D2 (the 5″ vertical line)
Select objects: 1 found	
Select objects:	D4 (the second 5″ vertical line)
Select objects: 1 found, 2 total	
Select objects:	<enter>
Select object to trim or shift-select to extend or [Fence/Crossing/ Project/Edge/eRase/Undo]:	**Click the two horizontal wall lines between D2 and D4.**
	<enter> (to complete the command; if you turned SNAP OFF to pick the lines, be sure to turn it back ON)

 NOTE: Press Enter to the Trim prompt "Select objects or <select all>:" to select all objects as possible cutting edges.

Watch the Trim prompts carefully. Not until all cutting edges have been selected and the Enter key is pressed, so that the prompt "Select object to trim or shift-select to extend or [Fence/Crossing/Project/Edge/eRase/Undo]:" appears, can you pick the objects to trim. If you are unable to trim an entity because it does not intersect a cutting edge, hold the Shift key down and click on the entity to extend while still in the Trim command.

Step 9. On your own:

See Figure 4–3.

1. Use Zoom–Window to zoom in on the lower right door area of the room. Use the Line command to draw a 3′ vertical door line. Snap (be sure SNAP is ON) to the upper right corner of the door opening to begin the door line. Draw the line using polar coordinates or direct distance entry.

2. Use the Arc-Start, Center, End method to draw the door swing arc, counter-clockwise. Note that the start of the arc is the top of the door line, the center is the bottom of the door line, and the end is the upper left corner of the door opening.

3. Change the current layer to Furniture. Use Zoom-Extents.

4. Use the Polyline command to draw a credenza (84″ long by 24″ deep) centered on the 15′ rear wall of the conference room, 2″ away from the wall. Locate an ID point by snapping to the inside upper left corner of the conference room. Start the Polyline @48,−2 (relative coordinates) away from the point. Finish drawing the credenza by using direct distance entry or polar coordinates. Use your own personal preference to enter feet or inches. Remember, AutoCAD defaults to inches in Architectural Units, so use the foot (′) symbol if you are using feet. Be sure to draw the credenza using one operation of Polyline so it is one continuous polyline. *Use the Close option for the last segment of the polyline.*

5. Draw a conference table 120″ long by 48″ wide using the Line command. You can determine the location of the first point by using ID Point or by using grid and snap increments. Use direct distance entry or polar coordinates to complete the table. Refer to Figure 4–3 for the location of the table in the room.

6. Use Zoom-Window to zoom in on the table.

NOTE: Remember to use the Zoom commands to move about your drawing.

Chamfer

A chamfer is an angle (usually 45°) formed at a corner. The following will use the Chamfer command to make the beveled corners of the conference table and credenza.

Step 10. Use Chamfer to bevel the corners of the table (Figure 4–4):

Prompt	Response
Command:	**Chamfer** (or TYPE: **CHA** <enter>)
(TRIM mode) Current chamfer Dist1 = 0′-0″ Dist2 = 0′-0″ Select first line or [Undo/Polyline/ Distance/Angle/Trim/mEthod/ Multiple]:	TYPE: **D** <enter>
Specify first chamfer distance <0′-0″>:	TYPE: **2** <enter>
Specify second chamfer distance <0′-2″>:	<enter>
Select first line or [Undo/Polyline/ Distance/Angle/Trim/mEthod/ Multiple]:	D1
Select second line:	D2
Command:	<enter> (repeat CHAMFER)

FIGURE 4–4
Bevel the Corners of the
Table and Credenza; Draw a
Rectangle Shape

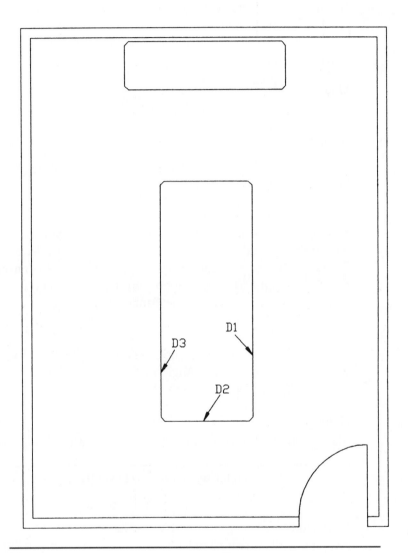

Prompt	Response
(TRIM mode) Current chamfer Dist1 = 0'-2", Dist2 = 0'-2"	
Select first line or [Undo/Polyline/ Distance/Angle/Trim/mEthod/ Multiple]:	**D2**
Select second line:	**D3**

TIP: TYPE: M <**enter**> (for Multiple) at the chamfer prompt so you do not have to repeat entering the Chamfer command.

Step 11. On your own:

1. Chamfer the other corners of the table (Figure 4–4).
2. Use Zoom-Dynamic to zoom in on the credenza.

Polyline

Because the credenza was drawn using one operation of the Polyline command, and the Close option was used to complete the credenza rectangle, it is treated as a single entity. The Chamfer command Polyline option chamfers all corners of a continuous polyline with one click.

Undo

Allows you to undo the previous chamfer.

Angle

This option of the Chamfer command allows you to specify an angle and a distance to create a chamfer.

Trim

This option of both the Chamfer and Fillet commands allows you to specify that the part of the original line removed by the chamfer or fillet remains as it was. To do this, TYPE: **T <enter>** at the Chamfer prompt and **N <enter>** at the Trim/No trim <Trim>: prompt. Test this option on a corner of the drawing so you know how it works. Be sure to return it to the Trim option.

mEthod

The mEthod option of the Chamfer command allows you to specify whether you want to use the Distance or the Angle method to specify how the chamfer is to be drawn. The default is the Distance method.

Multiple

Allows you to chamfer multiple corners without repeating the chamfer command.

Step 12. Use Chamfer distance 2″ to bevel the corners of the credenza (Figure 4–4):

Prompt	Response
Command:	**Chamfer**
(TRIM mode) Current chamfer Dist1 = 0′-2″, Dist2 = 0′-2″	
Select first line or [Undo/Polyline/ Distance/Angle/Trim/mEthod/ multiple]:	TYPE: **P <enter>** (accept 2″ distances as previously set)
Select 2D polyline:	CLICK: **anyplace on the credenza line.**
4 lines were chamfered	

NOTE: If the last corner of the credenza does not chamfer, this is because the Close option of the Polyline command was not used to complete the polyline rectangle. Explode the credenza and use the Chamfer command to complete the chamfered corner.

When setting the chamfer distance, you can set a different distance for the first and second chamfers. The first distance applies to the first line clicked, and the second distance applies to the second line clicked. You can also set the distance by clicking two points on the drawing.

You can set a chamfer distance of zero and use it to remove the chamfered corners from the table. Using a distance of zero will make 90° corners on the table. Then you can erase the old chamfer lines. This will change the table but not the credenza, because it does not work with a polyline. If you have two lines that do not meet to form an exact corner or that overlap, use the Chamfer command with 0 distance to form an exact corner. The Chamfer command will chamfer two lines that do not intersect. It automatically extends the two lines until they intersect, trims the two lines according to the distance entered, and connects the two trimmed ends with the chamfer line.

 NOTE: Save your drawing often so you do not lose your work.

Step 13. On your own:

See Figure 4–4.

1. Zoom in on a portion of the grid outside the conference room walls.
2. Draw a rectangle 26″ wide by 28″ deep using the Line command. Be sure to have SNAP ON when you draw the rectangle. You will now edit this rectangle using the Fillet command to create the shape of a chair.

 NOTE: Remember to turn Snap OFF and ON as needed. Turn Snap OFF when it interferes with selecting an entity. Turn it back on as needed.

Fillet

The Fillet command is similar to Chamfer, except the Fillet command creates a round instead of an angle.

Step 14. Use Fillet to edit the back of the rectangle to create the symbol of a chair (Figure 4–5):

Prompt	Response
Command:	**Fillet** (or TYPE: **F** <enter>)
Current settings: Mode = TRIM, Radius = 0′-0 1/2″	
Select first object or [Undo/ Polyline/Radius/Trim/Multiple]:	TYPE: **R** <enter>
Specify fillet radius <0′-0″>:	TYPE: **12** <enter>
Select first object or [Undo/ Polyline/Radius/Trim/Multiple]:	TYPE: **T** <enter>

FIGURE 4–5
Use Fillet to Create the
Chair Symbol

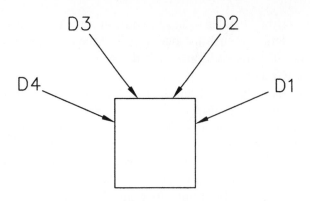

Prompt	Response
Enter Trim mode option [Trim/No trim]<Trim>:	TYPE: **T** **<enter>** (verify Trim option)
Select first object or [Undo/ Polyline/Radius/Trim/Multiple]:	**D1**
Select second object:	**D2**
Command:	**<enter>** (repeat Fillet)
Current settings: Mode = TRIM, Radius = 1'-0"	
Select first object or [Undo/ Polyline/Radius/Trim/Multiple]:	**D3**
Select second object:	**D4**

The Polyline option of Fillet automatically fillets an entire continuous polyline with one click. Remember to set the fillet radius first.

Fillet will also fillet two circles, two arcs, a line and a circle, a line and an arc, or a circle and an arc.

Copy and Osnap-Midpoint

The Copy command allows you to copy any part of a drawing either once or multiple times. Object Snap modes when combined with other commands help you to draw very accurately. As you become more familiar with the Object Snap modes you will use them constantly to draw with extreme accuracy. The following introduces the Osnap-Midpoint mode, which helps you to snap to the midpoint of a line or arc.

Step 15. **Use the Copy command, combined with Osnap-Midpoint, to copy three times the chair you have just drawn (Figure 4–6):**

Prompt	Response
Command:	**Copy** (or TYPE: **CP <enter>**)
Select objects:	CLICK: **the first corner of a window that will include the chair**
Specify opposite corner:	CLICK: **the other corner of the window to include the chair**
Select objects:	**<enter>**
Specify base point or [Displacement]<Displacement>:	TYPE: **MID <enter>**
Mid of	**D1**

FIGURE 4–6
Copy the Chair Three Times; Use
Rotate to Rotate the Chairs

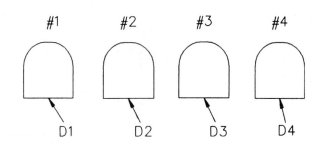

Prompt	Response
Specify second point or <use first point as displacement>:	**D2,D3,D4** (be sure SNAP is ON, and leave enough room to rotate the chairs, Figure 4–7)
Specify second point of displacement:	**<enter>**

The Osnap-Midpoint mode helped you snap very accurately to the midpoint of the line; you used the midpoint of the line that defines the front of the chair as the base point. When using the Copy command, carefully choose the base point so that it helps you easily locate the copies.

Rotate

The Rotate command rotates a selected drawing entity in the counterclockwise direction; 90° is to the left, and 270° (or −90°) is to the right. You select a base point of the entity to be rotated, and the entity rotates about that base point.

Step 16. Use the Rotate command to rotate chairs 2 and 3 (Figure 4–7):

Prompt	Response
Command:	**Rotate** (or TYPE: **RO <enter>**)
Select objects:	**Start the window to include chair 2.**
Specify opposite corner:	**Complete the window to include chair 2.**
Select objects:	**<enter>**
Specify base point:	TYPE: **MID <enter>**
Mid of	**D2** (Figure 4–6)
Specify rotation angle or [Copy/Reference]:	TYPE: **90 <enter>**
Command:	**<enter>** (Repeat ROTATE)
Select objects:	**Window chair 3**
Select objects:	**<enter>**

FIGURE 4–7
Rotated Chairs

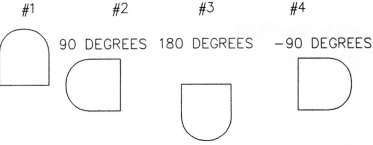

Prompt	Response
Specify base point: mid of Specify rotation angle or [Copy/Reference]:	TYPE: **MID** <enter> **D3** (Figure 4–6) TYPE: **180** <enter>

NOTE: If part of the entity that is to be rotated lies on the specified base point, that part of the entity remains on the base point while the entity's orientation is changed.

Step 17. On your own:

See Figure 4–7.

1. **Rotate chair 4 using a 270° (or −90°) rotation angle.**

Reference

The Reference option of the Rotate prompt is sometimes easier to use, especially if you do not know the rotation angle. It allows you to select the object to be rotated and click the base point. TYPE: **R** <enter> for Reference. Then you can enter the "Reference angle:" (current angle) of the object by typing it and pressing Enter. If you don't know the current angle, you can show AutoCAD the "Reference angle:" by picking the two endpoints of the line to be rotated. You can specify the "New angle:" by typing it and pressing Enter. If you don't know the new angle, you can show AutoCAD the "New angle:" by picking a point on the drawing.

Point

The Point command allows you to draw points on your drawing. Object Snap recognizes these points as nodes. The Osnap mode Node is used to snap to points.

There are many different types of points to choose from. The appearance of these points is determined by the Pdmode (point definition mode) and Pdsize (point definition size) options within the Point command.

Step 18. Use the Point Style... command to set the appearance of points:

Prompt	Response
Command: The Point Style dialog box appears (Figure 4–8):	**Point Style...** (or TYPE: **DDPTYPE** <enter>) CLICK: **the X box** CLICK: **Set Size in Absolute Units** TYPE: **6 in the Point Size: entry box**

You have just set the points to appear as an X, and they will be 6″ high. The Point Style dialog box shows the different types of points available. The size of the point may be set in a size relative to the screen or in absolute units. Your Point Style dialog box should appear as shown in Figure 4–8.

Prompt	Response
	CLICK: **OK**

FIGURE 4–8
Point Style Dialog Box

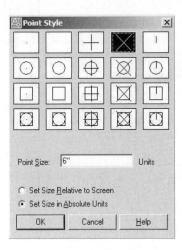

Step 19. On your own:

See Figure 4–9.

1. Use the Explode command on the table (so you can use the Offset command).
2. Use the Offset command to offset the two lines that define the long sides of the conference table. The chairs will be placed 6″ from the edge of the table, so set 6″ as the offset distance. Offset the lines on each side, outside the

FIGURE 4–9
Offset the Two Lines Defining the Long Sides of the Conference Table; Divide the Lines into Eight Equal Segments; Copy Chair 4

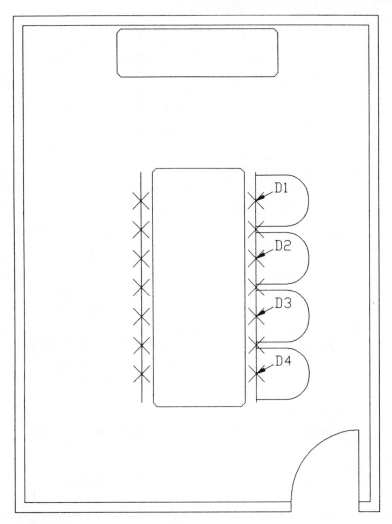

table as shown in Figure 4–9. These lines will be used as construction lines to help locate the chairs.

Divide

The Divide command divides an entity into equal parts and places point markers along the entity at the dividing points. The pdmode has been set to 3 (an X point), so an X will appear as the point marker when you use Divide.

Step 20. Use Divide to divide the offset lines into eight equal segments (Figure 4–9).

Prompt	Response
Command:	**Divide** (or TYPE: **DIV** <**enter**>)
Select object to divide:	CLICK: **anyplace on one of the offset lines.**
Enter the number of segments or [Block]:	TYPE: **8** <**enter**>

The X points divide the line into eight equal segments.

You can divide lines, circles, arcs, and polylines by selecting them. The Divide command also draws a specified Block at each mark between the equal segments. You will learn about Blocks in Chapter 8.

Step 21. On your own:

See Figure 4–9.

1. Continue with the Divide command and divide the other offset line into eight equal segments.
2. Make sure Ortho is OFF.

Copy, Osnap-Midpoint, Osnap-Node

Step 22. Use the Copy command (combined with Osnap-Midpoint and Osnap-Node) to copy chair 4 four times on the right side of the conference table (Figure 4–9):

Prompt	Response
Command:	**Copy** (or TYPE: **CP** <**enter**>)
Select objects:	CLICK: **below and to the left of chair 4**
Specify opposite corner:	**Window chair 4**
Select objects:	<**enter**>
Specify base point or [Displacement] <Displacement>:	TYPE: **MID** <**enter**>
_mid of	CLICK: **anyplace on the straight line that forms the front of the chair symbol**
Specify second point or <use first point as displacement>:	TYPE: **NOD** <**enter**>
of	**D1**
Specify second point or [Exit/Undo] <Exit>:	TYPE: **NOD** <**enter**>
of	**D2**

Prompt	Response
Specify second point or [Exit/Undo] <Exit>: of	TYPE: **NOD** <enter> D3
Specify second point or [Exit/Undo] <Exit>: of	TYPE: **NOD** <enter> D4
Specify second point or [Exit/Undo] <Exit>:	<enter>

The points act as nodes (snapping exactly on the center of the X) for Object Snap purposes.

Step 23. On your own:

See Figure 4–10.

1. Continue with the Copy, Osnap-Midpoint, and Osnap-Node commands, and place four chairs on the left side of the table.
2. Use the Copy command to place a chair at each end of the conference table. Because you will be copying each chair only once, go immediately to Osnap-Midpoint to specify the base point. Use the grid and snap to determine the "Second point of displacement:" for each chair.

FIGURE 4–10
Complete Exercise 4–1

3. TYPE: **PDMODE** <enter> at the Command: prompt. Set the Pdmode to 1, and the drawing is regenerated. The Xs will disappear. You have set the Pdmode to be invisible.
4. Erase the offset lines used to locate the chairs on each long side of the table. Use F7 to redraw when it looks like part of the chairs have been erased.
5. Erase the chairs you have drawn outside the conference room walls.
6. Exercise 4–1 is complete.

Help

If you have forgotten the name of a command or the options that are available for a specific command, the Help command is available to refresh your memory. The Help command provides a list of the AutoCAD commands as well as information about specific commands.

Measure

The Measure command is similar to the Divide command, except that with Measure you specify the distance. Divide calculates the interval to divide an entity into a specified number of equal segments. The Measure command places point markers at a specified distance along an entity.

The measurement and division of a circle start at the angle from the center that follows the current Snap rotation. The measurement and division of a closed polyline start at the first vertex drawn. The Measure command also draws a specified block at each mark between the divided segments.

Pickbox Size

The Pickbox Size slider bar on the Selection tab under Options... on the Tools menu (Figure 4–11) can be used to change the size of the target box, the small box that rides on the screen crosshair and appears when the Modify commands are used.

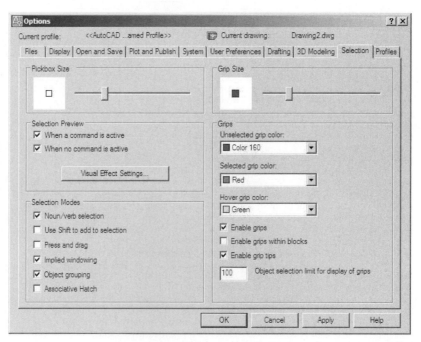

FIGURE 4–11
Options Dialog Box, Selection Tab, Pickbox Size Slider Bar

OSNAP

It is very important that you become familiar with and use Object Snap modes in combination with Draw, Modify, and other AutoCAD commands while you are drawing. When an existing drawing entity is not located on a snap point, it is impossible to connect a line or other drawing entity exactly to it. You may try, and you may think that the two points are connected, but a close examination (Zoom-Window) will reveal that they are not. Object Snap modes are used in combination with other commands to connect exactly to specific points of existing objects in a drawing. You need to use Object Snap modes constantly for complete accuracy while drawing.

Activating Osnap

An Osnap mode can be activated in four different ways:

1. Typing the Osnap abbreviation (first three letters of the Object Snap mode) from the keyboard.
2. Pressing Shift and right-clicking in the drawing area, then choosing an Object Snap mode from the Object Snap menu that appears (Figure 4–12).
3. Clicking from the Object Snap toolbar (Figure 4–13).
4. Right-clicking OSNAP on the status bar, then clicking Settings... (Figure 4–14) to access the Drafting Settings dialog box (Figure 4–15).

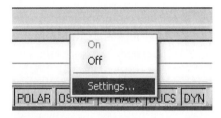

FIGURE 4–14
Activate Osnap by Right-Clicking OSNAP on the Status Bar, Then Clicking Settings ... to Access the Drafting Settings Dialog Box

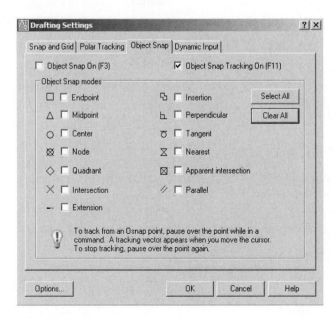

FIGURE 4–15
Drafting Settings Dialog Box, Object Snap Tab

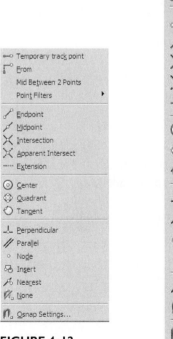

FIGURE 4–12
Activate the Osnap Menu by Pressing Shift and Right-Clicking in the Drawing Area

FIGURE 4–13
Activate Osnap by Using the Object Snap Toolbar

Osnap Modes That Snap to Specific Drawing Features

You have already used Osnap-Midpoint and Node. They are examples of Osnap modes that snap to specific drawing features. Midpoint snaps to the midpoint of a line or arc, and Node snaps to a point entity.

The following list describes other Osnap modes that snap to specific drawing features. AutoCAD Osnap modes treat each edge of a solid and each polyline segment as a line. 3D faces and viewports (described in later chapters) are treated in the same manner. You will use many of these Osnap modes while completing the exercises in this book.

Endpoint Snaps to the endpoint of a line or arc. The end of the line or arc nearest the point picked is snapped to.

Midpoint Snaps to the midpoint of a line or arc.

Mid Between 2 Points Snaps to a point that is halfway from one point to another.

Center Snaps to the center of an arc or circle.

Node Snaps to a point (POINT: command) entity.

Quadrant Snaps to the closest quadrant point of an arc or circle. These are the 0°, 90°, 180°, and 270° points on a circle or arc.

Intersection Snaps to the intersection of two lines, a line with an arc or circle, or two circles and/or arcs. You will use this mode often to snap to the intersection of two lines.

Extension Extends a line or arc. With a command and the extension mode active, pause over a line or arc, and after a small plus sign is displayed, slowly move along a temporary path that follows the extension of the line or arc. You can draw objects to and from points on the extension path line.

Insertion Snaps to the insertion point of text, attribute, or block entities. (These entities are described in later chapters.)

Perpendicular Snaps to the point on a line, circle, or arc that forms a 90° angle from that object to the last point. For example, if you are drawing a line, click the first point of the line, then use Perpendicular to connect the line to another line, circle, or arc. The new line will be perpendicular to form a 90° angle with the first pick.

Tangent Snaps to the point on a circle or arc that when connected to the last point entered forms a line tangent to (touching at one point) the circle or arc.

Nearest Snaps to the point on a line, arc, or circle that is closest to the position of the crosshair; also snaps to any point (POINT: command) entity that is visually closest to the crosshair. You will use this mode when you want to be sure to connect to a line, arc, circle, or point, and cannot use another Osnap mode.

Apparent intersection Snaps to what appears to be an intersection even though one object is above the other in 3D space.

Parallel Draws a line parallel to another line. With the Line command active, click the first point of the new line you want to draw. With the parallel mode active, pause over the line you want to draw parallel to, until a small parallel line symbol is displayed. Move the cursor away from but parallel to the original line, and an alignment path is displayed for you to complete the new line.

For the Line command, you can also use the Tangent and Perpendicular modes when picking the first point of the line. This allows you to draw a line tangent to, or perpendicular to, an existing entity.

Running Osnap Modes

You can use individual Osnap modes while in another command, as you did with Midpoint and Node. You can also set a running Osnap mode. A running Osnap mode is constantly in effect while you are drawing, until it is disabled. For example, if you have

FIGURE 4–16
Options Dialog Box, Drafting Tab

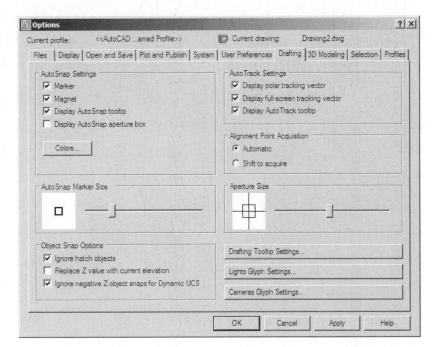

many intersections to which you are connecting lines, set the Intersection mode as a running mode. This saves time by eliminating your constant return to the Osnap command for each intersection pick.

You can set a running Osnap mode using Drafting Settings... from the Tools menu. When the Drafting Settings dialog box appears, Figure 4–15, make sure the Object Snap tab is active. You can also access this tab by holding your mouse over OSNAP in the status bar and right-clicking. Pick Settings... in the menu that appears. Click a check mark beside the desired Osnap mode or modes. Be sure to disable the running Osnap mode when you are through using it, as it will interfere with your drawing. Clicking OSNAP on in the status bar (or pressing function key F3) will activate any running Osnap modes you have set, and clicking it off will disable any running Osnap modes you have set.

Osnap Settings: Marker, Aperture, Magnet, Tooltip

Note the markers (small symbols) beside each Object Snap mode in the Drafting Settings dialog box, Object Snap tab (Figure 4–15). The display of the markers is controlled under the Drafting tab of the Options dialog box (Figure 4–16). A check mark beside Marker will add the marker symbol to the crosshair. The AutoSnap Marker Size slider bar near the bottom of the dialog box specifies the size of the marker.

When Osnap is activated, a small target box called an *aperture* can also be added to the screen crosshair. This small box shows the area within which AutoCAD will search for Object Snap candidates. The Aperture Size slider bar on the right side of the dialog box specifies the size of the box.

Step 24. When you have completed Exercise 4–1, save your work in at least two places. Exercise 4–1 is printed in Chapter 6.

Exercise 4–2:   Drawing a Rectangular Lecture Room, Including Furniture

A lecture room, including walls and furnishings, is drawn in Exercise 4–2. When you have completed Exercise 4–2, your drawing will look similar to Figure 4–17.

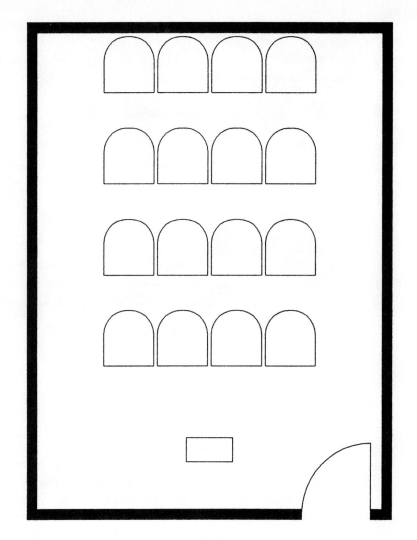

Step 1.   Use your workspace to make the following settings:

1.   **Use SaveAs... to save the drawing with the name CH4-EX2.**
2.   Set drawing Units: **Architectural**
3.   Set Drawing Limits: **25',35'**
4.   Set GRIDDISPLAY: **0**
5.   Set Grid: **12"**
6.   Set Snap: **6"**
7.   Create the following Layers:

LAYER NAME	COLOR	LINETYPE
Walls	White	Continuous
Furniture	Red	Continuous

8.   Set **Layer Walls** current.
9.   Use **Zoom-All** to view the limits of the drawing.

Solid Walls Using Polyline and Solid Hatch

In Exercise 4–1, a continuous polyline was used to draw the inside lines of the conference room walls, then Offset was used to draw the outside line showing the wall thickness. In Exercise 4–2 you will use the Line command to draw the lecture room walls, then you

FIGURE 4–18
Use Lines to Draw the
Lecture Room Walls

will use the Polyline Edit command to change the lines to a polyline before you offset the walls. After you have completed drawing the walls, you will use the Hatch command to make the walls solid.

Step 2. Use Line to draw the walls of the lecture room (Figure 4–18):

Prompt	Response
Command:	**Line** (or TYPE: **L <enter>**)
Specify first point:	TYPE: **5′,7′<enter>**
Specify next point or [Undo]:	**Turn ORTHO ON**
	Move your mouse to the right and TYPE: **15′<enter>**
Specify next point or [Undo]:	**Move your mouse straight up** and TYPE: **20′<enter>**
Specify next point or [Close/Undo]:	**Move your mouse to the left** and TYPE: **15′<enter>**
Specify next point or [Close/Undo]:	TYPE: **C<enter>**

Step 3. On your own:

1. **Use Zoom-Window to magnify the lower right corner of the lecture room where the door will be drawn.**

Break and From

The Break command can be used to erase a part of a drawing entity. The From option can be used to set a temporary reference point, similar to ID point.

Step 4. Use Break to create an opening for the lecture room door (Figure 4–19):

Prompt	Response
Command:	**Break** (or TYPE: **BR <enter>**)
Select object:	CLICK: **anyplace on the bottom horizontal line**
Specify second break point or [First point]:	TYPE: **F <enter>** (for first point)

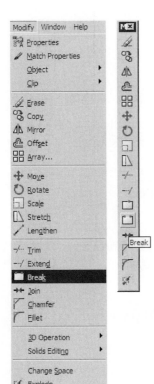

FIGURE 4-19
Use Break to Create an
Opening for the Lecture
Room Door

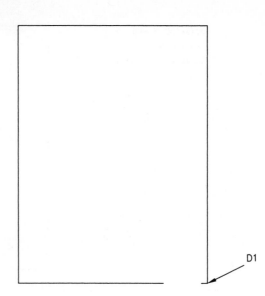

D1

Prompt	Response
Specify first break point:	TYPE: **FRO** **<enter>** (abbreviation for FROM)
Base point:	TYPE: **INT** **<enter>**
of	**D1** (Figure 4–22)
<Offset>	TYPE: **@6<180** **<enter>** (polar coordinate)
Specify second break point:	TYPE: **@36<180** **<enter>** (polar coordinate)

First

When selecting an entity to break, you may use the point entered in the selection process as the first break point, or you may TYPE: **F** **<enter>** to be able to select the first break point.

@

Sometimes you need only to break an entity and not erase a section of it. In that case, use @ as the second break point. The line will be broken twice on the same point; no segments will be erased from the line.

Edit Polyline

Edit Polyline is a special modify command used only to edit polylines or to change lines into polylines. It can also be used to change the width of an existing polyline. You will find many occasions to use the Polyline Edit command.

Step 5. **Use Polyline Edit to change the lines into a polyline:**

Prompt	Response
Command:	**Edit Polyline** (or TYPE: **PE<enter>**)
Select polyline or [Multiple]:	CLICK: **any of the lines drawn**
Object selected is not a polyline	
Do you want to turn it into	
one? <Y>	**<enter>** (to tell AutoCAD yes, you want to turn it into a polyline)
Enter an option [Close/Join/Width/	
Edit vertex/Fit/Spline/Decurve/	
Ltype gen/Undo]:	TYPE: **J<enter>** (for Join)

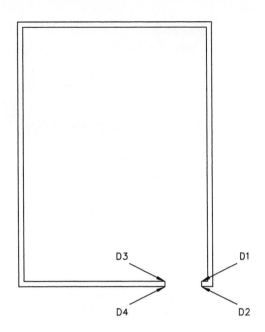

FIGURE 4–20
Use the Line Command to
Close the Ends of the
Polyline

D3 D1

D4 D2

Prompt	Response
Select objects:	TYPE: **ALL\<enter\>** (to select all the lines)
5 found	
Select objects:	\<enter\>
4 segments added to polyline	
Enter an option [Open/Join/ Width/Edit vertex/Fit/ Spline/Decurve/Ltype gen/Undo]:	\<enter\>

Step 6.   On your own:

1.   Use the Offset command to offset the polyline 5″ to the outside of the current polyline.
2.   Use the Line command with OSNAP endpoint to close the polyline. TYPE: L \<enter\> CLICK: **D1,D2** \<enter\> \<enter\> CLICK: **D3,D4** \<enter\> **as shown** in Figure 4–20.
3.   Use Zoom: Extents so you can see the entire drawing.

Hatch

The Hatch and Gradient dialog box is discussed in detail in Chapters 9 and 13. For now you will use a single hatch pattern to create solid walls as shown in Figure 4–17.

Step 7.   Use the Hatch command to make the walls solid:

Prompt	Response
Command:	Hatch... (or TYPE: H \<enter\>)
The Hatch and Gradient dialog box appears:	With the Hatch Tab selected: CLICK: **the Pattern: list and scroll up to the SOLID pattern** CLICK: **on it as shown in Figure 4–21** CLICK: **Add: Pick Points**

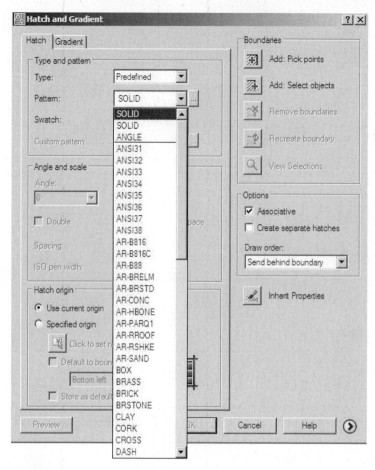

FIGURE 4–21
Select the SOLID Pattern from the Hatch and Gradient Dialog Box

Prompt	Response
Pick internal point or [Select objects/remove Boundaries]:	CLICK: **D1** (any point between polylines forming the wall, Figure 4–22)
Pick internal point or [Select objects/remove Boundaries]:	**<enter>**
The Hatch and Gradient dialog box or right-click menu appears:	CLICK: **Preview**
Pick or press Esc to return to dialog or <Right-click to accept hatch>:	**Right-click** (if the pattern looks correct) **or** PRESS: **Esc** (and fix the dialog box)
Command:	**<enter>**

Step 8. Draw the door and a chair:

On Your Own:

See Figure 4–23.

1. Use the Line command to draw a 3' vertical door line. Snap (be sure SNAP is ON) to the upper right corner of the door opening to begin the door line. Draw the line using polar coordinates or direct distance entry.
2. Use the Arc-Start, Center, End method to draw the counterclockwise door swing arc. Use Osnap-Endpoint for the start, center, and end connections.

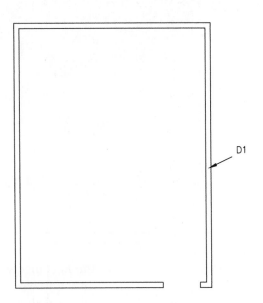

FIGURE 4–22
CLICK: Any Point Between the Two Polylines
Forming the Wall

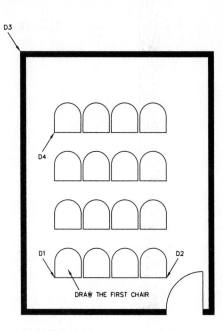

FIGURE 4–23
Draw the Chairs for the Lecture Room

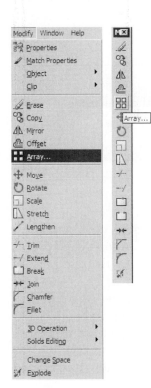

3. Set the current layer to Furniture. To draw the first chair in the group of chairs, zoom in on a portion of the grid inside the lecture room walls in the lower left area.
4. Use the Line command to draw a rectangle 26″ wide by 28″ deep. This chair shape will be used to draw the entire group of 16 chairs and will be moved to the correct position later. For now, just be sure it is located in the general area of the lower left corner of the room, shown in Figure 4–23.
5. Edit the rectangle, using the Fillet command, 12″ Radius to form the shape of the chair.
6. Zoom-Extents after you finish drawing the chair.

Array

Array allows you to make multiple copies of an object in a rectangular or polar (circular) array. The Rectangular option is used to draw all the chairs in the lecture room; the Polar option is described in Exercise 4–3.

Step 9. Use the Array command to make a rectangular pattern of 16 chairs (Figures 4–23 and 4–24):

Prompt	Response
Command:	**Array** (or TYPE: **AR** <enter>)
The Array dialog box appears:	CLICK: **the Select objects button**
Select objects:	PICK: **any point to locate the first corner of a window to include the entire chair**
Specify opposite corner:	**Window the chair just drawn**
Select objects:	**<enter>**

FIGURE 4–24
Array Dialog Box

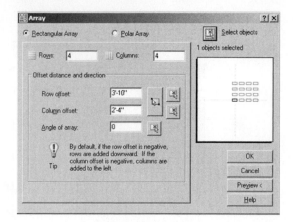

Prompt	Response
The Array dialog box appears:	CLICK: **the Rectangular Array button** TYPE: **4 in the Rows: input area** TYPE: **4 in the Columns: input area** TYPE: **46 in the Row offset: input area** TYPE: **28 in the Column offset: input area** TYPE: **0 in the Angle of array: input area** CLICK: **OK**

NOTE: In the Array command, include the original cornerstone item in the number of rows and columns.

Rectangular

The Rectangular option of Array allows you to make multiple copies of an object in a rectangular array. The array is made up of horizontal rows and vertical columns. The direction and spacing of the rows and columns are determined by the distance you specify between each. In the previous example we used the chair as the cornerstone element in the lower left corner of the array. Positive numbers were entered for the distance between the rows and columns, and the array was generated up and to the right. When a positive number is entered for the rows, they proceed up; when a negative number is entered, they proceed down. When a positive number is entered for the columns, they proceed to the right; when a negative number is entered, they proceed to the left.

NOTE: To rotate a rectangular array, set the Angle of array to the desired angle and then create the array.

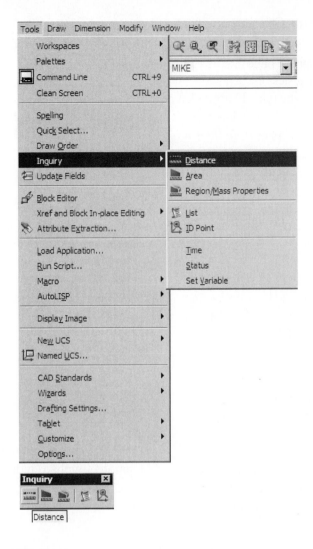

Distance

The Distance command can be used to determine measurements. We know the interior width of the room is 15′. To center the array of chairs accurately in the lecture room, we need to measure the width of the array. The depth appears to be fine for the room size.

Step 10. Use Distance to measure a specified distance (Figure 4–23):

Prompt	Response
Command:	**Distance** (or TYPE: **DIST <enter>**)
Specify first point:	TYPE: **INT <enter>**
int of	**D1**
Specify second point:	TYPE: **INT <enter>**
int of	**D2**
Distance = 9′-2″,Angle in XY	
Plane = 0,Angle from XY Plane = 0,	
Delta X = 9′-2″,Delta Y = 0′-0″,	
Delta Z = 0′-0″	

The room width, 180″, minus the array width, 110″, is 70″. You can leave 35″-wide aisles on each side of the array.

Position the Chair Array

To locate the chair array precisely, use Move and From as well as some Osnap modes. The array will be located 2″ away from the back wall of the lecture room and will have 35″-wide aisles on each side.

Using the outside upper left corner of the room as the base point, the aisle width of 35″, plus the 5″ wall, is 40″ on the X axis. The chair depth, 28″, plus the distance of the wall, 5″, and away from the wall, 2″, is 35″ on the Y axis. Make sure ORTHO is OFF.

Step 11. Locate the chair array (Figure 4–23):

Prompt	Response
Command:	**Move** (or TYPE: **M <enter>**)
Select objects:	CLICK: **any point to locate the first corner of a window to include the entire array**
Specify opposite corner:	**Window the entire array.**
Select objects:	**<enter>**
Specify base point or [Displacement] <Displacement>:	TYPE: **INT <enter>**
int of	**D4**
Specify second point or <use first point as displacement>:	TYPE: **FRO <enter>**
Base point:	TYPE: **INT <enter>**
Int of:	**D3**
<Offset>:	TYPE: **@40,-35 <enter>** (do not forget the minus (hyphen) in front of the 35)

Step 12. On your own:
See Figure 4–25.

1. Draw the lectern centered on the chair array, as shown.
2. Exercise 4–2 is complete.

Step 13. When you have completed Exercise 4–2, save your work in at least two places. Exercise 4–2 is printed in Chapter 6.

Exercise 4–3: Drawing a Curved Conference Room, Including Furniture

A conference room, including walls and furnishings, is drawn in Exercise 4–3. When you have completed Exercise 4–3, your drawing will look similar to Figure 4–26.

Step 1. Use your workspace to make the following settings:

1. **Use SaveAs... to save the drawing with the name CH4-EX3.**
2. Set drawing Units: **Architectural**
3. Set Drawing Limits: **25′,35′**
4. Set GRID DISPLAY: **0**
5. Set Grid: **12″**
6. Set Snap: **6″**

FIGURE 4–25
Complete Exercise 4–2

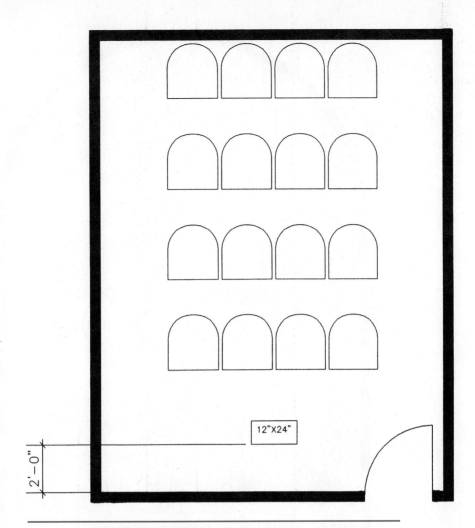

12"X24"

2'–0"

7. Create the following Layers:

LAYER NAME	COLOR	LINETYPE
Walls	White	Continuous
Furniture	Red	Continuous

8. Set **Layer Walls** current.
9. Use **Zoom-All** to view the limits of the drawing.

Polyline

The Polyline prompt is "Specify next point or [Arc/Close/Halfwidth/Length/Undo/Width]:". In Exercise 4–1, a continuous polyline was used to draw the inside lines of the conference room walls, then Offset was used to draw the outside line showing wall depth. The Width option of the Pline prompt allows you to specify a thickness for the polyline. The Width option is used to draw the lecture room walls in Exercise 4–3.

Width

The Width option allows you to draw wide polylines. In Exercise 4–3, a 5"-wide poly-line is used to draw the walls of the lecture room. The starting and ending points of the polyline are the *center* of the polyline's width. Because the starting and ending points of the wide polyline segments are the center of the line segment, 5" is added to each line length to compensate for the 2-1/2" wall thickness on each side of the center line.

When a wide polyline is exploded, the width information is lost and the polyline changes to a line segment.

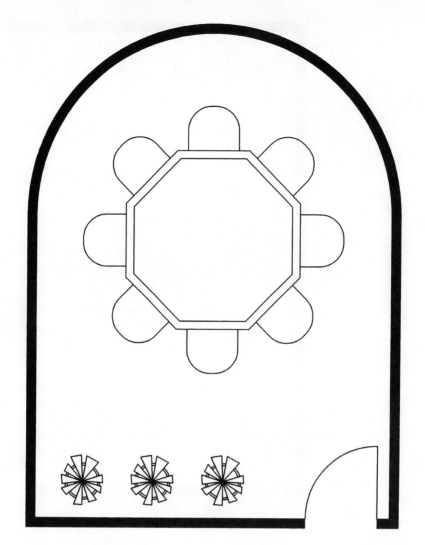

Length

The Length option in the Polyline prompt allows you to draw a polyline segment at the same angle as the previously drawn polyline segment, by simply specifying the length of the new segment. It also allows you to return to straight line segments after you have drawn a polyline arc.

Close

It is always best to use the Close option when you are completing a wide polyline. The effect of using Close is different from clicking or entering a point to complete the polyline. With the Close option, the last corner is completely closed.

Arc

The Polyline Arc command is similar to the Arc command in the Draw menu.

Step 2. **Draw the walls of the conference room, using a wide polyline and wide polyarc (Figure 4–27):**

Prompt	Response
Command:	**Polyline** (or TYPE: **PL** <enter>)
Specify start point:	TYPE: **4′9-1/2,4′9-1/2** <enter>
Current line-width is 0′-0″	

FIGURE 4–27
Draw Exercise 4–3

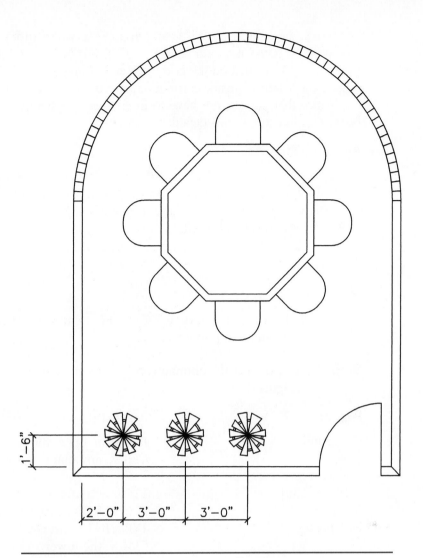

Prompt	Response
Specify next point or [Arc/ Halfwidth/Length/Undo/Width]:	TYPE: **W**
Specify starting width <0'-0">:	TYPE: **5 <enter>**
Specify ending width <0'-5">:	**<enter>**
Specify next point or [Arc/ Halfwidth/Length/Undo/Width]:	TYPE: **@15'5<0 <enter>**
Specify next point or [Arc/Close Halfwidth/Length/Undo/Width]:	TYPE: **@12'9<90 <enter>**
Specify next point or [Arc/Close/ Halfwidth/Length/Undo/Width]:	TYPE: **A <enter>**
Specify endpoint of arc or [Angle/ CEnter/CLose/Direction/ Halfwidth/Line/Radius/ Second pt/Undo/Width]:	TYPE: **@15'5<180 <enter>**
Specify endpoint of arc or [Angle/ CEnter/CLose/Direction/ Halfwidth/Line/Radius/Second pt/ Undo/Width]:	TYPE: **L <enter>**
Specify next point or [Arc/Close/ Halfwidth/Length/Undo/Width]:	TYPE: **C <enter>**

When you subtract 2-1/2″ (half the polyline width) from coordinates 5′,5′ to get your starting point of coordinates 4′9-1/2,4′9-1/2, the lower left inside corner of the lecture room is located on the grid mark at coordinates 5′,5′. Turn coordinates on and snap to the lower left inside corner of the lecture room to verify this.

Notice that you do not have to insert the inch symbol in the polar coordinates, because architectural units default to inches.

Fill On, Fill Off

The settings FILL ON and FILL OFF affect the appearance of the polyline and solid hatch. To have an outline of the polyline, TYPE: **FILL** <**enter**>, then **OFF** <**enter**> and regenerate the drawing. To have it appear solid again, TYPE: **FILL** <**enter**>, then TYPE: **ON** <**enter**> and regenerate the drawing (TYPE: **RE**<**enter**>).

Step 3. On your own:

See Figure 4–27.

1. TYPE: **FILL** <**enter**>, then TYPE: **OFF** <**enter**> and regenerate the drawing to create an open polyline.

Step 4. Use the Break command and From to create a 3′ door opening (Figure 4–27):

Prompt	Response
Command:	**Break** (or TYPE: **BR**<**enter**>)
Select Object:	CLICK: **any place on the polyline**
Specify second break point or [First point]:	TYPE: **F**<**enter**>
Specify first break point:	TYPE: **FRO**<**enter**> (abbreviation for FROM)
Base point:	TYPE: **INT**<**enter**>
of	CLICK: **the lower right intersection of the polylines**
<Offset>	TYPE: **@8-1/2**<**180**<**enter**>
Specify second break point:	TYPE: **@36**<**180**<**enter**>

Step 5. On your own:

See Figure 4–27.

1. **Use the Line command to draw a 3′ vertical door line. Start the door line at the inside corner of the door opening, with snap ON.**
2. **Use the Arc-Start, Center, End method to draw the door swing arc.**
3. **Set Layer Furniture current.**

Polygon

The Polygon command draws a polygon with 3 to 1024 sides. After the number of sides is specified, the Polygon prompt is "Specify center of polygon or [Edge]:". When the center of the polygon (default option) is specified, the polygon can then be inscribed in a circle or circumscribed about circle. When the polygon is inscribed in a circle, all the vertices lie on the circle, and the edges of the polygon are inside the circle. When the polygon is circumscribed about a circle, the midpoint of each edge of the polygon lies on the circle, and the vertices are outside the circle. A polygon, which is actually a closed polyline, must be exploded before it can be edited. Edit Polyline can be used to edit a polygon.

Step 6. Use the Polygon command to draw the conference table (Figure 4–27):

Prompt	Response
Command:	**Polygon** (or TYPE: **POL** <enter>)
Enter number of sides <4>:	TYPE: **8** <enter>
Specify center of polygon or [Edge]:	TYPE: **12′6,16′6** <enter>
Enter an option [Inscribed in circle/ Circumscribed about circle]<I>:	TYPE: **I** <enter> (or just <enter> if I is the default
Specify radius of circle:	TYPE: **48** <enter>

The method of specifying the radius controls the orientation of the polygon. When the radius is specified with a number, as above, the bottom edge of the polygon is drawn at the current snap angle—horizontal in the polygon just drawn. When the radius of an inscribed polygon is specified with a point, a vertex of the polygon is placed at the point location. When the radius of a circumscribed polygon is specified with a point, an edge midpoint is placed at the point's location.

Edge

When the Edge option of the prompt is selected, AutoCAD prompts "Specify first endpoint of edge:" and "Specify second endpoint of edge:". The two points entered to the prompts specify one edge of a polygon that is drawn counterclockwise.

Step 7. On your own:

See Figure 4–27.

1. To draw the first chair of the eight chairs that are placed around the conference table, zoom in on a portion of the grid inside the conference room walls.
2. Use the Line command to draw a rectangle 26″ wide by 28″ deep using polar coordinates or direct distance entry.
3. Edit one of the 26″-wide sides of the rectangle, using the Fillet command, 12″ Radius to form the back of the chair.
4. The chairs are located 6″ in from the outside edge of the table. Use the Move command, Osnap-Midpoint (to the front of the chair), and From to locate the front of the chair 6″ inside the midpoint of an edge of the conference table polygon.
5. Use the Trim and Erase commands to erase the part of the chair that is under the conference table.
6. Use the Offset command to offset the outside edge of the conference table 4″ to the inside, to form the 4″ band.
7. Zoom-Extents after you have finished step 7.

Array

Step 8. Use the Array command to make a polar (circular) pattern of eight chairs (Figure 4–27):

Prompt	Response
Command:	**Array** (or TYPE: **AR** <enter>)
The Array dialog box appears:	CLICK: **the Select objects button**
Select objects:	CLICK: **the first corner for a window to select the chair just drawn**

Prompt	Response
Specify opposite corner:	**Window the chair just drawn.**
Select objects:	**<enter>**
	CLICK: **the Polar Array button**
	CLICK: **the button that allows you to pick a center point**
Specify center point of array:	CLICK: **the center point of the polygon (or TYPE: 12'6,16'6 <enter>)**
	TYPE: **8 in the Total number of items input area**
	TYPE: **360 in the Angle to fill: input area Make sure there is a check in the Rotate items as copied check box.**
	CLICK: **OK**

Polar

The Polar option of Array allows you to make multiple copies of an object in a circular array. The 360° "Angle to fill" can be specified to form a full circular array. An angle less than 360° can be specified to form a partial circular array. When a positive angle is specified, the array is rotated counterclockwise (+=ccw). When a negative angle is specified, the array is rotated clockwise (−=cw).

AutoCAD constructs the array by determining the distance from the array's center point to a point on the entity selected. If more than one object is selected, the reference point is on the last item in the selection set. When multiple items are arrayed and are not rotated as they are copied, the resulting array depends on the reference point used.

If one of the two array parameters used above—the number of items in the array or the angle to fill—is not specified, AutoCAD will prompt for a third parameter—Angle between items:". Any two of the three array parameters must be specified to complete an array.

Step 9.   On your own:

See Figure 4–27.

1. Use Zoom-Window to zoom in on the area of the conference room where the plants and planters are located.
2. Use the Circle command, 9″ Radius, to draw the outside shape of one planter.
3. Use the Offset command, offset distance 1″, offset to the inside of the planter, to give a thickness to the planter.
4. Use the Line command to draw multisegmented shapes (to show a plant) in the planter.
5. Use Trim to trim any lines you need to remove. Window the entire planter to select the cutting edges, and then select the lines to trim.
6. Use the Copy command to draw the next two planters as shown in Figure 4–27.
7. Set FILL ON and regenerate the drawing to have the walls appear solid again.
8. Exercise 4–3 is complete.

Step 10.

When you have completed Exercise 4–3, save your work in at least two places. You can plot Exercise 4–3 after completing Chapter 5.

FIGURE 4–28
Exercise 4–4 Complete

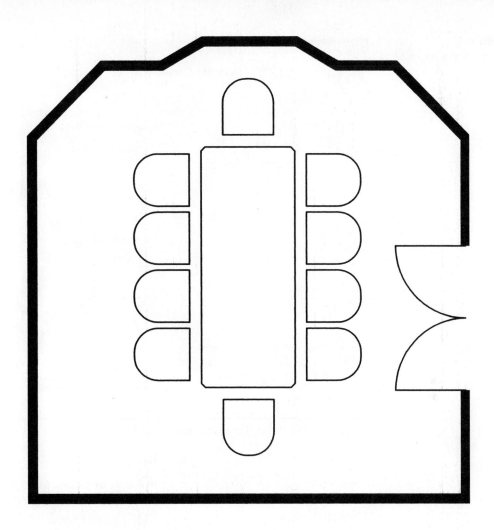

Exercise 4–4:   Drawing a Conference Room with Angles

In Exercise 4–4, Polar Tracking is used to draw lines at angles in 15° increments. The Polyline Edit command is used to join lines together and to change the width of the existing polyline. Zero Radius Fillet is used to join lines to form a square corner, and furniture is added.

When you have completed Exercise 4–4 your drawing will look similar to Figure 4–28.

Step 1.   **Use your workspace to make the following settings:**

1. **Use SaveAs… to save the drawing with the name CH4-EX4.**
2. Set drawing Units: **Architectural**
3. Set Drawing Limits: **25',35'**
4. Set GRIDDISPLAY: **0**
5. Set Grid: **12"**
6. Set Snap: **6"**
7. **Create the following Layers:**

LAYER NAME	COLOR	LINETYPE
Walls	White	Continuous
Furniture	Green	Continuous

8. Set **Layer Walls** current.

FIGURE 4–29
Set Polar Tracking Angles

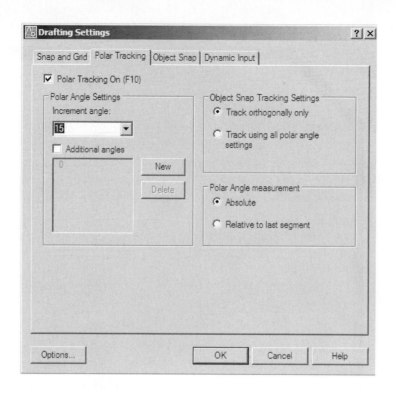

Step 2. Set Polar Tracking angles at 15°:

Prompt	Response
Command:	**Place your mouse over POLAR on the status bar and** RIGHT-CLICK
A shortcut menu appears:	CLICK: **Settings...**
The Drafting Settings dialog box appears with the Polar Tracking tab selected:	CLICK: **the list under Increment angle: and** CLICK: **15** as shown in Figure 4–29 CLICK: **OK**

Step 3. Use the Line command with direct distance entry and polar tracking to draw most of the wall symbols (Figure 4–30):

Prompt	Response
Command:	**Line** (or TYPE: **L**<enter>)
Specify first point:	TYPE: **11',7'**<enter>
Specify next point or [Undo]:	**Turn ORTHO ON**
	Move your mouse to the left and TYPE: **7'6**<enter>
Specify next point or [Undo]:	**Move your mouse straight up and** TYPE: **15'**<enter>
Specify next point or [Close/Undo]:	CLICK: **POLAR** (ORTHO turns OFF automatically)
	Move your mouse so that 45° shows and TYPE: **4'3**<enter>
Specify next point or [Close/Undo]:	**Move your mouse so that <0° shows and** TYPE: **2'6**<enter>

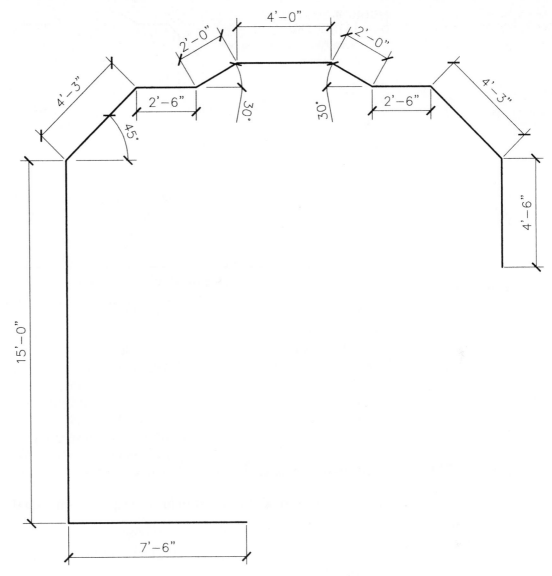

FIGURE 4–30
Measurements for the Walls

Prompt	Response
Specify next point or [Close/Undo]:	Move your mouse so that <30° shows and TYPE: **2'<enter>**
Specify next point or [Close/Undo]:	Move your mouse so that <0° shows and TYPE: **4'<enter>**
Specify next point or [Close/Undo]:	Move your mouse so that <330° shows and TYPE: **2'<enter>**
Specify next point or [Close/Undo]:	Move your mouse so that <0° shows and TYPE: **2'6<enter>**
Specify next point or [Close/Undo]:	Move your mouse so that <315° shows and TYPE: **4'3<enter>**
Specify next point or [Close/Undo]:	Move your mouse straight down so that <270° shows and TYPE: **4'6<enter>**
Specify next point or [Close/Undo]:	**<enter>**

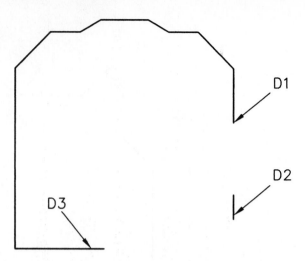

FIGURE 4–31
Draw the Door Opening and Use Zero Radius Fillet to Draw a Square Corner

D1

D2

D3

Step 4. Draw an opening for the double door (Figure 4–31):

Prompt	Response
Command:	<enter> (to repeat the Line command)
Specify first point:	TYPE: **FRO**<enter>
Base point:	TYPE: **END**<enter>
end of:	CLICK: **D1** (Figure 4–31)
<Offset>:	TYPE: **@6′<270**<enter>
Specify next point or [Undo]:	**Turn ORTHO ON**
	Move your mouse straight down and TYPE: **2′**<enter>
Specify next point or [Undo]:	<enter>

Step 5. Use Zero Radius Fillet to make a square corner on the lower left:

Prompt	Response
Command:	**FILLET** (or TYPE: **F**<enter>)
Current settings: Mode = TRIM, Radius = 0′-0″	TYPE: **R**<enter> (this is not necessary if the radius is already set at 0)
Specify fillet radius <default>:	TYPE: **0**<enter>
Select first object or [Undo/ Polyline/Radius/Trim/Multiple]:	CLICK: **D2** (Figure 4–31)
Select second object or shift-select to apply corner:	CLICK: **D3**

Step 6. Use Edit Polyline to join all lines into a single polyline and make it 5″ wide:

Prompt	Response
Command:	**Edit Polyline** (or TYPE: **PE**<enter>)
Select polyline or [Multiple]:	CLICK: **any of the lines**
Object selected is not a polyline Do you want to turn it into one? <Y>	<enter>
Enter an option [Close/Join/Width/ Edit vertex/Fit/Spline/Decurve/ Ltype gen/Undo]:	TYPE: **J**<enter>

Prompt	Response
Select objects:	TYPE: **ALL\<enter\>** (or use a crossing window to select all)
11 found	
Select objects:	\<enter\>
10 segments added to polyline	
Enter an option [Open/Join/ Width/Edit vertex/Fit/Spline/ Decurve/Ltype gen/Undo]:	TYPE: **W\<enter\>**
Specify new width for all segments:	TYPE: **5\<enter\>**
Enter an option [Open/Join/ Width/Edit vertex/Fit/Spline/ Decurve/Ltype gen/Undo]:	\<enter\>

Step 7. Draw the double door using the Line, Arc, and Mirror commands:

Prompt	Response
Command:	**Line** (or TYPE: **L\<enter\>**)
Specify first point:	TYPE: **END\<enter\>**
end of:	CLICK: **D1** (Figure 4–32)
Specify next point or [Undo]:	**Turn ORTHO ON** **Move your mouse to the left and** TYPE: **3′\<enter\>**
Specify next point or [Undo]:	\<enter\>
Command:	**Arc-Center, Start, End**
Specify center point of arc: (Figure 4–32)	CLICK: **with a running Osnap-Endpoint, D1**
Specify start point of arc:	CLICK: **D2**
Specify end point of arc or [Angle/ chord Length]:	**Move your mouse down and** CLICK: **D3**
Command:	**Mirror** (or TYPE: **MI\<enter\>**)
Select objects:	CLICK: **the line and the arc of the single door**
Select objects:	\<enter\>
Specify first point of mirror line:	CLICK: **D3** (Figure 4–32)
Specify second point of mirror line:	**With ORTHO ON** CLICK: **D4** (or any point directly to the left or right of D3)
Erase source objects? [Yes/No] \<N\>:	\<enter\> (to answer No, do not erase the first door)

FIGURE 4–32
Use Line, Arc, and Mirror to
Draw the Double Door

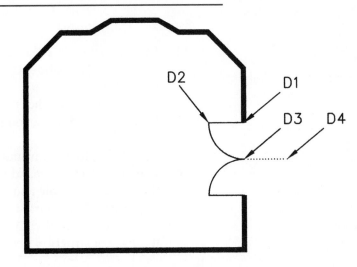

Rectangle

The Rectangle command allows you to draw a rectangle, chamfer or fillet the corners, and give width to the polyline that is created. To give you an idea of how the Rectangle command works, in the next part of this exercise, you will erase the table and redraw it with the Rectangle command and Osnap-Tracking.

Tracking

Tracking, which is similar to the ID Point command, allows you to specify points, except that you can activate Tracking anytime AutoCAD asks for a point. You can also specify as many points as you need until you arrive at the desired location, then you press Enter to end the tracking mode.

Step 8. Draw the table using Rectangle and Osnap-Tracking (Figure 4–28):

Prompt	Response
Command:	**Rectangle** (or TYPE: **REC** <enter>)
Specify first corner point or [Chamfer/Elevation/Fillet/Thickness/Width]:	TYPE: **C** <enter>
Specify first chamfer distance for rectangles <0'-0">:	TYPE: **2** <enter>
Specify second chamfer distance for rectangles <0'-2">:	<enter>
Specify first corner point or [Chamfer/Elevation/Fillet/Thickness/Width]:	TYPE: **TRACK** <enter>
First tracking point: int of	TYPE: **int**<enter> **the lower left inside corner of the room**
Next point (Press ENTER to end tracking):	**Move your mouse to the right and** TYPE: **7'3** <enter>
Next point (Press ENTER to end tracking):	**Move your mouse up and** TYPE: **4'6**<enter>
Next point (Press ENTER to end tracking):	<enter> (to end tracking)
Specify other corner point or [Area/Dimensions/Rotation]:	TYPE: **@48,120** <enter> (relative coordinates)

Step 9. On your own:

1. Draw a rectangle 26" wide and 28" deep using the Line command.
2. Use Fillet (12" radius) to edit the back of the rectangle to create the symbol of a chair.
3. Copy the chair symbol three times and rotate it 90°, 180°, and –90°.
4. Use the Point Style... command to set the appearance of points to X and size to 6".
5. Use the Explode command on the table (so you can use the Offset command).
6. Use the Offset command to offset the two lines that define the long sides of the conference table and the two lines that define the ends of the conference table. The chairs will be placed 6" from the edge of the table, so set 6" as the offset distance. Offset the lines outside the table. These lines will be used as construction lines to help locate the chairs.

7. Use Divide to divide the long offset lines into eight equal segments.
8. Use the Copy command (combined with Osnap-Midpoint and Osnap-Node) to copy the chairs on all four sides of the conference table.
9. Set Pdmode to 1 (invisible).
10. Erase the offset lines used to locate the chairs.
11. Exercise 4–4 is complete.

Step 10. Save your drawing in at least two places. You can plot Exercise 4–3 after completing Chapter 6.

Exercise 4–5: Drawing a Rectangular Conference Room, Including Furniture

A rectangular conference room including furniture (Figure 4–33) is drawn in Exercise 4–5.

Step 1. Use your workspace to make the following settings:

1. **Use SaveAs... to save the drawing with the name CH4-EX5.**
2. Set drawing Units: **Architectural**
3. Set Drawing Limits: **27',22'**
4. Set GRIDDISPLAY: **0**
5. Set Grid: **12"**

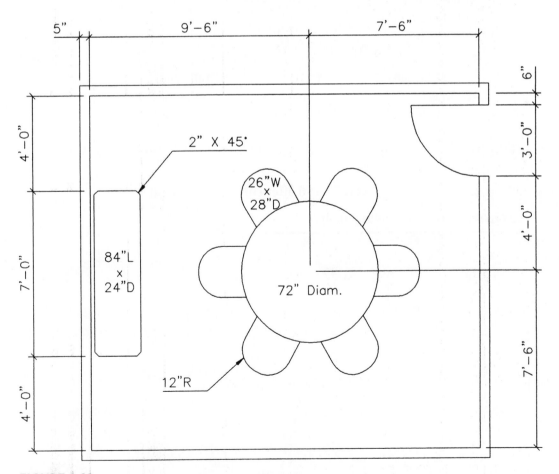

FIGURE 4–33
Exercise 4–5: Drawing a Rectangular Conference Room Including Furniture (Scale: 1/4″ = 1′-0″)

6. Set Snap: **6″**
7. Create the following Layers:

LAYER NAME	COLOR	LINETYPE
Walls	Blue	Continuous
Furniture	Red	Continuous

Step 2. Use the measurements shown in Figure 4–33 to draw the conference room full scale.

Step 3. You can plot Exercise 4–5 after completing Chapter 6.

Step 4. Save the drawing in at least two places.

Exercise 4–6:   ## Drawing a Rectangular Lecture Room, Including Furniture

A lecture room including furniture (Figure 4–34) is drawn in Exercise 4–6.

Step 1. Use your workspace to make the following settings:

1. **Use SaveAs... to save the drawing with the name CH4-EX6.**
2. Set drawing Units: **Architectural**
3. Set Drawing Limits: **25′,27′**
4. Set GRIDDISPLAY: **0**
5. Set Grid: **12″**
6. Set Snap: **6″**
7. Create the following Layers:

LAYER NAME	COLOR	LINETYPE
Walls	White	Continuous
Furniture	Magenta	Continuous

Step 2. Use the measurements shown in Figure 4–34 to draw the lecture room full scale.

Step 3. You can plot Exercise 4–6 after completing Chapter 6.

Step 4. Save the drawing in at least two places.

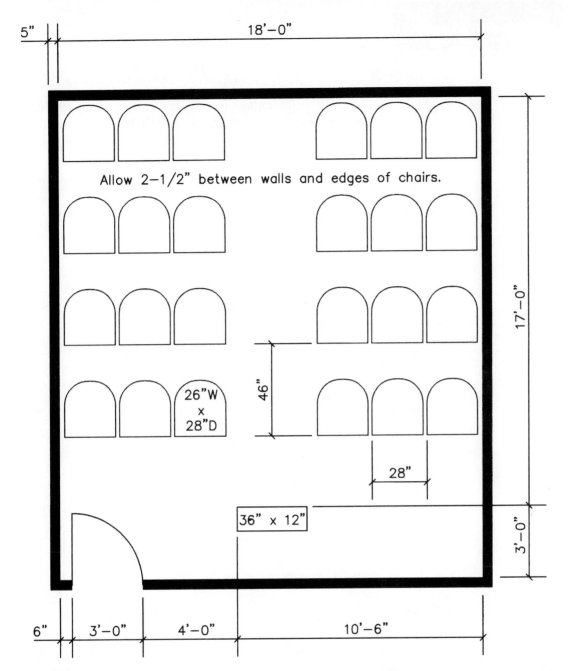

FIGURE 4–34

Exercise 4–6: Drawing a Rectangular Lecture Room Including Furniture (Scale: 1/4″ = 1′-0″)

1. When the outline of the walls of a room is drawn with a zero-width poly-line, which of the following commands can be used to draw most quickly the second line that shows the depth of the walls?
    a. Line
    b. Polyline
    c. Offset
    d. Copy
    e. Array

2. Which of the following commands is used to split a solid polyline into separate line segments?
    a. ID Point
    b. Offset
    c. Array
    d. Trim
    e. Explode

3. Which of the following commands is used to locate, on a drawing, a point that AutoCAD uses as the origin for a command?
    a. ID Point
    b. Inquiry
    c. First point
    d. Aperture
    e. Distance

4. The Chamfer command will chamfer two lines that do not intersect.
    a. True
    b. False

5. Which of the following commands can be used to draw a rounded corner?
    a. Chamfer
    b. Fillet
    c. Offset
    d. Trim
    e. Edit Polyline

6. Which of the following Osnap modifiers is used to snap to a point entity?
    a. Perpendicular
    b. Endpoint
    c. Node
    d. Midpoint
    e. Intersection

7. Which of the following rotation angles is the same as −90°?
    a. 90
    b. 180
    c. 270
    d. 300
    e. 330

8. Which of the following controls the appearance of the markers used in the Divide command?
    a. Aperture Size
    b. Point Style
    c. Osnap
    d. Pickbox Size
    e. ID Point

9. Which of the following settings is used to change the size of the target box that appears when Modify commands are used?
    a. Aperture Size
    b. Point Style
    c. Osnap
    d. Pickbox Size
    e. ID Point

10. Which of the following commands can be used to join lines or arcs together and make them a single polyline?
    a. Explode
    b. Edit Polyline
    c. Polyline
    d. Close
    e. Edit vertex

Complete.

11. Describe the difference between a square drawn with the Line command and a square drawn with the Polyline command when Offset is used to off-set the lines or polyline.

_____

_____

_____

12. Describe what the Trim prompt "Select cutting edges... Select objects:" means.

_____

_____

13. Describe how to chamfer the corners of a rectangle using only the Rectangle command.

_____

14. Describe how to change the width of an existing polyline.

_____

15. Which command is used to determine the exact distance from one point to another?

_____

16. Describe the difference between a polygon that has been inscribed in a circle and one that has been circumscribed about a circle.

Inscribed in a circle: _____

_____

Circumscribed about a circle _____

_____

17. When creating a counterclockwise polar array of six chairs arranged in a half circle, which "Angle to fill" would you use to form the array?

_____

18. Describe the use of the option From.

_____

19. Which Polyline Arc option allows you to draw a straight-line polyline after a polyline arc has been drawn?

_____

20. Describe the use of Tracking.

_____

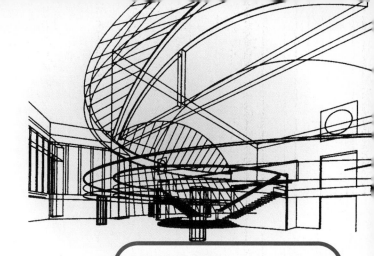

chapter

5

Adding Text, Tables, and Raster Images to the Drawing

Objectives

When you have completed this chapter, you will be able to:

Define the terms *style* and *font* and describe the function of each.

Use different fonts on the same drawing.

Place text on several different parts of the drawing with a single command.

Use the modifiers Center, Align, Fit, Middle, Right, Top, and Style.

Use the Text Style... setting to create condensed, expanded, rotated, backward, inclined, and upside-down text.

Use the Text Style... setting to change any style on the drawing to a different font.

Use standard codes to draw special characters such as the degree symbol, the diameter symbol, the plus and minus symbol, and underscored and overscored text.

Use Mtext (multiline text) to create paragraph text.

Spell check your drawing.

Use the Table... command to create door and window schedules.

Use Raster Image commands to insert pictures into AutoCAD drawings.

Exercise 5–1: Placing Text on Drawings

To make complete drawings with AutoCAD, you need to know how text is added to the drawings. The following AutoCAD commands, used to place lettering on drawings, are examined in Exercise 5–1.

Text Style...   Used to control the appearance of text.
Single Line Text (Dtext)   Used to draw text that is not in paragraph form.
Multiline Text (Mtext)   Used to draw text that is in paragraph form.

When you have completed Exercise 5–1, your drawing will look similar to the drawing in Figure 5–1.

The A-size drawing template, created in Chapter 2, will be used for this exercise.

**THIS WAS TYPED
WITH THE HEADING STYLE,
AND THE IMPACT FONT,
1/4" HIGH, CENTERED**

THIS WAS TYPED
WITH THE HANDLTR STYLE,
AND THE CITY BLUEPRINT FONT,
3/16" HIGH, CENTERED

STANDARD STYLE, FIT OPTION

V
E
R
T
I
C
A
L

S
T
Y
L
E

OVERSCORE WITH THE OVERSCORE STYLE

O̅V̅E̅R̅S̅C̅O̅R̅E̅ WITH THE STANDARD STYLE

U̲N̲D̲E̲R̲S̲C̲O̲R̲E̲ ̲W̲I̲T̲H̲ ̲T̲H̲E̲ ̲S̲T̲A̲N̲D̲A̲R̲D̲ ̲S̲T̲Y̲L̲E̲
STANDARD CODES WITH THE STANDARD STYHLE

±1/16"   45°   Ø1/2"

ᗡᴿ∀ANᗡ∀TS ꓒꓵᗡ∀ГИ∀TS ANᗡ ꓒꓵᗡ∀TS
[UPSIDEDOWN AND BACKWARD
WITH THE UPSIDEDOWN STYLE,
ARIAL FONT] *(displayed upside-down)*

THIS IS PARAGRAPH OR MULTILINE
TEXT TYPED WITH THE SANS
SERIF FONT, ⅛" HIGH IN AN AREA
THAT MEASURES 3" X 1"

THIS IS *PARAGRAPH OR MULTILINE*
TEXT TYPED WITH THE SANS
SERIF FONT, ⅛" HIGH IN AN AREA
THAT MEASURES 3" X 1"

Step I.   Use your workspace to make the following settings:

1. CLICK: **New**
2. LOOK: **in the drive and/or folder where you saved the A-size template**
3. CLICK: **A-size.dwt** (or DOUBLE-CLICK to open)
4. CLICK: **Open**
5. Use SaveAs... to save the drawing on the hard drive or network drive with the name **CH5–EX1**.
6. Set **Layer1** current.
7. Use **Zoom-All** to view the limits of the drawing.

 NOTE: If you cannot find your template, make the settings for this drawing using the settings described in Exercise 2–1.

Making Settings for Text Style...

It is very important to understand the difference between the terms *style name* and *font name* with regard to text:

Style name: This is a general category that can be assigned any name you choose. The style name is used to distinguish fonts. You may use the same name for the style as is used for the font, or you may use a different name, single number, or letter for the style name.

Font name: This is the name of a particular alphabet that you select to assign to a style name. A font has to be in the AutoCAD program before it can be selected and assigned to a style name.

You may have only one font per style, but you can have many styles with the same font. For example,

Style Name	Font Name
SIMPLEX	SIMPLEX
CLIENT NAME	ITALIC
NOTES	SIMPLEX
ITALIC	ITALIC
BANNER	MONOTEXT
COMPANY NAME	ROMAND
ROMAND	ROMAND

In the following procedure, the Text Style... setting is used.

Step 2. Make the setting for the STANDARD style (Figure 5–2):

Prompt	Response
Command:	**Text Style...** (or TYPE: **ST<enter>**)
The Text Style dialog box appears:	CLICK: **TechnicLite** (in the Font Name: list)
	CLICK: **Apply**

Any text typed while the STANDARD style is active will now contain the TechnicLite font. Notice the preview area in the lower right corner that shows you what the font looks like. Notice also that the vertical setting is grayed out, indicating that this font cannot be drawn running up and down.

The other settings should be left as they are. If you leave the text height set at 0, you will be able to draw different heights of the same style and you will be able to change the height of text if you need to. Leave the text height set to 0 in all cases. The Width Factor allows you to stretch letters so they are wider by making the width factor greater than 1, narrower by making the width factor less than 1. The Oblique Angle slants the letters to the right if the angle is positive and to the left if the angle is negative.

FIGURE 5–2
Select the TechnicLite Font
for the Standard Style

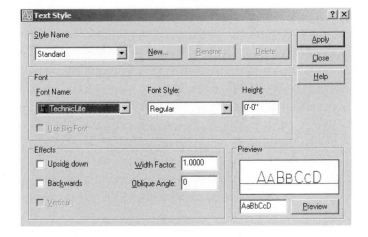

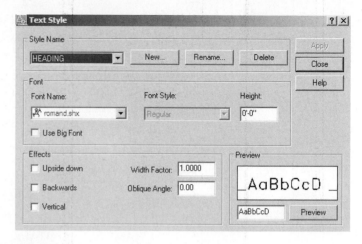

FIGURE 5–4
Select the romand.shx Font for the HEADING Style

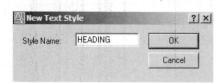

FIGURE 5–3
Name the Style, HEADING

 TIP: To locate a font in the Font Name: list, hold your cursor over any font name in the list and TYPE: the first letter of the desired font. You can also scroll through the Font Name: list by pressing the up or down key on the keyboard or using the wheel on your wheel mouse.

Step 3. Make the settings for a new style that will be used on the drawing (Figures 5–3 and 5–4):

Prompt	Response
The Text Style dialog box:	CLICK: **New...**
The New Text Style dialog box appears with a Style Name that AutoCAD assigns, style1:	TYPE: **HEADING** (to name the style, Figure 5–3) CLICK: **OK** (or PRESS: <**enter**>)
The Text Style dialog box appears:	CLICK: **romand.shx** (in the Font Name: list, Figure 5–4) CLICK: **Apply**

You now have two styles that have been defined on your drawing, STANDARD and HEADING.

Step 4. On your own (Figures 5–5 and 5–6):

1. Make the settings for the following new styles:

Style Name	Font Name:	Other Settings
HANDLTR	CityBlueprint	None
OVERSCORE	Arial	None
UPSIDEDOWN	Arial	Place checks in the Effects box labeled Upside down and the box labeled Backwards.
VERTICAL	romand.shx	Place a check in the Effects box labeled Vertical, Figure 5–5. Remove checks in Upside down and Backwards.

FIGURE 5–5
Make Setting for the VERTI-CAL Style

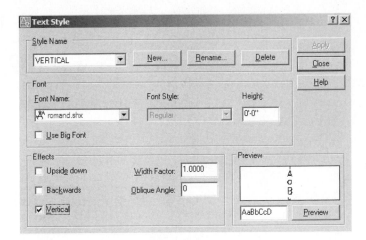

FIGURE 5–6
Check the Style Name List

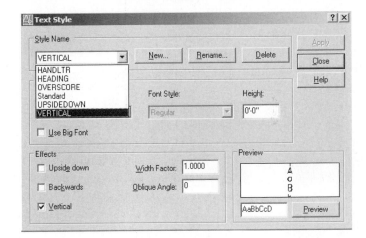

---

2. Click the down arrow in the Style Name list to determine if your list matches the one shown in Figure 5–6.
3. Click the HEADING style name to make it current.
4. Close the dialog box.

NOTE: If you make a mistake while making the settings for a new style, go back to the Text Style dialog box, highlight the style name, change or fix the settings, and CLICK: **Apply.**

Using the Single Line Text Command to Draw Text

The Single Line Text command (also known as Dtext) is used to draw text that is not in paragraph form. Although the name of the command might lead you to believe that only a single line can be drawn, such is not the case. To draw one line under another just PRESS: <**enter**>, and the next line will be ready to be drawn with the same settings as the first line. To demonstrate this, draw several of the lines of text on your current drawing.

If you are not happy with the location of the text, use the Move command to relocate it.

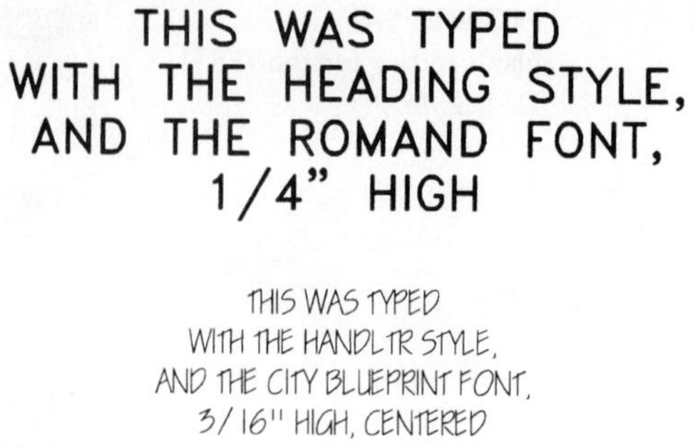

FIGURE 5–7
First Two Examples of Single
Line Text

THIS WAS TYPED
WITH THE HEADING STYLE,
AND THE ROMAND FONT,
1/4" HIGH

THIS WAS TYPED
WITH THE HANDLTR STYLE,
AND THE CITY BLUEPRINT FONT,
3/16" HIGH, CENTERED

Step 5. Draw the first two examples at the top of the page using single line text (Figure 5–7):

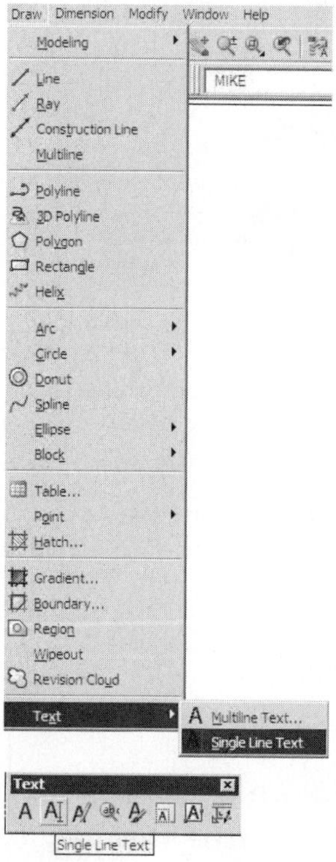

Prompt	Response
Command:	**Single Line Text** (or TYPE: **DT**<**enter**>)
Specify start point of text or [Justify/Style]:	TYPE: **C**<**enter**>
Specify center point of text:	TYPE: **4-1/4,10**<**enter**> (You are locating the center of the line of text using absolute coordinates, 4-1/4″ to the right and 10″ up)
Specify height <0′-0 3/16″>:	TYPE: **1/4**<**enter**>
Specify rotation angle of text <0>:	<**enter**>
The In-Place Text Editor appears ON the screen:	TYPE: **THIS WAS TYPED**<**enter**>
	TYPE: **WITH THE HEADING STYLE,** <**enter**>
	TYPE: **AND THE ROMAND FONT,** <**enter**>
	TYPE: **1/4″ HIGH**<**enter**>
	<**enter**> (to exit the Text Editor)
Command:	<**enter**> (repeat DTEXT)
Specify start point of text or [Justify/Style]:	TYPE: **S**<**enter**> (to change styles)
Enter style name or [?] <HEADING>:	TYPE: **HANDLTR**<**enter**>
Specify start point of text or [Justify/Style]:	TYPE: **C**<**enter**>
Specify center point of text:	TYPE: **4-1/4,8**<**enter**>
Specify height <0′-0 1/4″>:	TYPE: **3/16**<**enter**>
Specify rotation angle of text <0>:	<**enter**>
The In-Place Text Editor appears	TYPE: **THIS WAS TYPED**<**enter**>
	TYPE: **WITH THE HANDLTR STYLE,**<**enter**>
	TYPE: **AND THE CITY BLUEPRINT FONT,** <**enter**>
	TYPE: **3/16″ HIGH, CENTERED** <**enter**>
	<**enter**>

Step 6. Draw the next block of text using the Fit option of single line text with the STANDARD style (Figure 5–8):

Prompt	Response
Command:	**Single Line Text** (or TYPE: **DT**<**enter**>)

FIGURE 5–8
Using the Fit Option of Single Line Text

THIS WAS TYPED
WITH THE HEADING STYLE,
AND THE ROMAND FONT,
1/4" HIGH

THIS WAS TYPED
WITH THE HANDLTR STYLE,
AND THE CITY BLUEPRINT FONT,
3/16" HIGH, CENTERED

STANDARD STYLE, FIT OPTION

Prompt	Response
Specify start point of text or [Justify/Style]:	TYPE: **S<enter>** (to change styles)
Enter style name or [?] <HANDLTR>:	TYPE: **STANDARD<enter>**
Specify start point of text or [Justify/Style]:	TYPE: **F<enter>** (for Fit)
Specify first endpoint of text baseline:	TYPE: **1-1/2,6<enter>**
Specify second endpoint of text baseline:	TYPE: **7,6<enter>**
Specify height <0'-0 3/16">:	TYPE: **1/2<enter>**
The In-Place Text Editor appears:	TYPE: **STANDARD STYLE, FIT OPTION** <enter> <enter>

When you activate the Single Line Text command, the prompt is "Specify start point of text or [Justify/Style]:". The Style option allows you to select a different style (that has already been defined) for the text you are about to draw. If you TYPE: **J<enter>**, the prompt then becomes "Enter an option [Align/Fit/Center/Middle/ Right/TL/TC/TR/ML/ MC/MR/BL/BC/BR]:".

Align

Align draws the text between two points that you click. It does not condense or expand the font but instead adjusts the letter height so that the text fits between the two points.

Fit

Fit draws the text between two clicked points like the Align option, but instead of changing the letter height, Fit condenses or expands the font to fit between the points.

Center

Center draws the text so that the bottom of the line of lettering is centered on the clicked point. Centering is not displayed until the second return is pressed. You may also choose the top or the middle of the line of lettering by typing TC or MC at the justify prompt.

Middle

Middle draws the text so that the middle of the line of lettering is centered around a clicked point. This is very useful when a single line of text must be centered in an area such as a box. Middle is not displayed until the second return is pressed.

Right

Right draws the text so that each line of text is right justified (ends at the same right margin). Right justification is not displayed until the second return is pressed. The top or center of the line may also be selected by typing TR or MR at the justify prompt.

TL/TC/TR/ML/MC/MR/BL/BC/BR

These are alignment options: Top Left, Top Center, Top Right, Middle Left, Middle Center, Middle Right, Bottom Left, Bottom Center, Bottom Right. They are used with horizontal text.

Step 7. **Draw a line of text using the VERTICAL style (Figure 5–9):**
(Remember that you checked Vertical in the Text Style dialog box for this text style.)

Prompt	Response
Command:	<enter> (repeat DTEXT)
Specify start point of text or [Justify/Style]:	TYPE: S<enter>

FIGURE 5–9
Using the Vertical Option of
Single Line Text

THIS WAS TYPED
WITH THE HEADING STYLE,
AND THE ROMAND FONT,
1/4" HIGH

THIS WAS TYPED
WITH THE HANDLTR STYLE,
AND THE CITY BLUEPRINT FONT,
3/16" HIGH, CENTERED

STANDARD STYLE, FIT OPTION

V
E
R
T
I
C
A
L

S
T
Y
L
E

Prompt	Response
Enter style name or [?] <STANDARD>:	TYPE: **VERTICAL**<enter>
Specify start point of text or [Justify/Style]:	TYPE: **1,6** <enter>
Specify height <0'-0" 3/16">:	TYPE: **1/4** <enter>
Specify rotation angle of text <270>:	<enter>
The In-Place Text Editor appears:	TYPE: **VERTICAL STYLE**<enter> <enter>

Using Standard Codes to Draw Special Characters

Figures 5–10 through 5–14 show the use of codes to obtain several commonly used symbols, such as the degree symbol, the diameter symbol, the plus–minus symbol, and underscored and overscored text. The top line of Figure 5–10 shows the code that must be typed to obtain the degree symbol following the number 45. The top line is displayed until <enter> is pressed to obtain the degree symbol shown on the bottom line. Two percent symbols followed by the letter D produce the degree symbol.

Figure 5–11 illustrates that two percent symbols followed by the letter C produce the diameter symbol. Any text following the symbol must be typed immediately following the code.

Figure 5–12 shows the code for the plus–minus symbol.

Figure 5–13 shows the code for underscore: two percent symbols followed by the letter U. Notice that the first line contains only one code. The second line contains two codes: one to start the underline and one to stop it.

Figure 5–14 shows the code for overscored text. The same code sequence for starting and stopping the overscore applies.

Step 8. Draw five lines containing special codes for the overscore, underscore, plus–minus, degree, and diameter symbols (Figure 5–15):

Prompt	Response
Command:	<enter> (repeat DTEXT)
Specify start point of text or [Justify/Style]:	TYPE: **S**<enter>

45%%D

45˚

FIGURE 5–10
Degree Symbol Code

%%C.500

⌀.500

FIGURE 5–11
Diameter Symbol Code

%%P.005

±.005

FIGURE 5–12
Plus–Minus Symbol Code

%%UUNDERSCORE

UNDERSCORE

%%UUNDERSCORE%%U LETTERS

UNDERSCORE LETTERS

FIGURE 5–13
Underscore Code

%%OOVERSCORE

OVERSCORE

%%OOVERSCORE%%O LETTERS

OVERSCORE LETTERS

FIGURE 5–14
Overscore Code

Prompt	Response
Enter style name or [?] <VERTICAL>:	TYPE: **OVERSCORE**<enter>
Specify start point of text or [Justify/Style]:	TYPE: **1-1/2,5**<enter>
Specify height <0′-0 3/16″>:	TYPE: **3/16**<enter>
Specify rotation angle of text <0>:	<enter>
The In-Place Text Editor appears:	TYPE: **%%OOVERSCORE WITH THE OVER-SCORE STYLE**<enter><enter>
Command:	<enter> (repeat DTEXT)
Specify start point of text or [Justify/Style]:	TYPE: **S**<enter>
Enter style name or [?] <OVERSCORE>:	TYPE: **STANDARD**<enter>
Specify start point of text or [Justify/Style]:	TYPE: **1-1/2,4-1/2**<enter>
Specify height <0′-0 3/16″>:	TYPE: **3/16** <enter>
Specify rotation angle of text <0>:	<enter>
The In-Place Text Editor appears:	TYPE: **%%OOVERSCORE%%O WITH THE STANDARD STYLE** <enter> <enter>
Command:	<enter> (Repeat DTEXT)
Specify start point of text or [Justify/Style]:	TYPE: **1-1/2,4**<enter>
Specify height <0′-0 3/16″>:	TYPE: **3/16** <enter>

FIGURE 5–15
Using Single Line Text to Draw Symbols with Standard Codes

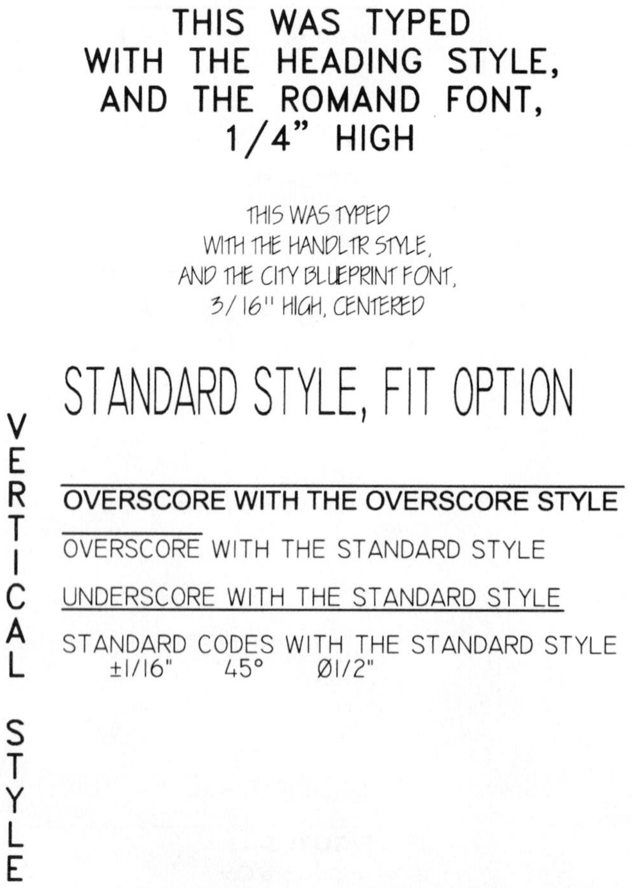

THIS WAS TYPED
WITH THE HEADING STYLE,
AND THE ROMAND FONT,
1/4" HIGH

THIS WAS TYPED
WITH THE HANDLTR STYLE,
AND THE CITY BLUEPRINT FONT,
3/16" HIGH, CENTERED

STANDARD STYLE, FIT OPTION

V
E
R
T
I
C
A
L

S
T
Y
L
E

OVERSCORE WITH THE OVERSCORE STYLE

OVERSCORE WITH THE STANDARD STYLE

UNDERSCORE WITH THE STANDARD STYLE

STANDARD CODES WITH THE STANDARD STYLE
±1/16"   45°   Ø1/2"

Prompt	Response
Specify rotation angle of text <0>	<enter>
The In-Place Text Editor appears:	TYPE: **%%UUNDERSCORE WITH THE STANDARD STYLE** <enter> <enter>
Command:	<enter> (Repeat DTEXT)
Specify start point of text or [Justify/Style]:	<enter>
The In-Place Text Editor appears:	TYPE: **STANDARD CODES WITH THE STANDARD STYLE** <enter> <enter>
Command:	<enter> (Repeat DTEXT)
Specify start point of text or [Justify/Style]:	CLICK: **a point in the approximate location ±1/16″ is shown in Figure 5–15**
Specify height <0′-0 3/16″>:	<enter> (to accept the 3/16″ default height)
Specify rotation angle of text <0>:	<enter>
The In-Place Text Editor appears:	TYPE: **%%P1/16″**<enter> <enter>
Command:	

Step 9. On your own:

1. Use Single Line Text (DTEXT) to add the following text (3/16 height) to your drawing as shown in Figure 5–15:

   45° (45 %%D)
   Ø1/2″ (%%C1/2″)

2. Make the Style Name UPSIDEDOWN current.
3. Use Single Line Text to draw the following phrase (3/16 height) upside down and backward with its start point at 7,2-1/2 (Figure 5–16):

UPSIDEDOWN AND BACKWARD <enter>
WITH THE UPSIDEDOWN STYLE, <enter>
ARIAL FONT <enter> <enter>

Using the Multiline Text Command to Draw Text Paragraphs

The Multiline Text command (also known as Mtext) is used to draw text in paragraph form. The command activates the Multiline Text Editor, which has many of the same features that other Windows Text Editors have. You can select a defined style, change the text height and case, boldface and italicize some fonts, select a justification style, specify the width of the line, rotate a paragraph, search for a word and replace it with another, undo, import text, number lines, insert bullets, and select symbols for use on your drawing. In this exercise you will create a paragraph using the sans serif font.

Step 10. Use Multiline Text to draw a paragraph (Figure 5–17), then copy it 3-1/4″ to the right:

Prompt	Response
Command:	TYPE: **ST**<enter> CLICK: **Standard** in the Style Name list and close the dialog box.
Command:	**Multiline Text** (or TYPE: **MT**<enter>)

FIGURE 5–16
Draw a Phrase Upside Down
and Backward with the
UPSIDEDOWN Style

THIS WAS TYPED
WITH THE HEADING STYLE,
AND THE ROMAND FONT,
1/4" HIGH, CENTERED

THIS WAS TYPED
WITH THE HANDLTR STYLE,
AND THE CITY BLUEPRINT FONT,
3/16" HIGH, CENTERED

STANDARD STYLE, FIT OPTION

V
E
R
T
I
C
A
L

S
T
Y
L
E

OVERSCORE WITH THE OVERSCORE STYLE

OVERSCORE WITH THE STANDARD STYLE

UNDERSCORE WITH THE STANDARD STYLE

STANDARD CODES WITH THE STANDARD STYLE
±1/16"   45°   Ø1/2"

UPSIDE DOWN AND BACKWARD
WITH THE UPSIDEDOWN STYLE,
ARIAL FONT

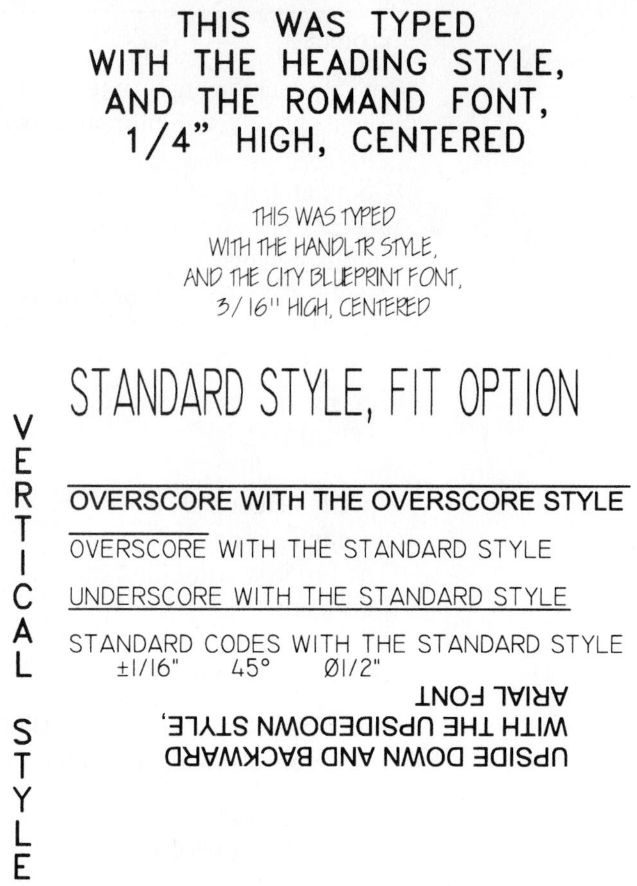

Prompt	Response
Specify first corner:	TYPE: **1-1/2,2<enter>**
Specify opposite corner or [Height/ Justify/Line spacing/Rotation/ Style/Width]:	TYPE: **@3,-1 <enter>** (Be sure to include the @ symbol and the minus (−) so the vertical side of the text box is down. This makes the paragraph box 3″ × 1″ tall)
The Text Formatting Editor appears:	**Change the text height to 1/8 and the font to SansSerif,** then TYPE: **the paragraph shown in Figures 5–17 and 5–19.** When you type 1/8 in the paragraph, the dialog box shown in Figure 5–18 appears. CHECK: **Enable AutoStacking** as shown so the fraction will be stacked with the numerator over the denominator. CLICK: **OK** to close the dialog box. After the paragraph is typed correctly, CLICK: **OK** to close the Text Formatting Editor and complete the paragraph.
Command:	TYPE: **CP<enter>**
Select objects:	CLICK: **any point on the paragraph**
Select objects:	**<enter>**

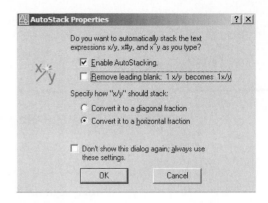

FIGURE 5–17
Multiline or Paragraph Text

FIGURE 5–18
Enable AutoStacking

Prompt	Response
Specify base point or [Displacement] <Displacement>:	CLICK: **any point**
Specify second point or <use first point as displacement>:	With ORTHO on: **move your mouse to the right** and TYPE: **3-1/4<enter>** (This copies the paragraph 3-1/4″ directly to the right, Figure 5–19.)
Specify second point or [Exit/Undo] <Exit>:	<enter>

FIGURE 5–19
Use Multiline Text to Type a
Paragraph, Then Copy It

THIS WAS TYPED
WITH THE HEADING STYLE,
AND THE ROMAND FONT,
1/4" HIGH

THIS WAS TYPED
WITH THE HANDLTR STYLE,
AND THE CITY BLUEPRINT FONT,
3/16" HIGH, CENTERED

STANDARD STYLE, FIT OPTION

<u>OVERSCORE WITH THE OVERSCORE STYLE</u>

OVERSCORE WITH THE STANDARD STYLE

UNDERSCORE WITH THE STANDARD STYLE
STANDARD CODES WITH THE STANDARD STYHLE

±1/16"   45°   Ø1/2"

ARIAL FONT
WITH THE UPSIDEDOWN STYLE,
UPSIDE DOWN AND BACKWARD

V
E
R
T
I
C
A
L

S
T
Y
L
E

THIS IS PARAGRAPH OR MULTILINE
TEXT TYPED WITH THE SANS
SERIF FONT, ⅜" HIGH IN AN AREA
THAT MEASURES 3" X 1"

THIS IS PARAGRAPH OR MULTILINE
TEXT TYPED WITH THE SANS
SERIF FONT, ⅜" HIGH IN AN AREA
THAT MEASURES 3" X 1"

If you have trouble getting the Multiline Text to change text height, cancel the command and TYPE: **DT** to activate Single Line Text and change the default text height to 1/8. The Multiline Text height will then be set at 1/8, and you can proceed with typing the paragraph. Be sure you do not cancel the Single Line Text command before you have changed the default text height.

Changing Text Properties

There will be occasions when you will need to change the text font, height, or content. AutoCAD has several commands that can be used to do these tasks:

Text Style...   Use this command to change the font of text within a text style that already exists on your drawing.

DDEDIT (Edit Text)   Use this command if you want to change the text contents only for Single Line Text. This command allows you to select multiline text and allows you to change its contents and several of its properties.

NOTE: Double-click on the text to edit it.

Properties   Use this command to change any of the text's characteristics: properties, origin, style, height, rotation angle, the text content, or any of several other properties.

Step 11. **Use the Text Style... command to change the font of text typed with the HEADING name from Romand to Impact (Figure 5–20):**

Prompt	Response
Command:	**Text Style...** (or TYPE: **ST<enter>**)
The Text Style dialog box appears:	CLICK: **HEADING** (in the Style Name list)
	CLICK: **Impact** (from the Font Name: list, Figure 5–20)
	CLICK: **Apply**
	CLICK: **Close**

FIGURE 5–20
Select the Impact Font for the HEADING Style

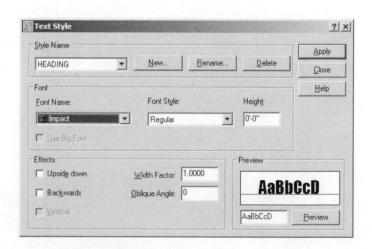

FIGURE 5–21
Change Text Using DDEDIT
(Edit Text)

**THIS WAS TYPED
WITH THE HEADING STYLE,
AND THE IMPACT FONT,
1/4" HIGH**

Notice that everything you typed with the HEADING style name is now still the HEADING style but changed to the Impact font.

Step 12. Use the DDEDIT (Edit Text) command to change "AND THE ROMAND FONT" at the top of the page to "AND THE IMPACT FONT" (Figure 5–21):

Prompt	Response
Command:	**Modify-Object-Text-Edit...** or TYPE: **ED<enter>**
Select an annotation object or [Undo]:	CLICK: **AND THE ROMAND FONT**
The In-Place Text Editor appears:	CLICK: **to the right of ROMAND, backspace over ROMAND** and TYPE: **IMPACT** (Figure 5–21)
Select an annotation object or [Undo]:	**<enter> <enter>**

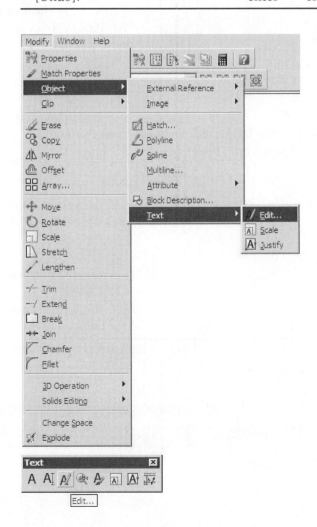

NOTE: Double-click on any text to edit it.

Step 13. On your own:

1. Use the Edit Text command or DOUBLE-CLICK on the line of text that reads "1/4″ HIGH" and change it to "1/4″ HIGH, CENTERED."

Step 14. Continue using the Edit Text command to change the words PARA-GRAPH OR MULTILINE TEXT in the copied paragraph to the italic font (Figure 5–22):

Prompt	Response
Command:	TYPE: **ED** <enter>
Select an annotation object or [Undo]:	CLICK: **any point on the copied paragraph**
The Text Formatting Editor (Figure 5–22) appears:	CLICK: **the left mouse button to the left of the word PARAGRAPH, hold it down, and drag to the end to the word TEXT so that PARAGRAPH OR MULTILINE TEXT is highlighted,** then CLICK: **I** (for italic)
	CLICK: **OK**
Select an annotation object or [UNDO]:	PRESS: **ESC** or <enter>

Step 15. Use the DDMODIFY (Properties) command to change the vertical line of text from Layer1 to Layer2 (Figure 5–23):

Prompt	Response
Command:	CLICK: **the vertical line of text (VERTICAL STYLE) and RIGHT-CLICK**
The right-click menu appears:	CLICK: **Properties**
The Properties dialog box appears:	CLICK: **Layer**
	CLICK: **the down arrow** (Figure 5–23)
	CLICK: **Layer2**
	CLICK: **the X in the upper left corner to close**
	PRESS: **Esc**

FIGURE 5–22
Changing Multiline Text to Italic

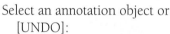

FIGURE 5–23
Change Text to Layer2

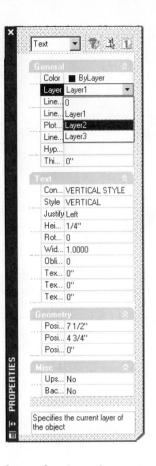

VERTICAL STYLE is now changed to Layer2.

Step 16. On your own:

1. Use Single Line Text, STANDARD style, 1/8″ high to place your name and class number in the upper left and upper right corners, respectively. The start point for your name is 1,10-1/2. Use right-justified text for class number (at the Dtext prompt "Specify start point of text or [Justify/Style]:" TYPE: R<enter>. The right endpoint of text baseline is 7-1/2,10-1/2.

Checking the Spelling

AutoCAD has a spell checker that allows you to accurately check the spelling on your drawing. If the word is correctly spelled but is not in the current dictionary, you can select Ignore All to ignore all instances of that word on the drawing. You can also add the word to the current dictionary. You can change the spelling of a single use of a word or all instances of the word on the drawing by picking Change All. AutoCAD also allows you to change dictionaries.

Step 17. On your own:

1. Purposely misspell the word TYPED. Use Edit Text... (or Properties) to change THIS WAS TYPED to THIS WAS TPYED.

Step 18. Use the Spelling command to check the spelling on your drawing (Figures 5–24 and 5–25):

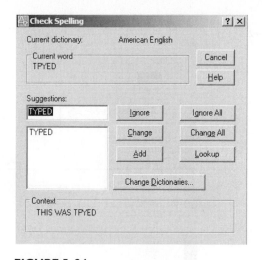

FIGURE 5–24
Change TPYED to TYPED Using the Spelling Command

FIGURE 5–25
CLICK: **OK** to Complete the Spell Check

Prompt	Response
Command:	**Spelling** (or TYPE: **SP**\<enter\>)
Select objects:	TYPE: **ALL**\<enter\> to select all the text on your drawing
Select objects:	\<enter\>
The Check Spelling dialog box appears (Figure 5–24):	CLICK: **Ignore All** for all font and command names until you reach the word TPYED
	CLICK: the word **TYPED** if it is not already highlighted in the Suggestions: box
	CLICK: **Change**
The AutoCAD Message appears:	CLICK: **OK** (Figure 5–25)

Step 19. When you have completed Exercise 5–1, save your work in at least two places.

Step 20. Print your drawing from the Model tab at a scale of 1 = 1 after completing Chapter 6.

Exercise 5–2: Using the Table... Command to Create a Door Schedule

Table...

The Table... command in AutoCAD 2007 gives us a tool to easily create professional appearing tables such as door schedules, tables for drawing sets, tabular drawings, window schedules, and similar items.

When you have completed Exercise 5–2 your drawing will look similar to Figure 5–26. This is a commonly used means of specifying the number and types of doors used in a commercial or residential building.

Step 1. Use your workspace to make the following settings:

1. Use Save As... to save the drawing with the name CH5-EX2.

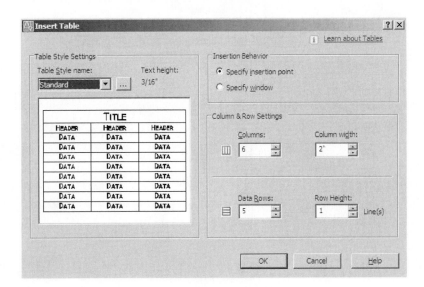

FIGURE 5–26
Door Schedule

DOOR SCHEDULE			
MARK	SIZE	QUANTITY	REMARKS
1	2'0" X 6'8	8	FLUSH DOOR
2	2'6" X 6'8"	2	FLUSH DOOR
3	2'6" X 6'8"	1	EXT FLUSH DOOR
4	3'0" X 7'0"	1	EXT FLUSH DOOR
5	4'0" X 6'8"	3	DOUBLE DOOR
6	3'0" X 6'8"	1	DOUBLE DOOR
7	9'4" X 6'8"	1	SLIDING GLASS

2. Set drawing Units: **Architectural**
3. Set Drawing Limits: **11,8–1/2**
4. Set GRIDDISPLAY: **0**
5. Set Grid: **1/4″**
6. Set Snap: **1/8″**
7. Create the following Layers:

LAYER NAME	COLOR	LINETYPE	LINEWEIGHT
Table	White	Continuous	Default
Text	Green	Continuous	Default

8. Set **Layer Table** current.
9. Use **Zoom-All** to view the limits of the drawing.

Step 2. Use the **Table...** command on the Draw menu to define the table:

Prompt	Response
Command:	CLICK: **Table** (or TYPE: **TABLE<enter>**)
The Insert Table dialog box, Figure 5–27 appears:	Make the settings shown in Figure 5–27: 6 columns (you will need only 4, but specify 6 anyway—you will delete two of them). Set Column width: at 2″ (you will change the column widths as you create the table).

FIGURE 5–27
Insert Table Dialog Box

FIGURE 5–28
Table Style Dialog Box

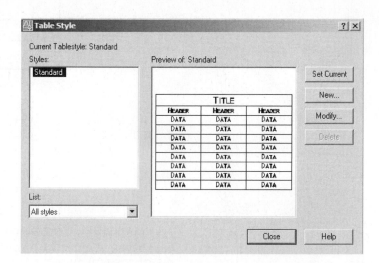

	Prompt	Response
		5 rows (you will need 7, but specify 5 for now—adding rows is very easy).
		Set Row Height: at 1 if it is not the default.
		CLICK: **the ellipsis (...) next to the Standard Table Style name:**
	The Table Style dialog box, Figure 5–28, appears:	At this point you could specify a New Table Style name, but for now just modify the Standard Table.
		CLICK: **Modify...**
	The Modify Table Style: Standard dialog box, Figure 5–29, appears:	There are three tabs: Data, Column Heads, and Title. The example figure to the right in the

FIGURE 5–29
Modify Table Style: Standard
Dialog Box

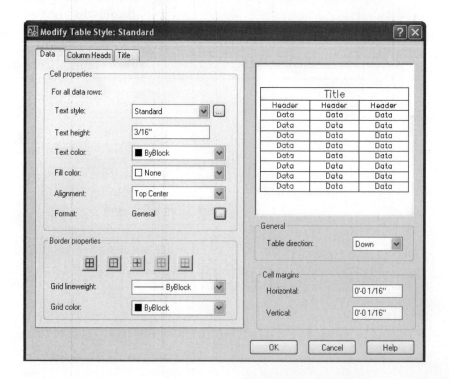

Prompt	Response
	dialog box shows you where the text for each tab is located in the table.
	In the Cell properties area you can choose a different text style for each tab if you desire. For this example only one will be used.
	CLICK: **the ellipsis (...) button to the right of the word Standard** (the Standard Text style name)
The Text Style dialog box appears:	**Change the font to Simplex.**
	CLICK: **Apply**
	CLICK: **Close** (Notice that the example table now shows the Simplex font.)
	Leave all other settings for Cell properties at the values shown in Figure 5–29. Notice that you can change the text height, text color, fill color, and alignment.
	The Border properties area allows you to set line thickness and line color and otherwise to vary the appearance of the table: **Leave all these settings as shown.**
	Table direction can go up or down. **Select Down for now.**
	Finally, the Cell margins allow you to specify how much space should be left between the text in the table and the lines forming the table. **Both settings should read 0′-0 1/16″.**
	CLICK: **the Column Heads tab**
The Column Heads tab, Figure 5–30, appears:	**Make settings or accept the defaults as shown in the figure.**
	CLICK: **the Title tab**

FIGURE 5–30
Column Heads Tab of the Modify Table Style: Standard Dialog Box

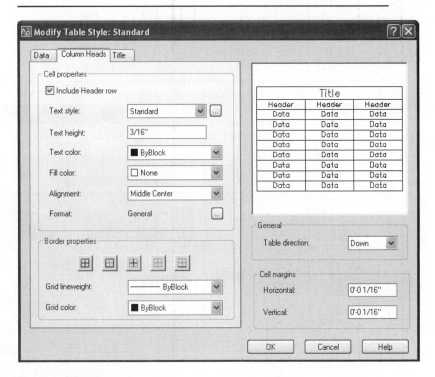

FIGURE 5–31
Title Tab of the Modify Table
Style: Standard Dialog Box

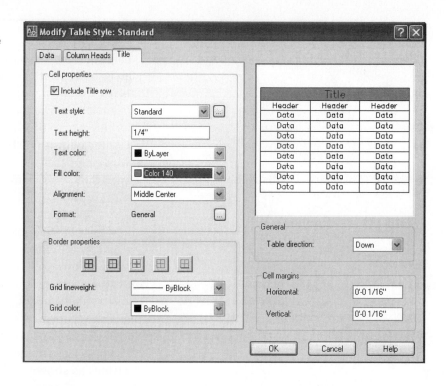

Prompt	Response
The Title tab, Figure 5–31, appears:	In the Cell properties area:
	Make sure a check appears in the Include Title row box.
	Text height: 1/4″
	CLICK: **the Text color: list and set it to ByLayer**
	CLICK: **the Fill color: list** and CLICK: **Select color...** at the bottom of the list
The Select Color dialog box appears:	CLICK: **color 140 in the area shown in Figure 5–32**
	CLICK: **OK**
The Title tab settings should appear as shown in Figure 5–31:	CLICK: **OK**
The Table Style dialog box appears:	CLICK: **Close**

FIGURE 5–32
Select Color Dialog Box

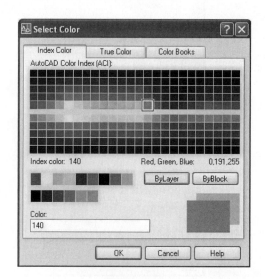

FIGURE 5–33
Door Schedule

DOOR SCHEDULE					
MARK					
1					
2					
3					
4					
5					

Step 3. Insert the table and type the title:

Prompt	Response
The Insert Table dialog box appears: The table appears attached to the cursor:	CLICK: **OK**
Specify insertion point:	CLICK: **a point to place the table in the approximate center of the page. (It will hang outside the drawing limits for now.)**
The Text Formatting dialog box appears with the cursor flashing in the center of the Title space:	TYPE: **DOOR SCHEDULE<enter>**

Step 4. Create column 1 head and all data in column 1:

Prompt	Response
The cursor begins flashing in the center of the first column head area:	TYPE: **MARK<enter>**
The cursor begins flashing in the center of the first data area:	TYPE: **1<enter>**
The cursor begins flashing in the center of the second data area:	TYPE: **2<enter>** **3<enter>** **through 5** so the table appears as shown in Figure 5–33

NOTE: If numbers in data cells are not in the center, CLICK: once on each number, then RIGHT-CLICK:, and CLICK: Cell Alignment - Top Center.

Prompt	Response
The table appears as shown in Figure 5–33:	CLICK: **once on the 5 data box as shown in Figure 5–34** **With the 5 box highlighted,** RIGHT-CLICK:
The right-click menu appears:	CLICK: **Insert Rows - Below**
With the 5 data box still highlighted:	**Hold down the Shift key,** CLICK: **the next row, release the Shift key, then** RIGHT-CLICK. CLICK: **Insert Rows - Below** (Figure 5–35) (to insert two rows at the same time)

Step 5. On your own:

1. DOUBLE-CLICK: **the blank box under item 5 and** Type: **6 <enter>, and 7
<enter>, then** CLICK: **OK.**
2. CLICK: **the blank row,** RIGHT-CLICK:, **and delete the 8th row.**

FIGURE 5–34
Insert Rows - Below

FIGURE 5–35
Door Schedule, Row 5
Highlighted

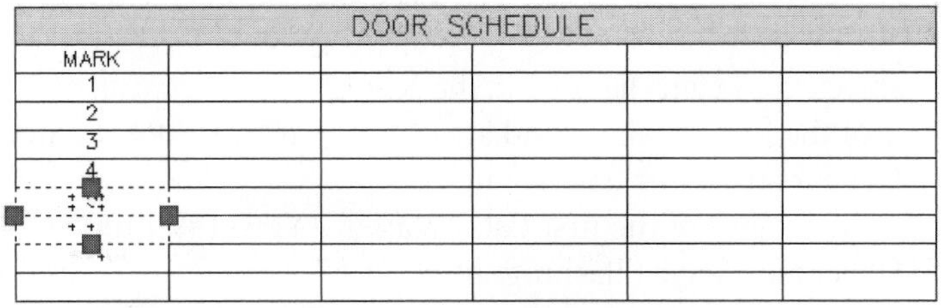

Step 6. Add remaining column heads (Figure 5–36):

Prompt	Response
	DOUBLE-CLICK: the second column head area
The Text Formatting Box appears with the cursor flashing in the center of the second column head:	TYPE: **SIZE** (do not press <enter>)
	PRESS: the Tab key
The cursor is flashing in the center of the third column head:	TYPE: **QUANTITY**
	PRESS: the Tab key
The cursor is flashing in the center of the fourth column head:	TYPE: **REMARKS** <enter>
	CLICK: **OK** (in the Text Formatting box)

FIGURE 5–36
Text Formatting Dialog Box
and Door Schedule

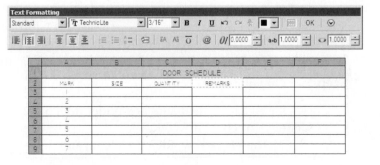

FIGURE 5–37
Delete Columns

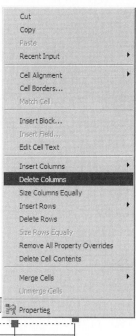

Step 7.   Delete unneeded columns (Figure 5–37):

Prompt   Response

                                          CLICK: **the two columns to the right of the
                                              REMARKS column.** (Hold down the Shift key
                                              to select the second column.)
                                          Release the Shift key.
                                          With the two blank columns highlighted,
                                              RIGHT-CLICK:
The right-click menu appears: CLICK: **Delete Columns**

Step 8.   Change the width of the columns to fit the data text (Figure 5–38):

Prompt   Response

                                          CLICK once on the first column head,
                                              (MARK) and RIGHT-CLICK:
The right-click menu appears: CLICK: **Properties**
The Properties palette appears: **Change Cell width to 1″ and Cell height to**
                                              5/8″, as shown.

Step 9.   On your own:

1. Change the width of the remaining columns (Figure 5–39):

    Column 2 (SIZE)—leave at 2″
    Column 3 (QUANTITY)—change to 1-1/2″
    Column 4 (REMARKS)—change to 2-3/4″

2. Close the Properties palette.

FIGURE 5–38
Properties Palette

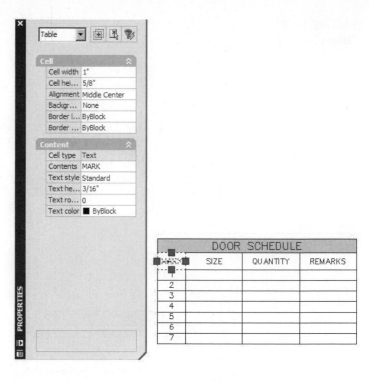

FIGURE 5–38
Properties Palette

Step 10. On your own (Figure 5–40):

1. DOUBLE-CLICK: the first cell under the SIZE column head and TYPE: 2′0″ × 6′8″ <enter>. TYPE: each door size.
2. DOUBLE-CLICK: the first cell under the QUANTITY column head and TYPE: each door quantity and PRESS: <enter>
3. DOUBLE-CLICK: the first cell under the REMARKS column head and TYPE: each door description and PRESS: <enter>

FIGURE 5–39
Properties Palette

FIGURE 5–40
Door Schedule

DOOR SCHEDULE			
MARK	SIZE	QUANTITY	REMARKS
1	2'0" X 6'8	8	FLUSH DOOR
2	2'6" X 6'8"	2	FLUSH DOOR
3	2'6" X 6'8"	1	EXT FLUSH DOOR
4	3'0" X 7'0"	1	EXT FLUSH DOOR
5	4'0" X 6'8"	3	DOUBLE DOOR
6	3'0" X 6'8"	1	DOUBLE DOOR
7	9'4" X 6'8"	1	SLIDING GLASS

FIGURE 5–41
Door Schedule

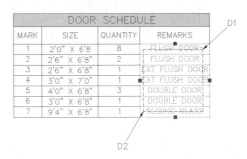

Everything is OK now except that the REMARKS data need to be aligned flush with the left side of the REMARKS column.

Step 11. Align data in the REMARKS column flush left (Figures 5–41, 5–42, and 5–43):

Prompt	Response
With no command active:	CLICK: **D1 (hold the mouse button down)** (Figure 5–41)
Specify opposite corner:	CLICK: **D2** RIGHT-CLICK:
The right-click menu, Figure 5–42, appears:	CLICK: **Cell Alignment - Middle Left** PRESS: **the Esc key**

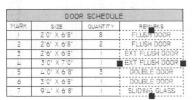

FIGURE 5–42
Cell Alignment

FIGURE 5–43
Completed Door Schedule Table

DOOR SCHEDULE			
MARK	SIZE	QUANTITY	REMARKS
1	2'0" X 6'8	8	FLUSH DOOR
2	2'6" X 6'8"	2	FLUSH DOOR
3	2'6" X 6'8"	1	EXT FLUSH DOOR
4	3'0" X 7'0"	1	EXT FLUSH DOOR
5	4'0" X 6'8"	3	DOUBLE DOOR
6	3'0" X 6'8"	1	DOUBLE DOOR
7	9'4" X 6'8"	1	SLIDING GLASS

Step 12. On your own:

1. Align SIZE column data - middle left.
2. TYPE: your name 1/8″ high in the lower right corner.

Step 13. When you have completed Exercise 5–2, save your work in at least two places.

Step 14. Print your drawing from the Model tab at a scale of 1 = 1 after completing Chapter 6.

FIGURE 5–44
Completed Window
Schedule Table

WINDOW SCHEDULE			
MARK	SIZE	QUANTITY	REMARKS
A	4′ 5–1/8″ X 4′ 2–5/8″	1	METAL FRAME
B	3′ 1–1/8″ X 4′ 2–5/8″	9	METAL FRAME
C	6′–0″ X 4′ 2–5/8″	1	METAL FRAME
D	5′–0″ X 4′ 2–5/8″	1	METAL FRAME
E	9′–0″ X 4′ 2–5/8″	1	METAL FRAME

Exercise 5–3: Using the Table... Command to Create a Window Schedule

When you have completed Exercise 5–3 your drawing will look similar to Figure 5–44. This is a commonly used means of specifying the number and types of windows used in a commercial or residential building. This window schedule describes the windows used in Exercise 5–4.

On Your Own:

1. Use the steps described in Exercise 5–2 to complete the window schedule shown in Figure 5–44.
2. You may copy CH5-EX2, save it as CH5-EX3 and change the column contents to make the new table. You will have to change the SIZE column (cell width) to 3-1/2″.

Exercise 5–4: Using Text and Raster Images to Make a Business Card

In this exercise you will use the text command and insert pictures (raster images) into the drawing to create a personalized business card. After you have drawn your business card, you will then make an array of the card so the card can be printed eight times on a single sheet of thick paper (card stock). The card stock is scored into sections 3-1/2″ wide by 2″ high so you get eight business cards from one sheet (Figure 5–45). The example shown here is for reference. You may select your own fonts for the text and your own pictures for the images. If you do not have access to a digital camera, you may select images from the Internet.

Step 1. On your own:

1. Look at existing business cards that measure 3-1/2″ by 2″ and plan approximately what you want your card to look like.
2. Use a digital camera to take pictures of yourself or other items you want to include on your business card.
3. Make a folder on the hard drive of your computer that will contain these pictures if you do not already have a folder of your drawings.
4. Save the pictures from the digital camera in .jpg format to the folder on the hard drive of your computer.

FIGURE 5–45
Exercise 5–4 Complete

The A-size drawing template, created in Chapter 2, will be used for this exercise.

Step 2.   Use your workspace to make the following setup:

1. CLICK: **New**
2. LOOK: **in the drive and/or folder where you saved the A-size template**
3. CLICK: **A-size.dwt** (or DOUBLE-CLICK to open) (or use settings from Exercise 2–1)
4. CLICK: **Open**
5. Use **SaveAs…** to save the drawing on the hard drive or network drive with the name **CH5-EX3.**
6. Set **Layer1** current
7. Set Drawing Units Precision: **1/32**
8. Use **Zoom-All** to view the limits of the drawing.

Step 3.   Draw a rectangle to define the limits of the business card and locate it at the correct point on the drawing:

Prompt	Response
Command:	**Rectangle** (or TYPE: **REC**<enter>)
Specify first corner point or [Chamfer/Elevation/Fillet/ Thickness/Width]:	TYPE: **1/2,3/4**<enter>
Specify other corner point or [Area/Dimensions/Rotation]:	TYPE: **@3-1/2,2**<enter>

FIGURE 5–46
Zoom in to the Rectangle

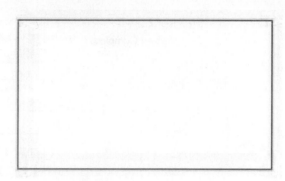

Step 4. Zoom in to the area defined by the rectangle (Figure 5–46):

Prompt	Response
Command:	**Zoom** (or TYPE: **Z<enter>**)
Specify corner of window, enter a scale factor (nX or nXP), or [All/Center/Dynamic/Extents/ Previous/Scale/Window/Object] <real time>:	CLICK: **one corner just outside the rectangle**
Specify opposite corner:	CLICK: **the diagonally opposite corner just outside the rectangle**

Step 5. Create the text styles, select a font for each style, and place the text on the card in the correct locations (Figures 5–47, 5–48, 5–49):

Prompt	Response
Command:	**Text Style...** (or TYPE: **ST<enter>**)
The Text Style dialog box appears:	CLICK: **New...**
The New Text Style dialog box appears with Style1 as the default style name:	CLICK: **OK**
	CLICK: **SansSerif in the Font Name: box and Regular in the Font Style: box, as shown in Figure 5–47.**
	CLICK: **Apply**
	CLICK: **New...**

FIGURE 5–47
Select the Font for style1

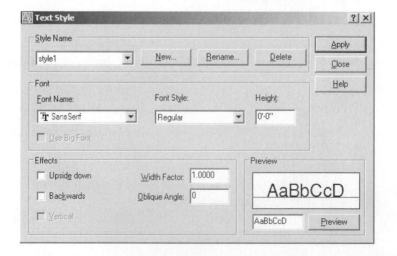

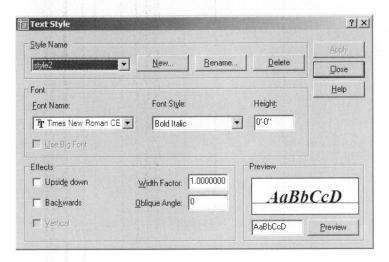

FIGURE 5–48
Select the Font for style2

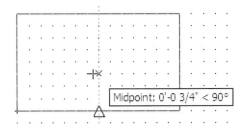

FIGURE 5–49
Center the First Line of Text 3/4″ from the
Midpoint of the Bottom Line of the Rectangle

Prompt	Response
The New Text Style dialog box appears with Style2 as the default style name:	CLICK: **OK**
	CLICK: **Times New Roman CE in the Font Name: box and Bold Italic in the Font Style: box, as shown in Figure 5–48**
	CLICK: **Apply**
Style2 is now the current text style:	CLICK: **Close**
Command:	**Single Line Text** (or TYPE: **DT<enter>**)
Current text style: "style2" Text height: 0′-0 3/16″ Specify start point of text or [Justify/Style]:	TYPE: **C<enter>**
Specify center point of text:	**With OTRACK ON and OSNAP-Midpoint selected in the Drafting Setting dialog box HOLD your mouse over the middle of the bottom line of the rectangle and move your mouse straight up until it reads 0′-3/4″<90°, as shown in Figure 5–49, and CLICK: that point**
Specify height <0′-0 3/16″>:	<enter> (or TYPE: **3/16** <enter> if the default is not 3/16)
Specify rotation angle of text <0>:	<enter>
The cursor is flashing at the center point:	TYPE: **MB STAINED GLASS<enter>** <enter>
Command:	<enter> (to repeat the Dtext command)
Current text style: "style2" Text height: 0′-0 3/16″ Specify start point of text or [Justify/Style]:	TYPE: **S<enter>**
Enter style name or [?]<style2>:	TYPE: **style1<enter>**
Current text style: "style1" Text height: 0′-0 3/16″ Specify start point of text or [Justify/Style]:	TYPE: **C<enter>**

Prompt	Response
Specify center point of text:	With OTRACK ON and OSNAP-Midpoint selected, HOLD your mouse over the middle of the bottom line of the rectangle and move your mouse straight up until it reads 0'-1/2"<90 and CLICK: that point
Specify height <0'-0 3/16">:	TYPE: **3/32<enter>**
Specify rotation angle of text <0>:	**<enter>**
The cursor is flashing at the center point:	TYPE: **MIKE AND BEVERLY KIRKPATRICK<enter> <enter>**
Command:	**<enter>** (to repeat the Dtext command)
Current text style: "style1" Text height: 0'-0 3/32" Specify start point of text or [Justify/Style]:	With SNAP ON, CLICK: **a point one snap to the right and one snap up from the lower left corner of the rectangle**
Specify height <0'-0 3/32">:	**<enter>**
Specify rotation angle of text <0>:	**<enter>**
The cursor is flashing at the left justification point:	TYPE: **PHONE: XXX-XXX-XXXX<enter> <enter>**
Command:	**<enter>** (to repeat the Dtext command)
Current text style: "style1" Text height: 0'-0 3/32" Specify start point of text or [Justify/Style]:	TYPE: **R<enter>** (for right justification)
Specify right endpoint of text baseline:	With SNAP ON, CLICK: **a point one snap to the left and one snap up from the lower right corner of the rectangle**
Specify height <0'-0 3/32">:	**<enter>**
Specify rotation angle of text <0>:	**<enter>**
The cursor is flashing at the right justification point:	TYPE: **EMAIL: mbkz@com.net<enter> <enter>**

The text appears as shown in Figure 5–50.

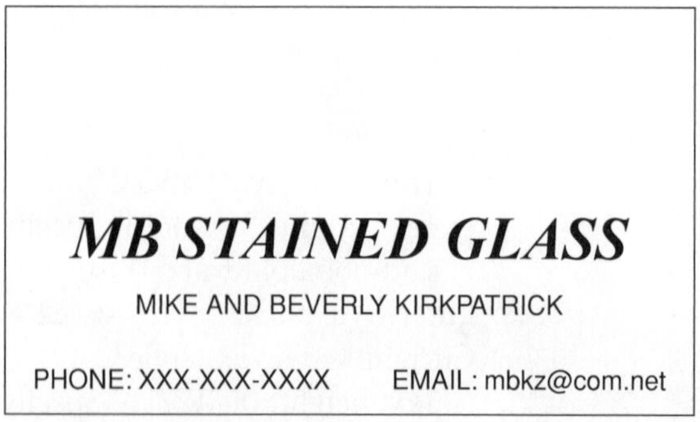

FIGURE 5–50
Text Complete

MB STAINED GLASS

MIKE AND BEVERLY KIRKPATRICK

PHONE: XXX-XXX-XXXX   EMAIL: mbkz@com.net

FIGURE 5–51
Select the First Picture
to Insert into Your
Drawing

Step 6. Insert the pictures you have selected using Raster Image commands to place the pictures (Figure 5–51):

Prompt	Response
Command:	RIGHT-CLICK: on any tool icon and display the Reference toolbar so you will have access to all the Raster Image commands
Command:	Raster Image…
The Select Image File dialog box appears:	Locate the folder that contains your digital pictures and CLICK: on the picture you want CLICK: **Open**
The Image dialog box appears:	CLICK: **OK**
Specify insertion point <0,0>:	CLICK: a point to locate the lower left corner of the image
Specify scale factor <1>:	Slowly move your mouse upward to the right to enlarge the image until you are satisfied it is about the correct size, then CLICK: that point

Step 7. Trim the image to get rid of the date and some of the surrounding background (Figures 5–52 and 5–53):

Prompt	Response
Command:	imageclip
Select image to clip:	CLICK: any point on the outside edge of the image (Figure 5–52)
Enter image clipping option [ON/OFF/Delete/New boundary] <New>:	<enter>
Enter clipping type [Polygonal/ Rectangular] <Rectangular>:	<enter>

FIGURE 5–52
Clip the Image after It Is
Inserted

FIGURE 5–53
The Image Is Clipped

MB STAINED GLASS

MIKE AND BEVERLY KIRKPATRICK

PHONE: XXX-XXX-XXXX   EMAIL: mbkz@com.net

Prompt	Response
Specify first corner point:	With **OSNAP** and **SNAP OFF**, CLICK: **one corner of a rectangle that will clip the image**
Specify opposite corner point:	CLICK: **the diagonally opposite corner of the clipping rectangle so the image appears similar to that shown in Figure 5–53**

Step 8. Adjust the brightness and contrast of the pictures you have selected using the Image Adjust command (Figure 5–54):

Prompt	Response
Command:	Image Adjust…
Select image(s):	CLICK: **any point on the outside edge of the image**
Select image(s):	<enter>
The Image Adjust dialog box appears:	Move the sliders so the brightness is 82 and the contrast is 72, as shown in Figure 5–54. (You may have to adjust your pictures to different values.) CLICK: **OK**

Step 9. On your own:
See Figure 5–55.

1. Use Raster Image commands to insert the remaining images (if you have others), and clip and adjust them.
2. If the pictures are not the correct size or in the correct location, use the Scale and Move commands to change their size and location.

FIGURE 5–54

Changing the Brightness and Contrast of the Image

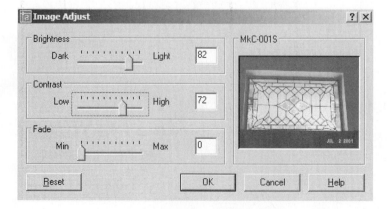

FIGURE 5–55
The Completed Business
Card

MB STAINED GLASS

MIKE and BEVERLY KIRKPATRICK

PHONE: XXX-XXX-XXXX   EMAIL: mbkz@com.net

3. You may also want to remove the frame around the pictures. To do that use the Image Frame command and turn it off by setting it to 0 after you have completed step 10.

Step 10. Check to be sure the lower left corner of the business card is 1/2″ to the right and 3/4″ up from 0,0 (the lower left corner of the page), then use the Array command to copy the finished business card to fill an entire 8-1.2″ × 11″ sheet (Figure 5–56):

Prompt	Response
Command:	TYPE: **ID**<enter>
Specify point:	CLICK: **the lower left corner of the business card**
X = 0′-0 1/2″ Y = 0′-0 3/4″ Z = 0′-0″	The point should read as shown. If it does not, use the Move command and move the entire card to the correct location. When AutoCAD asks for **Base point,** CLICK: **the lower left corner of the card.** When AutoCAD asks for second point, TYPE: **1/2,3/4**<enter>
Command:	**Array...** (or TYPE: **AR**<enter>)
The Array dialog box, Figure 5–56, appears:	CLICK: **Rectangular Array** TYPE: **4 in the Rows: input area** TYPE: **2 in the Columns: input area**

FIGURE 5–56
The Array Dialog Box

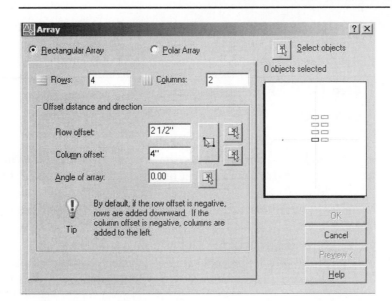

FIGURE 5–57
The Array of Eight Business
Cards

Prompt	Response
	TYPE: **2-1/2″ in the Row offset: input area**
	TYPE: **4″ in the Column offset: input area**
	CLICK: **Select objects**
Select objects:	**Use a window to select the entire business card.**
Select objects:	**<enter>**
	CLICK: **OK**

The drawing should appear as shown in Figure 5–57. Notice that there are three 1/4″ grid spaces at the bottom of the sheet and two grid spaces on each side of the sheet. This is the correct spacing for business card sheets available at many office supply stores.

Step 11. Complete the exercise.

On Your Own:

1. Save the drawing with the name CH5-EX4.
2. Make a check print (use the Model tab) of the drawing at 1 = 1 (full scale) on an 8-1/2″ × 11″ sheet of paper and check to see if the cards are properly aligned with the card stock after you complete Chapter 6.
3. Erase all the rectangles, so they do not appear on the individual business cards when you do the final printing.
4. Save the drawing again with the same name.
5. If the plot is properly aligned, put the card stock in the printer and print your business cards after completing Chapter 6.

1. The command used in this chapter to place line text (text not in paragraph form) on drawings is
   a. Single Line Text (Dtext)   d. DDedit
   b. TXT   e. MS-DOS Text Editor
   c. Multiline Text (Mtext)

2. The command used in this chapter to place paragraph text on drawings is
   a. Single Line Text (Dtext)   d. DDedit
   b. TXT   e. MS-DOS Text Editor
   c. Multiline Text (Mtext)

3. Which of the following could be used as a style name?
   a. SIMPLEX   d. A
   b. TITLE   e. All the above could be used as a style name.
   c. NAMES

4. Which of the following is a font name?
   a. SIMPLEX
   b. TITLE
   c. NAMES
   d. A
   e. All the above could be used as a font name.

5. You can change from one text style to another from within the Single Line Text command.
   a. True
   b. False

6. When you set the text style, which of the following text height settings will allow you to draw different heights of the same text style?
   a. 1/4   d. 1000
   b. 0'-0"   e. —
   c. 1

7. Which of the following Single Line Text options draws text between two clicked points and adjusts the text height so that it fits between the two points?
   a. Fit   d. Middle
   b. Align   e. Style
   c. Justify

8. Which of the following Single Line Text options draws text between two clicked points and condenses or expands the text to fit between the two points but does not change the text height?
   a. Fit   d. Middle
   b. Align   e. Style
   c. Justify

9. The justification letters MR stand for
   a. Middle, Right-justified   d. Bottom, Right-justified
   b. Margin, Right-justified   e. Margin Release
   c. Midpoint, Left-justified

10. Which of the following modifiers should be selected if you want the bottom of the line of text to end 1/2″ above and 1/2″ to the left of the lower right corner of the drawing limits?

    a. TL
    b. BR
    c. BL
    d. TR
    e. MR

Complete.

11. List three commands that can be used to change text.

    _____

    _____

    _____

12. List the command that allows you to change only the text contents for Single Line Text.

    _____

13. List the command that allows you to change text height, contents, properties, justification, style, and geometry.

    _____

14. List the command used to create a paragraph of text.

    _____

15. List the command that will spell check any line or paragraph of text you select.

    _____

16. List the command used to insert digital pictures into your drawing.

    _____

17. Describe how to delete columns in a table created with the Table... command.

    _____

18. List the command used to trim off unneeded parts of a digital picture.

    _____

    _____

19. Describe how to quickly change all the text on a drawing done in the STANDARD style, TXT font, to the SIMPLEX font.

    _____

    _____

20. List the standard codes for the following.

    a. Degree symbol: _____

    b. Plus–minus symbol: _____

    c. Diameter symbol: _____

    d. Underscore: _____

    e. Overscore: _____

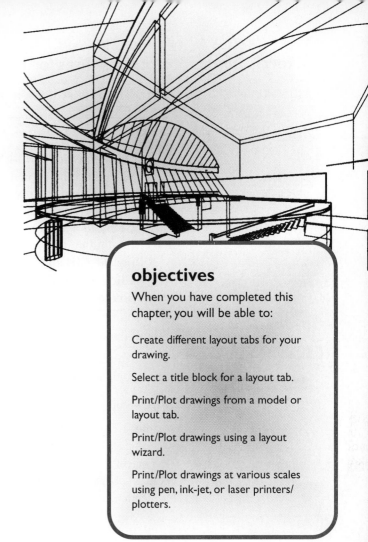

6

Printing and Plotting

objectives

When you have completed this chapter, you will be able to:

Create different layout tabs for your drawing.

Select a title block for a layout tab.

Print/Plot drawings from a model or layout tab.

Print/Plot drawings using a layout wizard.

Print/Plot drawings at various scales using pen, ink-jet, or laser printers/plotters.

Introduction

At the bottom of the drawing window are Model, Layout1, and Layout2 tabs. Model space is the 2D (and also 3D) environment in which you have been working to this point. Model space is where your 2D and 3D models (drawings) are created and modified.

When you start a new drawing AutoCAD provides a single Model tab and two Layout tabs. A Layout tab is similar to a piece of illustration board used to paste up a presentation; it helps you lay out your drawings for printing or plotting. You can create as many layouts for a drawing as you need. For example, one layout can be the floor plan, another the furniture plan, another the electrical plan, and so on. All the sheets (layouts) are in the one drawing and are identified with the Layout tab name. Sheets sets, which are described in a later chapter, allow you to group sheets that are in different drawings.

Exercise 6–1:   Plot Responses for Exercise 3–1, Using the Model Tab

The following is a hands-on, step-by-step exercise to make a hard copy of Exercise 3–1.

Step I.   On your own:

1. Open drawing CH3-EX1 on the hard drive or network drive so it is displayed on the screen. Remember, if your drawing has been saved on a disk, open it from the disk and save it on the hard drive.
2. Make sure the Model tab is current.
3. Click the Plot command from the Standard toolbar, or CLICK: **Plot...** from the File menu, or TYPE: PLOT<enter> to access the Plot dialog box. Pressing the Ctrl and P keys at the same time will also access the Plot dialog box.
4. Click the more options arrow in the lower right corner of the Plot dialog box to display the entire Plot dialog box (Figure 6–1).

Plot - Name

The strip at the top of the dialog box displays the current layout tab name or shows if the Model tab is current. It shows "Model" now, because the Model tab is current.

Page setup

Name: Layout settings (the settings that control the final plot output) are referred to as *page setups.* This list box displays any named or saved page setups that you can select to apply to the current page setup.

Add...   When this button is clicked, the Add Page Setup dialog box is displayed. You can specify a name for the new page setup.

FIGURE 6–1
Plot Dialog Box

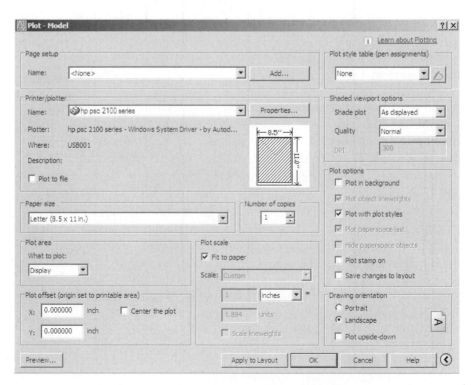

FIGURE 6–2
Plotter Configuration Editor
Dialog Box

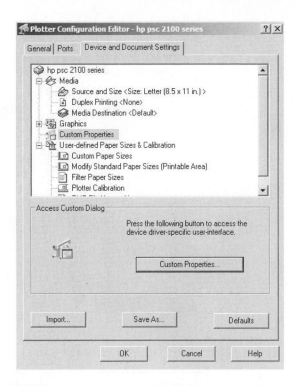

Step 2.   Set the Page setup to None.

Printer/plotter

The Name: line displays the current plot device (plotter or printer). When the down arrow is clicked, a list of the available plotting devices is displayed in the Name list. You can select the plot device that you want to use.

Properties...   When this button is clicked, the Plotter Configuration Editor (Figure 6–2) is displayed. The Plotter Configuration Editor allows you to view or to modify current plot device information.

Custom Properties...   When this button of the Plotter Configuration Editor is clicked, a Custom Properties dialog box for the configured plotter (or printer) appears. Each plotter (or printer) has a unique Custom Properties dialog box; you can customize settings for the vector colors, print quality, and raster corrections for your plotter (or printer) using the Properties dialog box.

Step 3.   Select the printer that you will use. If the Name: line does not show the correct plot device, click the down arrow and select the printer that you will use.

If you need to add a plot device, the Plotter Manager (under File in the menu bar) is used to add or modify plotter and printer configuration files.

Plot to File

If you do not check the Plot to file button, AutoCAD plots directly from your computer. If there is a cable leading from your computer to the printer or plotter, or if you are plotting from a network, do not check the Plot to file button.

If you do check the Plot to file button, a file is created with the extension .plt.

FIGURE 6–3
Plot Style Table

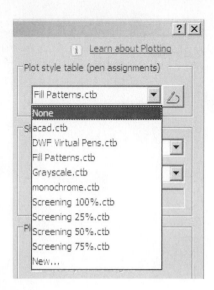

Browse for Plot File...

When Plot to file is selected, and OK is clicked, the Browse for Plot File dialog box is displayed. This box allows you to determine where the plot file is to be stored.

Step 4. Select the correct setting for the Plot to file check button, for your situation.

Plot style table (pen assignments)

Plot styles allow you to plot the same drawing in different ways; a plot style can be assigned to a layer or to an object. AutoCAD provides some plot styles, or you can create your own. A plot style contains settings that can override an object's color, linetype, and lineweight. Output effects that can be set in the plot style are pen assignments, dithering, gray scale, and screening. Line end styles, line join styles, and fill styles can also be set in plot styles.

The Plot style table list (Figure 6–3) can be used to create, edit, or store plot files. The Add Plot Style Table Wizard (Figure 6–4), located under Wizards in the Tools menu, leads you through creating a plot style. There are two types of plot styles: color dependent (stored with the extension .ctb) and named (stored with the extension .stb). With the color-dependent plot style, all objects of the same color will have the same

FIGURE 6–4
Add Plot Style Table Wizard

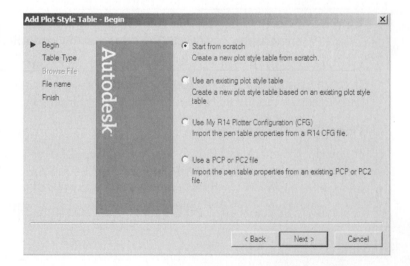

FIGURE 6–5
Plot Style Table Editor for the
acad.ctb Plot Style

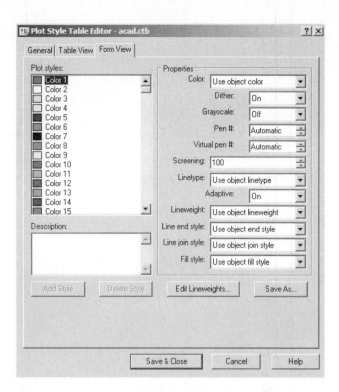

plot style that is assigned to that color. You can change the plot style of an object by changing the color of the object. With a named plot style, you can assign any plot style to any object regardless of color.

To use a plot style, you must attach it to the model or layout tabs by selecting it as described next.

Edit...   When a plot style other than None is selected in the plot style table list, and the Edit... icon (to the right of the list) is clicked, the Plot Style Table Editor (Figure 6–5) is displayed. This allows you to edit the selected plot style table that is assigned to the plot style selected in the Name line.

New...   When New... in the plot style table list is clicked, the Add Color-Dependent Plot Style Table wizard is displayed, which allows you to create a new plot style table.

> **TIP:** If you need to plot all layers black instead of the colors they have been assigned, CLICK: monochrome.ctb in the Plot style table (pen assignments) list in the Plot dialog box (or the Page Setup dialog box). CLICK: Edit to the right of the Plot style to make sure that the color selected is Black and Grayscale: is Off.

Step 5.   CLICK: the plot style acad.ctb in the Name: line.
CLICK: **No when AutoCAD asks "Assign this plot style table to all layouts?"**
CLICK: the Edit... button (to the right of the name) to view the Plot Style Table Editor for acad.ctb (Figure 6–5).
CLICK: the Cancel button to exit.
Do the same to view some of the other plot styles AutoCAD provides.

Step 6.   Set the Plot style table to None.

FIGURE 6–6

Paper Sizes for a Printer

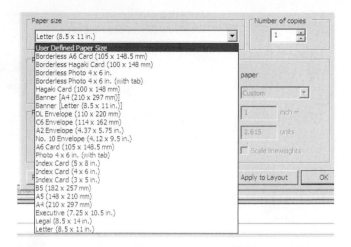

FIGURE 6–7

Paper Sizes for a Plotter

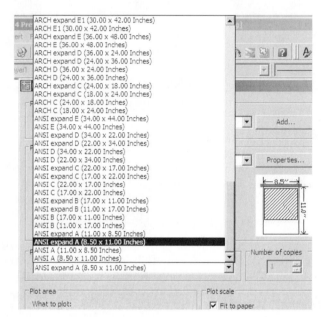

Paper Size

Paper size: The Paper size: line displays the current paper size. When the down arrow is clicked, it lists the paper sizes the printer (Figure 6–6) or plotter (Figure 6–7) can accommodate; the current size is highlighted. An A, B, D, or E displayed beside the size indicates a standard American National Standards Institute (ANSI) paper size. ARCH displayed beside the size indicates a standard architectural paper size.

Step 7. Select the Letter, 8-½″ × 11″ paper size, and 1 for the Number of copies.

Plot area

When you CLICK: the down arrow the following options are displayed (view will not be displayed because you have not named and saved a view in your drawing):

Limits This option plots the part of the drawing that lies within the drawing limits. The limits for drawing CH3-EX1 are 8-1/2,11.

Extents This option plots the drawing extents. The drawing extents are whatever graphics are actually drawn, including any graphics that lie outside the limits of the drawing area.

Display   This option plots the part of the drawing that is displayed on the screen at the time the plot is made.

View   This selection plots any view that has been named and saved with the View command. No view was named and saved for drawing CH3-EX1. If you have saved a view, click the View button and select the name of the view you want to print.

Window   This selection allows you to pick two corners of a window and plot only the part of the drawing that is within the window. When the **Window** < button is clicked, it clears the Plot dialog box so you can view your drawing and use your mouse to click the two corners of a window. AutoCAD then returns to the Plot dialog box.

Step 8.   **CLICK: Extents to select the drawing extents as part of the drawing that is to be printed.**

Plot scale

Scale: The Scale: line displays the scale at which the drawing will be plotted. If the scale list is gray, CLICK: the check mark in the Fit to paper box so a scale may be selected. When the down arrow is clicked, a list of available scales is displayed. You can select the scale that you want to use. To be able to measure a plotted drawing accurately using a scale, you must enter a specific plotting scale.

You may respond by selecting Fit to paper instead of entering a specific scale. When you select this option, AutoCAD scales the selected plot area as large as possible to fit the specified paper size.

Step 9.   **Select a scale of 1:1, which is 1 plotted inch = 1 drawing unit.**

Plot offset (origin set to printable area)

Center the Plot   To center the drawing on the paper, place a check in the Center the plot check box, and the plot will be automatically centered on the paper.

X and Y Offset   The plot offset specifies the location of the plot, on the paper, from the lower left corner of the paper. The X: input line moves the plotted drawing in the X direction on the paper, and the Y: input moves the drawing in the Y direction. You can enter either positive or negative values.

Step 10.   Place a check in the Center the plot check box.

Notice that the X and Y inputs are automatically calculated to center the selected plotting area (extents) in the paper size (8½″ × 11″).

Shaded viewport options

These options relate to 3D drawings and control how shaded and rendered viewports are plotted. This is described in Chapters 14 and 15.

Plot options

Plot in background   A check mark in this box allows you to continue working while your drawing is being plotted.

Plot object lineweights   A check mark in this box tells AutoCAD to plot the drawing using the lineweights you have assigned to any object in the drawing.

Plot with plot styles   This option allows you to use a plot style. Since you are not using a plot style, this box will not be checked.

Plot paperspace last   When this option is checked, model space will be plotted first. Usually, paper space drawings are plotted before model space drawings.

Hide paperspace objects   The Hide paperspace objects button refers to 3D objects only. When you use the Hide command, AutoCAD hides any surface on the screen that is behind another surface in 3D space. If you want to do the same on your paper space plot, you must click the Hide paper space objects check button so a check appears in the box. This shows only in the full plot preview window.

   Another way to hide in paper space is to select the viewport in which you want to have hidden lines, click Properties under Modify in the menu bar, and turn Shade plot to Hidden.

Plot stamp on   A check mark here allows you to place signatures and other stamps on the drawing.

Save changes to layout   Checking this box allows you to save any changes you have made in the plot dialog box.

Step 11.   **Do not put a check in any of these plot option boxes. (Plot paperspace last is grayed out because no layout tabs were used.)**

Drawing orientation

The paper icon represents the orientation of the selected paper size. The letter A icon represents the orientation of the drawing on the paper.

Portrait   This button allows you to specify a vertical orientation of the drawing on the page.

Landscape   This button allows you to specify a horizontal orientation of the drawing on the page. If a plot shows only half of what should have been plotted, the orientation may need to be changed.

Plot upside-down   This check box allows you to plot the drawing, in a portrait or landscape orientation, upside-down.

Step 12.   **Select the Portrait orientation.**

Preview...

The Preview... button shows you exactly how the final plot will appear on the sheet.

Step 13.   **Click the Preview... button.**

Preview your plot for Exercise 3–1, Figure 6–8. If there is something wrong with the plot, press the spacebar and make the necessary adjustments. If the preview looks OK, press the spacebar to end the preview. You may also click the right mouse button to access the menu shown in Figure 6–9.

Step 14.   **Click OK (or Exit from the right-click menu, then click OK.)**

The plot proceeds from this point. If you have not created a plot file, remove the completed plot from the printer or plotter. If you have created a .plt file, take your disk to the plot station or send your plot via a network.

Plotting for the Internet

The format of drawings that can be plotted to the Internet, and then viewed, must be different from that of the standard .dwg file. AutoCAD 2007 allows you to create

FIGURE 6–8
Plot Preview

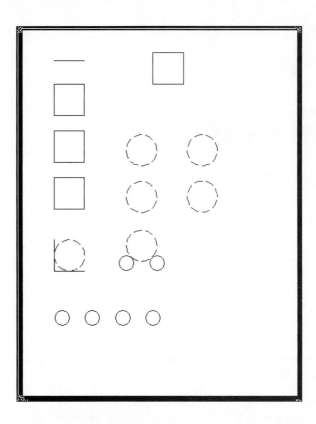

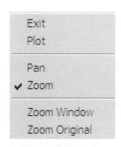

FIGURE 6–9
Preview Right-Click Menu

.DWF (drawing web format) and PublishToWeb files (.JPG and .PNG) from the Plot dialog box. To create any of these files do the following:

1. Start the Plot command.
2. Select a DWF or PublishToWeb (JPG or PNG) plotter for the plot device.
3. When you select a DWF or PublishToWeb (JPG or PNG) plotter, the Plot to file box is automatically checked.
4. When you select a DWF, JPG, or PNG plotter, to change the resolution, background color, layer information, or other properties, CLICK: **Properties...**, CLICK: **Custom Properties** in the plotter tree information, then CLICK: **Custom Properties...** when it appears on the tab.

The file is then created in the location you have specified. DWF or PublishToWeb (JPG and PNG) files can be viewed on the Internet.

Exercise 6–2: Print/Plot Responses for Exercise 4–1, Using a Layout Wizard

The following is a hands-on, step-by-step exercise to make a hard copy of Exercise 4–1 using a Layout wizard.

Step 1. On Your Own:

1. **Open drawing CH4-EX1 on the hard drive or network drive so it is displayed on the screen. Remember, if your drawing has been saved on a floppy disk, open it from the floppy disk and save it on the hard drive or network drive.**

Model, Layout1, and Layout2 Tabs

At the bottom of the drawing window are Model, Layout1, and Layout2 tabs. Model space is the 2D (and also 3D) environment in which you have been working to this point. Model space is where your 2D and 3D models (drawings) are created and modified.

FIGURE 6–10
Create Layout dialog box;
STEP 3. Enter a Name for
the Layout

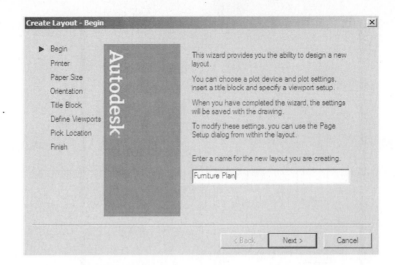

A layout tab is used to view paper space. Paper space simulates the actual printed or plotted drawing on a real size piece of paper. In Exercise 6–2, the Create Layout wizard creates a layout tab and is used to plot Exercise 4–1.

Step 2. On your own:

1. Make sure the Model tab is current.
2. Create a new layer named Viewport. Make its color green and set it current.
3. CLICK: Wizards (in the Tools menu in the menu bar). CLICK: **Create Layout...** (in the Wizards menu) to access the Create Layout dialog box (Figure 6–10).

Step 3. TYPE: "Furniture Plan" for the new layout name in the input box (Figure 6–10). CLICK: Next>.

Step 4. Select a configured printer or plotter for the new layout. CLICK: Next>.

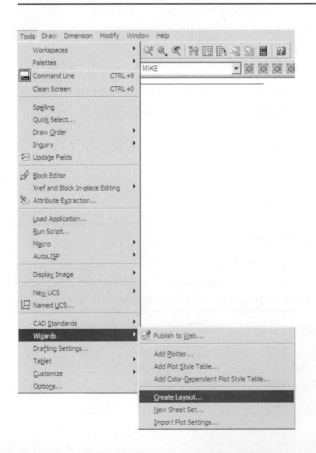

FIGURE 6–11
STEP 7. Select ANSI A title block Inserted as a Block

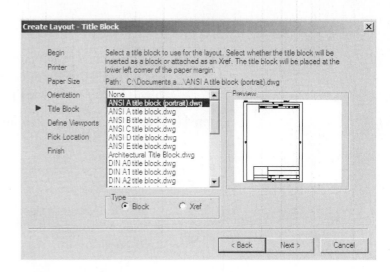

Step 5. Select a paper size of Letter, 8½″ × 11″. CLICK: Next>.

Step 6. Select the Portrait orientation of the drawing on the paper. CLICK: Next>.

Step 7. Select ANSI A title block (portrait).dwg for the layout. Select the Block radio button so the title block will be inserted as a block (Figure 6–11). CLICK: Next>.

 NOTE: It is not necessary to select a title block. You can select "None" in the Layout Wizard.

Step 8. Select the Single radio button so you will have a single viewport configuration. Select 1/4″ = 1′-0″ as the Viewport scale: (Figure 6–12). CLICK: Next>.

FIGURE 6–12
STEP 8. Select the Single Viewport and ¼″ = 1′0″ as the Viewport Scale

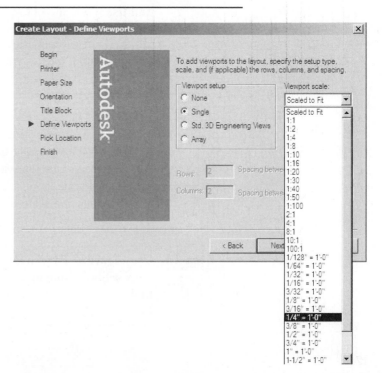

Step 9. CLICK: **Next>**. AutoCAD will locate the viewport.

Step 10. CLICK: **Finish.** The Layout tab named Furniture Plan is created with the CH4-EX1 conference room shown at 1/4′ = 1″-0″ scale. The title block is also in the viewport.

Step 11. The outline of the viewport (shown in green on your screen) needs to be turned off. Turn the Viewport layer off so it will not hide the dashed line or print.

> **NOTE:** If you can't click the green outline of the viewport without also selecting the title block, use Zoom-Window while in paper space to get closer in.

Step 12. If your conference room is not centered within the ANSI title block, change to model space (TYPE: **MS** <enter> or CLICK: **PAPER** on the status bar to switch to Model space). Use Pan to center the conference room. CLICK: **MODEL** on the status bar to return to paper space.
   You may also use the Move command *while in paper space* to move the title block.

> **NOTE:** It may be helpful to turn the grid off while in model space.

Step 13. Only the graphics that are within the dashed lines (printable area of your computer) will be plotted. If the title block is too large for the printable area of your printer, click the title block *while in paper space* and use the Scale command to reduce it. Specify 0,0 as the base point and TYPE: **.98** to reduce the title block 2%. Reduce the size as needed. You may also use the Move command while in paper space to center the title block within the dashed lines.

> **NOTE:** If you accidentally use a Zoom command while in Model space and change the scale of the drawing, turn the viewport layer on. Click on the viewport boundary line and then click on Properties. Locate the scale you want the drawing to be under Misc and the Standard scale input area. Zooming while you are in paper space will not change the scale of the drawing.

Step 14. Use Figure 6–13 as a guide. Use the Simplex font, 1/8″ high, to type your school name and title your drawing. Use the Simplex font, 1/16″ high, to type the scale and to type your name. Complete as shown in Figure 6–13.

FIGURE 6–13
Type Needed Information in
the Title Block

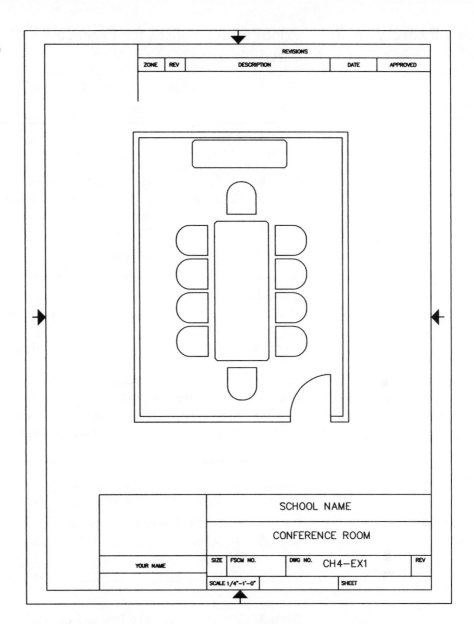

NOTE: When you type your name or anything else 1/8″ high in paper space, it will be printed 1/8″ high when the page is printed at a scale of 1:1.

Step 15. RIGHT-CLICK: the Furniture Plan tab. CLICK: Plot.... Make sure the scale is set 1:1. (The Viewport scale is already set to 1/4″ = 1′-0″; you are plotting the 8½ × 11 paper at 1:1.)

Step 16. CLICK: Preview... if the preview is OK, right-click and CLICK: Plot. If not, Exit and correct the problem.

The plot proceeds from this point. If you have not created a plot file, remove the completed plot from the printer or plotter. If you have created a .plt file, take your disk to the plot station or send your plot via a network.

Exercise 6–3: Print/Plot Responses for Exercise 4–2, Using a Layout Tab and Page Setup Manager

The following is a hands-on, step-by-step exercise to make a hard copy of Exercise 4–2, using Page Setup Manager.

Step 1. On your own:

1. Open drawing CH4-EX2 on the hard drive so it is displayed on the screen. Remember, if your drawing has been saved on a floppy disk, open it from the floppy disk and save it on the hard drive.
2. Create a new layer named Viewport. Make its color green and set it current.

Model, Layout1, and Layout2 Tabs

At the bottom of the drawing window are Model, Layout1, and Layout2 tabs. Model space is the 2D (and also 3D) environment in which you have been working to this point. Model space is where your 2D and 3D models (drawings) are created and modified. A layout tab is used to view paper space. Paper space shows the actual printed or plotted drawing on a real size piece of paper. Exercise 6–3 describes print/plot responses for Exercise 4–2 when a Layout tab is current and the Page Setup manager is used to plot.

Step 2. CLICK: the Layout1 tab at the bottom of drawing CH4-EX2. You are now in paper space. Notice that the far right tab on the status bar says PAPER. If you click it, it will change to MODEL. Make sure you are in paper space.

 NOTE: It may be helpful to turn the grid off while in MODEL space. Be sure to return to PAPER space.

Step 3. RIGHT-CLICK: the Layout1 tab and CLICK: **Page Setup Manager....** The Page Setup Manager, Figure 6–14, appears.

Step 4. With Layout1 in Page setups selected, CLICK: **Modify....** The Page Setup dialog box for Layout1 appears.

Step 5. Select the printer you will use.

Step 6. Set the Plot style table to None.

Step 7. Make the settings shown in Figure 6–15 in the Page Setup dialog box.

Step 8. Make sure the Plot scale is 1:1 (Figure 6–15).
Because you are plotting the layout tab that will be scaled using the viewport boundary line, use the Plot scale of 1:1 in the Page Setup dialog box.

Step 9. CLICK: OK. **The Page Setup Manager appears.**

Step 10. CLICK: **Close**

If you completed Step 1 and created a new layer with the color green, the viewport boundary line is green.

FIGURE 6–14
Page Setup Manager

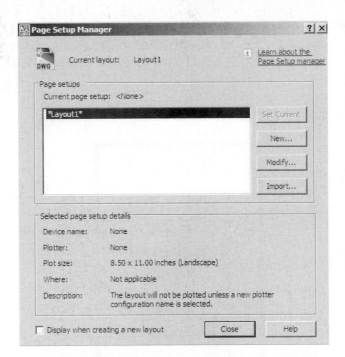

FIGURE 6–15
Page Setup Dialog Box for
Layout1

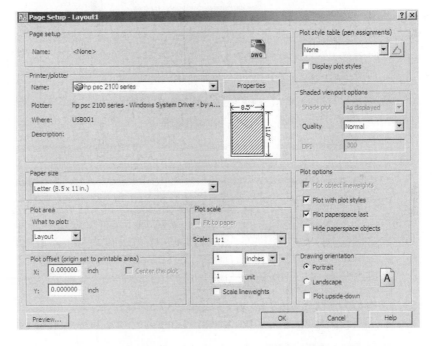

Step 11. CLICK: the green viewport boundary line to select it. If your viewport boundary line is not shaped as shown in Figure 6–16, CLICK: one of the small squares on each corner (called grips). It becomes red. Reshape the viewport by moving the grip. Be sure ORTHO is off.
You can reshape, resize, move, and copy the viewport. Information regarding the plotting of multiple viewports in 2D and 3D is covered in later chapters.

Step 12. If your drawing is not centered in the viewport, CLICK: PAPER in the status bar to return to model space. Use the Pan or Zoom commands to center the drawing. CLICK: MODEL to return to paper space before continuing with the plot setup.

FIGURE 6–16
Select the Viewport
Boundary

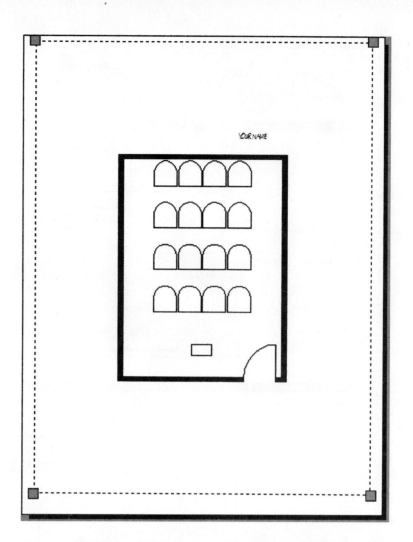

NOTE: The Viewport boundary line (green line) comes in on the layer that is current. That's why you created a layer named Viewport and assigned the green color to it.

Step 13. CLICK: the green viewport boundary line to select it (Figure 6–16).

Step 14. CLICK: Properties from the Modify menu.

Step 15. CLICK: Standard scale in the Properties dialog box (Figure 6–17). CLICK: the arrow to the right of Standard scale and scroll down to select 1/4″ = 1′-0″. This scale is applied to the drawing in the paper space viewport. CLICK: **Display locked** (above the scale) and CLICK: **Yes** to lock the display scale for this viewport. Close the Properties dialog box.

Step 16. Turn the Viewport layer off so the viewport boundary line will not print.

When the display is locked, you cannot accidentally zoom in or out while in model space and lose the 1/4″ = 1′-0″ scale. If you zoom in or out while in paper space, you do not change the scale, because you are zooming in or out on the paper only. When the display is locked, you cannot reposition the drawing. If you need to reposition or

FIGURE 6–17

Set Viewport Scale to ¼″ = 1′
= 0″ and Lock the Display

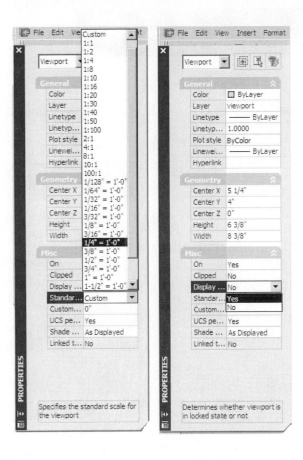

change the drawing in any way, you must turn the Viewport layer back on, select the viewport boundary line, select Properties, and unlock the display to make any changes.

Step 17. Create a text style using the CityBlueprint font and add your name in all capitals, 1/8″ high, to the paper (Figure 6–16).

Step 18. RIGHT-CLICK: **the Layout1 tab.** The right-click menu appears.

Step 19. CLICK: **Rename.** TYPE: **Furniture Plan** for the new layout name. CLICK: **OK**

Step 20. RIGHT-CLICK: **the Furniture Plan tab.** The right-click menu appears.

Step 21. CLICK: **Plot...** The Plot dialog box appears.

Step 22. CLICK: **Preview... If the preview is OK,** RIGHT-CLICK **and** CLICK: **Plot. If not, Exit and correct the problem.** The plot proceeds from this point.

Plotting Multiple Viewports

While in the Model tab you can use the command Viewports (VPORTS) to divide the display screen into multiple viewports. Model space is limited in that although multiple viewports may be visible on the display screen, only one viewport can be plotted, whereas in a Layout tab and in paper space, you can have multiple viewports. Each viewport can be treated as a single sheet of paper with a different part of the drawing showing and can be copied, stretched, erased, moved, or scaled. Paper space is not limited, in that you can plot all the viewports at the same time. Chapter 13 describes how to plot multiple viewports in paper space.

1. Which of the following pull-down menus contains the Plot... command?
   a. File
   b. Edit
   c. Format
   d. Tools
   e. Window

2. Output effects that can be set in a plot style table are
   a. Pen assignments
   b. Dithering
   c. Grayscale
   d. Screening
   e. All the above

3. Which of the following will produce a plot of the part of the drawing that is displayed on the screen?
   a. Display
   b. Extents
   c. Limits
   d. View
   e. Window

4. Which of the following will produce a plot of the entire drawing, even if part of it is outside the limits?
   a. All
   b. Extents
   c. Limits
   d. View
   e. Window

5. A plot file has which of the following extensions?
   a. .bak
   b. .dwg
   c. .plt
   d. .cfk
   e. .dwf

6. A plot that shows only half of what should have been plotted could probably be corrected by doing which of the following?
   a. Moving the origin .5
   b. Selecting View instead of Extents
   c. Writing the plot to a file
   d. Selecting Landscape instead of Portrait
   e. Selecting a smaller page

7. The Shaded viewport options part of the Plot dialog box relates to which of the following?
   a. 3D drawings
   b. Isometric drawings
   c. Hidden linetypes
   d. 2D drawings
   e. Slide files

8. A drawing that is to be plotted using the model tab so that it fits on a particular size sheet without regard to the scale requires which scale response?
   a. 1:1
   b. Full
   c. 1:2
   d. Fit to Paper
   e. MAX

9. Which of the following pull-down menus used in this chapter contains the command to create a Layout Wizard?
   a. File
   b. View
   c. Insert
   d. Tools
   e. Window

10. When you are using the Plot command to plot a layout tab that has a single viewport that is already scaled to 1/2″ = 1′0″, use a Plot scale of:
   a. 1/2″ =1′0″
   b. 1:1
   c. 1:2
   d. 1:48
   e. Scaled to Fit

Complete.

11. Name the three tabs that are at the bottom of the drawing window.

   _____   _____   _____

12. Describe why a Layout tab is used.

   _____

13. Describe why you would use different plot styles to plot the same drawing.

   _____

14. Describe the three different drawing orientations you can select when plotting.

   _____

15. Describe the difference between model space and a Layout tab (paper space).

   _____

16. List 11 commands that are on the right-click menu of a Layout tab when you are in paper space.

   _____   _____   _____

   _____   _____   _____

   _____   _____   _____

   _____   _____

17. Name the three types of files that can be viewed on the Internet.

   _____

   _____

   _____

18. When using a Layout Wizard, describe how to center your drawing within an ANSI title block.

    _____

19. When using a Layout Wizard, why do you turn off the outline of the paper space viewport?

    _____

20. List the 12 properties listed in the Plot Style Table Editor that can be set.

    _____   _____   _____

    _____   _____   _____

    _____   _____   _____

    _____   _____   _____

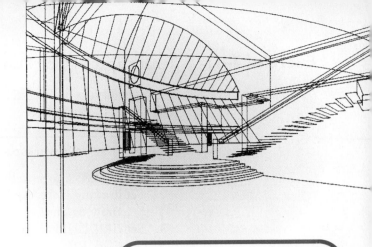

chapter

7

Drawing the Floor Plan: Walls, Doors, and Windows

objectives

When you have completed this chapter, you will be able to:

Correctly use the following commands and settings:

Aerial View	List
Block-Make...	Multiline
Color	Multiline Style...
Edit Multiline	Named Views
Extend	Properties...
Insert-Block...	View
Linetype	Wblock
Lineweight	

The Tenant Space Project

The Polyline or Multiline commands can be used to draw walls quickly. Polyline was described and used in Chapter 4. With Multiline, walls with up to 16 lines are drawn. Exercise 7–1 contains step-by-step instructions for using Multiline to draw the exterior and interior walls of a tenant space that is located in the northwest corner of a building. The exercise also contains step-by-step instructions for inserting windows and doors into the plan.

Chapters 8 through 11 provide step-by-step instructions to complete the tenant space project started in Chapter 7. Each chapter will use the building plan drawn in Chapter 7 to complete a part of the project as described next.

Chapter 8: The tenant space is dimensioned and the square feet calculated.

Chapter 9: Elevations, sections, and details are drawn.

Chapter 10: Furniture is drawn, attributes are assigned (furniture specifications), and the furniture is added to the plan.

Chapter 11: The reflected ceiling plan and power plan are drawn.

Exercise 7–1:   Tenant Space Floor Plan

When you have completed Exercise 7–1, the tenant space floor plan, your drawing will look similar to Figure 7–1.

Step I.   Use your workspace to make the following settings:

1. **Use SaveAs... to save the drawing on the hard drive with the name CH7-EX1.**
2. Set drawing Units: **Architectural**
3. Set Drawing Limits: **75′,65′**
4. Set GRIDDISPLAY: **0**
5. Set Grid: **12″**
6. Set Snap: **6″**

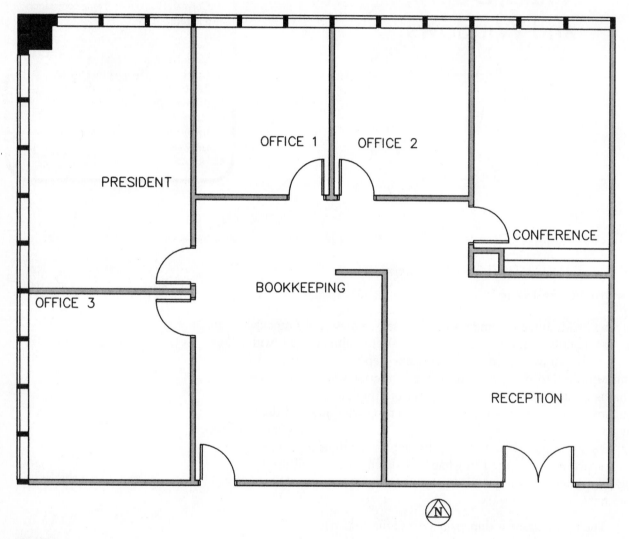

FIGURE 7–1
Exercise 7–1: Tenant Space Floor Plan (Scale: 1/8″ = 1′-0″)

7. **Create the following Layers.** Be sure to type and enter a comma after each layer name. The cursor will move to the next line so you can type the next layer name:

LAYER NAME	COLOR	LINETYPE
A-area	White	Continuous
A-clng	Green	Continuous
A-door	Cyan	Continuous
A-flor-iden	White	Continuous
A-flor-wdwk	White	Continuous
A-furn	Magenta	Continuous
A-glaz	White	Continuous
A-pflr-dims	Cyan	Continuous
A-wall-ext	Blue	Continuous
A-wall-int	Red	Continuous
E-lite	White	Continuous
E-powr	White	Continuous

The layers listed include those that will be used in Chapters 8, 10, and 11. The layer names are based on the guidelines provided by the document *CAD LAYER GUIDELINES Recommended Designations for Architecture, Engineering, and Facility Management Computer-Aided Design,* prepared by the Task Force on CAD Layer Guidelines.

8. Set **Layer A-wall-ext** current.
9. Use **Zoom-All** to view the limits of the drawing.

2D Solid

The 2D Solid command was described in Chapter 3. The following part of Exercise 7–1 uses the 2D Solid command to draw the window mullions and the 3′-square corner column located in the northwest corner of the tenant space.

Step 2.   Turn BLIPMODE on and use 2D Solid to draw the 3′-square corner column (Figure 7–2):

Prompt	Response
Command:	TYPE: **BLIPMODE**<enter>
Enter Mode [ON/OFF]<default>	TYPE: **ON**<enter>
Command:	**2D Solid** (or TYPE: **SO**<enter>)
Specify first point:	TYPE: **17′,51′** <enter>
Specify second point:	TYPE: **@3′<0** <enter>
Specify third point:	TYPE: **@-3′,-3′**<enter>
Specify fourth point or <exit>:	TYPE: **@3′<0**<enter>
Specify third point:	<enter>

FIGURE 7–2
Use the 2D Solid Command to Draw the Corner Column and Two Mullions

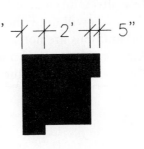

NOTE: When Blipmode is on when you use the Solid command, you can see where the points have been picked. Pressing F7 twice turns the grid off and on and cleans up the blips. Turn Blipmode off when you don't need it.

Step 3. On your own:

1. Zoom in close around the column, and use the 2D Solid command to draw the two separate mullions (5″ × 12″) that are on the east and south sides of the column just drawn, as shown in Figure 7–2. Use Snap, direct distance entry, and polar and relative coordinates to draw the mullions much like you just drew the corner column. Remember, with relative coordinates, enter the X axis first, then a comma, then the Y axis.

Array

The Array command was described in Chapter 4. The following part of Exercise 7–1 uses the Array command to draw the window mullions on the north and west exterior walls.

Step 4. Use Array to finish drawing the mullions on the north exterior wall (Figure 7–3):

Prompt	Response
Command:	**Array** (or TYPE: **AR**<enter>)
The Array dialog box appears:	CLICK: **the Select objects button**
Select objects:	CLICK: **the mullion located on the east side of the column**
Select objects: 1 found	
Select objects:	<enter>
	CLICK: **the Rectangular Array button**
	TYPE: **1 in the Rows: input area**
	TYPE: **13 in the Columns: input area**
	TYPE: **4′ in the Column offset: input area**
	TYPE: **0 in the Row offset: input area**
	TYPE: **0 in the Angle of array: input area**
	CLICK: **OK**

Step 5. On your own:

1. Use the Array command to draw the remaining mullions on the west exterior wall, as shown in Figure 7–3. Specify 10 rows, 1 column, −4′ in the Row offset: input area, and 0 in the Column offset: input area.
2. Next, you will draw the walls using Multiline. It is helpful if the column and mullions are not solid. Set FILL OFF and regenerate the drawing so that the columns and mullions are not solid.
3. Zoom-Extents to see the entire drawing.

Part II: Two-Dimensional AutoCAD

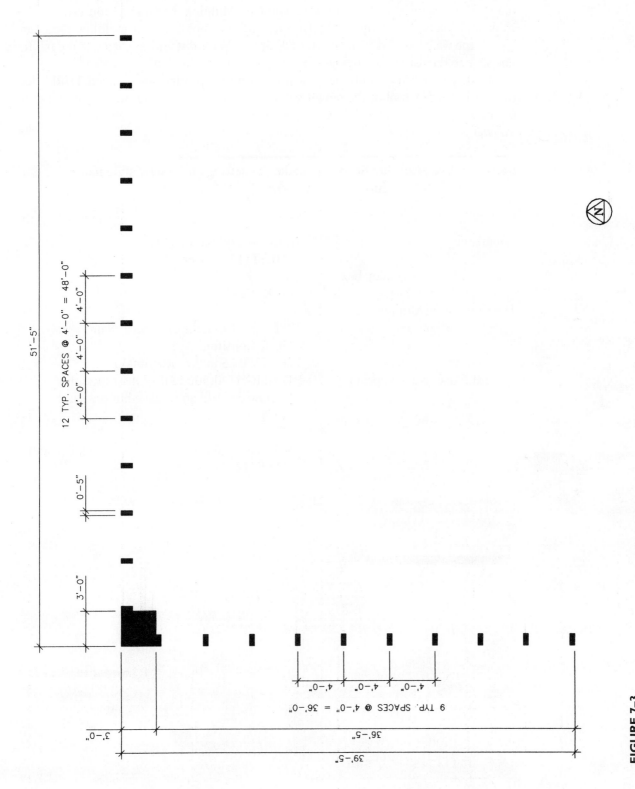

FIGURE 7-3

Use the Array Command to Finish Drawing the Mullions (Scale: 1/8" = 1'-0")

Multiline Style...

With the column and mullions now completed, you are ready to use Multiline to draw the walls. The Multiline Style... dialog box allows you to make the settings necessary to draw up to 16 lines at the same time with the Multiline command. You can specify color and linetype for any of the 16 lines and endcaps for each multiline. You can specify the walls as solid (background fill) or not. You must add the name of the multiline style to the list of current styles before you can draw with it.

Next, you will use Multiline Style... to create a multiline style named THREE for the north exterior wall of the tenant space. You will make settings to have one line at 0, one at 9″, and one at 12″ (the 3″ glass line is offset 3″ from the outside line of the 12″ wall).

Step 6. **Use Multiline Style... to make the settings for a new style named THREE (Figures 7–4 and 7–5):**

Prompt	Response
Command:	Multiline Style... (or TYPE: MLSTYLE<enter>)
The Multiline Styles dialog box appears (Figure 7–4):	CLICK: New...
The Create New Multiline Style dialog box appears:	TYPE: THREE in the New Style Name box CLICK: Continue
The New Multiline Style: THREE dialog box appears:	TYPE: WALLS in the Description: box HIGHLIGHT: 0.500 in the Offset input line (below the Add and Delete buttons) and TYPE: 9 CLICK: Add HIGHLIGHT: 0.000 in the Offset input line and TYPE: 12

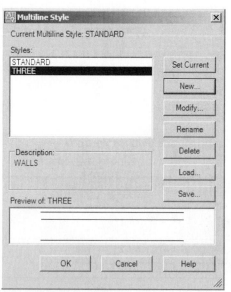

FIGURE 7–4
Multiline Style Named THREE

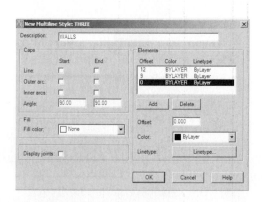

FIGURE 7–5
Element Properties with Offsets of 0, 9, and 12″

Prompt	Response
	CLICK: **Add**
	Do you have a scroll bar in the Elements list box that indicates more lines? If so, scroll down to look. If you have a −0.5 offset, CLICK: **−0.5** in the list and CLICK: **Delete** to delete an unnecessary offset.

You should now have a 12.0, a 9.0, and 0.0 in the Elements list as shown in Figure 7–5 and nothing else—no scroll bar to the right indicating more lines. You could now assign colors and linetypes to the lines. If you do not assign colors or linetypes, the lines will assume the color and linetype of the layer on which the multilines are drawn. Leave colors and linetypes assigned BYLAYER.

Prompt	Response
	CLICK: **OK**
The Multiline Style dialog box appears with THREE highlighted:	CLICK: **Set Current**
	CLICK: **OK**

Multiline

The Multiline prompt is "Specify start point or [Justification/Scale/STyle]:". The Multiline command uses the current Multiline Style to draw up to 16 lines at the same time with or without end caps.

Style   You can set any style current that has been defined with the Multiline Style... command if it is not already current (TYPE: **ST<enter>** to the Multiline prompt, then TYPE: **the style name<enter>** and begin drawing).

Justification   This option allows you to select Top, Zero, or Bottom lines to begin drawing multilines. The default is Top. In this case Zero and Bottom are the same because there are no negative offsets. If you have a positive 3 offset, a 0, and a negative 3 offset, your three lines will be drawn from the middle line with justification set to zero.

Scale   This option allows you to set the scale at which lines will be drawn. If your multiline style has a 10 offset, a 6 offset, and a 0, and you set the scale at .5, the lines will be drawn 5 and 3″ apart. The same style with a scale of 2 draws lines 20 and 12″ apart.

Step 7.   **Use Multiline to draw the north exterior wall of the tenant space (Figure 7–6):**

Prompt	Response
Command:	**Multiline** (or TYPE: **ML<enter>**)
Current settings: Justification = Top, Scale =1.00, Style = THREE	
Specify start point or [Justification/ Scale/STyle]:	TYPE: **INT<enter>**
of	**D1** (Figure 7–6)
Specify next point:	**Turn ORTHO ON. Move your mouse to the right and** TYPE: **48′<enter>**
Specify next point or [Undo]:	**<enter>**

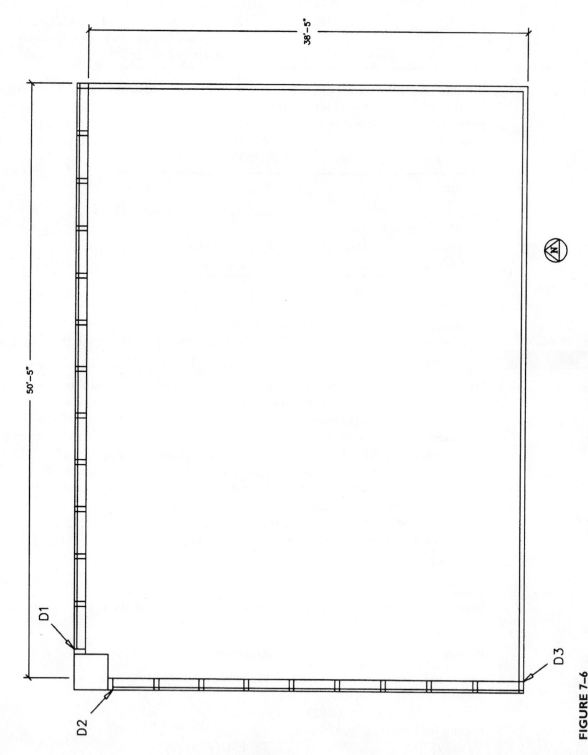

FIGURE 7–6

Use Multiline to Draw Exterior Walls with the Multiline Styles THREE, THREE-WEST, and TWO (Scale: 1/8" = 1'-0")

Step 8.   On your own (Figures 7–6, 7–7, and 7–8):

1. Create a new multiline style with the name THREE-WEST; start with THREE. Description: WALLS; and offsets of 0, 3, and 12. Just change the 9 to 3. Set this style current (Figure 7–7).

2. Use Multiline with a justification of Bottom to draw the west wall of the tenant space with the THREE-WEST multiline style. Use Osnap-Intersection and CLICK: D2 (Figure 7–6) to start the multiline and make the line 36′ long (subtract 2′5″ from the dimension on the right side of Figure 7–6 to account for the 3′-square corner column and the 5″ mullion).

3. Create a new multiline style with the name TWO; start with STANDARD Description: INTERIOR WALLS; and offsets of 0 and 5 (Figure 7–8). Set this style current.

4. Use Multiline with a justification of Bottom to draw the south and east walls of the tenant space. Use Osnap-Intersection and CLICK: D3 (Figure 7–6) and make the line to the right 50′5″ and the line up 38′5″.

5. Next, the interior walls are drawn. Remember to use transparent Zoom commands to move to different parts of the drawing while in the Multiline command. TYPE: ′Z from the keyboard and PRESS: <enter>. An apostrophe (′) must precede the Z, or use the Zoom commands from the View menu in the menu bar or from the Standard toolbar.

6. Keep layer A-WALL-EXT current. The layer on which the interior walls are drawn will be changed to A-WALL-INT in this exercise with the Properties... command.

 NOTE: You cannot have spaces in the style name, but spaces are OK in the Description.

Step 9.   Use Multiline with the Multiline Style TWO to draw 5″-wide horizontal and vertical interior walls inside the tenant space (Figure 7–9).

Prompt	Response
Command:	**Multiline** (or TYPE: **ML**<enter>)

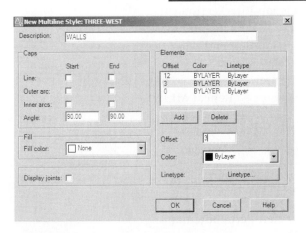

FIGURE 7–7
Make a New Multiline Style Named THREE-WEST

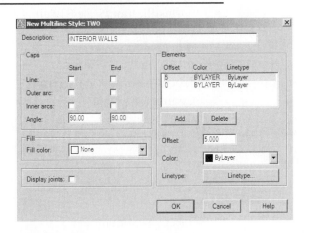

FIGURE 7–8
Make a New Multiline Style Named TWO

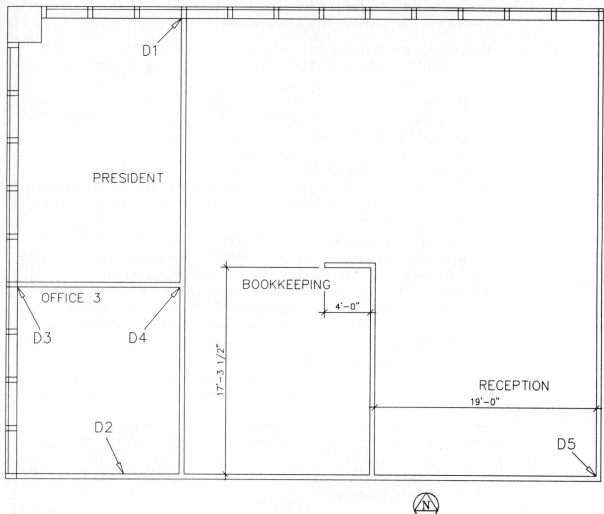

FIGURE 7–9
Use Multiline to Draw Interior Walls (Scale: 1/8″ = 1′-0″)

Prompt	Response
Current settings: Justification = Bottom, Scale = 1.00, Style = TWO	
Specify start point or [Justification/Scale/STyle]:	**Osnap-Intersection**
of	CLICK: **D1** (Figure 7–9)
Specify next point:	**Osnap-Perpendicular** (turn Snap off as needed)
to	**D2**
Specify next point or [Undo]:	**<enter>** (the intersection will be edited later)
Command:	**<enter> (Repeat MLINE)**
Current settings: Justification = Bottom, Scale = 1.00, Style = TWO:	
Specify start point or [Justification/Scale/STyle]:	**Osnap-Intersection**
of	**D3**
Specify next point:	**Osnap-Perpendicular**
to	**D4**
Specify next point or [Undo]:	**<enter>** (the intersection will be edited later)

FIGURE 7–10
Add an End Cap to the
Interior Walls

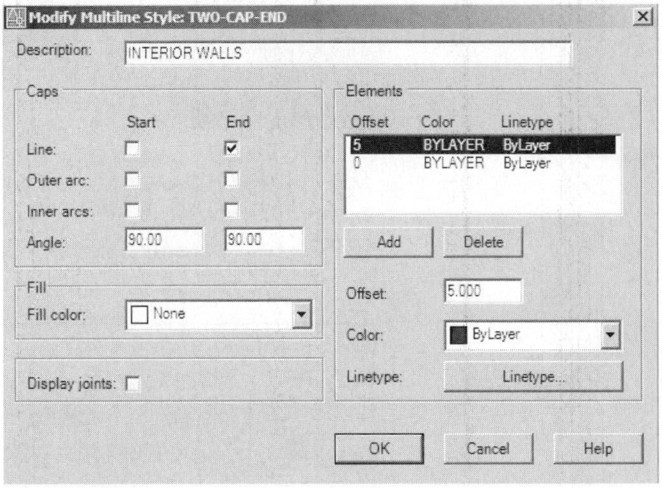

Modify Multiline Style: TWO-CAP-END

Description: INTERIOR WALLS

Caps
	Start	End
Line:	☐	☑
Outer arc:	☐	☐
Inner arcs:	☐	☐
Angle:	90.00	90.00

Fill
Fill color: ☐ None

Display joints: ☐

Elements
Offset	Color	Linetype
5	BYLAYER	ByLayer
0	BYLAYER	ByLayer

Add   Delete

Offset: 5.000
Color: ■ ByLayer
Linetype: Linetype...

OK   Cancel   Help

Step 10. Create a new multiline style that uses the settings of the TWO style but adds an end cap at the end of the line. Then use Multiline and Osnap-From to draw the wall that separates the reception and bookkeeping areas (Figures 7–9 and 7–10):

Prompt	Response
Command:	**Multiline Style...**
The Multiline Style dialog box appears:	CLICK: **TWO** and CLICK: **New...**
The Create New Multiline Style dialog box appears:	TYPE: **TWO-CAP-END** in the New Style Name box CLICK: **Continue**
The Modify Multiline Style: dialog box appears:	In the Caps area CLICK: **End** in the Line: row so a check appears in it as shown in Figure 7–10. CLICK: **OK**
The Multiline Styles dialog box appears with TWO-CAP-END highlighted:	CLICK: **Set Current**; CLICK: **OK**
Command:	TYPE: **ML<enter>**

Current settings:
    Justification = Bottom,
    Scale = 1.00,
    Style = TWO-CAP-END
Specify start point or
    [Justification/Scale/STyle]:
	Osnap-From (or TYPE: **FRO<enter>**)

Base point:	**Osnap-Endpoint**
of	**D5** (Figure 7–9)
<Offset>:	TYPE: **@19'<180<enter>**
Specify next point:	**Turn ORTHO ON. Move your mouse up and** TYPE: **17'3-1/2<enter>**
Specify next point or [Undo]:	**Move your mouse to the left and** TYPE: **4'<enter>**
Specify next point or [Close/Undo]:	**<enter>** (the intersection will be edited next)

Look at the check box marked On in the Fill color: area, Figure 7–10. When a color is selected from the list, the walls are drawn with a solid fill and can be filled with any color.

Edit Multiline

The Edit Multiline command allows you to change the intersections of multilines in a variety of ways as shown in Figure 7–11. Just CLICK: the change you want, and then CLICK: the two multilines whose intersection you want to change.

TIP: Use Zoom-Window, Zoom-Dynamic, and Zoom-Previous often to zoom in on parts of the drawing you are working on; drawing is easier, and you will be more accurate.

Step 11. Use Edit Multiline to trim the intersections of the multilines forming the interior walls to an Open Tee (Figures 7–11 and 7–12):

Prompt	Response
Command:	Under the Modify menu, CLICK: **Object**, then CLICK: **Multiline...** (or TYPE: **MLEDIT<enter>**)
The Multiline Edit Tools dialog box appears:	CLICK: **Open Tee**
Select first mline:	CLICK: **the vertical wall separating the reception and bookkeeping areas**
Select second mline:	CLICK: **the south horizontal exterior wall**
Select first mline (or Undo):	CLICK: **the interior vertical wall of office 3**
Select second mline:	CLICK: **the south horizontal exterior wall**
Select first mline (or Undo):	CLICK: **the interior horizontal wall of the president's office**
Select second mline:	CLICK: **the interior vertical wall of the president's office**
Select first mline (or Undo):	**<enter>**

If you made a mistake while drawing the walls, the next part of this exercise will show you how to explode the multiline and use a modify command to edit the multiline.

FIGURE 7–11
Edit Multiline Tools

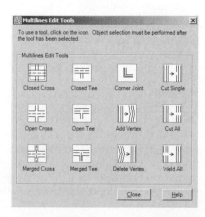

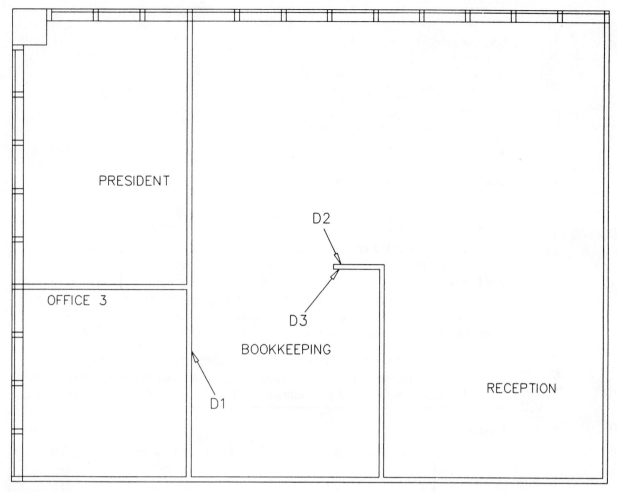

FIGURE 7–12
Practice Using the Extend Command (Scale: 1/8″ = 1′-0″)

Extend

The Extend command allows you to lengthen an existing line or arc segment to meet a specified boundary edge. You will find it very useful when drawing walls. In the following part of this exercise, a boundary edge will be selected, and the horizontal wall of the bookkeeping area will be extended. The Undo option will then be used to erase it.

Step 12. Practice using the Extend command, and then undo the practice session. You must first explode the multilines using the Explode command to make the separate lines (Figure 7–12):

Prompt	Response
Command:	**Explode** (or TYPE: **X<enter>**)
Select objects:	**D1**
Select objects:	**D2**
Select objects:	**<enter>**
Command:	**Extend** (or TYPE: **EX<enter>**)
Select boundary edges...	
Select objects or <select all>:	**D1**

FIGURE 7–13
Properties Palette

Prompt	Response
Select objects: 1 found	
Select objects:	<enter>
Select object to extend or shift-select to trim or [Fence/Crossing/ Project/Edge/Undo]:	D2
Select object to extend or shift-select to trim or [Fence/Crossing/ Project/Edge/Undo]:	D3
Select object to extend or shift-select to trim or [Fence/Crossing/ Project/Edge/Undo]:	<enter>

The points D2 and D3 were picked close to the left end of the line segment because the selected line (or arc) is extended from the end closest to the point picked. If you need to trim an entity that intersects the boundary edge, hold the Shift key down and click on the entity to be trimmed while still in the Extend command.

Step 13. On your own:

1. Use the Undo command to erase the practice session.
2. Before using the Properties command in the next part of this exercise, explode the outside wall line of the exterior north and west walls of the tenant space.

Properties...

The Properties command (Figure 7–13) allows you to change any property that can be changed.

Properties...

Step 14. Use the Properties... command to change the layer of the interior walls from the A-wall-ext layer to the A-wall-int layer:

Prompt	Response
Command:	Properties...
The Properties palette appears:	Use a crossing window to select all the interior walls.
The Properties palette lists all the interior wall properties:	CLICK: **Layer...** CLICK: **the down arrow** CLICK: **A-wall-int** Close the dialog box and PRESS: Esc twice.

To change a property using the Properties palette, select the object and then either enter a new value or select a new value from a list. You can leave the Properties palette open, and you can also right-click in the Properties palette to dock it.

Step 15. On your own:
1. Use the Properties command to change the layer property of the glass line (the middle line on the north and west walls) from the A-wall layer to the A-glaz layer.

TIP: You can also move an object to another layer by clicking on it and then clicking the new layer in the layer list.

List

After you have changed the property of an entity and would like to confirm the change, or if you need additional information about an entity, using the List command is very helpful. The List command provides a screen display of the data stored for an entity.

Step 16. Use the List command to examine the data stored for one line of an interior wall:

Prompt	Response
Command:	**List** (or TYPE: **LIST<enter>**)
Select objects:	CLICK: **only one line of an interior wall** **<enter>**

Depending on the type of entity selected, the List command displays data information for the entity. Use **Esc** to cancel the listing and return to the Command: prompt when the listing is longer than needed. PRESS: **F2** to return to the graphics screen.

Color

To access the Select Color dialog box (Figure 7–14), CLICK: **Color...** under Format in the menu bar.

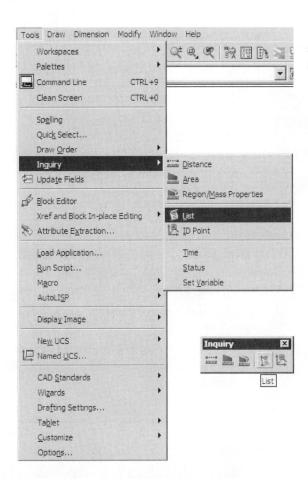

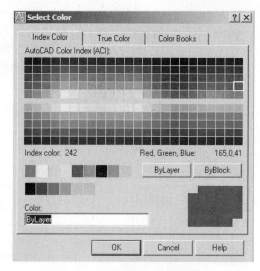

FIGURE 7–14
Select Color Dialog Box

Set Color ByLayer   We have discussed and used the entity property of Color as determined by the color assigned to a layer, thus controlling the entity color "ByLayer." The entity is drawn with a layer current and inherits the color assigned to the layer. The Select Color dialog box sets the color for drawing entities. When ByLayer is selected, the entities subsequently drawn inherit the color of the layer on which they are drawn.

Set Color Individually   The color property of entities can also be set individually. When a color, such as red, is selected from the Properties toolbar, or selected in the Select Color dialog box, the entities subsequently drawn inherit the color property red. The entities will be red regardless of the layer that is current when they are drawn.

To keep your drawing simple, when a new color is needed, create a layer and assign the new color to that layer.

Set Color By Block

Most library parts that are blocks need to be drawn on the 0 Layer, which is the same as setting the color property to ByBlock. The reason for this is explained in the following examples.

Example 1

A door (library part) is drawn on a layer named DOOR that is assigned the color property red, and a Wblock is made of the door. The door block is inserted into a new project. Because the block was originally drawn on a layer named DOOR (color red) the layer name is dragged into the new drawing layer listing, and the door will be red, regardless of the layer current in the new drawing.

Example 2

A door (library part) is drawn on the 0 Layer, Wblock is made of the door, and the door Wblock is inserted into a new project. Because the block was originally drawn on the 0 Layer, the door is generated on the drawing's current layer and inherits all properties of that layer.

Before any drawing entity that will be used as a block is drawn, you need to decide how it will be used in future drawings; that will determine the color property that it is assigned.

Linetype

When the Linetype command is typed and entered or selected from the Format menu, the Linetype Manager dialog box appears. Like the Color command, the linetype property can be set to ByLayer, individually, or ByBlock. Most library parts that are blocks should be drawn on the 0 Layer, which is the same as setting the linetype to ByBlock. When inserted as a block, the parts will inherit the linetype of the current layer.

Lineweight

When Lineweight... is selected from the Format menu, the Lineweight Settings dialog box (Figure 7–15) is displayed. Like the Color and Linetype commands, the lineweight property can be set to ByLayer or ByBlock or individually. It can also be set to default. The default value is initially set at .010 or .25 mm, which you can change. A lineweight value of 0 is displayed in model space as one pixel wide and plots the thinnest lineweight available on the specified plotter. CLICK: **LWT** on the status bar to display lineweight properties.

NOTE: You can set the color, linetype, and lineweight of an object using the Properties toolbar. Make sure you do not set these properties for objects individually. Create a new layer and assign the new color, linetype, or lineweight to the layer.

Make Object's Layer Current

This is another command that was very useful on the Layers toolbar. When you activate this command and pick any object, the layer that object is on becomes current.

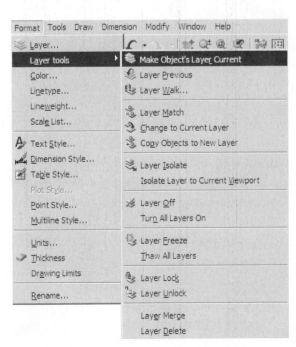

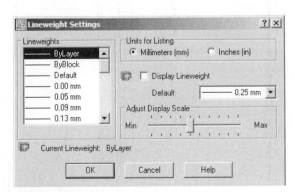

FIGURE 7–15
Lineweight Settings Dialog
Box

Step 17. On your own:

1. Set Layer A-wall-int current. Use Multiline with the correct Multiline Style current to finish drawing the interior walls of the tenant space. Use the dimensions shown in Figure 7–16. Remember that you can use the Modify commands (Extend, Trim, Edit Multiline, and so on) to fix the Multiline. To use Extend and Trim you must first explode the multiline.
2. Set FILL ON and regenerate the drawing.
3. Set 0 as the current layer. Use the dimensions shown in Figure 7–17 to draw the two door types—single door and double door—that will be defined

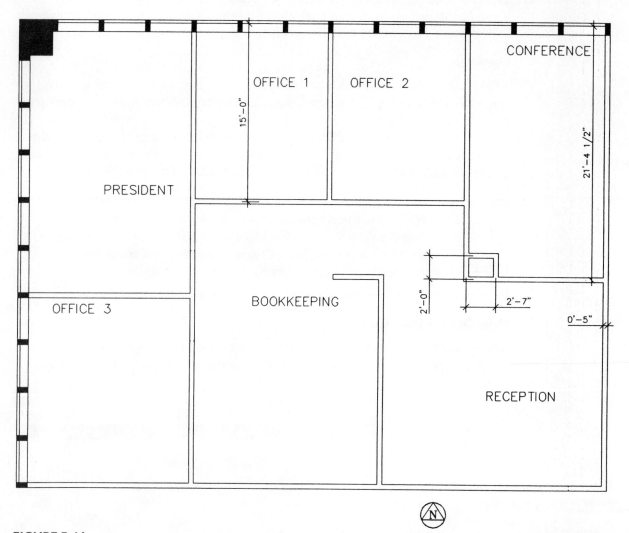

FIGURE 7–16
Use Multiline to Finish Drawing the Interior Walls (Scale: 1/8″ = 1′-0″)

FIGURE 7–17
Two Door Types That Will Be
Defined As Blocks and
Inserted into the Tenant Space

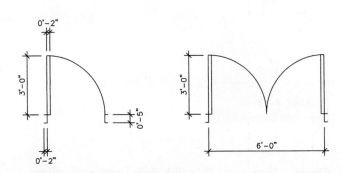

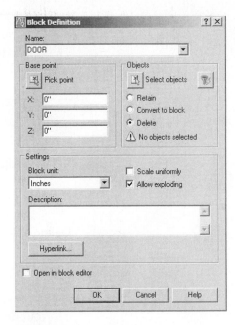

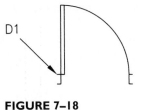

FIGURE 7–18
DOOR Block

FIGURE 7–19
Block Definition Dialog Box

as blocks and inserted into the tenant space. Pick any open space on your drawing and draw each door full size. In the following part of this exercise the Block and Wblock commands are used to define the doors as blocks.

Block-Make...

The Block-Make... command allows you to define any part of a current drawing as a block. Copies of the block can be inserted only into that drawing. Copies of a block defined with the Block-Make... command cannot be used in any other drawing without using the AutoCAD DesignCenter (described in Chapter 11).

Step 18. Use the Block-Make... command to define the single door drawing as a block named DOOR stored in the current drawing (Figures 7–18 and 7–19):

Prompt	Response
Command:	**Block-Make...** (or TYPE: **B\<enter\>**)
The Block Definition dialog box appears:	TYPE: **DOOR** in the Block name: box
	CLICK: **the Delete radio button under Objects**
	CLICK: **the Pick point button**
Specify insertion base point:	**Osnap-Endpoint**
of:	**D1** (Figure 7–18)
The Block Definition dialog box appears:	CLICK: **the Select objects button**
Select objects:	CLICK: **a point to locate the first corner of a selection window**
Specify opposite corner:	**Window only the single-door drawing.**
Select objects:	**\<enter\>**
The Block Definition dialog box appears:	CLICK: **OK**

Prompt	Response
The single door symbol is gone and is now defined as a block within your drawing.	

The three radio buttons in the Objects area of the Block Definition dialog box specify what happens to the selected object (in this instance, the door) after you create the block:

Retain   After the block is created, the door symbol will remain in the drawing but will not be a block.

Convert to Block   After the block is created, the door symbol will remain in the drawing and will be a block.

Delete   After the block is created, the door symbol will be deleted.

A Block name can be 1 to 255 characters long. It may include only letters, numbers, and three special characters—$ (dollar sign), - (hyphen), and _ (underscore).

The Insert command is used later in this exercise to insert copies of the DOOR block into your drawing. The "Specify insertion base point:" is the point on the inserted block to which the crosshair attaches. It allows you to position copies of the block exactly into the drawing. It is also the point around which the block can be rotated when it is inserted.

Step 19. **Use the Block-Make... command to view a listing of the block just created:**

Prompt	Response
Command:	**Block-Make...** (or TYPE: **B<enter>**)
The Block Definition dialog box appears:	CLICK: **the down arrow beside Name:**
The block name appears:	CLICK: **<cancel>**

Unless you use the DesignCenter, blocks defined with the Block command can be inserted only into the drawing in which they are defined. When you want to build a library of parts defined as blocks that can be inserted into any drawing, use the Wblock command, described next.

Wblock

The Wblock command allows you to define any part of a drawing or an entire drawing as a block. Blocks created with the Wblock command can be stored on a floppy disk, CD, DVD, or on the hard disk or network. Copies of the blocks can then be inserted into any drawing. These Wblocks become drawing files with a .dwg extension, just like any other AutoCAD drawing.

Step 20. **Use Wblock to save the double-door drawing as a block on your hard drive or on a network (Figures 7–20 and 7–21):**

Prompt	Response
Command:	TYPE: **W<enter>**
The Write Block dialog box appears:	TYPE: **DOORD** (to replace the "new block" name in the File name and path: box)
	CLICK: **the ... button** (to the right of File name and path:). This will allow you to Browse: for files or folders and select the path you want to save to.

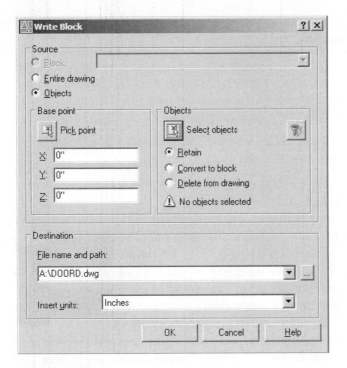

FIGURE 7–20
Write Block Dialog Box

FIGURE 7–21
DOORD Block

Prompt	Response
The Browse for Drawing File dialog box appears:	CLICK: **the down arrow in the Save in: box to select the folder you want to save the double door drawing in**
	CLICK: **Save**

NOTE: You may save the DOORD block to any folder or disk that is convenient.

The Write Block dialog box appears:	CLICK: **Delete from drawing button**
	CLICK: **Pick point button**
Specify insertion base point:	**Endpoint**
of	**D1** (Figure 7–21)
The Write Block dialog box appears:	CLICK: **the Select objects button**
Select objects:	**Window the entire double-door drawing.**
Select objects:	**<enter>**
The Write Block dialog box appears:	CLICK: **OK**

The double-door drawing disappears and is saved as a block.

The double-door drawing is now saved as a drawing file with a .DWG file extension. Copies of the DOORD drawing can be recalled and inserted into any other drawing. It is obvious that building a library of parts that can be inserted into any drawing saves time.

The three radio buttons in the Source area of the Write Block dialog box specify what you are defining as a Wblock:

Block   This helps define a block that is stored in a current drawing as a Wblock.

Entire Drawing   Not only parts of a drawing but also an entire drawing can be defined as a block. Use 0,0,0 as the base point when defining an entire drawing as a block.

Objects   Allows you to select an object to define as a block.

Step 21. On your own:

1. Use the Wblock command to write the DOOR block stored in your current drawing to a disk and folder of your choice.
2. In the following part of this exercise, the doors will be inserted into the tenant space. Before the doors are inserted, openings for all doors must be added to the drawing. Each single door is 3′4″ wide, including the 2″ frame, so each opening for a single door is 3′4″ wide. As shown in Figure 7–22, the dimension from the corner of each room to the outside edge of the single door frame is 3-1/2″. The dimensions shown in Figure 7–22 for the door to OFFICE 1 apply to all single-door openings.

   Use the dimensions shown in Figure 7–22 to draw the openings for the five single doors (Layer A-wall-int) and for the double-entry door (Layer A-wall-ext). A helpful hint: Use Osnap-From or ID with the Line command to draw the first door opening line, and Offset for the second door opening line. Then use Trim to complete the opening. If Trim does not work, explode the multiline first, then trim.
3. Set Layer A-DOOR current.

Insert-Block...

The Insert-Block... command allows you to insert the defined blocks into your drawing. It may be used to insert a block defined with either the Block-Make command or the Wblock command.

The Insert mode found in the Osnap menu allows you to snap to the insertion point of Text or a Block entity.

The following part of the exercise uses the Insert command to insert the DOOR block into the tenant space. Don't forget to zoom in on the area of the drawing on which you are working. Remember also that the insertion point of the DOOR block is the upper left corner of the door frame.

Step 22. Use the Insert command to insert the block named DOOR into OFFICE 2 (Figures 7–23 and 7–24):

Prompt	Response
Command:	**Insert-Block...** (or TYPE: **I<enter>**)
The Insert dialog box appears (Figure 7–23):	CLICK: **DOOR** (in the Name: box) (Be sure there is a check in the Specify On-screen box under Insertion point and in the Uniform Scale check box.)
	CLICK: **OK**
Specify insertion point or [Basepoint/ Scale/Rotate/PScale/PRotate]:	**Osnap-Intersection**
of	**D1** (Figure 7–24)

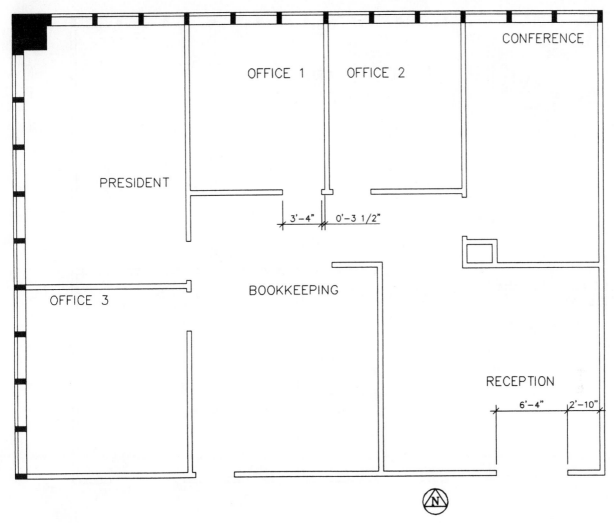

FIGURE 7–22
Use the Dimensions Shown to Draw the Openings for All Doors (Scale: 1/8″ = 1′-0″)

FIGURE 7–23
Insert Dialog Box

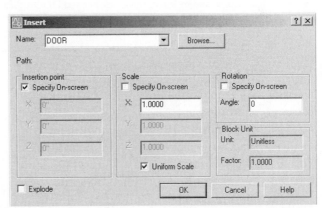

Step 23. Use the Insert-Block... command to insert the block named DOOR into the president's office (Figure 7–24).

Prompt	Response
Command:	**Insert-Block...** (or TYPE: **I<enter>**)
The Insert dialog box appears with DOOR in the Name: box:	TYPE: **90** (in the Rotation Angle: input box) CLICK: **OK**

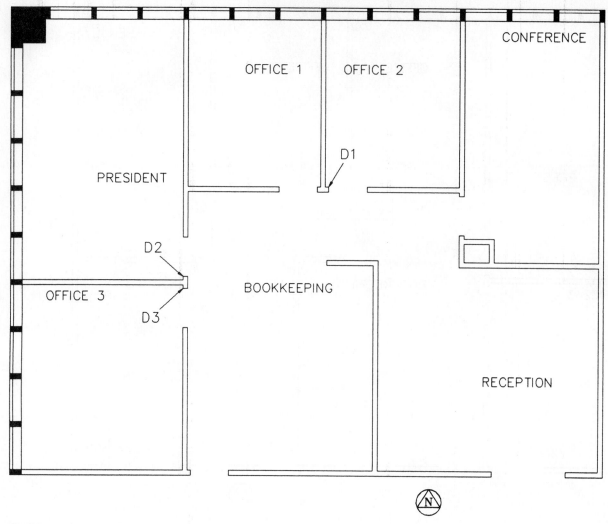

FIGURE 7–24
Use the Insert-Block... Command to Insert the Block Named DOOR (Scale: 1/8″ = 1′-0″)

Prompt	Response
Specify insertion point or [Basepoint/ Scale/Rotate/PScale/PRotate]:	**Osnap-Intersection**
of	**D2**

Because the doors were drawn on the 0 Layer, when inserted as blocks on the A-door Layer, they assumed the properties of the A-door Layer and are cyan.

When a copy of a block is inserted into the drawing, it is inserted as a single object. Before the Trim command can be used, or a copy of a block can be edited, the block must be exploded. When a block is exploded, it returns to separate entities; it also changes color because it returns to the 0 Layer.

If you want a block to be inserted retaining its separate objects, check the Explode box in the lower left corner of the Insert dialog box.

Insertion Point

The "Insertion point:" of the incoming block is the point where the "insertion base point" specified when the door was defined as a block will be placed. In the preceding exercises, the Osnap mode Intersection was used to position copies of the block exactly into the drawing. You can also use the ID command, or From (on the osnap menu) when inserting a block. Use the ID command to identify a point on the drawing, and then initiate the Insert-Block... command after the point has been located. You can then enter the "Insertion point:" of the block by using relative or polar coordinates to specify a distance from the established point location.

X Scale Factor, Y Scale Factor

The X and Y scale factors provide a lot of flexibility in how the copy of the block will appear when it is inserted. The default X and Y scale factor is 1. A scale factor of 1 inserts the block as it was originally drawn.

New scale factors can be typed and entered in response to the prompts. AutoCAD multiplies all X and Y dimensions of the block by the X and Y scale factors entered. By default, the Y scale factor equals the X scale, but a different Y scale factor can be entered separately. This is especially helpful when you are inserting a window block into a wall with windows of varying lengths. The block can be inserted, the X scale factor can be increased or decreased by the desired amount, and the Y scale factor can remain stable by being entered as 1.

Negative X or Y scale factors can be entered to insert mirror images of the block. When the X scale factor is negative, the Y scale factor remains positive. When the Y scale factor is negative, the X scale factor remains positive. Either a negative X or Y scale factor will work in the following example, but negative X will be used.

NOTE: The Measure command draws a specified block at each mark between divided segments. The Divide command also draws a specified block at each mark between equal segments.

Step 24. Use the Insert-Block... command and a negative X scale factor, and rotate the angle of the block to insert the block named DOOR into office 3 (Figure 7–24).

Prompt	Response
Command:	**Insert-Block...**
The Insert dialog box appears with DOOR in the Name: box:	UNCHECK: the Uniform Scale box
	TYPE: **–1** (in the X scale input box); TYPE: **90** (in the Rotation Angle: input box)
	CLICK: **OK**
Specify insertion point or [Basepoint/ Scale/Rotate/PScale/PRotate]:	**Osnap-Intersection**
of	**D3**

Step 25. On your own (Figure 7–25):

1. Use the Insert-Block... command to complete the insertion of all doors in the tenant space.
2. Set Layer A-flor-wdwk current. Draw two lines to show the cabinets in the conference room. The upper cabinets are 12″ deep.

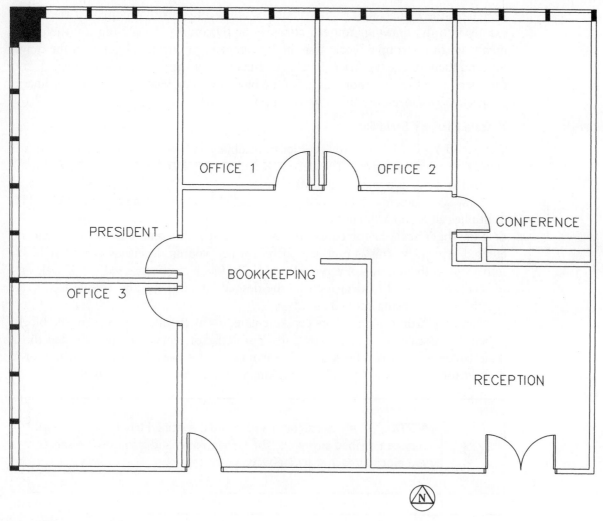

FIGURE 7–25
Exercise 7–1: Tenant Space Floor Plan (Scale: 1/8″ = 1′-0″)

3. Set Layer A-flor-iden current. Change the text style Standard so it uses the Simplex font. Use Dtext, height 9″, to type the identifying name in each room. Use the approximate locations as shown in Figure 7–25; the names can be moved as needed when furniture is inserted into the drawing.

Inserting Entire Drawings as Blocks

The Insert-Block... command can be used to insert into the current drawing any drawing that has not been defined as a block and to define it as a block within that drawing. Simply use the Insert-Block... command to insert the drawing. Use the Browse... button in the Insert dialog box to locate the drawing.

Redefining an Inserted Block Using the Block Command

The appearance of any block, defined as a block within a drawing, and all copies of the block within the drawing may be changed easily. As an example, we use the DOOR block that is defined as a block within the tenant space drawing. The following steps describe how to change the appearance of a block and all copies of the block that have already been inserted within a drawing. If you use this example to change the appearance of the DOOR block, **be sure to return it to the original appearance.**

1. Insert a copy of the DOOR block in an open space in the tenant space drawing.
2. Explode the DOOR block and edit it so that it is different from the original DOOR block.
3. Use the Block-Make... command to redefine the block as follows:

Prompt	Response
Command:	**Block-Make...**(or Type: **B <enter>**)
The Block Definition dialog box appears:	TYPE: **DOOR** in the Block name: box
	CLICK: **Pick Point**
Specify insertion base point:	**Pick the insertion base point.**
The Block Definition dialog box appears:	CLICK: **Select objects**
Select objects:	**Window the single door.**
Select objects:	**<enter>**
The Block Definition dialog box appears:	CLICK: **OK**
The AutoCAD Warning "DOOR is already defined. Block references already exist in the drawing. Update the definition and all of its references?"	CLICK: **Yes**

The DOOR block is redefined, and all copies of the DOOR block that are in the drawing are redrawn with the new definition of the DOOR block.

Advantages of Using Blocks

1. A library of drawing parts allows you to draw an often-used part once instead of many times.
2. Blocks can be combined with customized menus to create a complete applications environment around AutoCAD that provides the building and furnishings parts that are used daily.
3. Once a block is defined and inserted into the drawing, you can update all references to that block by redefining the block.
4. Because AutoCAD treats a block as a single object less disk space is used for each insertion of a block.

Aerial View

Aerial View works in all model space views. It displays a view of the drawing in a separate window that you can move or resize similar to Zoom Dynamic. When you keep Aerial View open, you can zoom or pan without choosing a command.

Named Views

Many of the drawings that architects and space planners work with are large. The Named Views command is useful when you are working with a complex drawing. It allows you to window a portion of the drawing and save it as a named view that can be recalled to the screen with the Named Views-Restore command. For example, you may View Window each room in the tenant space and assign a View Name; then you can recall each room for editing by using the Named Views-Restore command.

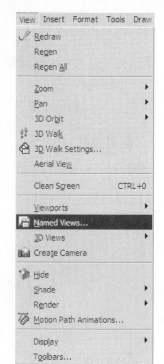

Use Zoom-All to view the entire tenant space drawing. Use the Named Views command to create, name, and restore a view of the president's office:

Prompt	Response
Command:	**Named Views...** (or TYPE: **V\<enter\>**)
The View Manager appears:	CLICK: **New...**
The New View dialog box (Figure 7–26) appears:	TYPE: **PRESIDENT** in the View name: box
	CLICK: **Define window** (radio button)
	CLICK: **Define View Window button** (with the small arrow on it)
Specify first corner:	**Window only the president's office.**
Specify opposite corner:	
Specify first corner:	**\<enter\>**
The New View dialog box appears:	CLICK: **OK**
The View Manager appears:	CLICK: **OK**
Command:	**\<enter\>** (Repeat Named Views...)
The View Manager appears:	CLICK: **PRESIDENT**
	CLICK: **Set current**
	CLICK: **OK**

The View named PRESIDENT
    appears on the screen.

When you first enter the Drawing Editor, you can recall a named view by using the Named View... command. You can also print or plot a portion of a drawing by supplying the view name.

Delete

Delete removes one or more views from the list of saved Views. CLICK: **the view name,** then PRESS: **the Delete button** on your keyboard.

FIGURE 7–26
New View Dialog Box

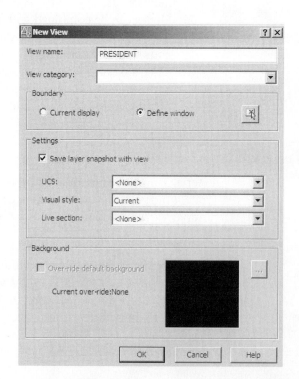

Step 26. When you have completed Exercise 7–1, save your work in at least two places.

Step 27. Use a Layout Wizard or Page Setup Manager to create a Layout tab named Floor Plan. Plot or print Exercise 7–1 to scale.

 TIP: If you need to plot all layers black instead of the colors they have been assigned, CLICK: **monochrome.ctb** in the Plot style table (pen assignments) list in the Plot dialog box (or the Page Setup dialog box). CLICK: **Edit** to the right of the Plot Style to make sure that the color selected is Black and Grayscale: is OFF.

Exercise 7–2: Hotel Room Floor Plan

In Exercise 7–2, the AutoCAD Design Center is used to insert existing fixtures such as a tub, toilet, sink, and faucet into the floor plan. Lineweights are used to make the drawing more attractive, and a solid hatch pattern with a gray color is used to make the walls solid. When you have completed Exercise 7–2 your drawing will look similar to Figure 7–27 without dimensions.

Step 1. Use your workspace to make the following settings:

1. **Use SaveAs… to save the drawing with the name CH7_EX2.**
2. Set drawing Units: **Architectural**
3. Set Drawing Limits: **30′,40′**
4. Set GRIDDISPLAY: **0**
5. Set Grid: **12″**
6. Set Snap: **6″**
7. Create the following Layers:

LAYER NAME	COLOR	LINETYPE	LINEWEIGHT
Bath	Magenta	Continuous	0.15mm
Center line	Cyan	CENTER	0.09mm
Dim	Cyan	Continuous	0.09mm
Door	White	Continuous	0.15mm
Faucet	Magenta	Continuous	0.05mm
Floor Plan Text	White	Continuous	Default
Furniture	Green	Continuous	0.15mm
Hatch	253	Continuous	default
Rod	White	HIDDEN	default
Walls	White	Continuous	0.30mm
Window	White	Continuous	0.15mm

8. Set **Layer Walls** current.

Step 2. Use Polyline to draw the outside walls:

Prompt	Response
Command:	**Polyline** (or TYPE: **PL**<enter>)
Specify start point:	TYPE: **24′,24′**<enter>

NOTE:
ALL WALLS ARE 5" WIDE EXCEPT FOR THE 6" OUTSIDE WINDOW WALL

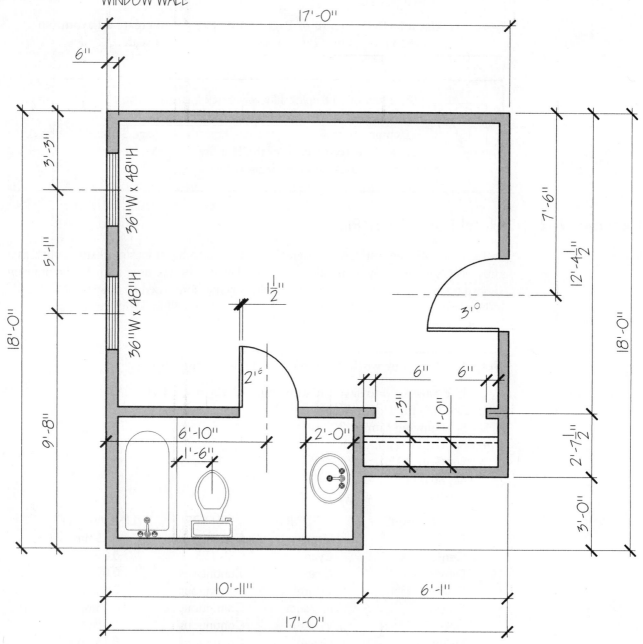

HOTEL ROOM FLOOR PLAN
SCALE: 1/ 4"=1'-0"

FIGURE 7–27
Dimensions for Exercise 7–2 Hotel Room Floor Plan (Scale: 1/4" = 1'-0")

Prompt	Response
Specify next point or [Arc/Halfwidth/ Length/Undo/Width]:	**Turn ORTHO ON, move your mouse straight up,** and TYPE: **6'<enter>**
Specify next point or [Arc/Close/ Halfwidth/Length/Undo/Width]:	**Move your mouse to the left,** and TYPE: **17'<enter>**

Prompt	Response
Specify next point or [Arc/Close/Halfwidth/Length/Undo/Width]:	**Move your mouse straight down,** and TYPE: **18′<enter>**
Specify next point or [Arc/Close/Halfwidth/Length/Undo/Width]:	**Move your mouse to the right,** and TYPE: **10′11<enter>**
Specify next point or [Arc/Close/Halfwidth/Length/Undo/Width]:	**Move your mouse straight up,** and TYPE: **3′<enter>**
Specify next point or [Arc/Close/Halfwidth/Length/Undo/Width]:	**Move your mouse to the right,** and TYPE: **6′1<enter>**
Specify next point or [Arc/Close/Halfwidth/Length/Undo/Width]:	**Move your mouse straight up,** and TYPE: **6′<enter>**
Specify next point or [Arc/Close/Halfwidth/Length/Undo/Width]:	**<enter>**

Step 3.   On your own (Figures 7–27 and Figure 7–28):

1. Offset the polyline just drawn 5″ to the inside.
2. Explode the offset polyline and move the inside line on the left 1″ to the right to make a 6″ wall on the window side. Trim where necessary, or use 0 distance chamfer to make square corners.
3. Draw the following:
    remaining walls
    closet shelf and rod (hidden line)
    door and window openings
    doors

Do not draw the window. It will be inserted as a block later.

4. **Change LTSCALE as needed to show the Hidden linetype of the rod.**

Hatch

Next you will add a solid hatch pattern to shade the walls of the hotel room. The most important aspect of using the Hatch command is to create a clear boundary for the hatch pattern. If the boundary of the hatching area is not clearly defined, the Hatch command will not work, or will not appear, as you want it to. Any small gap at intersections will cause an error message with the Hatch command.

Step 4.   Set Layer Hatch current.

Step 5.   Use the Hatch command to add shading to the walls of the hotel room:

Prompt	Response
Command:	**Hatch** (or TYPE: **H<enter>**)
The Hatch and Gradient dialog box appears:	CLICK: **Predefined** in the pattern Type area CLICK: **...** (to the right of the Pattern: list box) CLICK: **the Other Predefined tab**

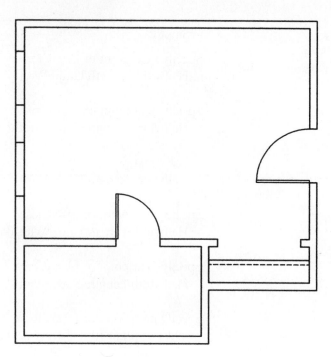

FIGURE 7–28
Complete Outside and Inside
Walls and Closet Details

Prompt	Response
	CLICK: **SOLID**
	CLICK: **OK**
	CLICK: **Add: Pick points**
Pick internal point or [Select objects/remove Boundaries]:	CLICK: **any point inside the lines defining the walls**
Pick internal point or [Select objects/remove Boundaries]:	**<enter>**
The Hatch and Gradient dialog box appears:	CLICK: **Preview** or **OK**

The walls are now hatched. If you get an error message, check that there are no gaps in the lines that form the boundaries for the walls.

Step 6. Set Layer Bath current.

Step 7. Open the AutoCAD DesignCenter and locate the House Designer drawing (Figure 7–29):

Prompt	Response
Command:	TYPE: **DC<enter>**
The DesignCenter appears;	CLICK: **the + to the left of House Designer .dwg (follow path shown in Figure 7–29)**
	CLICK: **Blocks**
The available blocks appear in the area to the right:	DOUBLE-CLICK: **Bath Tub = 26 × 60 in.**

FIGURE 7–29
Select the Bath Tub =
26 × 60 in. Block from the
DesignCenter and Insert It.

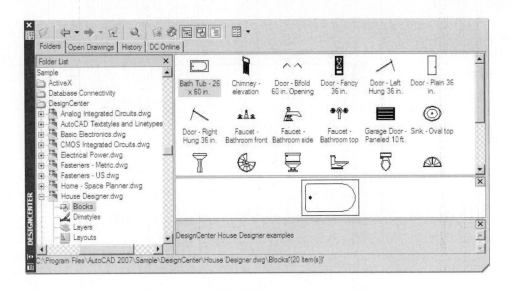

FIGURE 7–30
Insert the Bath Tub

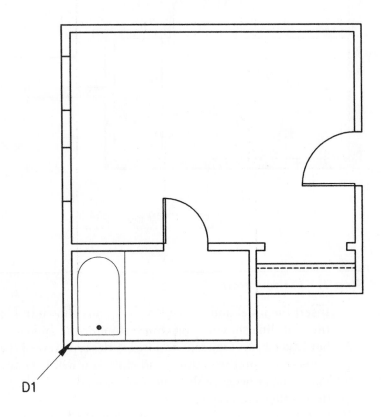

D1

Prompt	Response
The Insert dialog box appears;	TYPE: **90** in the Rotation - Angle: box CLICK: **OK**
Specify insertion point or [Basepoint/Scale/X/Y/Z/Rotate]:	CLICK: **D1** (Figure 7–30)

FIGURE 7–31
Exercise 7–2 Complete
(Scale: 1/4″ = 1′-0″)

YOUR NAME

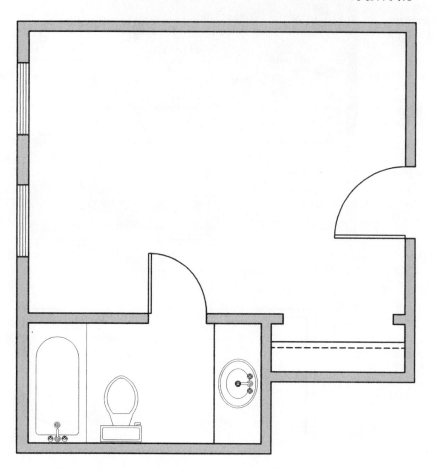

HOTEL ROOM FLOOR PLAN
SCALE: 1/ 4″=1′-0″

Step 8. On your own:

1. Insert the toilet and sink in the locations shown in Figure 7–31, and draw the 2′-0″ line showing the countertop for the sink.
2. Set Layer Faucet current and insert the top view of the faucet in the locations shown in the bathtub and sink. You will have to insert it on the Faucet layer because the faucet is so detailed the lines will flow together unless they are very thin.
3. Insert the 36″ wood frame windows in the location shown on the Window layer.
4. TYPE: the following in the City Blueprint font to complete the drawing:

   HOTEL ROOM FLOOR PLAN underscored, centered, 8″ high
   The scale, centered, 5″ high
   Your name, 5″ high

Step 9. Save your drawing in at least two places.

Step 10. Plot the drawing at a scale of 1/4″ = 1′-0″ centered vertically on an 8-1/2″ × 11″ sheet.

FIGURE 7–32
Log Cabin-Huntsman
(Courtesy of Tech Art)

Exercise 7–3: Log Cabin Floor Plan

1. Draw the floor plan of the log cabin shown in Figure 7–32. Use the dimensions shown in Figure 7–33 (Sheets 1 and 2), or use an architectural scale to measure the floor plan or fireplace detail and draw it full scale. Your drawing should look similar to Figure 7–33 without dimensions.
2. Use a Layout Wizard or Page Setup Manager to create a layout. Plot or print the drawing to scale.

Exercise 7–4: House Floor Plan

1. Draw the lower and upper levels of the house floor plan as shown in Figure 7–34 (Sheets 1 and 2). Use the dimensions shown, or use an architectural scale to measure the floor plan and draw it full scale. Your drawing should look similar to Figure 7–34 without dimensions.
2. Use a Layout Wizard or Page Setup Manager to create a layout. Plot or print the drawing to scale.

Exercise 7–5: Bank Floor Plan

1. Draw the bank floor plan as shown in Figure 7–35 (Sheets 1 and 2). Use the dimensions shown, or use an architectural scale to measure the floor plan and draw it full scale. Your drawing should look similar to Figure 7–35 without dimensions.
2. Use a Layout Wizard or Page Setup Manager to create a layout. Plot or print the drawing to scale.

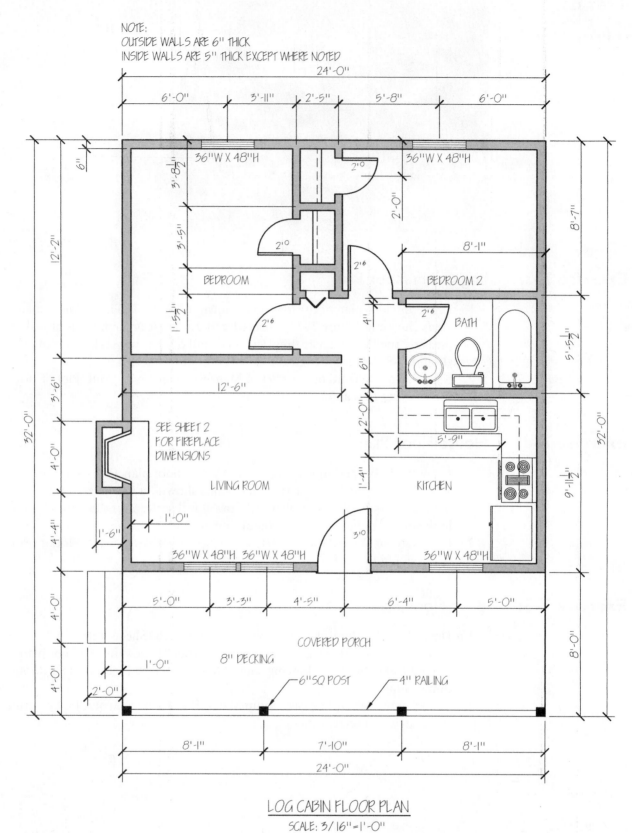

NOTE:
OUTSIDE WALLS ARE 6" THICK
INSIDE WALLS ARE 5" THICK EXCEPT WHERE NOTED

LOG CABIN FLOOR PLAN
SCALE: 3/16"=1'-0"

FIGURE 7–33
Sheet 1 of 2 Dimensions for Exercise 7–3 (Scale: 3/6″ = 1′-0″)
(Courtesy of Tech Art)

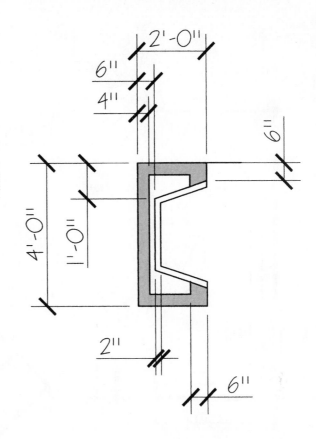

FIGURE 7–33
Sheet 2 of 2 Fireplace
Dimensions (Scale: 3/8″ =
1′-0″)

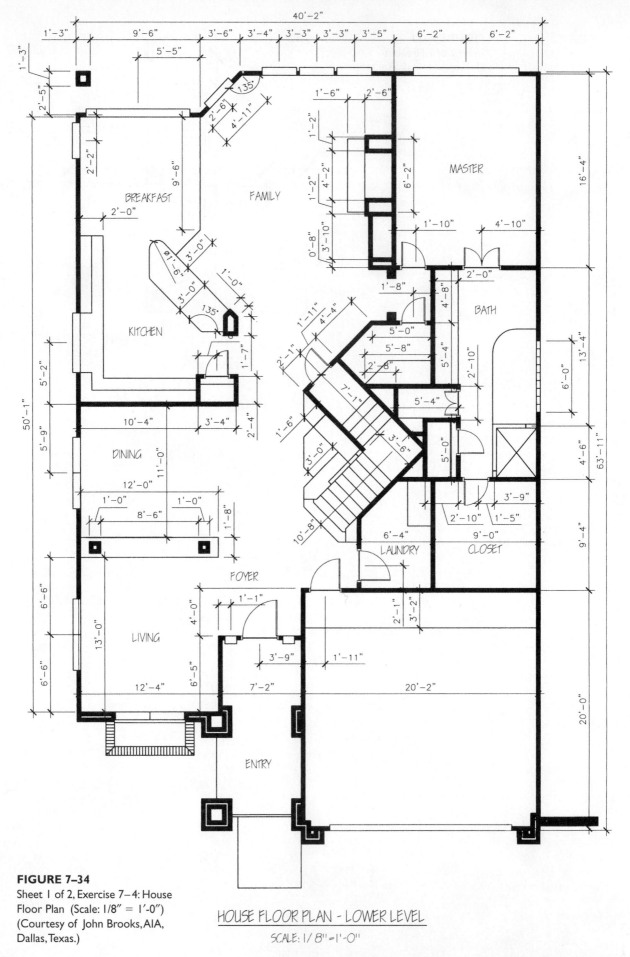

FIGURE 7-34

Sheet 1 of 2, Exercise 7-4: House
Floor Plan (Scale: 1/8" = 1'-0")
(Courtesy of John Brooks, AIA,
Dallas, Texas.)

HOUSE FLOOR PLAN - LOWER LEVEL

SCALE: 1/8"=1'-0"

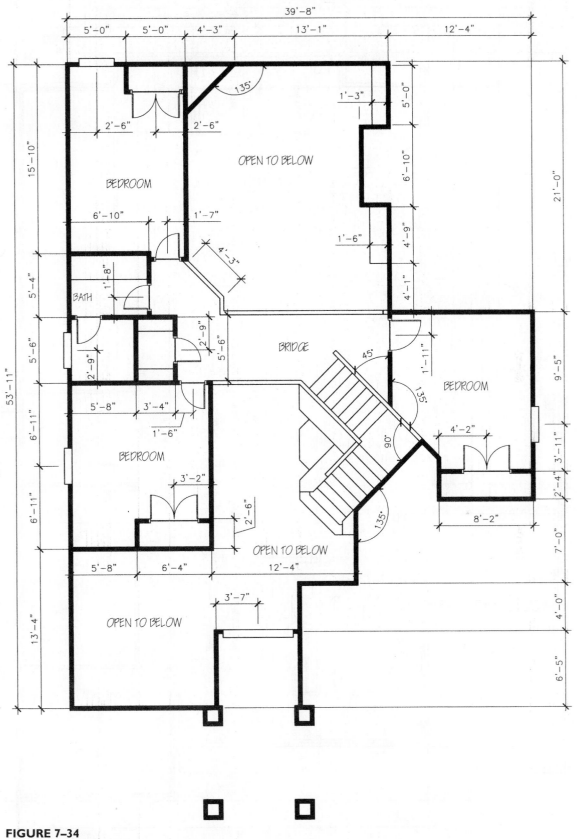

FIGURE 7–34
Sheet 2 of 2, Exercise 7–4: House
Floor Plan (Scale: 1/8″ = 1′-0″)
(Courtesy of John Brooks, AIA,
Dallas, Texas.)

HOUSE FLOOR PLAN - UPPER LEVEL
SCALE: 1/8″=1′-0″

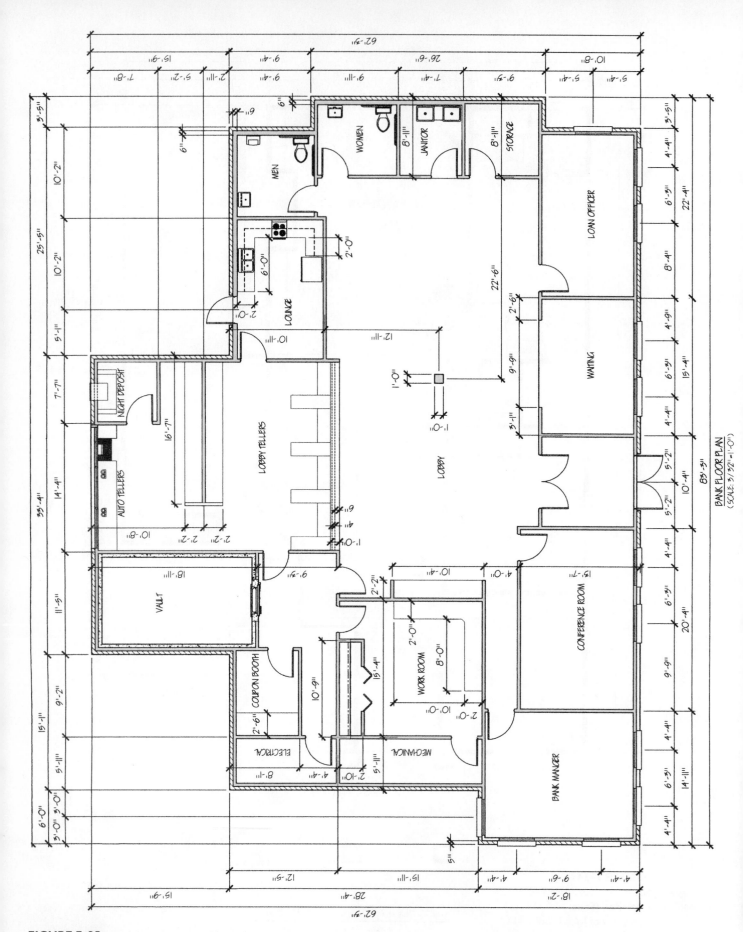

FIGURE 7–35

Sheet 1 of 2, Exercise 7–5: Bank Floor Plan (Scale: 3/32″ = 1′-0″)

(Courtesy of Benjamin Puente, Jr.)

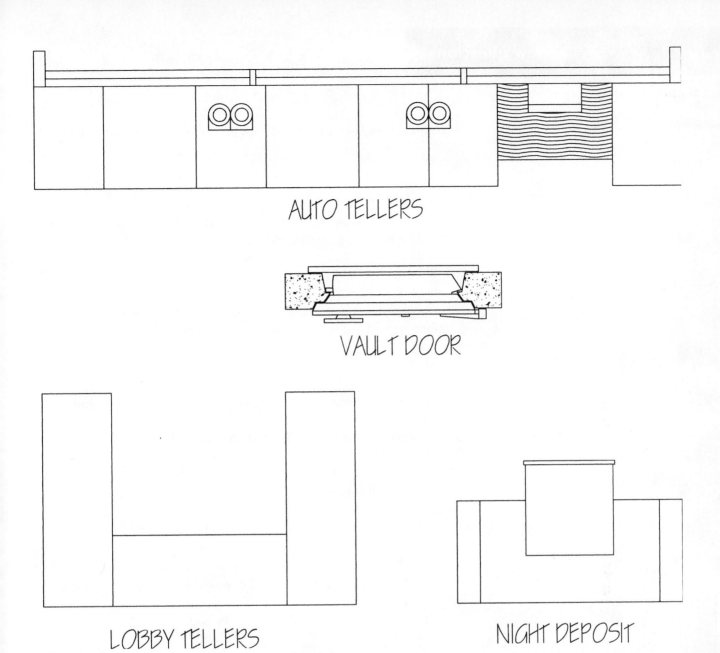

AUTO TELLERS

VAULT DOOR

LOBBY TELLERS

NIGHT DEPOSIT

FIGURE 7–35
Sheet 2 of 2, Exercise 7–5: Bank Floor Plan Details (Scale: 1/2″ = 1′-0″)
(Courtesy of Benjamin Puente, Jr.)

1. What is the maximum number of lines you can draw at the same time with Multiline?
   a. 2
   b. 4
   c. 8
   d. 12
   e. 16

2. Which of the following Multiline justification options can be used to draw a three-line wall using the middle line?
   a. Top
   b. Right
   c. Bottom
   d. Left
   e. Zero

3. When you are creating a new Multiline Style, what must you pick in the Multiline Style dialog box to set the new style current?
   a. Add
   b. Save...
   c. New
   d. Set Current
   e. Load...

4. Which of the following must be selected first when using the Extend command?
   a. The correct color
   b. The correct layer
   c. Object to be trimmed
   d. Object to extend
   e. Boundary

5. Which of the following may *not* be changed with the Properties... command?
   a. Color
   b. Layer
   c. Linetype
   d. Lineweight
   e. Drawing name

6. Which of the following commands tells you the layer a line is on and its length?
   a. Status
   b. Dist
   c. Area
   d. List
   e. Utility

7. On which layer should most blocks be constructed?
   a. 0 Layer
   b. Any layer with a color other than white
   c. Blocks Layer
   d. BL Layer
   e. Any layer other than the 0 Layer

8. If a block is inserted with a check in the Explode block, which of the following is true?
   a. The block must be exploded before it can be edited.
   b. Each element of the block is a separate object.
   c. The block assumes the color of the current layer.
   d. A Wblock is created with the same name.
   e. AutoCAD will not accept the block name.

9. The Wblock command does which of the following?
   a. Creates a block that can be used on the current drawing only
   b. Creates a drawing file on any disk
   c. Creates a drawing file on the hard disk only
   d. Creates blocks of parts of the current drawing only
   e. Uses only named blocks on the current drawing

10. Which scale factor can be used to create a mirror image of a block with the use of the Insert-Block... command?
    a. Negative X, Positive Y
    b. Positive X, Positive Y
    c. Negative X, Negative Y
    d. Mirrored images cannot be created with the Insert-Block... command.

Complete.

11. List the command you must use to create a new multiline style.

   _____

12. Describe how to edit a multiline with the Edit Multiline command.

   _____

   _____

   _____

13. List the command that allows you to change any property that can be changed.

   _____

14. Describe how to use the Block-Make... command to redefine, on the current drawing, seven insertions of the block DOOR using an updated drawing file named DOOR.

   _____

   _____

15. Describe the basic difference between Block-Make... and Wblock.

   _____

   _____

   _____

16. List the command that allows you to save and restore a view.

   _____

17. Describe what happens when a block is created using the Block-Make... command, and the Retain objects radio button is selected.

   _____

   _____

18. Describe how several entities drawn on a single layer may each be a different color.

   _____

   _____

19. List four advantages of using blocks.

    1. _____

       _____

    2. _____

       _____

    3. _____

       _____

    4. _____

       _____

20. What command can be used to change the scale of a Paper space viewport (a layout)?

    _____

    _____

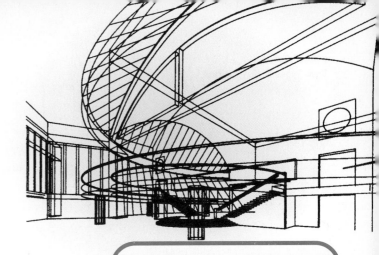

chapter

8

Dimensioning and Area Calculations

objectives

When you have completed this chapter, you will be able to:

Understand the function of dimensioning variables.

Set dimensioning variables.

Save and restore dimensioning styles.

Correctly use the following commands and settings:

Aligned Dimensioning
Align Text
Area
Baseline Dimensioning
Cal
Continue Dimensioning
DIMASSOC
Dimension Edit
Dimension Style...
Grips
Linear Dimensioning
Modify-Object-Text-Edit
Oblique
Override
QDIM
Status
Update

Six Basic Types of Dimensions

Six basic types of dimensions can be automatically created using Auto-CAD. They are linear (and arc length), aligned, ordinate, radius, diameter, and angular. They are listed in the Dimension menu and are shown on the Dimension toolbar. Each dimension type shown in Figure 8–1 can be activated by selecting one of the following:

Linear   For dimensioning the length of horizontal, vertical, and angled lines.

Arc Length   For dimensioning the length of an arc.

Aligned   For showing the length of features that are drawn at an angle.

Ordinate   To display the X or Y coordinate of a feature.

Radius   To create radius dimensioning for arcs and circles.

Diameter   To create diameter dimensioning for arcs and circles.

Angular   For dimensioning angles.

Additionally, leaders and center marks can be drawn by selecting Leader or Center Mark.

227

FIGURE 8–1
Basic Types of Dimensions

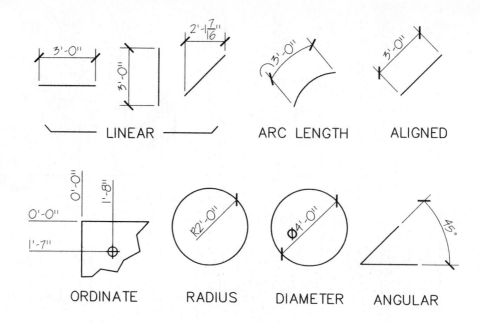

The appearance of these six basic types of dimensions, leaders, and center marks when they are drawn and plotted is controlled by settings called dimensioning variables.

Dimensioning Variables

Dimensioning variables are settings that determine what your dimensions look like on your drawing. For instance, as shown in Figure 8–2, setting the dimension variables will determine if a tick mark or arrow is used, how far the dimension line extends beyond the tick, how far the extension line extends beyond the dimension line, and so on.

A list of dimensioning variables and a brief description of each variable appears when STATUS is typed from the Dim: prompt. Figure 8–3 shows the list of dimensioning variables and the default setting for each as they appear when STATUS is typed from the Dim: prompt and Architectural units have been set. Some users of AutoCAD prefer to use the STATUS list to set dimensioning variables. Others like to use the Dimension Style Manager dialog box.

The Dimension Style Manager dialog box (Figure 8–4) allows you to set the dimensioning variables using a dialog box. It allows you to name the dimension style and change dimension variables using tabs on the dialog box. While dimensioning the same drawing, you may want some of the dimensions to have different variable settings from

FIGURE 8–2
Dimension Terms and
Variables

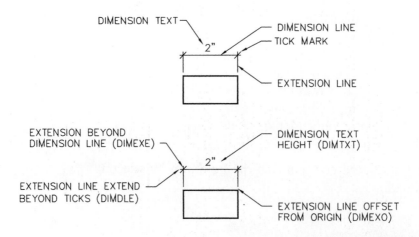

FIGURE 8–3

Dimensioning Variables

DIMASO	Off	Create dimension objects
DIMSTYLE	Standard	Current dimension style (read-only)
DIMADEC	0	Angular decimal places
DIMALT	Off	Alternate units selected
DIMALTD	2	Alternate unit decimal places
DIMALTF	25.4000	Alternate unit scale factor
DIMALTRND	0"	Alternate units rounding value
DIMALTTD	2	Alternate tolerance decimal places
DIMALTTZ	0	Alternate tolerance zero suppression
DIMALTU	2	Alternate units
DIMALTZ	0	Alternate unit zero suppression
DIMAPOST		Prefix and suffix for alternate text
DIMARCSYM	0	Arc length symbol
DIMASZ	3/16"	Arrow size
DIMATFIT	3	Arrow and text fit
DIMAUNIT	0	Angular unit format
DIMAZIN	0	Angular zero supression
DIMBLK	ClosedFilled	Arrow block name
DIMBLK1	ClosedFilled	First arrow block name
DIMBLK2	ClosedFilled	Second arrow block name
DIMCEN	1/16"	Center mark size
DIMCLRD	BYBLOCK	Dimension line and leader color
DIMCLRE	BYBLOCK	Extension line color
DIMCLRT	BYBLOCK	Dimension text color
DIMDEC	4	Decimal places
DIMDLE	0"	Dimension line extension
DIMDLI	3/8"	Dimension line spacing
DIMDSEP	.	Decimal separator
DIMEXE	3/16"	Extension above dimension line
DIMEXO	1/16"	Extension line origin offset
DIMFRAC	0	Fraction format
DIMFXL	1"	Fixed Extension Line
DIMFXLON	Off	Enable Fixed Extension Line
DIMGAP	1/16"	Gap from dimension line to text
DIMJOGANG	45	Radius dimension jog angle
DIMJUST	0	Justification of text on dimension line
DIMLDRBLK	ClosedFilled	Leader block name
DIMLFAC	1.0000	Linear unit scale factor
DIMLIM	Off	Generate dimension limits
DIMLTEX1	BYBLOCK	Linetype extension line 1
DIMLTEX2	BYBLOCK	Linetype extension line 2
DIMLTYPE	BYBLOCK	Dimension linetype
DIMLUNIT	2	Linear unit format
DIMLWD	-2	Dimension line and leader lineweight
DIMLWE	-2	Extension line lineweight
DIMPOST		Prefix and suffix for dimension text
DIMRND	0"	Rounding value
DIMSAH	Off	Separate arrow blocks
DIMSCALE	1.0000	Overall scale factor
DIMSD1	Off	Suppress the first dimension line
DIMSD2	Off	Suppress the second dimension line
DIMSE1	Off	Suppress the first extension line
DIMSE2	Off	Suppress the second extension line
DIMSOXD	Off	Suppress outside dimension lines
DIMTAD	0	Place text above the dimension line
DIMTDEC	4	Tolerance decimal places
DIMTFAC	1.0000	Tolerance text height scaling factor
DIMTFILL	0	Text background enabled
DIMTFILLCLR	BYBLOCK	Text background color
DIMTIH	On	Text inside extensions is horizontal
DIMTIX	Off	Place text inside extensions
DIMTM	0"	Minus tolerance
DIMTMOVE	0	Text movement
DIMTOFL	Off	Force line inside extension lines
DIMTOH	On	Text outside horizontal
DIMTOL	Off	Tolerance dimensioning
DIMTOLJ	1	Tolerance vertical justification
DIMTP	0"	Plus tolerance
DIMTSZ	0"	Tick size
DIMTVP	0.0000	Text vertical position
DIMTXSTY	Standard	Text style
DIMTXT	3/16"	Text height
DIMTZIN	0	Tolerance zero suppression
DIMUPT	Off	User positioned text
DIMZIN	0	Zero suppression

FIGURE 8–4

Dimension Style Manager
Dialog Box

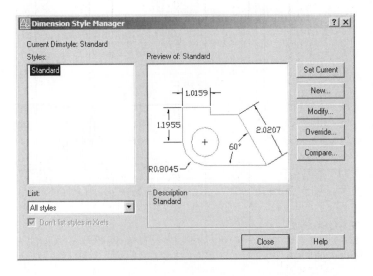

the rest of the dimensions. Two or more distinct styles of dimensioning can be used in the same drawing. Each style (and the variable settings for that style) may be saved separately and recalled when needed.

Exercise 8–1: Dimensioning the Tenant Space Floor Plan Using Linear Dimensions

Exercise 8–1 provides instructions for setting the dimensioning variables for the tenant space floor plan drawn in Exercise 7–1, saving the dimensioning variables, and dimensioning the exterior and interior of the tenant space floor plan using linear dimensions. When you have completed Exercise 8–1, your drawing will look similar to Figure 8–5.

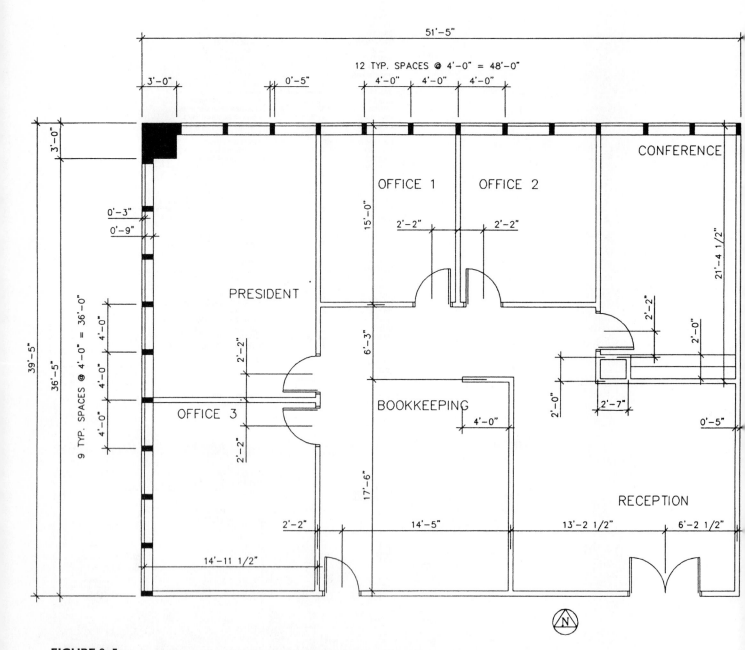

FIGURE 8–5

Exercise 8–1: Dimensioning the Tenant Space Floor Plan Using Linear Dimensions
(Scale: 1/8″ = 1′-0″)

Part II: Two-Dimensional AutoCAD

Step 1. Begin drawing CH8-EX1 by opening existing drawing CH7-EX1 and saving it as CH8-EX1 on the hard drive or network drive:

Prompt	Response
Command:	CLICK: **Open...**
The Select File dialog box appears:	LOCATE: **CH7-EX1**
	DOUBLE-CLICK: **CH7-EX1**
CH7-EX1 is opened.	
Command:	**SaveAs...**
The Save Drawing As... dialog box is displayed:	TYPE: **CH8-EX1** (replace CH7-EX1 in the File Name: input box)
	CLICK: the correct drive and folder
	CLICK: **Save**

You are now working on the hard drive or network with a drawing named CH8-EX1.

Step 2. Verify that UNITS is set to Architectural:

Prompt	Response
Command:	TYPE: **UNITS<enter>**
The Drawing Units dialog box appears:	SELECT: **Architectural** in the Type: box
	SELECT: **0'-0 1/32"** in the Precision: box
	CLICK: **OK**

 NOTE: Be sure to select 32 as the denominator of the smallest fraction to display when setting drawing Units so that the dimensioning variable settings may display the same fraction if they are set in 32nds.

There are two different ways the dimensioning variables can be set. They can be set using the Dim: prompt, or by using the Dimension Style Manager dialog box. The following describes the two ways to set dimensioning variables.

Set the Dimensioning Variables Using the Dim: Prompt

Step 3. Use STATUS to view the current status of all the dimensioning variables and change the setting for DIMDLE:

Prompt	Response
Command:	TYPE: **DIM<enter>**
Dim:	TYPE: **STATUS<enter>**
(The dimension variables appear on the screen.)	CLICK: **the maximize button** (You can see how the variables are currently set.)

Prompt	Response
Dim:	TYPE: **DLE**<enter> (dimension line extension)
Dim: dle	
Enter new value for dimension variable <default>:	TYPE: **1/16**<enter> < enter> (The second <enter> is so the variables will scroll and you can see the new setting.)
Dim:	PRESS: **F2** PRESS: **Esc**

NOTE: When the Dim: prompt is current, you can type the dimensioning variable name without the "DIM" prefix (example: DLE). When the Command: prompt is current, you must type the "DIM" prefix (example: DIMDLE).

Set the Dimensioning Variables Using the Dimension Style Manager Dialog Box

The Dimension Style Manager dialog box (Figure 8–6) allows you to change dimension variables using tabs on the dialog box. The default dimension style is Standard. Notice that there is a *style override* to the Standard dimension style. The override was created when you just typed a new setting for DIMDLE, using the command line. You can also create an override using the dialog box (see the Override... button). A dimension style override changes a dimensioning system variable without changing the current dimension style. All dimensions created in the style include the override until you delete the override, save the override to a new the style, or set another style current.

You can use the Modify... button to modify the existing Standard style, or you can name a new style and make that style current when you begin dimensioning. In this exercise you will create a new style that has several dimensioning variables that are different from the Standard style.

FIGURE 8–6
Dimension Style Manager Dialog Box Showing a Style Override

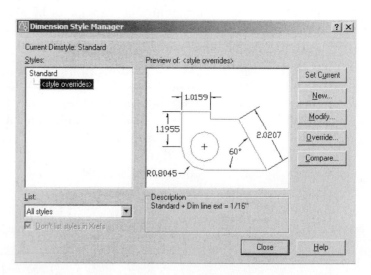

Part II: Two-Dimensional AutoCAD

FIGURE 8–7
Create New Dimension Style
Dialog Box

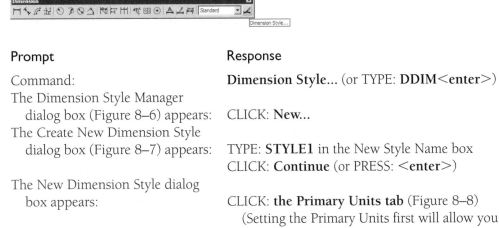

Step 4. Use the Dimension Style Manager to create a new style (Figures 8–6 through 8–28).

Prompt	Response
Command:	**Dimension Style...** (or TYPE: **DDIM**<enter>)
The Dimension Style Manager dialog box (Figure 8–6) appears:	CLICK: **New...**
The Create New Dimension Style dialog box (Figure 8–7) appears:	TYPE: **STYLE1** in the New Style Name box CLICK: **Continue** (or PRESS: <enter>)
The New Dimension Style dialog box appears:	CLICK: **the Primary Units tab** (Figure 8–8) (Setting the Primary Units first will allow you to view how dimensions will appear as you set other variables.)
The Primary Units tab is shown:	SELECT: **Architectural** in the Unit format: box SELECT: **0'-0 1/2"** in the Precision box **Set all other variables for this tab as shown in Figure 8–8.** CLICK: **the Symbols and Arrows tab** (Figure 8–9)

FIGURE 8–8
Primary Units Tab of the
New Dimension Style Dialog
Box

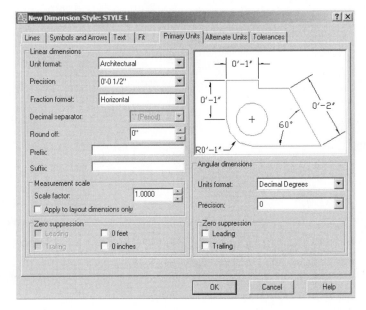

FIGURE 8–9
Symbols and Arrows Tab

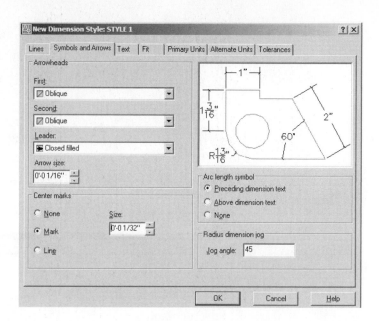

Prompt	Response
The Symbols and Arrows tab is shown:	CLICK: **Oblique** in the Arrowheads First: list SELECT: **0'-0 1/16″** in the Arrow size: list SELECT: **0'-0 1/32″** in the Center marks Size: list **Set all other variables for this tab as shown in Figure 8–9.** CLICK: **the Lines tab** (Figure 8–10)
The Lines tab is shown:	CLICK: **the down arrow so that 0'-0 1/16″ appears in the Extend beyond dim lines box** CLICK: **the down arrow so that 0'-0 1/16″ appears in the Extend beyond ticks: box** **Set all other variables for this tab as shown Figure 8–10** CLICK: **the Text tab**

FIGURE 8–10
Lines Tab

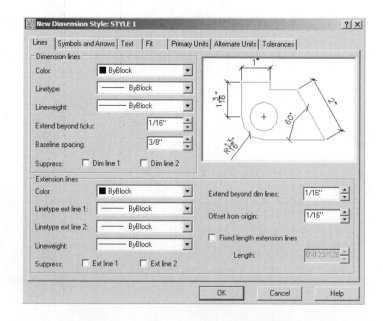

NOTE: If you want a thicker tick, select Architectural tick in the Arrowheads First: list.

Prompt	Response
The Text tab is shown:	CLICK: **1/16″** in the Text height: box (Figure 8–11)
	CLICK: **1/32″** in the Offset from dim line: box in the Text placement area
	CLICK: **Above** in the Vertical: box of the Text placement area (This places dimension text above the dimension line.)
	CLICK: the **Aligned with dimension line** radio button in the Text alignment area
	CLICK: **the three dots (ellipsis) to the right of the Standard Text style: box**
The Text Style dialog box appears:	CLICK: **simplex.shx** in the Font Name: box
	CLICK: **Apply** and **Close** (or **Cancel** if Simplex is already the font)
	Set all other variables for this tab as shown in Figure 8–11.

FIGURE 8–11
Text Tab and Text Style Dialog Box

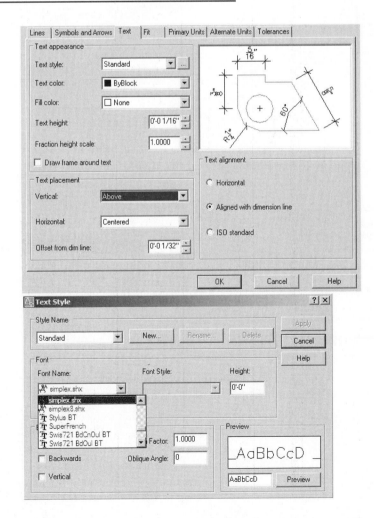

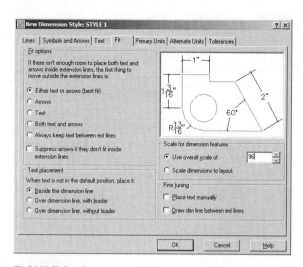

FIGURE 8–12
Fit Tab

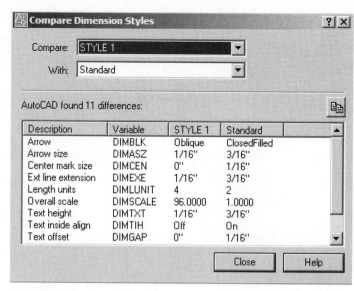

FIGURE 8–13
Compare Dimension Styles Dialog Box

Prompt	Response
	CLICK: **the Fit tab**
The Fit tab is shown:	CLICK: the **Either text or arrows (best fit)** radio button in the Fit Options area (Figure 8–12)
	CLICK: the **Use overall scale of:** radio button
	HIGHLIGHT: **the text** in the Use overall scale of: text box and Type: **96** (This sets a dimscale of 1/8″ = 1′ (8 × 12) so that all dimensioning variables are multiplied by 96. For example, as you are dimensioning the drawing, the text height, originally set at 1/16″, will actually measure 1/16 × 96, or 6″. When the layout is created using 1/8″ = 1′ scale, all variables will be the size set originally. For example, text height will be 1/16″ (or 6″ ÷ 96).)
	Set all other variables for this tab as shown in Figure 8–12.
	CLICK: **OK**
The Dimension Style Manager appears with STYLE1 highlighted:	CLICK: **Set Current** (to set STYLE1 current)
The AutoCAD Alert dialog box appears:	CLICK: **OK**
	CLICK: **Compare...**
The Compare Dimension Styles dialog box appears (Figure 8–13):	CLICK: **Standard** in the With: box
	Check to see which variables have changed from the Standard default setting.
	CLICK: **Close**
The Dimension Style Manager appears:	CLICK: **Close**

Alternate and Tolerances Tabs

The remaining tabs in the New Dimension Style dialog box contain variables for alternate units and tolerances. Alternate dimensions are usually metric dimensions that are displayed with decimal dimensions on mechanical drawings. Tolerances are also associated with mechanical drawings. Because both of these are seldom used on architectural drawings, neither tab will be discussed here.

Dimensioning Value for Overall Scale (DIMSCALE)

The preceding section set dimensioning variables that govern the sizes, distances, and offsets of dimensioning elements. It is important to understand how the value that is entered for a variable that governs a size, distance, or offset of a dimensioning element relates to your drawing as it appears on the screen and when the drawing is plotted.

When a building that is drawn full scale is displayed on the screen, the dimensioning elements will be drawn in a larger scale and will thus measure larger than when plotted at a scale of 1/8″ = 12″. DIMSCALE is the variable that controls the overall scale factor, or how the dimensioning parts appear on the screen display while you are drawing full scale and how they appear when plotted. For example, if you decide that the dimensioning text (DIMTXT) will be 1/8″ high when a drawing is plotted, enter 1/8″ for the DIMTXT value. If you plan to plot the drawing at 1/2″ = 12″, set DIMSCALE to 24. While you are drawing full scale, the text height will be 1/8″ × 24″, or 3″ high, on the screen. When the drawing is plotted at 1/2″ = 12″, the entire drawing including the dimensioning is reduced by a scale factor of 24 (1/2 = 12, 1 = 24).

The DIMSCALE for a drawing that is plotted at 1/4″ = 12″ is 48 (1/4 = 12, 1 = 48), and for a plotting ratio of 1/8″ = 12″ the DIMSCALE is 96 (1/8 = 12, 1 = 96).

Step 5.   On your own:

You have just completed setting the dimensioning variables for dimensioning the tenant space floor plan. On the Primary Units tab of the Dimension Style dialog box, you set the Overall scale to 96 (Figure 8–12). If you TYPE: **STATUS** to the DIM: prompt, you will see this setting as DIMSCALE in the dimensioning variable list (Figure 8–14).

If you plan to plot or print CH8-EX1 at a scale of 1/8″ = 12″, using an 8-1/2″ × 11″ paper size, then an Overall scale (DIMSCALE) of 96 is correct.

1. **If you plan to plot CH8-EX1 at a scale of ¼″ = 12″, using an 18″ × 24″ paper size, change the Overall scale (DIMSCALE) variable to 48.**

> **NOTE:** Start a drawing, set the dimensioning variables, and save the drawing as a template for future dimensioning projects.

Step 6.   On your own:

1. **Set Layer A-pflr-dims current.**
2. **Use Zoom-All to view the entire drawing.**

FIGURE 8–14

Dimensioning Variables with
DIMSCALE Set to 96

DIMASO	Off	Create dimension objects
DIMSTYLE	STYLE1	Current dimension style (read-only)
DIMADEC	0	Angular decimal places
DIMALT	Off	Alternate units selected
DIMALTD	2	Alternate unit decimal places
DIMALTF	25.40000	Alternate unit scale factor
DIMALTRND	0"	Alternate units rounding value
DIMALTTD	2	Alternate tolerance decimal places
DIMALTTZ	0	Alternate tolerance zero suppression
DIMALTU	2	Alternate units
DIMALTZ	0	Alternate unit zero suppression
DIMAPOST		Prefix and suffix for alternate text
DIMARCSYM	0	Arc length symbol
DIMASZ	1/16"	Arrow size
DIMATFIT	3	Arrow and text fit
DIMAUNIT	0	Angular unit format
DIMAZIN	0	Angular zero supression
DIMBLK	ArchTick	Arrow block name
DIMBLK1	ClosedFilled	First arrow block name
DIMBLK2	ClosedFilled	Second arrow block name
DIMCEN	1/32"	Center mark size
DIMCLRD	BYBLOCK	Dimension line and leader color
DIMCLRE	BYBLOCK	Extension line color
DIMCLRT	BYBLOCK	Dimension text color
DIMDEC	1	Decimal places
DIMDLE	1/16"	Dimension line extension
DIMDLI	3/8"	Dimension line spacing
DIMDSEP	.	Decimal separator
DIMEXE	1/16	Extension above dimension line
DIMEXO	1/16"	Extension line origin offset
DIMFRAC	0	Fraction format
DIMFXL	1"	Fixed Extension Line
DIMFXLON	Off	Enable Fixed Extension Line
DIMGAP	1/32"	Gap from dimension line to text
DIMJOGANG	45	Radius dimension jog angle
DIMJUST	0	Justification of text on dimension line
DIMLDRBLK	ClosedFilled	Leader block name
DIMLFAC	.00000	Linear unit scale factor
DIMLIM	Off	Generate dimension limits
DIMLTEX1	BYBLOCK	Linetype extension line 1
DIMLTEX2	BYBLOCK	Linetype extension line 2
DIMLTYPE	BYBLOCK	Dimension linetype
DIMLUNIT	4	Linear unit format
DIMLWD	-2	Dimension line and leader lineweight
DIMLWE	-2	Extension line lineweight
DIMPOST		Prefix and suffix for dimension text
DIMRND	0"	Rounding value
DIMSAH	Off	Separate arrow blocks
DIMSCALE	96.00000	Overall scale factor
DIMSD1	Off	Suppress the first dimension line
DIMSD2	Off	Suppress the second dimension line
DIMSE1	Off	Suppress the first extension line
DIMSE2	Off	Suppress the second extension line
DIMSOXD	Off	Suppress outside dimension lines
DIMTAD	1	Place text above the dimension line
DIMTDEC	1	Tolerance decimal places
DIMTFAC	1.00000	Tolerance text height scaling factor
DIMTFILL	0	Text background enabled
DIMTFILLCLR	BYBLOCK	Text background color
DIMTIH	Off	Text inside extensions is horizontal
DIMTIX	Off	Place text inside extensions
DIMTM	0"	Minus tolerance
DIMTMOVE	0	Text movement
DIMTOFL	Off	Force line inside extension lines
DIMTOH	Off	Text outside horizontal
DIMTOL	Off	Tolerance dimensioning
DIMTOLJ	1	Tolerance vertical justification
DIMTP	0"	Plus tolerance
DIMTSZ	0"	Tick size
DIMTVP	0.00000	Text vertical position
DIMTXSTY	Standard	Text style
DIMTXT	1/16"	Text height
DIMTZIN	0	Tolerance zero suppression
DIMUPT	Off	User positioned text
DIMZIN	1	Zero suppression

Linear and Continue Dimensioning

Step 7. Using Linear, dimension the column and one mullion on the north exterior wall of the tenant space floor plan (Figure 8–15).

Prompt	Response
Command:	**Linear** (or Type: **HOR<enter>** from the Dim: prompt)

FIGURE 8–15
Linear Dimensioning

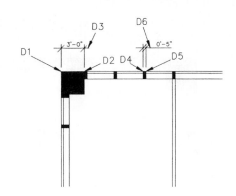

Prompt	Response
Specify first extension line origin or <select object>:	**D1** (with Snap ON)
Specify second extension line origin:	**View, Zoom-Window** (from the menu bar or Standard toolbar)
>>Specify first corner:	**Window the northwest corner of the**
>>Specify opposite corner:	**president's office.**
Specify second extension line origin:	**D2**
Specify dimension line location or [Mtext/Text/Angle/Horizontal/ Vertical/Rotated]:	**D3** (on snap, three grid marks up, with 12″ grid)
Command:	<enter> (repeat Linear)
Specify first extension line origin or <select object>:	TYPE: **INT**<enter>
of	**D4**
Specify second extension line origin:	TYPE: **INT**<enter>
of	**D5**
Specify dimension line location or [Mtext/Text/Angle/Horizontal/ Vertical/Rotated]:	**D6** (on snap, three grid marks up)

In the Linear command, after the second extension line origin is selected, the prompt reads: Specify dimension line location or [Mtext/Text/Angle/Horizontal/Vertical/Rotated]:

Before you pick a dimension line location, you may type the first letter of any of the options in the brackets and press <enter> to activate it. These options are as follows:

Mtext   To activate the multiline text command for dimensions requiring more than one line of text.

Text   To replace the default text with a single line of text. To suppress the text entirely, press the space bar.

Angle   To rotate the text of the dimension to a specific angle.

Horizontal   To specify that you want a horizontal dimension; this is normally not necessary.

Vertical   To specify that you want a vertical dimension; this is normally not necessary.

Rotated   To specify that you want to rotate the entire dimension.

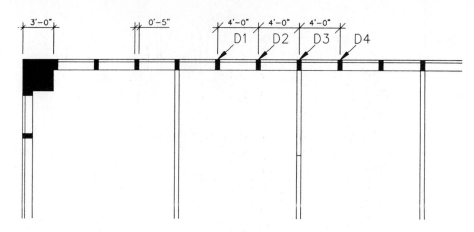

Step 8. Using Linear and Continue, dimension horizontally (center to center) the distance between four mullions on the north exterior wall of the tenant space (Figure 8–16). (Before continuing, Zoom in or Pan over to the four mullions to be dimensioned.)

Prompt	Response
Command:	**Linear** (from the Dimension menu)
Specify first extension line origin or <select object>:	TYPE: **MID**<enter>
of	**D1**
Specify second extension line origin:	TYPE: **MID**<enter>
of	**D2**
Specify dimension line location or [Mtext/Text/Angle/Horizontal/ Vertical/Rotated]:	CLICK: **a point on snap, three grid marks up, to align with previous dimensions.**
Command:	**Continue** (from the Dimension menu)
Specify a second extension line origin or [Undo/Select]<Select>:	TYPE: **MID** <enter>
of	**D3**
Specify a second extension line origin or [Undo/Select]<Select>:	TYPE: **MID**<enter>
of	**D4**
Specify a second extension origin or [Undo/Select]<Select>:	**<enter>**
Select continued dimension:	**<enter>** (to complete the command)

NOTE: You may change the dimension string at the prompt "Specify dimension line location," by typing **T**<**enter**>, then typing new dimensions from the keyboard and pressing the Enter key.

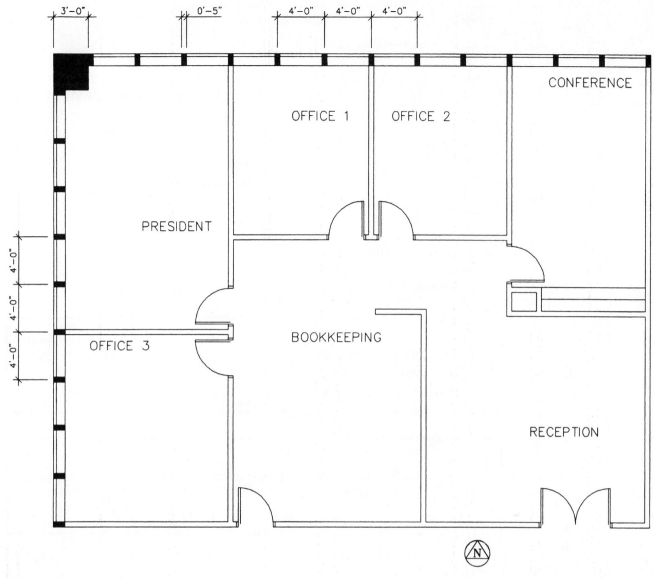

FIGURE 8–17
Linear Dimensioning with the Continue Command to Draw Vertical Dimensions
(Scale: 1/8″ = 1′-0″)

Step 9. Using Linear and Continue, dimension vertically (center to center) the distance between four mullions on the west exterior wall of the tenant space (Figure 8–17). (Before continuing, Zoom in on the four mullions to be dimensioned.)

Prompt	Response
Command:	**Linear** (or TYPE: **VER**<enter> from the Dim: prompt)
Specify first extension line origin or <select object>:	TYPE: **MID**<enter>
of	CLICK: **the first mullion** (Dimension south to north)
Specify second extension line origin:	TYPE: **MID**<enter>
of	PICK: **the second mullion**

Prompt	Response
Specify dimension line location or [Mtext/Text/Angle/Horizontal/ Vertical/Rotated]:	PICK: **a point on snap, three grid marks to the left, similar to previous dimension line locations**
Command:	**Continue** (on the Dimension menu)
Specify a second extension line origin or [Undo/Select]<Select>:	TYPE: **MID<enter>**
of	PICK: **the third mullion**
Specify a second extension line origin or [Undo/Select]<Select>:	TYPE: **MID<enter>**
of	PICK: **the fourth mullion**
Specify a second extension line origin or [Undo/Select]<Select>:	**<enter>**
Select continued dimension:	**<enter>**

TIP: Use Osnap commands to select extension line origins. Set a running Osnap mode.

NOTE: You can use the default dimension text, supply your own text, or suppress the text entirely.

Aligned Dimensioning

When Aligned is used, you can select the first and second extension line origin points of a line that is at an angle, and the dimension line will run parallel to the origin points. Figure 8–18 shows an example of aligned dimensioning.

Baseline Dimensioning

With linear dimensioning, after the first segment of a line is dimensioned, picking the Baseline command in the Dimension menu automatically continues the next linear dimension from the baseline (first extension line) of the first linear dimension. The new dimension line is offset to avoid drawing on top of the previous dimension. The DIMDLI variable controls the size of the offset. Figure 8–19 shows linear dimensioning with the Baseline command.

TIP: Use the transparent Zoom and Pan commands while in the Dim: mode. You will find them very helpful.

ALIGNED

FIGURE 8–18
Dimensioning with the Aligned Command

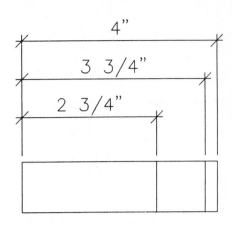

FIGURE 8–19
Linear Dimensioning with the Baseline Command

CAUTION: When erasing construction lines, avoid selecting definition points; otherwise the dimension associated with that point will be erased.

NOTE: When stacking dimension lines, locate the first dimension line farther from the object being dimensioned than subsequent dimension lines are from each other. For example, locate the first dimension line three grid marks from the object and the second dimension line two grid marks from the first dimension line.

Step 10. On your own (Figure 8–20):

1. Use Dtext, centered, to add the text "12 TYP. SPACES @4'-0" = 48'-0"" to the plan. Place it two grid marks (on a 12" grid) above the dimension line of the mullions dimension. Set the text height to 6".

2. Use Linear to dimension the overall north exterior wall of the tenant space. You may snap to the tick (intersection) of a previous dimension.

3. Use Dtext, centered, to add the text "9 TYP. SPACES @ 4'-0" = 36'-0"" to the plan. Place it two grid marks (on a 12" grid) above the dimension line of the mullions dimension. Set the text height to 6".

4. Use Linear to dimension from the southwest corner of the tenant space to the southern corner of the column. Use Continue to continue the dimension to the outside northwest corner of the building.

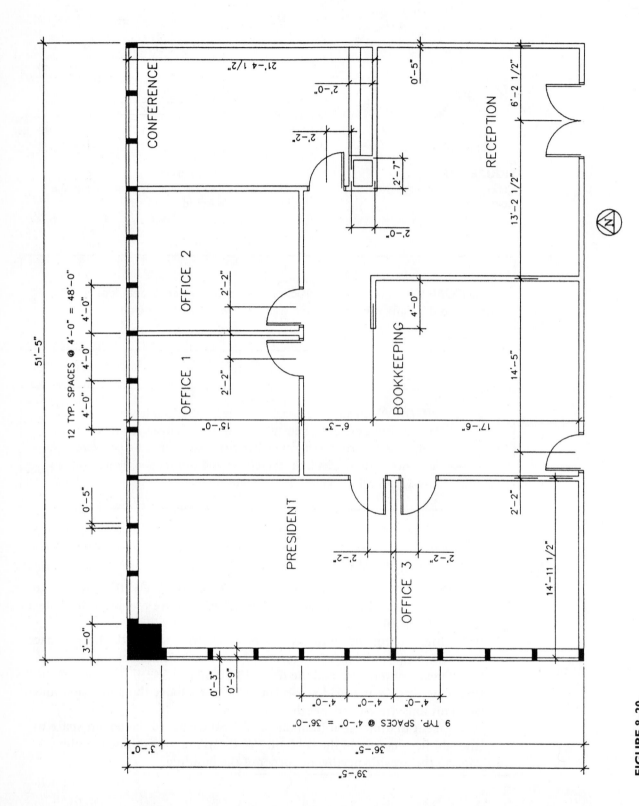

FIGURE 8-20

Complete Exercise 8–1 (Scale: 1/8″ = 1′-0″)

5. Use Linear to dimension the overall west exterior wall of the tenant space.
6. Complete the dimensioning using the Linear dimension commands. Use the Line command and appropriate Osnap modifiers to draw a temporary line across any doorways or wall that is dimensioned to the center. Using Osnap-Midpoint, pick the lines to locate the extension line origin of the dimensions.

    When you are dimensioning from left to right, any outside dimension line and text will be placed to the right. Dimensioning from right to left draws any outside dimension line and text to the left.
7. **Erase the temporary lines drawn in the doorways and walls.** Be careful not to pick a *defpoint* (small points on the drawing used to create associative dimensions); otherwise an entire dimension will be erased. Zoom in closely when you are erasing to avoid defpoints.

Step 11. **When you have completed Exercise 8–1, save your work in at least two places.**

Step 12. **Use a Layout Wizard or Page Setup Manager to create a Layout tab named Dimensioning Plan1. Select a scale to correspond with the specified DIMSCALE setting. Plot or print Exercise 8–1.**

Exercise 8–2:   Associative Dimension Commands and Grips

DIMASSOC System Variable

This setting is not one of the dimensioning variables and is not stored in a dimension style, but it does affect how dimensions behave in relation to the object being dimensioned. It has three states:

0   DIMASSOC is OFF. This setting creates exploded dimensions. Each part of the dimension (arrowheads, lines, text) is a separate object.

1   DIMASSOC is ON. This setting creates dimensions that are single objects but are not associated with the object being dimensioned. When the dimension is created, definition points are formed (at the ends of extension lines, for example). If these points are moved, as with the Stretch command, the dimension changes, but it is not directly associated with the object being dimensioned.

2   DIMASSOC is ON. This setting creates associative dimension objects. The dimensions are single objects, and one or more of the definition points on the dimension are linked to association points on the object. When the association point on the object moves, the dimension location, orientation, and text value of the dimension change. For example: Check DIMASSOC to make sure the setting is 2 (TYPE: **DIMASSOC<enter>**. If the value is not 2, TYPE: **2<enter>**). Draw a 2″ circle and dimension it using the diameter dimensioning command. With no command active, CLICK: any point on the circle so that grips appear at the quadrants of the circle. CLICK: any grip to make it hot and move the grip. The dimension changes as the size of the circle changes.

Exercise 8–2 describes the dimensioning commands that can be used only when DIMASSOC is ON. When you have completed Exercise 8–2, your drawing will look similar to Figure 8–21.

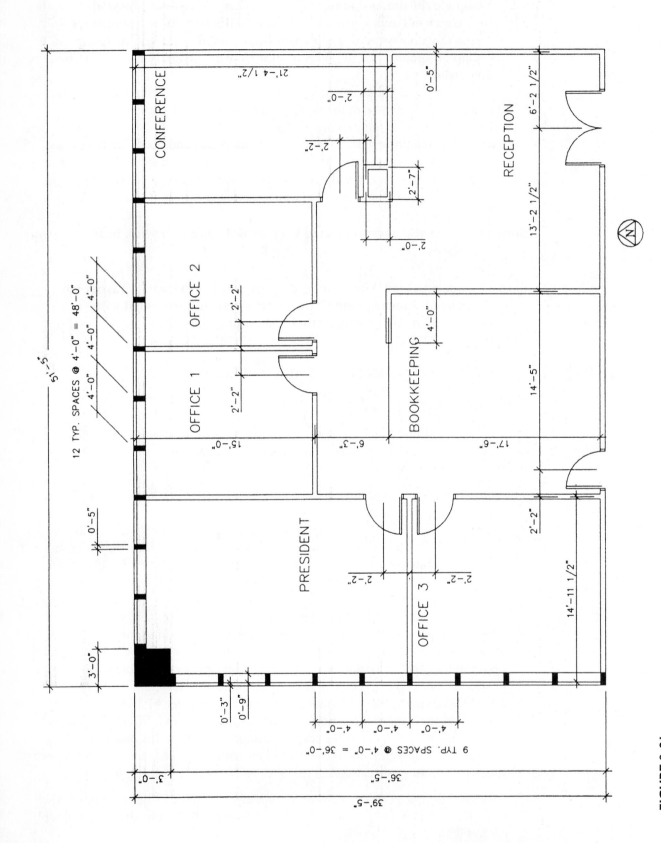

FIGURE 8-21

Exercise 8-2: Associative Dimension Commands (Scale: 1/8" = 1'-0")

Step 1. Open drawing CH8-EX1 and save it as CH8-EX2 to the hard drive or network drive.

Associative Dimension Commands

When the DIMASSOC variable is on, each dimension that is drawn is created as a block. That means that the extension lines, dimension lines, ticks or arrows, text, and all other parts of the dimensions are entered as a single object. When DIMASSOC is ON and set to 2, the dimensions drawn are called *associative dimensions*. When DIMASSOC is OFF, the extension lines, dimension lines, and all other parts of the dimension are drawn as separate entities.

Five dimension commands—Oblique, Align Text, Dimension Edit, Override, and Update—can be used only if DIMASSOC was ON while you drew the dimensions. The following describes those commands.

Oblique

Step 2. Create an oblique angle for the extension lines of the four mullions on the north exterior wall of the tenant space (Figure 8–22):

Prompt	Response
Command:	**Oblique** (or TYPE: **OB<enter>** from the DIM: prompt)
Select objects:	PICK: **the extension lines of the mullion dimensions on the North exterior wall until they are all highlighted.**
Select objects:	**<enter>**
Enter obliquing angle (press ENTER for none):	TYPE: **45<enter>**

The extension lines of the mullion dimensions appear as shown in Figure 8–22.

Align Text–Angle

Step 3. Rotate the text for the overall dimension on the north exterior wall of the tenant space (Before continuing, Zoom in on the dimension text, 51′-5″.) (Figure 8–23):

Prompt	Response
Command:	**Align Text–Angle**
Select dimension:	PICK: **the dimension text, "51′-5″"**
Specify angle for dimension text:	TYPE: **30<enter>**

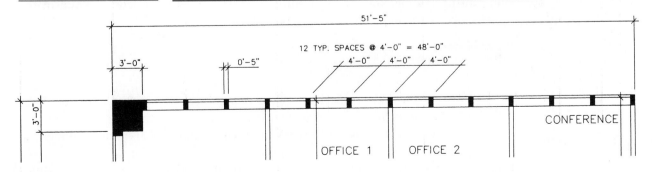

FIGURE 8–22
Using the Oblique Command

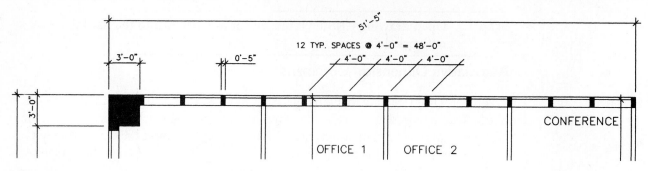

FIGURE 8–23
Using the Align Text–Angle Command

The text is rotated as shown in Figure 8–23.

Align Text-Home-Left-Center-Right (Dimension Text Edit from the Dimension toolbar)

Step 4. **Change the placement of the text for the overall dimension on the west exterior wall of the tenant space to flush right, and return it to the center position:**

Prompt	Response
Command:	**Align Text–Right**
Select dimension:	PICK: **the dimension text, 39′-5″**
The text moves to the right side of the dimension line (if the dimension line was drawn bottom to top, the dimension moves to the left).	
Command:	**Align Text–Center**
Select objects:	PICK: **the same dimension<enter>**
The text moves back to the center of the dimension line.	

The Left option left justifies the text along the dimension line. The Angle option allows you either to type a new text angle (and PRESS: <enter>) or to pick two points to show Auto-CAD the new text angle. The Home option returns the dimension text to its home position.

Dimension Edit

When Dimension Edit is clicked from the Dimension toolbar or **DIMED** <enter> is typed at the Command: prompt, the Dimension Edit prompt is "Enter type of dimension editing [Home/New/Rotate/Oblique]<Home>:" To activate any one of the options type the first letter:

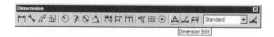

Home   Returns the dimension to its default (original) location in the dimension line.
New   Allows you to change the existing text using the Text Formatting Editor. Delete the angle brackets, type the new text, PRESS: <enter>, then click the dimension whose text you want to change.
Rotate   Allows you to rotate existing text to a specified angle.
Oblique   Allows you to make an existing dimension into an oblique one.

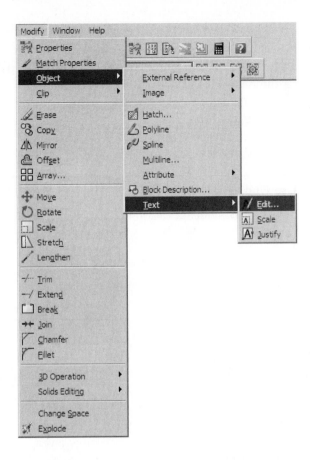

Override

The Override command is helpful when you are in the middle of dimensioning a project or have completed dimensioning a project and decide that one or more of the dimension variables in a named style needs to be changed. The Override command can be used to change one or more dimension variables for selected dimensions but does not affect the current dimension style.

Step 5. Use Override to change the DIMTXT variable of STYLE1 from 1/16″ to 1/8″:

Prompt	Response
Command:	**Override** (from the Dimension menu or toolbar) (or Type: **OV\<enter>** from the DIM: prompt)
Enter dimension variable name to override or [Clear overrides]:	TYPE: **DIMTXT\<enter>**
Enter new value for dimension variable \<1/16″>:	TYPE: **1/8\<enter>**
Enter dimension variable name to override:	**\<enter>**
Select objects:	PICK: **any dimension entity on the drawing**
Select objects:	**\<enter>** (see the text size change)
Command:	TYPE: **DIMTXT \<enter>**
Enter new value for dimension variable \<1/16″>:	**\<enter>**

The DIMTXT of 1/16″ setting has not changed.

Update

Update differs from Override in that it updates dimensions using the current settings of the dimension style. For example, if you decide a dimension variable needs to be changed in a dimension style, change the variable. You may click the Save button in the Dimension Styles dialog box to save the changed variable to the dimension style. If you do not save the changed variable, AutoCAD prompts you with an ALERT dialog box, "Save changes to current style?" when you change dimension styles. Use Update to include the new variable settings in all or part of the dimensions within the drawing.

Step 6. **Use Update to change the 1/8″ DIMTXT back to 1/16″:**

Because the Override command did not change DIMTXT within the STYLE1 settings, it is still set at 1/16″.

Prompt	Response
Command:	**Update** (from the Dimension menu or toolbar) (or TYPE: **UP<enter>** from the DIM: prompt)
Select objects:	CLICK: **the dimension entity on the drawing changed with Override**
Select objects:	**<enter>** (The text changes back to 1/16″ H.)

Defpoints Layer

When DIMASSOC is on, a special layer named Defpoints is also created. Definition points for dimensions are drawn on the Defpoints layer. They are small points on the drawing that are not plotted but are used to create the dimension. When the dimension is updated or edited, the definition points are redefined.

Modify-Object-Text-Edit...

Modify-Object-Text-Edit from the menu bar works when DIMASSOC is ON or OFF. It activates the Text Formatting Editor and allows you to change the existing dimension text.

Properties

The Properties command on the Modify menu can be used to change the properties of any dimension, as shown in Figure 8–24. Begin by selecting the dimension to be modified, then CLICK: **Properties** from the Modify menu. The Properties palette appears. Clicking the arrows to the right of the Property group displays a list of those items that can be changed. To change dimension text, CLICK: the ∀ to the right of Text, then CLICK: **Text Override** and TYPE: **the new text** in the box to the right.

Grips

Grips are small, solid-filled squares that appear on an object when the object is clicked. Grips are particularly useful in modifying the placement of dimension text and the location of extension and dimension lines.

Step 7. **Use grips to modify a dimension:**

Prompt	Response
Command:	CLICK: **the 14′-11 1/2″ dimension in OFFICE 3**
Five squares appear on the dimension; one at the end of each	

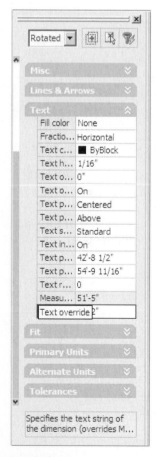

FIGURE 8–24
Properties Palette

Prompt	Response
extension line, one at the center of each tick, and one in the center of the dimension text:	CLICK: **the grip in the center of the dimension text**

 NOTE: To use multiple grips and to keep the shape of the dimension or any object you are using grips with, hold down the Shift key as you select the grips to make them hot.

Prompt	Response
The grip changes color (becomes HOT): Specify stretch point or [Base point/Copy/Undo/eXit]:	**With SNAP ON move your mouse up and CLICK: a point two grid marks up**
The dimension is stretched up two grid marks:	**CLICK: the same grip to make it hot, move your mouse to the right, and CLICK: a point two grid marks to the right**
The dimension text moves two grid marks to the right:	**CLICK: the grip at the origin of the first extension line to make it hot, and move your mouse up two grid marks**
The origin of the first extension line moves up two grid marks:	**CLICK: the grip in the center of the dimension text to make it hot, and press: the space bar one time**
The prompt changes to Specify move point or [Base point/Copy/Undo/eXit]:	**Move your cursor two grid marks down and CLICK: a point**
The entire dimension moves down two grid marks:	PRESS: **Esc**
The grips disappear:	TYPE: **U<enter>, and continue pressing <enter> until the dimension is returned to its original state**

To use grips, select a grip to act as the base point. Then select one of the grip modes—stretch, move, rotate, scale, or mirror. You can cycle through these modes by pressing <enter> or the space bar, or right-click to see all the modes and options.

Step 8. When you have completed Exercise 8–2, save your work in at least two places.

Step 9. Use a Layout Wizard or Page Setup to create a Layout tab named Dimensioning Plan2. Select a scale to correspond with the specified DIMSCALE setting. Plot Exercise 8–2.

Exercise 8–3: Tenant Space Total Square Feet

Exercise 8–3 provides step-by-step instructions for using the Area command to compute the total square feet of the tenant space floor plan. It also provides instructions for using the Cal (calculator) command. When you have completed Exercise 8–3, your drawing will look similar to Figure 8–25.

Step 1. Open drawing CH8-EX1 and save it as CH8-EX3 to the hard drive.

Area

In order for the total square feet of any space to be computed, the exact area that is to be included must be identified. In the tenant space, the face of the exterior building glass on the north and west walls is used as the building's exterior measuring points, and the center of the south and east walls will be used as the interior measuring points.

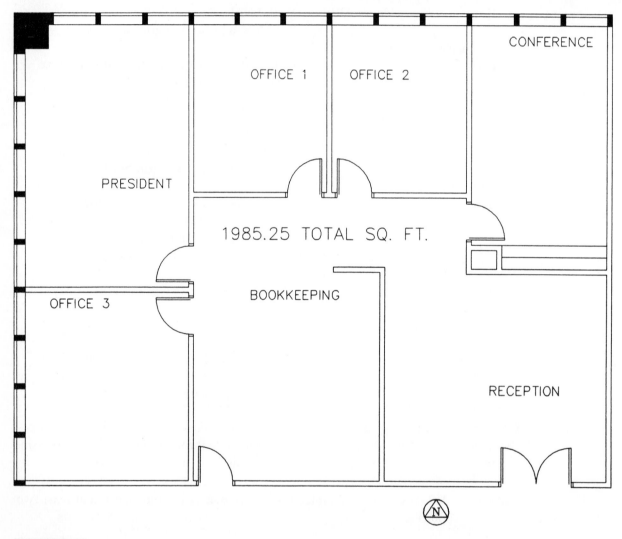

FIGURE 8–25
Exercise 8–3: Tenant Space Total Square Feet

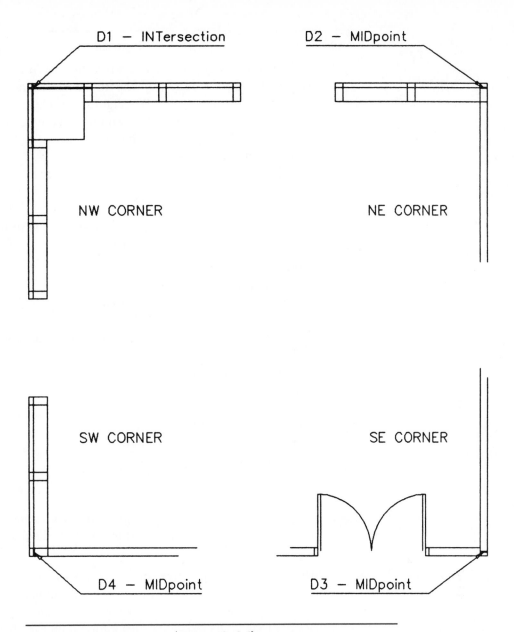

FIGURE 8–26
Defining Points of the Exact Area Included in the Total Square Feet of the Tenant Space

D1 — INTersection

D2 — MIDpoint

NW CORNER

NE CORNER

SW CORNER

SE CORNER

D4 — MIDpoint

D3 — MIDpoint

Step 2. On your own (Figure 8–26):

1. Freeze Layers A-pflr-dims and Defpoints, and set Layer A-area current.
2. TYPE: FILL<enter> then OFF<enter> so that the column and mullions are not solid. Regenerate the drawing (TYPE: RE<enter>).
3. To be able to select the defining points of the exact area, as described above, use the Line command to draw separate lines in each corner of the tenant space to which you can snap using Osnap-Intersection and Osnap-Midpoint. Each corner with the added lines is shown in Figure 8–26.

Step 3. Compute the total square feet of the tenant space (Figure 8–26).

Prompt	Response
Command:	**Area** (or TYPE: **AREA**<enter>)
Specify first corner point or [Object/ Add/Subtract]:	TYPE: **INT**<enter>

Prompt	Response
	Use View-Zoom-Window to window around the northwest corner.
of	D1 (Figure 8–26)
	Use Zoom-Dynamic to window the northeast corner.
Specify next corner point or press ENTER for total:	TYPE: **MID**<enter>
of	**D2**
	Use Zoom-Dynamic to window the southeast corner.
Resuming AREA command. Specify next corner point or press ENTER for total:	TYPE: **MID**<enter>
of	**D3**
	Use Zoom-Dynamic to window the southwest corner.
Specify next corner point or press ENTER for total:	TYPE: **MID**<enter>
of	**D4**
Specify next corner point or press ENTER for total:	<enter>
Area = 285876.25 square in. (1985.2517 square ft), Perimeter = 179'-10"	
Command:	Use the Dtext command (12″ high) to write the number of total square feet of the drawing.

Add   When Add is picked, the Area command is placed in an add mode. Add must be picked before the first space (of all the spaces to be added together) is specified. When the first space is specified, the area information is displayed. When the second space is specified, its individual area information is displayed along with the total area information of the two spaces together. Each subsequent space specified is displayed as an individual area total and is added to the running total.

Subtract   When Subtract is picked, each subsequent space specified is displayed as an individual area total and is subtracted from the running total.

Object   Object allows you to compute the area of a selected circle ellipse, polygon, solid, or polyline. For a circle, the area and circumference are displayed. When a wide, closed polyline is picked, the area defined by the center line of the polyline is displayed (the polyline width is ignored). Object is the fastest way to find the area of a closed polyline.

Step 4.   On your own:

1. **When you have completed practicing with the Area command, turn FILL ON.**
2. Regenerate the drawing (TYPE: **RE**<enter>).

CAL

AutoCAD provides a handy calculator function that functions much like many hand-held calculators. The following uses the add and divide features of the calculator. You may want to try other features on your own.

Use CAL to add three figures:
+ = add
− = subtract
× = multiply
/ = divide

Prompt	Response
Command:	TYPE: **CAL<enter>**
>>Expression:	TYPE: **2′6″ + 6′2″ + 4′1″<enter>**
12′-9″	

QuickCalc

AutoCAD also has a calculator that can be used for scientific calculations, unit conversion, and basic calculations.

 TIP: CAL can be used within any command, such as Line or Move, to specify a point. This avoids having to add and subtract dimensions beforehand.

Step 5. When you have completed Exercise 8–3, save your work in at least two places.

Step 6. Use a Layout Wizard or Page Setup Manager to create a layout tab named Dimensioning Plan 3. Select a scale to correspond with the specified DIMSCALE setting. Plot or print Exercise 8–3.

Exercise 8–4:   Use QDIM to Dimension the Conference Room from Exercise 4–1

Exercise 8–4 gives you practice in using the QDIM command from the Dimension menu or toolbar. QDIM allows you to select the objects you want to dimension and to specify which type of dimensioning you want to use and then automatically dimensions the geometry for you. Although you can select any areas to be automatically dimensioned, the more complex the geometry (for example, a complex floor plan), the more careful you have to be in selecting objects because QDIM dimensions everything.

Step 1. On your own:

1. Begin this exercise by opening CH4-EX1 and saving it as CH8-EX4 to the hard drive.
2. Erase the furniture from the drawing so the drawing appears as shown in Figure 8–27.
3. Set dimensioning variables as shown in 8–8, 8–9, 8–10, 8–11, and 8–12.

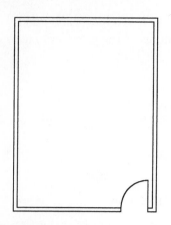

FIGURE 8–27
CH4-EX1 with Furniture Erased

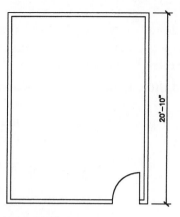

FIGURE 8–28
Use Quick Dimension to
Dimension the Right Side

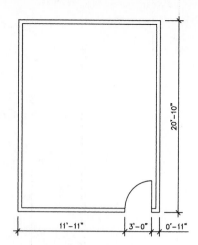

FIGURE 8–29
Use Quick Dimension to
Dimension the Bottom

Step 2. Use Quick Dimension to dimension the drawing (Figures 8–28 and 8–29):

Prompt	Response
Command:	**Quick Dimension** (from the Dimension menu or toolbar) (or TYPE: **QDIM** from the Command: prompt)
Select geometry to dimension:	CLICK: **on the outside right side of the floor plan**
Select geometry to dimension:	<enter>
Specify dimension line position, or [Continuous/Staggered/Baseline/ Ordinate/Radius/Diameter/ datumPoint/Edit/seTtings] <Continuous>:	CLICK: **a point two grid marks to the right of the right side**
The drawing is dimensioned as shown in Figure 8–28.	
Command:	<enter> (repeat QDIM)
Select geometry to dimension:	CLICK: **the bottom line of the floor plan including the door opening**
Select geometry to dimension:	<enter>
Specify dimension line position, or [Continuous/Staggered/Baseline/ Ordinate/Radius/Diameter/ datumPoint/Edit/seTtings] <Continuous>:	CLICK: **a point two grid marks below the bottom of the floor plan**

The plan is dimensioned as shown in Figure 8–29.

Step 3. When you have completed Exercise 8–4, save your work in at least two places.

Step 4. Use a Layout Wizard or Page Setup Manager to create a layout tab named Dimensioning Plan 4. Select a scale to correspond to the specified DIMSCALE setting. Plot or print Exercise 8–4.

Exercise 8–5: Hotel Room Dimension Plan

1. Set dimensioning variables for the hotel room floor plan completed in Exercise 7–2.
2. Dimension the hotel room floor plan (Figure 8–30) on the Dim layer.

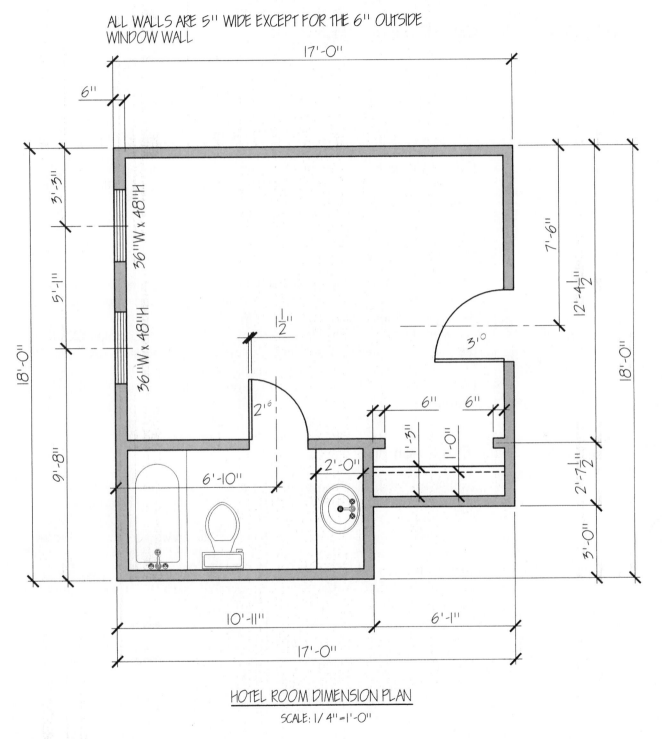

HOTEL ROOM DIMENSION PLAN
SCALE: 1/ 4"=1'-0"

FIGURE 8–30
Exercise 8–5: Hotel Room Dimension Plan (Scale: ¼″ = 1′-0″)

3. Locate the first row of dimensions farther from the drawing (example: 2′) than the first row of dimensions is from the second row of dimensions (example: 1′6″). Consistently space each row of dimensions on all four sides of the drawing.

4. Use a Layout Wizard or Page Setup Manager to create a layout. Plot or print the drawing to scale.

Exercise 8–6:   ## Log Cabin Dimension Plan

1. Set dimensioning variables for the log cabin floor plan completed in Exercise 7–3.
2. Create a new layer for dimensions, and dimension the log cabin floor plan (Figure 8–31).
3. Locate the first row of dimensions farther from the drawing (example: 2′) than the first row of dimensions is from the second row of dimensions (example: 1′6″). Consistently space each row of dimensions on all four sides of the drawing.
4. Use a Layout Wizard or Page Setup Manager to create a layout. Plot or print the drawing to scale.

Exercise 8–7:   ## House Dimension Plan

1. Set dimensioning variables for the house floor plan completed in Exercise 7–4.
2. Create a new layer for dimensions, and dimension the house floor plan (Figure 8–32, Sheets 1 and 2).
3. Locate the first row of dimensions farther from the drawing (example: 2′) than the first row of dimensions is from the second row of dimensions (example:1′6″). Consistently space each row of dimensions on all four sides of the drawing.
4. Use a Layout Wizard or Page Setup Manager to create a layout. Plot or print the drawing to scale.

Exercise 8–8:   ## Bank Dimension Plan

1. Set dimensioning variables for the bank plan completed in Exercise 7–5:
2. Create a new layer for dimensions, and dimension the bank floor plan (Figure 8–33).
3. Locate the first row of dimensions farther from the drawing (example: 2′) than the first row of dimensions is from the second row of dimensions (example: 1′6″). Consistently space each row of dimensions on all four sides of the drawing.
4. Use a Layout Wizard or Page Setup Manager to create a layout. Plot or print the drawing to scale.

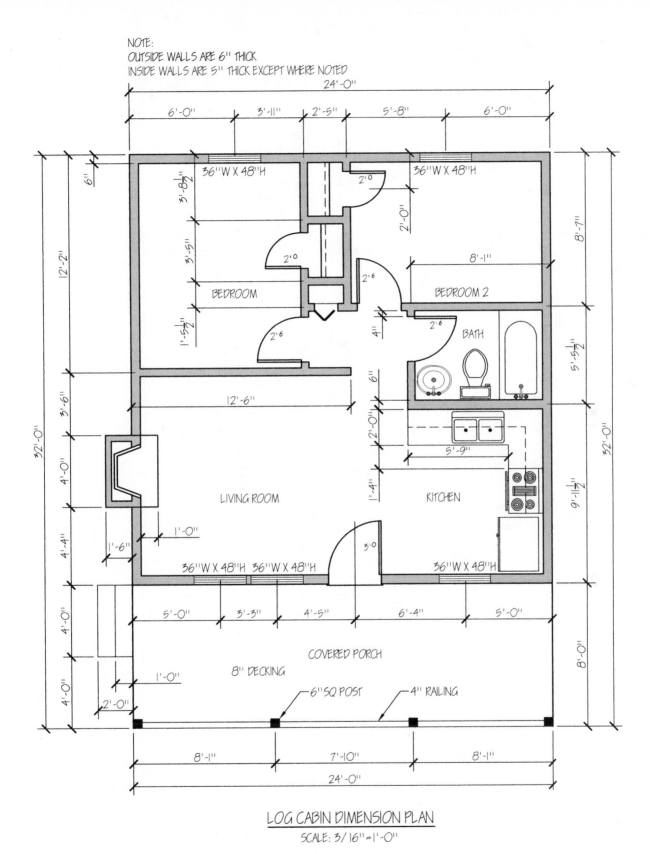

NOTE:
OUTSIDE WALLS ARE 6" THICK
INSIDE WALLS ARE 5" THICK EXCEPT WHERE NOTED

LOG CABIN DIMENSION PLAN
SCALE: 3/16"=1'-0"

FIGURE 8-31
Exercise 8-6: Log Cabin Dimension Plan (Scale: 3/16" = 1'-0")

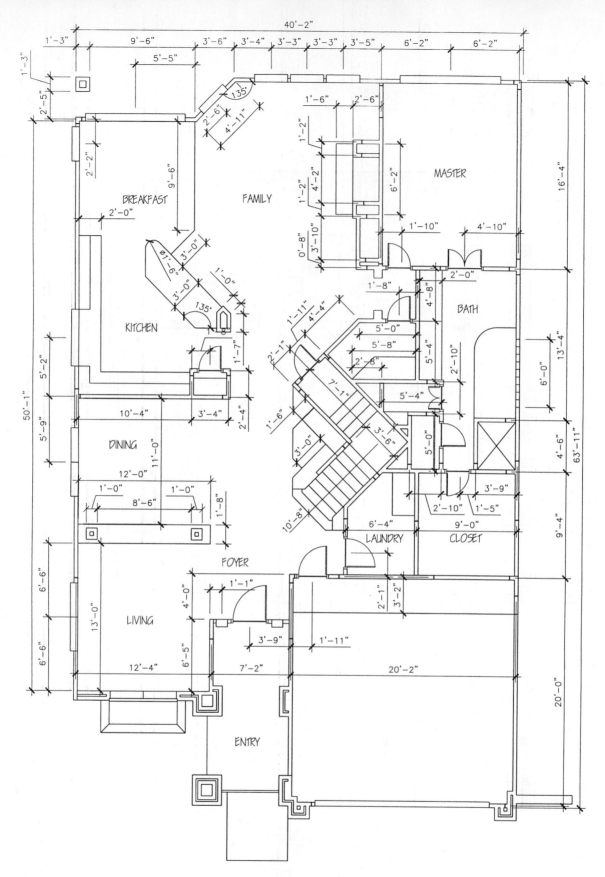

HOUSE DIMENSION PLAN - LOWER LEVEL

SCALE: 1/8" = 1'-0"

FIGURE 8–32

Exercise 8–7: House Dimension Plan (Scale: 1/8″ = 1′-0″) (Sheet 1 of 2)
(Courtesy of John Brooks, AIA, Dallas, Texas)

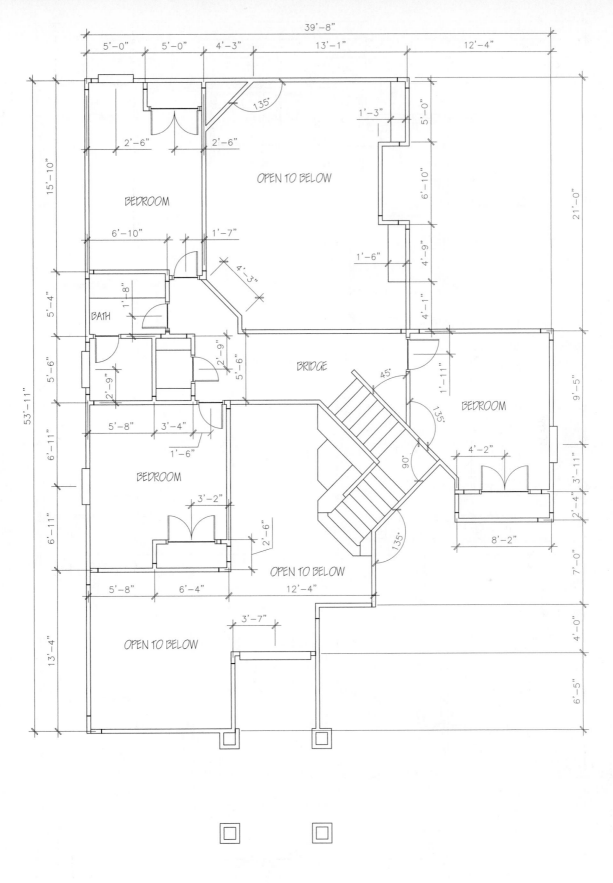

HOUSE DIMENSION PLAN - UPPER LEVEL

SCALE: 1/8" = 1'-0"

FIGURE 8–32

Exercise 8–7: House Dimension Plan (Scale: 1/8″ = 1′-0″) (Sheet 2 of 2)
(Courtesy of John Brooks, AIA, Dallas, Texas.)

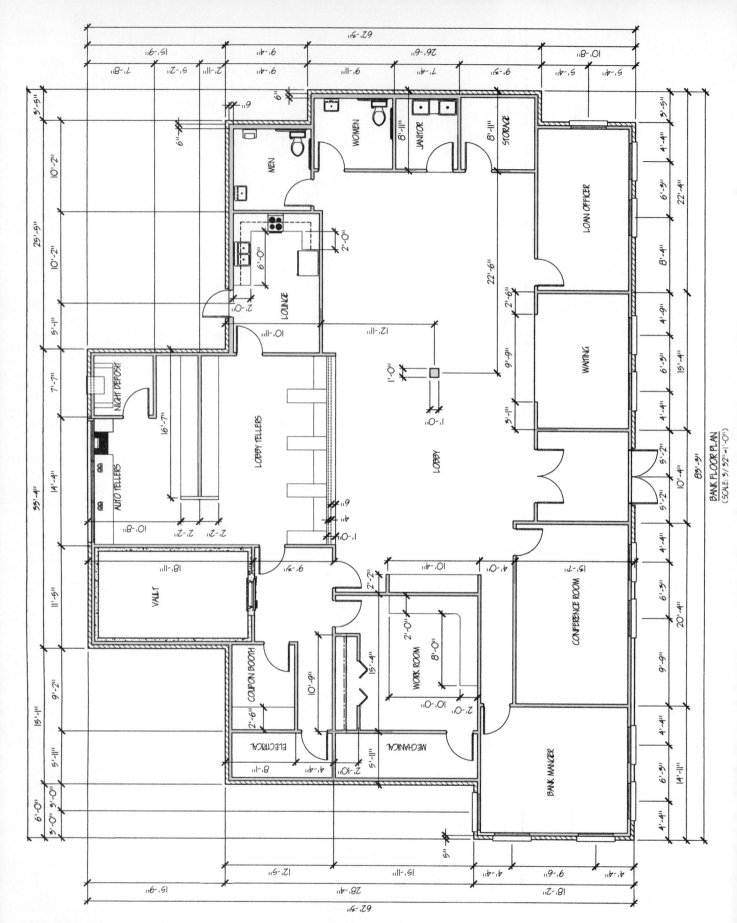

FIGURE 8–33

Exercise 8–8: Bank Dimension Plan (Scale: 3/32″ = 1′-0″)

1. A complete list of current dimensioning variables and settings is displayed when which of the following is typed from the Dim: prompt?
   a. LINEAR
   b. DIM VARS
   c. STATUS
   d. DIMSTYLE
   e. UPDATE

2. Which of the following dimensioning variables controls the height of text used in the dimension?
   a. DIMSTYLE
   b. DIMTSZ
   c. DIMASZ
   d. DIMTXT
   e. DIMTIX

3. Which tab on the New Dimension Style dialog box would you use to change a tick to a closed, filled arrowhead?
   a. Lines
   b. Symbols and Arrows
   c. Text
   d. Fit
   e. Primary Units
   f. Alternate Units

4. Which tab on the New Dimension Style dialog box would you use to change the appearance of the dimension text from one text style to another?
   a. Lines
   b. Symbols and Arrows
   c. Text
   d. Fit
   e. Primary Units
   f. Alternate Units

5. Which tab on the New Dimension Style dialog box would you use to change the overall scale factor from 96 to 48?
   a. Lines
   b. Symbols and Arrows
   c. Text
   d. Fit
   e. Primary Units
   f. Alternate Units

6. Which tab on the New Dimension Style dialog box would you use to set the distance that the dimension line extends beyond the tick?
   a. Lines
   b. Symbols and Arrows
   c. Text
   d. Fit
   e. Primary Units
   f. Alternate Units

7. Which tab on the New Dimension Style dialog box would you use to make a setting that will have the dimension text always appear horizontal on the page?
   a. Lines
   b. Symbols and Arrows
   c. Text
   d. Fit
   e. Primary Units
   f. Alternate Units

8. If a full-size drawing is to be plotted at a plotting ratio of $1/8'' = 12''$, the DIMSCALE value should be set to
   a. 1
   b. 12
   c. 24
   d. 48
   e. 96

9. Which of the following commands can be used only when DIMASSOC is ON?
   a. Linear
   b. Diameter
   c. Ordinate
   d. Oblique
   e. Angular

10. Which of the following commands can be used to change the dimension text string for any dimension?
   a. Update
   b. Change
   c. Trotate
   d. Modify-Object-Text-Edit
   e. Hometext

11. A Defpoints layer is created when a dimension is drawn with which of the following variables set to ON?
   a. DIMSTYLE
   b. DIMTOH
   c. DIMTAD
   d. DIMASSOC
   e. DIMTIH

12. To find the area of a closed polyline most quickly, which of the Area options should be used?
   a. Object
   b. Poly
   c. Add
   d. Subtract
   e. First point

Complete.

13. List the seven tabs in the New Dimension Style dialog box:

   1. _____

   2. _____

   3. _____

   4. _____

   5. _____

   6. _____

   7. _____

14. Which setting must be made for dimensioning variable values to be displayed in 32nds of an inch?

   _____

   _____

15. Describe the use of the Continue command for linear dimensioning.

   _____

   _____

16. Describe what the Defpoints layer is.

   _____

17. Describe what happens to the dimension of a 2″-diameter circle when the circle is enlarged to 40″ if DIMASSOC is set to 2.

   _____

   _____

18. Describe how the Update command differs from the Override command.

_____

_____

_____

_____

19. Describe the use of the Quick Dimension command.

_____

_____

_____

_____

20. Describe the use of grips to move dimensioning text.

_____

_____

_____

_____

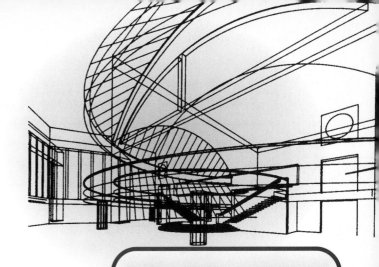

chapter

9

Drawing Elevations, Wall Sections, and Details

objectives

When you have completed this chapter, you will be able to:

Correctly use the following commands and settings:

Edit Hatch	Point Filters
Editing Hatch Patterns	Rename…
Hatch…	Stretch
Mirror	UCS
Named UCS… (DDUCS)	UCS Icon
OTRACK	

Introduction

The AutoCAD program makes it possible to produce clear, accurate, and impressive drawings of elevations, sections, and details. Many of the commands you have already learned are used in this chapter, along with some new commands.

Exercise 9–1: Tenant Space: Elevation of Conference Room Cabinets

In Exercise 9–1, an elevation of the south wall of the tenant space conference room is drawn. The south wall of the tenant space conference room has built-in cabinets that include a refrigerator and a sink. When you have completed Exercise 9–1, your drawing will look similar to Figure 9–1.

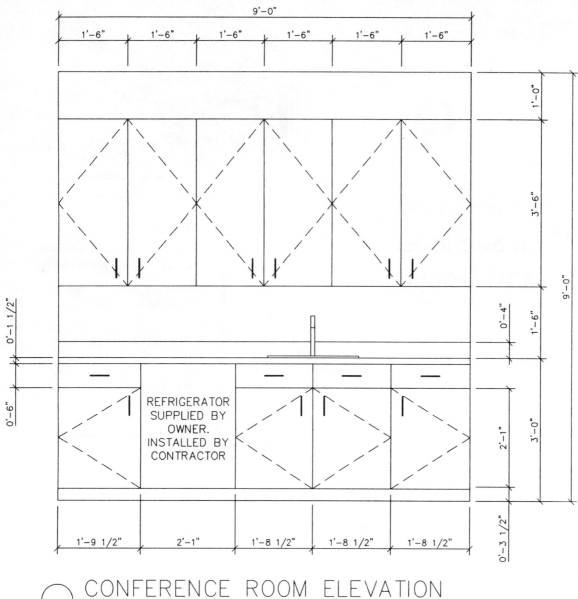

CONFERENCE ROOM ELEVATION

SCALE: 1/2"=1'-0"

FIGURE 9–1

Exercise 9–1: Tenant Space, Elevation of Conference Room Cabinets (Scale: 1/2″ = 1′-0″)

Step 1. Use your workspace to make the following settings:

1. Use SaveAs... to save the drawing on the hard drive with the name **CH9-EX1.**
2. Set drawing Units: **Architectural**
3. Set Drawing Limits: **25′,24′**
4. Set GRIDDISPLAY: **0**
5. Set Grid: **12″**
6. Set Snap: **6″**
7. Create the following Layers:

LAYER NAME	COLOR	LINETYPE	LINEWEIGHT
A-elev	Red	Continuous	Default
A-elev-hid	Green	Hidden	Default
A-elev-text	White	Continuous	Default
A-elev-dim	Blue	Continuous	Default

8. Set **Layer A-elev** current.
9. **Zoom-All**

UCS

While you were drawing with AutoCAD in previous chapters, the UCS (user coordinate system) icon was located in the lower left corner of your drawings. A coordinate system is simply the X, Y, and Z coordinates used in your drawings. For two-dimensional drawings, only the X and Y coordinates are meaningful. The Z coordinate is used for a three-dimensional model.

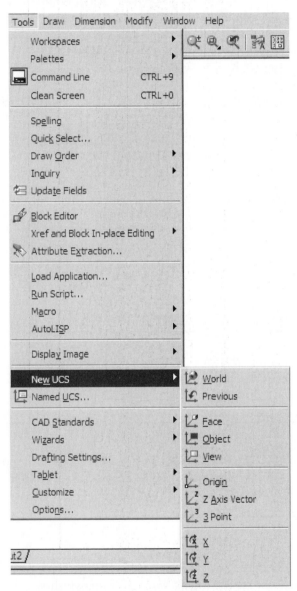

Notice that the 2D UCS icon (Figure 9–2) has a W on it. The W stands for *world coordinate system*. This is the AutoCAD fixed coordinate system, which is common to all AutoCAD drawings.

The UCS command is used to set up a new user coordinate system. When UCS is typed from the Command: prompt, the prompt is "Specify origin of UCS or [Face/NAmed/OBject/Previous/View/World/X/Y/Z/ZAxis] <World>". The Z coordinate is described and used extensively in the chapters that cover three-dimensional modeling. The UCS command options that apply to two dimensions are listed next.

FIGURE 9–2
2D Model Space, 3D Model
Space, and Paper Space UCS
Icons

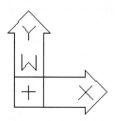

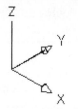

2D MODEL SPACE ICON   3D MODEL SPACE ICON   PAPER SPACE ICON

Specify origin of UCS   Allows you to create a new UCS by selecting a new origin and
a new X axis. If you select a single point, the origin of the current UCS moves
without changing the orientation of the X and Y axes.

NAmed   When this option is entered, the prompt "Enter an option
[Restore/Save/Delete/?]" appears. It allows you to restore, save, delete, and list
named user coordinate systems.

OBject   Allows you to define a new UCS by pointing to a drawing object such as an
arc, point, circle, or line.

Previous   Makes the previous UCS current.

World   This is the AutoCAD fixed coordinate system, which is common to all Auto-
CAD drawings. In most cases you will want to return to the world coordinate system before plotting any drawing.

Step 2.   Use the UCS command to change the origin of the current UCS:

Prompt	Response
Command:	TYPE: **UCS** <enter>
Specify origin of UCS or [Face/NAmed/OBject/Previous/View/World/X/Y/Z/ZAxis] <World>	TYPE: **8′,12′** <enter>
Specify point on X-axis or <Accept>:	<enter>

The origin for the current user coordinate system is now 8′ in the X direction and 12′
in the Y direction. The UCS icon may not have moved from where 0,0 was originally
located. The UCS Icon command, described next, is used to control the orientation
and visibility of the UCS icon.

 NOTE: You can change the UCS so you can move 0,0 to any point on
your drawing to make it more convenient to locate points.

UCS Icon

There are two model space UCS icons that you can choose to use: one for 2D drawings and
one for 3D drawings. The default is the 3D icon, which you will probably use for both 2D
and 3D. The UCS Icon command is used to control the visibility and orientation of the UCS
icon (Figure 9–2). The UCS icon appears as arrows (most often located in the lower left corner of an AutoCAD drawing) that show the orientation of the X, Y, and Z axes of the current
UCS. It appears as a triangle in paper space. The UCS Icon command options are
"ON/OFF/All/Noorigin/ORigin/Properties:". The UCS Icon command options are listed next.

ON   Allows you to turn on the UCS icon if it is not visible.

OFF   Allows you to turn off the UCS icon when it gets in the way. This has nothing to
do with the UCS location—only the visibility of the UCS icon.

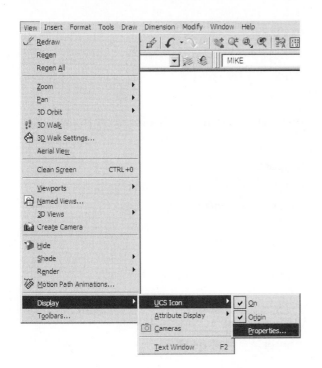

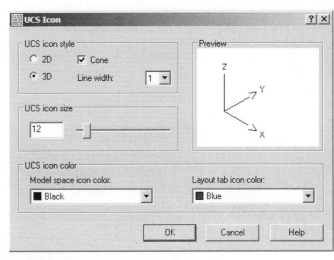

FIGURE 9–3
UCS Icon Dialog Box

All Allows you to apply changes to the UCS icon in all active viewports. (The Viewports command, which allows you to create multiple viewports, is described in Chapter 13.)

Noorigin When Noorigin is current, the UCS icon is displayed at the lower left corner of the screen.

ORigin Forces the UCS icon to be displayed at the origin of the current UCS. For example, when USC Icon-Origin is clicked, the new UCS that you just created will appear in its correct position. If the origin of the UCS is off the screen, the icon is still displayed in the lower left corner of the screen.

Properties When Properties is selected, the UCS Icon dialog box apppears (Figure 9–3). This box allows you to select the 2D or 3D model space icon, and to change the size and color of model space and paper space (Layout tab) icons.

Step 3. Use the UCS Icon command to force the UCS icon to be displayed at the origin of the new, current UCS:

Prompt	Response
Command:	TYPE: **UCSICON**<enter>
Enter an option [ON/OFF/All/ Noorigin/ORigin/Properties] <ON>:	TYPE: **OR**<enter>

The UCS icon now moves to the 8′,12′ coordinate location. You can now begin to draw the cabinets using the new UCS location.

Step 4. Using absolute coordinates, draw the lines forming the first upper cabinet door. Start the drawing at the 0,0 location of the new UCS (Figure 9–4):

Prompt	Response
Command:	**Line** (or TYPE: **L**<enter>)
Specify first point:	TYPE: **0,0**<enter>
Specify next point or [Undo]:	TYPE: **18,0**<enter>

FIGURE 9–4
Draw the Lines Forming the
First Upper Cabinet Door

Prompt	Response
Specify next point or [Undo]:	TYPE: **18,3'6<enter>**
Specify next point or [Close/Undo]:	TYPE: **0,3'6<enter>**
Specify next point or [Close/Undo]:	TYPE: **C<enter>**

Step 5. Use Polyline to draw the door hardware using absolute coordinates (Figure 9–4):

Prompt	Response
Command:	**Polyline** (or TYPE: **PL<enter>**)
Specify start point:	TYPE: **15,2<enter>**
Specify next point or [Arc/ Halfwidth/Length/Undo/Width]:	TYPE: **W<enter>**
Specify starting width <0'-0">:	TYPE: **1/4<enter>**
Specify ending width <0'-0 1/4">:	**<enter>**
Specify next point or [Arc/ Halfwidth/Length/Undo/Width]:	TYPE: **15,7<enter>**
Specify next point or [Arc/Close/ Halfwidth/Length/Undo/Width]:	**<enter>**

Step 6. Set Layer A-elev-hid current and draw the dashed lines of the door using absolute coordinates (Figure 9–4):

Prompt	Response
Command:	**Line** (or TYPE: **L<enter>**)
Specify first point:	TYPE: **18,3'6<enter>**
Specify next point or [Undo]:	TYPE: **0,21<enter>**
Specify next point or [Undo]:	TYPE: **18,0<enter>**
Specify next point or [Close/Undo]:	**<enter>**

Step 7. Change the linetype scale of the Hidden linetype to make it appear as dashes, change the linetype to Hidden2, or both. A large linetype scale such as 12 is needed. (TYPE: **LTSCALE <enter>**, then TYPE: **12 <enter>**.)

Mirror

The Mirror command allows you to mirror about an axis any entity or group of entities. The axis can be at any angle.

Step 8. Draw the second cabinet door, using the Mirror command to copy part of the cabinet door just drawn. The top and bottom lines of the cabinet door are not mirrored (Figure 9–5):

Prompt	Response
Command:	**Mirror** (or TYPE: **MI<enter>**)
Select objects:	**D1**
Specify opposite corner:	**D2**
Select objects:	**<enter>**
Specify first point of mirror line:	**D3** (with ORTHO and SNAP ON)
Specify second point of mirror line:	**D4**
Erase source objects? [Yes/No] <N>:	**<enter>** (to complete command)

FIGURE 9–5
Use the Mirror Command to
Copy Part of the Cabinet
Door

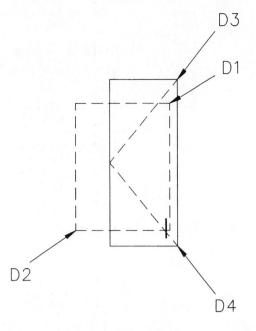

NOTE: If you want to mirror a part of a drawing containing text but do not want the text to be a mirror image, change the MIRRTEXT system variable setting to 0. This allows you to mirror the part and leave the text "right reading." When MIRRTEXT is set to 1 the text is given a mirror image. To change this setting TYPE: **MIRRTEXT <enter>**, then TYPE: **0<enter>**.

Step 9. On your own:

1. **Use the Mirror command to draw the inside and the right vertical cabinet edge of the next two sets of doors.** When this step is completed, your drawing will look like Figure 9–6.

Later you will extend the lines forming the top and bottom of the first cabinet so that you do not have 12 small lines instead of 2 long lines. Having extra line segments increases the size of your drawing file and creates a drawing that is sometimes difficult to change.

FIGURE 9–6
Use the Mirror Command to
Draw the Inside of the Cabinet Doors and the Right Vertical Edge of the Next Two
Sets of Doors

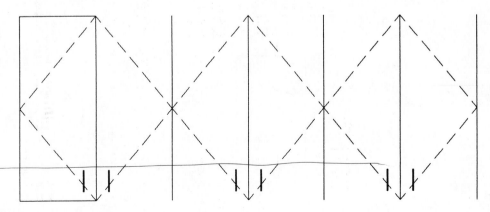

NOTE: A crossing window is clicked right to left. The default color for the crossing window is green.

Step 10. Use the Mirror command to draw the first lower cabinet door (Figure 9–7):

Prompt	Response
Command:	**Mirror** (or TYPE: **MI<enter>**)
Select objects:	**D2** (left to right)
Specify opposite corner:	**D1**

Prompt	Response
Select objects:	**<enter>**
Specify first point of mirror line:	**D3** (with ORTHO and SNAP ON; the lower cabinets will be moved to the accurate location later)
Specify second point of mirror line:	**D4**
Erase source objects? [Yes/No] <N>:	**<enter>**

The lower cabinet door is now too high and too narrow. The Stretch command can be used to shrink the cabinet to the correct height and stretch it to the correct width.

FIGURE 9–7

Use the Mirror Command to Draw the First Lower Cabinet Door

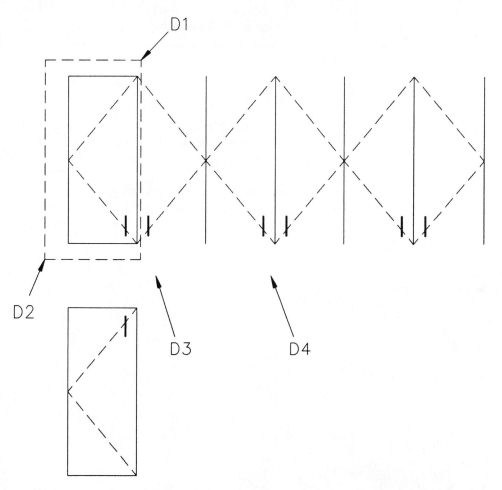

Stretch

The Stretch command can be used to stretch entities to make them longer or shorter. It can also be used to move entities that have other lines attached to them without removing the attached lines (described later in this exercise). Stretch requires you to use a crossing window to select objects. As with many other Modify commands, you may select objects initially, then remove or add objects to the selection set before you perform the stretch function.

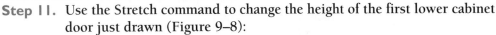

Step 11. Use the Stretch command to change the height of the first lower cabinet door just drawn (Figure 9–8):

Prompt	Response
Command:	**Stretch** (or TYPE: **S** <enter>)
Select objects to stretch by crossing-window or crossing-polygon...	
Select objects:	**D1**
Specify opposite corner:	**D2**
Select objects:	<enter>
Specify base point or [Displacement] <Displacement>:	**D3** (any point)
Specify second point or <use first point as displacement>:	TYPE: **@8-1/2<270**<enter> (or with ORTHO ON move your mouse down and TYPE: **8.5**<enter>) (the upper door height, 3′6″, minus the lower door height, 2′1″, divided by 2; take half off the top of the door and half off the bottom)
Command:	**Stretch** (OR PRESS: <enter>)
Select objects to stretch by crossing-window or crossing-polygon...	
Select objects:	**D4**
Specify opposite corner:	**D5**
Select objects:	<enter>

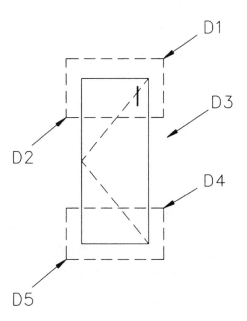

FIGURE 9–8
Use the Stretch Command to Change the Height of the First Lower Cabinet Door

Prompt	Response
Specify base point or [Displacement] <Displacement>:	**D3** (any point)
Specify second point or <use first point as displacement>:	TYPE: **@8-1/2<90<enter>** (or move your mouse up and TYPE: **8.5 <enter>**)

The lower cabinet door should now be 17″ shorter than the upper cabinet door from which it was mirrored (3′6″ minus 17″ equals 2′1″, the cabinet door height). Next, use Stretch to make the door the correct width.

Step 12. Use the Stretch command to change the width of the cabinet door (Figure 9–9):

Prompt	Response
Command:	**Stretch**
Select objects to stretch by crossing-window or crossing-polygon…	
Select objects:	**D1**
Specify opposite corner:	**D2**
Select objects:	**<enter>**
Specify base point or [Displacement] <Displacement>:	**D3** (any point)
Specify second point or <use first point as displacement>:	TYPE: **@3-1/2<0<enter>** (or move the mouse to the right and TYPE: **3.5 <enter>**) (the upper door width, 1′6″, plus 3-1/2″, equals the lower door width, 1′9-1/2″)

Step 13. Save the current UCS used to draw the upper cabinets:

Prompt	Response
Command:	TYPE: **UCS<enter>**
Specify origin of UCS or [Face/ NAmed/OBject/Previous/View/ World/X/Y/Z/ZAxis] <World>:	TYPE: **S<enter>**
Enter name to save current UCS or [?]:	TYPE: **UPPER<enter>**

Step 14. Create a new UCS origin for drawing the lower cabinets by moving the existing UCS origin –4′6″ in the Y direction:

Prompt	Response
Command:	**<enter>** (repeat UCS)
Specify origin of UCS or [Face/ NAmed/OBject/Previous/View/ World/X/Y/Z/ZAxis] <World>:	TYPE: **O<enter>**
Specify new origin point <0,0,0>:	TYPE: **0,-4′6<enter>** (be sure to include the minus)

Step 15. Move the lower cabinet door to a point 3-1/2″ (the base height) above the origin of the current UCS (Figure 9–10):

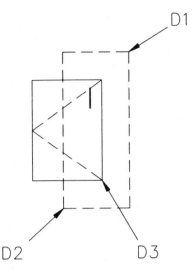

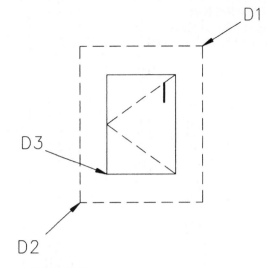

FIGURE 9–9
Use the Stretch Command to Change
the Width of the Cabinet Door

FIGURE 9–10
Move the Lower Cabinet Door to a Point 3-1/2″
above the Origin of the Current UCS

Prompt	Response
Command:	**Move** (or TYPE: **M**<enter>)
Select objects:	**D1**
Specify opposite corner:	**D2**
Select objects:	<enter>
Specify base point or [Displacement]	
<Displacement>:	Osnap-Intersection
of	**D3**
Specify second point or <use first	
point as displacement>:	TYPE: **0,3-1/2**<enter>

Step 16. On your own:

1. Copy part of the lower cabinet 3′10-1/2″ to the right, as shown in Figure 9–11.
2. Stretch the right side of the copied door 1″ to the left, making it 1″ narrower.
3. Use Mirror and Copy to draw the remaining doors, as shown in Figure 9–12.
4. Use Extend to extend the top and bottom lines of both the upper and lower cabinets to the right edges of the cabinets, as shown in Figure 9–13.
5. Use Offset to draw the bottom line of the base, the top and bottom (top of the drawers line) lines of the countertop, and the backsplash line (Figure 9–14).
6. Use Erase and Extend to connect the sides of the upper and lower cabinets and the base with one line on each side (Figure 9–14).
7. Set A-elev Layer current, set snap to 1/2″, and use Extend, Polyline, and Copy to draw the lower cabinet drawers and their 5″ × 1/4″ handles. Use Trim to trim the line out of the area where the refrigerator is located (Figure 9–14). Turn SNAP ON to draw the handles with the 1/4″-wide polyline.

Step 17. Draw the sink in the approximate location shown in Figure 9–15 (the Stretch command will be used later to move the sink to the correct location):

Prompt	Response
Command:	**Line** (or TYPE: **L**<enter>)
Specify first point:	**D1** (with SNAP on)

FIGURE 9–11
Copy Part of the Lower Cabinet 3'9-1/2" to the Right

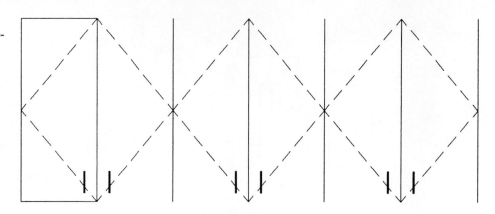

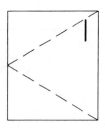
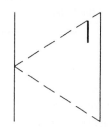

FIGURE 9–12
Use Mirror and Copy to Draw the Remaining Doors

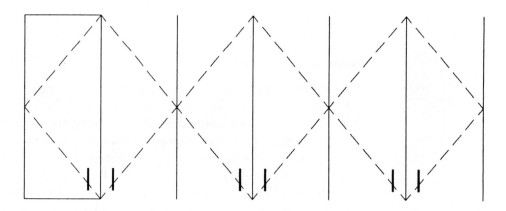

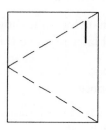
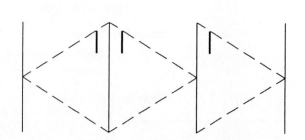

FIGURE 9–13
Use Extend to Extend the
Top and Bottom Lines of
Both the Upper and Lower
Cabinets

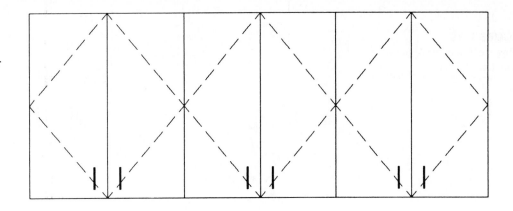

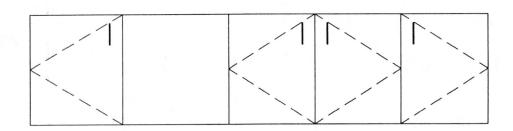

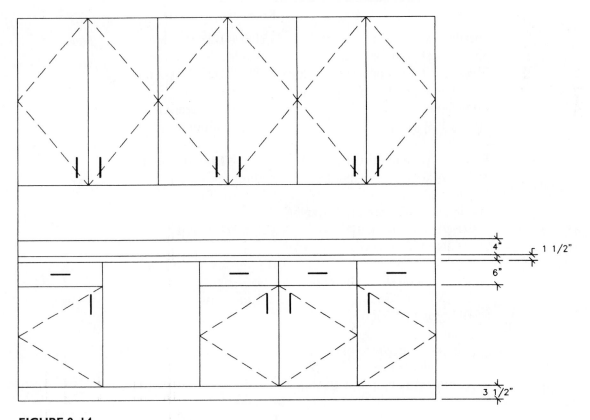

FIGURE 9–14
Finish Drawing the Cabinets As Shown

FIGURE 9–15
Draw the Sink in the Approximate Location Shown

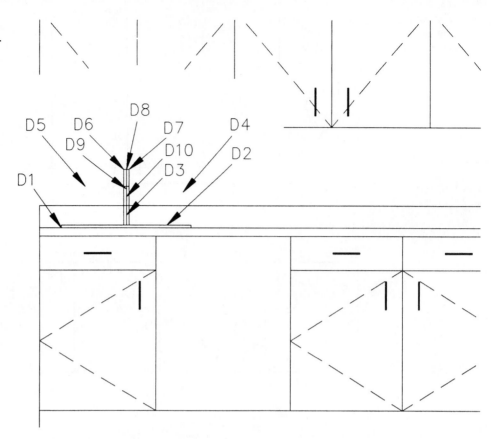

Prompt	Response
Specify next point or [Undo]:	TYPE: @1/2<90<enter>
Specify next point or [Undo]:	TYPE: @25<0<enter>
Specify next point or [Close/Undo]:	TYPE: @1/2<270<enter>
Specify next point or [Close/Undo]:	<enter>
Command:	<enter> (Repeat LINE)
Specify first point:	**Osnap-Midpoint**
of	**D2**
Specify next point or [Undo]:	TYPE: @10<90<enter>
Specify next point or [Undo]:	<enter>
Command:	**Offset** (or TYPE: **O**<enter>)
Specify offset distance or [Through/ Erase/Layer]<default>:	TYPE: **1/2**<enter>
Select object to offset or [Exit/Undo] <Exit>:	**D3** (the line just drawn)
Specify point on side to offset or [Exit/Multiple/Undo] <Exit>:	**D4** (to the right)
Select object to offset or [Exit/Undo] <Exit>:	**D3**
Specify point on side to offset or [Exit/Multiple/Undo] <Exit>:	**D5** (to the left)
Select object to offset or [Exit/Undo] <Exit>:	<enter>
Command:	**Line**
Specify first point:	**Osnap-Endpoint**
of	**D6**
Specify next point or [Undo]:	**Osnap-Endpoint**

Prompt	Response
of	**D7**
Specify next point or [Undo]:	<**enter**> (to complete the command)
Command:	**Offset**
Specify offset distance or [Through/ Erase/Layer] <0'-1/2">:	TYPE: **3**<**enter**>
Select object to offset or [Exit/Undo] <Exit>:	**D8**
Specify point on side to offset or [Exit/Multiple/Undo] <Exit>:	**D4**
Select object to offset or [Exit/Undo] <Exit>:	<**enter**>
Command:	**Erase** (or TYPE: **E**<**enter**>)
Select objects:	**D9** (the center vertical line)
Select objects:	<**enter**>

Step 18. Trim out the line of the backsplash where it crosses the faucet.

Step 19. Set SNAP to 1".

Step 20. You can use the Stretch command to move entities that have other lines attached to them without removing the attached lines. Use Stretch to move the sink to its correct location (Figure 9–16):

Prompt	Response
Command:	**Stretch** (or TYPE: **S**<**enter**>)
Select objects to stretch by crossing-window or crossing-polygon...	
Select objects:	**D2**
Specify opposite corner:	**D1**
Select objects:	<**enter**>

FIGURE 9–16
Use Stretch to Move the Sink to Its Correct Location

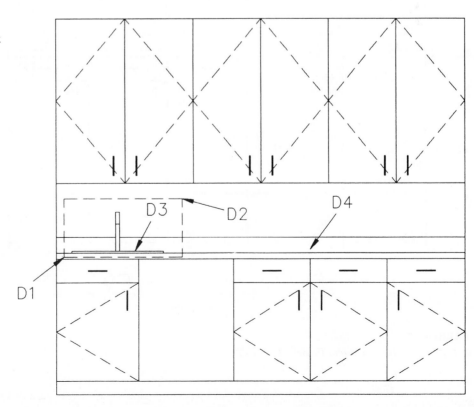

Prompt	Response
Specify base point or [Displacement] <Displacement>:	**Osnap-Midpoint**
of	**D3**
Specify second point or <use first point as displacement>:	**D4** (with ORTHO and SNAP ON, PICK: **a point directly above where the two doors meet**)

Step 21. Use Offset and Extend to draw the ceiling line above the cabinets (Figure 9–17).

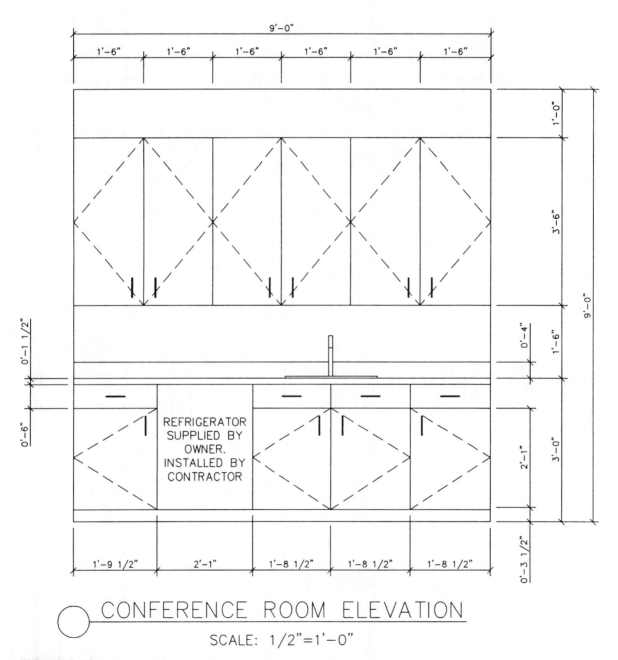

CONFERENCE ROOM ELEVATION

SCALE: 1/2"=1'-0"

FIGURE 9–17
Complete the Elevation Drawing (Scale: 1/2" = 1'-0")

Step 22. Set the A-elev-text Layer current, and use Simplex lettering, 2″ high, to place the note on the refrigerator, to write the name of the elevation, 4″ high, and to write the scale 2-1/2″ high.

Step 23. Use the UCS command to save the current UCS, and name it LOWER. Set the UCS to World.

Step 24. Set the A-elev-dim Layer current, set the dimensioning variables as described in Exercise 8–1 (with DIMSCALE set to 24), and add the dimensions as shown in Figure 9–17. You may want to change the GRID and SNAP settings to do the dimensioning.

Step 25. When you have completed Exercise 9–1, save your work in at least two places.

Step 26. Use Layout Wizard or Page Setup Manager to create a layout at a scale of 1/2″ = 1′, and plot or print Exercise 9–1.

Exercise 9–2: Tenant Space: Section of Conference Room Cabinets with Crosshatching

In Exercise 9–2, a sectional view of the built-in cabinets on the south wall of the tenant space conference room is drawn. The sectional view of the south wall of the cabinets (Figure 9–18) shows many construction details that elevation and plan views cannot. Sectional views are imaginary cuts through an area. Crosshatched lines are used to show where the imaginary saw used to make these imaginary cuts touches the cut objects. This crosshatching is done in AutoCAD by drawing hatch patterns. Exercise 9–2 will describe the Hatch command, used to draw hatch patterns.

When you have completed Exercise 9–2, your drawing will look similar to Figure 9–18.

Step 1. Use your workspace to make the following settings:

1. Begin drawing CH9-EX2 on the hard drive or network drive by opening existing drawing CH9-EX1 and saving it to the hard drive or network drive with the name CH9-EX2. You can use all the settings created for Exercise 9–1.
2. Reset Drawing Limits, Grid, and Snap as needed.
3. Create the following Layers by renaming the existing layers and changing the Hidden linetype to Continuous:

LAYER NAME	COLOR	LINETYPE	LINEWEIGHT
A-sect	Red	Continuous	Default
A-sect-patt	Green	Continuous	Default
A-sect-text	White	Continuous	Default
A-sect-dim	Blue	Continuous	Default

4. Set Layer A-sect current.
5. After looking closely at Figure 9–18, you may want to keep some of the conference room elevation drawing parts. Use Erase to eliminate the remainder of the drawing.
6. The cabinet section must be drawn before you use the Hatch command to draw the crosshatching. Draw the sectional view of the south wall of the tenant space conference room full size (measure features with an architectural scale of 3/4″ = 1′ to find the correct size) as shown in Figure 9–19.

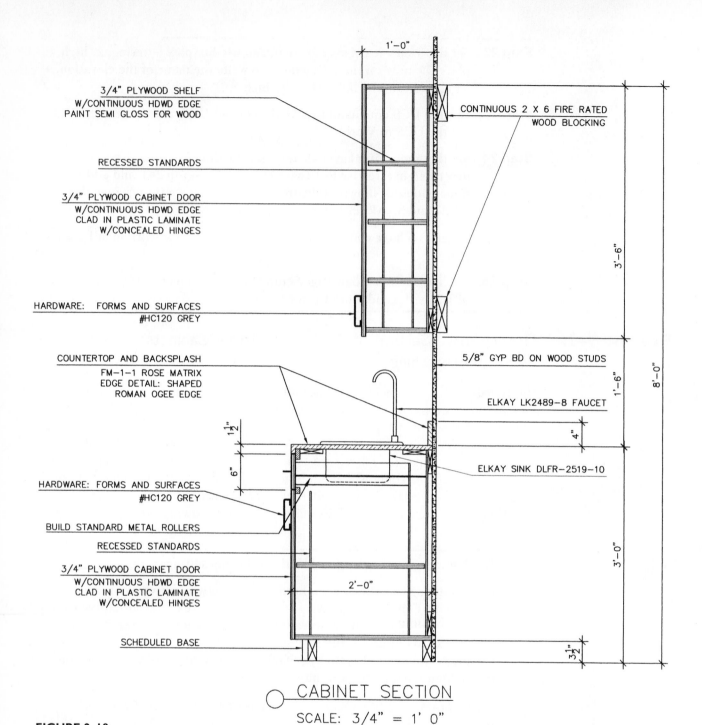

3/4" PLYWOOD SHELF
W/CONTINUOUS HDWD EDGE
PAINT SEMI GLOSS FOR WOOD

RECESSED STANDARDS

3/4" PLYWOOD CABINET DOOR
W/CONTINUOUS HDWD EDGE
CLAD IN PLASTIC LAMINATE
W/CONCEALED HINGES

HARDWARE: FORMS AND SURFACES
#HC120 GREY

COUNTERTOP AND BACKSPLASH
FM-1-1 ROSE MATRIX
EDGE DETAIL: SHAPED
ROMAN OGEE EDGE

HARDWARE: FORMS AND SURFACES
#HC120 GREY

BUILD STANDARD METAL ROLLERS

RECESSED STANDARDS

3/4" PLYWOOD CABINET DOOR
W/CONTINUOUS HDWD EDGE
CLAD IN PLASTIC LAMINATE
W/CONCEALED HINGES

SCHEDULED BASE

1'-0"

CONTINUOUS 2 X 6 FIRE RATED
WOOD BLOCKING

3'-6"

5/8" GYP BD ON WOOD STUDS

ELKAY LK2489-8 FAUCET

ELKAY SINK DLFR-2519-10

1'-6"

8'-0"

4"

3'-0"

1 1/2"

6"

2'-0"

3 1/2"

CABINET SECTION
SCALE: 3/4" = 1' 0"

FIGURE 9–18

Exercise 9–2: Tenant Space, Section of Conference Room Cabinets with Crosshatching (Scale: 3/4″ = 1′-0″)

Include the text and the dimensions. Use Layer A-sect to draw the view, Layer A-sect-text for the text and leaders, and Layer A-sect-dim for the dimensions. Hatch patterns as shown in Figure 9–18 will be drawn on Layer A-sect-patt.

7. When the cabinet section is complete with text and dimensions, freeze Layers A-sect-text and A-sect-dim so that they do not interfere with drawing the hatch patterns.

TIP: The dimensioning leader command draws leaders. It can be used to show dimensions or place notes on a drawing. TYPE: **DIM**<**enter**>, then **L**<**enter**> or CLICK: Leader from the Dimension menu or toolbar and follow the prompts.

Preparing to Use the Hatch Command
with the Select Objects Boundary Option

The most important aspect of using the Hatch command when you use "Select Objects" to create the boundary is to have the boundary of the area to be hatched defined clearly on the drawing. If the boundary of the hatching area is not clearly defined, the hatch pattern will not appear as you want it to. For example, some of the hatch pattern may go outside the boundary area, or the boundary area may not be completely filled with the hatch pattern.

Before you use the Hatch command in this manner, all areas to which hatching will be added must be prepared so that none of their boundary lines extend beyond

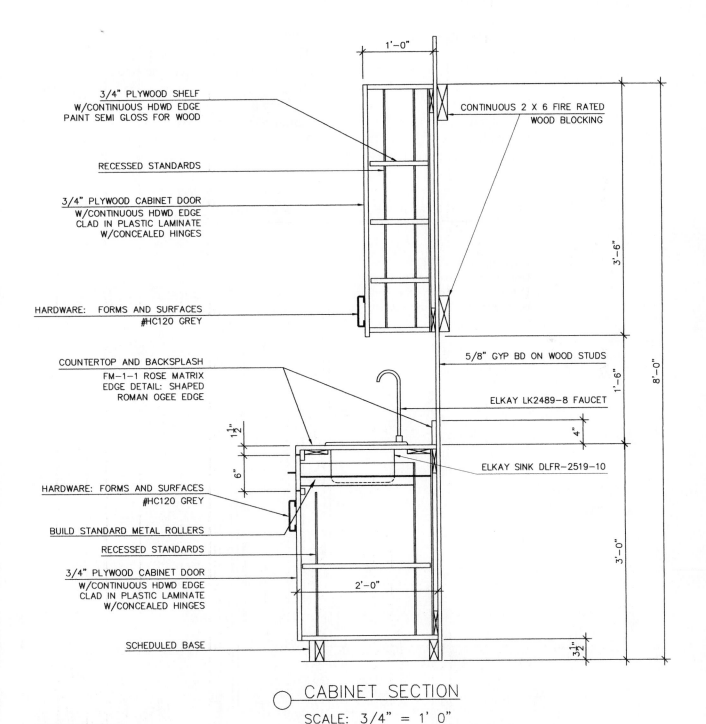

3/4" PLYWOOD SHELF
W/CONTINUOUS HDWD EDGE
PAINT SEMI GLOSS FOR WOOD

RECESSED STANDARDS

3/4" PLYWOOD CABINET DOOR
W/CONTINUOUS HDWD EDGE
CLAD IN PLASTIC LAMINATE
W/CONCEALED HINGES

HARDWARE: FORMS AND SURFACES
#HC120 GREY

COUNTERTOP AND BACKSPLASH
FM−1−1 ROSE MATRIX
EDGE DETAIL: SHAPED
ROMAN OGEE EDGE

HARDWARE: FORMS AND SURFACES
#HC120 GREY

BUILD STANDARD METAL ROLLERS

RECESSED STANDARDS

3/4" PLYWOOD CABINET DOOR
W/CONTINUOUS HDWD EDGE
CLAD IN PLASTIC LAMINATE
W/CONCEALED HINGES

SCHEDULED BASE

1'−0"

CONTINUOUS 2 X 6 FIRE RATED
WOOD BLOCKING

3'−6"

5/8" GYP BD ON WOOD STUDS

ELKAY LK2489−8 FAUCET

1'−6"

8'−0"

4"

ELKAY SINK DLFR−2519−10

1 1/2"

6"

2'−0"

3'−0"

3 1/2"

CABINET SECTION
SCALE: 3/4" = 1' 0"

FIGURE 9–19
Exercise 9–2: Tenant Space, Section of Conference Room Cabinets Before Crosshatching (Scale: 3/4″ = 1′-0″)

the area to be hatched. When the views on which you will draw hatching have already been drawn, it is often necessary to use the Break command to break the boundary lines into line segments that clearly define the hatch boundaries. The Break command is used to break any of the lines that define the area to be hatched so that those lines do not extend beyond the boundary of the hatching area.

Step 2. Use the Break command to help clearly define the right edge of the horizontal plywood top of the upper cabinets (Figure 9–20):

Prompt	Response
Command:	**Break** (or TYPE: **BR**<enter>)
Select object:	**D1** (to select the vertical line)
Specify second break point or [First point]:	TYPE: **F**<enter>
Specify first break point:	**D2** (use Osnap-Intersection)
Specify second break point:	TYPE: **@**<enter> (places the second point exactly at the same place as the first point, and no gap is broken out of the line)
Command:	<enter> (repeat BREAK)
Select object:	**D3** (to select the vertical line)
Specify second break point or [First point]:	TYPE: **F**<enter>
Specify first break point:	**D4** (use Osnap-Intersection)
Specify second break point:	TYPE: **@**<enter>

FIGURE 9–20
Use the Break Command to Clearly Define the Right Edge of the Horizontal Top Area of the Upper Cabinets

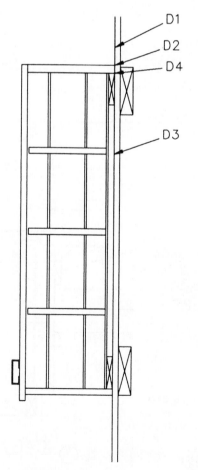

You have just used the Break command with the @ option to break the vertical line so that it is a separate line segment that clearly defines the right edge of the plywood top area.

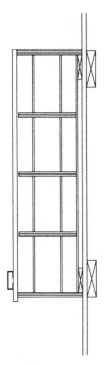

> **TIP:** You can also use the Break at Point command from the Modify toolbar and eliminate typing F for first point.

The Break command can also be used to erase or break a gap out of an entity. To break a gap out of an entity, simply click the first and second points of the desired gap at the command prompts. As shown in the prompt, "Enter second point (or F for first point):", the point used to "Select object:" can be used as the first point of the break.

Before using the Hatch command to hatch the plywood top, the three plywood shelves, and the plywood bottom of the upper cabinet as shown in Figure 9–21, you need to define clearly the boundaries of those areas.

FIGURE 9–21
Upper Cabinets with Hatch Patterns Drawn

Step 3. On your own (Figure 9–21):

1. Use the Break command to break the vertical line at the intersection of the bottom of the left edge of the plywood top boundary.
2. When the boundary of the plywood top is clearly defined, the top, bottom, right, and left lines of the top are separate line segments that do not extend beyond the boundary of the plywood top. To check the boundary, use the Erase command to pick and highlight each line segment. When each line is highlighted, you can see clearly if it needs to be broken. Use the Esc key to cancel the Erase command so that the lines are not actually erased. Use the Break command on the top horizontal line of the plywood top, if needed.
3. Use the Break command to prepare the three plywood shelves and the plywood bottom of the upper cabinet boundaries for hatching.
4. The Hatch command will also not work properly if the two lines of an intersection do not meet, that is, if there is any small gap. If you need to check the intersections of the left side of the plywood shelves to make sure they intersect properly, do this before continuing with the Hatch command.

> **TIP:** You may prefer to draw lines on a new layer over the ones existing to form the enclosed boundary area instead of breaking, as described in this procedure. These additional lines may be erased easily with a window after you turn off all layers except the one to be erased. This is sometimes faster and allows the line that was to be broken to remain intact.

> **TIP:** Use the Chamfer command (0 distance) or the Fillet command (0 radius) to connect two lines to form a perfect 90° angle.

Hatch... Hatch and Gradient Dialog Box; Hatch Tab

Type and pattern

When the Hatch command is activated (TYPE: **H<enter>**), the Hatch and Gradient dialog box with the Hatch tab selected appears (Figure 9–22). As listed in the Type and pattern: list box, the pattern types can be as follows:

Predefined   Makes the Pattern... button available.
User-defined   Defines a pattern of lines using the current linetype.
Custom   Specifies a pattern from the ACAD.pat file or any other PAT file.

To view the predefined hatch pattern options, CLICK: **the ellipsis (...)** to the right of the Pattern: list box. The Hatch Pattern Palette appears (Figure 9–23). Other parts of the Hatch and Gradient dialog box are as follows:

Pattern   Specifies a predefined pattern name.
Custom pattern   This list box shows a custom pattern name. This option is available when Custom is selected in the Type area.

Angle and scale

Angle   Allows you to specify an angle for the hatch pattern relative to the X axis of the current UCS.
Scale   This allows you to enlarge or shrink the hatch pattern to fit the drawing. It is not available if you have selected User-defined in the Type list box.
Double   When you check this box the area is hatched with a second set of lines at 90° to the first hatch pattern (available when User-defined pattern type is selected).
Relative to paper space   Scales the pattern relative to paper space so you can scale the hatch pattern to fit the scale of your paper space layout.

FIGURE 9–22
Hatch and Gradient Dialog Box, Hatch Tab

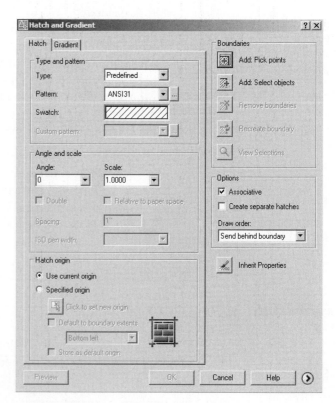

FIGURE 9–23
Hatch Pattern Palette

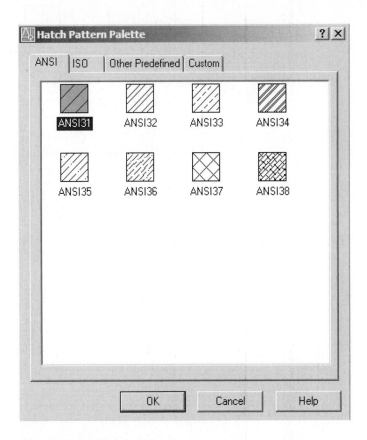

Spacing   Allows you to specify the space between lines on a user-defined hatch pattern.

ISO pen width   If you select one of the 14 ISO (International Organization of Standardization) patterns at the bottom of the list of hatch patterns and on the ISO tab of the Hatch Pattern Palette, this option scales the pattern based on the selected pen width. Each of these pattern names begins with ISO.

Hatch origin

Controls where the hatch pattern originates. Some hatch patterns, such as brick, stone and those used as shingles, need to start from a particular point on the drawing. By default, all hatch origins are the same as the current UCS origin.

Use current origin   Uses 0,0 as the origin by default. In most cases this will be what you want.

Specified origin   Specifies a new hatch origin. When you CLICK: this option the following options become available.

Click to set new origin   When you CLICK: this box you are then prompted to pick a point on the drawing as the origin for the hatch pattern.

Default to boundary extents   This option allows you to select a new origin based on the rectangular extents of the hatch. Choices include each of the four corners of the extents and its center.

Store as default origin   This option sets your specified origin as the default.

Preview button   Allows you to preview the hatch pattern before you apply it to a drawing.

Boundaries

Add: Pick points   Allows you to pick points inside a boundary to specify the area to be hatched.

Add: Select objects   Allows you to select the outside edges of the boundary to specify the area to be hatched.

Remove boundaries   Allows you to remove from the boundary set objects defined as islands by the Pick Points< option. You cannot remove the outer boundary.

Recreate boundary   Allows you to create a polyline or a region around the hatch pattern.

View Selections   Displays the currently defined boundary set. This option is not available when no selection or boundary has been made.

Options

Associative   When a ✓ appears in this button, the hatch pattern is a single object and stretches when the area that has been hatched is stretched.

Create separate hatches   When this button is clicked so that a ✓ appears in it, you can create two or more separate hatch areas by using the Hatch command only once. You can erase those areas individually.

Draw order: The Draw order: list allows you to place hatch patterns on top of or beneath existing lines to make the drawing more legible.

Inherit Properties   Allows you to pick an existing hatch pattern to use on another area. The pattern picked must be associative (attached to and defined by its boundary).

More Options

When the More Options arrow in the lower right corner is clicked, the following options, Figure 9–24, appear.

Islands

Island display style:

The following Island display style options are shown in Figure 9–24:

Normal   When Normal is clicked (and a selection set is composed of areas inside other areas), alternating areas are hatched, as shown in the Island display style area.

Outer   When Outer is clicked (and a selection set is composed of areas inside other areas), only the outer area is hatched, as shown in the Island display style area.

Ignore   When Ignore is clicked (and a selection set is composed of areas inside other areas), all areas are hatched, as shown in the Island display style area.

Boundary retention

Retain boundaries   Specifies whether the boundary objects will remain in your drawing after hatching is completed.

Object type: Allows you to select either a polyline or a region if you choose to retain the boundary.

FIGURE 9–24
Hatch and Gradient Dialog
Box, More Options

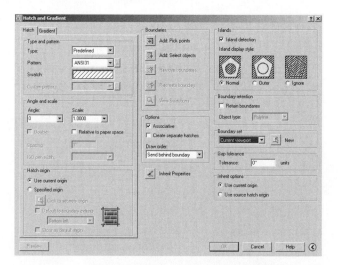

Boundary set

List box   This box allows you to select a boundary set from the current viewport or
an existing boundary set.

New   When New is clicked, the dialog box temporarily closes and you are prompted
to select objects to create the boundary set. AutoCAD includes only objects that
can be hatched when it constructs the new boundary set. AutoCAD discards any
existing boundary set and replaces it with the new boundary set. If you don't select
any objects that can be hatched, AutoCAD retains any current set.

Gap tolerance

Allows a gap tolerance between 0 and 5000 units to hatch areas that are not completely enclosed.

Inherit options

Allows you to choose either the current hatch origin or the origin of the inherited
hatch for the new hatch pattern.

Hatch... Hatch and Gradient Dialog Box; Gradient Tab

The gradient tab (Figure 9–25) is discussed fully in Chapter 12.

Step 4.   **Set Layer A-sect-patt current.**

Step 5.   **Use the Hatch command with the Select Objects boundary option to
draw a uniform horizontal-line hatch pattern on the plywood top of the
upper cabinets (Figure 9–26):**

Prompt	Response
Command:	**Hatch** (or TYPE: **H\<enter>**)

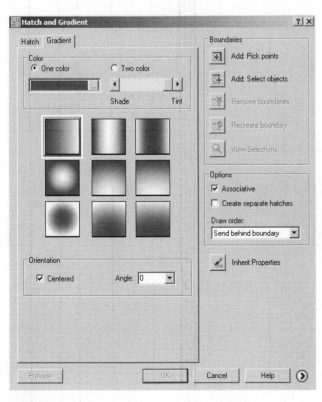

FIGURE 9–25
Gradient Tab

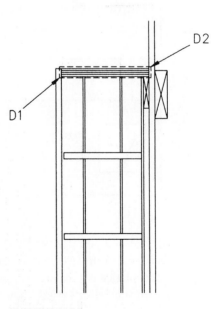

FIGURE 9–26
Use the Hatch Command with the Select
Objects< Boundary Option to Draw a
Uniform Horizontal-Line Hatch Pattern on
the Plywood Top of the Upper Cabinets

Prompt	Response
The Hatch and Gradient dialog box appears:	CLICK: **User-defined** in the pattern Type: area Angle: **0** Spacing: **1/4″** CLICK: Add: **Select objects**
Select objects or [picK internal point/remove Boundaries]:	CLICK: **D1**
Specify opposite corner:	CLICK: **D2**
Select objects or [picK internal point/remove Boundaries]:	**<enter>**
The Hatch and Gradient dialog box appears:	CLICK: **Preview**
Pick or press Esc to return to dialog or <Right-click to accept hatch>: (A preview of your hatching appears)	**RIGHT-CLICK** (if the correct hatch pattern was previewed; if not, CLICK: **Esc** and fix the problem)

The plywood top of the upper cabinet is now hatched.

Step 6. Use the same hatching procedure to draw a hatch pattern on the three plywood shelves and the plywood bottom of the upper cabinet, as shown in Figure 9–27.

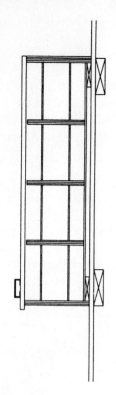

FIGURE 9–27
Draw a Hatch Pattern on the Three Plywood Shelves and the Plywood Bottom of the Upper Cabinet

 NOTE: Although the "Pick Points" method of creating hatch boundaries is often much easier, you must know how to use "Select Objects" as well. There are instances when "Pick Points" just does not work.

 TIP: Turn off or freeze the text and dimension layers if they interfere with hatching.

When you use the Pick Points boundary option to create a boundary for the hatch pattern, AutoCAD allows you to pick any point inside the area, and the boundary is automatically created. You do not have to prepare the boundary of the area as you did with the Select Objects boundary option, but you have to make sure there are no gaps in the boundary.

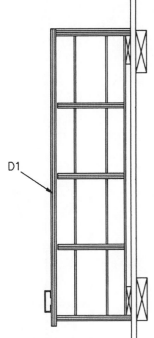

FIGURE 9–28
Use the Hatch Command with the Pick Points Boundary Option to Draw a Uniform Vertical-Line Hatch Pattern on the Upper Cabinet Door

D1

Step 7. Use the Hatch command with the Pick Points boundary option to draw a uniform vertical-line hatch pattern on the upper cabinet door (Figure 9–28):

Prompt	Response
Command:	**Hatch** (or TYPE: **H<enter>**)
The Hatch and Gradient dialog box appears:	CLICK: **User-defined** in the pattern TYPE: area
	Angle: **90**
	Spacing: **1/4**
	CLICK: Add: **Pick points**
Pick internal point or [Select objects/remove Boundaries]:	CLICK: **D1** (inside the door symbol)
Pick internal point or [Select objects/remove Boundaries]:	**<enter>**
The Hatch and Gradient dialog box appears:	CLICK: **Preview**
Pick or press Esc to return to dialog or <Right-click to accept hatch>:	
(A preview of your hatching appears):	RIGHT CLICK (if the correct hatch pattern was previewed; if not, CLICK: **Esc** and fix the problem)

TIP: You may have to draw a line across the top of the 5/8″ gypsum board to create the hatch pattern on the gypsum board.

Step 8. Use the Hatch command with the Pick Points boundary option to draw the AR-SAND hatch pattern on the 5/8″ gypsum board (Figures 9–29, 9–30, and 9–31):

Prompt	Response
Command:	**Hatch**
The Hatch and Gradient dialog box appears:	CLICK: **Predefined**
	CLICK: **...** (to the right of the Pattern: list box)
The Hatch pattern palette appears:	CLICK: **the Other Predefined tab**
	CLICK: **AR-SAND** (Figure 9–29)
	CLICK: **OK**

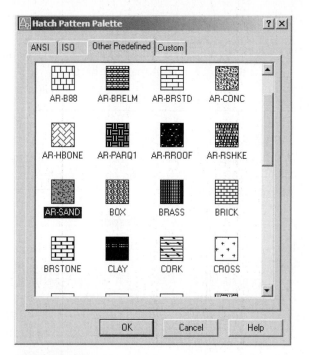

FIGURE 9–29
Select AR-SAND

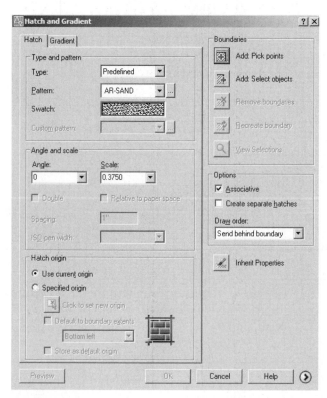

FIGURE 9–30
Specify Scale for AR-SAND

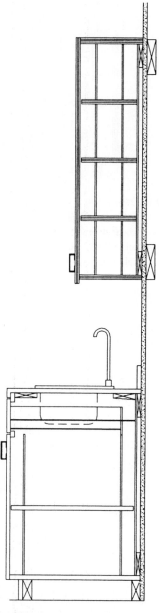

FIGURE 9–31
Use the Hatch Command to Draw the AR-SAND Hatch Pattern on the 5/8″ Gypsum Board

Prompt	Response
The Hatch and Gradient dialog box appears (Figure 9–30):	CLICK: **0** (in the Angle box) TYPE: **3/8″** (in the Scale: box) CLICK: **Add: Pick points**

 NOTE: Remember when you use the Pick Points button, often the complete boundary of the area to be hatched must be visible on the screen.

Prompt	Response
Pick internal point or [Select objects/remove Boundaries]:	CLICK: **any point inside the lines defining the 5/8″ gypsum board boundary**
Pick internal point or [Select objects/remove Boundaries]:	**<enter>**
The Hatch and Gradient dialog box appears:	CLICK: **OK**

The 5/8″ gypsum board is now hatched. (If you get an error message, try 1/2″ for scale in the Scale box or draw a line across the top of the gypsum board.)

 NOTE: Be sure to preview your hatch patterns to make sure they are correct.

Editing Hatch Patterns

Select **Modify-Object-Hatch...** or TYPE: **HE<enter>** or DOUBLE-CLICK: **on a hatch pattern** to access the Hatch Edit dialog box (Figure 9–32). You can edit the pattern, angle, scale, origin, and draw order of the hatch pattern.

If you already have an associative hatch pattern on a drawing that has one or two lines extending outside the hatch area, if necessary, explode the hatch pattern. The lines may then be trimmed, because they are individual lines.

Step 9. On your own:

1. Using the patterns described in Figure 9–33, draw hatch patterns by using the Pick Points option on the lower cabinets.
2. Thaw Layers A-sect-text and A-sect-dim.

Step 10. When you have completed Exercise 9–2, save your work in at least two places.

Step 11. Use Layout Wizard or Page Setup Manager to create a layout at a scale of 3/4″ = 1′ and plot or print Exercise 9–2.

FIGURE 9–32
Hatch Edit Dialog Box

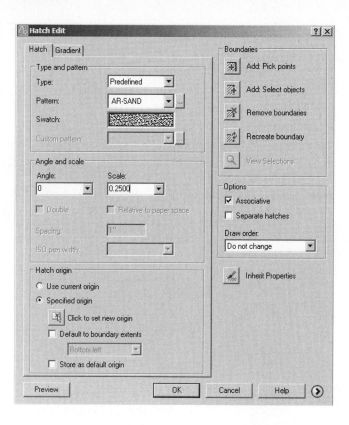

FIGURE 9–33
Draw the Hatch Patterns on the Lower Cabinets as Shown

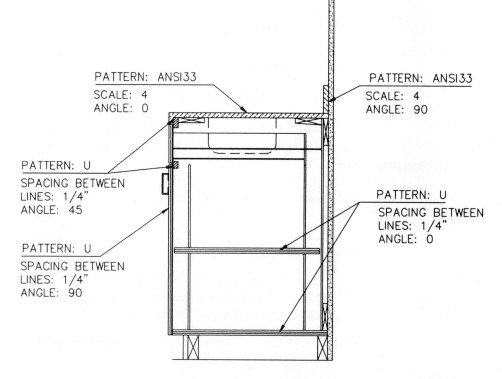

PATTERN: ANSI33
SCALE: 4
ANGLE: 0

PATTERN: ANSI33
SCALE: 4
ANGLE: 90

PATTERN: U
SPACING BETWEEN LINES: 1/4"
ANGLE: 45

PATTERN: U
SPACING BETWEEN LINES: 1/4"
ANGLE: 0

PATTERN: U
SPACING BETWEEN LINES: 1/4"
ANGLE: 90

Exercise 9–3: Detail of Door Jamb with Crosshatching

In Exercise 9–3, a detail of a door jamb is drawn. When you have completed Exercise 9–3, your drawing will look similar to Figure 9–34.

Step 1. Use your workspace to make the following settings:

1. Use SaveAs… to save the drawing on the hard drive with the name CH9-EX3.
2. Set Drawing Units, Limits, Grid, and Snap.
3. Create the following Layers:

LAYER NAME	COLOR	LINETYPE	LINEWEIGHT
A-detl	Red	Continuous	Default
A-detl-patt	Green	Continuous	Default
A-detl-text	White	Continuous	Default
A-detl-dim	Blue	Continuous	Default

4. Set Layer A-detl current.

Step 2. Using the dimensions shown in Figure 9–34, draw all the door jamb components. Drawing some of the components separately and copying or moving them into place will be helpful. Measure any dimensions not shown with a scale of 3″ = 1′-0″.

FIGURE 9–34
Exercise 9–3: Detail of a Door Jamb with Crosshatching (Scale: 3″ = 1′-0″)

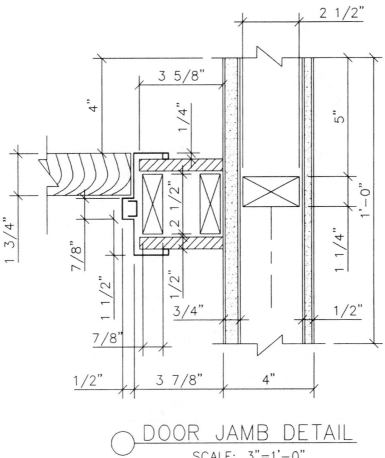

DOOR JAMB DETAIL
SCALE: 3"=1'-0"

FIGURE 9–35
Exercise 9–3: Hatch Patterns

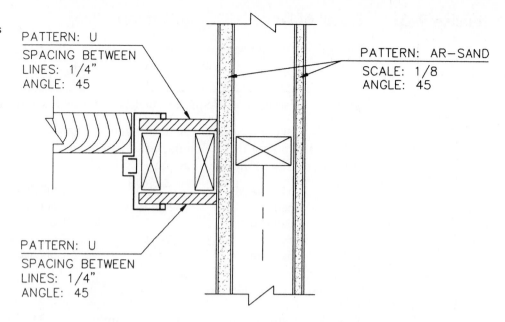

PATTERN: U
SPACING BETWEEN
LINES: 1/4"
ANGLE: 45

PATTERN: AR–SAND
SCALE: 1/8
ANGLE: 45

PATTERN: U
SPACING BETWEEN
LINES: 1/4"
ANGLE: 45

Step 3. Set Layer A-detl-patt current, and draw the hatch patterns as described in Figure 9–35. Use a Spline and array it to draw the curved wood grain pattern.

Step 4. Set Layer A-detl-dim current, set the dimensioning variables, and draw the dimensions as shown in Figure 9–34.

Step 5. Set Layer A-detl-text current, and add the name of the detail as shown in Figure 9–34.

Step 6. Save the drawing in two places.

Step 7. Create a layout at a scale of 3"=1'-0", and plot or print the drawing.

Exercise 9–4: Using POINT FILTERS and OTRACK to Draw an Orthographic Drawing of a Conference Table

In Exercise 9–4, the AutoCAD features called Point Filters and Otrack are used. These features are especially helpful when you are making 2-dimensional drawings showing the top, front, and side views of an object. All of the features in these views must line up with the same features in the adjacent view. When you have completed Exercise 9–4 your drawing will look similar to Figure 9–36.

Step 1. Use your workspace to make the following settings:

1. Set drawing Units: **Architectural**
2. Set Drawing Limits: **12', 9'**
3. Set Grid: **2"**
4. Set Snap: **1"**
5. Set GRIDDISPLAY: **0**

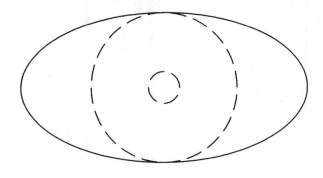

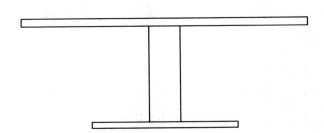

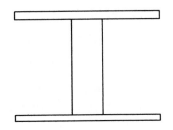

CONFERENCE TABLE

SCALE 1/2"=1'-0"

FIGURE 9–36
Exercise 9–4: Using Point Filters and OTRACK to Draw Three Views of a Conference Table

6. Create the following Layers:

LAYER NAME	COLOR	LINETYPE	LINEWEIGHT
A-furn-s	Red	Continuous	Default
A-furn-h	Green	HIDDEN	Default
A-furn-text	White	Continuous	Default

7. Set **Layer A-furn-h** current.
8. Set LTSCALE: **16**

Step 2. **Draw the base and column of the table (HIDDEN Line), as shown in the top view (Figure 9–37):**

Prompt	Response
Command:	**Circle-Center, Diameter** (not Radius)
Specify center point for circle or [3P/2P/Ttr (tan tan radius)]:	TYPE: **4',6'<enter>**
Specify diameter of circle <default>:	TYPE: **3'1-1/2<enter>**
Command:	**Circle-Center, Diameter** (not Radius)
Specify center point for circle or [3P/2P/Ttr (tan tan radius)]:	TYPE: **4',6'** (The same center as the first circle)
Specify diameter of circle <default>:	TYPE: **8<enter>**

Step 3. **Set Layer A-furn-s current.**

FIGURE 9–37
Draw the Top View of the
Base, Column, and Top of the
Table

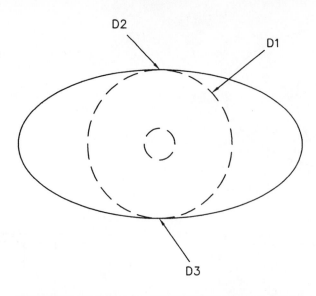

Step 4. Draw the elliptical top of the table (Continuous Linetype), as shown in the top view (Figure 9–37).

Prompt	Response
Command:	Ellipse-Axis, End
Specify axis endpoint of ellipse or [Arc/Center]:	Osnap-Quadrant
of	D2
Specify other endpoint of axis:	Osnap-Quadrant
of	D3
Specify distance to other axis or [Rotation]:	TYPE: 36-3/4<enter>

Step 5. Use Point Filters to draw the front view of the top of this odd-size elliptical table (Figure 9–38):

Prompt	Response
Command:	Line
Specify first point:	TYPE: .X<enter>
of	Osnap-Quadrant
of	D1 (Figure 9–38)

FIGURE 9–38
Draw the Front View of the
Table Using Point Filters

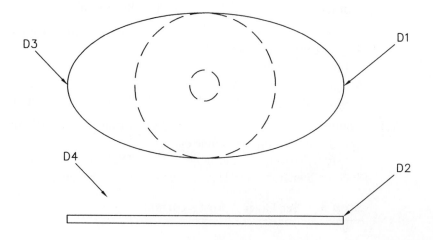

Prompt	Response
(need YZ):	**D2** (with SNAP ON, **pick a point in the approximate location shown in Figure 9–38**)
Specify next point or [Undo]:	TYPE: **.X<enter>**
of	**Osnap-Quadrant**
of	**D3**
(need YZ):	**D4** (with ORTHO ON, **pick any point to identify the Y component of the point;** ORTHO makes the Y component of the new point the same as the Y component of the previous point)
Specify next point or [Close/Undo]:	With ORTHO ON, **move your mouse straight down,** and TYPE: **2<enter>**
Specify next point or [Close/Undo]:	TYPE: **.X<enter>**
of	**Osnap-Endpoint**
of	**D2**
(need YZ):	With ORTHO ON, **move your mouse to the right, and pick any point**
Specify next point or [Close/Undo]:	TYPE: **C<enter>**

Step 6. Set running Osnap modes of Endpoint, Quadrant, and Intersection and turn OSNAP and OTRACK ON.

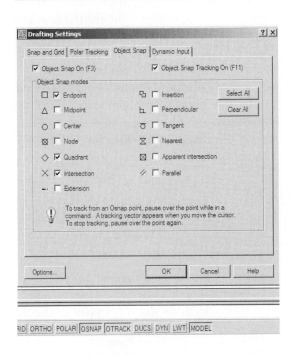

Step 7. Use OTRACK and Offset to draw the front view of the column (Figure 9–39):

Prompt	Response
Command:	**Line**
Specify first point:	**Move your mouse to the quadrant shown as D1** (Figure 9–39) but do not CLICK:

FIGURE 9–39
Use OTRACK to Draw the
Front View of the Column

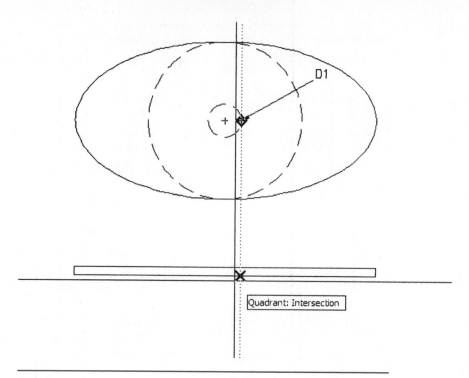

Quadrant: Intersection

Prompt	Response
	Hold it until the Quadrant symbol shows, then move your mouse straight down until the dotted line shows the intersection symbol on the bottom line of the table top as shown, then CLICK: the intersection point.
Specify next point or [Undo]:	With ORTHO ON move your mouse straight down and TYPE: **24<enter>**
Specify next point or [Undo]:	**<enter>**
Command:	**Offset** (or TYPE: **O<enter>**)
Specify offset distance or [Through/ Erase/Layer] <Through>:	TYPE: **8<enter>**
Select object to offset or [Exit/Undo] <Exit>:	CLICK: **D1** (Figure 9–40)
Specify point on side to offset or [Exit/Multiple/Undo] <Exit>:	CLICK: **D2 (any point to the left of the 24″ line)**
Select object to offset or [Exit/Undo] <Exit>:	**<enter>**

Step 8. Use OTRACK to draw the front view of the base (Figure 9–40):

Prompt	Response
Command:	**Line**
Specify first point:	Move your mouse to the quadrant shown as D3 (**Figure 9–40**) but do not CLICK. Hold it until the Quadrant symbol shows, then move your mouse to D4 (do not CLICK) (the dotted line shows the endpoint symbol), then move your mouse back to the vertical dotted line and CLICK:

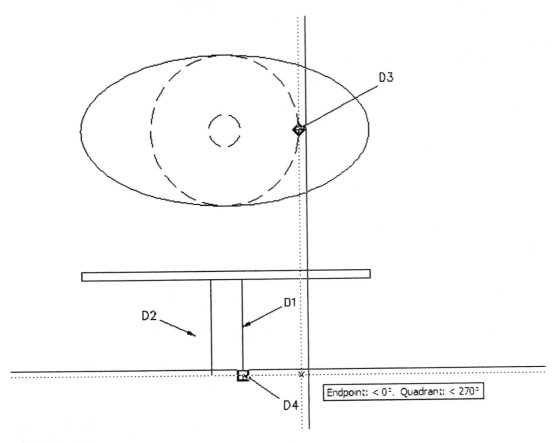

FIGURE 9–40
Use OTRACK to Draw the Front View of the Base

Prompt	Response
Specify next point or [Undo]:	**With ORTHO ON move your mouse straight down** and TYPE: **1-1/2<enter>**
Specify next point or [Undo]:	**With ORTHO ON, move your mouse to the left** and TYPE: **3'1-1/2<enter>**
Specify next point or [Close/Undo]:	With ORTHO ON, **move your mouse straight up,** and TYPE: **1-1/2<enter>**
Specify next point or [Close/Undo]:	TYPE: **C<enter>**

Step 9. On your own:

1. Use OTRACK to draw the right side view of the table with the Line and Copy commands (Figure 9–41). Be sure to get depth dimensions from the top view.

Step 10. Save your drawing in two places.

Step 11. Create a layout at a scale of $1/2'' = 1'\text{-}0''$ and plot or print the drawing.

Exercise 9–5: Different Hatch Styles

1. Draw the figure (without hatching) shown in Figure 9–42. Use an Architectural scale of $1/2'' = 1''$ to measure the figure, and draw it full scale. Copy it two times, leaving 1" between figures.

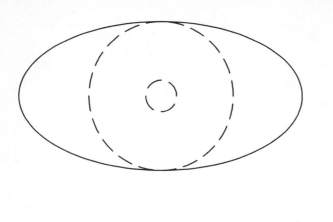

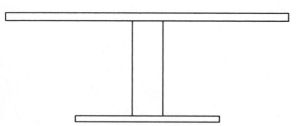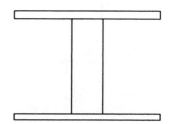

FIGURE 9–41
Draw the Right Side View Using Copy, Line, and OTRACK

2. Shade each figure with a different Hatch Style (CLICK: the More Options arrow in the lower right corner of the Hatch and Gradient dialog box) as shown: Normal, Outer, and Ignore. Use the same hatch pattern: User-defined, 1/8 spacing, 45 angle.
3. Save the drawing in two places, and plot or print the drawing to scale.

Exercise 9–6: Drawing a Mirror from a Sketch

1. Use the dimensions shown to draw the figure shown in Figure 9–43 using AutoCAD.
2. Set your own drawing limits, grid, and snap. Create your own layers as needed.
3. Do not place dimensions on this drawing, but do show the cutting plane lines and label them as shown.

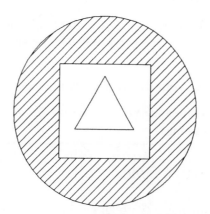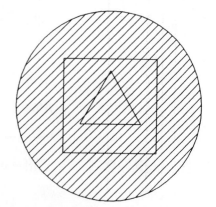

FIGURE 9–42
Practice Exercise 9–5: Different Hatch Styles (Scale: 1/2″ = 1″)

4. Do not draw Detail A. This information is shown so you can draw that part of the mirror.
5. Draw and label sections A-A, B-B, and C-C in the approximate locations shown on the sketch. Use the ANSI31 hatch pattern for the sectional views, or draw splines and array them to show wood. Do not show dimensions on this part of the drawing either.
6. Save the drawing in two places, create a layout at an appropriate scale, and print the drawing.

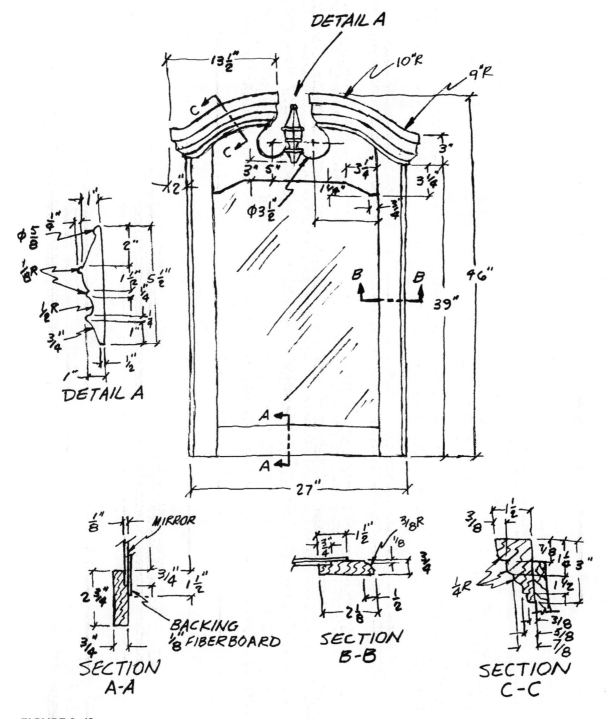

FIGURE 9–43
Exercise 9–6: Mirror

Exercise 9–7: Elevation 1 of the Log Cabin Kitchen

Figure 9–44 shows the floor plan of the log cabin kitchen with two elevations indicated. Figure 9–45 shows where the Kitchen drawing is located in the AutoCAD DesignCenter. The front view of the dishwasher, faucet, range-oven, and refrigerator are blocks contained within this drawing. Just DOUBLE-CLICK: on any of these blocks to activate the Insert command, and insert these blocks into your elevation drawing as needed.

Draw elevation 1 of the log cabin kitchen as shown in Figure 9–46. Use the dimensions shown or use an Architectural scale of 1/2″=1′0″ to measure elevation 1, and draw it full scale without dimensions. Use lineweights to make the drawing more attractive and a solid hatch pattern with a gray color to make the walls solid.

When you have completed Exercise 9–7 your drawing will look similar to Figure 9–46 with dimensions.

1. **Use your workspace to make the following settings:**
   1. Set drawing Units: **Architectural**
   2. Set Drawing Limits: **15′,19′**
   3. Set GRIDDISPLAY: **0**
   4. Set Grid: **12″**
   5. Set Snap: **3″**

FIGURE 9–44
Plan View of the Log Cabin Kitchen

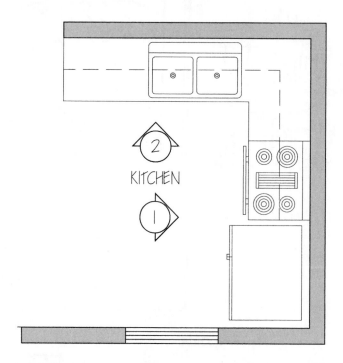

FIGURE 9–45
DesignCenter with the Kitchen Drawing Blocks Displayed

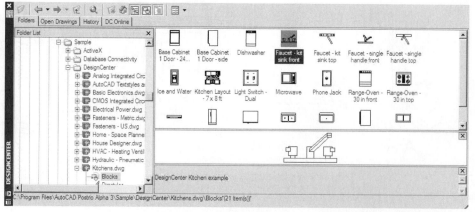

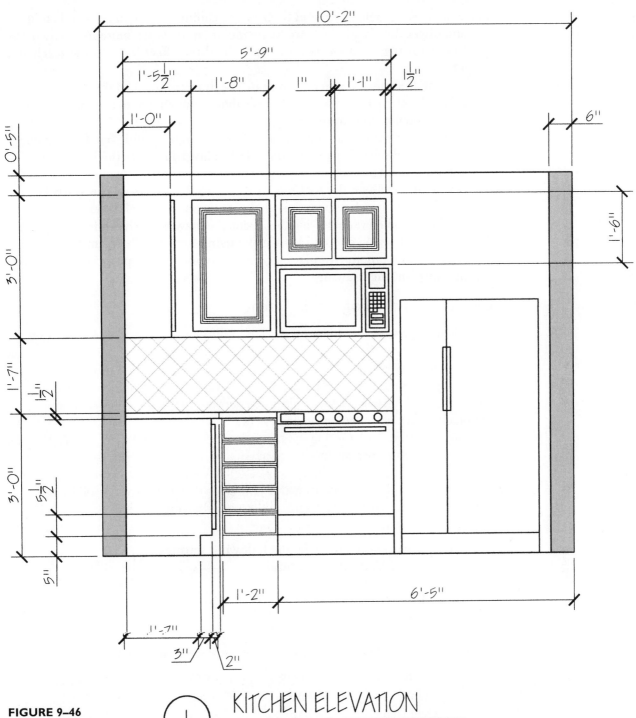

FIGURE 9–46
Elevation 1 of the Log Cabin
Kitchen (Scale: 1/2″ = 1′ – 0″)

KITCHEN ELEVATION

1

SCALE: 1/ 2″ = 1′-0″

6. Create the following layers:

LAYER NAME	COLOR	LINETYPE	LINEWEIGHT
Kitchen	White	Continuous	default
Kitchen Thin	White	Continuous	0.15mm
Faucet	Magenta	Continuous	0.05mm
Text	White	Continuous	default
Hatch	253	Continuous	default
Walls	White	Continuous	0.30mm

2. Use the Rectangle command to draw the cabinet doors on the Kitchen layer, and offset the rectangle 2″ to the inside, then ½″ twice more to get the three lines showing the door pattern. Place the three offset lines on the Kitchen Thin layer.

3. Use the Rectangle command to draw the drawers (next to the range-oven) on the Kitchen Thin layer, and offset that rectangle ½″ to the inside. Leave ½″ between each drawers.

4. Use a user-defined hatch pattern with a 45° angle, double hatch, 4″ spacing, and create the hatch pattern on the Hatch layer to create the backsplash behind the range-oven.

5. Insert all blocks on the Kitchen layer. Put wall outlines on the Walls layer and the solid hatch pattern inside the walls on the Hatch layer.

6. Set dimensioning variables and dimension the drawing as shown in Figure 9–46.

7. Label the drawing and add your name using the City Blueprint font.

8. Save the drawing in two places, create a layout at an appropriate scale, and plot or print the drawing.

Exercise 9–8: ## Elevation 2 of the Log Cabin Kitchen

Figure 9–44 shows the floor plan of the log cabin kitchen with arrows indicating the line of sight for two elevations of this room. Figure 9–45 shows where the Kitchen drawing is located in the AutoCAD DesignCenter. The front view of the dishwasher, faucet, range-oven, and refrigerator are blocks contained within this drawing. Just DOUBLE-CLICK: on any of these blocks to activate the Insert command, and insert these blocks into your elevation drawing as needed.

Draw elevation 2 of the log cabin kitchen as shown in Figure 9–47. Use the dimensions shown or use an Architectural scale of 1/2″=1′0″ to measure elevation 2, and draw it full scale without dimensions. Use lineweights to make the drawing more attractive and a solid hatch pattern with a gray color to make the walls solid.

When you have completed Exercise 9–8 your drawing will look similar to Figure 9–47 with dimensions.

1. Use your workspace to make the following settings:
   1. Set drawing Units: **Architectural**
   2. Set Drawing Limits: **15′,19′**
   3. Set GRIDDISPLAY: **0**
   4. Set Grid: **12″**
   5. Set Snap: **3″**
   6. Create the following Layers (if you do not have them already):

LAYER NAME	COLOR	LINETYPE	LINEWEIGHT
Kitchen	White	Continuous	default
Kitchen Thin	White	Continuous	0.15mm
Faucet	Magenta	Continuous	0.05mm
Text	White	Continuous	default
Hatch	253	Continuous	default
Walls	White	Continuous	0.30mm
Dim	White	Continuous	default

2. Use the Rectangle command to draw the cabinet doors on the Kitchen layer, and offset the rectangle 2″ to the inside, then ½″ twice more to get the three lines showing the door pattern. Place the three offset lines on the Kitchen Thin layer.

3. Use a user-defined hatch pattern with a 45° angle, double hatch, 4″ spacing, and create the hatch pattern on the Hatch layer to create the backsplash behind the sink.

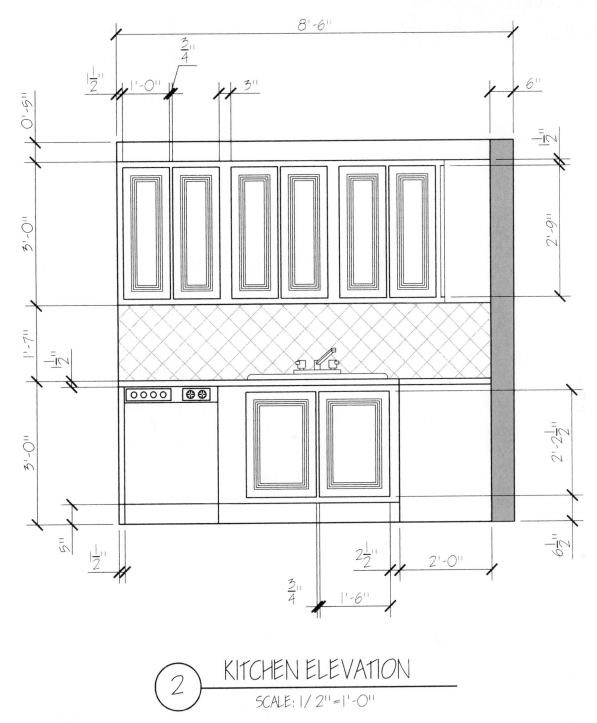

$$\underset{2}{\bigcirc} \quad \underline{\text{KITCHEN ELEVATION}}$$

SCALE: 1/2" = 1'-0"

FIGURE 9–47
Elevation 2 of the Log Cabin Kitchen (Scale: 1/2" = 1' – 0")

4. Insert all blocks except the faucet on the Kitchen layer. Put the faucet on the Faucet layer, wall outlines on the Walls layer, and the solid hatch pattern inside the walls on the Hatch layer.

5. Set dimensioning variables and dimension the drawing as shown in Figure 9–47.

6. Label the drawing and add your name using the City Blueprint font.

7. Save the drawing in two places, create a layout at an appropriate scale, and plot or print the drawing.

1. Which of the following patterns produces evenly spaced dots?
   a. U
   b. DOTS
   c. ANSI34
   d. DOLMIT
   e. LINE

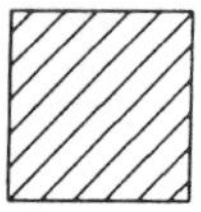

FIGURE 9–48

2. Which of the following angles produces the User-defined pattern shown in Figure 9–48?
   a. 45
   b. 90
   c. 0
   d. 135
   e. 105

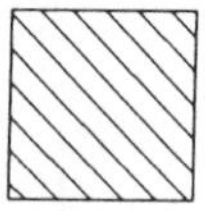

FIGURE 9–49

3. Which of the following angles produces the User-defined pattern shown in Figure 9–49?
   a. 45
   b. 90
   c. 0
   d. 135
   e. 105

4. Which of the following commands can be used to correct a hatch pattern that extends outside a hatch boundary, after it has been exploded?
   a. Array
   b. Copy
   c. Move
   d. Trim
   e. Break

FIGURE 9–50

5. Which of the following describes the User-defined pattern shown in Figure 9–50?
   a. X pat
   b. 45,145
   c. Double
   d. Double section
   e. Line-two

6. Which of the following in the Spacing: input area in the Hatch and Gradient dialog box produces hatch lines 1/4″ apart (User-defined pattern)?
   a. 1/4″
   b. 1
   c. 1-4
   d. 4
   e. Depends on the size of the drawing.

7. After a Hatch command that spaced lines 1/8″ apart has been performed, what is the default setting in the Spacing: input area for the next hatch pattern?
   a. 0″
   b. 1/4″
   c. 1/8″
   d. 1″
   e. Depends on the size of the drawing.

8. Which setting allows an image to be Mirrored without mirroring the text?
   a. MIRRTEXT = 1
   b. MIRRTEXT = 0
   c. MIRRTXT = 1
   d. MIRRTXT = 0
   e. DTEXT-STYLE = 0

9. The Stretch command is best used for
   a. Stretching an object in one direction
   b. Shrinking an object in one direction
   c. Moving an object along attached lines
   d. All the above
   e. None of the above

10. Which Hatch option allows you to hatch only the outermost boundary of multiple areas within a selection window?
   a. Pattern
   b. Scale
   c. Outer
   d. Normal
   e. Ignore

Complete.

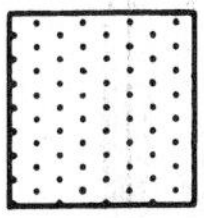

FIGURE 9–51

11. What is the correct name of the pattern in Figure 9–51?

   _____

12. How can the predefined Hatch pattern options (Hatch Pattern Palette) be called up on the screen?

   _____

   _____

FIGURE 9–52

13. Correctly label the User-defined pattern shown in Figure 9–52. Show angle and spacing at full scale.

   Angle_____ Spacing _____

14. Correctly label the Predefined pattern shown in Figure 9–53. Show pattern and angle.

   Pattern_____ Angle _____

FIGURE 9–53

15. How can a hatch pattern line that extends outside a hatch boundary be corrected?

   _____

   _____

   _____

16. What is the name of the UCS Icon command option that forces the UCS icon to be displayed at the 0,0 point of the current UCS?

   _____

17. How can all the lines of an associative 35-line hatch pattern be erased?

   _____

18. List the command that allows you to change a hatch pattern from Associative to individual lines.

   _____

19. Describe a practical use for the UCS command for two-dimensional drawing.

   _____

   _____

   _____

   _____

20. List the prompts and responses for getting the UCS icon to move to the UCS origin after the UCS has been moved.

   Prompt   Response

   Command: _____

   _____   _____

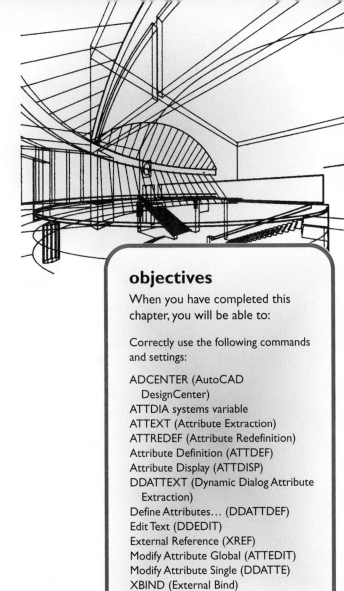

chapter

10

Drawing the Furniture Plan, Adding Specifications, and Extracting Data

Introduction

This chapter describes the AutoCAD commands that allow specifications to be added to furnishings and how the specifications are extracted from the drawing. These commands are especially important because they reduce the amount of time it takes to add furniture to the plan, and to count large amounts of like furniture pieces (with specifications) from the plan. There are many software programs available that can be used with AutoCAD to save even more time. These programs provide furniture symbols already drawn and programs that extract specification information in a form that suits your individual needs. Although you may ultimately combine one of these programs with the AutoCAD program, learning the commands included in this chapter will help you to understand how they interact with AutoCAD.

Exercise 10–1: Tenant Space Furniture Plan with Furniture Specifications

When you have completed Exercise 10–1, your drawing will look similar to Figure 10–1.

Step 1. Use your workspace to make the following settings:

1. Begin drawing CH10-EX1 on the hard drive or network drive by opening existing drawing CH8-EX1 and saving it as CH10-EX1.
2. Set Layer 0 current.
3. Freeze Layers A-pflr-dims, Defpoints, and A-area.
4. Use Zoom-All to view the limits of the drawing.

Step 2. On your own:

1. The furniture symbols must be drawn in plan view before you use the -ATTDEF (Attribute Definition) command to add specifications. Draw the tenant space reception furniture symbols as shown in Figure 10–2. Use a 1/4″ = 1′-0″ architectural scale to measure the symbols, and draw each piece full scale on your drawing. Pick any open space on your drawing to draw the furniture. Draw each symbol on the 0 Layer. Blocks will be made of each symbol after you use the Define Attributes… command, so it does not matter where the furniture is drawn on the plan. Use short, straight sections of a polyline to draw the plant inside the planter.

FIGURE 10–1
Exercise 10–1: Tenant Space Furniture Plan with Furniture Specifications (Scale: 1/8″ = 1′-0″)

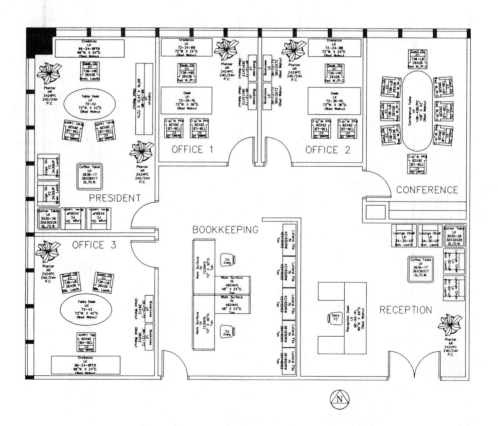

TENANT SPACE – RECEPTION

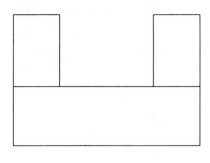

DESC: Reception Desk
MFG: LK
PROD: 96–66–RL
SIZE: 96"W. X 66"D.
FINISH: Oiled Walnut

DESC: Sec. Chair
MFG: FC
PROD: 467–PC–T
SIZE: 20"D. X 18"W.
FINISH: Red Wool Uph./P.C. Base

DESC: Lounge Chair
MFG: LK
PROD: 34–30–UP
SIZE: 34"W. X 30" D.
FINISH: Black Leather Uph.

DESC: Corner Table
MFG: LK
PROD: 3030–26
SIZE: 30"W. X 30"D. X 26"H.
FINISH: Glass/Oiled Walnut

DESC: Coffee Table
MFG: LK
PROD: 3636–17
SIZE: 36"W. X 36"D. X 17"H.
FINISH: Glass/Oiled Walnut

DESC: Planter
MFG: AR
PROD: 2424PC
SIZE: 24"Diam./24"H.
FINISH: P.C.

FIGURE 10–2
Reception Furniture Symbols and Specifications (Scale:1/4″ = 1′-0″)

-ATTDEF and Define Attributes... (ATTDEF)

The -ATTDEF (Attribute Definition) command allows you to add attributes (furniture specifications) to the furniture symbols drawn in plan view using prompts from the command line. Define Attributes... (ATTDEF) allows you to do the same thing using a dialog box. In this exercise you will use both commands. After the attributes are added, a block is made of the symbol. When the block is inserted into a drawing, the specifications appear on the drawing if they have been defined as visible (attributes can be visible or invisible). You can then extract the attribute information from the drawing using the Attribute Extraction dialog box (ATTEXT).

As shown in Figure 10–2, each piece of furniture in the reception area has five attributes. An attribute is made up of two parts, the tag and the value. The tag is used to help define the attribute but does not appear on the inserted drawing. It does appear on the drawing while attributes are being defined and before it is made into a block. The tags on the reception area furnishings are DESC., MFG., PROD., SIZE, and FINISH. The tag is used when the attribute information is extracted from the drawing. The ATTEXT command lists each occurrence of an attribute in the drawing. The attribute tag may contain any characters, but no spaces, and it is automatically converted to uppercase.

The value is the actual specification, such as Reception Desk, LK, 96-66-RL, 96″W × 66″D, and Oiled Walnut. The attribute value may contain any characters, and it may also have spaces. The value appears on the drawing after it is inserted as a block. It appears exactly as it was entered.

There are six optional modes for the value of -ATTDEF; these are set at the beginning of the attribute definition:

Invisible   This value is not displayed on the screen when the block is inserted. You may want to use the Invisible mode for pricing, or you may want to make some attributes invisible so that the drawing does not become cluttered.

Constant   This value is fixed and cannot be changed. For example, if the same chair is used throughout a project but the fabric varies, then the furniture manufacturer value of the chair will be constant, but the finish value will vary. A Constant value cannot be edited.

Verify   This mode allows the value to be variable and allows you to check (verify) the value you have entered. Changes in the value may be entered as needed when the block is inserted. A second set of prompts appears while you are inserting the block. These prompts allow you to verify that the value you entered is correct.

Preset   This mode allows the value to be variable, but the changes are not requested as the block is inserted. It is similar to Constant in that fewer prompts appear. But unlike a Constant value, the Preset value can be changed with ATTEDIT, DDATTE, DDEDIT, and Properties... commands.

Variable   If none of the above modes is selected, the value is Variable. The Variable mode allows the value to be changed and prompts you once when the block is inserted to type any value other than the default value.

Lock Position   This option locks the attribute inside the block. This is useful when dynamic blocks are used as described in Exercise 10–4.

Step 3.   On your own:

1. Keep the 0 Layer current.
2. Zoom in on the reception desk.

FIGURE 10–3
Use -ATTDEF to Define the Attributes of the Reception Desk

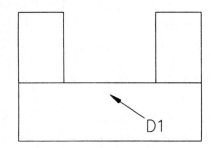

Step 4. Use -ATTDEF to define the attributes of the reception desk. Make all the attributes of the reception desk Constant (Figure 10–3):

Prompt	Response
Command:	TYPE: **-ATT** <enter> (be sure to include the hyphen)
Current attribute modes: Invisible=N Constant=N Verify=N Preset=N Lock position=Y	
Enter an option to change [Invisible/ Constant/Verify/Preset/ Lock position] <done>:	TYPE: **C**<enter> (to set the mode to Constant)
Current attribute modes: Invisible=N Constant=Y Verify=N Preset=N Lock position=Y	
Enter an option to change [Invisible/ Constant/Verify/Preset/ Lock position]<done>: (NOTE: The "N" after Constant has changed to "Y.")	<enter>
Enter attribute tag name:	TYPE: **DESC**<enter>
Enter attribute value:	TYPE: **Reception Desk**<enter>
Specify start point of text or [Justify/Style]:	TYPE: **C**<enter>
Specify center point of text:	**D1** (Figure 10–3)
Specify height <default>:	TYPE: **3**<enter>
Specify rotation angle of text <0>:	<enter>
(The first attribute is complete; the Attribute tag appears on the drawing.)	
Command:	<enter> (repeat -ATTDEF)
Current attribute modes: Invisible=N Constant=Y Verify=N Preset=N Lock position=Y	
Enter an option to change [Invisible/Constant/Verify/Preset/ Lock position] <done>:	<enter> (to keep the Constant mode)
Enter attribute tag name:	TYPE: **MFG**<enter>
Enter attribute value:	TYPE: **LK**<enter>

Prompt	Response
Specify start point of text or [Justify/Style]:	\<enter\> (AutoCAD automatically aligns each new definition below the previous attribute definition)
(The second attribute is complete.)	
Command:	\<enter\> (to return the ATTDEF prompt)
Current attribute modes: Invisible=N Constant=Y Verify=N Preset=N Lock position=Y Enter an option to change [Invisible/Constant/Verify/Preset/Lock position] \<done\>:	\<enter\>
Enter attribute tag name:	TYPE: **PROD**\<enter\>
Enter attribute value:	TYPE: **96-66-RL**\<enter\>
Specify start point of text or [Justify/Style]:	\<enter\>
Command:	\<enter\> (repeat -ATTDEF)
(The third attribute is complete.)	
Current attribute modes: Invisible=N Constant=Y Verify=N Preset=N Lock position=Y Enter an option to change [Invisible/Constant/Verify/Preset/Lock position] \<done\>:	\<enter\>
Enter attribute tag name:	TYPE: **SIZE**\<enter\>
Enter attribute value:	TYPE: **96″W X 66″D**\<enter\>
Specify start point of text or [Justify/Style]:	\<enter\>
(The fourth attribute is complete.)	
Command:	\<enter\>
Current attribute modes: Invisible=N Constant=Y Verify=N Preset=N Lock position=Y Enter an option to change [Invisible/Constant/Verify/Preset/Lock position] \<done\>:	\<enter\>
Enter attribute tag name:	TYPE: **FINISH**\<enter\>
Enter attribute value:	TYPE: **Oiled Walnut**\<enter\>
Specify start point of text or [Justify/Style]:	\<enter\>
(The fifth attribute is complete.)	
Command:	

When you have completed defining the five attributes, your drawing of the reception desk will look similar to the desk in Figure 10–4.

In the next part of this exercise, you will see how the ATTDEF prompts for a Constant attribute differ from an attribute defined with the Verify mode.

FIGURE 10–4
Reception Desk with
Attribute Tags

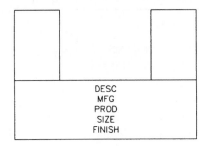

DESC
MFG
PROD
SIZE
FINISH

> **NOTE:** If you are not happy with the location of the Attribute Tags, use the Move command to relocate them before using the Block command.

Step 5. On your own:

1. Keep the 0 Layer current.
2. Zoom in on the corner table.

Step 6. Use -ATTDEF to define the attributes of the corner table. Make the DESC. and MFG. attributes of the corner table Constant, and use the Verify mode for the PROD., SIZE, and FINISH attributes (Figure 10–5):

D1

FIGURE 10–5
Use -ATTDEF to Define the
Attributes of the Corner
Table

Prompt	Response
Command:	TYPE: **-ATT**<enter>
Current attribute modes:	
Invisible=N Constant=Y	
Verify=N Preset=N	
Lock position=Y	
Enter an option to change	
[Invisible/Constant/Verify/Preset/	
Lock position] <done>:	
(*Note:* The "Y" indicates Constant is	
still the current mode.)	<enter>
Enter attribute tag name:	TYPE: **DESC**<enter>
Enter attribute value:	TYPE: **Corner Table**<enter>
Specify start point of text or	
[Justify/Style]:	TYPE: **C**<enter>
Specify center point of text:	**D1** (Figure 10–5)
Specify height <0'-3">:	<enter>
Specify rotation angle of text <0>:	<enter>
(The first attribute is complete;	
the Attribute tag appears on	
the drawing.)	
Command:	<enter> (repeat -ATTDEF)
Current attribute modes:	
Invisible=N Constant=Y	

Prompt	Response
Verify=N Preset=N Lock position=Y Enter an option to change [Invisible/Constant/Verify/Preset/ Lock position] <done>:	<enter> (to keep the Constant mode)
Enter attribute tag name:	TYPE: **MFG**<enter>
Enter attribute value:	TYPE: **LK**<enter>
Specify start point of text or [Justify/Style]:	<enter>
(The second attribute is complete.)	
Command:	<enter>
Current attribute modes: Invisible=N Constant=Y Verify=N Preset=N Lock position=Y	
Enter an option to change [Invisible/Constant/Verify/Preset/ Lock position] <done>:	TYPE: **C**<enter> (to cancel the Constant mode)

 NOTE: The Constant mode must be canceled for the Verify and Pre set modes to function. The Constant mode overrides the other two.

Current attribute modes: Invisible=N Constant=N Verify=N Preset=N Lock position=Y Enter an option to change [Invisible/Constant/Verify/Preset/ Lock position] <done>:	TYPE: **V**<enter> (to set the Verify mode)
Current attribute modes: Invisible=N Constant=N Verify=Y Preset=N Lock position=Y Enter an option to change [Invisible/Constant/Verify/Preset/ Lock position] <done>:	<enter>
Enter attribute tag name:	TYPE: **PROD**<enter>
Enter attribute prompt:	TYPE: **Enter product number**<enter>

 NOTE: The "Attribute prompt:" line will say whatever you want it to say.

Enter default attribute value:	TYPE: **30-30-26**<enter>
Specify start point of text or [Justify/Style]:	<enter>

Prompt	Response
(The third attribute is complete.)	
Command:	\<enter>
Current attribute modes:	
Invisible=N Constant=N	
Verify=Y Preset=N Lock position=Y	
Enter an option to change	
[Invisible/Constant/Verify/Preset/	
Lock position] \<done>:	\<enter>
Enter attribute tag name:	TYPE: **SIZE**\<enter>
Enter attribute prompt:	TYPE: **Enter product size**\<enter>
Enter default attribute value:	TYPE: **30″W X 30″D X 26″H**\<enter>
Specify start point of text or	
[Justify/Style]:	\<enter>
(The fourth attribute is complete.)	
Command:	\<enter>
Current attribute modes:	
Invisible=N Constant=N	
Verify=Y Preset=N	
Lock position=Y	
Enter an option to change	
[Invisible/Constant/Verify/Preset/	
Lock position] \<done>:	\<enter>
Enter attribute tag name:	TYPE: **FINISH**\<enter>
Enter attribute prompt:	TYPE: **Enter product finish**\<enter>
Enter default attribute value:	TYPE: **Glass/Oiled Walnut**\<enter>
Specify start point of text or	
[Justify/Style]:	\<enter>
(The fifth attribute is complete.)	
Command:	

When the attribute mode is set to Verify, two additional prompts appear—"Attribute prompt:" and "Default attribute value:". The attribute prompt information that is typed and entered will appear when the block of the corner table is inserted into the drawing; it will appear and prompt you to enter the product finish, size, and number. The default attribute value appears if a different value is not typed and entered. These prompts do not appear while you are defining Constant attributes, because a Constant attribute value cannot vary.

In the following part of this exercise, you will use ATTDEF and notice that the prompts for the Variable and Preset modes are the same as for the Verify mode. If none of the modes—Constant, Verify, or Preset—is set, the mode is Variable. You will also use the Invisible mode to define attributes.

FIGURE 10–6
Use ATTDEF to Define the Attributes of the Secretarial Chair

Step 7. **On your own:**

1. **Keep the 0 Layer current.**
2. **Zoom in on the secretarial chair.**
3. **If you need to, rotate your secretarial chair to appear oriented like the chair in Figure 10–6.**

FIGURE 10–7
Defining the First Attribute
for the Secretarial Chair

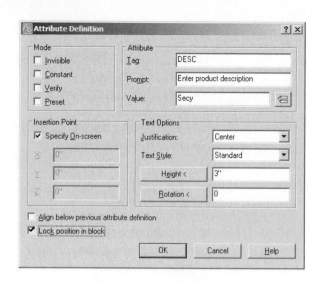

Step 8. Use Define Attributes... (ATTDEF) to define the attributes of the secretarial chair. Make the DESC. and MFG. attributes of the secretarial chair variable. Use the Preset and Invisible modes for the PROD., SIZE, and FINISH attributes (Figures 10–6, 10–7, 10–8, 10–9, 10–10, and 10–11):

Prompt	Response
Command: The Attribute Definition dialog box appears:	**Define Attributes...** or TYPE: **ATT\<enter\>** **Clear all the checks in the Mode area** (the attribute will now be variable) TYPE: **DESC** in the Tag: box TYPE: **Enter product description** in the Prompt: box TYPE: **Secy** in the Value: box CLICK: **the down arrow** in the Justification: box and CLICK: **Center**

All other parts of the dialog box should be as shown in Figure 10–7.

 NOTE: The icon to the right of the value is the Insert field command, which allows you to insert dates, sheet numbers, and many other commonly used items.

Prompt	Response
	CLICK: **OK**
Specify start point: The first attribute is complete; the Attribute Tag appears on the drawing. Command:	**D1** (Figure 10–6) **\<enter\>** (repeat ATTDEF)

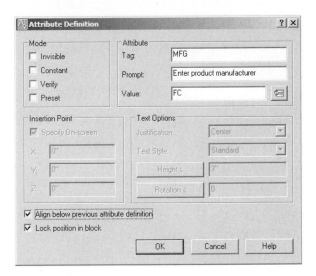

FIGURE 10-8
Defining the Second Attribute for the Secretarial Chair

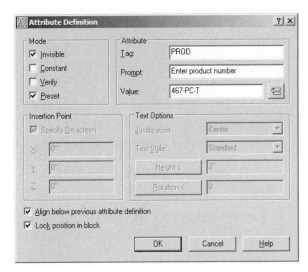

FIGURE 10-9
Defining the Third Attribute for the Secretarial Chair

Prompt	Response
The Attribute Definition dialog box appears:	Complete the dialog box as shown in Figure 10–8. Notice that the Align below previous attribute definition button is checked, so the Insertion Point and Text Options areas are grayed out. CLICK: **OK**
The second attribute is complete; the Attribute Tag appears on the drawing aligned below the first attribute. Command:	<enter> (repeat ATTDEF)
The Attribute Definition dialog box appears:	Complete the dialog box as shown in Figure 10–9. Notice that the Align below previous attribute definition button is checked again and that the Preset and Invisible modes are checked. CLICK: **OK**
The third attribute is complete; the Attribute Tag appears on the drawing aligned below the second attribute. Command:	<enter> (repeat ATTDEF)
The Attribute Definition dialog box appears:	Complete the dialog box as shown in Figure 10–10. Notice that the Align below previous attribute definition button is checked again and that the Preset and Invisible modes are checked. CLICK: **OK**

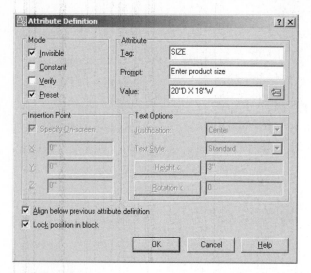

FIGURE 10–10
Defining the Fourth Attribute for the Secretarial Chair

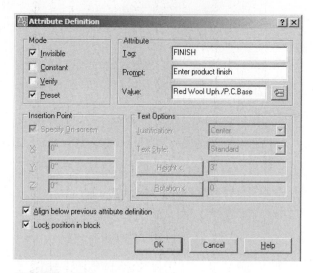

FIGURE 10–11
Defining the Fifth Attribute for the Secretarial Chair

Prompt	Response
The fourth attribute is complete; the Attribute Tag appears on the drawing aligned below the third attribute.	
Command:	**\<enter\>** (repeat ATTDEF)
The Attribute Definition dialog box appears:	**Complete the dialog box as shown in Figure 10–11. Notice that the Align below previous attribute definition button is checked again and that the Preset and Invisible modes are checked.**
	CLICK: **OK**
The fifth attribute is complete; the Attribute Tag appears on the drawing aligned below the fourth attribute.	

Edit Text (DDEDIT)

Did you make a mistake while responding to the "Attribute tag," "Attribute prompt," or "Default attribute value" prompts? The Edit Text command allows you to use the Edit Attribute Definition dialog box (Figure 10–12) to correct any typing mistakes you may have made while defining the attributes. The Edit Text prompt is "Select an

FIGURE 10–12
Edit Attribute Definition
Dialog Box

Edit Attribute Definition	? ×
Tag:	SIZE
Prompt:	Enter product size
Default:	20"D X 18"W

OK   Cancel   Help

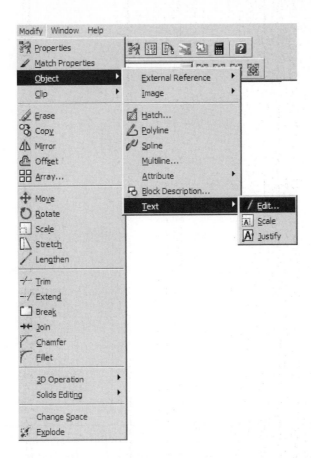

annotation object or [Undo]:". When you pick a tag, the Edit Attribute Definition dialog box appears and allows you to change the attribute tag, prompt, or default value for a Variable, Verify, or Preset attribute. The tag and the default (actually the Value) can be changed for a Constant attribute; adding a prompt for an attribute defined as Constant does not change the attribute mode, and the prompt does not appear.

 TIP: You can double-click any attribute tag to activate the Edit Attribute Definition dialog box.

The Edit Text command can be used only before the symbol is made into a block.

Step 9. On your own:

1. Use Wblock to save the reception desk as a Wblock (a drawing). Save the Wblock to a disk, a CD, or the drive you are working in. Name the Wblock RDSK. Use the insertion base point as shown in Figure 10–13. Have the desk oriented as shown in Figure 10–13.

2. Use Wblock to save the corner table as a Wblock (a drawing). Save the Wblock to a disk, a CD, or the drive you are working in. Name the Wblock CRTBL. Use the insertion base point as shown in Figure 10–13. If the table was drawn on snap, you can use the snap point of the two sides of the table as if they met at a 90° angle.

FIGURE 10–13
Save the Reception Desk and
the Corner Table as a Wblock
(a Drawing) on a Disk

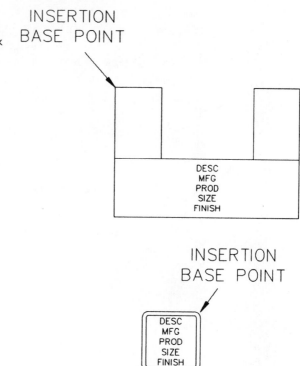

3. Use Wblock to save the secretarial chair as a Wblock. Save the Wblock to a disk, a CD, or the drive you are working in. Name the block SECY. Pick the center of the chair as the insertion base point.

Inserting a Block with Attributes—Using the Command: Prompt Line

The Insert command is used to insert the blocks with attributes into the tenant space floor plan. Let's insert the reception desk into the drawing. Remember, all five attribute values were defined as Constant. They will appear on the drawing as you entered them.

Step 10. Set the A-furn Layer current.

Step 11. Use the Insert command to insert the RDSK block into the tenant space floor plan. Use the ID command to help position the block (Figure 10–14):

Prompt	Response
Command:	TYPE: **ID<enter>**
Specify point:	**Osnap-Intersection**
of	**D1**
ID Point: Int of	
X = 49'-0" Y = 12'-0" Z = 0'-0"	
Command:	**Insert-Block...** (or TYPE: **I<enter>**)
The Insert dialog box appears:	CLICK: **Browse...**
The Select Drawing File dialog box	
appears:	LOCATE **and** CLICK: **the RDSK drawing file**
	CLICK: **Open**

FIGURE 10–14
Use the Insert Command to
Insert the RDSK Block into
the Tenant Space Floor Plan

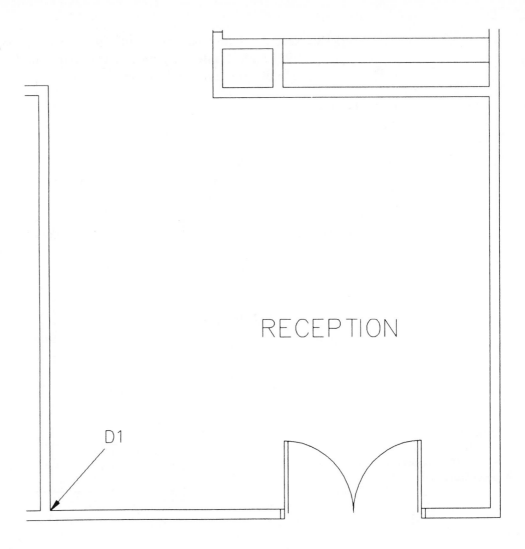

RECEPTION

D1

Prompt	Response
The Insert dialog box appears with RDSK in the Name: box:	**Place a check mark in the two Specify On-screen boxes for Insertion Point and Rotation.** CLICK: **OK**
Specify insertion point or [Basepoint/ Scale/Rotate/PScale/PRotate]:	TYPE: **@24,30<enter>**
Specify rotation angle <0>:	TYPE: **90<enter>** (the RDSK block is inserted; the Values appear on the block)

Next, you will insert the corner table into the drawing. Remember, the Description and Manufacturer attribute values of the corner table were defined with the Constant mode. The Product, Size, and Finish attribute values were defined with the Verify mode. The prompts entered during the ATTDEF command for the values defined with Verify will appear while you insert the CRTBL block. Those prompts allow you to change the attribute value or accept the Default attribute value that was also entered during the ATTDEF command.

Step 12. Keep the A-furn Layer current. Use the Insert command to insert the CRTBL block into the tenant space floor plan. Use the From option to help position the block (Figure 10–15):

Prompt	Response
Command:	Insert-Block... (or TYPE: **I**<enter>)
The Insert dialog box appears:	CLICK: **Browse...**
The Select Drawing File dialog box appears:	LOCATE **and** CLICK: **the CRTBL drawing file**
	CLICK: **Open**
The Insert dialog box appears with CRTBL in the Name: box:	**Place a check mark in the two Specify On-screen boxes for Insertion point and Rotation.**
	CLICK: **OK**
Specify insertion point or [Basepoint/ Scale/Rotate/PScale/PRotate]:	TYPE: **FRO**<enter>
Base point:	**Osnap-Intersection**
of	**D1**
<Offset>	TYPE: **@-2,-2**<enter>

FIGURE 10–15
Use the Insert Command to Insert the CRTBL Block into the Tenant Space Floor Plan

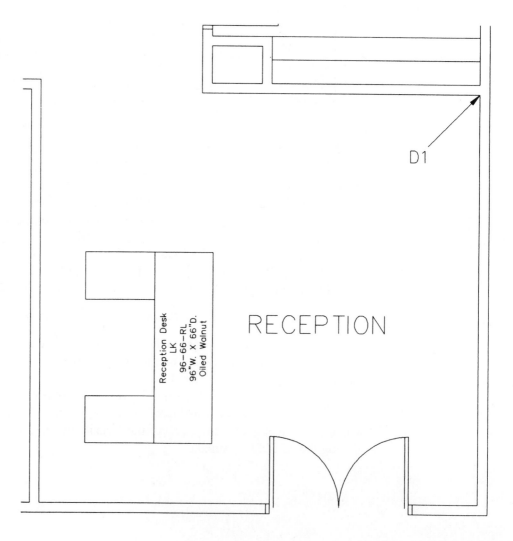

Reception Desk
LK
96–66–RL
96"W. x 66"D.
Oiled Walnut

RECEPTION

D1

Prompt	Response
Specify scale factor <1>:	<enter>
Enter attribute values enter product finish <Glass/Oiled Walnut>:	<enter> (to accept the default)
enter product size <30″W × 30″D × 26″H>:	<enter>
enter product number <30-30-26>:	<enter>
Verify attribute values enter product finish <Glass/Oiled Walnut>:	<enter>
enter product size <30″W × 30″D × 26″H>:	<enter>
enter product number <30-30-26>:	<enter>

 TIP: If you are not happy with a Block location after insertion, use the Move command to relocate it.

Some of the values that appeared on the corner table are too long; they go outside the table symbol. We will fix this later in the exercise with the ATTEDIT command.

When you insert a block with attributes defined using the Verify mode, you may type and enter a new value or accept the default value at the first prompt. A second prompt appears, allowing you to verify that the attribute values you entered by accepting the default or typing from the keyboard are correct.

Inserting a Block with Attributes—Using an Enter Attributes Dialog Box

The Enter Attributes dialog box (Figure 10–16) can be used to insert blocks with attributes. The dialog box allows you to change or accept the default values of the attributes you defined using the Variable, Verify, or Preset modes. Its appearance is controlled by the ATTDIA system variable.

Step 13. Set the ATTDIA system variable to 1 to make the dialog box appear while you insert blocks with attributes:

Prompt	Response
Command:	TYPE: **ATTDIA**<enter>
Enter new value for ATTDIA <0>:	TYPE: **1**<enter>

Insert the secretarial chair into the drawing. Remember, the DESC and MFG attributes were defined as Variable, and PROD, SIZE, and FINISH attributes were defined as Preset and Invisible.

FIGURE 10–16
Edit Attributes Dialog Box

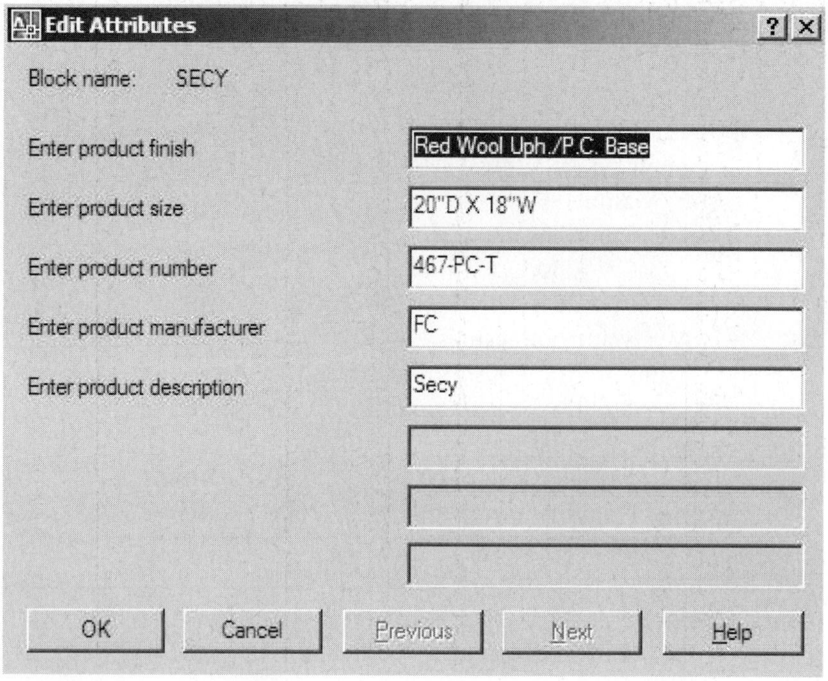

Step 14. Keep the A-furn Layer current. Use the Insert command to insert the SECY block into the tenant space reception area:

Prompt	Response
Command:	**Insert Block...** (or TYPE: **I<enter>**)
The Insert dialog box appears:	CLICK: **Browse...**
The Select Drawing File dialog box appears:	LOCATE and CLICK: **the SECY drawing file**
	CLICK: **Open**
The Insert dialog box appears with SECY in the Name: box.	CLICK: **OK**
Specify insertion point or [Basepoint/ Scale/X/Y/Z/Rotate]:	**The block is dragged in with the crosshair on the insertion point of the chair. CLICK: a point behind the reception desk close to the location of the center of the chair.**
Specify rotation angle <0>:	**<enter>**
(The Edit Attributes dialog box appears, Figure 10–16)	CLICK: **OK**

The last three attributes, because they were defined using the Invisible mode, are not visible on the inserted chair.

Using the dialog box, you may change the values for attributes defined using the Verify, Preset, or Variable modes. Prompts do not appear in the Command: prompt area for the values defined with the Preset mode, but with a dialog box, the Preset mode values can be changed as they are inserted.

NOTE: The Preset ATTDEF mode is used to eliminate prompts and save time but still allows you to edit the attributes after insertion.

Attribute Display (ATTDISP)

The Attribute Display (ATTDISP) command allows you to turn on the Invisible attributes of the secretarial chair. The prompt is "Enter attribute visibility setting [Normal/ON/ OFF] <OFF>:".

ON   Pick ON to make the Invisible attributes appear. Try this, and you will be able to see the Invisible attributes of the secretarial chair.

OFF   Pick OFF to make all the attributes on the drawing Invisible. Try this, and you will see that all the attributes are not visible.

Normal   Pick Normal to make visible attributes defined as Visible and to make invisible attributes defined as Invisible. Set Normal as the default.

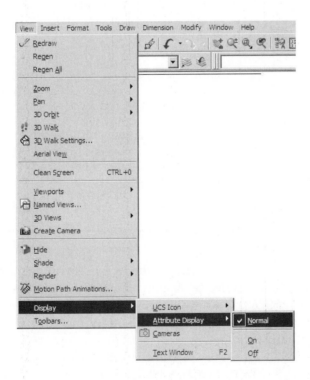

Modify-Object-Attribute-Single

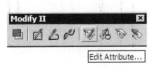

The Modify-Object-Attribute-Single command uses the Enhanced Attribute Editor dialog box (Figure 10–17) to edit Variable, Verify, and Preset Attributes values of an inserted block. Attributes defined with the Constant mode cannot be edited.

Some of the values on the corner table are too long. Let's use the Modify-Object-Attribute-Single command to make them shorter.

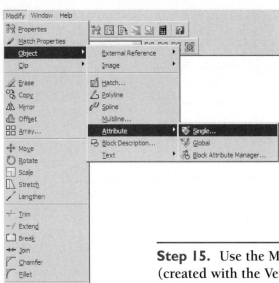

FIGURE 10–17
Enhanced Attribute Editor Dialog Box

Step 15. Use the Modify-Object-Attribute-Single command to edit the values (created with the Verify mode) on the inserted corner table:

Prompt	Response
Command:	**Modify-Object-Attribute-Single** (or TYPE: **EATTEDIT<enter>**)
Select a block: The Enhanced Attribute Editor dialog box appears.	PICK: **any place on the corner table.** Use the dialog box to insert the following two new values: (highlight the attribute, then change the value in the Value: text box, then CLICK: Apply) Enter product finish: **GL/O.W.** Enter product size..: **30X30X26** CLICK: **OK**

The values that appear on the corner table now fit within the table symbol.

Step 16. On your own:

1. Set the 0 Layer current. Use the Define Attributes... command to add to the lounge chair, coffee table, and planter the attributes shown in Figure 10–2. Make each attribute Variable and Visible. Set the text height at 3″. Refer to the inserted blocks in Figure 10–18 for the value text (may be abbreviated to fit) and location.
2. Use Wblock to save the lounge chair, coffee table, and planter as blocks. Name the blocks LGCH, CFTBL, and PLANT. Look at the location of each inserted block in Figure 10–18, and select a point for the insertion base point of each block.
3. Set the A-furn Layer current. Use the Insert command to complete the insertion of all furniture in the tenant space reception area. Changing the SNAP setting to 2″ may help with insertion of the blocks. Remember, once a block is inserted, it can be moved to a new location.

Modify-Object-Attribute-Global (-ATTEDIT-Attribute Edit)

The Modify-Object-Attribute-Global (Attribute Edit) command allows you to edit inserted attribute values, independent of their block reference. It allows you to edit

FIGURE 10–18
Tenant Space Reception Area
(Scale: 1/4″ = 1′-0″)

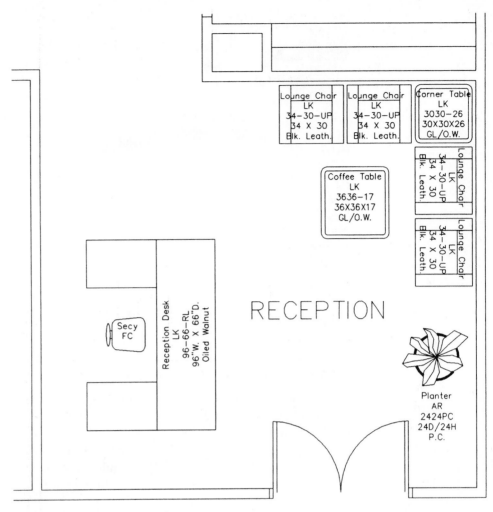

one at a time the text string, text string position, text height, text angle, text style, layer, or color of inserted attribute values. It also provides prompts that allow you globally to edit the value text strings of many attributes all at once. Constant values cannot be edited.

The Modify-Object-Attribute-Global prompts allow you to narrow the value selection by entering a specific block name, tag specification, and value specification.

Only visible attributes can be edited when you respond with "Yes" to the prompt "Edit attributes one at a time?". If you respond with "No" to the prompt, visible and invisible attribute value text strings can be edited.

Let's use the Modify-Object-Attribute-Global command to edit all at once a value on the four lounge chairs.

Step 17. **Use the Modify-Object-Attribute-Global command to edit the text string of the finish value on all the chairs at once:**

Prompt	Response
Command:	**Modify-Object-Attribute-Global** (or TYPE: **-ATTEDIT**<enter>)
Edit attributes one at a time? [Yes/No] <Y>	TYPE: **N**<enter>
Edit only attributes visible on screen? [Yes/No] <Y>	<enter>

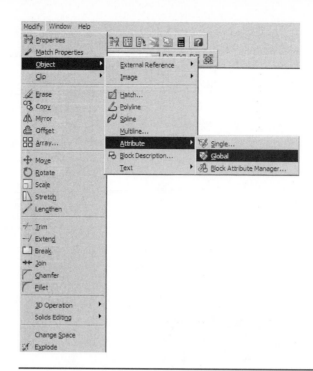

Prompt	Response
Enter block name specification <*>:	TYPE: **LGCH<enter>**
Enter attribute tag specification <*>:	TYPE: **FINISH<enter>**
Enter attribute value specification <*>:	TYPE: **Black Leather Uph. <enter>**
Select Attributes:	**Window all four chairs and the coffee table<enter>**
4 attributes selected.	
Enter string to change:	TYPE: **Black Leather Uph. <enter>**
Enter new string:	TYPE: **Brwn. Leath.<enter>**

When you use this option of the Modify-Object-Attribute-Global command, the wild-card character "*" is interpreted literally by AutoCAD, so it cannot be used. Type and enter the block name, tag, and value exactly. You may also enter "No" in response to the prompt "Edit only attributes visible on screen?" and invisible attribute values may also be changed.

ATTREDEF

Any drawing defined as a block with the Wblock command and inserted into a drawing then becomes available for use as a block in the current drawing. Once inserted, these blocks are similar to blocks defined with the Block command.

The ATTREDEF command allows you to redefine a block within the drawing and updates all previous insertions of the block in your drawing. In the following part of this exercise, the LGCH block will be redefined. Before redefining the block, you must complete a new definition of the block attributes.

Step 18. On your own:

1. Select "?" from the Command: line Block prompt (TYPE: -B<enter>), and view the list of blocks available within the drawing.
2. Set 0 Layer current.

Part II: Two-Dimensional AutoCAD

3. Insert a copy of the LGCH block in an open space in the tenant space drawing.
4. Explode the LGCH block and erase the tags.
5. Use the ATTDEF command to create the following new attributes. Make all the attributes variable.

Tag	Value
DESC	Lnge. Ch.
MFG	FC
PROD	34-30-UP
UPH	Nat. Leath.

Step 19. Use ATTREDEF to redefine the LGCH block:

Prompt	Response
Command:	TYPE: **ATTREDEF<enter>**
Enter name of block you wish to redefine:	TYPE: **LGCH<enter>**
Select objects for new Block…	
Select objects:	**Window the newly drawn lounge chair.**
Other corner: 11 found	
Select objects:	**<enter>**
Specify insertion base point of new Block:	**Select the same insertion base point you previously selected.**

TIP: Be consistent with the position of the "Insertion base point" location of the furniture symbol blocks. For example, always pick up the upper right or upper left corner. This helps you to remember the "Insertion base point" location when inserting the furniture symbols. It is especially necessary to be consistent when using ATTREDEF so the newly redefined block is oriented correctly.

The drawing is regenerated and all previous insertions of the LGCH block are redefined (Figure 10–19). The values on the block may not have changed exactly as you thought they would. When ATTREDEF is used to redefine a block:

1. New attributes to existing block references are given their default values.
2. Old attributes to existing block references retain their old values.
3. Old attributes not included in the new block definition are deleted from the existing block references.

The shape of the block can also be changed with ATTREDEF. If the lounge chair needed to be smaller, it could have been redrawn before you redefined the block. Future insertions of the block will use the redefined variable attribute tags and values.

FIGURE 10–19
Redefined LGCH Block

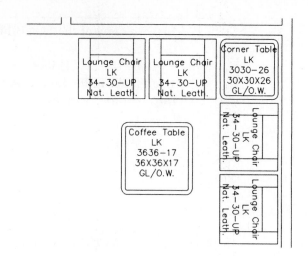

Redefining an Inserted Block with Attributes Using the Block Command

As described in Chapter 7, you can redefine a block using the Block command. When a block that has attributes assigned is redefined using the Block command, previous insertions of the block are affected as follows:

1. Old constant attributes are lost, replaced by new constant attributes, if any.
2. Variable attributes remain unchanged, even if the new block definition does not include those attributes.
3. New variable attributes are not added.

Future insertions of the block will use the new attributes. The previous insertions of the block must be erased and inserted again to use the new attributes.

Step 20. On your own:

1. Set the 0 Layer current. Draw the remaining furniture symbols as shown in Figures 10–20 through 10–24 for the tenant space. Be sure to note furniture pieces that are repeated, and draw them only once. For example, the planter and secretarial chair symbols have already been drawn, attributes have been added, and a block has been made.

```
DESC:    Conference Table
MFG:     LK
PROD:    108-42B/PC
SIZE:    108" X 42"
FINISH:  Oiled Walnut
```

```
DESC:    Conference Chair
MFG:     FC
PROD:    T36-LB
SIZE:    26"W. X 26"D.
FINISH:  Red Wool Uph./P.C. Base
```

FIGURE 10–20
Conference Room Furniture Symbols and Specifications (Scale: 1/4″ = 1′-0″)

TENANT SPACE — OFFICE 1 and OFFICE 2

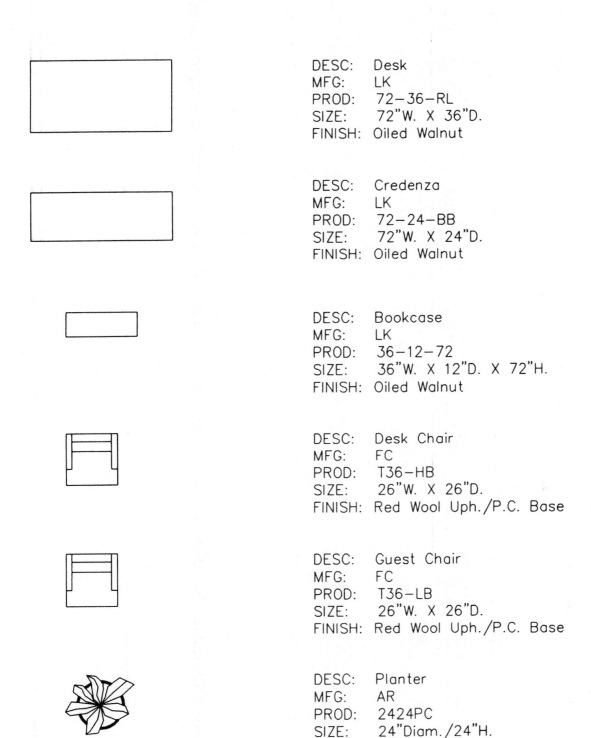

DESC: Desk
MFG: LK
PROD: 72—36—RL
SIZE: 72"W. X 36"D.
FINISH: Oiled Walnut

DESC: Credenza
MFG: LK
PROD: 72—24—BB
SIZE: 72"W. X 24"D.
FINISH: Oiled Walnut

DESC: Bookcase
MFG: LK
PROD: 36—12—72
SIZE: 36"W. X 12"D. X 72"H.
FINISH: Oiled Walnut

DESC: Desk Chair
MFG: FC
PROD: T36—HB
SIZE: 26"W. X 26"D.
FINISH: Red Wool Uph./P.C. Base

DESC: Guest Chair
MFG: FC
PROD: T36—LB
SIZE: 26"W. X 26"D.
FINISH: Red Wool Uph./P.C. Base

DESC: Planter
MFG: AR
PROD: 2424PC
SIZE: 24"Diam./24"H.
FINISH: P.C.

FIGURE 10–21
Office 1 and Office 2 Furniture Symbols and Specifications (Scale: 1/4″ = 1′-0″)

TENANT SPACE — OFFICE 3

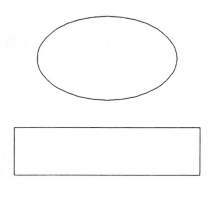

DESC: Table Desk
MFG: LK
PROD: 72—42
SIZE: 72"W. X 42"D.
FINISH: Oiled Walnut

DESC: Credenza
MFG: LK
PROD: 96—24—BFFB
SIZE: 96"W. X 24"D.
FINISH: Oiled Walnut

DESC: Bookcase
MFG: LK
PROD: 36—12—72
SIZE: 36"W. X 12"D. X 72"H.
FINISH: Oiled Walnut

DESC: Desk Chair
MFG: FC
PROD: T36—HB
SIZE: 26"W. X 26"D.
FINISH: Black Leather

DESC: Guest Chair
MFG: FC
PROD: T36—LB
SIZE: 26"W. X 26"D.
FINISH: Black Leather

DESC: Planter
MFG: AR
PROD: 2424PC
SIZE: 24"Diam./24"H.
FINISH: P.C.

FIGURE 10–22
Office 3 Furniture Symbols and Specifications (Scale: 1/4" = 1'-0")

TENANT SPACE – BOOKKEEPING

DESC: Panel
MFG: TK
PROD: T4812TS
SIZE: 48" X 2" X 62"H.
FINISH: Rose Fabric

DESC: Panel
MFG: TK
PROD: T3612TS
SIZE: 36" X 2" X 62"H.
FINISH: Rose Fabric

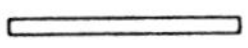

DESC: Panel
MFG: TK
PROD: T3012TS
SIZE: 30" X 2" X 62"H.
FINISH: Rose Fabric

DESC: Panel
MFG: TK
PROD: T2412TS
SIZE: 24" X 2" X 62"H.
FINISH: Rose Fabric

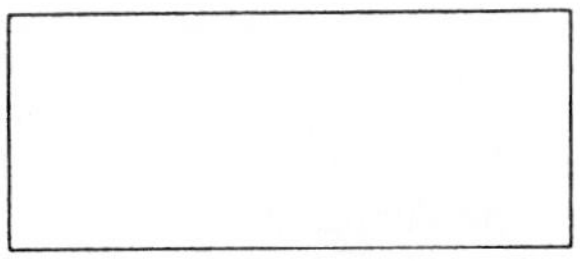

DESC: Work Surface
MFG: TK
PROD: 7230HS
SIZE: 72" X 30"D.
FINISH: Tan

DESC: Work Surface
MFG: TK
PROD: 4824HS
SIZE: 48" X 24"D.
FINISH: Tan

FIGURE 10–23
Bookkeeping Furniture Symbols and Specifications (Scale: 1/4″ = 1′-0″)

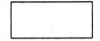

DESC: Lateral File
MFG: TK
PROD: 42185DRW
SIZE: 42" X 18" X 62"H.
FINISH: Tan

DESC: Lateral File
MFG: TK
PROD: 36185DRW
SIZE: 36" X 18" X 62"H.
FINISH: Tan

DESC: Sec. Chair
MFG: FC
PROD: 467—PC—T
SIZE: 20"D. X 18"W.
FINISH: Red Wool Uph./P.C. Base

FIGURE 10–23 *continued*

2. Use the -ATTDEF command to add the attributes shown in Figure 10–20 through 10–24 to the furniture symbols. Make all attributes Variable. Make all the attributes Visible, except the attributes of the bookkeeping systems panels, which need to be Invisible. Set the Text height at 3". Refer to the inserted blocks in Figure 10–25 for the value text (may be abbreviated to fit) and location.

TIP: To save time while using the -ATTDEF command, press the Enter key at the "Attribute prompt:" prompt line. The Attribute prompt will then automatically be the same as the tag.

3. Use Wblock to save the new furniture symbols as blocks. Create a name for each new block. Look at the location of each inserted block in Figure 10–25, and select a point for the insertion base point of each block.
4. Set the A-furn Layer current, and use the Insert command to complete the insertion of all furniture symbols in the tenant space reception plan.

TIP: If the furniture symbols are inserted on the wrong layer, use the Properties... command to change the symbols to the correct layer.

TENANT SPACE — PRESIDENT

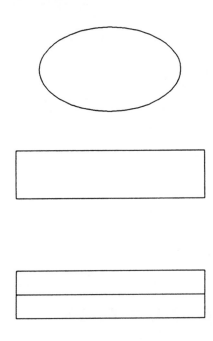

DESC: Table Desk
MFG: LK
PROD: 72—42
SIZE: 72"W. X 42"D.
FINISH: Oiled Walnut

DESC: Credenza
MFG: LK
PROD: 96—24—BFFB
SIZE: 96"W. X 24"D.
FINISH: Oiled Walnut

DESC: Cabinet
MFG: LK
PROD: 96—24—BK
SIZE: 96"W. X 24"D. X 72"H.
FINISH: Oiled Walnut

DESC: Desk Chair
MFG: FC
PROD: T36—HB
SIZE: 26"W. X 26"D.
FINISH: Brown Leather

DESC: Guest Chair
MFG: FC
PROD: T36—LB
SIZE: 26"W. X 26"D.
FINISH: Brown Leather

DESC: Planter
MFG: AR
PROD: 2424PC
SIZE: 24"Diam./24"H.
FINISH: P.C.

DESC: Corner Table
MFG: LK
PROD: 3030—26
SIZE: 30"W. X 30"D. X 26"H.
FINISH: Glass/Oiled Walnut

FIGURE 10–24
President's Furniture Symbols and Specifications (Scale: 1/4″ = 1′-0″)

TENANT SPACE – PRESIDENT (CONT.)

DESC: Coffee Table
MFG: LK
PROD: 3636–17
SIZE: 36"W. X 36"D. X 17"H.
FINISH: Glass/Oiled Walnut

DESC   Lounge Chair
MFG: FC
PROD: 3430UP
FINISH: Brown Leather

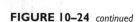

FIGURE 10–24 *continued*

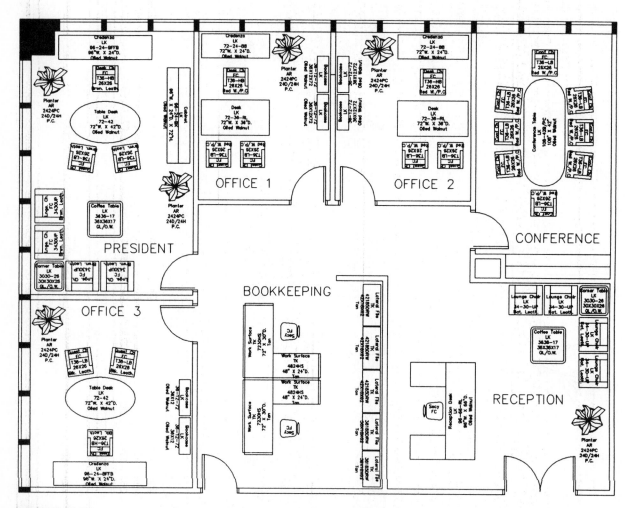

FIGURE 10–25
Exercise 10–1: Tenant Space Furniture Plan with Furniture Specifications (Scale: 1/8" = 1'-0")

Extracting Attributes

The Attribute Extraction wizard in AutoCAD 2007 can be used to produce a parts list or bill of materials directly from a drawing that contains blocks with attributes. The drawing you made in this chapter is an excellent example of this type of drawing. With the Attribute Extraction Wizard you can extract existing attributes and create a table as described in Exercise 10–2.

Step 21. When you have completed Exercise 10–1, save your work in at least two places.

Step 22. Use a Layout Wizard or Page Setup Manager to create a layout tab named Furniture Plan. Plot or print Exercise 10–1 to scale.

Exercise 10–2: Extracting Attributes from the Tenant Space Furniture Plan

When you have completed Exercise 10-2, your drawing will look similar to Figure 10–26.

Step 1. Begin drawing CH10-EX2 on the hard drive or network drive by opening existing drawing CH10-EX1 and saving it as CH10–EX2.

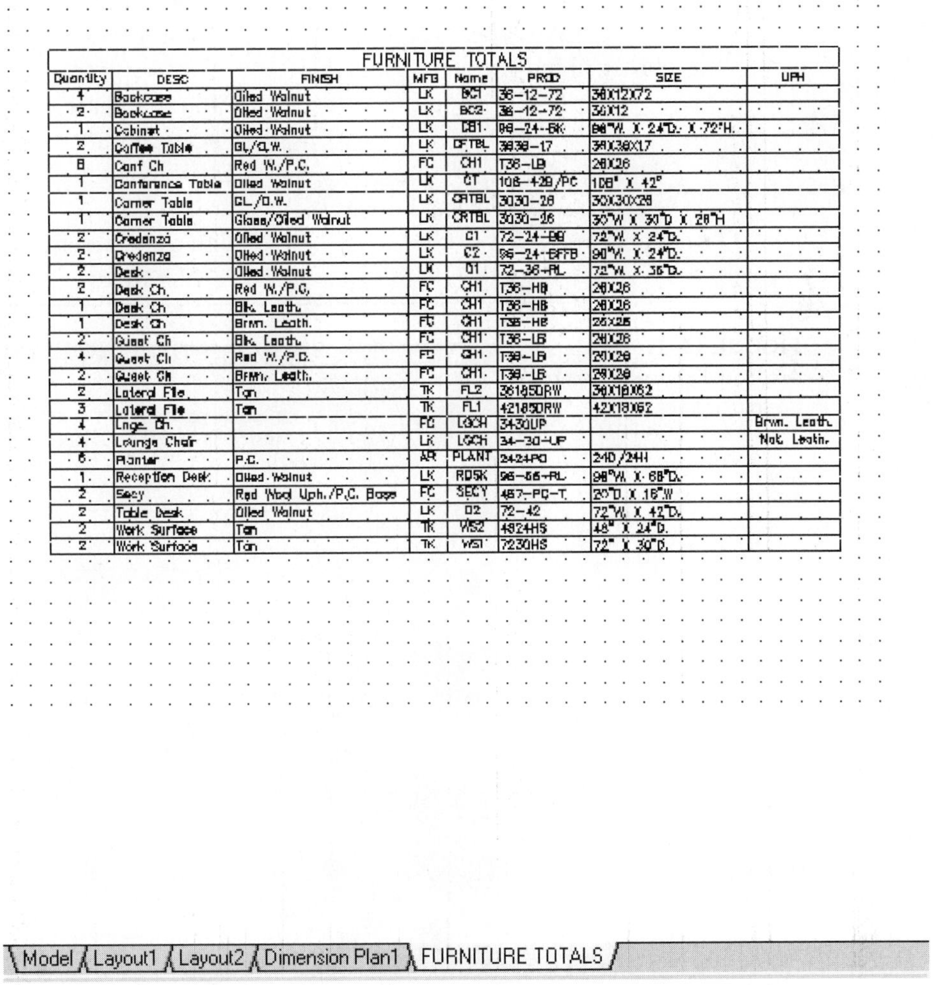

FIGURE 10–26
Exercise 10–2, Complete

FURNITURE TOTALS

Quantity	DESC	FINISH	MFG	Name	PROD	SIZE	UPH
4	Bookcase	Oiled Walnut	LK	BC1	36–12–72	36X12X72	
2	Bookcase	Oiled Walnut	LK	BC2	36–12–72	36X12	
1	Cabinet	Oiled Walnut	LK	CB1	96–24–6K	96"W. X 24"D. X 72"H.	
2	Coffee Table	GL/O.W.	LK	CFTBL	3636–17	36X36X17	
8	Conf Ch	Red W./P.C.	FC	CH1	T36–LB	26X26	
1	Conference Table	Oiled Walnut	LK	CT	108–42B/PC	108" X 42°	
1	Corner Table	GL./O.W.	LK	CRTBL	3030–28	30X30X28	
1	Corner Table	Glass/Oiled Walnut	LK	CRTBL	3030–28	30"W X 30"D X 28"H	
2	Credenza	Oiled Walnut	LK	C1	72–24–96	72"W. X 24"D.	
2	Credenza	Oiled Walnut	LK	C2	96–24–6FFB	96"W. X 24"D.	
2	Desk	Oiled Walnut	LK	D1	72–36–RL	72"W. X 36"D.	
2	Desk Ch.	Red W./P.C.	FC	CH1	T36–HB	26X26	
1	Desk Ch	Blk. Leath.	FC	CH1	T36–HB	26X26	
1	Desk Ch	Brwn. Leath.	FC	CH1	T36–HB	26X26	
2	Guest Ch	Blk. Leath.	FC	CH1	T36–LB	26X26	
4	Guest Ch	Red W./P.C.	FC	CH1	T36–LB	20X26	
2	Guest Ch	Brwn. Leath.	FC	CH1	T36–LB	26X26	
2	Lateral File	Tan	TK	FL2	361850RW	36X18X62	
3	Lateral File	Tan	TK	FL1	421850RW	42X18X62	
4	Lnge. Ch.		FC	LGCH	3430UP		Brwn. Leath.
4	Lounge Chair		LK	LGCH	34–30–UP		Nat Leath.
6	Planter	P.C.	AR	PLANT	2424PO	24D /24H	
1	Reception Desk	Oiled Walnut	LK	RDSK	96–66–RL	96"W. X 66"D.	
2	Secy	Red Wool Uph./P.C. Base	FC	SECY	467–PC–T.	20"D. X 16"W	
2	Table Desk	Oiled Walnut	LK	D2	72–42	72"W. X 42"D.	
2	Work Surface	Tan	TK	WS2	4824HS	48" X 24"D.	
2	Work Surface	Tan	TK	WS1	7230HS	72" X 30"D.	

Model / Layout1 / Layout2 / Dimension Plan1 \ FURNITURE TOTALS /

Step 2. On your own:

Prepare the drawing to accept the extracted attributes in a tabular form as follows:

1. Make a new layout using the Create Layout Wizard (on the Insert menu):

   Name it FURNITURE TOTALS.
   CLICK: **Letter (8.5″×11″)** for the page size.
   CLICK: **Landscape** for the orientation.
   CLICK: **None** for the Title Block.
   CLICK: **Single** for the Viewports.
   CLICK: **Next >** for Pick Locations
   CLICK: **Finish**

2. Select the viewport border and erase this viewport created on the new layout so this layout will contain nothing but the table with the extracted attributes (Figure 10–26).

3. Make sure the FURNITURE TOTALS layout is selected, to continue.

Step 3. Extract attributes from this drawing using the Attribute Extraction... command and create a table on the blank FURNITURE TOTALS layout (Figures 10–27, 10–28, 10–29, and 10–30):

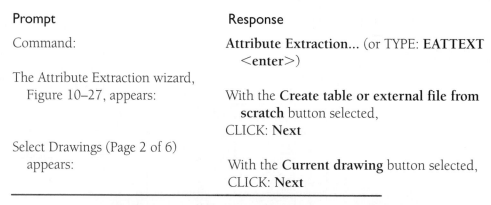

Prompt	Response
Command:	**Attribute Extraction...** (or TYPE: **EATTEXT** <enter>)
The Attribute Extraction wizard, Figure 10–27, appears:	With the **Create table or external file from scratch** button selected, CLICK: **Next**
Select Drawings (Page 2 of 6) appears:	With the **Current drawing** button selected, CLICK: **Next**

FIGURE 10–27
Attribute Extraction Wizard -
Begin (Page 1 of 6)

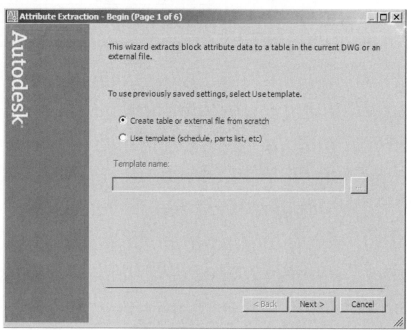

FIGURE 10–28
Attribute Extraction - Select
Attributes (Page 3 of 6)

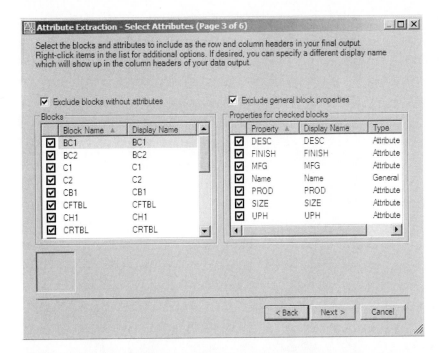

FIGURE 10–29
Attribute Extraction -
Finalize Output (Page 4 of 6)
Sort Ascending the DEC
Column to Put the List in
Alphabetical Order

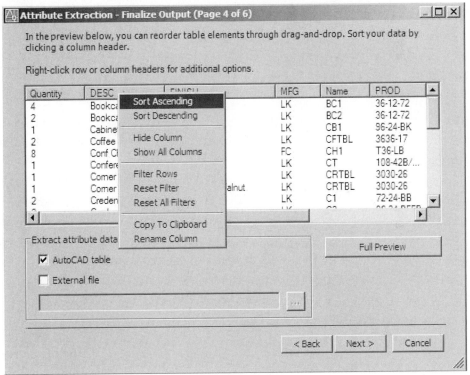

Prompt	Response
Select Attributes (Page 3 of 6) appears:	With checks in **Exclude blocks without attributes** and **Exclude general block properties** (Figure 10–28)
	CLICK: **Next**
Finalize Output (Page 4 of 6) appears:	RIGHT-CLICK: **on the column heading DESC** and CLICK: **Sort Ascending** (Figure 10–29) (to put the list in alphabetical order)

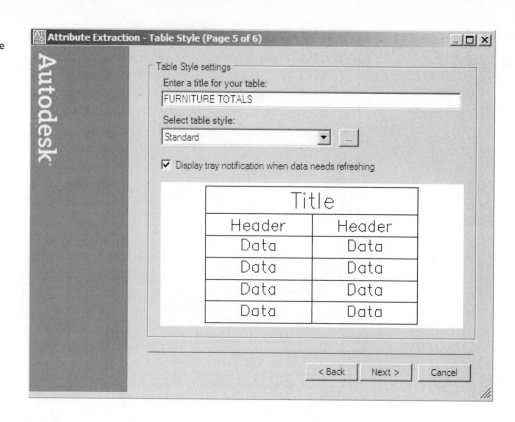

Prompt	Response
	CLICK: **Next**
Table Style (Page 5 of 6) appears:	TYPE: **FURNITURE TOTALS in the Enter a title for your table: text box** (Figure 10–30)
	CLICK: **Next**
Finish (Page 6 of 6) appears:	CLICK: **Finish**
Attribute Extraction - Insert Table appears: Continue inserting table:	CLICK: **Yes**
Specify insertion point:	TYPE: **1/2,8<enter>**
The completed table appears:	**Zoom-All** (to view the entire table)

Step 4. Align DESC, FINISH, Name, PROD, and SIZE columns Middle Left (Figure 10–31):

Prompt	Response
Command:	CLICK: **the open area to the right in the first cell under the DESC column to start a crossing window and move your mouse to the left and down so your crossing window selects all cells in the DESC column but DOES NOT CROSS THE BOTTOM LINE OF THE TABLE**
	Then, RIGHT-CLICK:
The right-click menu appears:	SELECT: **Cell Alignment - Middle Left** (Figure 10–31)

FIGURE 10–31

Extracted Attributes in a Table, Aligning Columns Middle Left

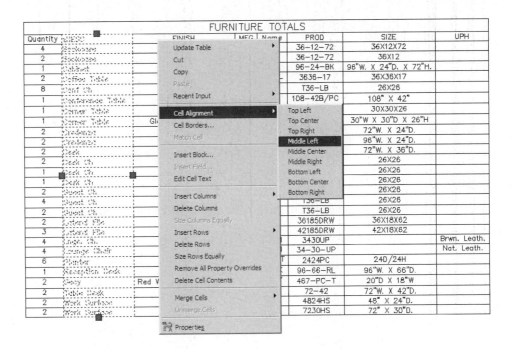

Step 5. On your own:

1. Align the FINISH, Name, PROD, and SIZE middle left.
2. Set the grid for the FURNITURE TOTALS layout to 1/4″ (so it is visible).
3. Use the Reference option of the SCALE command to scale the long side (the horizontal side) of the table to 10″.
4. Move the table if necessary so it fits the grid as shown in Figure 10–26.

Step 6. When you have completed Exercise 10–2, save your work in at least two places.

Step 7. Plot or print the FURNITURE TOTALS layout at a scale of 1:1 on an 11″ × 8-1/2″ sheet.

Exercise 10–3: Reception Area Furniture Plan Using the AutoCAD DesignCenter

When you have completed Exercise 10–3, your drawing will look similar to Figure 10–34 without dimensions.

Step 1. Use your workspace to make the following settings:

1. Use SaveAs… to save the drawing with the name CH10–EX3.
2. Set drawing Units: **Architectural**
3. Set Drawing Limits 44′,34′
4. Set GRIDDISPLAY: **0**
5. Set Grid: **12″**
6. Set Snap: **6″**

You will now use several of the features of the AutoCAD DesignCenter to set up and draw Exercise 10–3.

The AutoCAD DesignCenter

The AutoCAD DesignCenter allows you to do several things that can save you a great deal of time:

Use several existing blocks arranged in categories that AutoCAD has provided.

Use blocks, layers, linetypes, text and dimension styles, and external references from any existing drawing using drag and drop.

Examine drawings and blocks as either drawing names or pictures.

Search for drawings and other files.

Step 2. Open the DesignCenter and examine it:

Prompt	Response
Command:	**DesignCenter** (or TYPE: **DC<enter>**)
The DesignCenter appears:	DOUBLE-CLICK: **Load** (the icon on the top of the DesignCenter on the extreme left)
The Load dialog box appears:	**Look at the bottom of Figure 10–32. Use the same or similar path to locate the Design-Center folder** DOUBLE-CLICK: **DesignCenter** CLICK: **Home-Space Planner.dwg** CLICK: **Open**
The DesignCenter appears, showing the Blocks and other items in the Home-Space Planner.dwg (Figure 10–32). Your DesignCenter may appear different, depending on what is selected in the Views icon or Tree View toggle at the top of the DesignCenter.	DOUBLE-CLICK: **Blocks**
All the predefined blocks for this drawing appear.	

You can now click on any of these drawings, hold down the left mouse button, drag the drawing into the current drawing, and drop it. Do not do that for this exercise. You

FIGURE 10–32
The DesignCenter Home - Space Planner Drawing

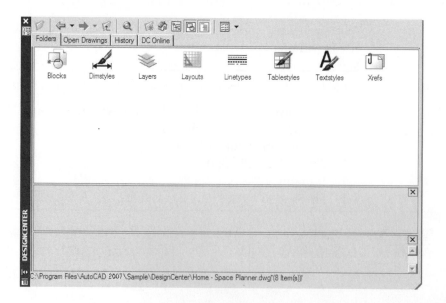

will use layers and blocks from CH10-EX1 to complete CH10-EX3. Let's look at the parts of the DesignCenter.

DesignCenter Tabs

The tabs at the top of the DesignCenter allow you to access all the following options of the DesignCenter:

Folders Tab   Clicking this button shows you the folders existing on the hard drive of your computer.

Open Drawings Tab   Shows you the drawing that is currently open.

History Tab   Shows you a list of the most recently opened drawings.

DC Online Tab   Gives you access to the DesignCenter online where thousands of pictures (blocks) are available.

DesignCenter Buttons

Now examine the buttons above the tabs. They are listed below, starting from the first one on the left. Click the Folders tab to display all the icons.

Load   Allows you to load drawings and other items that you want to use in your current drawing.

Back   Returns you to the previous screen.

Forward   Sends you forward from a screen obtained from clicking back.

Up   Sends you to the next higher folder structure.

Search   Allows you to search for and locate data you need.

Favorites   Shows what you have in the Favorites folder. You can save your most-often-used items here.

Home   Returns you to the default starting folder.

Tree View Toggle   Displays and hides the tree view. The tree view shows the structure of the files and folders in the form of a chart.

Preview   Allows you to look at a preview of any selected item. If there is no preview image saved with the selected item, the Preview area will be empty.

Description   Shows a text description of any selected item.

Views   Provide you with different display formats for the selected items. You can select a view from the View list or choose the View button again to cycle through display formats.

> **Large Icons**   Show the names of loaded items with large icons.
> **Small Icons**   Show the names of loaded items with small icons.
> **List**   Shows a list of loaded items.
> **Details**   Places a name for each item in an alphabetical list.

Next, use the DesignCenter to complete your drawing.

Step 3.   **Use the A-FURN, A-DOOR, and A-WALL-INT layers from CH10–EX1 in the new drawing:**

Prompt	Response
Command:	CLICK: **Load**
	CLICK: **Locate drawing CH10–EX1 and DOUBLE-CLICK: CH10–EX1**
	DOUBLE-CLICK: **Layers**
The display (Figure 10–33) appears:	CLICK: **Layer A-DOOR, hold down the pick button, drag it into the current drawing**

FIGURE 10–33

Layers in CH10-EX1

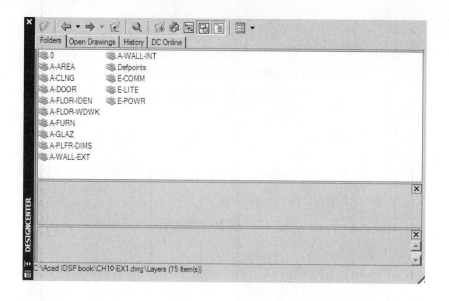

Prompt	Response
	(to the right of the DesignCenter), and release the pick button
	Repeat the previous for Layers A-FURN and A-WALL-INT
	Close the DesignCenter

Step 4. On your own:

1. Set Layer A-WALL-INT current.
2. Use Multiline to draw the outside walls of the reception area using the dimensions from Figure 10–34. Set an offset of 5″ for the wall thickness.
3. Set Layer A-DOOR current.
4. Open the DesignCenter and CLICK: Blocks under CH10–EX1, find the block named DOOR, and drag and drop it into the current drawing.
5. Use the Mirror and Rotate commands if necessary to correctly position the door.
6. Place doors in the correct location using the dimensions from Figure 10–34.
7. Explode the doors and walls and use the Trim command to trim the walls from the door openings.
8. Set Layer A-FURN current.
9. CLICK: Blocks under CH10–EX1, find the blocks named PLANT, CRTBL, RDSK, SECY, and LGCHAIR, and drag and drop them into the currrent drawing.
10. Use the Mirror and Rotate commands if necessary to correctly position each item.
11. Place furniture in the approximate locations shown in Figure 10–34.

Step 5. When you have completed Exercise 10–3 save your work in at least two places.

Step 6. Plot Exercise 10–3 to scale.

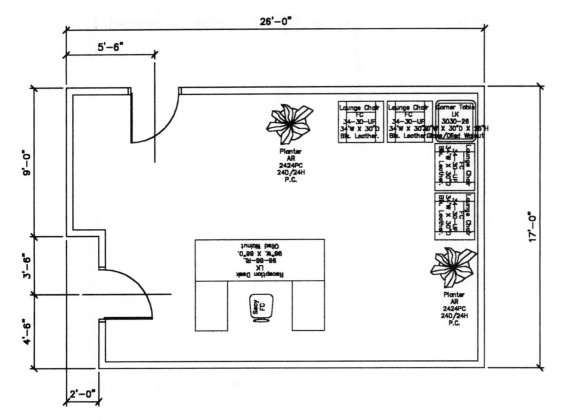

26'-0"

5'-6"

9'-0"

3'-6"

4'-6"

2'-0"

17'-0"

Planter
AR
2424PC
24D/24H
P.C.

Lounge Chair
FC
34-30-UP
34"W X 30"D
Blk. Leather

Lounge Chair
FC
34-30-UP
34"W X 30"D
Blk. Leather

Corner Table
LK
3030-26
30"W X 30"D X 26"H
Glass/Oiled Walnut

Lounge Chair
FC
34-30-UP
34"W X 30"D
Blk. Leather

Lounge Chair
FC
34-30-UP
34"W X 30"D
Blk. Leather

Reception Desk
LK
96-66-RL
96"W. X 66"D.
Oiled Walnut

Secy
FC

Planter
AR
2424PC
24D/24H
P.C.

FIGURE 10–34
Dimensions for Exercise 10–3

Exercise 10–4: Training Room Furniture Plan Using the AutoCAD DesignCenter

When you have completed Exercise 10–4 your drawing will look similar to Figure 10–35.

Step 1. Use your workspace to make the following settings:

1. Open Drawing CH4-EX2 and save it to the hard drive with the name CH10-EX4.
2. Erase all furniture and the door so that only the walls remain.
3. Set Layer Walls current.

Step 2. Use a block from the DesignCenter-House Designer drawing to draw a new door.

Prompt	Response
Command:	**DesignCenter** (or TYPE: **DC<enter>**)
The DesignCenter appears:	CLICK: **the Folders tab**
	CLICK: **the Load button** (first button on the left—above the Folders tab)
The Load dialog box appears:	CLICK: the **UP button** to the [C:] drive, then CLICK: **Program Files/AutoCAD 2007/ Sample/DesignCenter** folder, as shown in Figure 10–36
	In the DesignCenter folder, DOUBLE-CLICK: **House Designer.dwg**

FIGURE 10–35
Exercise 10–4: Training
Room, Complete

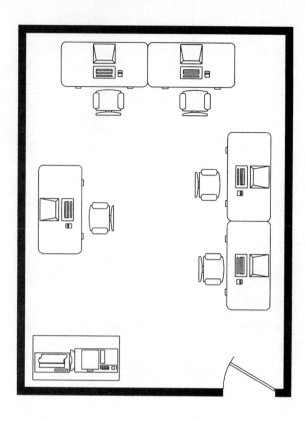

FIGURE 10–36
Locate House Designer
Blocks

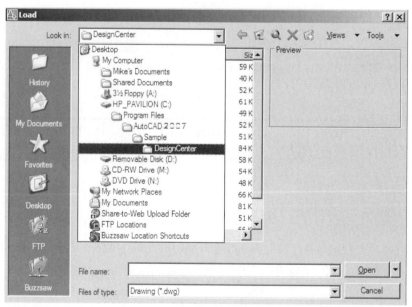

The available items in the House
Designer drawing appear:

DOUBLE-CLICK: **Blocks** and CLICK: **Large
Icons on the Views list as shown in Figure
10–37**
CLICK: **on the Door - Right Hung 36 in. icon
and continue to hold down the left mouse
button, Figure 10–38. Drag the Door off the
DesignCenter and use Osnap-Endpoint to
place it as shown in Figure 10–39.**

FIGURE 10–37
CLICK: Blocks and Large
Icons in the Views List

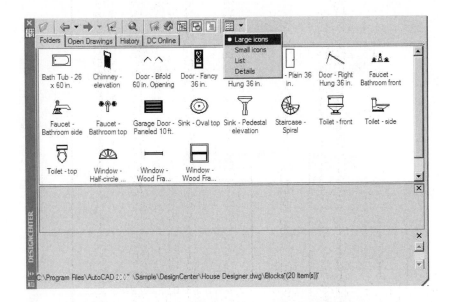

FIGURE 10–38
CLICK: The Door - Right
Hung 36 in., Hold Down the
Pick Button, and Drag the
Door off the DesignCenter

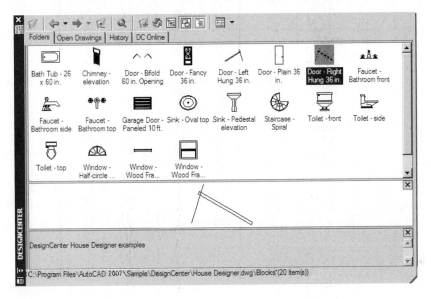

FIGURE 10–39
Use Osnap-Endpoint to Place
the Door in the Opening

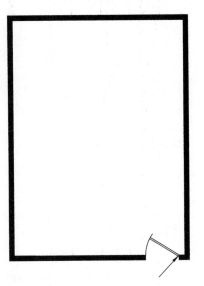

FIGURE 10–40

Open Home - Space Planner
Drawing

Step 3.   Set the Furniture layer current.

Step 4.   Drag and drop blocks from the Home-Space Planner to create furniture
in the Training Room:

Prompt	Response
Command:	Move your mouse back to the DesignCenter palette.
The DesignCenter opens up again:	CLICK: **the Load button again** and DOUBLE-CLICK: **Home-Space Planner.dwg**, Figure 10–40
The available items in the Home - Space Planner.dwg appear:	DOUBLE-CLICK: **Blocks** CLICK: **on the Desk 30 × 60 in. icon** and continue to hold down the left mouse button as you drag the desk off the DesignCenter and place it on the drawing

---

 TIP: To minimize the DesignCenter, CLICK: on the Auto-hide button in the lower left corner.

Step 5.   On your own:

1. Drag and drop the following blocks from the Home-Space Planner drawing,
Figure 10–41:

Chair - Desk   Computer terminal   Desk = 30 × 60 in.   Table - Rectangular Woodgrain 60 × 30

2. Explode the Table - Rectangular Woodgrain and erase the wood grains so
you can see the items you are going to place on top of it.

FIGURE 10–41

Home - Space Planner
Drawing Blocks

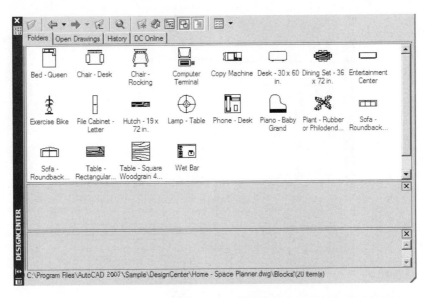

FIGURE 10–42

Desk, Computer, Chair, and
Rectangular Wood Grain
Table

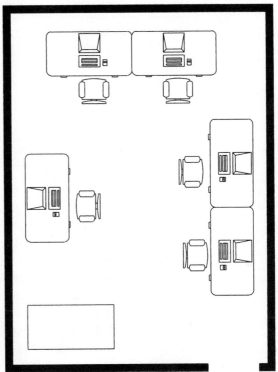

3. Move the computer terminal on top of the Desk = 30 × 60 in. and place the chair in front of the desk.
4. Place the wood grain table in the drawing. Copy and rotate the desk, computer, and chair so your drawing looks like Figure 10–42.
5. Drag and drop the copy machine from the Home - Space Planner drawing and place it on top of the wood grain table (Figure 10–35).

Step 6. Locate a printer in the DesignCenter Online and drag and drop it on top of the wood grain table to complete the drawing:

Prompt	Response
Command:	Move your mouse back to the DESIGNCEN-TER palette

FIGURE 10–43
DC Online-2D Architectural-Office

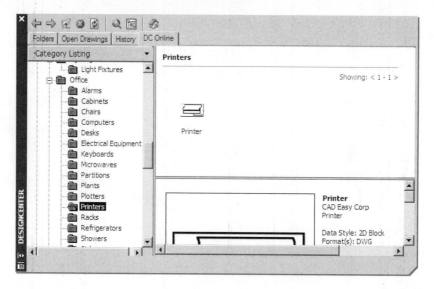

The DesignCenter opens up again: CLICK: **the DC Online tab**
The Category Listing appears: CLICK: **the + to the left of 2D Architectural,**
Figure 10–43
SCROLL: **down to the Office category**
CLICK: **the + to the left of Office**
Find the Printer and drag and drop it on top
of the wood grain table to complete the
Training Room, Figure 10–35

Dynamic Blocks

Part of an inserted dynamic block such as a chair can be moved within the dynamic block (such as a chair-and-desk combination) without exploding the block. A dynamic inserted block can be changed without exploding it. A standard inserted block must be exploded before it can be changed. The size of the dynamic block can also be changed as you work. For example, if the desk is available in a variety of sizes, you can define it as a dynamic block that has a parameter (a feature) that allows the width, depth, or both to be changed without exploding the block or redefining it. The shape or location of a feature in a dynamic block is changed through grips or custom properties. This allows you to adjust the block in place as necessary rather than searching for another block to insert or redefining the existing one.

For example, if you insert a door as a block into a drawing, you may discover that you need to change the size of the door as the drawing is being completed. If the block is dynamic and you have defined it to have an adjustable size, you can change the size of the door by dragging the custom grip or by specifying a different size in the Properties palette. You may also need to change the angle showing how open the door is. You can do that by adding a polar parameter. The door block may also contain an alignment grip, which allows you to align the door block to a wall at a different angle from the original position of the block in the drawing.

You use the Block Editor to create dynamic blocks. The Block Editor allows you to add the elements that make a block dynamic. You can create a block from scratch, or you can add dynamic features to an existing block.

Creating Dynamic Blocks

This book does not contain information on how to create dynamic blocks. Companies that use a great many blocks that are similar will find dynamic blocks useful. If you are interested in creating a dynamic block, use the steps described in the new features workshop or the index (dynamic block) located on the Help menu.

Step 7. When you have completed Exercise 10–4, save your work in at least two places.

Step 8. Use a Layout Wizard or Page Setup Manager to create a layout tab. Plot or print Exercise 10–4 to scale.

External Reference (XREF)

The External Reference command allows you to attach an external reference (xref) (drawing) to a primary drawing. For each drawing, the data is stored in its own separate file. Any changes made to the external reference drawing are reflected in the primary drawing each time the primary drawing is loaded into the Drawing Editor.

There are three distinct advantages to using external references:

1. The primary drawing always contains the most recent version of the external reference.
2. There are no conflicts in layer names and other similar features (called *named objects*), such as linetypes, text styles, and block definitions. AutoCAD automatically precedes the external reference layer name or other object name with the drawing name of the xref and a slash (/). For example, if the primary drawing and the external reference (named CHAIR) have a layer named Symbol, then the current drawing layer retains the name Symbol, and the external reference layer in the current drawing becomes Chair/symbol.
3. Drawing files are often much smaller.

External references are used, for example, for drawing a large furniture plan containing several different levels of office types, such as assistant, associate, manager, vice president, and president. Each office typical (furniture configuration used in the office) is attached to the current drawing as an external reference. When changes are made to the external reference drawing of the manager's office (as a result of furniture substitution, for example), the change is reflected in each instance of a manager's office in the primary large furniture plan when it is loaded into the Drawing Editor.

When the External Reference command is activated, the Select Reference File dialog box appears. After you attach a drawing to your current drawing, the following options are available in the Xref Manager dialog box:

Attach The Attach option allows you to attach as an external reference any drawing to the current drawing. There is no limit to the number of external references that you can attach to your drawing.

Detach The Detach option lets you remove unneeded external references from your drawing.

Reload The Reload option allows you to update the current drawing with an external reference that has been changed since you began the current drawing. You do not have to exit from the current drawing to update it with an external reference that you or someone else changed while in the current drawing.

Unload   Temporarily clears the external reference from the current drawing until the drawing is reloaded.

Bind...   The Insert option in the Bind dialog box creates a block of the external reference in the current drawing and erases any reference to it as an external reference. The Bind option binds the selected xref to the drawing and renames layers in a manner similar to that of the attached xref.

Reference Type

The External Reference dialog box allows you to specify whether the xref will be an attachment or an overlay.

Attachment   An attached xref that is then attached to another drawing becomes a nested xref with all its features fully recognized.

Overlay   An overlay is ignored when the drawing it is overlayed on is then attached as an xref to another drawing.

Features of External References

1. An external reference cannot be exploded.
2. An external reference can be changed into a block with the Bind-Insert option and then exploded. The advantage of using the external reference is then lost. The Bind option would be used if you wanted to send a client a disk containing only the current drawing without including external references on the same disk.
3. External references can be nested. That means that a current drawing containing external references can itself be used as an external reference on another current drawing. There is no limit to the number of drawings you can nest like this.

XBIND

The XBIND (External Bind) command allows you to bind a selected subset of an external reference's dependent symbols to the current drawing. For example, if you did not want to create a block of the entire external reference but wanted permanently to add only a dimension style of the external reference to the drawing, you could use XBIND.

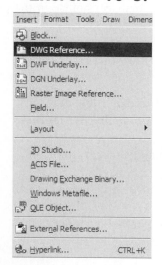

Exercise 10–5:   Attach an External Reference to an Office Floor Plan

Step 1.   On your own:

1. Draw the floor plan shown in Figure 10–44 and save it as CH10-EX5.
2. Draw the typical workstation shown in Figure 10–45 and save it as WS10-1. Estimate any dimensions not shown.

Step 2.   Open drawing CH10-EX5.

Step 3.   Attach the workstation to the current drawing:

Prompt	Response
Command:	DWG Reference...

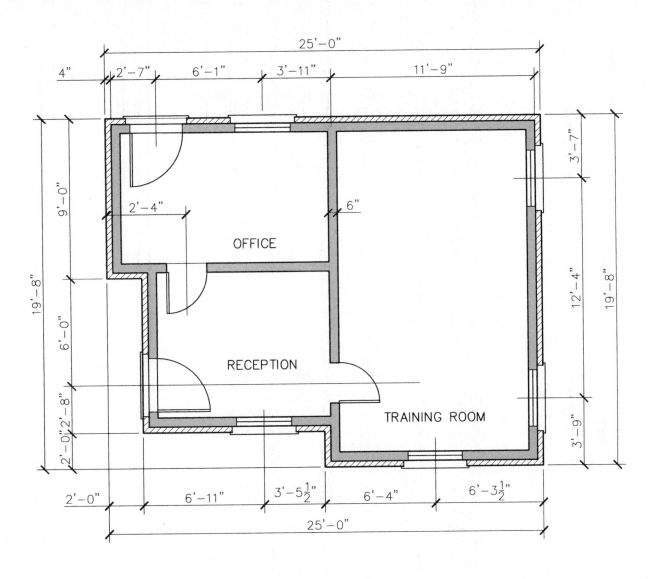

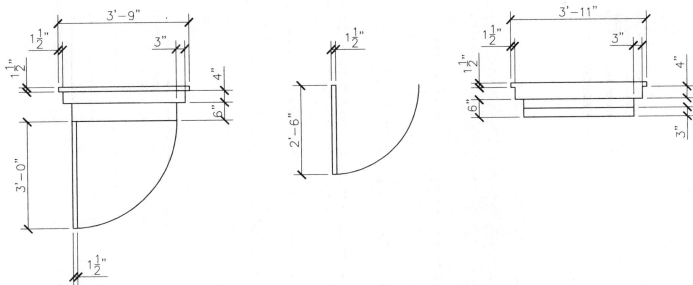

FIGURE 10–44

Floor Plan Dimensions for Exercise 10–5 (Scale: 3/16″ = 1′-0″)

FIGURE 10–45

Exercise 10–5: Typical Workstation Dimensions

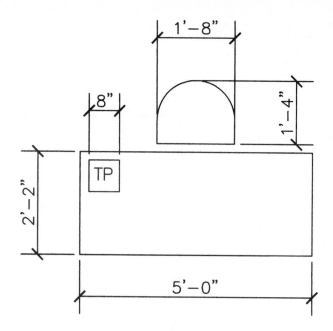

Prompt	Response
The Select Reference File dialog box (Figure 10–46) appears:	**Locate drawing WS10-1 and** CLICK: **on it** CLICK: **Open**
The External Reference dialog box (Figure 10–47) appears:	CLICK: **OK**
Specify insertion point or [Scale/X/Y/Z/Rotate/PScale/ PX/PY/PZ/PRotate]:	CLICK: **D1** (Figure 10–48)

That's all there is to attaching an external reference to another drawing.

FIGURE 10–46

Locate Drawing WS10-1, and
Select It

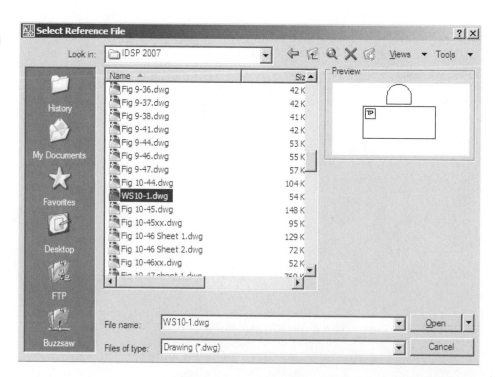

FIGURE 10–47
External Reference Dialog
Box with WSIO-1 Selected

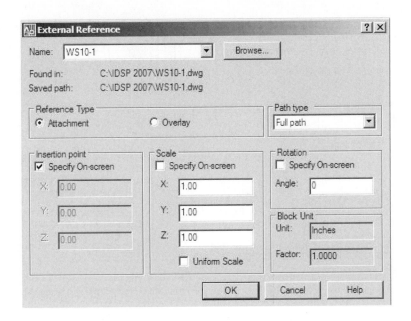

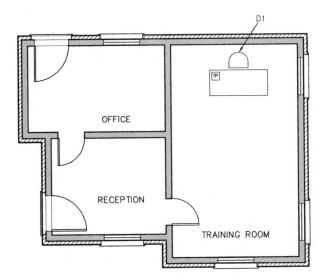

FIGURE 10–48
Insert the External Reference

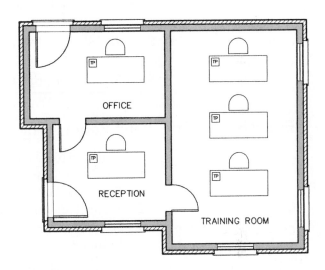

FIGURE 10–49
Copy the External Reference to Four Other Locations

Step 4. On your own:

1. Copy the external reference to four other locations on the floor plan as shown in Figure 10–49 (the exact location is not important).
2. Save your drawing (CH10-EX5) to the same folder or disk as WS10-1.

You have been informed that all of the workstations must now have a computer.

Step 5. On your own:

1. Open drawing WS10-1 and draw a computer approximately the size shown in Figure 10–50 and label it. Save the new workstation drawing in the same place from which it came.

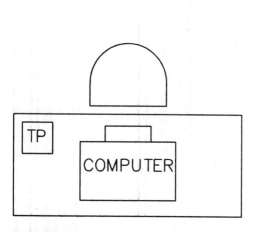

FIGURE 10–50
The New Workstation

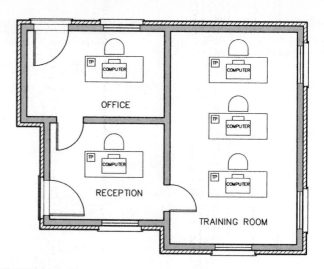

FIGURE 10–51
The Office Floor Plan with New Workstations

Step 6. Open drawing CH10-EX5. It should appear as shown in Figure 10–51.

Step 7. Save CH10-EX5 in the same folder or disk from which it came.

Step 8. Plot or print the drawing to scale.

Exercise 10–6:   Hotel Room Furniture Plan

1. Begin CH10-EX6 on the hard drive or network drive by opening existing drawing CH7-EX2 and saving it as CH10-EX6. Your final drawing will look similar to Figure 10–52.
2. Set the Furniture Layer current and turn off any layers that are not needed.
3. Select furniture from the Design Center, and insert it by double-clicking on the furniture symbol. Place the furniture in the approximate locations shown in Figure 10–52. You will find all this furniture in the Home - Space Planner drawing.
4. Save the drawing in two places, and plot or print the drawing to scale.

Exercise 10–7:   Log Cabin Furniture Plan

1. Begin CH10-EX7 by opening existing drawing CH7-EX3 and saving it as CH10-EX7. Your final drawing will look similar to Figure 10–53.
2. Set the Furniture Layer current and turn off any layers that are not needed.
3. Select furniture from the Design Center, and insert it by double-clicking on the furniture symbol. Place the furniture in the approximate locations shown in Figure 10–53. You will find this furniture in the Home - Space Planner drawing and 2D Architectural On-Line. Use a 3/16″ = 1′-0″ architectural scale to measure any furniture you do not find, and draw it full scale.
4. Save the drawing in two places, and plot or print the drawing to scale.

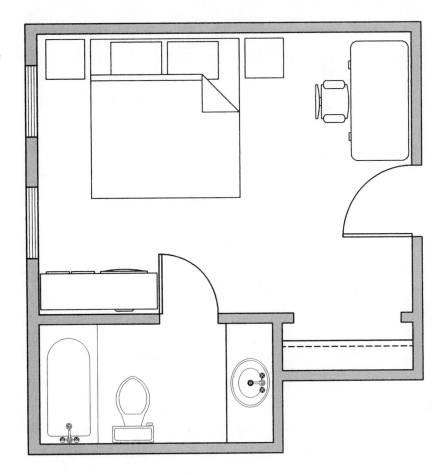

FIGURE 10–52

Exercise 10–6: Hotel Room Furniture Plan (Scale: 1/4″ = 1′-0″)

HOTEL ROOM FURNITURE PLAN

SCALE: 1/ 4″=1′-0″

Exercise 10–8: House Furniture Plan

1. Begin CH10-EX8 by opening existing drawing CH7-EX4 and saving it as CH10-EX8.
2. Create a new layer for furniture and set it current. Turn off any layers that are not needed.
3. Your final drawing will look similar to Figure 10–54, Lower and Upper Levels. Use a 1/8″ = 1′-0″ architectural scale to measure the furniture, and draw it full scale.
4. Save the drawing in two places, and plot or print the drawing to scale.

Exercise 10–9: Bank Furniture Plan

1. Begin CH10-EX9 by opening existing drawing CH7-EX5 and saving it as CH10-EX9.
2. Create a new layer for furniture and set it current. Turn off any layers that are not needed.
3. Your final drawing will look similar to Figure 10–55, Sheet 1. Select furniture from the Design Center, and insert it by double-clicking on the furniture symbol.

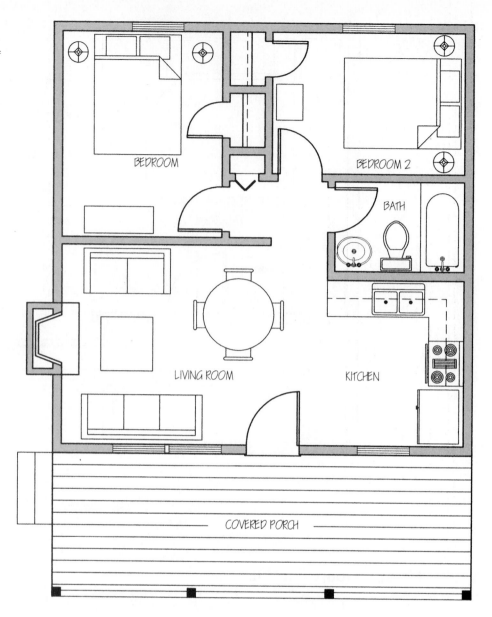

LOG CABIN FURNITURE PLAN
SCALE: 3/16″=1′-0″

Place the furniture in the approximate locations shown in Figure 10–55. You will find this furniture in the Home - Space Planner drawing and 2D Architectural On-Line. Use a 3/32″ = 1′-0″ architectural scale to measure any furniture you do not find, and draw it full scale.

4. Measure the two areas shown on Figure 10–55, Sheet 2 with a ¼″ = 1′-0″ architectural scale, and draw them full size in the approximate location shown on Sheet 1.

5. Save the drawing in two places, and plot or print the drawing to scale.

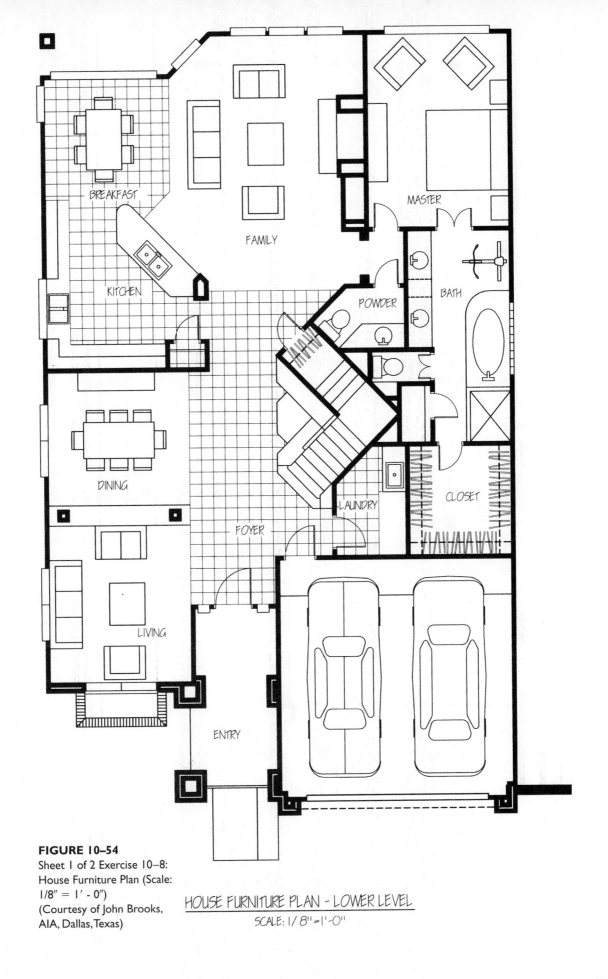

FIGURE 10–54
Sheet 1 of 2 Exercise 10–8:
House Furniture Plan (Scale:
1/8″ = 1′ - 0″)
(Courtesy of John Brooks,
AIA, Dallas, Texas)

HOUSE FURNITURE PLAN - LOWER LEVEL
SCALE: 1/ 8″=1′-0″

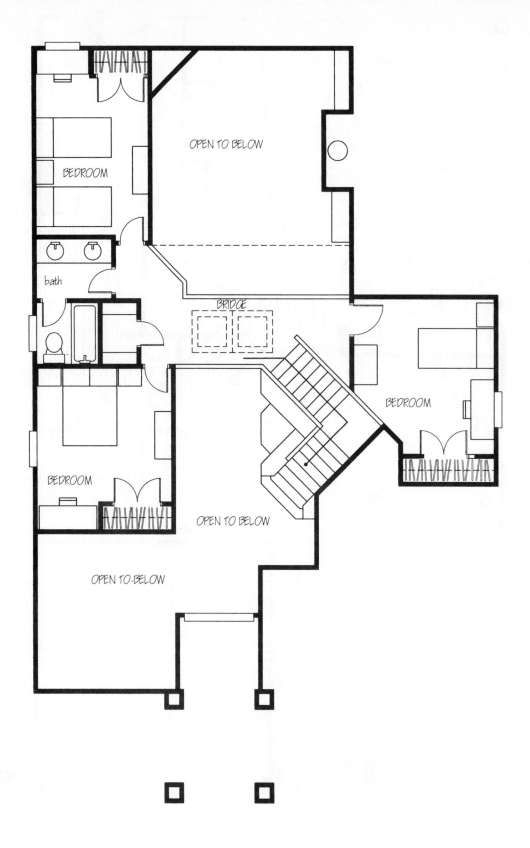

OPEN TO BELOW

BEDROOM

bath

BRIDGE

BEDROOM

BEDROOM

OPEN TO BELOW

OPEN TO·BELOW

HOUSE FURNITURE PLAN - UPPER LEVEL
SCALE: 1/ 8" = 1'-0"

FIGURE 10–54
Sheet 2 of 2 Exercise 10–8: House Furniture Plan (Scale: 1/8″ = 1′ - 0″)
(Courtesy of John Brooks, AIA, Dallas, Texas)

Part II: Two-Dimensional AutoCAD

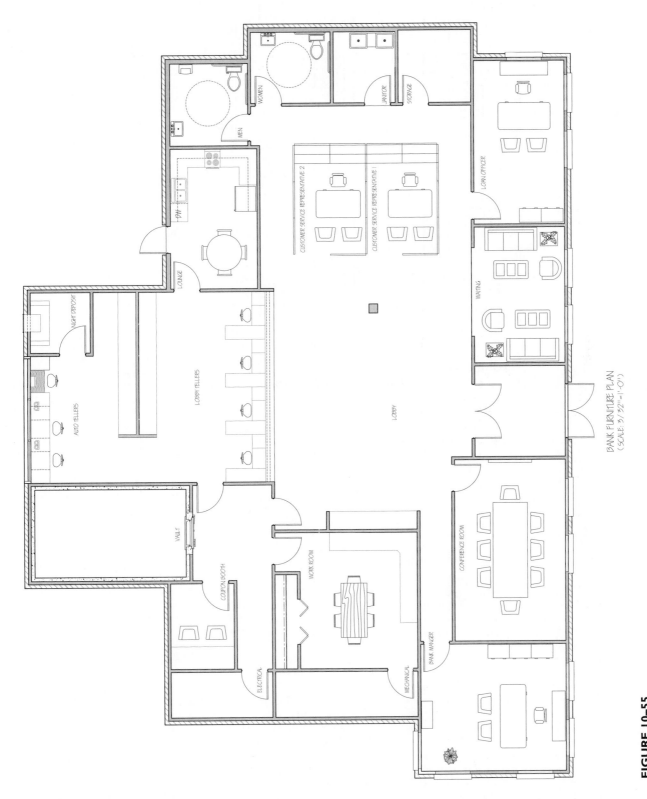

BANK FURNITURE PLAN
(SCALE: 3/32"=1'-0")

FIGURE 10-55

Sheet 1 of 2 Exercise 10-8: Bank Furniture Plan (Scale: 1/8" = 1' - 0")

367

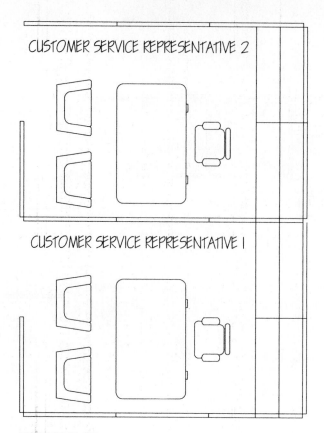

FIGURE 10–55
Sheet 2 of 2 Exercise 10–8: Bank Furniture Plan (Scale: 1/4″ = 1′ - 0″)

1. Which of the following modes must be selected to create a variable attribute that gives you two chances to type the correct value?
   a. Invisible
   b. Constant
   c. Verify
   d. Preset
   e. Do not select any of these.

2. The prompt "Current attribute modes: Invisible=Y Constant=Y Verify=N Preset=N Lock position=Y" indicates which of the following?
   a. Verify mode is active.
   b. Preset mode is active.
   c. Invisible and Constant modes are active.
   d. Verify and Preset modes are active.
   e. Invisible mode only is active.

3. To change the prompt in Question 2 to "Current attribute modes: Invisible=N Constant=N Verify=N Preset=N Lock position=Y" you must:
   a. TYPE: IC, then N
   b. TYPE: I, then CI, then N
   c. TYPE: I, then C
   d. TYPE: IC, then OFF
   e. TYPE: IC, then Y

4. In which of the following may spaces *not* be used?
   a. Value
   b. Default Value
   c. Prompt
   d. Tag
   e. Spaces may be used in all the above.

5. AutoCAD automatically places an attribute definition below one that was defined with the previous -ATTDEF command.
   a. True
   b. False

6. Which of the following part of an attribute appears on the inserted furniture symbol when the attribute mode is *not* Invisible?
   a. Tag
   b. Prompt
   c. Value
   d. Mode
   e. Block name

7. If you insert a block with attributes into a drawing and no attribute prompts occur, which of the following is true?
   a. All attributes are Constant.
   b. All attributes are Variable.
   c. All attributes are Verify.
   d. All attributes are Invisible.
   e. The block has not been inserted on the correct layer.

8. To use the Enter Attributes dialog box to change or accept default values of attributes, which of the following system variables must be set to 1?
   a. ATTREQ
   b. ATTDIA
   c. ATTMODE
   d. ANGDIR
   e. AUPREC

9. Which of the following commands can be used to make invisible all the visible attributes on the drawing?
   a. DDATTE
   b. ATTEXT
   c. ATTDEF
   d. ATTEDIT
   e. ATTDISP

10. Which of the following commands can be used to edit Variable, Verify, Preset, and Constant attribute values of an inserted block using a dialog box?
    a. ATTEXT
    b. ATTDEF
    c. ATTEDIT
    d. ATTDISP
    e. Constant attributes cannot be edited.

Complete.

11. List the command that allows you to edit the value of many attributes simultaneously.

   _____

12. After you have selected several attribute values for editing using -ATTEDIT, how do you know which attribute you are currently editing?

   _____

13. Which command will change all the attribute values "Black" to "Brown" on all occurrences of the Tag "COLOR" at the same time, independent of the block reference?

   _____

14. The command that allows you to redefine a block within a drawing and update all previous insertions of the block in your drawing is:

   _____

15. When a block that has attributes assigned is redefined with the Block command, what happens to existing Variable attributes on the drawing?

   _____

16. The command used to extract attributes from a drawing is:

   _____

17. How many external references can be attached to a primary drawing?

   _____

18. Which External Reference option allows you to make a block of an external reference on the present drawing?

   _____

19. Describe how a dynamic block differs from a standard block.

   _____

   _____

20. List three advantages of using external references.

   _____

   _____

   _____

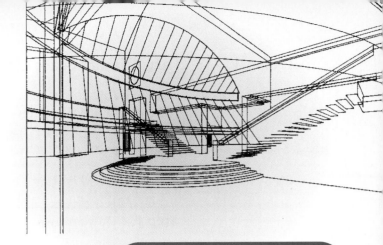

objectives

When you have completed this chapter, you will be able to:

Draw a lighting legend.

Draw a reflected ceiling plan.

Draw voice/data/power legends.

Draw a voice/data/power plan.

Introduction

Previously learned commands are used to draw the tenant space reflected ceiling plan in Exercise 11–1, Part 1, and the voice/data/power plan in Exercise 11–1, Part 2. Helpful guidelines for drawing Exercise 11–1, Parts 1 and 2, are provided.

The reflected ceiling plan shows all the lighting symbols and other items such as exit signs that attach to the ceiling in their correct locations in the space. The plan also shows all the switching symbols needed to turn the lights on and off.

The voice/data/power plan shows symbols for telephones (voice), computers (data), and electrical outlets (power).

Exercise 11–1: Part 1, Tenant Space Lighting Legend and Reflected Ceiling Plan

In Exercise 11–1, Part 1, two separate drawings are drawn—a lighting legend and a reflected ceiling plan for the tenant space. The lighting legend is drawn first and then inserted into the tenant space reflected ceiling plan. When you have completed Exercise 11–1, Part 1, your reflected ceiling plan drawing will look similar to Figure 11–1.

Tenant Space Lighting Legend Drawing

Step 1. On your own:

1. Begin the lighting legend drawing on the hard drive or network drive.
2. Create a Layer named E-lite-txt, color Green.
3. Draw the lighting legend as shown in Figure 11–2, full scale. Draw the lighting symbols on the 0 Layer, and the text and the two arrows on the E-lite-txt Layer. Typically, the lighting symbols and related circuitry have heavier lineweights than the floor plan. You may accomplish this by drawing the lighting symbols and circuitry on a layer to which you have assigned a thicker lineweight.

 NOTE: When you draw the lighting symbols on the 0 Layer, they will inherit the property of the layer that is current when you insert the lighting legend into the reflected ceiling plan drawing.

---

4. Wblock the lighting legend drawing with the name LIGHTING.

Tenant Space Reflected Ceiling Plan

Step 2. On your own:

1. Begin drawing CH11-EX1 on the hard drive or network drive by opening existing drawing CH10-EX1 and saving it as CH11-EX1.
2. Freeze the following layers that have objects drawn that are not needed to draw the reflected ceiling plan:

   A-area
   A-door
   A-flor-iden
   A-furn
   A-pflr-dims

3. Create a layer named E-lite-d, color Red, lineweight Default, and make it current. Draw lines across the door openings as shown in Figure 11–1 (A-door Layer is frozen) on Layer E-lite-d.

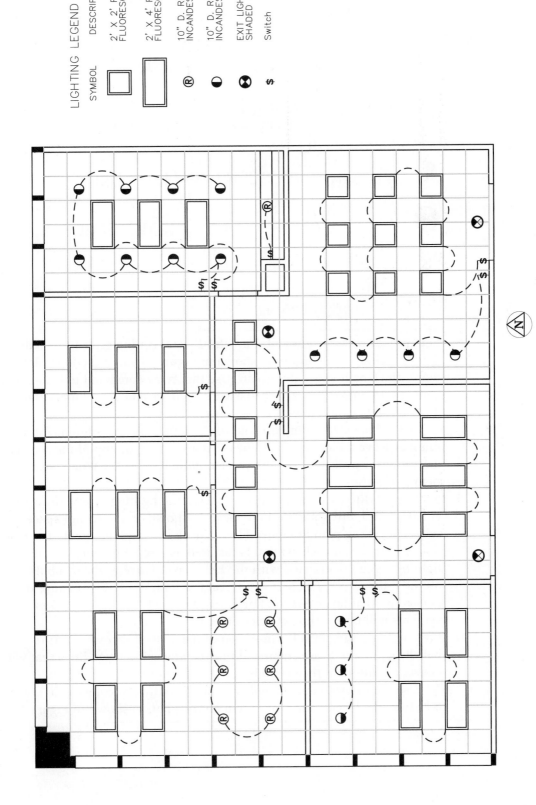

LIGHTING LEGEND

SYMBOL	DESCRIPTION
☐	2' X 2' RECESSED FLUORESCENT FIXTURE
▭	2' X 4' RECESSED FLUORESCENT FIXTURE
ℝ	10" D. RECESSED INCANDESCENT DOWN LIGHT
◖	10" D. RECESSED INCANDESCENT WALLWASHER
⊗	EXIT LIGHT SHADED AREAS DENOTE FACES
$	Switch

FIGURE 11–1

Exercise 11–1, Part 1: Tenant Space Reflected Ceiling Plan (Scale: 1/8" = 1'-0")

FIGURE 11–2
Tenant Space Lighting Legend
(Scale: 1/4″ = 1′-0″)

LIGHTING LEGEND

SYMBOL   DESCRIPTION

2' X 2' RECESSED
FLUORESCENT FIXTURE

2' X 4' RECESSED
FLUORESCENT FIXTURE

Ⓡ

10" D. RECESSED
INCANDESCENT DOWN LIGHT

◐

10" D. RECESSED
INCANDESCENT WALLWASHER

⊗

EXIT LIGHT
SHADED AREAS DENOTE FACES

$

Switch

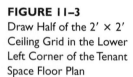

FIGURE 11–3
Draw Half of the 2′ × 2′
Ceiling Grid in the Lower
Left Corner of the Tenant
Space Floor Plan

4. Set Layer A-clng current and draw the 2′ × 2′ ceiling grid: Draw half of a 2′ × 2′ ceiling tile symbol, as shown in Figure 11–3, in the lower left corner of the tenant space floor plan. Use the Array command to complete the ceiling grid, making it rectangular with 19 rows and 25 columns and having 2′ distance between rows and columns.

   Erase the extra ceiling line out of the larger corner column. You may erase or leave the ceiling grid lines that are drawn on top of the south and west interior wall lines (giving you a double line) of the tenant space floor plan.

5. Set Layer E-lite current and Insert-Block... the lighting legend drawing (LIGHTING), full scale, into the location shown on the tenant space reflected ceiling plan in Figure 11–1. Check the Explode box in the Insert dialog box so that each symbol is inserted as a separate entity. When the lighting legend is inserted with the E-lite layer current, the symbols will be on the E-lite Layer. The text will be on the E-lite-txt Layer because it was created on that layer. Set the lineweight for the E-lite Layer to .3 mm so the symbols will have a thicker lineweight.

6. Prepare the ceiling grid for insertion of the 2′ × 4′ recessed fixture symbols by using the Erase command to erase the ceiling grid lines that will cross the centers of the symbols.

   Use the Copy command and an Osnap modifier to copy the lighting symbols from the legend and place them on the plan, as shown in Figure 11–1.

The wallwasher, 2′ × 4′ fixture, and switch symbols appear on the reflected ceiling plan in several different orientations. Copy each symbol and Rotate the individual symbols into the various positions, then use Copy to draw the additional like symbols in the correct locations on the plan.

7. Create an E-lite-w Layer, color white, with a DASHEDX2 linetype, lineweight .3 mm, and set it current. Use the Arc command to draw the symbol for the circuitry. Adjust LTSCALE as needed (try 6) so lines appear as dashed.

8. When you have completed Exercise 11–1, Part 1, save your work in at least two places.

9. Use a Layout Wizard or Page Setup Manager to create a Layout tab named Reflected Ceiling Plan. Set the appropriate viewport scale for your printer or plotter. You may need to reset LTSCALE to a smaller value (1, 1/2, or even smaller) in paper space for dashed lines to appear dashed. Plot or print Exercise 11–1, Part 1.

TIP: If you need to plot all layers black instead of the colors they have been assigned, CLICK: **monochrome.ctb** in the Plot style table (pen assignments) lists in the Plot dialog box (or the Page Setup dialog box). CLICK: **Edit** to the right of the Plot Style to make sure that the color selected is Black and Grayscale: is OFF.

Exercise 11–1: Part 2, Tenant Space Voice/Data/Power Plan

In Exercise 11–1, Part 2, two separate drawings are made—a voice/data/power legend and a voice/data/power plan for the tenant space project. The legend is drawn first and then inserted into the tenant space voice/data/power plan. When you have completed Exercise 11–1, Part 2, your tenant space voice/data/power plan drawing will look similar to Figure 11–4.

Tenant Space Voice/Data/Power Legend Drawing

Step 1. On your own:

1. Begin the drawing of the voice/data/power legend on the hard drive or network drive.
2. Create a Layer named E-power-txt, color Green.
3. Draw the voice/data/power legend as shown in Figure 11–5, full scale. Draw the symbols on the 0 Layer, and the text on the E-power-txt Layer.
4. Wblock the voice/data/power legend drawing with the name VDP.

Tenant Space Voice/Data/Power Plan

Step 2. On your own:

1. Open drawing CH11-EX1 on the hard drive or network drive.
2. Freeze all layers that are not required to draw the voice/data/power plan.

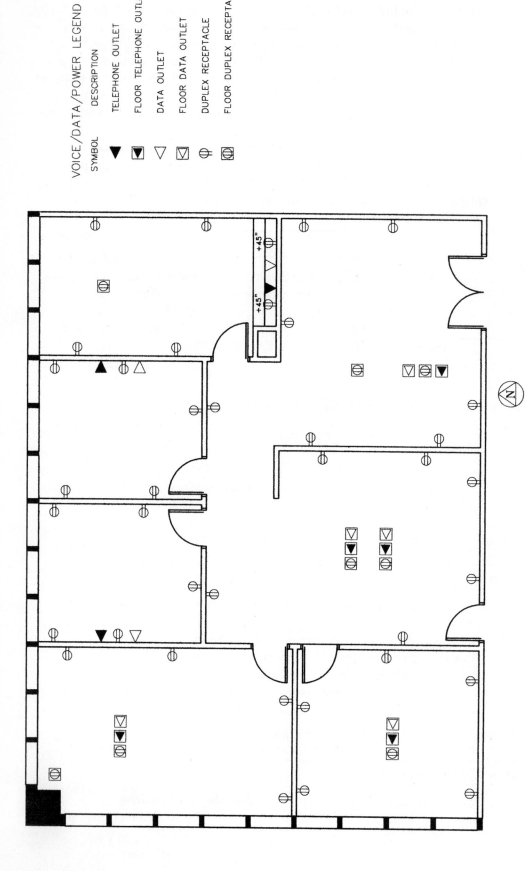

FIGURE 11–4

Exercise 11–1, Part 2: Tenant Space Voice/Data/Power Plan (Scale: 1/8" = 1'-0")

FIGURE 11–5
Tenant Space Voice/Data/
Power Legend (Scale: 1/4″ =
1′-0″)

VOICE/DATA/POWER LEGEND

SYMBOL   DESCRIPTION

◀   TELEPHONE OUTLET

◨   FLOOR TELEPHONE OUTLET

◁   DATA OUTLET

◁̲   FLOOR DATA OUTLET

⏀   DUPLEX RECEPTACLE

◫   FLOOR DUPLEX RECEPTACLE

3. Set Layer E-powr current and Insert-Block... the voice/data/power legend drawing (VDP) full scale in the location shown on the tenant space voice/data/power plan in Figure 11–4. Check the Explode box in the Insert dialog box to separate the symbols into individual entities.

4. Use the Copy command and an Osnap modifier to copy the symbols from the legend and place them on the plan as shown in Figure 11–4.

   The duplex receptacle symbol appears on the plan in several different orientations. Copy the symbol, and use Rotate to obtain the rotated positions as shown on the plan. Use the Copy command to draw like rotated symbols in the correct locations on the plan.

   It is helpful to draw a line connecting the two endpoints of the two lines in the duplex receptacle. Use the midpoint of this line to locate the duplex receptacle along the walls. Do not include this line in the selection set of the Copy command. Use Osnap-Center to help locate the floor receptacle symbol.

5. When you have completed Exercise 11–1, Part 2, save your work in at least two places.

6. Use a Layout Wizard or Page Setup Manager to create a Layout tab named Voice/Data/Power Plan. Set the appropriate viewport scale for your printer or plotter. Plot or print Exercise 11–1, Part 2.

 NOTE: You can freeze different layers on each layout tab. This is explained in Chapter 13.

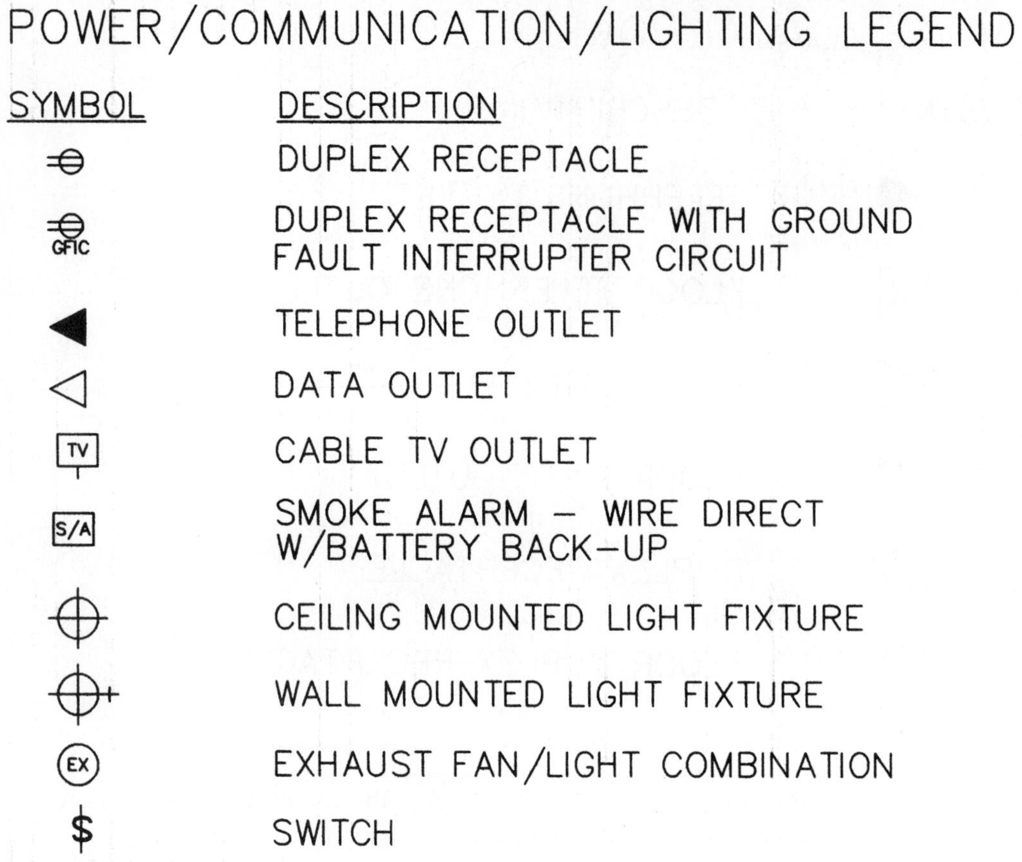

POWER/COMMUNICATION/LIGHTING LEGEND

SYMBOL	DESCRIPTION
⊖	DUPLEX RECEPTACLE
⊖ GFIC	DUPLEX RECEPTACLE WITH GROUND FAULT INTERRUPTER CIRCUIT
◀	TELEPHONE OUTLET
◁	DATA OUTLET
TV	CABLE TV OUTLET
S/A	SMOKE ALARM – WIRE DIRECT W/BATTERY BACK–UP
⊕	CEILING MOUNTED LIGHT FIXTURE
⊕⊢	WALL MOUNTED LIGHT FIXTURE
EX	EXHAUST FAN/LIGHT COMBINATION
$	SWITCH

FIGURE 11–6
Hotel Room Power/Communication/Lighting Legend (Scale: 1/4″ = 1′-0″)

Exercise 11–2: Hotel Room Power/Communication/Lighting Plan

1. Draw the hotel room power/communication/lighting legend as shown in Figure 11–6. Use an architectural scale to measure the symbols and draw them full scale on a separate layer.
2. Complete the hotel room power/communication/lighting plan as shown in Figure 11–7. Create a new layer for the HIDDENX2 linetype. The 45″ notation on the receptacles in the bathroom shows the distance from the floor to the receptacles.
3. Use a Layout Wizard or Page Setup Manager to create a layout. Plot or print the drawing to scale.

POWER/COMMUNICATION/LIGHTING LEGEND

SYMBOL	DESCRIPTION
⌽	DUPLEX RECEPTACLE
⌽_{GFIC}	DUPLEX RECEPTACLE WITH GROUND FAULT INTERRUPTER CIRCUIT
▼	TELEPHONE OUTLET
▽	DATA OUTLET
TV	CABLE TV OUTLET
S/A	SMOKE ALARM – WIRE DIRECT W/BATTERY BACK–UP
⊕	CEILING MOUNTED LIGHT FIXTURE
⊕	WALL MOUNTED LIGHT FIXTURE
EX	EXHAUST FAN/LIGHT COMBINATION
$	SWITCH

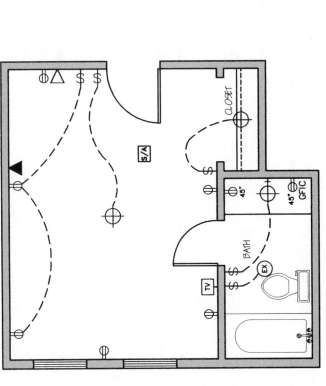

HOTEL ROOM POWER/ COMMUNICATION/ LIGHTING PLAN

SCALE: 3/16" = 1'-0"

FIGURE 11–7

Exercise 11–2: Hotel Room Power/Communication/Lighting Plan (Scale: 3/16" = 1'0")

379

LIGHTING LEGEND

SYMBOL   DESCRIPTION

Ⓡ   RECESSED LIGHT FIXTURE

      CEILING MOUNTED LIGHT FIXTURE

      WALL MOUNTED LIGHT FIXTURE

      RECESSED WALL WASHER LIGHT FIXTURE

Ⓔ🅧   EXHAUST FAN/LIGHT COMBINATION

Ⓞ   CEILING FAN WITH INTEGRAL LIGHT(S)
           PROVIDE SEPARATE SWITCHING FOR
           FAN AND LIGHT(S)

$ SWITCH

$₃   3–WAY SWITCH

Exercise 11–3:   Log Cabin Lighting Plan

1. Draw the log cabin lighting legend as shown in Figure 11–8. Use an architectural scale to measure the symbols and draw them full scale on a separate layer.
2. Complete the log cabin lighting plan as shown in Figure 11–9. Create a new layer for the HIDDENX2 linetype. Three-way switches are used when two switches turn on the same lights.
3. Use a Layout Wizard or Page Setup Manager to create a layout. Plot or print the drawing to scale.

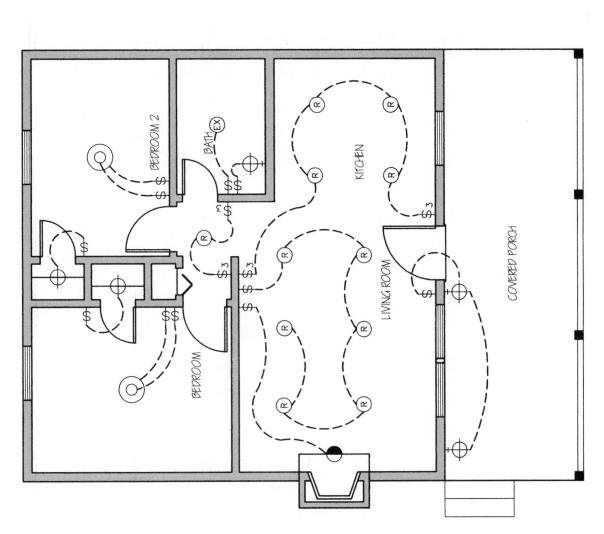

LIGHTING LEGEND

SYMBOL	DESCRIPTION
(R)	RECESSED LIGHT FIXTURE
⊕	CEILING MOUNTED LIGHT FIXTURE
⊕	WALL MOUNTED LIGHT FIXTURE
◐	RECESSED WALL WASHER LIGHT FIXTURE
(EX)	EXHAUST FAN/LIGHT COMBINATION
◉	CEILING FAN WITH INTEGRAL LIGHT(S) PROVIDE SEPARATE SWITCHING FOR FAN AND LIGHT(S)
$	SWITCH
$₃	3-WAY SWITCH

LOG CABIN LIGHTING PLAN
SCALE: 3/16" = 1'-0"

FIGURE 11-9

Exercise 11-3: Log Cabin Lighting Plan (Scale: 3/16" = 1'0")

381

POWER/COMMUNICATION LEGEND

SYMBOL	DESCRIPTION
⊖	DUPLEX RECEPTACLE
⊖ GFIC	DUPLEX RECEPTACLE WITH GROUND FAULT INTERRUPTER CIRCUIT
R⊖	RANGE OUTLET
◀	TELEPHONE OUTLET
◁	DATA OUTLET
TV	CABLE TV OUTLET
S/A	SMOKE ALARM WIRE DIRECT W/BATTERY BACKUP
$	SWITCH

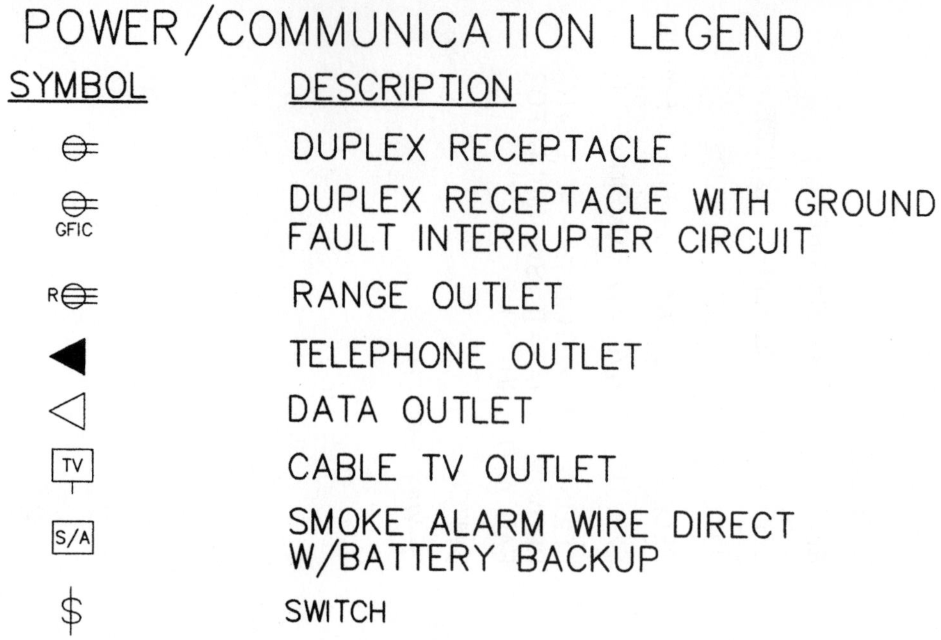

Exercise 11–4: Log Cabin Power/Communication Plan

1. Draw the log cabin power/communication legend as shown in Figure 11–10. Use an architectural scale to measure the symbols and draw them full scale.
2. Complete the log cabin power/communication Plan as shown in Figure 11–11. The 45″ notation on three of the receptacles shows the distance from the floor to the receptacle.
3. Use a Layout Wizard or Page Setup Manager to create a layout. Plot or print the drawing to scale

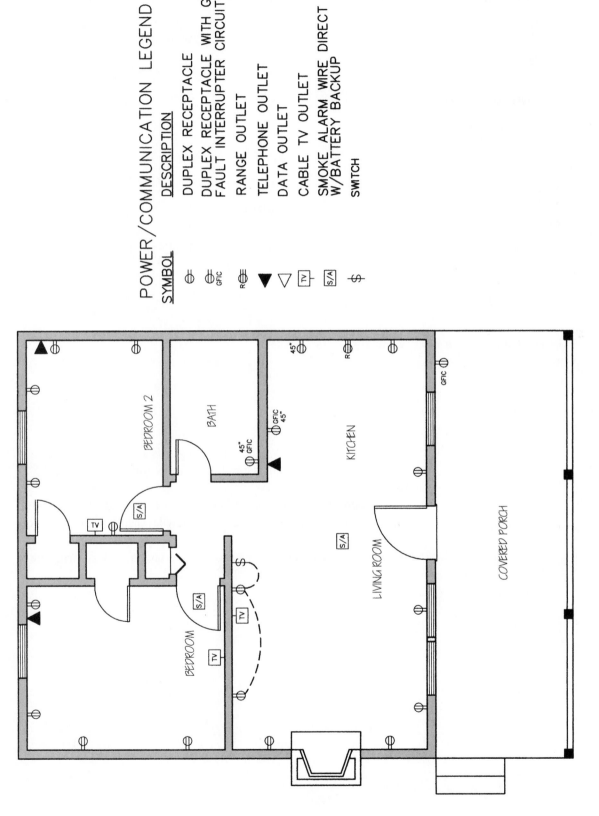

POWER/COMMUNICATION LEGEND

SYMBOL | DESCRIPTION

DUPLEX RECEPTACLE

DUPLEX RECEPTACLE WITH GROUND
FAULT INTERRUPTER CIRCUIT

RANGE OUTLET

TELEPHONE OUTLET

DATA OUTLET

CABLE TV OUTLET

SMOKE ALARM WIRE DIRECT
W/BATTERY BACKUP

SWITCH

POWER/ COMMUNICATION PLAN

SCALE: 3/16" = 1'-0"

FIGURE 11–11

Exercise 11–4: Log Cabin Power/Communication Plan (Scale: 3/16" = 1'-0")

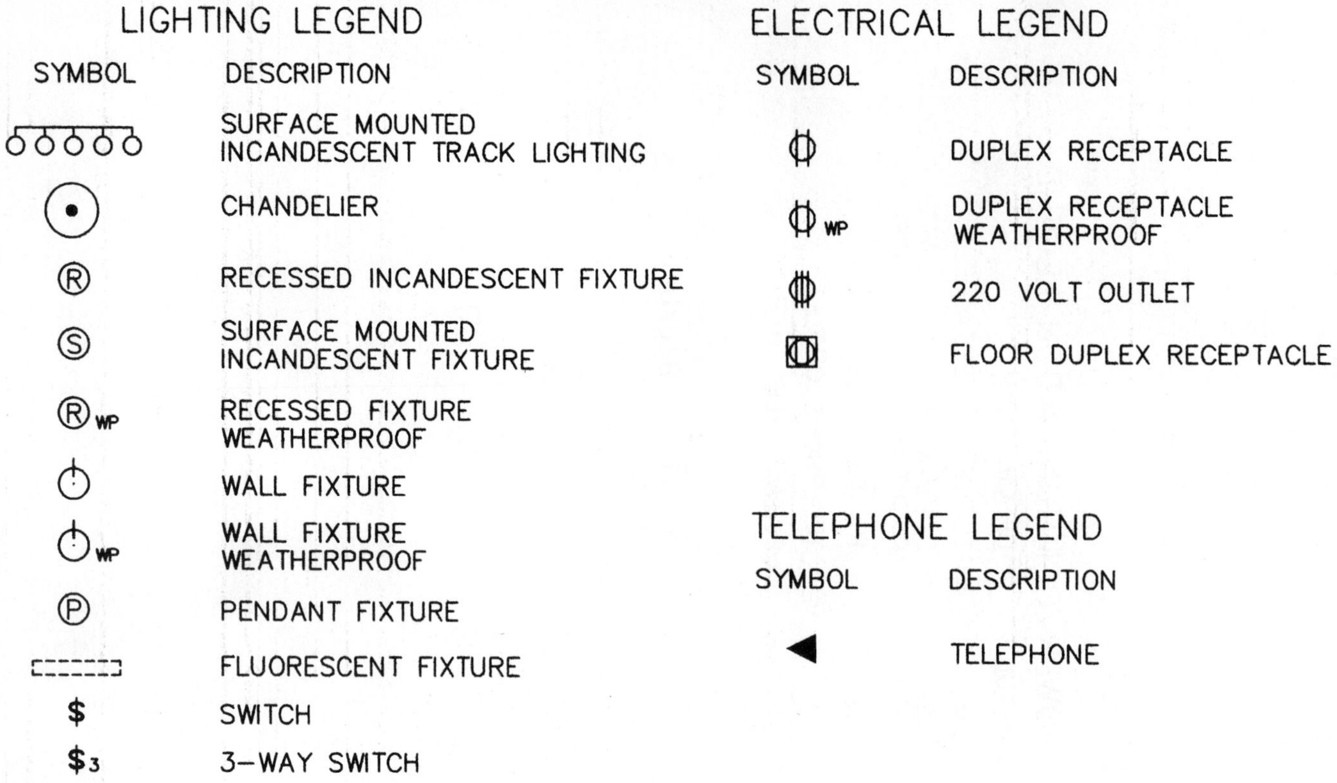

LIGHTING LEGEND

SYMBOL	DESCRIPTION
⟨o o o o o⟩	SURFACE MOUNTED INCANDESCENT TRACK LIGHTING
(•)	CHANDELIER
(R)	RECESSED INCANDESCENT FIXTURE
(S)	SURFACE MOUNTED INCANDESCENT FIXTURE
(R) wp	RECESSED FIXTURE WEATHERPROOF
(↓)	WALL FIXTURE
(↓) wp	WALL FIXTURE WEATHERPROOF
(P)	PENDANT FIXTURE
⊏┅┅┅┅┅⊐	FLUORESCENT FIXTURE
$	SWITCH
$₃	3—WAY SWITCH

ELECTRICAL LEGEND

SYMBOL	DESCRIPTION
⏀	DUPLEX RECEPTACLE
⏀ wp	DUPLEX RECEPTACLE WEATHERPROOF
⏀	220 VOLT OUTLET
◫	FLOOR DUPLEX RECEPTACLE

TELEPHONE LEGEND

SYMBOL	DESCRIPTION
◀	TELEPHONE

FIGURE 11–12
Exercise 11–5: House Lighting, Electrical, and Telephone Legends (Scale: 3/16″ = 1′-0″)

Exercise 11–5:   House Lighting and Electrical Plan

1. Draw the house lighting, electrical, and telephone legends as shown in Figure 11–12. Use an architectural scale to measure the symbols and draw them full scale on a separate layer.
2. Complete the house lighting and electrical plan—Lower Level and Upper Level as shown in Figure 11–13 Sheets 1 and 2. Create a new layer for the HIDDENX2 linetype.
3. Use a Layout Wizard or Page Setup Manager to create a layout. Plot or print the drawing to scale.

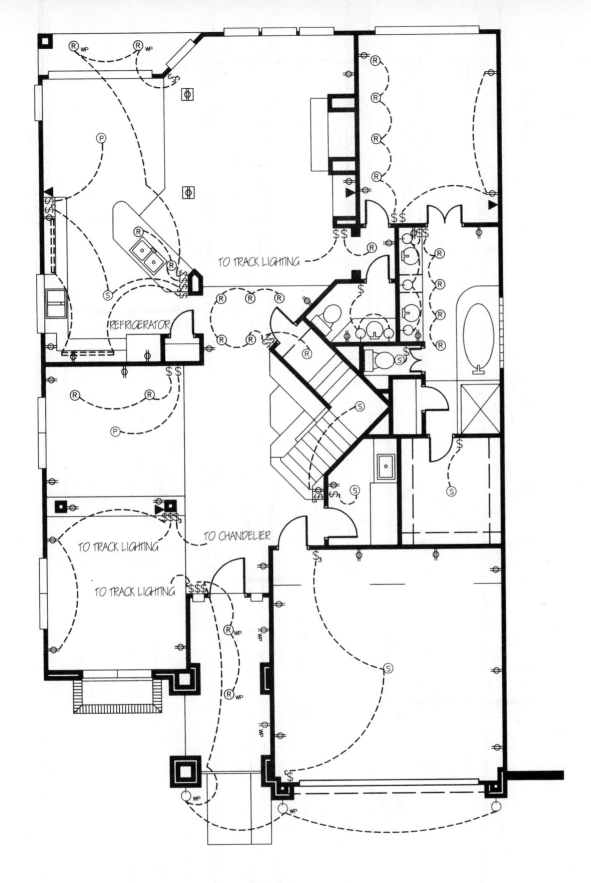

TO TRACK LIGHTING

REFRIGERATOR

TO TRACK LIGHTING

TO CHANDELIER

TO TRACK LIGHTING

HOUSE LIGHTING AND ELECTRICAL PLAN - LOWER LEVEL
(SCALE: 1/8"=1'-0")

FIGURE 11–13

Sheet 1 of 2

Exercise 11–5: House Lighting and Electrical Plan (Scale: 1/8″ = 1'-0″)

(Courtesy of John Brooks, AIA, Dallas, Texas)

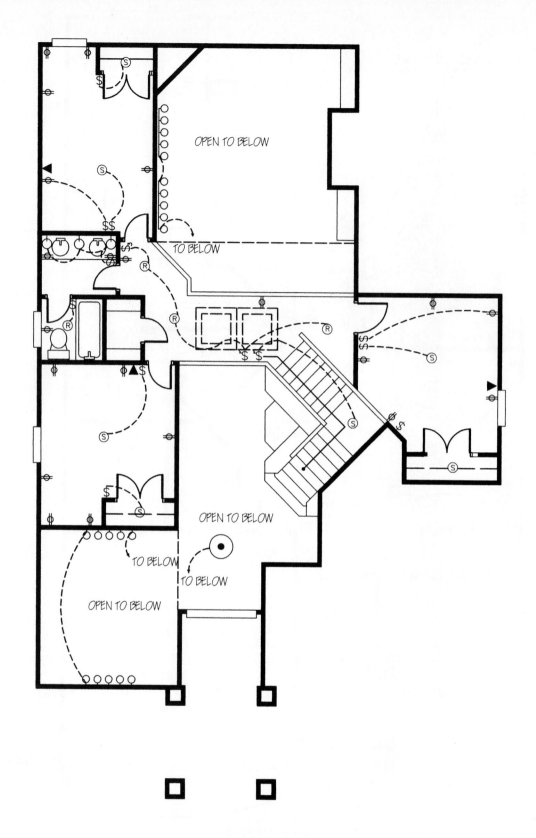

OPEN TO BELOW

TO BELOW

OPEN TO BELOW

TO BELOW

TO BELOW

TO BELOW

OPEN TO BELOW

OPEN TO BELOW

HOUSE LIGHTING AND ELECTRICAL PLAN -UPPER LEVEL
(SCALE: 1/8"=1'-0")

FIGURE 11–13
Sheet 2 of 2
Exercise 11–5: House Lighting and Electrical Plan (Scale: 1/8″ = 1′-0″)
(Courtesy of John Brooks, AIA, Dallas, Texas)

FIGURE 11–14
Exercise 11–6: Bank Lighting
Legend (Scale: 1/4″ = 1′-0″)

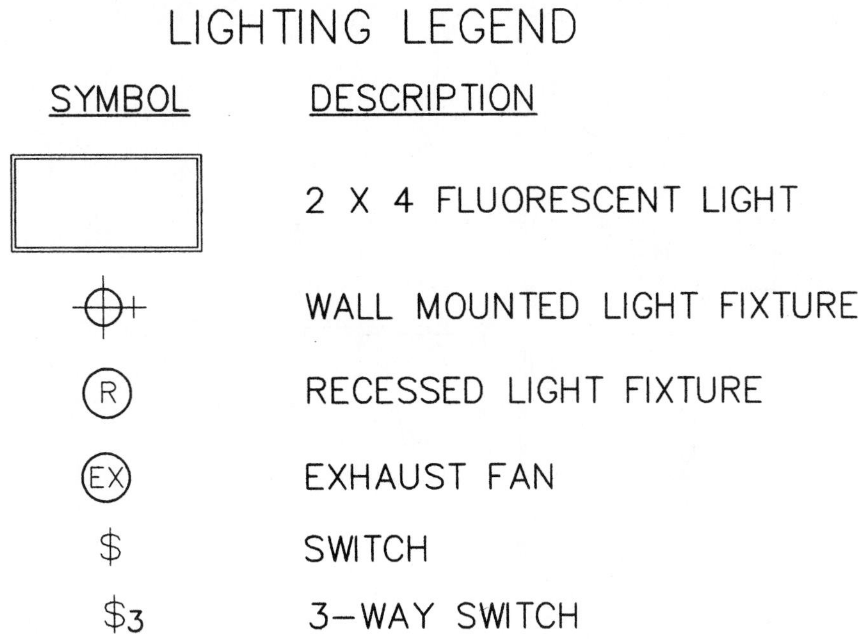

LIGHTING LEGEND

SYMBOL   DESCRIPTION

2 X 4 FLUORESCENT LIGHT

WALL MOUNTED LIGHT FIXTURE

RECESSED LIGHT FIXTURE

EXHAUST FAN

SWITCH

3—WAY SWITCH

Exercise 11–6:   Bank Lighting Plan

1. Draw the bank lighting legend as shown in Figure 11–14. Use an architectural scale to measure the symbols and draw them full scale on a separate layer.
2. Complete the bank lighting plan as shown in Figure 11–15. Create a new layer for the HIDDENX2 linetype.
3. Use a Layout Wizard or Page Setup Manager to create a layout. Plot or print the drawing to scale.

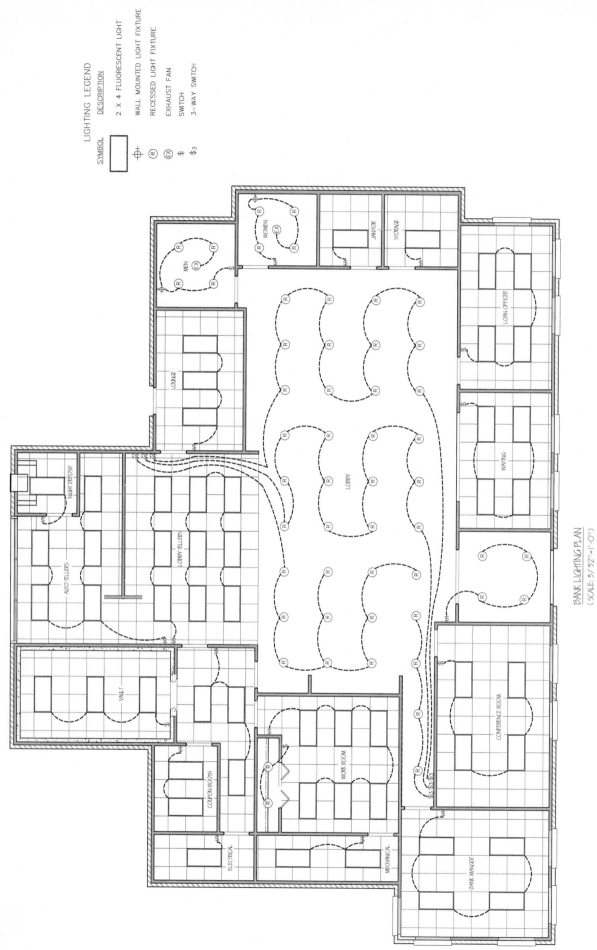

LIGHTING LEGEND

SYMBOL	DESCRIPTION
▭⊕	2 X 4 FLUORESCENT LIGHT
⊕	WALL MOUNTED LIGHT FIXTURE
Ⓡ	RECESSED LIGHT FIXTURE
ⒺⓍ	EXHAUST FAN
$	SWITCH
$₃	3-WAY SWITCH

BANK LIGHTING PLAN
(SCALE: 3/32" = 1'-0")

FIGURE 11-15

Exercise 11-6: Bank Lighting Plan (Scale: 3/32" = 1'-0")

388

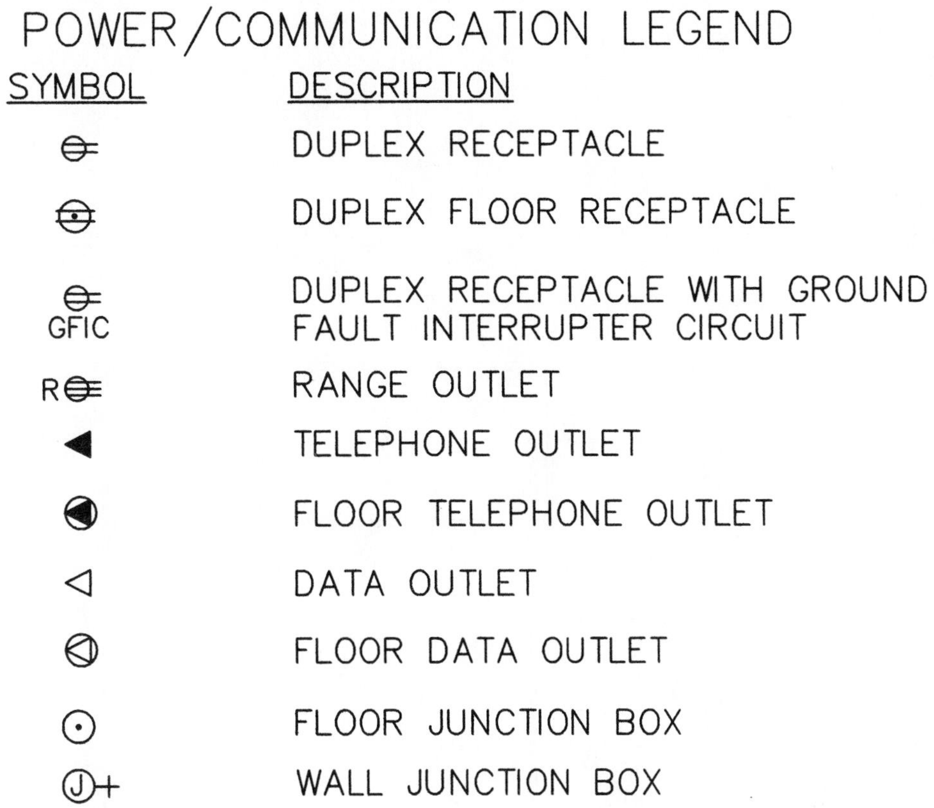

POWER/COMMUNICATION LEGEND

SYMBOL	DESCRIPTION
⊖	DUPLEX RECEPTACLE
⊖	DUPLEX FLOOR RECEPTACLE
⊖ GFIC	DUPLEX RECEPTACLE WITH GROUND FAULT INTERRUPTER CIRCUIT
R⊖	RANGE OUTLET
◀	TELEPHONE OUTLET
◉	FLOOR TELEPHONE OUTLET
◁	DATA OUTLET
◉	FLOOR DATA OUTLET
⊙	FLOOR JUNCTION BOX
Ⓙ+	WALL JUNCTION BOX

Exercise 11–7:   Bank Power/Communication Plan

1. Draw the bank power/communication legend as shown in Figure 11–16. Use an architectural scale to measure the symbols and draw them full scale.
2. Complete the bank power/communication plan as shown in Figure 11–17.
3. Use a Layout Wizard or Page Setup Manager to create a layout. Plot or print the drawing to scale.

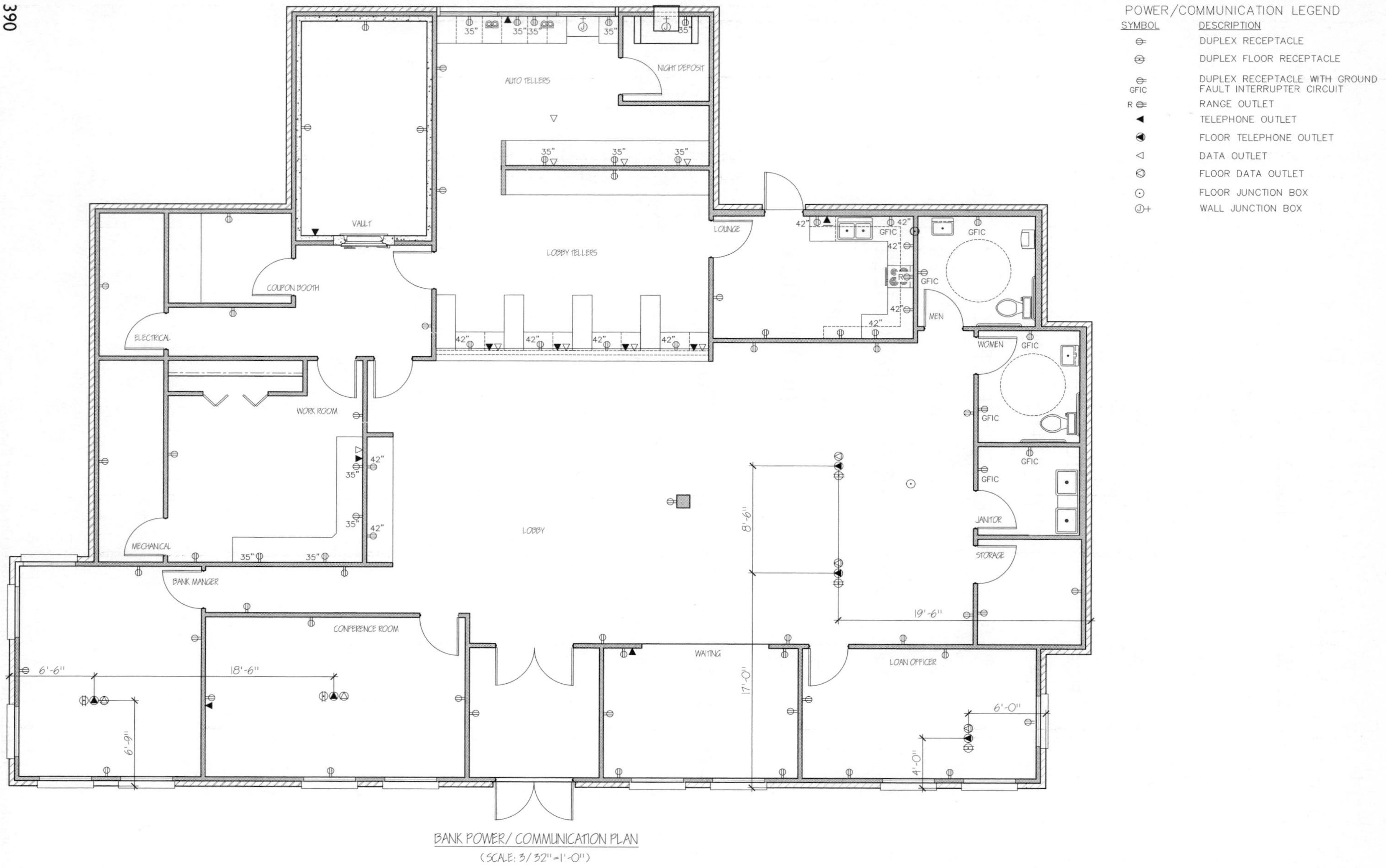

POWER/COMMUNICATION LEGEND

SYMBOL   DESCRIPTION

⊕   DUPLEX RECEPTACLE

⊕   DUPLEX FLOOR RECEPTACLE

GFIC   DUPLEX RECEPTACLE WITH GROUND
              FAULT INTERRUPTER CIRCUIT

R ⊕   RANGE OUTLET

▼   TELEPHONE OUTLET

▼   FLOOR TELEPHONE OUTLET

▽   DATA OUTLET

⊙   FLOOR DATA OUTLET

⊙   FLOOR JUNCTION BOX

⊕⊣   WALL JUNCTION BOX

BANK POWER/COMMUNICATION PLAN
(SCALE: 3/32" = 1'-0")

FIGURE 11-17

Exercise 11-6: Bank Power/Communication Plan (Scale: 3/32" = 1'-0")

1. Describe how to make the lighting symbols and related circuitry have heavier lineweights than the floor plan when plotted.

    _____

    _____

2. Why do you draw lighting legend symbols on the 0 layer?

    _____

3. How do you use an existing drawing to create a new drawing?

    _____

4. Describe how to set a viewport scale.

    _____

5. Describe what checking the Explode box in the Insert dialog box does when a drawing is inserted into another drawing, using the Insert-Block... command.

    _____

    _____

6. Why do you freeze layers instead of turning them off ?

    _____

    _____

7. List the numbers of rows and columns and the spacing used to create an array of the ceiling grid for the Tenant space.

    Rows _____

    Row spacing _____

    Columns _____

    Column spacing _____

8. List the setting that controls the sizes of linetypes as they appear on the screen.

    _____

9. If a Wblock is created on a layer that has the color property green, what color does it assume when it is inserted on a layer with the color property red?

    _____

10. How do you insert a block so that all its lines are separate objects?

    _____

11. Which of the following plans would most likely contain a symbol for a 3-way switch?
    a. Lighting
    b. Power
    c. Voice
    d. Data
    e. None of the above

12. Which of the following plans would most likely contain a symbol for a telephone?
    a. Lighting
    b. Power
    c. Voice
    d. Data
    e. None of the above

13. Which of the following plans would most likely contain a symbol for a duplex receptacle?
    a. Lighting
    b. Power
    c. Voice
    d. Data
    e. None of the above

14. Which of the following plans would most likely contain a symbol for a ceiling fan?
    a. Lighting
    b. Power
    c. Voice
    d. Data
    e. None of the above

15. Which of the following plans would most likely contain a symbol for a fluorescent fixture?
    a. Lighting
    b. Power
    c. Voice
    d. Data
    e. None of the above

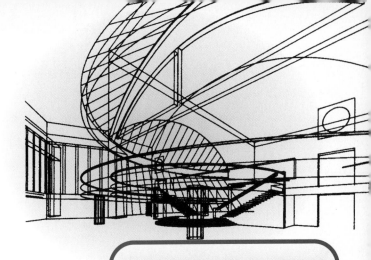

chapter

12

Isometric Drawing and Gradient Hatch Rendering

objectives

When you have completed this chapter, you will be able to:

Make isometric drawings to scale from two-dimensional drawings.

Correctly use the following commands and settings:

ELLIPSE-Isocircle
SNAP-Style Iso

Use the Ctrl-E or F5 keys to change from one isoplane to another.

Use gradient hatch patterns to render isometric drawings.

Axonometric Drawing

The forms of axonometric drawing are isometric, dimetric, and trimetric, as shown in Figure 12–1. The trimetric form has the most pleasing appearance because each of the three axes uses a different scale. Dimetric uses the same scale on two axes, and isometric uses the same scale on all three axes. Isometric drawing is the axonometric drawing form covered in this book.

Isometric Drawing

Isometric drawing is commonly used to show how objects appear in three dimensions. This drawing method is a two-dimensional one (you are drawing on a flat sheet of paper) that is used to give the appearance of three dimensions. It is not a 3D modeling form such as those that are covered in later chapters. In 3D modeling you actually create three-dimensional objects that can be viewed from any angle and can be placed into a perspective mode.

FIGURE 12–1
Axonometric Drawing Forms

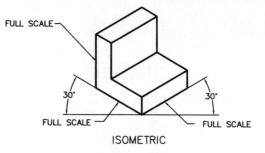

ISOMETRIC

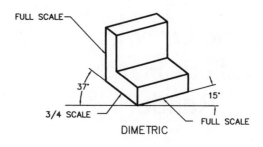

DIMETRIC

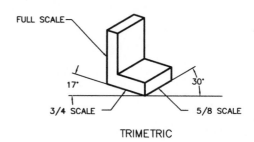

TRIMETRIC

You can make isometric drawings quickly and easily using AutoCAD software. Once the proper Grid and Snap settings are made, the drawing itself proceeds with little difficulty. The three isometric axes are 30° right, 30° left, and vertical.

Exercise 12–1:   Fundamentals of Isometric Drawing

Seven isometric shapes are drawn in this exercise to acquaint you with the fundamentals of making isometric drawings using AutoCAD. We will begin with a simple isometric box so that you can become familiar with drawing lines on an isometric axis. All seven of these shapes are drawn on the same sheet and plotted on one 8 1/2″ × 11″ sheet. When you have completed Exercise 12–1, your drawing will look similar to Figure 12–2.

Step 1.   Use your workspace to make the following settings:

1. **Use SaveAs. . . to save the drawing with the name CH12-EX1.**
2. Set drawing Units: **Architectural**
3. Set Drawing Limits: **11′, 8′6″** (be sure to use the foot symbol)
4. Set Snap as follows.

Set Snap for an isometric grid:

Prompt	Response
Command:	TYPE: **SN** <enter>

FIGURE 12-2
Exercise 12-1 Complete

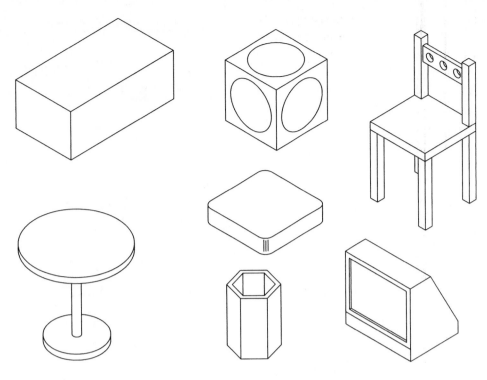

Prompt	Response
Specify snap spacing or [ON/OFF/ Aspect/Style/Type] <0'-0 ½">:	TYPE: **S<enter>**
Enter snap grid style [Standard/ Isometric] <S>:	TYPE: **I<enter>** (I for isometric)
Specify vertical spacing <0'-6">:	TYPE: **1<enter>** (if 1" is not the default)

When you want to exit the isometric grid, TYPE: **SN<enter>** and then TYPE: **S<enter>**, then TYPE: **S<enter>** again to select the standard grid. Keep the isometric grid for this exercise.

5. Set Griddisplay: **0**
6. Set Grid: **3"**
7. Create the following Layers:

LAYER NAME	COLOR	LINETYPE	LINEWEIGHT
A-furn-iso-r	Red	Continuous	Default
A-furn-iso-g	Green	Continuous	Default

8. Set **Layer A-furn-iso-g** current.
9. **Zoom-All.**

Drafting Settings Dialog Box

When the isometric 1" snap and 3" grid are set, and GRIDDISPLAY is set to 0, the Drafting Settings dialog box will appear as shown in Figure 12-3.

Shape 1: Drawing the Isometric Rectangle

Drawing shape 1 (Figure 12-4) helps you become familiar with drawing lines using isometric polar coordinates.

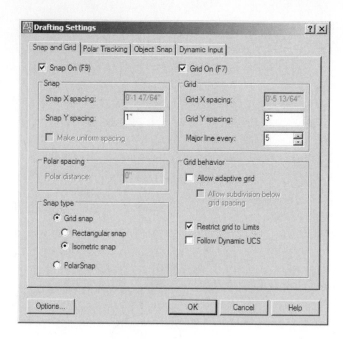

FIGURE 12–3
Drafting Settings Dialog Box

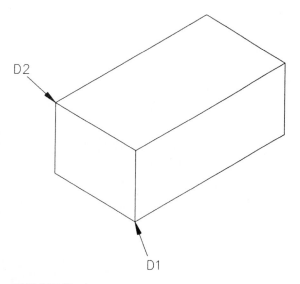

D2

D1

FIGURE 12–4
Shape 1: Drawing the Isometric Rectangle

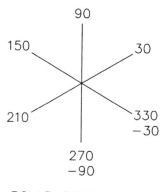

POLAR COORDINATES
FOR ISOMETRIC DRAWING

Step 2. Draw the right face of an isometric rectangular box measuring 12″ × 16″ × 30″ using isometric polar coordinates:

Prompt	Response
Command:	**Line** (or TYPE: **L<enter>**)
Specify first point:	**D1** (Figure 12–4) (absolute coordinates 1′7-1/16, 4′11″)
Specify next point or [Undo]:	TYPE: **@30<30<enter>**
Specify next point or [Undo]:	TYPE: **@12<90<enter>**
Specify next point or [Close/Undo]:	TYPE: **@30<210<enter>**
Specify next point or [Close/Undo]:	TYPE: **C<enter>**

Step 3. Draw the left face of the isometric rectangular box.

Prompt	Response
Command:	<enter> (Repeat LINE)
Specify first point:	**D1 (Osnap-Endpoint)**
Specify next point or [Undo]:	TYPE: **@16<150<enter>**
Specify next point or [Undo]:	TYPE: **@12<90<enter>**
Specify next point or [Close/Undo]:	TYPE: **@16<330<enter>**
Specify next point or [Close/Undo]:	<enter>

Step 4. Draw the top of the isometric rectangular box.

Prompt	Response
Command:	<enter> (Repeat LINE)
Specify first point:	**D2**
Specify next point or [Undo]:	TYPE: **@30<30<enter>**
Specify next point or [Undo]:	TYPE: **@16<-30<enter>**
Specify next point or [Close/Undo]:	<enter>

Shape 2: Drawing Isometric Ellipses

When using polar coordinates to draw lines in isometric, you can ignore Isoplanes. Isoplanes are isometric faces—Top, Right, and Left. Pressing two keys, Ctrl and E, at the same time toggles your drawing to the correct Isoplane—Top, Right, or Left. The function key F5 can also be used to toggle to the correct Isoplane.

Shape 2 (Figure 12–5) has a circle in each of the isometric planes of a cube. When drawn in isometric, circles appear as ellipses. You must use the isoplanes when drawing isometric circles using the Ellipse command. The following part of the exercise starts by drawing a 15″ isometric cube.

Step 5. Draw the right face of a 15″ isometric cube using direct distance entry.

Prompt	Response
Command:	**Toggle to the right isoplane** (PRESS: **F5** until <Isoplane Right> appears) **and** CLICK: **Line** (or TYPE: **L<enter>**)

FIGURE 12–5
Shape 2: Drawing Isometric Ellipses

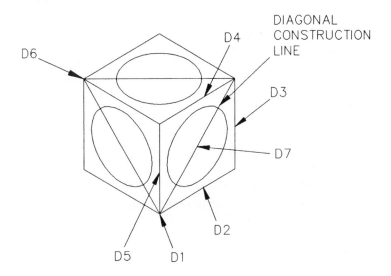

Prompt	Response
Specify first point:	**D1** (absolute coordinates 6'3/4", 5'3")
Specify next point or [Undo]:	**With ORTHO ON, move your mouse upward 30° to the right, and** TYPE: **15<enter>**
Specify next point or [Undo]:	**Move the mouse straight up, and** TYPE: **15<enter>**
Specify next point or [Close/Undo]:	**Move the mouse downward 210° to the left, and** TYPE: **15<enter>**
Specify next point or [Close/Undo]:	TYPE: **C,<enter>.**

 NOTE: When Ortho is ON, the movement of the crosshair is restricted to the isoplane currently active.

Step 6. Use the Mirror command to draw the left face of the isometric cube:

Prompt	Response
Command:	**Mirror** (or TYPE: **MI<enter>**)
Select objects:	**D2,D3,D4<enter>**
Specify first point of mirror line:	**D1** (be sure Ortho is ON) **(Osnap-Endpoint)**
Specify second point of mirror line:	**D5** (PRESS: **F5** to be sure you are in either the right or left isoplane.)
Erase source objects? [Yes/No]<N>:	**<enter>**

Step 7. Complete the top face of the isometric cube:

Prompt	Response
Command:	**Toggle to the top isoplane and** CLICK: **Line** (or TYPE: **L<enter>**)
Specify first point:	**D6 (Osnap-Endpoint)**
Specify next point or [Undo]:	**Move the mouse upward 30° to the right, and** TYPE: **15<enter>**
Specify next point or [Undo]:	**Move the mouse downward 330° to the right, and** TYPE: **15<enter>**
Specify next point or [Close/Undo]:	**<enter>**

Step 8. Locate centers of ellipses:

On Your Own:

1. Draw construction lines, as shown in Figure 12–5, across diagonally opposite corners in each of the visible surfaces. Be sure a running Osnap-Endpoint is ON and ORTHO is OFF. The construction lines will be used to locate accurately the centers of the ellipses.

Step 9. Draw an isometric ellipse (6″ radius) that represents a circle in the RIGHT ISOPLANE:

Prompt	Response
Command:	**Ellipse** (or TYPE: **EL<enter>**)
Specify axis endpoint of ellipse or [Arc/Center/Isocircle]:	TYPE: **1<enter>**
Specify center of isocircle:	**Osnap-Midpoint**
mid of	**D7**
Specify radius of isocircle or [Diameter]:	PRESS: **the F5 function key until the command line reads <Isoplane Right>, then TYPE: 6<enter>**

When you type and enter **D** in response to the prompt "Specify radius of Isocircle or Diameter:", you can enter the diameter of the circle. The default is radius.

Step 10. On your own:

1. Follow a similar procedure to draw ellipses in the left and top isoplanes. Be sure to specify Isocircle after you have selected the Ellipse command, and be sure you are in the correct isoplane before you draw the ellipse. Use F5 to toggle to the correct isoplane.
2. Erase the construction lines.

When you have completed this part of the exercise, you have the essentials of isometric drawing. Now you are going to apply these essentials to a more complex shape.

TIP: After you become familiar with isometric angles and toggling to isoplanes, use direct distance entry with Ortho ON to draw lines. Just move your mouse in the isometric direction and TYPE: the number that tells AutoCAD how far you want to go. You may choose to watch the dynamic display of distance and polar angles and simply pick the desired point.

Shape 3: Drawing a Chair with Ellipses That Show the Thickness of a Material

Step 11. Draw the right side of the front chair leg:

Prompt	Response
Command:	**Toggle to the right isoplane and** CLICK: **Line** (or TYPE: **L<enter>**) (be sure Ortho is ON)
Specify first point:	**D1** (Figure 12–6) (pick a point in the approximate location (**9'-7/8",4'11"**) shown in Figure 12–2)

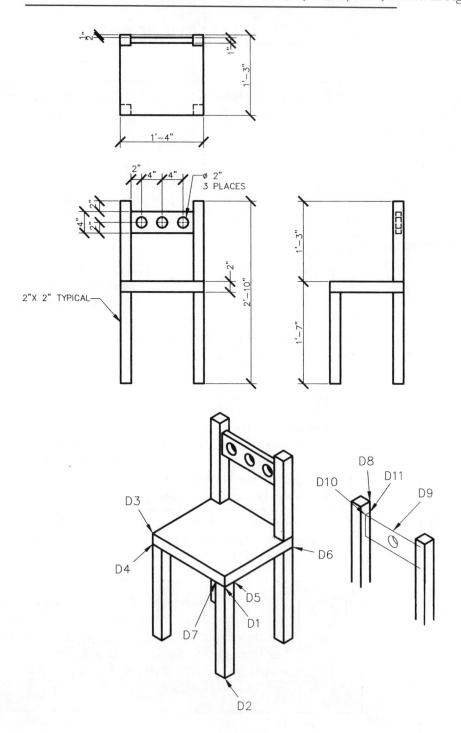

Prompt	Response
Specify next point or [Undo]:	With Ortho ON, move your mouse straight down 270° and TYPE: 1′5<enter>
Specify next point or [Undo]:	Move your mouse upward 30° to the right and TYPE: 2<enter>
Specify next point or [Close/Undo]:	Move your mouse straight up 90° and TYPE: 1′5<enter>
Specify next point or [Close/Undo]:	<enter>

Step 12. Draw the left side of the front chair leg:

Prompt	Response
Command:	Toggle to the left isoplane and CLICK: Line (or TYPE: L<enter>)
Specify first point:	D2 (Osnap-Endpoint) (Figure 12–6)
Specify next point or [Undo]:	Move your mouse upward 150° to the left, and TYPE: 2<enter>
Specify next point or [Undo]:	Move your mouse straight up 90° and TYPE: 1′5<enter>
Specify next point or [Close/Undo]:	<enter>

Step 13. Draw the chair seat:

Prompt	Response
Command:	Line (or TYPE: L<enter>)
Specify first point:	D1 (Osnap-Endpoint) (Figure 12–6)
Specify next point or [Undo]:	Move your mouse 150° upward to the left and TYPE: 1′4<enter>
Specify next point or [Undo]:	Move your mouse straight up and TYPE: 2<enter>
Specify next point or [Close/Undo]:	Move your mouse 330° downward to the right and TYPE: 1′4<enter>
Specify next point or [Close/Undo]:	TYPE: C<enter>
Command:	<enter> (to begin the line command)
Specify first point:	D1 (Osnap-Endpoint)
Specify next point or [Undo]:	Toggle to the right isoplane and with Ortho ON, Move your mouse 30° upward to the right and TYPE: 1′3<enter>
Specify next point or [Undo]:	Move your mouse straight up and TYPE: 2<enter>
Specify next point or [Close/Undo]:	Move your mouse 210° downward to the left and TYPE: 1′3<enter>
Specify next point or [Close/Undo]:	<enter> (to end the line command)
Command:	<enter> (to begin the line command)
Specify first point:	D3 (Osnap-Intersection)
Specify next point or [Undo]:	Toggle to the top isoplane and with Ortho ON, move your mouse 30° upward to the right and TYPE: 1′3<enter>
Specify next point or [Close/Undo]:	Move your mouse 330° downward to the right and TYPE: 1′4<enter>
Specify next point or [Close/Undo]:	<enter>

Step 14. On your own:

Copy the front leg to the other three positions.

1. Using the Copy command, select the lines of the front leg. Use D5 (Osnap-Endpoint) (Figure 12–6) as the base point and D6 (Osnap-Intersection) as the second point of displacement.
2. Using the Copy command, select both legs on the right side. Use D7 (Osnap-Endpoint) (Figure 12–6) as the base point and D4 (Osnap-Intersection) as the second point of displacement.
3. Use the Trim and Erase commands to delete any unnecessary lines.

Step 15. On your own:

1. Use the Line command to draw one of the upright posts, and use the Copy command to copy it to the other position. Follow the dimensions shown in Figure 12–6.

Step 16. Draw the 1″ × 4″ × 12″ piece containing the three holes.

Prompt	Response
Command:	Line (or TYPE: L<enter>)
Specify first point:	TYPE: FRO<enter>
Base point:	CLICK: D8 (Osnap-Intersection) (Figure 12–6)
<Offset>:	TYPE: @2<-90<enter>
Specify next point or [Undo]:	TYPE: @1<210<enter>
Specify next point or [Undo]:	TYPE: @12<-30<enter>
Specify next point or [Close/Undo]:	<enter>
Command:	Toggle to the left isoplane, and with Ortho OFF, Ellipse (or TYPE: EL<enter>)
Specify axis endpoint of ellipse or [Arc/Center/Isocircle]:	TYPE: I<enter>
Specify center of isocircle:	TYPE: FRO<enter>
Base point:	CLICK: D9 (Osnap-Midpoint)
<Offset>:	TYPE: @2<-90<enter>
Specify radius of isocircle or [Diameter]:	TYPE: 1<enter>
Command:	COPY (or TYPE: CP<enter>)
Select objects:	CLICK: the ellipse just drawn
Select objects:	<enter>
Specify base point or [Displacement] <Displacement>:	CLICK: D10 (Osnap-Endpoint)
Specify second point or <use first point as displacement>:	CLICK: D11 (Osnap-Endpoint)
Specify second point or [Exit/Undo] <Exit>:	<enter>

Step 17. On your own:

1. Trim the copied ellipse so that only the part within the first ellipse remains.
2. Copy the hole described by the ellipses 4″ 330° downward to the right, and 4″ 150° upward to the left.
3. Draw a 4″ line straight down from D10 (Endpoint) and a 12″ line 330° downward to the right from the end of the 4″ line.
4. Draw a 12″ line 330° downward to the right from D11 (Endpoint).
5. Use the Move command to move the 1″ × 4″ × 12″ piece and three holes 210° downward to the left 1/2″.
6. Trim to complete the drawing.

Shape 4: Drawing a Shape That Has a Series of Ellipses Located on the Same Centerline

Shape 4 (Figure 12–7), similar to a round table, will help you become familiar with drawing a shape that has a series of ellipses located on the same centerline. Five ellipses must be drawn. The centers of two of them, the extreme top and bottom ellipses, can be located by using endpoints of the centerline.

The following part of the exercise begins by drawing a centerline through the entire height of the object.

FIGURE 12–7

Shape 4: Drawing a Shape That Has a Series of Ellipses Located on the Same Centerline

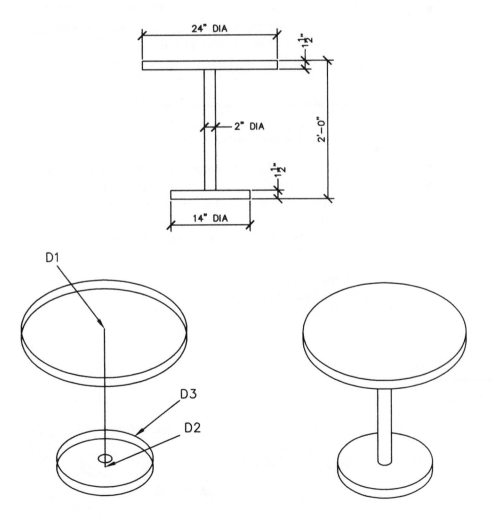

Step 18. Begin to draw a shape containing several ellipses of different sizes located on the same centerline by drawing the centerline:

Prompt	Response
Command:	**Line** (or TYPE: **L**<enter>)
Specify first point:	**D1** (1'11-7/16,1'4-1/2)
Specify next point or [Undo]:	TYPE: **@24<90**<enter>
Specify next point or [Undo]:	<enter>

Step 19. On your own:

Draw five ellipses:

1. Toggle to the top isoplane and use Endpoint to locate the center of the uppermost isometric ellipse on the endpoint of the vertical line. Draw it with a diameter of 24".
2. Draw a second 24"-diameter isometric ellipse by copying the 24" ellipse 1-1/2" straight down.
3. Draw the 14"-diameter ellipse using the bottom Endpoint of the vertical line as its center. Copy the 14"-diameter ellipse 1-1/2" straight up.
4. Draw the 2"-diameter ellipse at the center of the copied 14"-diameter ellipse using Osnap-Center to locate its center.

 NOTE: Although Osnap-Nearest can be used to end an isometric line on another line, the position is not exact. A more exact method is to draw the line beyond where it should end and trim it to the correct length.

Step 20. On your own:

1. To draw the 2" column, toggle to the right or left isoplane (the top isoplane does not allow you to draw vertical lines using a mouse if Ortho is ON). Turn Ortho (F8) ON. Draw a vertical line from the quadrant of one side of the 2"-diameter ellipse to just above the first 24"-diameter ellipse. Draw a similar line to form the other side of the column.

FIGURE 12–8
Shape 4: Drawing Tangents to the Ellipses

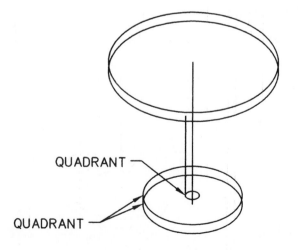

QUADRANT

QUADRANT

2. With Ortho (F8) ON and toggled to the right or left isoplane, draw vertical lines from the quadrants of the ellipse segments to connect each side of the top and bottom ellipses as shown in Figure 12–8.

3. Use Trim and Erase to remove unneeded lines. The drawing is complete as shown in the lower right corner of Figure 12–7.

Shape 5: Isometric Detail with Rounded Corners

The fifth drawing (Figure 12–9) in this exercise is a shape that has rounded corners. Rounded corners are common in many items. In two-dimensional drawing, the Fillet command allows you to obtain the rounded corners quickly and easily. This is not so in isometric. Drawing Shape 5 will help you become familiar with how rounded corners must be constructed with isometric ellipses.

Step 21. Turn Ortho and Snap ON, and toggle to the top isoplane. Draw an 18″ × 18″ square shape in the top isoplane (Figure 12–9):

Prompt	Response
Command:	**Line** (or TYPE: **L**<enter>)
Specify first point:	**D1** (on a grid mark) (5′11, 3′3)
Specify next point or [Undo]:	TYPE: **@18<30**<enter>
Specify next point or [Undo]:	TYPE: **@18<150**<enter>
Specify next point or [Close/Undo]:	TYPE: **@18<210**<enter>
Specify next point or [Close/Undo]:	TYPE: **C**<enter>

Step 22. On your own:

Copy the 18″ × 18″ square 4″ down:

1. Copy the front two edges of the square to form the bottom of the shape. Copy using @4<270 (4″ is the depth) as the polar coordinates for the second point of displacement.

FIGURE 12–9
Shape 5: Isometric Detail with Rounded Corners

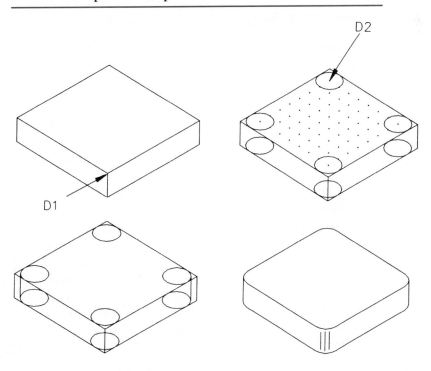

2. **Draw lines connecting the top and bottom edges.** (These lines are for reference only. You may skip this step if you choose.)

Step 23. Draw a 2″ radius ellipse in the top isoplane:

Prompt	Response
Command:	**Ellipse** (or TYPE: **EL**<**enter**>) (toggle to the top isoplane)
Specify axis endpoint of ellipse or [Arc/Center/Isocircle]:	TYPE: **I**<**enter**>
Specify center of isocircle:	**D2** (Count 2″ in both the 330 and 210 directions from the corner to locate the center of the ellipse. Make sure snap is ON.)
Specify radius of isocircle or [Diameter]:	TYPE: **2**<**enter**>

Step 24. On your own:

1. Copy the ellipse just drawn to the other four top corners, locating them in a similar manner.
2. Copy the front three ellipses 4″ in the 270 direction to form corners in the bottom plane. Make sure snap is ON.
3. Draw lines connecting the two outside ellipses using Osnap-Quadrant.
4. Use the Trim and Erase commands to remove the extra lines.
5. Add highlights on the front corner to complete the drawing.

Shape 6: A TV Shape with an Angled Back

While drawing in isometric, you will often need to draw angles. To do that you will need to locate both ends of the angle and connect them. You will not be able to draw any angle otherwise, such as the 62° angle in Figure 12–10.

Step 25. Draw the right side of Figure 12–10:

Prompt	Response
Command:	**Line** (or TYPE: **L**<**enter**>)
Specify first point:	**D1** (8′9-5/8″,9″)
Specify next point or [Undo]:	**Toggle to the right isoplane and with Ortho ON, move your mouse 30° upward to the right and** TYPE: **1′2**<**enter**>
Specify next point or [Undo]:	**Move your mouse straight up and** TYPE: **3**<**enter**>
Specify next point or [Close/Undo]:	<**enter**>
Command:	<**enter**> (to get the Line command back)
Specify first point:	**D1** (again) (**Endpoint**)
Specify next point or [Undo]:	**Move your mouse straight up and** TYPE: **1′6**<**enter**>
Specify next point or [Close/Undo]:	**Move your mouse 30° upward to the right and** TYPE: **6**<**enter**>
Specify next point or [Undo]:	**D3** (**Endpoint**)
Specify next point or [Close/Undo]:	<**enter**>

FIGURE 12–10
Shape 6: Drawing a TV Shape
with an Angle in One Plane

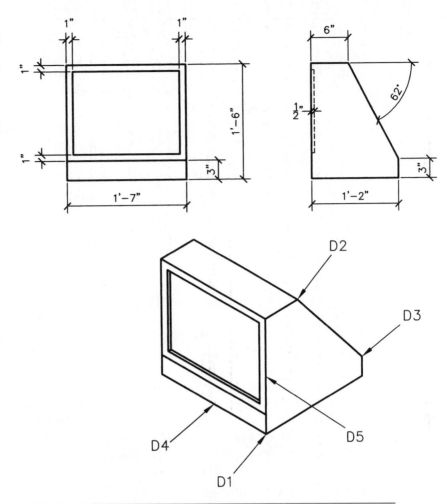

Step 26. Draw the left side and top of Figure 12–10:

Prompt	Response
Command:	**Line** (or TYPE: **L**<enter>)
Specify first point:	CLICK: **D1** (Figure 12–10)
Specify next point or [Undo]:	**Toggle to the left isoplane and with Ortho ON, move your mouse 150° upward to the left and** TYPE: **1′7**<enter>
Specify next point or [Undo]:	**Move your mouse straight up and** TYPE: **1′6**<enter>
Specify next point or [Close/Undo]:	**Toggle to the top isoplane and move your mouse 30° upward to the right and** TYPE: **6**<enter>
Specify next point or [Close/Undo]:	CLICK: **D2**
Specify next point or [Close/Undo]:	<enter>
Command:	**COPY** (or TYPE: **CP**<enter>)
Select objects:	CLICK: **D4**
Select objects:	<enter>
Specify base point or [Displacement] <Displacement>:	CLICK: **any point**
Specify second point or <use first point as displacement>:	**Toggle to the left isoplane and move your mouse straight up and** TYPE: **3**<enter>

Prompt	Response
Specify second point or [Exit/Undo] <Exit>:	Move your mouse straight up and TYPE: 4<enter>
Specify second point or [Exit/Undo] <Exit>:	Move your mouse straight up and TYPE: 1'5<enter>
Specify second point or [Exit/Undo] <Exit>:	Move your mouse straight up and TYPE: 1'6<enter>
Specify second point or [Exit/Undo] <Exit>:	<enter>
Command:	<enter>(to repeat the COPY command)
Select objects:	CLICK: **D5**
Select objects:	<enter>
Specify base point or [Displacement] <Displacement>:	CLICK: **any point**
Specify second point or <use first point as displacement>:	Move your mouse 150° upward to the left and TYPE: 1<enter>
Specify second point or [Exit/Undo] <Exit>:	Move your mouse upward 150° to the left and TYPE: 1'6<enter>
Specify second point or [Exit/Undo] <Exit>:	<enter>

Step 27. On your own:

1. Use the Trim command to trim unnecessary lines.
2. Use the Copy command to draw the two lines forming the inside edge of the TV screen.
3. Draw a line at the intersection of those copied lines.
4. Use the Trim command to trim unnecessary lines. The drawing is complete.

Shape 7: Isometric Detail—A Hexagonal-Shaped Vase

The final shape in this exercise combines several features (Figure 12–11).

Step 28. Draw the hexagonal shape of the vase (Figure 12–11A):

Prompt	Response
Command:	**Polygon** (or TYPE: **POL**<enter>)
Enter number of sides <4>:	TYPE: **6**<enter>
Specify center of polygon or [Edge]:	CLICK: **a point on a grid mark, in the approximate location shown in Figure 12–2 (with SNAP ON)**
Enter an option [Inscribed in circle/ Circumscribed about circle] <1>:	TYPE: **C**<enter>
Specify radius of circle:	TYPE: **6**<enter>

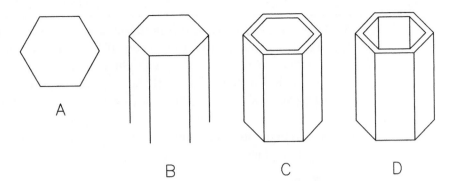

FIGURE 12–11

Shape 7: Drawing a Hexagonal-Shaped Vase

A

B   C   D

Now you have a hexagon that cannot be used in isometric drawing. To use it, you must block the hexagon and then insert it with different X and Y values. **Be sure to toggle to the top isoplane when you insert the hexagonal block.**

Step 29. Block and insert the hexagon (Figure 12–11B):

Prompt	Response
Command:	**Block** (or TYPE: **B**<enter>)
The Block Definition dialog box appears:	TYPE: **HEX** in the Name: box. **Make sure Delete is selected.** CLICK: **Pick point**
Specify insertion base point:	CLICK: **the center of the hexagon**
The Block Definition dialog box appears:	CLICK: **Select objects**
Select objects:	CLICK: **any point on the hexagon**
Select objects:	<enter>
The Block Definition dialog box appears:	CLICK: **OK**
The hexagon disappears:	
Command:	**Insert-Block…** (or TYPE: **I**<enter>)
The Insert dialog box appears:	CLICK: **the down arrow in the Name: box**
	CLICK: **HEX** (if it is not already in the Name: box)
	CHANGE: **Y: in the Scale area to .58** (This is a very close approximation to the isometric scale factor.)
	CLICK: **OK**
Specify insertion point or [Basepoint/ Scale/X/Y/X/Rotate]:	PICK: **the location of the isometric hexagon as shown in Figure 12–2** (ON SNAP) (5′7-9/16″, 2′-4″)
Specify rotation angle:	<enter>

Step 30. On your own:

1. Draw 1′-3″ vertical lines from each of the visible corners of the hexagon in the 270 direction (Figure 12–11B). (You can draw one line, then copy it three times.)
2. Using Osnap-Endpoint, draw lines to form the bottom of the hexagon (Figure 12–11C).

---

3. Copy the HEX block and pick the same point for base point and second point of displacement so that the copied HEX lies directly on top of the first HEX.

4. Use the Scale command to scale the copied HEX to a .8 scale factor. Be sure to CLICK: the center of the HEX block as the base point.

5. Draw vertical lines on the inside of the vase as shown in Figure 12–11D.

Step 31. When you have completed Exercise 12–1, save your work in at least two places.

Step 32. Plot or print the drawing on an 8-1/2″ × 11″ sheet of paper; use Fit to paper.

Exercise 12–2: Tenant Space Reception Desk in Isometric

The tenant space reception desk is drawn in isometric in Exercise 12–2. When you have completed Exercise 12–2, your drawing will look similar to Figure 12–12.

Step 1. Use your workspace to make the following settings:

1. Use SaveAs… to save the drawing on the hard drive with the name CH12-EX2.
2. Set drawing Units: **Architectural**
3. Set Drawing Limits: **15′,15′**
4. Set Snap: **Style-Isometric-1″**
5. Set GRIDDISPLAY: **0**
6. Set Grid: **4″**

FIGURE 12–12
Exercise 12–12: Tenant Space
Reception Desk in Isometric

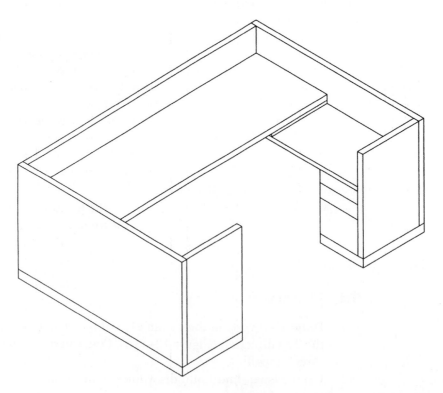

Part II: Two-Dimensional AutoCAD

7. Create the following Layer:

LAYER NAME	COLOR	LINETYPE	LINEWEIGHT
A-furn-iso-g	Green	Continuous	Default

8. Set **Layer A-furn-iso-g** current.
9. **Zoom-All.**

This exercise is a series of straight lines, all of which are on the isometric axes. It is suggested that you follow the step-by-step procedure described next so that you get some ideas about what you can and cannot do when using the isometric drawing method. To draw an isometric view of the reception desk (Figure 12–12) use the dimensions shown in Figure 12–14.

Step 2. Set Snap and Ortho ON. Toggle to the top isometric plane. Draw the top edge of the panels (Figure 12–13):

Prompt	Response
Command:	**Line** (or TYPE: **L<enter>**)
Specify first point:	**D1** (Figure 12–13) (absolute coordinates 8'1,7'4)
Specify next point or [Undo]:	TYPE: **@24<210<enter>** (or **move the mouse downward 30° to the left and** TYPE: **24<enter>**)

FIGURE 12–13
Drawing the Top Edge of the Panels

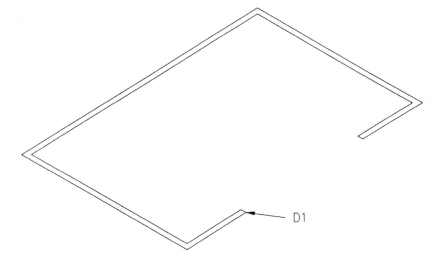

D1

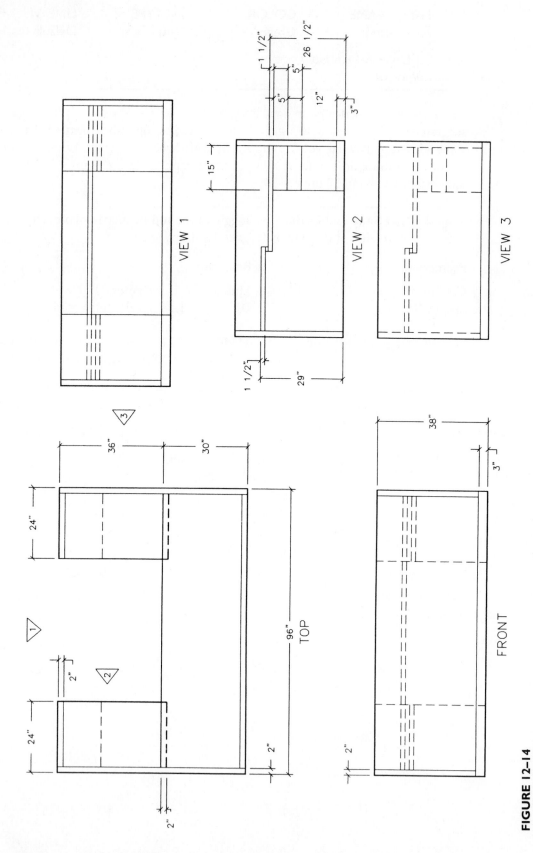

FIGURE 12-14
Dimensions of the Tenant Space Reception Desk (Scale: 3/8" = 1'-0")

412

Prompt	Response
Specify next point or [Undo]:	TYPE: @66<150<enter>
Specify next point or [Close/Undo]:	TYPE: @96<30<enter>
Specify next point or [Close/Undo]:	TYPE: @66<-30<enter>
Specify next point or [Close/Undo]:	TYPE: @24<210<enter>
Specify next point or [Close/Undo]:	TYPE: @2<150<enter>
Specify next point or [Close/Undo]:	TYPE: @22<30<enter>
Specify next point or [Close/Undo]:	TYPE: @62<150<enter>
Specify next point or [Close/Undo]:	TYPE: @92<210<enter>
Specify next point or [Close/Undo]:	TYPE: @62<330<enter>
Specify next point or [Close/Undo]:	TYPE: @22<30<enter>
Specify next point or [Close/Undo]:	TYPE: C<enter>

Step 3. Use the Extend command to extend the inside lines of the panels to form the separate panels (Figure 12–15):

Prompt	Response
Command:	**Extend** (or TYPE: **EX<enter>**)
Select objects or <select all>:	**<enter>** (enter Select all objects as boundary edges)
Select object to extend or shift-select to trim or [Fence/Crossing/Project/Edge/Undo]:	**D3,D4,D5,D6<enter>**

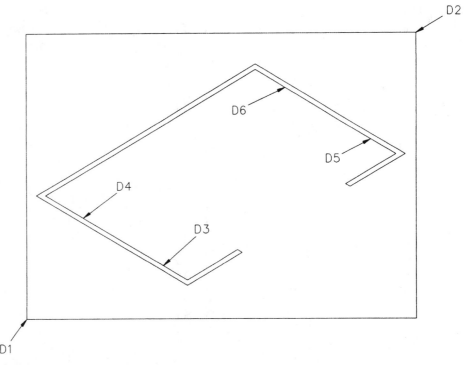

FIGURE 12–15
Extend Lines to Form the Separate Panels

Step 4. Copy the top edges of the panels to form the lower kickplate surfaces (Figure 12–16):

 TIP: You can also use direct distance entry to specify distances when you copy if you toggle to the correct isoplane.

Prompt	Response
Command:	**Copy** (or TYPE: **CP<enter>**)
Select objects:	**D1,D2,D3,D4**
Select objects:	**<enter>**
Specify base point or [Displacement] <Displacement>:	**D1** (any point is OK)
Specify second point or <use first point as displacement>:	TYPE: **@35<270<enter>**
Specify second point or [Exit/Undo] <Exit>:	TYPE: **@38<270<enter>**
Specify second point or [Exit/Undo] <Exit>:	**<enter>**

FIGURE 12–16
Copy the Top Edges to Form the Lower Kickplate Surfaces and the Edge of the Main Work Surface

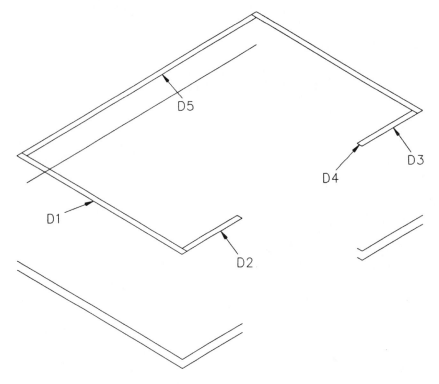

Step 5. Repeat the Copy command to draw the edge of the main work surface against the inside of the panel (Figure 12–16):

Prompt	Response
Command:	<enter>
Select objects:	**D5**
Select objects:	<enter>
Specify base point or [Displacement] <Displacement>:	**D5** (any point is OK)
Specify second point or <use first point as displacement>:	TYPE: **@9<270<enter>**

Step 6. On your own:

See Figure 12–17.

1. Set a running Osnap mode of Endpoint and draw vertical lines connecting top and bottom outside lines and the inside corner above the work surface. Next, you will draw the work surface.

Step 7. Draw the work surfaces (Figure 12–17).

Prompt	Response
Command:	**Line** (or TYPE: **L<enter>**)
Specify first point:	**Osnap-Endpoint, D1**
Specify next point or [Undo]:	TYPE: **@28<330<enter>**

FIGURE 12–17
Draw the Vertical Lines Connecting Top and Bottom Edges; Draw the Work Surfaces

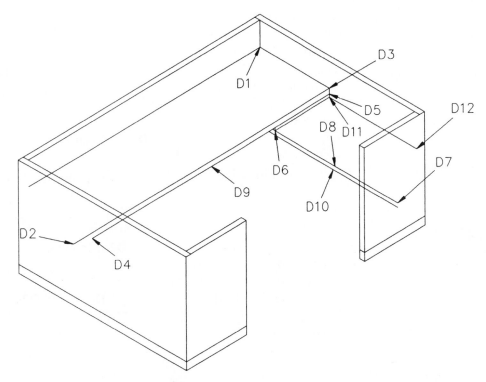

Prompt	Response
Specify next point or [Undo]:	**D2** (With Ortho ON and the top isoplane active, move your mouse downward 30° to the left and pick any point beyond the inside of the left partition; you can Trim these later.)
Specify next point or [Close/Undo]:	**\<enter\>**
Command:	**\<enter\>** (repeat LINE)
Specify first point:	**Osnap-Endpoint, D3**
Specify next point or [Undo]:	TYPE: **@1-1/2\<270\<enter\>**
Specify next point or [Undo]:	**D4** (pick another point outside the left partition)
Specify next point or [Close/Undo]:	**\<enter\>**
Command:	**\<enter\>** (repeat LINE)
Specify first point:	**Osnap-Endpoint, D5**
Specify next point or [Undo]:	TYPE: **@1\<270\<enter\>**
Specify next point or [Undo]:	TYPE: **@22\<210\<enter\>**
Specify next point or [Close/Undo]:	TYPE: **@1\<90\<enter\>**
Specify next point or [Close/Undo]:	**\<enter\>**
Command:	**\<enter\>** (repeat LINE)
Specify first point:	**Osnap-Endpoint, D6 (Figure 12–17)**
Specify next point or [Undo]:	**D7** (move the mouse downward 30° to the right and pick a point outside the right rear panel)
Specify next point or [Undo]:	**\<enter\>**
Command:	**\<enter\>** (Repeat LINE)
Specify first point:	**Osnap-Endpoint, D11**
Specify next point or [Undo]:	**D12** (pick a point outside the right rear panel) **\<enter\>**
Command:	**Copy** (or TYPE: **CP\<enter\>**)
Select objects:	**D8**
Select objects:	**\<enter\>**
Specify base point or [Displacement] \<Displacement\>:	**D8 (any point)**
Specify second point or \<use first point as displacement\>:	TYPE: **@1-1/2\<270\<enter\>**
Command:	**Extend** (or TYPE: **EX\<enter\>**)
Select objects or \<select all\>:	**D9\<enter\>**
Select object to extend or [Fence/Crossing/Project/ Edge/Undo]:	**D8,D10\<enter\>**

Step 8. Trim lines that extend outside the panels (Figure 12–18):

Prompt	Response
Command:	**Trim** (or TYPE: **TR\<enter\>**)
Select objects or \<select all\>:	**D1,D2,D3\<enter\>**
Select object to trim or shift-select to extend or [Fence/Crossing/ Project/Edge/eRase/Undo]:	**D4,D5,D6,D7,D8,D9\<enter\>**

FIGURE 12–18
Trim Lines and Draw the
Drawer Pedestal

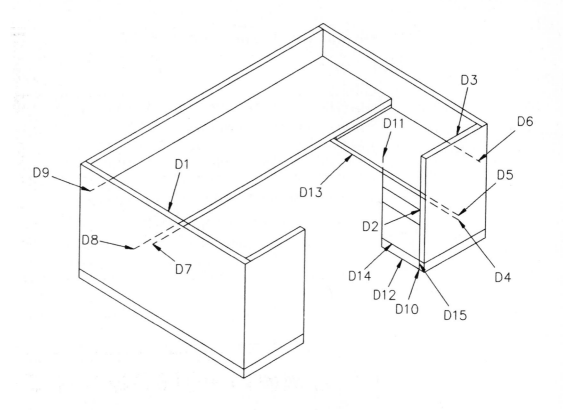

Step 9. Draw the drawer pedestal (Figure 12–18):

Prompt	Response
Command:	**Line** (or TYPE: **L\<enter>**)
Specify first point:	**Osnap-Endpoint, D10**
Specify next point or [Undo]:	**Toggle to the left isoplane and** TYPE: **@15<150\<enter>**
Specify next point or [Undo]:	**D11** (with Ortho ON, pick a point above the bottom edge of the desktop)
Specify next point or [Close/Undo]:	**\<enter>**
Command:	**Copy** (or TYPE: **CP\<enter>**)
Select objects:	**D12** (Figure 12–18)
Select objects:	**\<enter>**
Specify base point or [Displacement] \<Displacement>:	**D12 (any point)**
Specify second point or \<use first point as displacement>:	TYPE: **@3<90\<enter>**
Specify second point or [Exit/Undo] \<Exit>:	TYPE: **@15<90\<enter>**
Specify second point or [Exit/Undo] \<Exit>:	TYPE: **@20<90\<enter>**
Specify second point or [Exit/Undo] \<Exit>:	**\<enter>**

Step 10. Trim the extra lines:

Prompt	Response
Command:	**Trim** (or TYPE: **TR**<enter>)
Select objects or <select all>:	**D13,D14**<enter>
Select object to trim or shift-select to extend or [Fence/Crossing/ Project/Edge/eRase/Undo]:	**D15,D11**<enter>

Dimensioning in Isometric

You can resolve the problem of placing dimensions on an isometric drawing by buying a third-party software dimensioning package designed specifically for isometric. Other methods, such as using the aligned option in dimensioning and using an inclined font with the style setting, solve only part of the problem. Arrowheads must be constructed and individually inserted for each isoplane. If you spend a little time blocking the arrowheads and customizing your menu, you can speed up the process significantly.

 NOTE: You will find it quick to CLICK: the Layout viewport boundary, RIGHT-CLICK: and Select **Properties** from the right-click menu.

Step 11. When you have completed Exercise 12–2, save your work in at least two places.

Step 12. CLICK: **Layout1**, CLICK: **the viewport boundary**, RIGHT-CLICK, **and use Properties menu to set a standard scale of 1/2″ = 1′. Plot or print the drawing on an 8-1/2″ × 11″ sheet of paper.**

Gradient Hatch

Gradient (the tab on the Hatch and Gradient dialog box) can be used to render two-dimensional drawings such as the isometric drawings in this chapter (Figure 12–19). The appearance of these renderings is very similar to air brush renderings. The three means you can use to change the pattern appearance are

1. Select one of the nine pattern buttons.
2. Check: Centered (or Uncheck: centered).
3. Change the angle of the pattern.

In addition, you can select a color and vary its shade.
In general follow these guidelines:

1. When selecting a gradient pattern those on left and right isoplanes should be placed at a 60° angle to a horizontal line. Top isoplanes can vary from a horizontal pattern (90° of rotation) to 30°.
2. Use the center pattern on the top row to shade holes. This pattern should be at a 0° angle in the top isoplane, 120° in the left isoplane, and 60° in the right isoplane. The Centered button should be unchecked so that the pattern shows a darker area on one side of the hole than on the other side.

FIGURE 12–19
Exercise 12–3 Complete

419

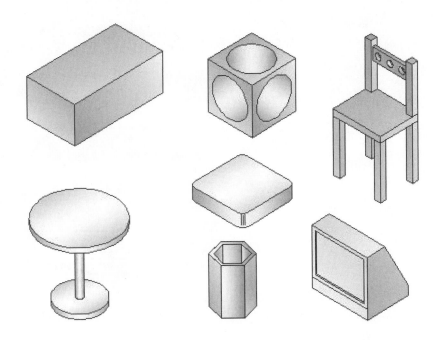

3. Do not be too concerned about where the light is coming from. Consider that there are varying sources of light. Just try to keep light areas next to dark ones and do not be afraid to experiment with any of the nine patterns. Some figures will be challenging and will require several trys before the rendering looks right.

4. Use the Draw order: command to "Send to back" all your gradient patterns so that the lines of the drawing show in front of the gradient patterns.

Exercise 12–3: Using Gradient Patterns to Render the Shapes of Exercise 12–1

Step 1. Open drawing CH12-EX1.

Step 2. Save the drawing as CH12-EX3.

Step 3. Open the Hatch and Gradient dialog box and select a color:

Prompt	Response
Command:	Hatch… (or TYPE: H<enter>)
The Hatch and Gradient dialog box appears:	With the Gradient tab selected: CLICK: the ellipsis (the three dots) to the right of the one color swatch
The Select Color dialog box (Figure 12–20) appears:	CLICK: the Index Color tab CLICK: a color (for now, number 42) CLICK: OK

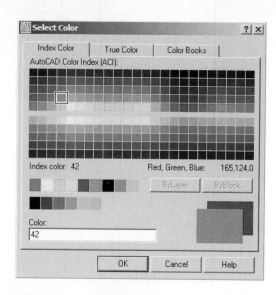

FIGURE 12–20
Select a Color for Gradient Hatch

Step 4. Hatch the top plane of Shape 1, Figure 12–21.

Prompt	Response
The Hatch and Gradient dialog box appears:	CLICK: **the first pattern from the left on the top row to select it** **Uncheck the Centered box** **Change the Angle to 300** CLICK: **Send to back** (in the Draw order: list) so the lines are visible CLICK: **Add: Pick points**
Pick internal point or [Select objects/remove Boundaries]:	CLICK: **any point inside the top plane of Shape 1**
Pick internal point or [Select objects/remove Boundaries]:	**<enter>**
The Hatch and Gradient dialog box appears:	CLICK: **Preview**
Pick or press Esc to return to dialog or <Right-click to accept hatch>:	**RIGHT-CLICK** (if the pattern looks right) or PRESS: **Esc and fix the dialog box**
Command:	**<enter>** (Repeat Hatch)

Step 5. Hatch the left plane of Shape 1, Figure 12–21:

Prompt	Response
The Hatch and Gradient dialog box appears:	CLICK: **the first pattern from the left on the top row to select it.** **Uncheck the Centered box** **Change the Angle to 255** CLICK: **Send to back** CLICK: **Add: Pick Points**
Pick internal point or [Select objects/remove Boundaries]:	CLICK: **any point inside the left plane of Shape 1**

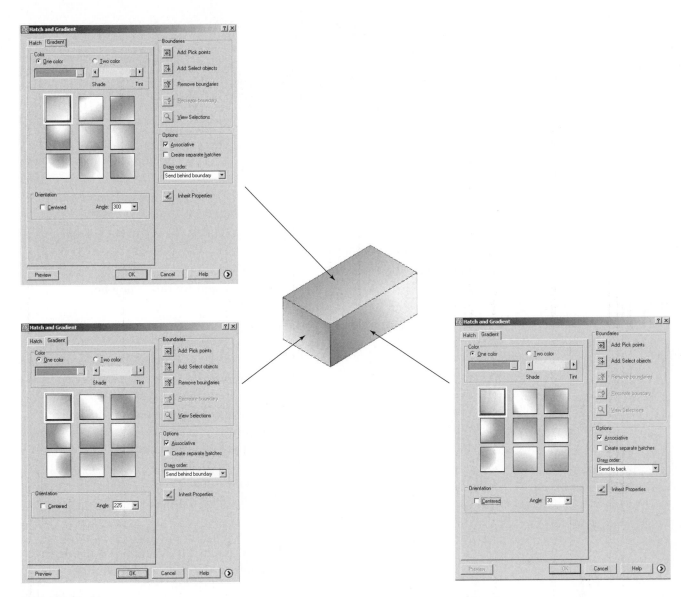

FIGURE 12–21
Apply Gradient Hatch Patterns to Shape 1

Prompt	Response
Pick internal point or [Select objects/remove Boundaries]:	<enter>
The Hatch and Gradient dialog box appears:	CLICK: **Preview**
Pick or press Esc to return to dialog or <Right-click to accept hatch>:	**RIGHT-CLICK** (if the pattern looks right) or PRESS: **Esc and fix the dialog box**
Command:	<enter>(Repeat Hatch)

Step 6. Hatch the right plane of Shape 1, Figure 12–21:

Prompt	Response
The Hatch and Gradient dialog box appears:	CLICK: **the first pattern from the left on the top row to select it**

Prompt	Response
	Uncheck the Centered box
	Change the Angle to 30
	CLICK: **Send to back**
	CLICK: **Add: Pick Points**
Pick internal point or [Select objects/remove Boundaries]:	CLICK: **any point inside the right plane of Shape 1**
Pick internal point or [Select objects/remove Boundaries]:	<enter>
The Hatch and Gradient dialog box appears:	CLICK: **Preview**
Pick or press Esc to return to dialog or <Right-click to accept hatch>:	**RIGHT-CLICK** (if the pattern looks right) or PRESS: **Esc and fix the dialog box**

Step 7. Hatch the top planes of Shape 4, Figure 12–22:

Prompt	Response
Command:	TYPE: **H**<enter>
The Hatch and Gradient dialog box appears:	CLICK: **the second pattern from the left on the top row to select it**
	Uncheck the Centered box
	Change the Angle to 300
	CLICK: **Send to back**
	CLICK: **Add: Pick Points**
Pick internal point or [Select objects/remove Boundaries]:	CLICK: **any point inside the top plane of Shape 4**, then CLICK: **any point inside the top plane of the base**, as shown in Figure 12–22.

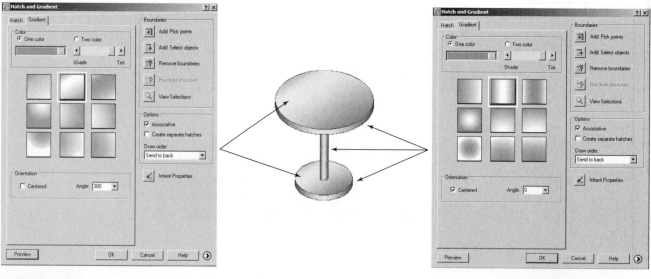

FIGURE 12–22
Gradient Hatch Patterns for Shape 4

Prompt	Response
Pick internal point or [Select objects/remove Boundaries]:	<enter>
The Hatch and Gradient dialog box appears:	CLICK: **Preview**
Pick or press Esc to return to dialog or <Right-click to accept hatch>:	**RIGHT-CLICK** (if the pattern looks right) or PRESS: **Esc and fix the dialog box**

Step 8. Hatch the cylindrical planes of Shape 4, Figure 12–22:

Prompt	Response
Command:	TYPE: **H**<enter>
The Hatch and Gradient dialog box appears:	CLICK: **the second pattern from the left on the top row to select it**
	Check the Centered box
	Change the Angle to 0
	CLICK: **Send to back**
	CLICK: **Add: Pick Points**
Pick internal point or [Select objects/remove Boundaries]:	CLICK: **any point inside the top edge of the table top, Figure 12–22.**
Pick internal point or [Select objects/remove Boundaries]:	<enter>
The Hatch and Gradient dialog box appears:	CLICK: **Preview**
Pick or press Esc to return to dialog or <Right-click to accept hatch>:	**RIGHT-CLICK** (if the pattern looks right) or PRESS: **Esc and fix the dialog box**

Step 9.   On your own:

1. Use the same settings in the Hatch and Gradient dialog box to apply patterns to the post and the base edge. You will have to do each one separately because the areas to be hatched are much different in size.

Step 10. Use the Inherit Properties option to Hatch Shape 5, Figure 12–23:

FIGURE 12–23
Use Inherit Properties to
Hatch Shape 5—Select
Associative Hatch Object

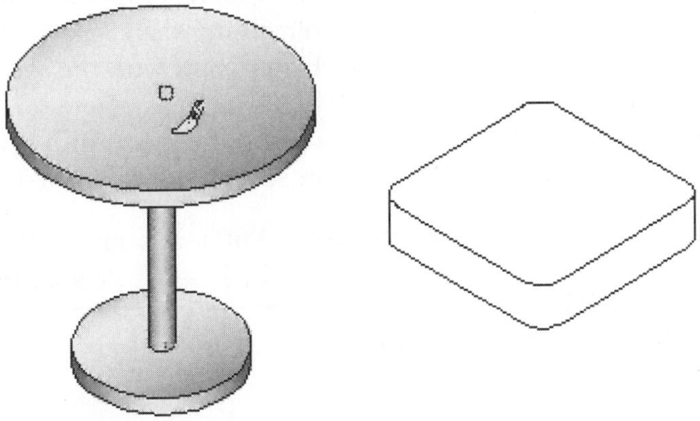

FIGURE 12–24
Select Internal Point

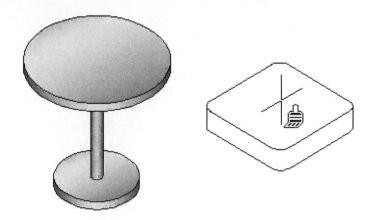

Prompt	Response
Command:	TYPE: **H<enter>**
The Hatch and Gradient dialog box appears:	CLICK: **Inherit Properties**
Select hatch object:	CLICK: **the top surface of Shape 4, Figure 12–23.**
Pick internal point or [Select objects/remove Boundaries]:	CLICK: **the top surface of Shape 5, Figure 12–24**
Pick internal point or [Select objects/remove Boundaries]:	**<enter>**
	CLICK: **Send to back**
	CLICK: OK
Command:	**<enter>**(Repeat Hatch)
The Hatch and Gradient dialog box appears:	CLICK: **Inherit Properties**
Select hatch object:	CLICK: **The post pattern of Shape 4**
Pick internal point or [Select objects/remove Boundaries]:	CLICK: **The unshaded surface of Shape 5**
Pick internal point or [Select object/remove Boundaries]:	**<enter>**
	CLICK: OK

Step 11. On your own:

1. Use the gradient hatch patterns shown in Figure 12–25 to hatch five of the areas of Shape 3. Use Inherit Properties to select hatch patterns from Shapes 1 and 5 to complete Shape 3.
2. Use Inherit Properties and any other patterns you need to shade the remaining shapes so your final drawing looks similar to Figure 12–19.
3. Experiment with the Wipeout command on the Draw menu to create highlights in areas where no hatch pattern should appear. Wipeout completely covers any image hiding any part or all of it. You will find uses for Wipeout in several types of illustrating.

Step 12. Put your name in the lower right corner and plot the drawing at a scale of 1″ = 1′. Be sure the Shade plot: box shows: As Displayed.

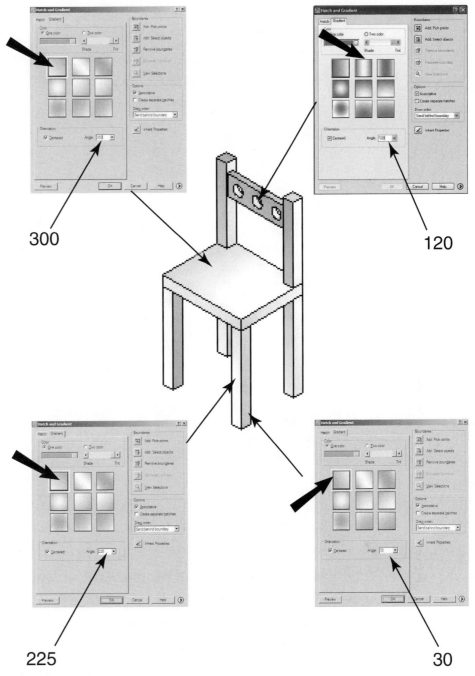

300

120

225

30

FIGURE 12–25
Gradient Hatch Patterns for Shape 3

FIGURE 12–26
Exercise 12–4, Completed

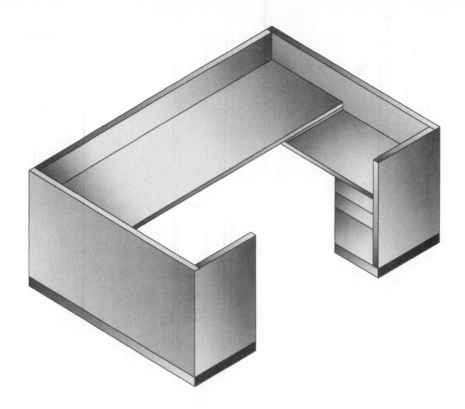

Exercise 12–4: Using Gradient Patterns to Render the Reception Desk of Exercise 12–2.

Open CH12-EX2 and use gradient hatch patterns to shade this drawing so it looks similar to Figure 12–26. When you have completed the hatching put your name in the lower right corner and plot this drawing at a scale of 1/2″ = 1′-0″. Be sure the Shade plot: box shows: As Displayed.

Exercise 12–5: Tenant Space Reception Seating Area in Isometric

1. Make an isometric drawing, full size, of the chairs, coffee table, and corner table to show the entire reception room seating area. Use the dimensions shown in Figure 12–27.
2. CLICK: **Layout1**, CLICK: **the viewport boundary,** and use Properties from the Modify menu to set a standard scale of 1/2″ = 1′. Plot or print the drawing on an 8-1/2″ × 11″ sheet of paper.

Exercise 12–6: Tenant Space Conference Chair in Isometric

1. Make an isometric drawing, full size, of the conference room chair. Use the dimensions shown in Figure 12–28.
2. CLICK: **Layout1**, CLICK: **the viewport boundary,** and use Properties from the Modify menu to set a standard scale of 1/2″ = 1′. Plot or print the drawing on an 8-1/2″ × 11″ sheet of paper.

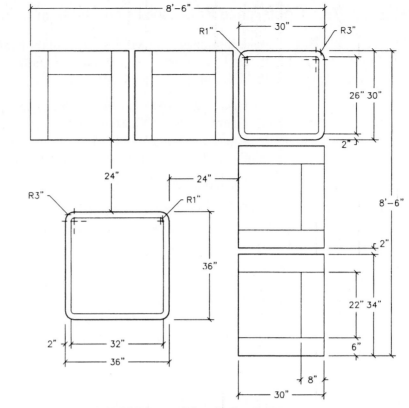

RECEPTION AREA FURNITURE
PLAN VIEW

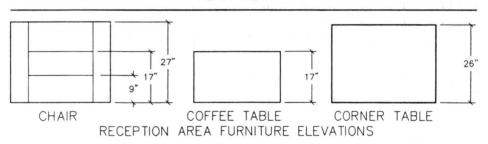

CHAIR   COFFEE TABLE   CORNER TABLE
RECEPTION AREA FURNITURE ELEVATIONS

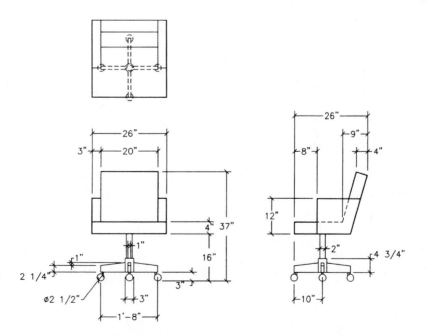

Chapter 12: Isometric Drawing and Gradient Hatch Rendering

427

Exercise 12–7: Conference Room Walls and Table in Isometric

1. Make an isometric drawing, full size, of the conference room shown in Figure 12–29. Draw a view from the direction shown by the arrow in Figure 12–29(A). The following figures provide the information needed to complete Exercise 12–7:

   ☐ Figure 12–29(A): Plan view of the conference room.
   ☐ Figure 12–29(B): Elevation of the north wall of the conference room.
   ☐ Figure 12–29(C): Elevation of the east wall of the conference room.
   ☐ Figure 12–29(D): Plan and elevation views of the conference table.

   Your final drawing should look similar to Figure 12–29(E).

2. CLICK: **Layout1**, CLICK: **the viewport boundary,** and use Properties from the Modify menu to set a standard scale of 1/4″ = 1′. Plot or print the drawing on an 8-1/2″ × 11″ sheet of paper.

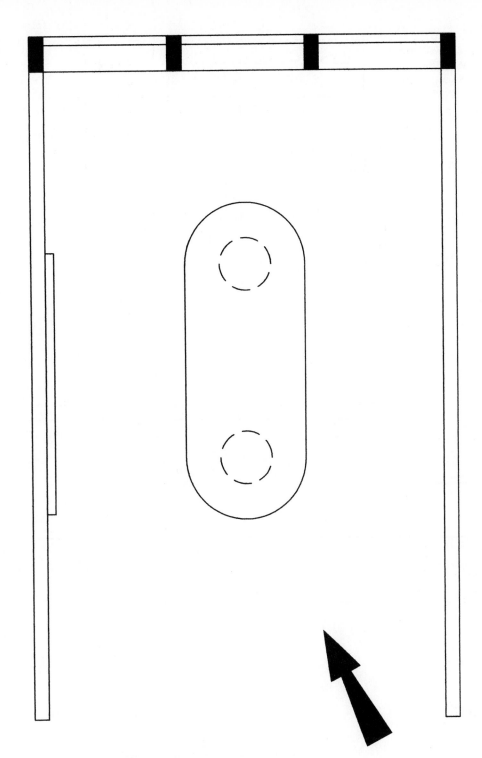

FIGURE 12–29(A)
Exercise 12–7: Plan View of
the North Part of the
Conference Room
(Scale: 3/8″ = 1′-0″)
(Courtesy of Micaela
Charabie)

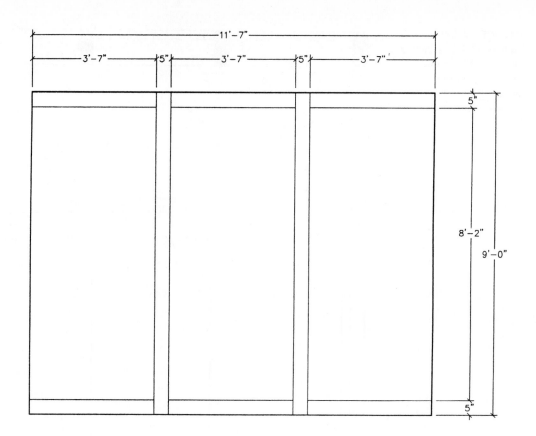

FIGURE 12–29(B)
Exercise 12–7: Elevation of
the North Wall of the
Conference Room
(Scale: 3/8″ = 1′-0″)

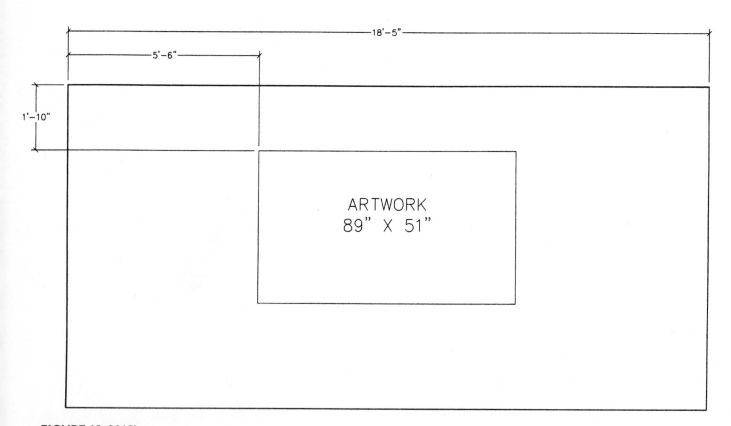

FIGURE 12–29(C)
Exercise 12–7: Elevation of the East Wall of the Conference Room (Scale: 3/8″ = 1′-0″)

ARTWORK
89″ X 51″

FIGURE 12–29(D)
Exercise 12–7: Plan and
Elevation Views of the
Conference Table
(Scale: 3/8″ = 1′-0″)

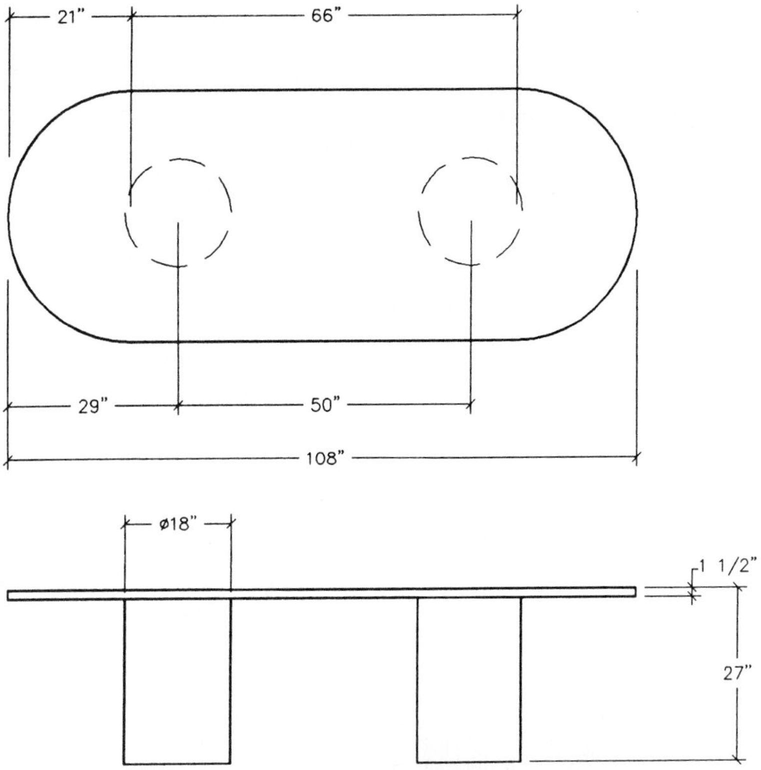

21″

66″

29″

50″

108″

Ø18″

1 1/2″

27″

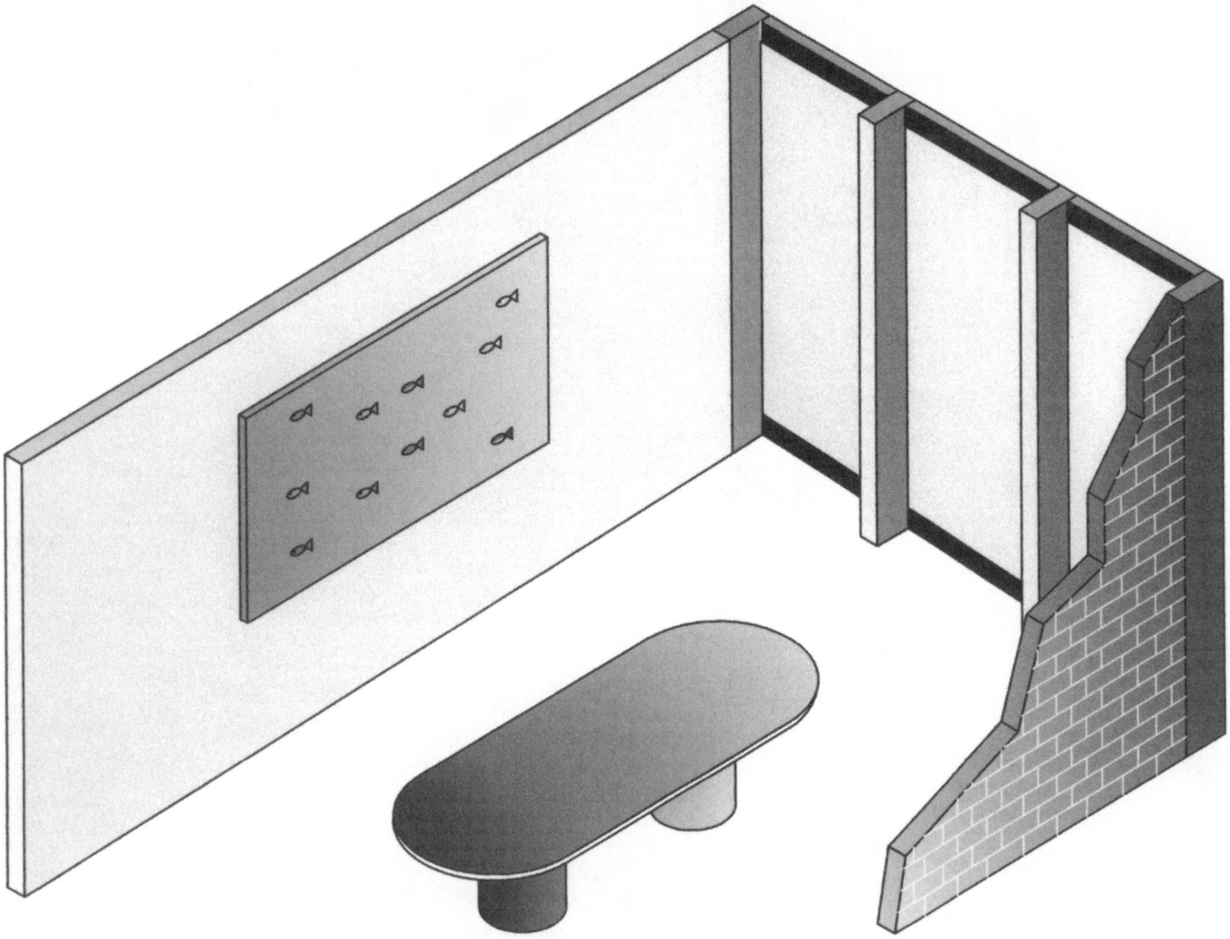

FIGURE 12–29(E)
Exercise 12–7: Gradient Hatch Isometric View of the North Part of the Conference Room
(Scale: 1/4″ = 1′ = 0″)

Chapter 12: Isometric Drawing and Gradient Hatch Rendering

Exercise 12–8:   Log Cabin Kitchen Isometric Cutaway Drawing

Exercise 12–8 is an isometric cutaway drawing of the log cabin kitchen, Figure 12–30. When you have completed Exercise 12–8 your drawing will look similar to Figure 12–30, but your drawing will be in color.

Use the dimensions from Figures 12–32 and 12–33, and if necessary, measure some of the features in the isometric drawings (Figures 12–30 and 12–31) using the scales indicated.

1. Use your workspace to make the following settings:

   1. **Use SaveAs… to save the drawing with the name CH12-EX8.**
   2. Set drawing Units: **Architectural**
   3. Set Drawing Limits: **30′,40′**

FIGURE 12–30
Exercise 12–8: Log Cabin
Kitchen Cutaway
(Scale: 3/8″ = 1′-0″)

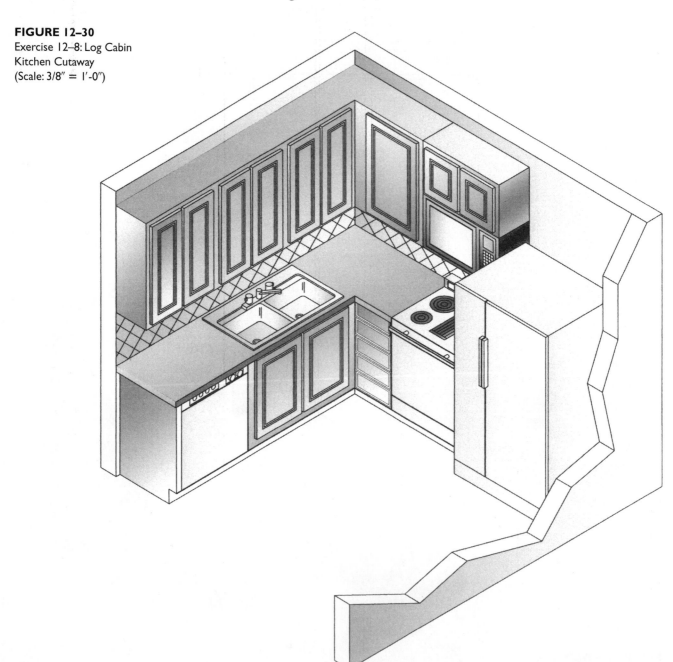

FIGURE 12–31
Log Cabin Kitchen Sink
(Scale: 1″ = 1′-0″)

4. Set GRIDDISPLAY: **0**
5. Set Grid: **12″**
6. Set Isometric Snap: **3″**
7. Create the following Layers:

LAYER NAME	COLOR	LINETYPE	LINEWEIGHT
Kitchen	White	Continuous	0.15mm
Kitchen Thin	Magenta	Continuous	0.05mm
Text	White	Continuous	Default
Hatch	Varies	Continuous	Default
Walls	White	Continuous	0.30mm

2. You will be able to draw one of the doors as a polyline, offset it to the inside 2″ once, ½″ twice, and then copy it and stretch it to make all the other doors. It may be helpful to block the doors and insert them as you are drawing.

3. Use different colors in the gradient hatch box (CLICK: the ellipsis… in the Color area) to apply gradient hatch patterns to each of the areas such as wood, appliances, and sink.

4. The backsplash is a combination of two hatch patterns, a gradient pattern (send to back) and a double, user-defined 60° angle with 4″ spacing on the left side and a double, user-defined 120° angle with 4″ spacing on the right side.

5. You can also insert the appliances from the DesignCenter that you used in Exercises 9–7 and 9–8 to get measurements of many of the details.

6. Plot the drawing at a scale of 3/8″ = 1′-0″ centered vertically on an 8-1/2″ × 11″ sheet.

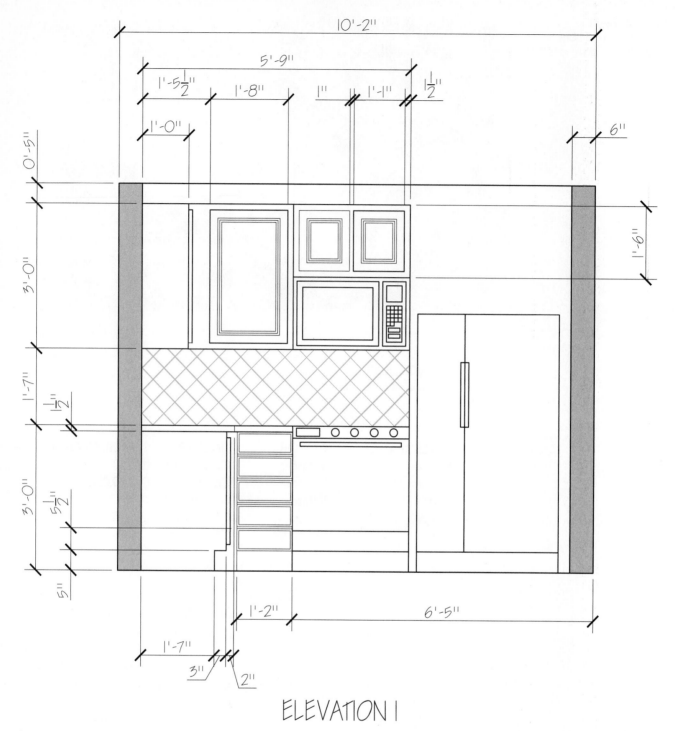

ELEVATION 1

FIGURE 12–32
Dimensions for Elevation 1

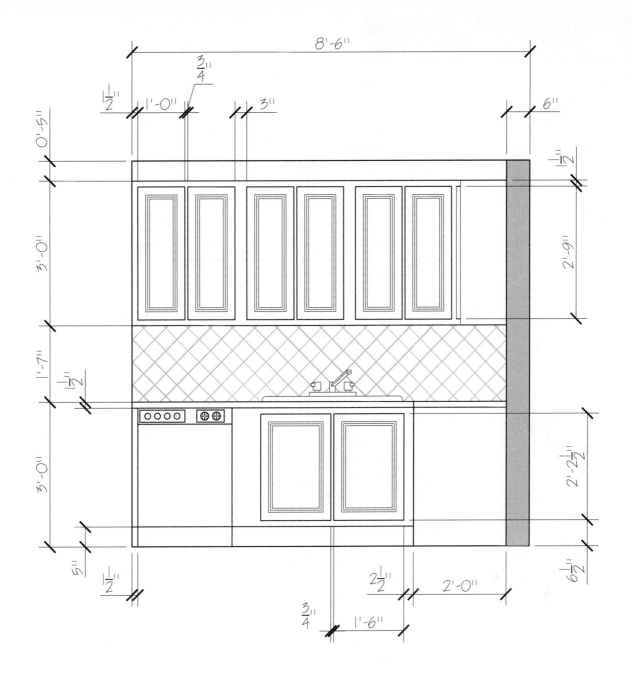

ELEVATION 2

FIGURE 12–33
Dimensions for Elevation 2

1. From which of the following selections on the Tools menu on the menu bar are the isometric snap and grid obtained?
    a. Layer Control…
    b. Drafting Settings…
    c. Set SysVars
    d. Grid On/Off
    e. UCS Control…

2. From which of the Snap options is the isometric snap obtained?
    a. ON
    b. OFF
    c. Aspect
    d. Rotate
    e. Style

3. Which of the following is *not* one of the normal isometric axes?
    a. 30
    b. 60
    c. 90
    d. 210
    e. 330

4. From which of the Ellipse prompts is the isometric ellipse obtained?
    a. <Axis endpoint 1>
    b. Center
    c. Isocircle
    d. Axis endpoint 2
    e. Rotation

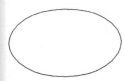

FIGURE 12–34

5. Which isoplane is used to draw the ellipse shown in Figure 12–34?
    a. Top
    b. Left
    c. Right

6. Which isoplane is used to draw the ellipse shown in Figure 12–35?
    a. Top
    b. Left
    c. Right

7. Which isoplane is used to draw the ellipse shown in Figure 12–36?
    a. Top
    b. Left
    c. Right

FIGURE 12–35

8. Which key(s) toggle from one isoplane to another?
    a. Ctrl-C
    b. F9
    c. F7
    d. F5
    e. Alt-F1

9. Which of the following is the same as −30°?
    a. 60°
    b. 150°
    c. 180°
    d. 210°
    e. 330°

FIGURE 12–36

10. Which tab on the Hatch and Gradient dialog box allows you to apply patterns shown in Figure 12–19?
    a. Gradient
    b. Advanced
    c. Hatch

Complete.

11. Which function key is used to turn the isometric grid ON and OFF?

_____

12. Write the correct syntax (letters and numbers) to draw a line 5.25″ at a 30° angle upward to the right.

_____

FIGURE 12–37

13. Write the correct sequence of keystrokes, using polar coordinates, to draw the right side of the isometric rectangle shown in Figure 12–37, after the first point (lower left corner) has been picked. Draw to the right and up.

   1. _____

   2. _____

   3. _____

   4. _____

14. In Exercise 12–2, why were lines drawn beyond where they should stop and then trimmed to the correct length?

_____

_____

15. Which of the isoplanes will not allow vertical lines to be drawn with a mouse when ORTHO is ON?

_____

16. List the six angles used for polar coordinates in drawing on isometric axes.

_____

17. Describe how to draw an angled line that is *not* on one of the isometric axes.

_____

_____

18. Describe how to use the Draw order: option in the Hatch and Gradient dialog box to make lines appear more prominent than a gradient hatch pattern.

_____

_____

19. Describe two problems that must be solved to place dimensions on an isometric drawing.

_____

_____

20. Describe the difference between isometric drawing and 3D modeling.

_____

_____

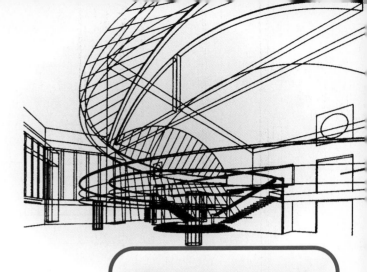

chapter

13

Creating Presentations with Layouts and Sheet Sets

objectives

When you have completed this chapter, you will be able to:

Correctly use the following commands and settings:

EDIT	RegenAll
Model Space	RESUME
MSLIDE	SCRIPT
MVIEW	SLDSHOW
MVSETUP	Tilemode
Paper Space	Viewports (VPORTS)
Redraw	VPLAYER
RedrawAll	VSLIDE
Regen	

Model Space and Paper Space

This chapter presents the details of how to use model space and paper space and how to plot multiple viewports. It also describes how to write a script file and prepare a slide presentation of your work. Let's begin with the concepts of model space and paper space.

Model Space

Model space is the 2D environment (and also 3D, as you will discover in Chapters 14 and 15) in which you have been working to this point. While in model space you can use the Viewports (VPORTS) command to divide the display screen into multiple viewports, as shown in Figure 13–1. Model space is limited in that although several viewports may be visible on the display screen, only one viewport can be active on the display screen at a time and only one viewport can be plotted. Model space is where your 2D or 3D model (drawing) is created and modified. When you start a new drawing, you are in model space. When the Model tab is clicked, you are in model space.

FIGURE 13–1
Viewports Created in Model
Space

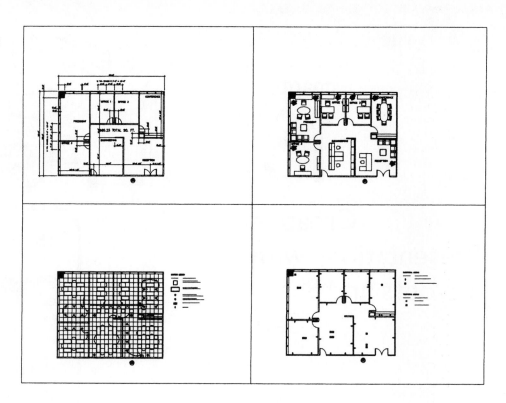

Paper Space

Paper space is similar to a piece of illustration board used to paste up a presentation. The MVIEW command, which operates only when Tilemode is OFF (0), is used to create and control viewport display; the display screen can be divided into multiple viewports. Each viewport can be treated as a single sheet of paper (on the illustration board) and can be copied, stretched, erased, moved, or scaled, as shown in Figure 13–2. You cannot edit the drawing within the viewport while it is in paper space; however, you can draw something over the viewport—for example, you can add dimensions or labels to a drawing. You can even overlap a viewport over one or more of the other viewports. You can also place the viewports into a single architectural format sheet, and you can plot all the viewports at the same time. When you click any of the Layout tabs, your drawing is placed into paper space.

Exercise 13–1: Creating a Printed Presentation of the Tenant Space Project by Combining Multiple Plans on One Sheet of Paper

When you have completed Exercise 13–1, your drawing will look similar to Figure 13–3.

Step 1. Open existing drawing CH11-EX1 and save it as CH13-EX1.

Step 2. Use Zoom-All to view the limits of the drawing.

Viewports (VPORTS)

Begin by dividing the screen into four viewports. Remember that while it is in model space the model (drawing) is the same in each viewport. If you edit the model in any

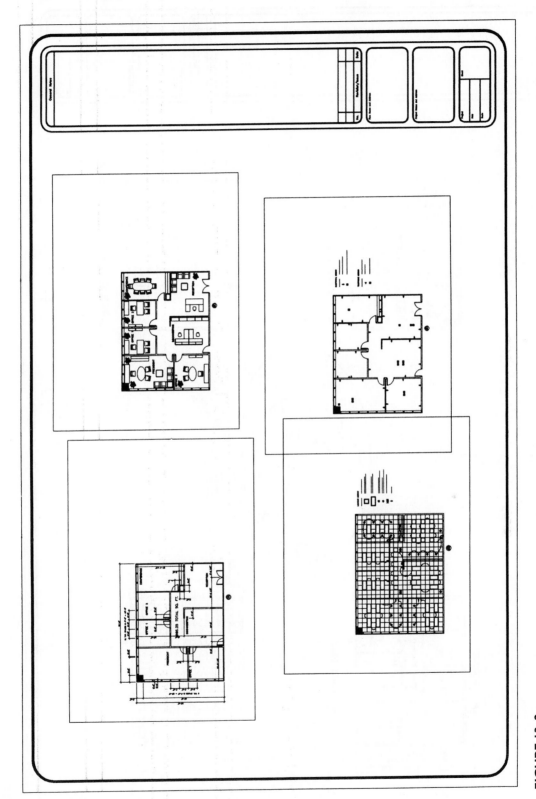

FIGURE 13-2
Viewports Modified in Paper Space

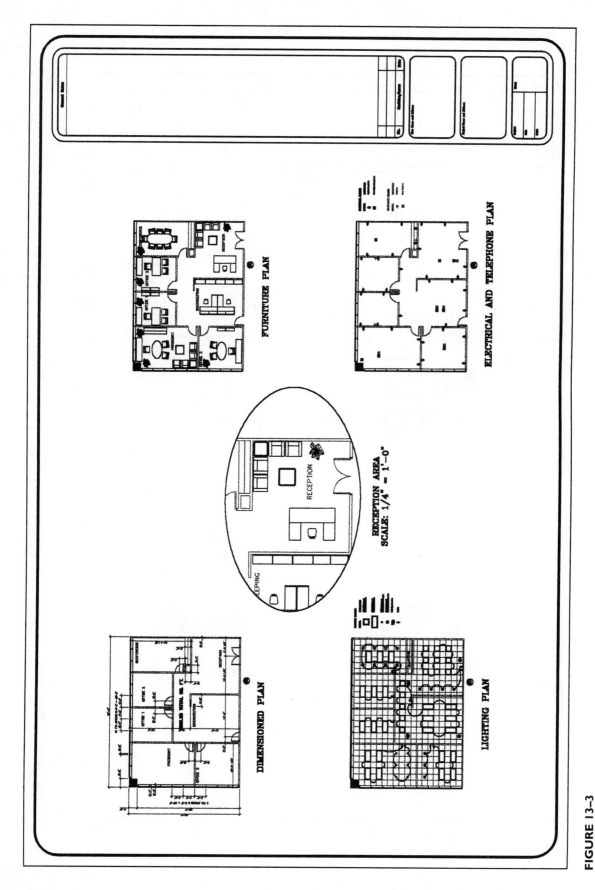

FIGURE 13–3

Exercise 13–1: Creating a Printed Presentation of the Tenant Space by Combining Multiple Plans on One Sheet of Paper

one viewport, you are doing it in all viewports. You may, however, freeze different layers in each viewport, which you will do later in this exercise; display a different UCS in each viewport; and you may zoom in or out in a viewport without affecting other viewport magnification.

Step 3. **Divide the screen into four viewports:**

Prompt	Response
Command:	TYPE: **-VPORTS**<**enter**>
Enter an option [Save/Restore/Delete/ Join/SIngle/?/2/<3>/4]<3>:	TYPE: **4**<**enter**> (or CLICK: **Viewports:4 viewports**) (or CLICK: **Viewports-New Viewports. . .** then CLICK: **Four Equal**)

The screen is now divided into four viewports. The active viewport, outlined with a solid line, displays the lines of the cursor when the cursor is moved into it. Inactive viewports display an arrow when the cursor is moved into those areas. To make a different viewport active, position the arrow in the desired viewport and press the click button on your mouse. The options of the viewports command are:

Save Allows you to name a set of viewports and save it for future use. Restore recalls the saved viewports. Any number of sets of viewports may be named, saved, and recalled.

Restore Restores a saved set of viewports. AutoCAD prompts you for the name of the saved viewport.

Delete Deletes a named viewport set. AutoCAD prompts you for the name of the saved viewport set to be deleted.

Join Joins two viewports into a larger one. The resulting view is the dominant viewport. AutoCAD prompts for the following when Join is picked:

Prompt	Response
Select dominant viewport <current viewport>:	<**enter**> (to accept the current active viewport, or click the one you want)
Select viewport to join:	CLICK: **the other viewport**

SIngle Returns the display to a single viewport. The resulting view is the current active viewport before single was selected.

? Lists the identification numbers and the screen positions of the current arrangement of viewports and all previously saved viewports by name if you accept the default <*> when AutoCAD prompts you for the viewport configuration to list.

2,3,4 Divides the current viewport into two, three, or four viewports with the same view, snap, grid, and layer settings. Selections 2 and 3 also allow you to select a vertical or horizontal arrangement. Selection 3 allows for two smaller viewports to the left or right of one larger one. You can divide the screen into as many as 64 viewports depending on your display.

On Your Own:

See Figure 13–4. Experiment with the viewports so that you can get an idea of how viewports can be useful in drawing as well as in presentation:

1. **Click the upper left viewport to make it active, and zoom a window around the lower right corner of the building in the upper left viewport.**

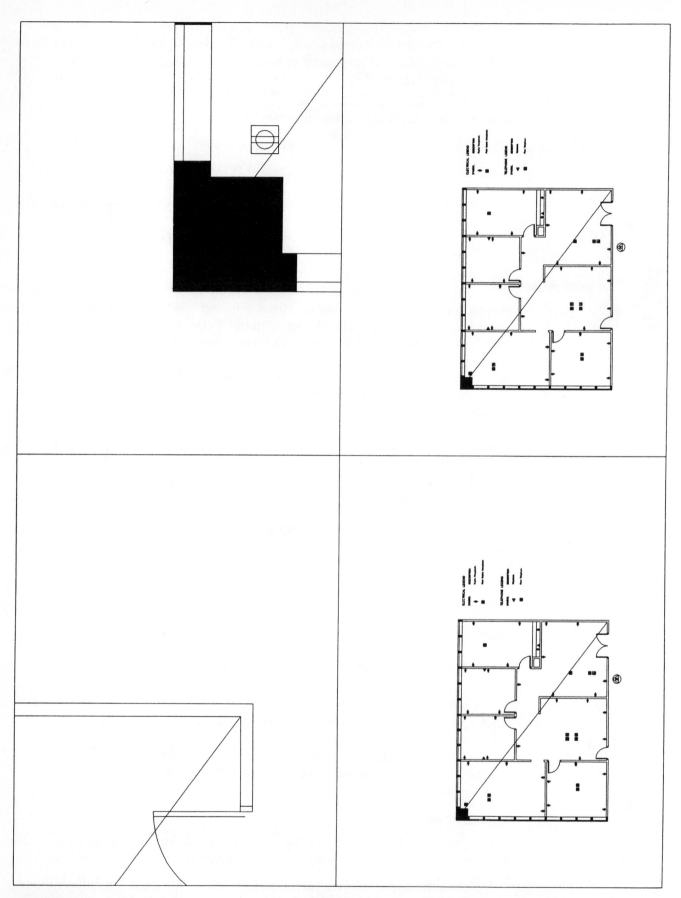

FIGURE 13–4
Start a Command in One Viewport and End It in Another

2. Click the upper right viewport to make it active, and zoom a window around the upper left corner of the building in the upper right viewport.

3. Draw a line from the lower right corner of the building to the upper left corner. Click the upper left viewport to make it active, start the Line command in the upper left viewport, and then click the upper right viewport to make it active, ending the line in the upper right viewport. (Be sure Ortho is OFF.)

When you begin a command in any viewport you must first click the viewport to make it active, so ending the line in the upper right viewport requires two picks: one to make the viewport active and one to complete the Line command. Experiment with this a little, and then use Undo to erase the line and Zoom-All in each viewport to return all displays to their original magnification. Use Redraw in the View menu to refresh the display in all viewports at the same time.

Redraw, Redrawall, Regen, and Regenall

The Redraw and Regen commands redraw or regenerate the drawing in the current viewport only. The RedrawAll and RegenAll commands redraw or regenerate the drawing in all viewports at the same time. When you TYPE: **R<enter>** you activate Redraw. When you CLICK: **Redraw** on the View menu you activate RedrawAll.

Tilemode

Two types of viewports, tiled and nontiled, are available to you in AutoCAD.

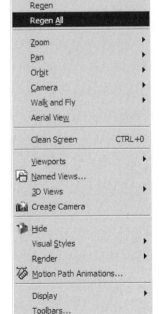

Tiled Viewport Characteristics   (When you CLICK: **the Model tab,** Tilemode is ON.) Tiled viewports are those that exist in model space with Tidemode ON. They have the following characteristics:

☐ They fill the graphics screen, lie side-by-side like ceramic tiles, and cannot be moved.
☐ They are fixed and cannot overlap.
☐ They can be deleted only by changing the viewport configuration.
☐ Only one tiled viewport can be active at a time.
☐ Only the active viewport can be plotted.
☐ Nothing drawn in a tiled viewport can be edited in a nontiled viewport.

Nontiled Viewport Characteristics   (When you CLICK: **the Layout tab,** Tilemode is OFF.) Nontiled viewports are those that exist in paper space or model space. They have the following characteristics:

☐ They may or may not fill the graphics screen.
☐ They can overlap.
☐ They can be moved, copied, scaled, stretched, or erased while they are in paper space.
☐ They can have different layers frozen in any viewport.
☐ All nontiled viewports can be plotted at the same time when they are in paper space.
☐ Nothing drawn in paper space can be edited in model space.

Tilemode Settings   Settings for Tilemode are 1 (ON) and 0 (OFF). The Tilemode setting determines whether the viewports displayed are tiled (1—ON) or nontiled (0—OFF).

☐ You can work in model space with Tilemode set either to 1 (ON) or 0 (OFF). You can move from paper space to model space with Tilemode OFF by clicking PAPER on the status bar at the bottom of your display or typing **MS<enter>**.

☐ Tilemode must be 0 (OFF) for you to work in paper space.

☐ The default for Tilemode is 1 (ON).

MVIEW

The MVIEW command operates only when Tilemode is set to 0 (OFF) and is used to create and control viewport display in model space and paper space. When you TYPE: **MV<enter>**, the Tilemode setting must first be set to 0 (OFF). The MVIEW options are:

OFF   Think of each viewport as a single sheet of paper (on the illustration board). The viewport can be copied, stretched, erased, moved, or scaled. The drawing within the viewport cannot be edited while it is in paper space. The OFF option turns off the views inside the viewport and saves regeneration time while you are editing the viewports. When the viewports are located so that you are pleased with the format, you can turn the views back on.

ON   Turns ON the model space view (drawing inside the viewport).

Shadeplot   Allows you to choose from four options: Wireframe, As displayed, Hidden, and Rendered. These options are discussed in the 3D chapters.

Lock   Allows you to lock the scale of a viewport so it does not change when you zoom in or out.

Object   Allows you to create a new viewport by selecting an existing object such as a circle.

Polygonal   Allows you to draw an irregular-shaped viewport using polyline lines and arcs.

Fit   Creates a single viewport to fill current paper space limits. Other viewports can be erased before or after the Fit option is used.

2,3,4   Creates two, three, or four viewports in a specified area or to fit the current paper space limits.

Restore   Restores saved model space viewports (saved with the Viewports (VPORTS) command) into paper space.

<First point>   Creates a new viewport defined by picking two corners or by typing the X and Y coordinates of lower left and upper right corners.

Step 4.   **The Layout Wizard combines most of the MVIEW options, so use the Layout Wizard to save the current viewport configuration in model space and restore it in paper space in an architectural format measuring 24″ × 36″ with all viewports at a scale of 1/8″ = 1′:**

Prompt	Response
Command:	CLICK: **Create-Layout Wizard** (from the Insert-Layout menu)
The Layout Wizard appears with the name Layout2:	CLICK: **Next**
The Printer option appears:	CLICK: **DWF6 ePlot.pc3** (or a plotter that plots ARCH D size [24.00 × 36.00 inches])
	CLICK: **Next**
The Paper size option appears:	LOCATE: **ARCH D [24.00 × 36.00 inches] in the paper size list and** CLICK: **it**
	CLICK: **Next**
The Orientation option appears:	CLICK: **Landscape**
	CLICK: **Next**
The Title block option appears:	CLICK: **Architectural Title Block.dwg**
	CLICK: **Next**

FIGURE 13-5
Defining Viewports in the
Layout Wizard

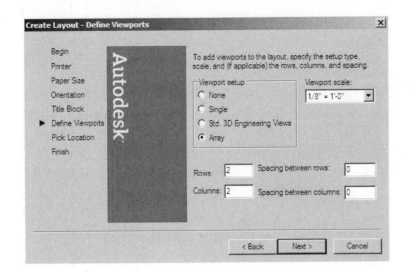

Prompt	Response
The Define Viewports option appears:	CLICK: **Array in the Viewport setup box** (Figure 13–5)
	CLICK: **1/8″=1′ in the Viewport scale: box**
	TYPE: **2 in the Rows: box**
	TYPE: **2 in the Columns: box**
	TYPE: **0 in the Spacing between rows: box**
	TYPE: **0 in the Spacing between columns: box**
	CLICK: **Next**
The Pick Location option appears:	CLICK: **Select location:**
Specify first corner:	TYPE: **2,2<enter>**
Specify opposite corner:	TYPE: **28,22<enter>**
The Finish option appears:	CLICK: **Finish**
Command:	**Paper Space** (or TYPE: **PS<enter>** or CLICK: **MODEL** on the status bar if you are not already in paper space)

 Note: The UCS icon appears as a triangle in paper space.

The Model Space command (with Tilemode OFF) switches you from paper space to model space with paper space viewports active. You may work in model space with Tilemode either ON or OFF.

Since you are presently in paper space, you know that Tilemode is 0 because paper space cannot be active unless Tilemode is 0. To return to model space, TYPE: **MS<enter>** or CLICK: **PAPER** on the status bar (not the Model tab).

Step 5. **Return to model space with Tilemode set to 0:**

Prompt	Response
Command:	TYPE: **MS<enter>** (or CLICK: **PAPER** on the status bar)

Step 6. On your own:

In the next part of this exercise, the VPLAYER command is used to freeze different layers in each viewport, to create a unique drawing in each viewport.

1. **Before continuing with the VPLAYER command, thaw all frozen layers. When all layers are thawed, they will all be visible in each viewport.**
2. **Set Attribute Display (TYPE: ATTDISP<enter>, then TYPE: OFF<enter>) to OFF so that the attributes will not appear on the furniture symbols.**
3. **CLICK: each model space viewport and Zoom-All so that all viewports show the entire drawing.**

VPLAYER

The VPLAYER command allows you to freeze different layers in any viewport. It works in either paper space or model space. To use the VPLAYER command, you must set TILEMODE to 0 (OFF) (CLICK: **any Layout tab**).

In model space, you can use the Layer Properties Manager dialog box to freeze layers in individual viewports by clicking the Freeze/Thaw button under the current heading beside the layer name. When you click the Freeze/Thaw button under the New heading, that layer is frozen for all new viewports created. Both of these buttons should be picked to freeze layers for newly created viewports.

The VPLAYER command options are:

? Lists layers frozen in selected paper space viewports.
Freeze Prompts you to list the names of layers you want to freeze, then prompts you for the viewports in which you want to freeze the layers. The viewport options are:

All—All viewports, while in model space or paper space.
Select—Switches to paper space (when you are in model space) and allows you to pick viewports for layer freeze.
Current—Selects the current viewport while in model space for layer freeze.

Thaw Prompts you as before to name the layers you want to thaw, then prompts you for the viewports in which you want to thaw the layers.
Reset After you use the Freeze or Thaw option to change a layer's visibility, you can use the Reset option to restore the default visibility setting for a layer in a selected viewport.
Newfrz Creates new layers that are frozen in all viewports. If you then want to thaw a layer in a single viewport, use the Thaw option.
Vpvisdflt If a layer is frozen in some viewports and thawed in others, you can use the Vpvisdflt option to set the default visibility per viewport for any layer. This default setting then determines the layer's visibility in any new viewport created with the MVIEW command.

Step 7. Use the VPLAYER command to freeze layers in the upper left viewport.

Prompt	Response
Command:	CLICK: **the upper left viewport to make it active**
Command:	TYPE: **VPLAYER<enter>**
Enter an option [?/Freeze/Thaw/Reset/	
Newfrz/Vpvisdflt]:	TYPE: **F<enter>**

TIP: You can PRESS: <**enter**> at the "Enter Layer name(s) to freeze or <select objects>" prompt and CLICK: objects that are on the layers you wish to freeze.

Prompt	Response
Enter layer name(s) to freeze or <select objects>:	TYPE: **A-AREA,A-FURN,A-CLNG,E-LITE, E-LITE-D,E-LITE-W,E-POWR,E-COMM, E-POWER-TXT**<**enter**>
Enter an option [All/Select/Current] <Current>:	<**enter**> (the current viewport)
Enter an option [?/Freeze/Thaw/ Reset/Newfrz/Vpvisdflt]:	<**enter**>

Step 8. On your own:

1. CLICK: the upper right viewport to make it active. Use the Layer Properties Manager dialog box to freeze layers in the current viewport. CLICK: the Freeze/Thaw icons in the Current. . . column so snowflakes appear as shown in Figure 13–6. CLICK: OK.

 TIP: If you cannot see the Current column, hold the cursor over the right border of the dialog box and when the double arrow appears hold down the left mouse button and drag the border to the right so the current column is visible.

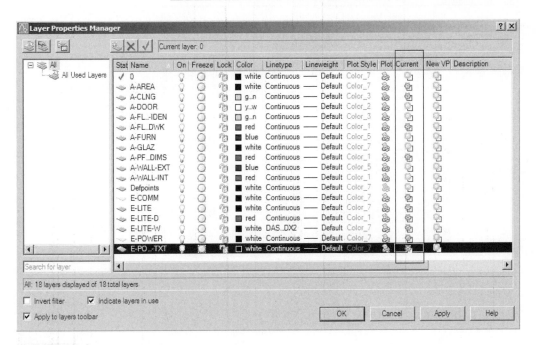

FIGURE 13–6
Frozen Layers in the Upper Right Viewport

The layers to be frozen in the upper right viewport (just in case you cannot identify them in the illustration) are:

A-AREA
A-CLNG
A-FLOR-WDWK
A-PFLR-DIMS
E-COMM
E-LITE
E-LITE-D
E-LITE-W
E-POWR
E-POWER-TXT

2. CLICK: the lower left viewport to make it active. Use the Layer Properties Manager dialog box to freeze layers in the current viewport. CLICK: "the Freeze/Thaw icons" in the Current. . . column as shown in Figure 13–7. CLICK: OK.

The layers to be frozen in the lower left viewport (just in case you cannot identify them in the illustration) are:

A-AREA
A-DOOR
A-FLOR-WDWK
A-FLOR-IDEN
A-FURN
A-PFLR-DIMS
E-COMM
E-POWR
E-POWER-TXT

3. CLICK: the lower right viewport to make it active. Use the Layer Properties Manager dialog box to freeze layers in the current viewport. CLICK: "the

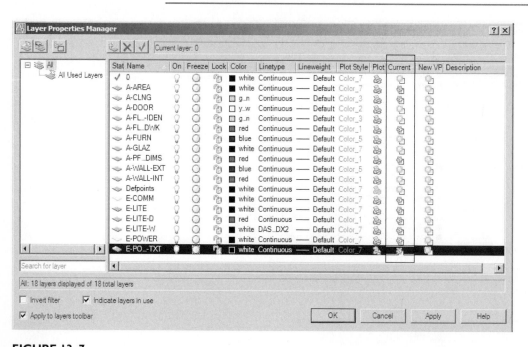

FIGURE 13–7
Frozen Layers in the Lower Left Viewport

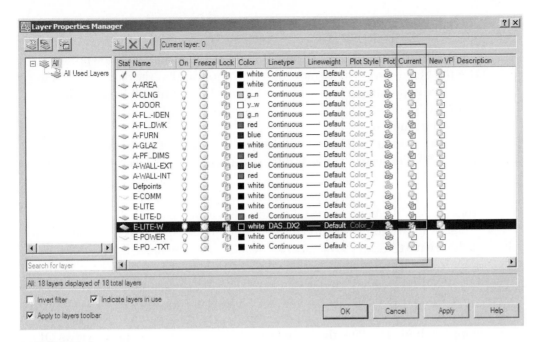

FIGURE 13–8
Frozen Layers in the Lower Right Viewport

Freeze/Thaw icons" in the Current... column as shown in Figure 13–8.
CLICK: **OK.**

The layers to be frozen in the lower right viewport (just in case you cannot identify them in the illustration) are:

A-AREA
A-CLNG
A-FLOR-IDEN
A-FLOR-WDWK
A-FURN
A-PFLR-DIMS
E-LITE
E-LITE-D
E-LITE-W

There will be occasions when you will want to select or deselect all Layers at the same time. To do that, position the cursor in an open area in the dialog box and PRESS: **the right mouse button,** then CLICK: **Select All** or **Clear All.**

Paper Space

The Paper Space command switches you from model space to paper space. Tilemode must be 0 (OFF) for Paper Space to work. Tilemode is still set to 0. You have been working in model space with Tilemode set to 0.

Step 9.   **Use the Paper Space command to return to paper space:**

Prompt	Response
Command:	**Paper Space** (or TYPE: **PS<enter>**) (or CLICK: **MODEL** on the status bar—not the Model tab)

Step 10. On your own:

1. You now have a 36″ × 24″ architectural format with the four viewports in it. Use the Move command to move the viewports so that they are centered in the space approximately as shown in Figure 13–9. You will have to pick the outside edge of any viewport to move it, or select all four viewports by using a crossing window.

2. Make sure you are still in PAPER SPACE. In the next part of this exercise the Modify Properties command is used to make sure each viewport is still a standard size of 1/8″ = 1′-0″.

3. CLICK: the boundary of all paper space viewports, then CLICK: Properties from the Modify menu and set a standard scale of 1/8″ = 1′ in all four viewports, as shown in Figure 13–10. Use Pan in model space to center images in each viewport. CLICK: Properties and CLICK: Display locked - Yes so the scale of the viewports is set until unlocked. Use Pan to center images in each viewport.

4. Use the MVIEW command (TYPE: MV<enter>) to turn off the model space views (drawings inside the viewports), as shown in Figure 13–10. Turning the viewports off decreases regeneration time and allows you to work faster on complex drawings. Pick the boundary of the viewport to turn the views OFF.

5. Use the Move command to move all viewports to the approximate locations as shown in Figure 13–11.

6. Use the Mview command (TYPE: MV<enter>) to turn ON the model space views.

Mvsetup

Because the viewports have been moved, it is possible that your model space views are not lined up vertically and horizontally. The Mvsetup command can be used to align the views (drawings) within each viewport.

Step 11. Use the Mvsetup command to align viewports in model space (Figure 13–12):

(You will have to **UNLOCK THE DISPLAY** in the Properties palette before using Mvsetup.)

Prompt	Response
Command:	TYPE: **MVSETUP**<enter>
Enter an option [Align/Create/ Scale viewports/Options/Title block/Undo]:	TYPE: **A**<enter>
Enter an option [Angled/Horizontal/ Vertical alignment/Rotate view/ Undo]:	TYPE: **H**<enter> (AutoCAD changes to model space)
Specify basepoint:	CLICK: **the lower right viewport to make it active**
	Osnap-Intersection
of	**D1**
Specify point in viewport to be panned:	CLICK: **the lower left viewport to make it active**
	Osnap-Intersection
of	**D2**

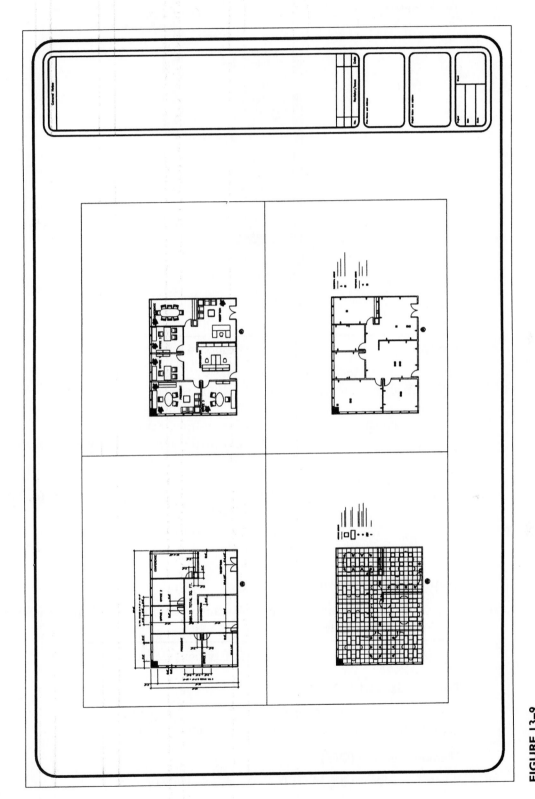

FIGURE 13-9
Position the Paper Space Viewports in the Architectural Format

453

FIGURE 13-10
Use Modify Properties to Set
a Scale of 1/8" = 1' for All
Four Viewports

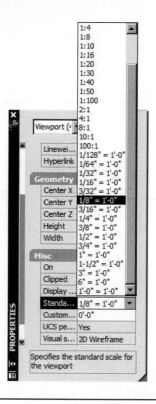

Prompt	Response
Enter an option [Angled/Horizontal/ Vertical alignment/Rotate view/ Undo]:	TYPE: **V\<enter\>**
Specify basepoint:	**Osnap-Intersection**
of	CLICK: **the upper right viewport to make it active** **D3**
Specify point in viewport to be panned:	CLICK: **the lower right viewport to make it active** **Osnap-Intersection**
of	**D1**

Step 12. On your own:

1. **Align, horizontally and vertically, any remaining model space views that need to be aligned.**

A brief description of the MVSETUP options follows:

Tilemode Set to 1 (ON)

When Tilemode is ON, MVSETUP acts just like SETUP in earlier versions of AutoCAD. You set Units, Scale, and Paper Size using prompts for each setting.

Tilemode Set to 0 (OFF)

When Tilemode is OFF, MVSETUP has the following options:

Align   This option lets you pan the view so that it aligns with a basepoint in another viewport. You may align viewports horizontally and vertically; you may align them at a specified distance and angle from a basepoint in another viewport; and you may rotate the view in a viewport about a basepoint. This option also has an undo feature.

FIGURE 13–11
Turn Off the Model Space Views and Move the Viewports

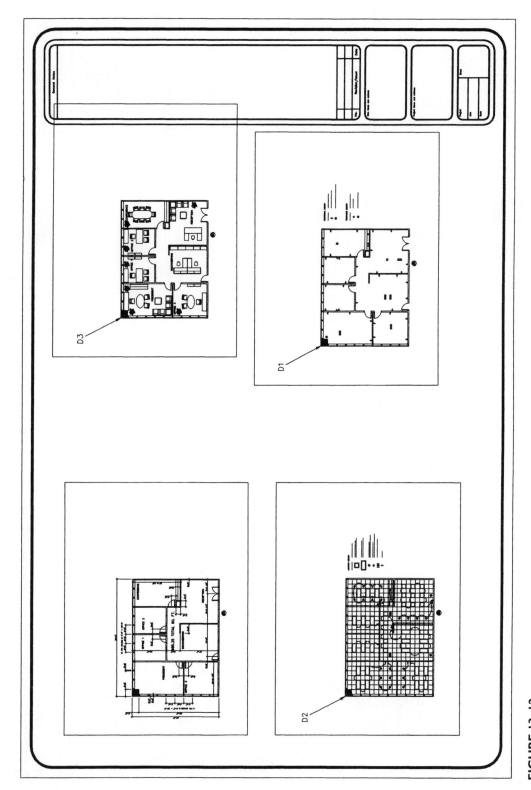

FIGURE 13–12
Use MVSETUP to Align the Views within Each Viewport

Create   This option allows you to delete existing viewports. It also allows you to create one or more standard-size viewports. If more than one is created, this option allows you to specify the distance between viewports. It also allows you to create an array of viewports. This option also has an undo feature.

Scale Viewports   This option allows you to set the scale of the drawing displayed in the viewports. The Properties command is now used for scaling viewports.

Options   This option allows you to specify a layer for the title block, reset paper space limits, change different units, or attach an Xref as the title block.

Title block   This option allows you to delete objects from paper space and to select the origin point for this sheet. It then prompts you to select one of 13 standard formats. This option also has an undo feature.

Undo   This is an undo option for the major routine.

Adding Details and Annotating Paper Space Viewports

Step 13.   **On your own:**

Add another viewport.

1. Draw an ellipse in paper space the approximate size and location of the one in Figure 13–13.

Step 14.   Now use the MVIEW command to make a new viewport of the ellipse:

Prompt	Response
Command:	TYPE: **MV**<enter>
Specify corner of viewport or [ON/ OFF/Fit/Shadeplot/Lock/Object/ Polygonal/Restore/2/3/4] <Fit>:	TYPE: **O**<enter>
Select object to clip viewport:	CLICK: **the ellipse**
	CLICK: **PAPER to move to MODEL space**

You are now in model space and have a viewport containing a view of the active model space viewport. All the layers are turned on. Later in the exercise, the borders of the large viewports will be frozen.

Step 15.   **On your own:**

1. Use Zoom-Window to obtain a view of the reception area of the tenant space.

Step 16.   Return to paper space and use the Modify Properties command to scale the view:

Prompt	Response
Command:	CLICK: **MODEL**
Command:	CLICK: **the elliptical viewport boundary; select Properties from the Modify menu**
	CLICK: **1/4″ = 1′-0″ from the Standard scale list**
	CLICK: **Yes from the Display locked list**

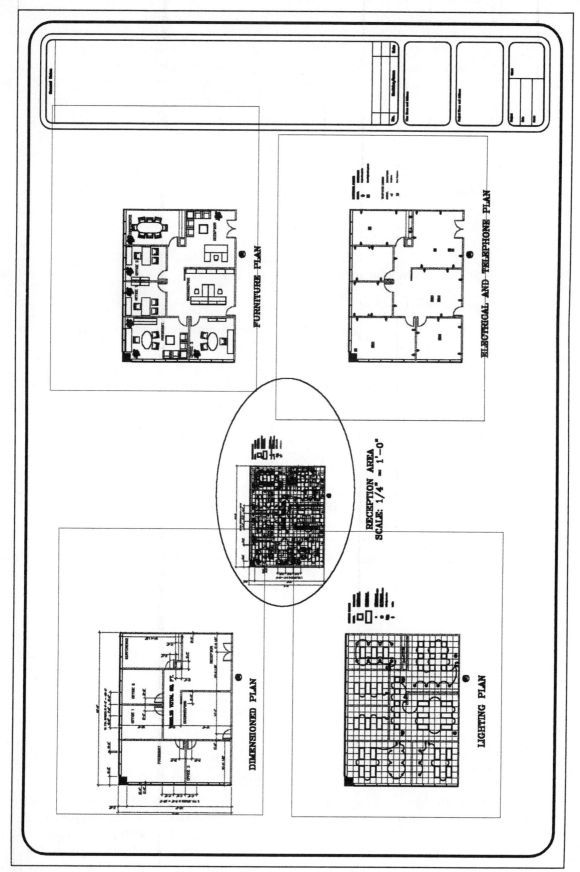

FIGURE 13–13
Use MVIEW to Create Another Viewport

TIP: If the list at the top of the Properties Palette shows "All (2)," CLICK: **Viewport (1)** to select only the viewport.

Step 17. On your own:

1. Use the Layer Properties Manager dialog box to freeze layers in the newly added, current viewport. Freeze the same layers as you did for the upper right viewport. Go back to model space to do this (CLICK: PAPER).
2. If needed, use the Move command to locate the views in paper space so that they are located approximately as shown in Figure 13–14. Align them as needed.
3. Create a new layer named VPORT. While in paper space change the outside edges of the four large viewports to the VPORT layer. Do not select the outside edge of the viewport that has the detail of the reception area in it. Use the Layer list to turn the VPORT Layer OFF. The outside edges of the viewports will no longer be visible.
4. Label the views using Dtext (single line text) with the STYLE name Label, FONT—Complex, HEIGHT—1/4, as shown in Figure 13–14. Use the Zoom-Window command to zoom in on the viewports so that the text is visible.
5. Fill in the title block information as appropriate using the Dtext (single line text) command.

TIP: Use the viewport Navigation control to maximize a viewport, then return it to its previous scale with a click on the same icon.

Step 18. When you have completed Exercise 13–1, save your work in at least two places.

Step 19. Plot or print Exercise 13–1 at a plotting ratio of 1 = 1. You will be plotting on a 36″ × 24″ sheet.

Exercise 13–2: Creating a Slide Show of the Tenant Space Project Drawings

Another means of creating a presentation is with the use of slides. A slide is made of a drawing while it is active on the display screen; it is a file containing a "snapshot" (a raster image) of the display on the screen. A script file is used to display the slides in the correct order and with an appropriate amount of delay between slides.

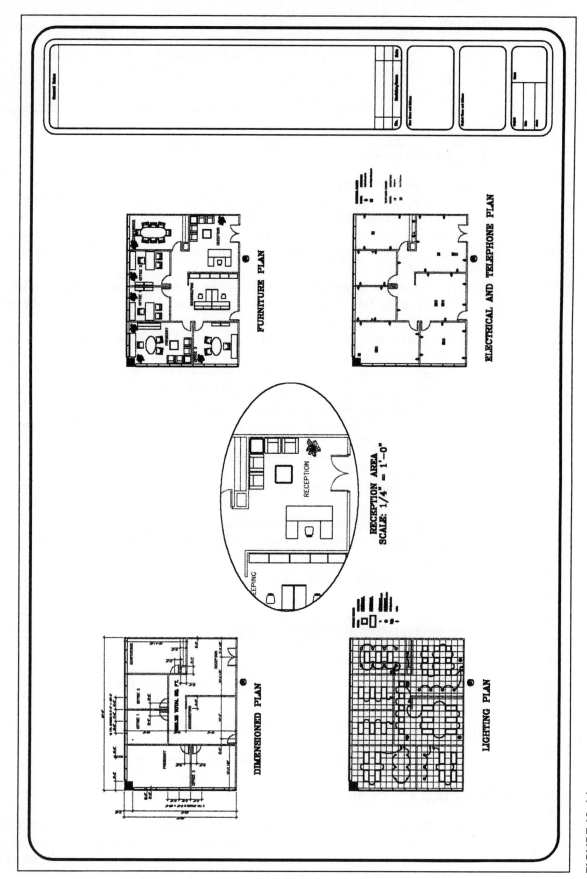

FIGURE 13–14

Exercise 13–1 Complete

Use the following steps to create a slide show:

Step 1.   Select and organize the drawings to be included in the slide show.

Decide which drawings you wish to include in your slide show. Make a storyboard consisting of quick sketches of the drawings in the order in which you want them to appear. Identify each drawing by the name under which you have it stored. You may include as many drawings as you want (for this exercise use a minimum of 10).

Step 2.   Use MSLIDE to make slides of each drawing:

Using AutoCAD, open each drawing to be included in the slide show on the hard drive or network drive, one at a time. Zoom a window around a drawing so that it fills the screen. Inserting drawings into a blank area may be the fastest means of accomplishing this. Insert, make the slide, then Undo to get rid of the drawing.

   You may also use the Layer Properties Manager dialog box to control the display of different layers to create different drawings and make slides of each drawing. The view of the drawing as displayed on the screen is what your slide will look like.

   Make slides of each displayed drawing by using the following procedure:

Prompt	Response
Command:	TYPE: **MSLIDE**<enter>
The Create Slide File dialog box appears:	TYPE: **A:SLIDE1** in the File name: input area (use an empty disk so that all your slides and the script file will fit on it; label each slide with a different consecutive number. Substitute the readable disk letter for A if needed.)
	CLICK: **Save**

Continue this procedure for each drawing until all slides are made. Number each slide with a different consecutive number. Be sure to save the slides on the disk in drive A or D by including A: or D: as the destination.

Step 3.   Use VSLIDE to view any slide that you have created:

When the VSLIDE command is used, the slide recalled replaces the current drawing on the display screen. View any slide that you have created by using the following procedure:

Prompt	Response
Command:	TYPE: **VSLIDE**<enter>
The Select Slide File dialog box appears:	CLICK: **SLIDE1** (on the disk containing your slides)
	CLICK: **Open** (to view Slide1)

Step 4.   Make a script file for your slide show:

AutoCAD provides the Script command, which allows other commands to be read and executed from a script file. The following procedure describes how to use the Edit command to make a script file for 10 slides while you are in the drawing editor. Read through the description first, and if you have more than 10 slides, you will be able to add to the script file.

Prompt	Response
Command:	Open: **Notepad** (in Windows-Accessories)

Save the file as **A:SLDSHOW.SCR<enter>**
(SLDSHOW is the name of your script file—it can be any standard eight characters, the SCR extension identifies this as a script file to AutoCAD)

Type the following exactly as described:

TYPE: **VSLIDE A:SLIDE1<enter>** (VSLIDE is the VSLIDE command that tells AutoCAD to display a slide; A:SLIDE1 tells AutoCAD where the slide is located and its name)

NOTE: Leave one space only between the following:
VSLIDE and **A:**
VSLIDE and ***A:**
DELAY and **2500**
PRESS: <**enter**> only once at the end of each line, otherwise your script file will not work.

TYPE: **VSLIDE *A:SLIDE2<enter>** (tells AutoCAD to load the next file—* means load; A:SLIDE2 is the name of the slide located on a floppy disk in drive A)

TYPE: **DELAY 2500<enter>** (tells AutoCAD to delay 2500 milliseconds before proceeding to the next line)

TYPE: **VSLIDE<enter>** (tells AutoCAD to display the slide that was loaded with line 2—Slide 2)

TYPE: **VSLIDE *A:SLIDE3<enter>**
TYPE: **DELAY 2500<enter>**
TYPE: **VSLIDE<enter>**
TYPE: **VSLIDE *A:SLIDE4<enter>**
TYPE: **DELAY 2500<enter>**
TYPE: **VSLIDE<enter>**
TYPE: **VSLIDE *A:SLIDE5<enter>**
TYPE: **DELAY 2500<enter>**
TYPE: **VSLIDE<enter>**
TYPE: **VSLIDE *A:SLIDE6<enter>**
TYPE: **DELAY 2500<enter>**
TYPE: **VSLIDE<enter>**
TYPE: **VSLIDE *A:SLIDE7<enter>**
TYPE: **DELAY 2500<enter>**
TYPE: **VSLIDE<enter>**
TYPE: **VSLIDE *A:SLIDE8<enter>**
TYPE: **DELAY 2500<enter>**
TYPE: **VSLIDE<enter>**
TYPE: **VSLIDE *A:SLIDE9<enter>**
TYPE: **DELAY 2500<enter>**

Prompt	Response
	TYPE: **VSLIDE**<enter>
	TYPE: **VSLIDE *A:SLIDE10**<enter>
	TYPE: **DELAY 2500**<enter>
	TYPE: **VSLIDE**<enter>
	TYPE: **RSCRIPT**<enter> (tells AutoCAD to rerun the script file)

Step 5. **Check each line of your file to be sure it contains no errors.**

Check each line of your script file to be sure there are no extra spaces or returns.

Step 6. **Save your script file.**

Prompt	Response
	CLICK: **File-Save**
	CLICK: **File-Exit**

You now have a disk containing your script file named Sldshow.Scr and 10 (or more) slides named SLIDE1.sld through SLIDE10.sld.

Step 7. **Test our slide show and script file.**

Prompt	Response
Command:	TYPE: **SCRIPT**<enter>
(The Select Script File dialog box appears.)	CLICK: **SLDSHOW.SCR** (on the disk containing all the slide show files)
	CLICK: **Open**

If all is well, your slide show will run uninterrupted until you decide to stop it. To stop the slide show at any point, PRESS: **Esc.** To start it again, TYPE: **RESUME**<enter>.

If the file does not run, make sure the script file and your slide files are on the same disk and your script file is correct. Also make sure you have typed the script file name correctly. If the delay period is not what you want, you may edit your script file and make the delay longer or shorter as you wish.

Step 8. **Edit your script file.**

Prompt	Response
Command:	Open: **Notepad** (Windows-Accessories)
	CLICK: **File-Open**
	Change the default File name: to ***.SCR**
	Locate: **SLDSHOW.SCR and open it**

Exercise 13–3: **Creating a Four-Sheet Drawing with Different Layers Frozen on Each Sheet (Figure 13–15)**

When you have completed Exercise 13–3 your drawing will look similar to Figure 13–15.

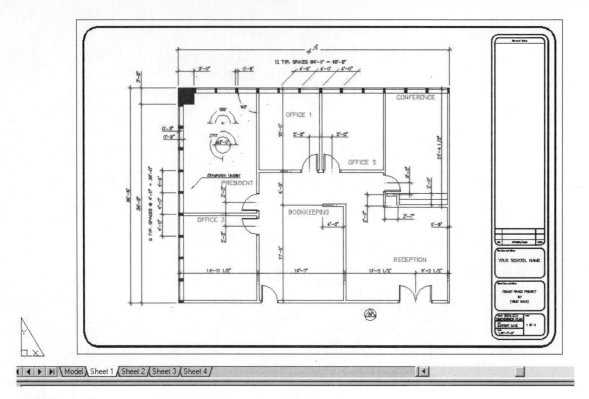

FIGURE 13–15
Exercise CH13-EX3 Complete

Step 1. Use your workspace to make the following settings:

1. Open drawing CH11-EX1 and save it with the name CH13-EX3.
2. Check to make sure the settings and layer structure are the same as shown in CH11-EX1. Thaw all frozen layers.
3. In model space return the view to a single viewport.

Step 2. Delete any existing layouts. CLICK: the layout name, RIGHT-CLICK: to get the right-click menu, and CLICK: **Delete**.

NOTE: You may not be able to delete Layout 1 at this time. If not, delete it after you create the layout named Sheet 1.

Step 3. Add a new layout named Sheet 1:

Prompt	Response
Command:	CLICK: **Create Layout Wizard** (from the Insert-Layout menu)
The Create Layout Wizard appears with the name Layout 1 (or Layout 2 if Layout 1 could not be deleted):	TYPE: **Sheet 1** CLICK: **Next**

Prompt	Response
The Printer option appears:	CLICK: **the appropriate printer configured for your computer**
	CLICK: **Next**

> **NOTE:** If your printer does not print a 24″ × 36″ sheet, use the DWF6ePlot.pc3 printer.

Prompt	Response
The Paper size option appears:	LOCATE: **ARCH D (24 × 36 inches)** in the paper list and CLICK: **on it**
	CLICK: **Next**
The Orientation option appears:	CLICK: **Landscape**
	CLICK: **Next**
The Title block option appears:	CLICK: **Architectural Title block.dwg**
	CLICK: **Next**
The Define viewports option appears:	CLICK: **Single**
	CLICK: **3/8″ = 1′-0″** (in the Viewport Scale list)
	CLICK: **Next**
The Pick Location option appears:	CLICK: Select location<
Specify first corner:	TYPE: **3,1<enter>**
Specify other corner:	TYPE: **28,22<enter>**
The Finish option appears:	CLICK: **Finish**

Step 4. On your own:

1. CLICK: PAPER to go to MODEL space. Use the Layer Properties Manager to freeze the following layers in the Current column, then use PAN to center your drawing:
   A-AREA
   A-FURN
   A-CLNG
   E-LITE
   E-LITE-D
   E-LITE-W
   E-POWER
   E-COMM
   E-POWER-TXT

2. **Return to paper space** (CLICK: MODEL), CLICK: any point on the viewport boundary, select Properties, check to make sure 3/8″ = 1′-0″ scale is selected, then CLICK: **Display locked...**, and select Yes to lock this viewport at that scale.

3. **Create a new layer named VP**, place the viewport boundary on that layer, and turn the new layer off.

4. **Return to paper space** (CLICK: MODEL), make a new layer named FOR-MAT TEXT, color white, set it current, and complete the title block (Figure 13–16) using the following:

Use DTEXT, 3/16″ high, for SCHOOL NAME, 1/8″ high simplex font for all other text.

FIGURE 13–16
Format Text

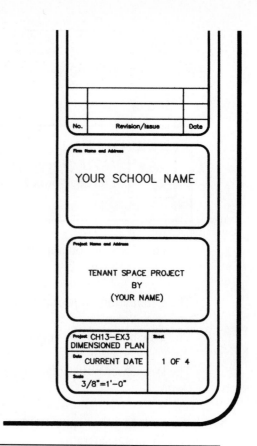

Firm Name and Address:	**YOUR SCHOOL NAME**
Project Name and Address:	**TENANT SPACE PROJECT**
	by
	(YOUR NAME)
Project:	**CH13-EX3**
	DIMENSIONED PLAN
Date:	**Current date**
Scale:	**3/8″ = 1′-0″**
Sheet:	**1 of 4**

 NOTE: Now is the time to delete Layout 1 if you have not done so.

Step 5. Add a new layout named Sheet 2:

Prompt	Response
Command:	CLICK: **Create Layout Wizard** (from the Insert-Layout menu)
The Create Layout Wizard appears with the name Layout 1	TYPE: **Sheet 2**
	CLICK: **Next**
The Printer option appears:	CLICK: **the appropriate printer configured for your computer**
	CLICK: **Next**

NOTE: If your printer does not print a 24″ × 36″ sheet, use the DWF6ePlot.pc3 printer.

Prompt	Response
The Paper size option appears:	LOCATE: **ARCH D (24 × 36 inches)** in the paper list and CLICK: **on it**
	CLICK: **Next**
The Orientation option appears:	CLICK: **Landscape**
	CLICK: **Next**
The Title block option appears:	CLICK: **Architectural Title block.dwg**
	CLICK: **Next**
The Define viewports option appears:	CLICK: **Single**
	CLICK: **3/8″ = 1′-0″** (in the Viewport Scale list)
	CLICK: **Next**
The Pick Location option appears:	CLICK: **Select location<**
Specify first corner:	TYPE: **3,1<enter>**
Specify other corner:	TYPE: **28,22<enter>**
The Finish option appears:	CLICK: **Finish**

Step 6.   On your own:

1. CLICK: **PAPER to go to MODEL space.** Use the Layer Properties Manager to freeze the following layers in the Current column, then use PAN to center your drawing:
    A-AREA
    A-CLNG
    A-FLOR-WDWK
    A-PFLR-DIMS
    E-COMM
    E-LITE
    E-LITE-D
    E-LITE-W
    E-POWER
    E-POWER-TXT

2. **Return to paper space (CLICK: MODEL), CLICK: any point on the viewport boundary, select Properties, check to make sure 3/8″ = 1′-0″ scale is selected, then CLICK: Display Locked..., and select Yes to lock this viewport at that scale.**

3. **Place the viewport boundary on the VP layer that is turned off.**

4. **Return to paper space (CLICK: MODEL) and complete the title block using the following:**

Use DTEXT, 3/16″ high, for SCHOOL NAME, 1/8″ high simplex font for all other text.

Firm Name and Address:	**YOUR SCHOOL NAME**
Project Name and Address:	**TENANT SPACE PROJECT**
	by
	(YOUR NAME)

Project:	**CH13-EX3**
	FURNITURE PLAN
Date:	**Current date**
Scale:	**3/8″ = 1′-0″**
Sheet:	**2 of 4**

Step 7. Add a new layout named Sheet 3:

Prompt	Response
Command:	CLICK: **Create Layout Wizard** (from the Insert-Layout menu)
The Create Layout Wizard appears with the name Layout 1:	TYPE: **Sheet 3**
	CLICK: **Next**
The Printer option appears:	CLICK: **the appropriate printer configured for your computer**
	CLICK: **Next**

 NOTE: If your printer does not print a 24″ × 36″ sheet, use the DWF6ePlot.pc3 printer.

The Paper size option appears:	LOCATE: **ARCH D (24 × 36 inches) in the paper list and** CLICK: **on it**
	CLICK: **Next**
The Orientation option appears:	CLICK: **Landscape**
	CLICK: **Next**
The Title block option appears:	CLICK: **Architectural Title block.dwg**
	CLICK: **Next**
The Define viewports option appears:	CLICK: **Single**
	CLICK: **3/8″ = 1′-0″** (in the Viewport Scale list)
	CLICK: **Next**
The Pick Location option appears:	CLICK: **Select location<**
Specify first corner:	TYPE: **3,1<enter>**
Specify other corner:	TYPE: **28,22<enter>**
The Finish option appears:	CLICK: **Finish**

Step 8. On your own:

1. CLICK: **PAPER** to go to **MODEL** space. Use the Layer Properties Manager to freeze the following layers in the Current column, then use PAN to center your drawing. After you have frozen the following layers you may have to return to paper space and use grips to stretch the viewport so it contains the lighting legend.

   A-AREA
   A-DOOR
   A-FLOR-WDWK
   A-FLOR-IDEN
   A-FURN

A-PFLR-DIMS
E-COMM
E-POWER
E-POWER-TXT

2. Return to paper space (CLICK: MODEL) and CLICK: any point on the viewport boundary, select Properties, check to make sure 3/8″ = 1′-0″ scale is selected, then CLICK: Display locked..., and select Yes to lock this viewport at that scale.

3. Place the viewport boundary on the VP layer that is turned off.

4. Return to paper space (CLICK: MODEL) and complete the title block using the following:

Use DTEXT, 3/16″ high, for SCHOOL NAME, 1/8″ high simplex font for all other text.

Firm Name and Address: **YOUR SCHOOL NAME**
Project Name and Address: **TENANT SPACE PROJECT**
                                            by
                                (YOUR NAME)
Project: **CH13-EX3**
                                LIGHTING PLAN
Date: **Current date**
Scale: **3/8″ = 1′-0″**
Sheet: **3 of 4**

Step 9.   Add a new layout named Sheet 4:

Prompt	Response
Command:	CLICK: **Create Layout Wizard** (from the Insert-Layout menu)
The Create Layout Wizard appears with the name Layout 1:	TYPE: **Sheet 4** CLICK: **Next**
The Printer option appears:	CLICK: **the appropriate printer configured for your computer** CLICK: **Next**

 NOTE: If your printer does not print a 24″ × 36″ sheet, use the DWF6ePlot.pc3 printer.

The Paper size option appears:	LOCATE: **ARCH D (24 × 36 inches)** in the paper list and CLICK: **on it** CLICK: **Next**
The Orientation option appears:	CLICK: **Landscape** CLICK: **Next**
The Title block option appears:	CLICK: **Architectural Title block.dwg** CLICK: **Next**
The Define viewports option appears:	CLICK: **Single** CLICK: **3/8″ = 1′-0″** (in the Viewport Scale list) CLICK: **Next**

Prompt	Response
The Pick Location option appears:	CLICK: **Select location<**
Specify first corner:	TYPE: **3,1<enter>**
Specify other corner:	TYPE: **28,22<enter>**
The Finish option appears:	CLICK: **Finish**

Step 10. On your own:

1. CLICK: **PAPER to go to MODEL space.** Use the Layer Properties Manager to freeze the following layers in the Current column, then use PAN to center your drawing. After you have frozen the following layers you may have to return to paper space and use grips to stretch the viewport so it contains the legends.

   A-AREA
   A-CLNG
   A-FLOR-IDEN
   A-FLOR-WDWK
   A-FURN
   A-PFLR-DIMS
   E-LITE
   E-LITE-D
   E-LITE-W

2. **Return to paper space** (CLICK: **MODEL**) and CLICK: any point on the viewport boundary, select Properties, check to make sure 3/8″ = 1′-0″ scale is selected, then CLICK: **Display Locked...**, and select Yes to lock this viewport at that scale.
3. Place the viewport boundary on the VP layer that is turned off.
4. **Return to paper space** (CLICK: **MODEL**) and complete the title block using the following:

Use DTEXT, 3/16″ high, for SCHOOL NAME, 1/8″ high simplex font for all other text.

Firm Name and Address:	YOUR SCHOOL NAME
Project Name and Address:	TENANT SPACE PROJECT
	by
	(YOUR NAME)
Project:	CH13-EX3
	ELECTRICAL AND TELEPHONE PLAN
Date:	Current date
Scale:	3/8″ = 1′-0″
Sheet:	4 of 4

Step 11. Save your drawing in at least two places.

Step 12. Plot each layout of the drawing on 24″ × 36″ sheets full scale, or plot half-size on 12″ × 18″ sheets.

Sheet Sets

The Sheet Sets command in this version of AutoCAD allows you to organize drawing layouts from several drawings into a single set that may easily be transmitted to a client. Any drawing to be used in a sheet set must contain one or more paper space layouts. The layouts are used to make up the sheet set. In Exercise 13–4 you will need three drawings. Two of them, CH13-EX3 and CH9-EX3, contain layouts already and will require no additional work. The third drawing, which is to be the TITLE PAGE, will simply be a blank drawing with a layout titled TITLE PAGE. The Sheet Set Manager will automatically create a table that will be inserted into that blank layout. For simplicity, all these drawings will be placed in a separate folder on the C: drive of your computer. Exercise 13–4 will lead you step-by-step through the creation of a sheet set and its preparation for transmitting as a .zip file attached to an email.

Exercise 13–4: Making a Sheet Set Containing Five Drawing Layouts and a Title Page

When you have completed Exercise 13–4 your Sheet Set Manager will look similar to Figure 13–17.

Step 1. On your own:

1. Use Windows Explorer to make a new folder on the C: drive labeled C:\Tenant Space Project.
2. Copy drawings CH13-EX3 (the drawing containing four layouts), CH10-EX1, CH10-EX2, and CH10-EX3 from Chapter 9 into folder C:\Tenant Space Project.
3. Exit Windows Explorer.

Now, make a new drawing with a layout named Title Page, and save it in the C:\Tenant Space Project folder.

Step 2. Use your workspace to make the following settings:

1. Set Units: **Architectural**
2. Set Drawing Limits: **36, 24**
3. Set GRIDDISPLAY: **0**
4. Set Grid: **1**
5. Set Snap: **1/2**

FIGURE 13–17
Sheet Set Manager for CH13-EX4

6. Make the following layers:

LAYER NAME	COLOR	LINETYPE	LINEWEIGHT
TABLE	White	Continuous	Default

7. Set **Layer TABLE** current.

Step 3. Make the layout named Title Page and save the drawing with the name TITLE PAGE:

Prompt	Response
Command:	CLICK: **Create Layout Wizard** (from the Insert menu-Layout)
The Create Layout dialog box appears:	TYPE: **Title Page** in the name box CLICK: **Next**
The Printer tab appears:	CLICK: **DWF6 ePlot pc3** CLICK: **Next**
The Paper Size tab appears:	CLICK: **ARCH D(36.00 × 24.00 inches)** CLICK: **Next**
The Orientation tab appears:	CLICK: **Landscape** CLICK: **Next**
The Title Block tab appears:	CLICK: **Architectural Title Block.dwg** CLICK: **Next**
The Define Viewports tab appears:	CLICK: **Single** CLICK: **Next**
The Pick Location tab appears:	CLICK: **Next**
The Finish tab appears:	CLICK: **Finish**
The Title Page layout appears:	RIGHT-CLICK: **on all other layouts** and CLICK: **Delete** so that no other paper space layouts exist
Command:	CLICK: **Save As... and save the drawing with the Name TITLE PAGE in the folder labeled C:\Tenant Space Project, Figure 13–18**

FIGURE 13–18
Save TITLE PAGE Drawing in the Tenant Space Project Folder

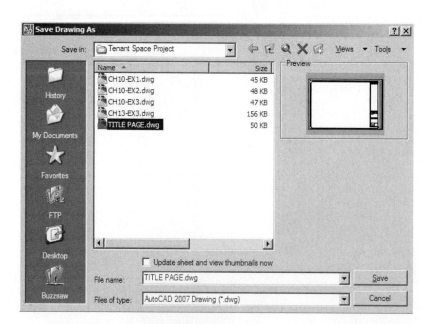

Part II: Two-Dimensional AutoCAD

FIGURE 13–19
Create Sheet Set - Name of
New Sheet Set

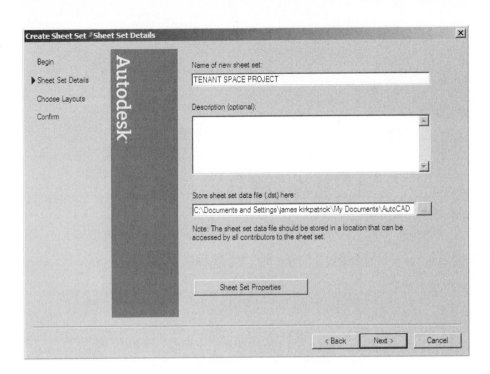

Step 4. Make a new sheet set with the name TENANT SPACE PROJECT:

Prompt	Response
Command:	**New Sheet Set...**
The Create Sheet Set-Begin tab appears:	CLICK: **Existing drawings** in the Create a sheet set using area
	CLICK: **Next**
The Sheet Set Details tab appears:	TYPE: **TENANT SPACE PROJECT** in the Name of new sheet set: box, Figure 13–19
	CLICK: **the ellipsis (three dots) button** to the right of Store sheet set data file (.dst) here:
	CLICK: **the Tenant Space Project folder on the C: drive**
	CLICK: **Open**
	CLICK: **Next**
The Choose Layouts tab appears:	CLICK: **Browse**
The Browse for Folder dialog box appears:	CLICK: **the Tenant Space Project folder,** Figure 13–20
	CLICK: **OK**
The layouts in drawings in that folder appear as shown in Figure 13–21.	CLICK: **Next**
The Confirm tab, Figure 13–22, appears:	CLICK: **Finish** (if all the layouts shown in Figure 13–22 are there. If not, you may need to open and save one or more of the drawings so the layouts are in the list.)

FIGURE 13–20
CLICK: The Tenant Space
Project Folder

FIGURE 13–21
Choose Layouts

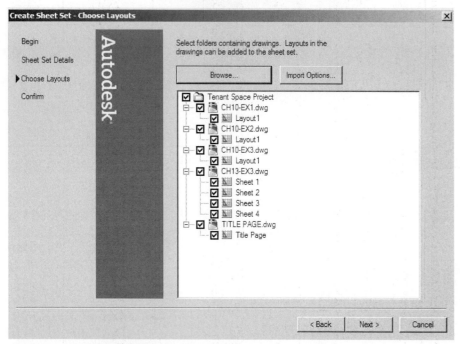

FIGURE 13–22
Confirm Layouts

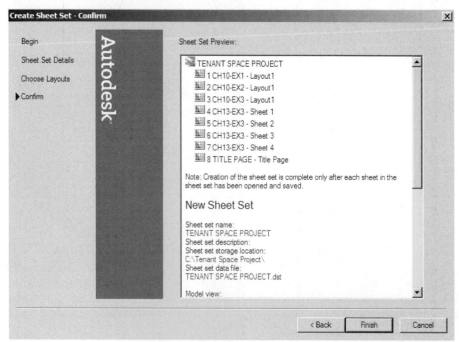

FIGURE 13–23
Rename & Renumber Sheet
Dialog Box

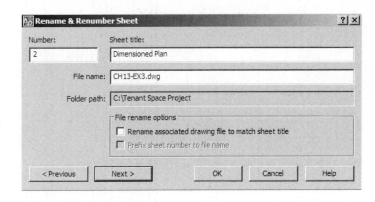

Step 5. Rename and renumber all the layouts so you can identify each layout:

Prompt	Response
With the SHEET SET MANAGER open:	RIGHT-CLICK: on CH13-EX3-Sheet 1.
The right-click menu appears:	CLICK: **Rename and Renumber...**
The Rename & Renumber Sheet dialog box, Figure 13–23, appears:	TYPE: **2** (in the Number: box)
	TYPE: **Dimensioned Plan** (in the Sheet title: box)
	CLICK: **Next** (in the lower left)
CH13-EX3-Sheet 2 appears in the dialog box:	TYPE: **3** (in the Number: box)
	TYPE: **Furniture Plan** (in the Sheet title: box)

On Your Own:

1. Rename and renumber the remaining layouts as shown in Figure 13–24.

    No. 6: Rename to 4 - Lighting Plan
    No. 7: Rename to 5 - Electrical and Telephone Plan
    No. 1: Rename to 6 - Conference Room Elevation
    No. 2: Rename to 7 - Cabinet Section
    No. 3: Rename to 8 - Door Jamb Detail
    CLICK: **OK**

FIGURE 13–24
Sheets Renamed and
Renumbered

FIGURE 13–25
Move Title Page So It Is the
First Sheet in the List

Step 6. Move the sheet labeled 1-Title Page to its correct location, Figure 13–25:

Prompt	Response
With the SHEET SET MANAGER open:	CLICK: **1-Title Page and hold down the** CLICK: **button as you move your mouse up so a black line appears at the top of the list as shown in Figure 13–25** **Release the** CLICK: **button**
The Title Page sheet is now the first sheet in the list:	**Rearrange the remaining Sheets so they are in numerical order**

Step 7. Make a table showing the contents of the sheet set on the TITLE PAGE; change font to simplex:

Prompt	Response
With the SHEET SET MANAGER open:	RIGHT-CLICK **the Sheet Set Title, TENANT SPACE PROJECT**
The right-click menu, Figure 13–26, appears:	CLICK: **Insert Sheet List Table...** (If this command is grayed out, save the TITLE PAGE drawing to the Tenant Space Project folder and try again.)
The Insert Sheet List Table dialog box appears:	CLICK: **OK**
The Sheet List Table warning box appears:	CLICK: **OK**
The Sheet List Table is attached to your cursor:	CLICK: **a point to place the table in the approximate center of the space on the Title Page layout, Figure 13–27.**
Command:	TYPE: **ST<enter>**
The Text Style dialog box appears:	**Change the font from txt to simplex**

FIGURE 13–26
RIGHT-CLICK: on the TEN-
ANT SPACE PROJECT Title
and CLICK: Insert Sheet List
Table...

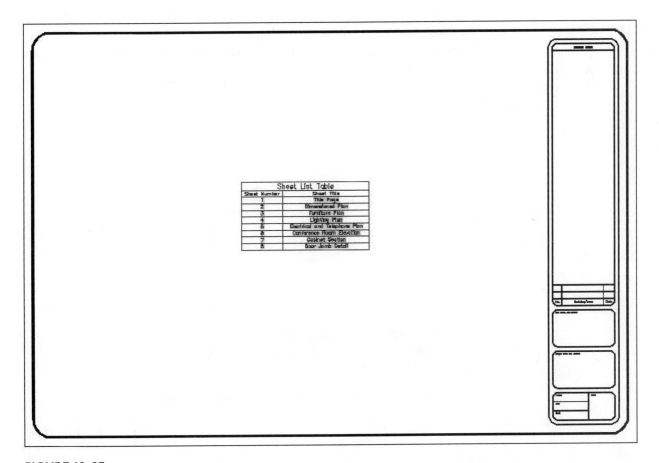

FIGURE 13–27
Place Sheet List Table in the Center of the Sheet

FIGURE 13-28
CLICK: eTransmit on the right-click menu

Step 8.   On your own:

1.   Save the TITLE PAGE drawing to C:\Tenant Space Project.
2.   Test your sheet set by double-clicking on each sheet in the drawing set with the Sheet Set Manager open and make sure each sheet has the correct name. If not, rename and number as needed.

Step 9.   Use eTransmit... to save all layouts to a .zip file (so they can be attached to an email and electronically transmitted):

Prompt	Response
With the SHEET SET MANAGER open:	RIGHT-CLICK: the Sheet Set Title, TENANT SPACE PROJECT
The right-click menu, Figure 13–28, appears:	CLICK: eTransmit...

 TIP: If you get a message telling you that some drawings need to be saved, CLICK: on the sheet that is contained within the drawing and save the drawing.

The Create Transmittal dialog box appears:	CLICK: **OK**
The Specify Zip file dialog box, Figure 13–29 appears:	CLICK: **on the Tenant Space Project folder** and CLICK: **Save**

FIGURE 13–29
Specify Zip File Dialog Box

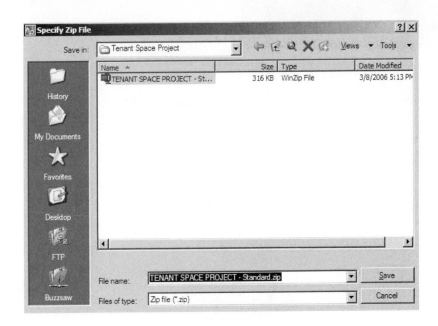

Step 10. The sheet set is now saved as a .zip file and can be attached to an email and sent to anyone you choose. If you are an on-line student, attach the .zip file to an email and send it to your instructor.

The Sheet Set Manager can also be used to publish these sheet sets to a Web site by using one of the icons above the sheet set title.

1. Which of the following is a characteristic of paper space?
   a. Viewports are tiled.
   b. Tilemode is set to 1.
   c. Viewports can overlap.
   d. Models are created.
   e. The VPORTS command will work.

2. How many model space viewports can be created on any one drawing?
   a. 2
   b. 4
   c. 16
   d. 64
   e. Unlimited

3. The Create Layout Wizard does *not* do which of the following?
   a. Turn viewport on and off
   b. Scale viewports
   c. Allow you to specify the corners of a viewport's location
   d. Allow you to name the Layout
   e. Allow you to create an array of viewports

4. Which command shows you all the viewport options on the New Viewports tab of the Viewports dialog box?
   a. Named Views
   b. Named Viewports
   c. New Viewports
   d. MView
   e. Aerial View

5. A command can be started in one viewport and completed in a different viewport.
   a. True
   b. False

6. Which of the following is a characteristic of a nontiled viewport?
   a. Fills the graphics screen and touches all other viewports.
   b. Is fixed and cannot overlap.
   c. Can be erased or moved.
   d. Only one of these viewports may be plotted at one time.
   e. Only one viewport may be active at one time.

7. Model space may be active with Tilemode set at either 0 or 1.
   a. True
   b. False

8. Which of the following MVIEW options creates several viewports at the same time?
   a. ON
   b. OFF
   c. Fit
   d. 2,3,4
   e. <First point>

9. Which command can be used to set a standard scale of 1/4" = 1' in paper space viewports?
   a. Paper Space
   b. Tilemode
   c. Properties
   d. Scale
   e. Model Space

10. Which of the following can be used to align viewports accurately in model space?

    a. MVIEW   d. MVSETUP

    b. VPORTS   e. Align

    c. Move

Complete.

11. Which option of the MVSETUP command is used to obtain a 24″ × 36″ architectural format?

    _____

12. List the command and its option that will insert a set of saved model space viewports into paper space.

    _____

13. List the prompts and responses needed to freeze layers A-AREA and A-FURN in one of four model space viewports (Tilemode is OFF). The viewport is active.

Prompt	Response
Command:	TYPE: **VPLAYER**<enter>
_____	TYPE: _____
_____	TYPE: _____
_____	_____

14. List the command used to switch from model space to paper space when Tilemode is OFF.

    _____

15. List the setting in the Properties palette that is used to lock the scale of a viewport.

    _____

16. List the prompts and responses needed to create a slide named SLD1 on a disk in drive D.

Prompt	Response
Command:	TYPE: _____
_____	TYPE: _____
	CLICK: _____

17. Write the command used to view a slide.

    _____

18. Describe how to make a title page table listing all the sheets in a sheet set.

    _____

    _____

19. Describe how to move a sheet in the Sheet Set Manager to another location.

_____

_____

_____

_____

20. Describe how to make a .zip file of a sheet set using the Sheet Set Manager.

_____

_____

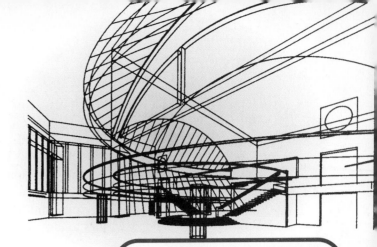

chapter

14

Solid Modeling of Simple Shapes

objectives

When you have completed this chapter, you will be able to

Use the dashboard palette and the 3D workspace to create solids.

Draw the following primitive solids: box, sphere, wedge, cone, cylinder, torus.

Make settings to display solids smoothly.

Draw extruded solids.

Draw revolved solids.

Rotate solids about the X, Y, or Z axis.

Form chamfers and fillets on solid edges.

Join two or more solids.

Subtract one or more solids from another solid.

Use the Solidedit command to change existing solids.

Form a solid model from the common volume of two intersecting solids.

Obtain a perspective view of a complex solid model.

Use 3D Orbit and Render to render solids and print the rendered model.

Introduction

AutoCAD provides three means of creating 3D models: basic 3D using elevation and thickness, surface modeling, and solid modeling. Basic 3D has very limited uses. Surface modeling uses commands similar to those used in solid modeling but requires a wire frame on which surfaces are placed to give the illusion of a solid model. Models cannot be subtracted from other models when surface modeling is used, nor can they be joined to form a composite model. Neither Basic 3D nor surface modeling is covered in this book. Solid modeling creates solids that are much more useful and easier to modify than basic 3D or surface models. A solid may be a single object called a *primitive,* or it may be a combination of objects called a *composite.*

Solids Commands Used to Create Basic Shapes

A primitive solid is a single solid shape that has had nothing added to or subtracted from it. There are six solid primitives (box, sphere, wedge, cone, cylinder, torus) that are the basic shapes often used in solid modeling. They are drawn by using nine commands:

Box   Polysolid
Cone   Sphere
Cylinder   Torus
Helix   Wedge
Planar Surface

AutoCAD also allows you to form solids by extruding (adding height) sweeping (extruding along a path), lofting (selecting cross-sectional areas), and revolving (rotating about an axis) two-dimensional drawing entities such as polylines, circles, ellipses, rectangles, polygons, and donuts. The commands that extrude sweep, loft, and revolve drawing entities to form solids are:

Extrude   Sweep
Revolve   Loft

Solids Commands Used to Create Composite Solids

Composite solids are formed by joining primitive solids, other solids, or a combination of the two. These combinations may also be added to or subtracted from other solids to form the composite model needed. The following commands used to create composite solids are described in this chapter:

Union   Allows you to join several solids to form a single solid.
Intersect   Allows you to create composite solids from the intersection of two or more solids. Intersect creates a new solid by calculating the common volume of two or more existing solids.
Subtract   Allows you to subtract solids from other solids.
Interfere   Does the same thing as Intersect except it retains the original objects.

Solids Commands Used to Edit Solids

Slice   Used to create a new solid by cutting the existing solid into two pieces and removing or retaining either or both pieces.
Section   Used to create the cross-sectional area of a solid. That area may then be hatched using the Hatch command with any pattern you choose. Be sure the section is parallel with the current UCS when you hatch the area.
Thicken   Used to make a surface thicker.

SOLIDEDIT

The SOLIDEDIT command has several options that allow you to change features of 3D solid objects. These options are shown as separate tools on the Solids Editing toolbar and as separate commands on the Solids Editing menu from the Modify menu on the menu bar.

With SOLIDEDIT, you can change solid objects by extruding, moving, rotating, offsetting, tapering, copying, coloring, separating, shelling, cleaning, checking, or deleting features such as holes, surfaces, and edges.

When you TYPE: **SOLIDEDIT <enter>, the following prompt appears:**

Enter a solids editing option [Face/Edge/Body/Undo/eXit] <eXit>:

When you TYPE: **F<enter> for face, the following options appear for changing surfaces:**

Extrude   Allows you to extrude an existing surface or surfaces on a solid along a path.
Move   Allows you to move surfaces such as holes or objects in the solid from one point to another.

Rotate   Allows you to rotate surfaces in a solid such as slots, or other shapes.

Offset   Allows you to create new surfaces by offsetting existing ones.

Taper   Allows you to taper surfaces on a solid along a path.

Delete   Allows you to delete surfaces (such as holes and other features) from the solid.

Copy   Allows you to copy existing surfaces from a solid model.

coLor   Allows you to assign a color to any surface of the solid model.

mAterial   Allows you to attach materials to solids.

All these options are similar to commands you have already used.

When you TYPE: E<enter> for Edge, the following options appear for changing edges:

Copy   Allows you to copy existing edges from a solid model.

coLor   Allows you to assign a color to any edge of the solid model.

When you TYPE: B<enter> for Body, the following options appear for changing the body of the model:

Imprint   Allows you to imprint a shape onto a solid. The object to be imprinted must intersect one or more faces on the selected solid in order for imprinting to be successful. You can imprint the following objects: arcs, circles, lines, 2D and 3D polylines, ellipses, splines, regions, and 3D solids.

seParate solids   Allows you to separate some solids that have been joined together to form a composite solid.

Shell   Creates a hollow, thin wall with a specified thickness. You can specify a constant wall thickness for all the faces. You can also exclude faces from the shell by selecting them. A 3D solid can have only one shell.

cLean   Removes any unused or duplicated geometry from the model.

Check   Allows you to verify that the object is a valid solid.

Controlling UCS in Three Dimensions

Understanding and controlling the UCS is extremely important in creating three-dimensional models. The UCS is the *location and orientation* of the origin of the X, Y, and Z axes. If you are going to draw parts of a 3D model on a slanted surface, you can create a slanted UCS. If you are going to draw a 3D object, such as the handles on the drawer pedestal, you can locate your UCS so that it is flush with the front plane of the pedestal. An extrusion is then made from that construction plane, and the handles are easily created in the correct location.

The UCS command options Origin, OBject, Previous, Restore, Save, Delete, World, and ? were described in Chapter 9. The options described in this chapter are Move, Origin, 3point, OBject, View, and X/Y/Z. All these options can be selected directly from the menu bar or the UCS toolbar.

Dynamic UCS

You can draw on any face of a 3D solid without changing the UCS orientation with one of the UCS options by activating DUCS on the status bar. The UCS then changes automatically when your cursor is over a face of an object, and dynamic UCS is on.

Commands to View Solids

3D Views Menu Options

Viewpoint Presets   The Viewpoint Presets dialog box, Figure 14–1, appears when 3D Views-Viewpoint Presets is clicked from the View menu in the menu bar.

FIGURE 14–1
Selecting 3D Views

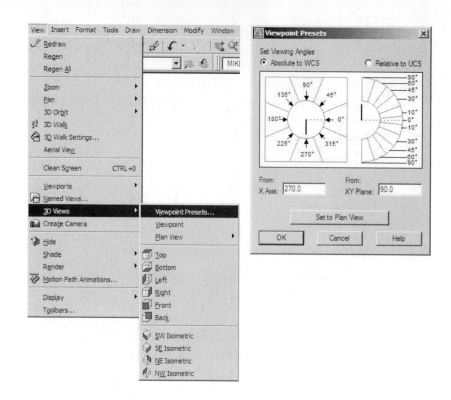

Absolute to WCS—When this button is selected, the resulting viewpoint is relative to the World UCS.

Relative to UCS—When this button is selected, the resulting viewpoint is relative to the UCS that is current in the drawing at the time.

From X Axis: Button and Chart—Specifies the viewing angle from the X axis. The button allows you to type the angle; the chart above it allows you to specify a new angle by clicking the inner region on the circle. The chart, consisting of a square with a circle in it, may be thought of as a viewpoint looking down on the top of an object:

270	Places your view directly in front of the object.
315	Places your view to the right and in front of the object.
0	Places your view on the right side of the object.
45	Places your view to the right and behind the object.
90	Places your view directly behind the object.
135	Places your view to the left and behind the object.
180	Places your view on the left side of the object.
225	Places your view to the left and in front of the object.

From XY Plane: Button and Chart—Specifies the viewing angle from the X-Y plane. The button allows you to type the angle, and the chart above it allows you to specify a new angle by clicking the inner region on the half circle. Consisting of two semicircles, the chart allows you to specify whether the viewpoint is to be above or below the object:

0	Places your view directly perpendicular to the chosen angle. For example, a view of 270 on the left chart and 0 on the right chart places the viewpoint directly in front of the object.
10 to 60	Places your view above the object.
90	Places your view perpendicular to the top view of the chosen angle.
−10 to −60	Places your view below the object.
−90	Places your view perpendicular to the bottom view of the chosen angle.

Set to Plan View—Sets the viewing angles to plan view (270,90) relative to the selected UCS.

Now, let's look at other 3D Views options:

Viewpoint　The AutoCAD compass and Axis tripod appear.

Plan View　Allows you to select the plan view of the current UCS, the World UCS, or a saved and named UCS.

Top　Gives you the top view of the model.

Bottom　Gives you the bottom view of the model.

Left　Gives you the left side view of the model.

Right　Gives you the right side view of the model.

Front　Gives you the front view of the model.

Back　Gives you the back view of the model.

SW Isometric　Gives you an isometric view from the front, to the left, above.

SE Isometric　Gives you an isometric view from the front, to the right, above.

NE Isometric　Gives you an isometric view from the back, to the right, above.

NW Isometric　Gives you an isometric view from the back, to the left, above.

> **NOTE:** The front view is a 90° clockwise rotation of the plan view of the object looking straight into it. Left side, right side, and rear views are also 90° rotations.

3DFLY　Changes your view of a 3D model so that it is as if you were flying through the model.

3DFORBIT　Allows you to control the viewing of a 3D model using a free orbit.

3DORBIT　Allows you to control the viewing of a 3D model using a constrained orbit.

3DWALK　Changes your view of a 3D model so that it is as if you were walking through the model.

Other Commands That Can Be Used to Edit Solids

3D Move　Moves solids easily.

3D Array　Used to create three-dimensional arrays of objects.

3D Rotate　Used to rotate solids about X, Y, or Z axis.

3D Scale　Used to scale solids.

3D Mirror　Used to create mirror images of solids about a plane specified by three points.

Trim　Used to trim lines, polylines and similar entities in 3D space, but this command will not trim a solid shape.

Extend　Used to extend lines, polylines, and similar entities in 3D space, but this command will not extend a solid shape.

Fillet　Used to create fillets and rounds. Specify the radius for the fillet and then click the edge or edges to be filleted.

Chamfer　Used to create chamfers. Specify the distances for the chamfer and then click the edge or edges to be chamfered.

Align　Used to move a solid so that a selected plane on the first solid is aligned with a selected plane on a second solid.

Explode　Used to explode a solid into regions or planes. (Example: An exploded solid box becomes six regions: four sides, a top, and a bottom.) Use care with Explode. When you explode a solid you destroy it as a solid shape.

Interference Checking　Alerts you if your camera is about to bump into something.

All the following commands may be used to edit or view solids in the same manner as you have used them previously:

Move	Scale	Zoom
Properties	Mview	Pan
Erase	3D orbit	

Settings That Control How the Solid Is Displayed

FACETRES Used to make shaded solids and those with hidden lines removed appear smoother. Values range from 0.01 to 10.0. The default value is 0.5. Higher values take longer to regenerate but look better. Four is a good compromise. If you change this value, you can update the solid to the new value by using the Shade or Hide command again.

ISOLINES Sets the number of lines on rounded surfaces of solids. Values range from 0 to 2047. The default value is 4. Twenty is a good middle ground. If you change this value, you can update the solid to the new value by regenerating the drawing.

Exercise 14–1: Part 1, Drawing Primitive Solids

Exercise 14–1, Parts 1 through 6, provides step-by-step instructions for using the solid commands just described. These basic commands will also be used to create complex solid models in Exercise 14–2. Upon completion of this chapter, and mastery of the commands included in the chapter, you will have a sound foundation for learning solid modeling.

When you have completed Exercise 14–1, Parts 1 through 6, your drawing will look similar to Figure 14–2.

In Part 1 of this exercise you will set FACETRES and ISOLINES and use Box, Sphere, Wedge, Cone, Cylinder, and Torus to draw primitive solids.

Step 1. Use your workspace to make the following settings:

1. **Use SaveAs... to save the drawing on the hard drive with the name CH14-EX1.**
2. Set drawing Units: **Architectural**
3. Set Drawing Limits: **11, 8-1/2**
4. Set GRIDDISPLAY: **0**
5. Set Grid: **1/2**
6. Set Snap: **1/16**
7. Create the following Layers:

LAYER NAME	COLOR	LINETYPE	LINEWEIGHT
3d-w	253 (one of the grays)	Continuous	Default
3d-r	Red	Continuous	Default
3d-g	Green	Continuous	Default

FIGURE 14–2
Exercise 14–1 Complete

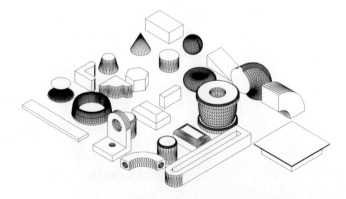

8. Set **Layer 3d-w** current.

9. **Use the Vports command to make two vertical viewports. Zoom-All in both viewports to start, then Zoom in closer so your view is similar to the figures shown.** Either viewport may be active as you draw. You will need to Zoom-All occasionally in both viewports to see the entire drawing.

10. CLICK: **SE Isometric from 3D Views on the View menu to set a viewpoint for the right viewport.**

11. **Open the Dashboard palette (on the Tools-Palettes Menu).** RIGHT-CLICK: **on the Dashboard and** CLICK: <Anchor-Right>.

FACETRES and ISOLINES

Step 2. Set the FACETRES and ISOLINES variables:

Prompt	Response
Command:	TYPE: **FACETRES**<enter>
Enter new value for FACETRES <0.5000>:	TYPE: **4**<enter>
Command:	TYPE: **ISOLINES**<enter>
Enter new value for ISOLINES <4>:	TYPE: **20**<enter>

Box

Step 3. Draw a solid box, 1.2 × .8 × .5 height (Figure 14–3):

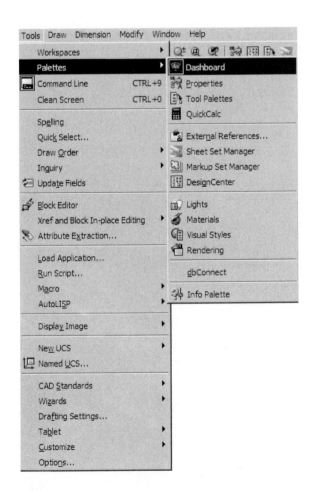

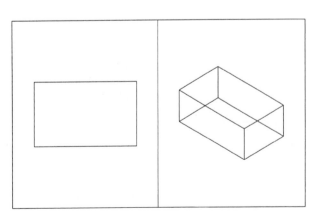

FIGURE 14–3
Draw a Solid Box

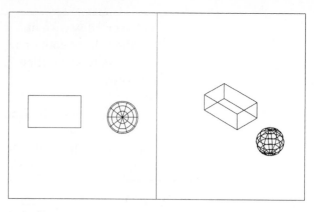

FIGURE 14–4
Draw a Solid Sphere

Prompt	Response
Command:	**Box** (or TYPE: **BOX\<enter>**)
Specify corner of box or [Center] \<0,0,0>:	TYPE: **1/2,7-1/2\<enter>**
Specify other corner or [Cube/Length]:	TYPE: **1-3/4,8-1/4\<enter>**
Specify height or [2 Point]:	TYPE: **1/2\<enter>**

Center   Allows you to draw a box by first locating its center.
Cube   Allows you to draw a cube by specifying the length of one side.
Length   Allows you to draw a box by specifying its length (X), width (Y), and height (Z).

Sphere

Step 4.   **Draw a solid sphere, 3/8 radius (Figure 14–4):**

Prompt	Response
Command:	**Sphere** (or TYPE: **SPHERE\<enter>**)
Specify center point or [3P/2P/Ttr]:	TYPE: **2-3/4,7-3/4\<enter>**
Specify radius of sphere or [Diameter]:	TYPE: **3/8\<enter>**

Wedge

Step 5.   **Draw a solid wedge, 3/4 × 1-1/4 × 1/2 height (Figure 14–5):**

Prompt	Response
Command:	**Wedge** (or TYPE: **WEDGE\<enter>**)

FIGURE 14–5
Draw a Solid Wedge

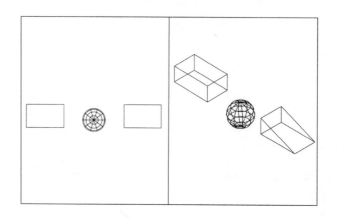

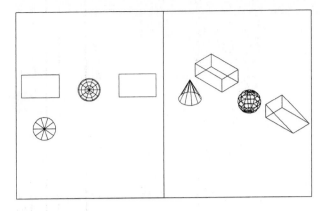

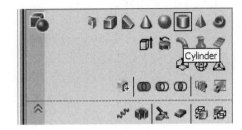

FIGURE 14–6
Draw a Solid Cone

Prompt	Response
Specify first corner or [Center]:	TYPE: **3-3/4,7-1/2<enter>**
Specify other corner or [Cube/Length]:	TYPE: **5,8-1/4<enter>**
Specify height:	TYPE: **1/2<enter>**

Cone

Step 6.   Draw a solid cone, 3/8 radius, 3/4 height (Figure 14–6):

Prompt	Response
Command:	**Cone** (or TYPE: **CONE<enter>**)
Specify center point for base of cone or [Elliptical]<0,0,0>:	TYPE: **1-1/4,6-1/2<enter>**
Specify radius for base of cone or [Diameter]:	TYPE: **3/8<enter>**
Specify height of cone or [Apex]:	TYPE: **3/4<enter>**

Cylinder

Step 7.   Draw a solid cylinder, 3/8 radius, 1/2 height (Figure 14–7):

Prompt	Response
Command:	**Cylinder** (or TYPE: **CYLINDER<enter>**)
Specify center point for base or [3P/2P/Ttr/Elliptical]:	TYPE: **2-3/4,6-1/2<enter>**
Specify base radius [Diameter]<default>:	TYPE: **3/8<enter>**
Specify height or [2point/Axis endpoint]<default>:	TYPE: **1/2<enter>**

Torus

Step 8.   Draw a solid torus (a 3D donut), 3/8 torus radius, 1/4 tube radius (Figure 14–8):

Prompt	Response
Command:	**Torus** (or TYPE: **TORUS<enter>**)
Specify center point or [3P/2P/Ttr]:	TYPE: **4-3/8,6-1/2<enter>**

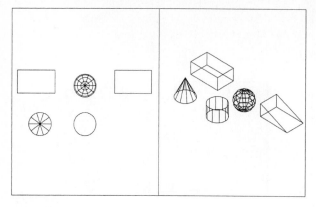

FIGURE 14–7
Draw a Solid Cylinder

FIGURE 14–8
Draw a Solid Torus

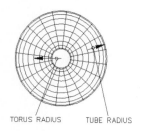

TORUS RADIUS   TUBE RADIUS

FIGURE 14–9
Radius of the Tube and
Radius of the Torus

Prompt	Response
Specify radius or [Diameter]:	TYPE: **3/8<enter>**
Specify tube radius or [2 point/Diameter]:	TYPE: **1/4<enter>**

The radius of the torus is the distance from the center of the 3D donut to the center of the tube that forms the donut. The radius of the tube is the radius of the tube forming the donut (Figure 14–9).

Exercise 14–1: Part 2, Using Extrude to Draw Extruded Solids

Draw an Extruded Circle

Step 9. Draw a circle (Figure 14–10):

Prompt	Response
Command:	TYPE: **C<enter>**
Specify center point for circle or [3P/2P/Ttr (tan tan radius)]:	TYPE: **1-1/4,5<enter>**
Specify radius of circle or [Diameter]:	TYPE: **3/8<enter>**

Step 10. Extrude the circle, 1/2 height, 15° extrusion taper angle (Figure 14–10).

Prompt	Response
Command:	**Extrude** (or TYPE: **EXT<enter>**)
Select objects to extrude:	CLICK: **the circle**
Select objects to extrude:	**<enter>**
Specify height of extrusion or [Direction/Path/Taper angle] <0'-0 1/2">:	TYPE: **T<enter>**
Specify angle of taper for extrusion <0:>	TYPE: **15<enter>**
Specify height of extrusion or [Direction/Path/Taper angle] <0'-0 1/2":>	TYPE: **1/2<enter>**

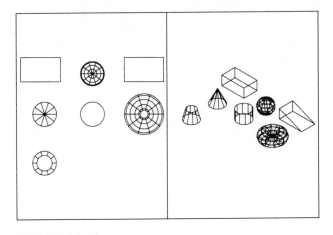

FIGURE 14-10
Extruding and Tapering a Circle

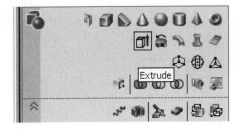

Draw an Extruded Polygon

Step 11. Draw a polygon (Figure 14–11):

Prompt	Response
Command:	**Polygon** (or TYPE: **POL<enter>**)
Enter number of sides <4>:	TYPE: **6<enter>**
Specify center of polygon or [Edge]:	TYPE: **2-3/4,5<enter>**
Enter an option [Inscribed in circle/ Circumscribed about circle] <I>:	TYPE: **C<enter>**
Specify radius of circle:	TYPE: **3/8<enter>**

Step 12. Extrude the polygon, 1/2 height, 0° extrusion taper angle (Figure 14–11):

Prompt	Response
Command:	**Extrude** (or TYPE: **EXT<enter>**)
Select objects to extrude:	CLICK: **the hexagon**
Select objects to extrude:	**<enter>**
Specify height of extrusion or [Direction/Path/Taper angle] <0'-0 1/2">:	TYPE: **1/2<enter>**

FIGURE 14-11
Extruding a Polygon

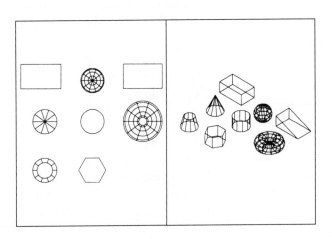

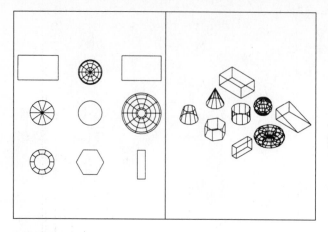

FIGURE 14–12
Extruding a Rectangle

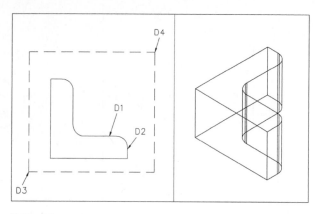

FIGURE 14–13
Extruding a Structural Steel Angle

Draw an Extruded Rectangle

Step 13. Draw a rectangle (Figure 14–12):

Prompt	Response
Command:	**Rectangle** (or TYPE: **REC<enter>**)
Specify first corner point or [Chamfer/ Elevation/Fillet/Thickness/Width]:	TYPE: **4-1/4,4-1/2<enter>**
Specify other corner point or [Area/Dimensions/Rotation]:	TYPE: **4-1/2,5-3/8<enter>**

Step 14. Extrude the rectangle, 1/2 height, 0° extrusion taper angle (Figure 14–12):

Prompt	Response
Command:	**Extrude** (or TYPE: **EXT<enter>**)
Select objects to extrude:	CLICK: **the rectangle**
Select objects to extrude:	**<enter>**
Specify height of extrusion or [Direction/Path/Taper angle] <0'-0 1/2">:	TYPE: **1/2<enter>**

Draw an Extruded Structural Angle

Step 15. Draw the outline of the cross section of a structural angle (Figure 14–13):

Prompt	Response
Command:	TYPE: **L<enter>**
Specify first point:	TYPE: **1,3<enter>**
Specify next point or [Undo]:	TYPE: **@7/8,0<enter>** (or turn ORTHO ON and use direct distance entry)
Specify next point or [Undo]:	TYPE: **@0,1/4<enter>**
Specify next point or [Close/Undo]:	TYPE: **@-5/8,0<enter>**
Specify next point or [Close/Undo]:	TYPE: **@0,5/8<enter>**
Specify next point or [Close/Undo]:	TYPE: **@-1/4,0<enter>**
Specify next point or [Close/Undo]:	TYPE: **C<enter>**

Step 16. Add a 1/8 radius fillet to the outline (Figure 14–13):

Prompt	Response
Command:	**Fillet** (or TYPE: **F<enter>**)
Current settings: Mode = TRIM, Radius = 0'-0 1/2"	
Select first object or [Undo/Polyline/ Radius/Trim/Multiple]:	TYPE: **R<enter>**
Specify fillet radius <0'-0 1/2">:	TYPE: **1/8<enter>**

Select first object or [Undo/Polyline/
    Radius/Trim/Multiple]:
	D1 (Use the Zoom-Window command if needed
	    to allow you to pick the necessary lines.)

Select second object or shift-select to apply corner:	**D2**

Step 17. On your own (Figure 14–13):

1. Draw 1/8 radius fillets at the other two intersections shown.

Step 18. Use Edit Polyline (Pedit) to combine all the lines and fillets into a single entity (Figure 14–13):

Prompt	Response
Command:	**Edit Polyline** (or TYPE: **PE<enter>**)
Select polyline or [Multiple]:	CLICK: **one of the lines forming the structural angle**
Object selected is not a polyline Do you want to turn it into one? <Y>	**<enter>**

Enter an option [Close/Join/Width/
    Edit vertex/Fit/Spline/Decurve/
    Ltype gen/Undo]:
	TYPE: **J<enter>** (to select the Join option)

Select objects:	**D3**
Specify opposite corner:	**D4**
Select objects:	**<enter>**

7 segments added to polyline
Enter an option [Open/Join/Width/
    Edit vertex/Fit/Spline/Decurve/
    Ltype gen/Undo]:
	<enter> (to exit from the Pedit command)

Step 19. Extrude the cross section of the structural angle, 1/2 height, 0° extrusion taper angle (Figure 14–13):

Prompt	Response
Command:	**Extrude** (or TYPE: **EXT<enter>**)
Select objects to extrude:	CLICK: **the polyline**
Select objects to extrude:	**<enter>**
Specify height of extrusion or [Direction/Path/Taper angle] <0'-0 1/2">:	TYPE: **1/2<enter>**

FIGURE 14–14
Extruding a Molding Shape

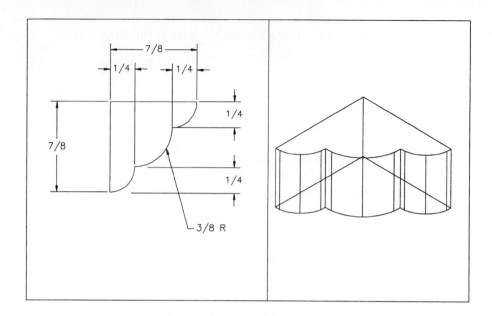

Draw an Extruded Shape

Step 20. On your own (Figure 14–14):

1. Draw the shape shown as Figure 14–14 in the approximate location shown in Figure 14–2. When you draw the shape, be sure that you draw only what is needed. If you draw extra lines, the Edit Polyline command cannot join the lines into a single polyline.
2. Use the Edit Polyline command to join all lines and arcs into a single polyline.
3. Extrude the figure to a height of 1/2.

Exercise 14–1: Part 3, Using Revolve to Draw Revolved Solids; Using Rotate 3D to Rotate Solids about the X, Y, and Z Axes

Draw Revolved Shape 1

Step 21. Draw two circles (Figure 14–15):

Prompt	Response
Command:	TYPE: **C**<enter>
Specify center point for circle or [3P/2P/Ttr (tan tan radius)]:	TYPE: **6-1/4,7-3/4**<enter>
Specify radius of circle or [Diameter]:	TYPE: **1/2**<enter>
Command:	<enter>
Specify center point for circle or [3P/2P/Ttr (tan tan radius)]:	TYPE: **6-1/4,8-1/4**<enter>
Specify radius of circle or [Diameter] <0'-1/2">:	TYPE: **1/8**<enter>

FIGURE 14–15
Revolving a Shape 90°

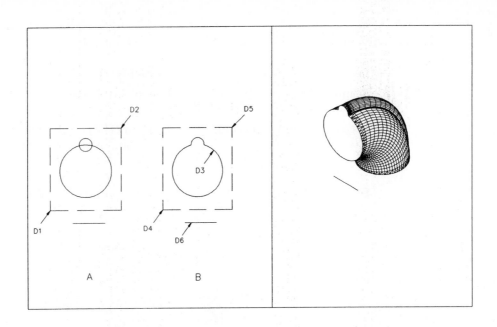

Step 22. Use the Trim command to trim parts of both circles (Figures 14–15A and 14–15B):

Prompt	Response
Command:	**Trim** (or TYPE: **TR<enter>**)
Select cutting edges...	
Select objects or <select all>:	**<enter>**
Select object to trim or shift-select to extend or [Fence/Crossing/ Project Edge/eRase/Undo]:	**Trim the circles as shown in Figure 14–15B.** (Zoom-Window to get in closer if needed.) **<enter>**

Step 23. Join all segments of the circles into one polyline (Figure 14–15B):

Prompt	Response
Command:	**Edit Polyline** (or TYPE: **PE<enter>**)
Select polyline:	**D3<enter>**
Object selected is not a polyline	
Do you want to turn it into one? <Y>	**<enter>**
Enter an option [Close/Join/Width/ Edit vertex/Fit/Spline/Decurve/ Ltype gen/Undo]:	TYPE: **J<enter>**
Select objects:	**D4**
Specify opposite corner:	**D5**
Select objects:	**<enter>**
1 segment added to polyline	
Enter an option [Open/Join/Width/ Edit vertex/Fit/Spline/Decurve/ Ltype gen/Undo]:	**<enter>** (to exit from the Edit Polyline command)

Step 24. Draw the axis of revolution (Figure 14–15):

Prompt	Response
Command:	**Line** (or TYPE: **L<enter>**)
Specify first point:	TYPE: **6,6-3/4<enter>**
Specify next point or [Undo]:	**With ORTHO ON move your mouse to the right and TYPE: 5/8<enter>**
Specify next point or [Undo]:	**<enter>**

Step 25. Use Revolve to form a revolved solid created by revolving a single poly-line 90° counterclockwise about an axis (Figure 14–15B):

Prompt	Response
Command:	**Revolve** (or TYPE: **REV<enter>**)
Select objects to revolve:	**D3**
Select objects to revolve:	**<enter>**
Specify axis start point or define axis by [Object/X/Y/Z]<Object>:	**<enter>**
Select an object:	**D6** (Be sure to click the left end of the line for counterclockwise rotation.)
Specify angle of revolution or [Start angle]<360>:	TYPE: **90<enter>**

Draw a Revolved Rectangle

Step 26. Draw a rectangle (Figure 14–16):

Prompt	Response
Command:	**Rectangle** (or TYPE: **REC<enter>**)
Specify first corner point or [Chamfer/Elevation/Fillet/Thickness/Width]:	TYPE: **7-3/8,7-3/8<enter>**
Specify other corner point or [Area/Dimensions/Rotation]:	TYPE: **8-1/4,8-1/8<enter>**

Step 27. Draw the axis of revolution (Figure 14–16):

Prompt	Response
Command:	TYPE: **L<enter>**
Specify first point:	TYPE: **7-3/8,6-3/4<enter>**
Specify next point or [Undo]:	**Move your mouse to the right and TYPE: 3/4<enter>** (Be sure ORTHO is ON.)
Specify next point or [Undo]:	**<enter>**

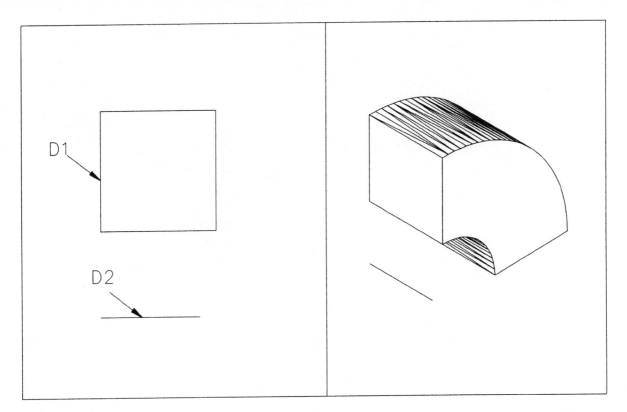

FIGURE 14–16
Revolving a Rectangle

Step 28. Use the Revolve command to form a revolved solid created by revolving the rectangle 90 counterclockwise about an axis (Figure 14–16):

Prompt	Response
Command:	**Revolve**
Select objects to revolve:	**D1\<enter>**
Select objects to revolve:	**\<enter>**
Specify axis start point or define axis by [Object/X/Y/Z] \<Object>:	**\<enter>**
Select an object:	**D2**
	(CLICK: **the left end of the line**)
Specify angle of revolution or [Start angle] \<360>:	TYPE: **90\<enter>**

Draw a Revolved Paper Clip Holder

Step 29. On your own (Figures 14–17 and 14–18):

1. Draw the cross-sectional shape of the object shown in Figures 14–17 using the Line and Arc commands in the approximate locations shown in Figure 14–2.
2. Use the Edit Polyline command to join all entities of the shape into a single closed polyline.
3. Locate the axis of revolution for the shape in the position shown.
4. Use Revolve to revolve the shape full circle about the axis.

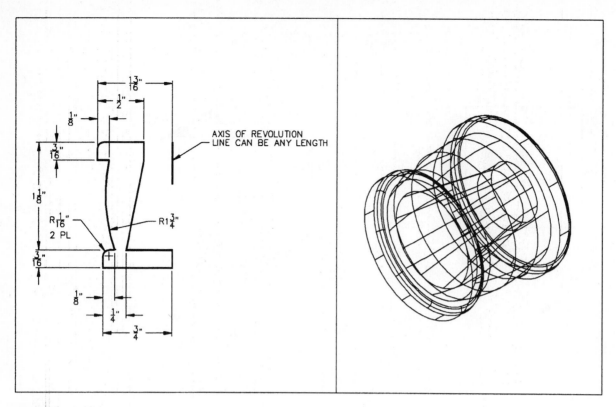

FIGURE 14–17
Revolving a Paper Clip Holder

Rotate 3D

Step 30. Use Rotate 3D to rotate the paper clip holder 90° about the X axis so that it assumes the position shown in Figure 14–18:

Prompt	Response
Command:	(TYPE: **ROTATE3D<enter>**)
Select objects:	CLICK: **the paper clip holder**
Select objects:	**<enter>**
Specify first point on axis or define axis by [Object/Last/View/Xaxis/Yaxis/Zaxis/2points]:	TYPE: **X<enter>**
Specify a point on the X axis <0,0,0>:	TYPE: **CEN<enter>**

FIGURE 14–18
Rotating an Object about the X Axis

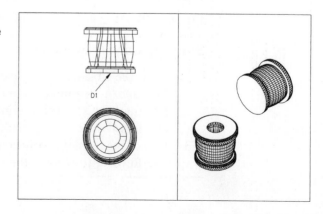

Prompt	Response
of	**D1**
Specify rotation angle or [Reference]:	TYPE: **90<enter>**

Exercise 14–1: Part 4, Using Chamfer and Fillet to Form Chamfers and Fillets on Solid Edges

Chamfer and Fillet the Top Four Edges of Two Separate Boxes

Step 31. On your own (Figure 14–2):

1. Use Box to draw two boxes measuring 1-1/4″ × 3/4″ × 1/2″ H each, in the approximate locations shown in Figure 14–2.

Step 32. Chamfer the top four edges of the first box (Figure 14–19):

Prompt	Response
Command:	**Chamfer** (or TYPE: **CHA<enter>**)
(TRIM mode) Current chamfer Dist1 = 0′-0 1/2″, Dist2 = 0′-0 1/2″ Select first line or [Undo/Polyline/ Distance/Angle/Trim/mEthod/ Multiple]:	TYPE: **D<enter>**
Specify first chamfer distance <0′-0 1/2″>:	TYPE: **3/16<enter>**
Specify second chamfer distance <0′-0 3/16″>:	**<enter>**
Select first line or [Undo/Polyline/ Distance/Angle/Trim/mEthod/ Multiple]:	**D1** (Figure 14–19)
Base surface selection... Enter surface selection option [Next/OK (current)] <OK>:	

If the top surface of the box turns dotted, showing it as the selected surface, continue. If one of the side surfaces is selected, TYPE: **N<enter>** until the top surface is selected.

FIGURE 14–19
Chamfering and Filleting Solid Edges

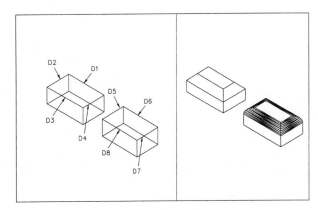

Prompt	Response
Enter surface selection option [Next/OK (current)] <OK>:	<enter>
Specify base surface chamfer distance <0'-0 3/16">:	<enter>
Specify other surface chamfer distance <0'-0 3/16">:	<enter>
Select an edge or [Loop]:	**D1, D2, D3, D4**
Select an edge or [Loop]:	<enter>

Step 33. Fillet the top four edges of the second box (Figure 14–19):

Prompt	Response
Command:	**Fillet** (or TYPE: **F<enter>**)
Current settings: Mode = TRIM, Radius = 0'−0 1/8"	
Select first object or [Undo/Polyline/ Radius/Trim/Multiple]:	**D5** (Figure 14–19)
Enter fillet radius <0'-0 1/8">:	TYPE: **3/16<enter>**
Select an edge or [Chain/Radius]:	**D6,D7,D8**
Select an edge or [Chain/Radius]:	<enter>

Chamfer and Fillet on the Top Edge of Two Separate Cylinders

Step 34. On your own (Figure 14–20):

1. Draw two cylinders using Cylinder with a radius of 3/8 and a height of 3/4 in the approximate location shown in Figure 14–20.
2. Chamfer the top edge of the first cylinder (Figure 14–20) using chamfer distances of 1/16. CLICK: **D1** when you select edges to be chamfered.
3. Fillet the top edge of the second cylinder (Figure 14–20) using a fillet radius of 1/16. CLICK: **D2** when you select edges to be filleted.

The edges of the cylinders should appear as shown in Figure 14–21.

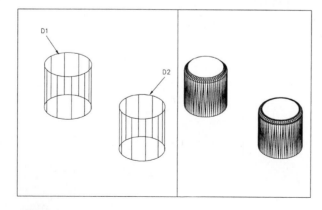

FIGURE 14–20
Chamfering and Filleting Cylinders

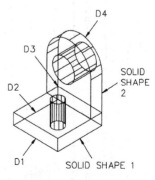

FIGURE 14–21
Drawing a Composite Solid

Exercise 14–1: Part 5, Using Union to Join Two Solids; Using Subtract to Subtract Solids from Other Solids

Draw Solid Shape 1

Step 35. Draw solid shape 1 (the base of the shape), and a cylinder that will be the hole in the base (Figure 14–21) with UCS set to World:

Prompt	Response
Command:	TYPE: **UCS<enter>**
Specify origin of UCS or [Face/ NAmed/OBject/Previous/View/ World/X/Y/Z/ZAxis] <World>:	**<enter>**
Command:	**Box**
Specify corner of box or [Center] <0,0,0>:	TYPE: **4-1/2,3/4<enter>**
Specify corner or [Cube/Length]:	TYPE: **@1,1<enter>**
Specify height:	TYPE: **1/4<enter>**
Command:	**Cylinder** (or TYPE: **CYLINDER<enter>**)
Specify center point of base or [3P/2P/Ttr/Elliptical]:	TYPE: **.X<enter>**
of	TYPE: **MID<enter>**
of	**D1**
(need YZ):	TYPE: **MID<enter>**
of	**D2**
Specify base radius or [Diameter]:	TYPE: **1/8<enter>**
Specify height or [2 Point/Axis endpoint/Center of other end]:	TYPE: **1/2<enter>** (Make the height of the hole tall enough so you can be sure it goes through the model.)

Draw Solid Shape 2

Step 36. On your own:

Set the UCS Icon command to ORigin so you will be able to see the USC icon move when the origin is relocated (TYPE: UCSICON<enter>, then OR<enter>).

Step 37. Rotate the UCS 90° about the X axis, and move the origin of the UCS to the upper left rear corner of the box (Figure 14–21):

Prompt	Response
Command:	TYPE: **UCS<enter>**
Specify origin of UCS or [Face/ NAmed/OBject/Previous/View/ World/X/Y/Z/ZAxis] <World>:	TYPE: **X<enter>**
Specify rotation angle about X axis <90>:	**<enter>**
Command:	TYPE: **UCS<enter>**
Specify origin of UCS or [Face/ NAmed/OBject/Previous/View/ World/X/Y/Z/ZAxis] <World>:	TYPE: **O<enter>**

Prompt	Response
Specify new origin point <0,0,0>:	endpoint
Of	D3

Step 38. Draw solid shape 2 (the vertical solid) and a cylinder that will be the hole in the vertical solid (Figure 14–21):

Prompt	Response
Command:	Polyline
	(or TYPE: **PL<enter>**)
Specify start point:	TYPE: **0,0<enter>**
Specify next point or [Arc/Close/ Halfwidth/Length/Undo/Width]:	With **ORTHO ON** move your mouse **right** and TYPE: **1<enter>**
Specify next point or [Arc/Close/ Halfwidth/Length/Undo/Width]:	Move your mouse **up** and TYPE: **3/4<enter>**
Specify next point or [Arc/Close/ Halfwidth/Length/Undo/Width]:	TYPE: **A<enter>**
Specify endpoint of arc or [Angle/ CEnter/CLose/Direction/ Halfwidth/Line/Radius/ Second pt/Undo/Width]:	Move your mouse **left** and TYPE: **1<enter>**
Specify endpoint of arc or [Angle/ CEnter/CLose/Direction/ Halfwidth/Line/Radius/ Second pt/Undo/Width]:	TYPE: **CL<enter>**
Command:	**Extrude** (or TYPE: **EXT<enter>**)
Select objects to extrude:	CLICK: **the polyline just drawn.**
Select objects to extrude:	**<enter>**
Specify height of extrusion or [Direction/Path/Taper angle]:	TYPE: **1/4<enter>**
	<enter>
Command:	**Cylinder**
Specify center point of base or [3P/2P/Ttr/Elliptical]:	TYPE: **CEN<enter>**
of	**D4**
Specify base radius or [Diameter]:	TYPE: **1/4<enter>**
Specify height or [2point/Axis endpoint]:	TYPE: **1/2<enter>**

The cylinder is longer than the thickness of the upright piece so you can be sure that the hole goes all the way through it.

Make sure the base of the cylinder is located on the back surface of the upright piece. If the cylinder is located on the front surface of the upright piece, move the cylinder 3/8 in the negative Z direction.

Union

Step 39. Join the base and the vertical shape together to form one model:

Prompt	Response
Command:	**Union** (from Modify-Solids Editing)
	(or TYPE: **UNION<enter>**)

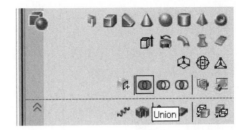 

Prompt	Response
Select objects:	CLICK: the base (shape 1) and the vertical solid (shape 2).
Select objects:	\<enter\>

Subtract

Step 40. Subtract the holes from the model:

Prompt	Response
Command:	**Subtract** (from Modify-Solids Editing) (or TYPE: **SU\<enter\>**)
Select solids and regions to subtract from...	
Select objects:	CLICK: any point on the model.
Select objects:	\<enter\>
Select solids and regions to subtract...	
Select objects:	CLICK: the two cylinders.
Select objects:	\<enter\>

Hide

Step 41. Perform a Hide to be sure the model is correct (Figure 14–22):

Prompt	Response
Command:	Hide (or TYPE: HI\<enter\>)

The model should appear as shown in Figure 14–22.

Step 42. On your own:
1. Return to the World UCS.

FIGURE 14–22
The Completed Model After a Hide

Exercise 14–1: Part 6, Using Sweep, Loft, Planar Surface, Thicken, and Polysolid to Draw Solid Shapes

The commands in this part of Exercise 14–1 are new to AutoCAD 2007 and are extremely powerful. Sweep is used in the first shape.

Sweep

The Sweep command gives you the ability to create a new solid by sweeping an object along a path. You have the options of selecting a base point, scaling the object as it is swept along the path, and twisting the object as it is swept.

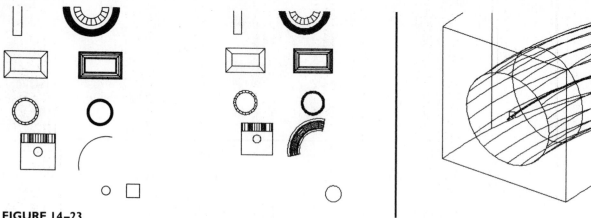

FIGURE 14–23
Draw an Arc, a Circle, and a
Square

FIGURE 14–24
Zoom in Close to CLICK: the Arc in the Center of the Swept Circle

Step 43. On your own:

1. Draw an arc in the approximate location shown in Figure 14–23. It should be about 1-1/2″ long and approximately the shape shown.
2. Draw a 1/8″ radius circle in the approximate location shown in Figure 14–23.
3. Draw a 3/8″ square using the rectangle command in the approximate location shown.

Step 44. Use the Sweep command to create the shape shown in Figure 14–24:

Prompt	Response
Command:	**Sweep** (or TYPE: **SWEEP**<enter>)
Select objects to sweep:	CLICK: **any point on the circle**
Select objects to sweep:	<enter>
Select sweep path or Alignment/ Base point/Scale/Twist]:	CLICK: **any point on the arc**
Command:	<enter> (repeat the Sweep command)
Select objects to sweep:	CLICK: **any point on the square**
Select objects to sweep:	<enter>
Select sweep path or Alignment/ Base point/Scale/Twist]:	CLICK: **any point on the arc**

You will have to CLICK: in the 3D view, then zoom in close to CLICK: the arc as shown in Figure 14–24.

Step 45. Use the Subtract command to create a hole throughout the swept square and use the Hide command to check the shape (Figure 14–25):

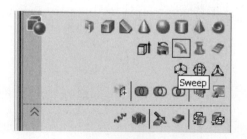

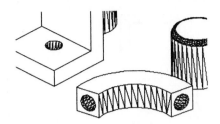

FIGURE 14–25
Use Subtract to Create a Hole
in the Swept Square

Prompt	Response
Command:	**Subtract** (or TYPE: **SU**<enter>)
Select solids and regions to subtract from:	
Select objects:	CLICK: **any point on the swept square**
Select solids and regions to subtract:	
Select objects:	CLICK: **any point on the swept circle**
Command:	**Hide** (or TYPE: **HI**<enter>)

Loft

The Loft command gives you the ability to create a 3D solid or surface selecting a set of two or more cross-sectional areas.

If you select two or more closed cross-sectional areas, a solid is created.

If you select two or more open cross-sectional areas, a surface is created.

You cannot use both open and closed cross-sectional areas in a set. You have to choose one or the other.

When you make a lofted shape, you can use the Loft Settings dialog box to control the shape of the surface or solid.

Step 46. On your own:

1. Draw three circles (1/2″ radius, 3/8″ radius, and 1/4″ radius) in the approximate location shown in Figure 14–26.
2. Move the 1/4″ radius circle up 1/4″ in the Z direction. You may use the Move command and TYPE: @0,0,1/4 <enter> for the second point of displacement OR in the 3D view (with ORTHO ON) CLICK: on the circle, move your mouse up, and TYPE: 1/4 <enter>.
3. Move the 3/8″ radius circle up 1/2″ in the Z direction.

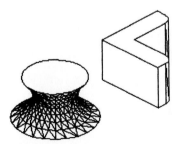

FIGURE 14–26
Draw 1/4″, 3/8″, and 1/2″
Radius Circles

Step 47. Use the Loft command to create a lofted solid and use the Hide command to check it (Figure 14–27):

Prompt	Response
Command:	**Loft** (or TYPE: **LOFT**<enter>)
Select cross-sections in lofting order:	CLICK: **the 1/2″ radius circle** (the one on the bottom)
Select cross-sections in lofting order:	CLICK: **the 1/4″ radius circle** (the next one up)
Select cross-sections in lofting order:	CLICK: **the 3/8″ radius circle** (the one on top)
Select cross-sections in lofting order:	<**enter**>

FIGURE 14–27
Lofted Shape Complete

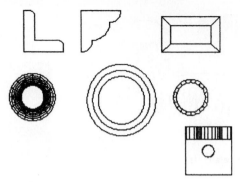

FIGURE 14–28
Draw 1/2″, 5/8″, and 3/4″ Radius Circles

FIGURE 14–29
Lofted Bowl Shape Complete

Prompt	Response
Enter an option [Guides/Path/ Cross-sections only] <Cross-sections only>:	<enter>
The Loft Settings dialog box appears;	CLICK: OK
Command:	**Hide** (or TYPE: **HI**<enter>)

Step 48. Create a lofted shape similar to a bowl:

On Your Own:

1. Draw three circles (3/4″ radius, 5/8″ radius, and 1/2″ radius) in the approximate location shown in Figure 14–28.
2. Move the 1/2″ radius circle up 1/8″ in the Z direction.
3. Move the 5/8″ radius circle up 1/2″ in the Z direction.
4. Use the Loft command to create the bowl but pick the circles in a different order: CLICK: the one on the bottom first, the one on the top next, and the one in between the two others last.
5. Use the Hide command to check its shape, Figure 14–29.

Planar Surface

You can use the Planar Surface (PLANESURF) command to make a surface using one of the following:

Select one or more objects that form an enclosed area.
Draw a rectangle so that the surface is created parallel to the rectangle.

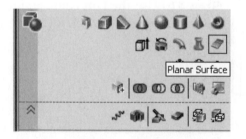

FIGURE 14–30
Draw the Planar Surface and
Thicken It

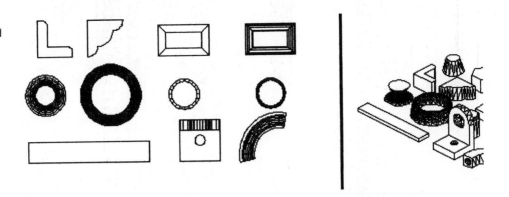

Step 49. Draw a planar surface and thicken it (Figure 14–30):

Prompt	Response
Command:	**Planar Surface** (or TYPE: **PLANESURF**<enter>)
Specify first corner or [Object] <Object>:	CLICK: **the lower left corner in the approximate location shown in Figure 14–30.**
Specify other corner:	TYPE: **@3,1/2<enter>**
Command:	**Thicken** (or TYPE: **THICKEN**<enter>)
Select surfaces to thicken:	CLICK: **the planar surface**
Select surfaces to thicken:	**<enter>**
Specify thickness <0'-0">:	TYPE: **1/8<enter>**

Polysolid

You can use the Polysolid command to draw walls by specifying the wall width and its height. You can also create a polysolid from an existing line, polyline, arc, or circle. If the width and height have been set, clicking on the object from the polysolid prompt such as a line or an arc will change it to a polysolid that is the height and width of the polysolid setting.

Step 50. Draw a polysolid that has a height of 1/2″ and a width of 1/4″ (Figure 14–31):

Prompt	Response
Command:	**Polysolid** (or TYPE: **POLYSOLID**<enter>)
Specify start point or [Object/ Height/Width/Justify] <Object>:	TYPE: **H<enter>**
Specify height <0'-0">:	TYPE: **1/2<enter>**
Specify start point or [Object/ Height/Width/Justify] <Width>:	TYPE: **W<enter>**
Specify width <0'-0 ">:	TYPE: **1/4<enter>**
Specify start point or [Object/ Height/Width/Justify] <Width>:	TYPE: **8-1/2,4<enter>**
Specify next point or [Arc/Undo]: <Ortho on>	**Move your mouse down 3″ and** CLICK:
Specify next point or [Arc/Undo]:	TYPE: **A<enter>**
Specify endpoint of arc or [Close/ Direction/Line/Second point/ Undo]:	**Move your mouse to the left 1/2″ and** CLICK:

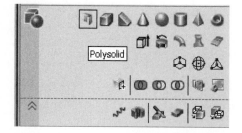

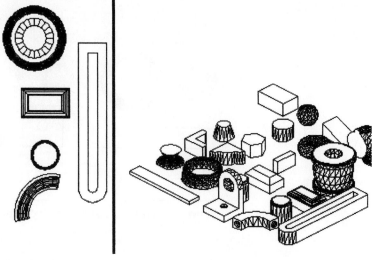

FIGURE 14–31
Draw a Polysolid with a Height of 1/2″ and a Width of 1/4″

Prompt	Response
Specify next point or [Arc/Close/Undo]:	
Specify endpoint of arc or [Close/Direction/Line/Second point/Undo]:	TYPE: **L<enter>**
Specify next point or [Arc/Close/Undo]:	**Move your mouse up 3″ and** CLICK:
Specify next point or [Arc/Close/Undo]:	TYPE: **C<enter>**
Command:	**Hide** (or TYPE: **HI<enter>**)

Exercise 14–1: Part 7, Using Intersection to Form a Solid Model from the Common Volume of Two Intersecting Solids

Drawing the solid model in Exercise 14–1, Part 7, demonstrates another powerful tool that can be used to form complex models.

In this exercise two separate solid shapes are drawn (in this case the same shape is copied and rotated so the two shapes are at right angles to each other) and moved so that they intersect. Intersection is used to combine the shapes to form one solid model from the common volume of the two intersecting solids. Figure 14–32 shows the two separate solid shapes, and the solid model that is formed from the common volume of the two solid shapes.

This shape will also be used in Exercise 14–4 to form the cornices at the top of the columns (Figure 14–66).

Draw Two Extruded Shapes at Right Angles to Each Other:

Step 51. On your own:

1. Zoom out so you can draw the full size shape shown in Figure 14–33 (Zoom .25) in the left viewport. In an open area of the screen draw Figure 14–33 using Line and Arc or Circle commands.

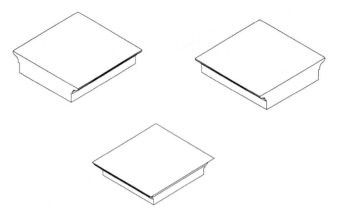

FIGURE 14–32
Two Shapes and the Shape Formed from the Intersected Volume of the Two Shapes

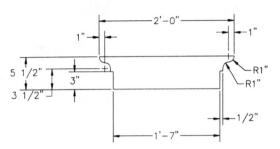

FIGURE 14–33
Dimensions for the Extruded Shapes

2. Use Edit Polyline to join all parts of Figure 14–33 to form a single polyline.
3. Use the Scale command to scale the polyline to 1/12 its size. (This is a scale of 1″ = 1′. In Exercise 14–3 you will scale this model to its original size.)
4. In the right viewport, set UCS to World, copy the shape, and use Rotate 3D to rotate both shapes 90° about the X axis.
5. Use Rotate 3D to rotate the shape on the right 90° about the Z axis (Figure 14–34).
6. Extrude the shape on the left 2″ (Figure 14–35).
7. Extrude the shape on the right 2″.

Step 52. Use the Move command to move the solid on the left to intersect with the other solid (Figure 14–36):

Prompt	Response
Command:	**Move**
Select objects:	CLICK: **the shape on the left**
Select objects:	<enter>
Specify base point or [Displacement] <Displacement>:	TYPE: **END**<enter>
of	**D1**
Specify second point or <use first point as displacement>:	TYPE: **END**<enter>
of	**D2**

FIGURE 14–34
Two Shapes Rotated 90° to Each Other

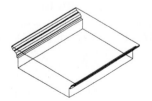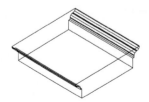

FIGURE 14–35
Both Shapes Extruded

FIGURE 14-36
Moving One Shape to
Intersect with the Other

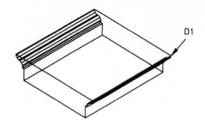
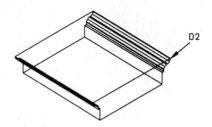

Intersect

Step 53. Use Intersect to form a solid model from the common volume of the two intersecting solids (Figure 14–37):

Prompt	Response
Command:	**Intersect** (from Modify-Solids Editing) (or TYPE: **IN<enter>**)
Select objects:	CLICK: **both shapes**
2 solids intersected	

FIGURE 14-37
The Shape Formed from the
Intersected Shapes

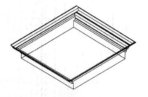

The display should appear as shown in Figure 14–37.

Step 54. Perform a Hide to be sure the solid model is correct (Figure 14–38):

Prompt	Response
Command:	**Hide** (or TYPE: **HI<enter>**)

The display should appear as shown in Figure 14–38.

FIGURE 14-38
The Intersected Solid After a
Hide

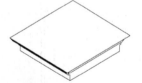

Step 55. On your own:

1. Return the UCS to World so you will not be surprised at the position the model will assume when it is inserted.

Wblock the Intersected Model

You should now Wblock the intersected model so you can use it in Exercise 14–2 to form the cornices at the tops of the columns (see Figure 14–4).

Step 56. Use Wblock to save the model to a disk (Figure 14–39):

Prompt	Response
Command:	TYPE: **W<enter>**
The Write Block dialog box appears:	**Locate the Removable Disk:** (CLICK: **the three dots to the far right of the location box**)

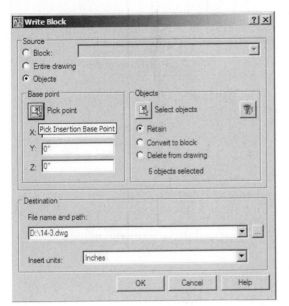

FIGURE 14–39
Wblocking the Intersected Shape

FIGURE 14–40
Rendered Image of Exercise 14–1

Prompt	Response
	(Substitute the letter for the correct drive if you do not have a removable disk.)
The Browse for Drawing File dialog box appears:	TYPE: **14–3** in the File name: box, then CLICK: **Save**
	CLICK: **Pick Point**
Specify insertion base point:	TYPE: **END**<enter>
of	CLICK: **the bottom corner of the intersected shape using Osnap-Endpoint. It will be the lowest point on the display.**
The Write Block dialog box appears:	CLICK: **Select Objects**
Select objects:	CLICK: **the intersected shape**
Select objects:	<enter>
The Write Block dialog box appears:	**If Retain is not on,** CLICK: **that radio button**
	CLICK: **OK**

The shape now exists on your disk as 14–3.dwg, and it is also on the current drawing.

Complete Exercise 14–1

Step 57. On your own:

1. Use the Move command to move the intersected shape to the approximate location shown in Figure 14–2.
2. Use the Vports command to return to a single viewport of the 3D viewport (Figure 14–2).
3. Use the Render command (TYPE: RENDER <enter>) to shade the drawing as shown in Figure 14–40.
4. Close the Render window.

Step 58. Save the drawing in two places.

Step 59. Plot the 3D viewport from the Model tab on a standard size sheet of paper. Be sure to click Rendered from the Shade plot: list in the Plot dialog box so the final plot appears as shown in Figure 14–40.

Exercise 14–2: Using Grips to Modify Solid Shapes

Grips for solids are new to AutoCAD 2007 and make changing the size and shape of solids much easier. In this exercise you will draw some solid shapes and use grips to change them.

Step 1. Use your workspace to make the following settings:

1. Use SaveAs… to save the drawing on the hard drive with the name CH14-EX2.
2. Set drawing Units: **Architectural**
3. Set Drawing Limits: **8-1/2,11**
4. Set GRIDDISPLAY: **0**
5. Set Grid: **1/4**
6. Set Snap: **1/8**
7. Create the following Layers:

LAYER NAME	COLOR	LINETYPE	LINEWEIGHT
3d-r	Red	Continuous	Default
3d-m	Magenta	Continuous	Default
3d-g	Green	Continuous	Default

8. Set **Layer 3d-m** current
9. Use the Viewports command to make two vertical viewports. Zoom-All in both viewports to start, then Zoom in closer as needed.
10. CLICK: **SE Isometric** from 3D Views for the right viewport.
11. Set FACETRES to 2, ISOLINES to 10.

Step 2. Draw the following solids in the approximate locations shown in Figure 14–41:

FIGURE 14–41
Draw Solids in This Approximate Location

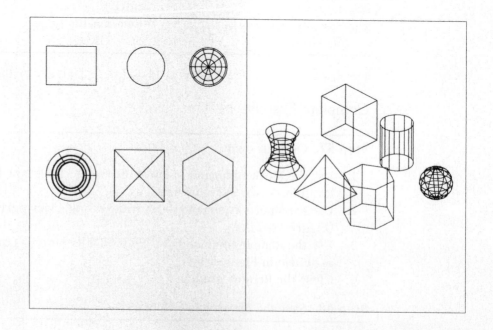

1. Use the Box command to draw a box 2″ long × 1-1/2″ deep × 2″ high.
2. Use the Cylinder command to draw a cylinder with a radius of 3/4″ × 2″ high.
3. Use the Sphere command to draw a 3/4″ radius sphere.
4. Use the Circle command to draw three circles; 1″ radius, 3/4″ radius, 1/2″ radius. Move the 1/2″ radius circle up 1″ in the Z direction and the 3/4″ radius circle up 2″ in the Z direction. Use the Loft command to create the shape shown.
5. Use the Pyramid command to draw a pyramid with a 1″ radius base, 2″ high.
6. Use the Polygon command to draw a 6 sided polygon with a 1″ radius circumscribed.
7. Use the Extrude command to extrude the polygon 2″.

Step 3.   Use grips to change the box to make it 2″ taller and 1″ deeper:

1. With no command active CLICK: any point on the box.
2. CLICK: the up grip to make it active (it changes color) and move your mouse up (in the Z direction) until the dynamic input reads 2″ as shown in Figure 14–42, then CLICK: to choose 2″ (or TYPE: 2<enter>). Then PRESS: ESC.
3. With no command active CLICK: any point on the box.
4. CLICK: the grip in front to make it active and move your mouse forward (in the Y direction) until the dynamic input reads 1″ as shown in Figure 14–43, then CLICK: to choose 1″ (or TYPE: 1<enter>).
5. Then PRESS: ESC.

Step 4.   Use grips to make the cylinder 4″ taller with a radius of 1/2″:

1. With no command active CLICK: any point on the cylinder.
2. CLICK: the up grip to make it active, and move your mouse up (in the Z direction) until the dynamic input reads 4″, as shown in Figure 14–44, then CLICK: to choose 4″ (or TYPE: 4<enter>). Then PRESS: ESC.
3. With no command active CLICK: any point on the cylinder.
4. CLICK: one of the grips on the quadrants to make it active and move your mouse in until the dynamic input reads 1/4″, as shown in Figure 14–45, then CLICK: to choose 1/4″ (or TYPE: 1/4<enter>).
5. Then PRESS: ESC.

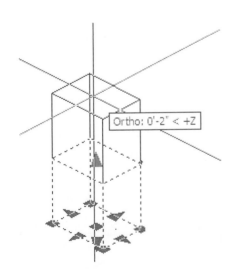

FIGURE 14–42
Use Grips to Make the Box 2″ Taller

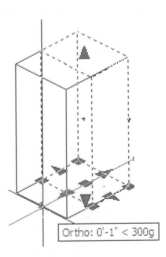

FIGURE 14–43
Use Grips to Make the Box 1″ Deeper

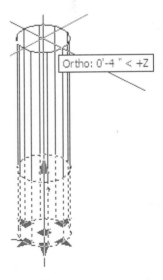

FIGURE 14–44
Use Grips to Make the Cylinder 4″ Taller

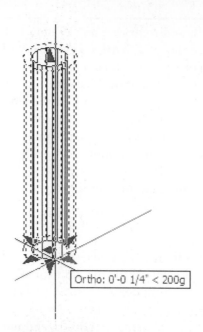

FIGURE 14–45
Use Grips to Make the Cylinder
Radius 1/4" Smaller

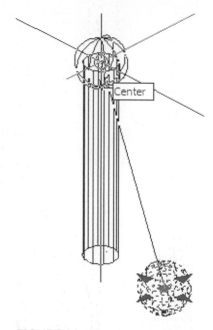

FIGURE 14–46
Use Grips to Move the Sphere to the
Top of the Cylinder

Step 5. Use grips to move the sphere to the top of the cylinder:

1. With no command active CLICK: **any point on the sphere.**
2. CLICK: **the grip in the center to make it active, turn ORTHO OFF, activate Osnap-Center, and** CLICK: **the top of the cylinder, as shown in Figure 14–46.** Then, PRESS: **ESC.**

Step 6. Use grips to move the extruded polygon back 4":

1. With no command active CLICK: **any point on the extruded polygon.**
2. CLICK: **one of the grips to make it active, turn ORTHO ON, PRESS: the space bar or toggle to the MOVE grip mode, and move your mouse back in the Y direction until the dynamic input reads 4", as shown in Figure 14–47.**

Step 7. Use grips to make the extruded polygon 4" taller:

1. With no command active CLICK: **any point on the extruded polygon.**

FIGURE 14–47
Use Grips to Make the
Extruded Polygon Back 4" in
the Y Direction

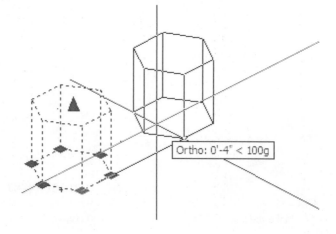

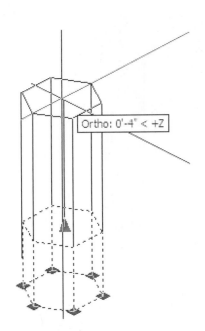

FIGURE 14–48
Use Grips to Make the Extruded
Polygon 4″ Taller

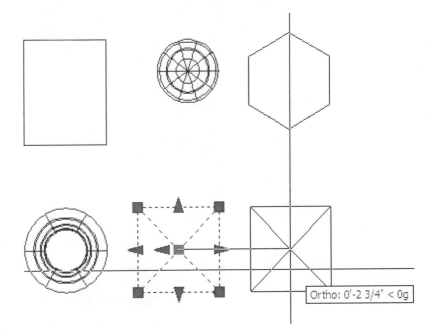

FIGURE 14–49
Use Grips to Move the Pyramid 2-3/4″ to the Right

2. CLICK: the up grip to make it active (and move your mouse up (in the Z direction) until the dynamic input reads 4″, as shown in Figure 14–48, then CLICK: to choose 4″ (or TYPE: 4<enter>). Then, PRESS: ESC.

Step 8. Use grips to move the pyramid 2-3/4″ to the right:

1. CLICK: the left viewport to make it active, and with no command active CLICK: any point on the pyramid.
2. CLICK: the grip in the center to make it active, turn ORTHO ON, and move your mouse to the right until the dynamic input reads 2-3/4″, as shown in Figure 14–49. CLICK: to choose 2-3/4″ (or TYPE: 2-3/4<enter>). Then, PRESS: ESC.

Step 9. Use grips to make the pyramid 4″ taller:

1. With no command active CLICK: any point on the extruded polygon.
2. CLICK: the up grip to make it active, move your mouse up (in the Z direction) until the dynamic input reads 4″, as shown in Figure 14–50, then CLICK: to choose 4″ (or TYPE: 4<enter>). Then, PRESS: ESC.

Step 10. Use grips to scale the lofted solid 1-1/4 larger than it is:

1. With no command active CLICK: any point on the lofted solid.
2. CLICK: the grip in the center to make it active, PRESS: the space bar several times to toggle to the SCALE grip mode, and TYPE: 1-1/4<enter>. Then, PRESS: ESC.

Step 11. On your own:

1. CLICK: the 3D viewport to make it active, and change the display to a single viewport.
2. Use the Hide command to remove hidden lines, as shown in Figure 14–51.

Step 12. Save your drawing in two places.

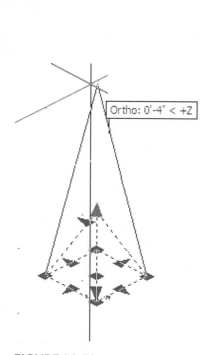

FIGURE 14–50
Use Grips to Make the Pyramid 4″ Taller

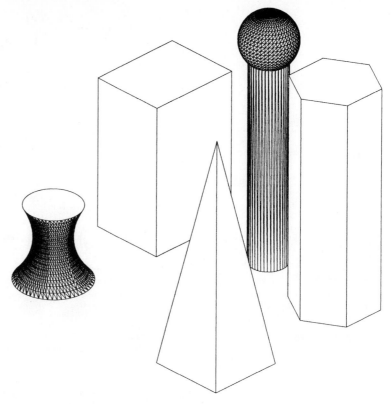

FIGURE 14–51
Exercise CH14-EX2 Complete

Step 13. Plot the drawing on an 11″ × 8-1/2″ sheet, scale: 1:2, as a display in the shadeplot area.

Exercise 14–3: Creating a Solid Model of Chair 1

In this exercise you will create a solid model of chair 1 (Figure 14–52) using many of the commands you used in Exercise 14–1 and many of the options of the SOLIDEDIT command.

Step 1. Use your workspace to make the following settings:

1. Use SaveAs... to save the drawing on the hard drive with the name CH14-EX3.
2. Set drawing Units: **Architectural**
3. Set Drawing Limits: **50,50**
4. Set GRIDDISPLAY: **0**
5. Set Grid: **1**
6. Set Snap: **1/2**
7. Create the following Layers:

LAYER NAME	COLOR	LINETYPE	LINEWEIGHT
3d-r	Red	Continuous	Default
3d-m	Magenta	Continuous	Default
3d-g	Green	Continuous	Default

8. Set **Layer 3d-r** current.
9. **Use the Viewports command to make two vertical viewports. Zoom-All in both viewports to start, then Zoom in closer as needed.** You will need both viewports as aids in creating this model.

FIGURE 14–52
Exercise 14–3 Complete

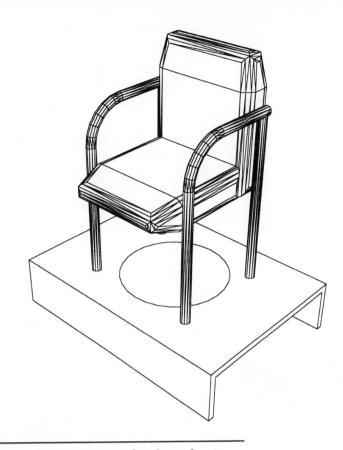

10. CLICK: **SE Isometric** from **3D Views** for the right viewport.
11. Set **FACETRES** to 4, **ISOLINES** to 20.

Draw One Side of the Chair Legs and Arms

Step 2. Define a UCS that is parallel to the side of the chair legs and arms in the right viewport:

Prompt	Response
Command:	TYPE: **UCS\<enter\>**
Specify origin of UCS or [Face/ NAmed/OBject/Previous/View/ World/X/Y/Z/ZAxis] \<World\>:	TYPE: **X\<enter\>**
Specify rotation angle about X axis \<90\>:	\<enter\>
Command:	TYPE: **UCS\<enter\>**
Specify origin of UCS or [Face/ NAmed/OBject/Previous/View/ World/X/Y/Z/ZAxis] \<World\>:	TYPE: **Y\<enter\>**
Specify rotation angle about Y axis \<90\>:	\<enter\>

Step 3. In the right viewport draw a path for the chair arm and front leg (two lines and a fillet and join them together using Pedit). Draw a circle to form the metal tube, and sweep it along the path:

Prompt	Response
Command:	TYPE: **L\<enter\>**
Specify first point:	TYPE: **8,12\<enter\>**

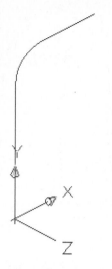

FIGURE 14–53
Draw a Path to Sweep a
Circle

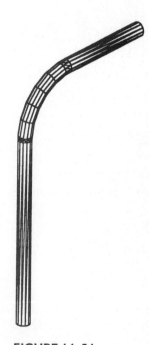

FIGURE 14–54
Chair Leg–Arm Extrusion
Complete

Prompt	Response
Specify next point or [Undo]:	TYPE: **@0,27<enter>**
Specify next point or [Undo]:	TYPE: **@16.5,0<enter>**
Specify next point or [Close/Undo]:	**<enter>**
Command:	TYPE: **F<enter>**
Select first object or [Undo/Polyline/ Radius/Trim/Multiple]:	TYPE: **R<enter>**
Specify fillet radius <0'-0">:	TYPE: **5<enter>**
Select first object or [Undo/Polyline/ Radius/Trim/Multiple] to apply corner:	CLICK: **one of the lines**
Select second object or shift-select:	CLICK: **the other line**
Command:	TYPE: **PE<enter>**
Select polyline or [Multiple]:	CLICK: **one of the lines** (Figure 14–53)
Object selected is not a polyline	
Do you want to turn it into one? <Y>	**<enter>**
Enter an option [Close/Join/Width/ Edit vertex/Fit/Spline/Decurve/ Ltype gen/Undo]:	TYPE: **J<enter>**
Select objects:	TYPE: **ALL<enter>**
Select objects:	**<enter>**
2 segments added to polyline	
Enter an option [Close/Join/Width/ Edit vertex/Fit/Spline/Decurve/ Ltype gen/Undo]:	**<enter>**
Command:	TYPE: **C<enter>**
Specify center point for circle or [3P/2P/Ttr (tan tan radius)]:	TYPE: **END<enter>**
of	CLICK: **the lower end of the vertical line**
Specify radius of circle or [Diameter]:	TYPE: **1<enter>**
Command:	**Sweep** (or TYPE: **SWEEP<enter>**)
Select objects to sweep:	CLICK: **the circle**
Select objects to sweep:	**<enter>**
Select sweep path or [Alignment/ Base point/Scale/Twist]:	CLICK: **the polyline**

The right viewport should appear as shown in Figure 14–54.

Draw the Cushion of the Chair

Step 4. Set a new UCS that is parallel to the World UCS (the cushion of the chair) that has an origin at the bottom of the chair leg:

Prompt	Response
Command:	TYPE:**UCS<enter>**
Specify origin of UCS or [Face/ NAmed/OBject/Previous/View/ World/X/Y/Z/ZAxis] <World>:	**<enter>**
Command:	**<enter>**
Specify origin of UCS or [Face/ NAmed/OBject/Previous/View/ World/X/Y/Z/ZAxis] <World>:	**Osnap-Center**

FIGURE 14–55
Move the UCS

Prompt	Response
of	CLICK: **the bottom of the chair leg** (Figure 14–55)
Specify point on X-axis or <Accept>:	<enter>

Step 5. Set Layer 3d-m current. Draw a box for the chair cushion and extrude and taper the front of it:

On Your Own:

1. Set Layer 3d-m current.

Prompt	Response
Command:	**Box** (or TYPE: **BOX**<enter>)
Specify corner of box or [Center]:	TYPE: **.75,13,14**<enter>
Specify corner or [Cube/Length]:	TYPE: **@18,-13** (Be sure to include the minus.)
Specify height:	TYPE: **5**<enter>
Command:	TYPE: **SOLIDEDIT**<enter>
Enter a solids editing option [Face/ Edge/Body/Undo/eXit] <eXit>:	TYPE: **F**<enter> (for face or surface)
Enter a face editing option [Extrude/Move/Rotate/Offset/ Taper/Delete/Copy/coLor/Undo/ eXit] <eXit>:	TYPE: **E**<enter>
Select faces or [Undo/Remove]:	CLICK: **D1**(Figure 14–56)
Select faces or [Undo/Remove/ALL]:	TYPE: **R**<enter> (to remove any surfaces that you do not want to extrude. You will probably have one that needs to be removed.)
Remove faces or [Undo/Add/ALL]:	CLICK: **any extra faces so the model appears as shown in Figure 14–57**

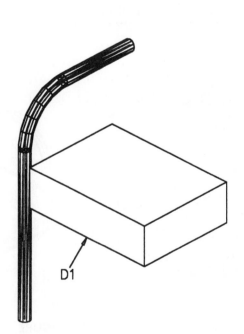

FIGURE 14–56
CLICK: the Face to Extrude

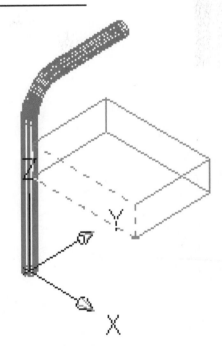

FIGURE 14–57
Select the Front Face to Extrude

Prompt	Response
Remove faces or [Undo/Add/ALL]:	<enter>
Specify height of extrusion or [Path]:	TYPE: **5**<enter>
Specify angle of taper for extrusion <0>:	TYPE: **15**<enter>
Enter a face editing option [Extrude/ Move/Rotate/Offset/Taper/Delete/ Copy/coLor/Undo/eXit] <eXit>:	<enter>
Enter a solids editing option [Face/ Edge/Body/Undo/eXit] <eXit>:	<enter>

The model appears as shown in Figure 14–58.

Draw the Back of the Chair

Step 6. Draw a box for the back of the chair:

Prompt	Response
Command:	**Box** (or TYPE: **BOX**<enter>)
Specify corner of box or [Center]	TYPE: **END**<enter> (or CLICK: **Osnap-endpoint**)
of	CLICK: **D1** (Figure 14–59)
Specify corner or [Cube/Length]:	TYPE: **@20,5**<enter>
Specify height:	TYPE: **16**<enter>

Oops, the back is too long. Correct it by moving the right surface of the box 2″ to the left using SOLIDEDIT, then Extrude the top face of the back 5″ with a 15° taper as shown in Figure 14–60 and use the Fillet command to round all the box edges.

Step 7. On your own:

1. Use the Move Faces option of the Solids Editing (SOLIDEDIT) command to move the right side of the back of the chair 2″ to the left. Be sure that only

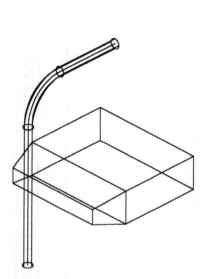

FIGURE 14–58
Cushion Extruded

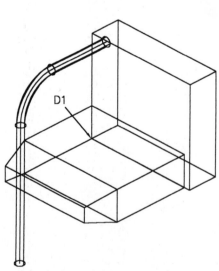

D1

FIGURE 14–59
Draw the Box for the Back of the Chair

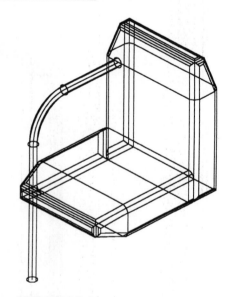

FIGURE 14–60
Correct the Back, Extrude Its Top Surface, and Fillet All Sharp Edges 1″

the right side of the box is selected. Select any point as a base point, then TYPE: @2<180 as the second point of displacement. You can skip several prompts by using either the Solids Editing toolbar or Solids Editing-Move Faces from the Modify menu on the menu bar. Typing the command shows you the complete structure of the SOLIDEDIT command.

2. Use the Extrude Faces option of the Solids Editing (SOLIDEDIT) command to extrude the top of the chair back 5″ with a 15° taper. You can skip several prompts by using either the Solids Editing toolbar or Solids Editing-Extrude Faces from the Modify menu on the menu bar.

3. Use the Fillet command to round all sharp edges of the chair cushion and back. TYPE: F <enter> for fillet, then TYPE: R <enter> for radius, then TYPE: 1 <enter> to set the radius, then select edges when you get the prompt: "Select an edge or [Chain/Radius]:". Pick the edges of the right side of the cushion, for example, then PRESS: <enter>. If you try to select all edges at the same time you will get an error message.

Complete the Leg and Arm Assembly

Step 8. Draw a circle for one of the back legs, extrude it, and combine front and back legs into a single object using the Union command (Figure 14–61):

On Your Own:

1. Set Layer 3d-g current:

Prompt	Response
Command:	TYPE: **C**<enter>
Specify center point for circle or [3P/2P/Ttr (tan tan radius)]:	TYPE: **0,15−1/2**<enter> (This makes the center point of the circle 15½″ in the Y direction from the UCS origin.)
Specify radius of circle or [Diameter]:	TYPE: **1**<enter>
Command:	TYPE: **EXT**<enter>
Select objects to extrude:	CLICK: **the circle you just drew**
Select objects to extrude:	<enter>

FIGURE 14–61
Draw a Circle for the Back
Leg, Extrude It, and Union It
with the Front Leg and Arm

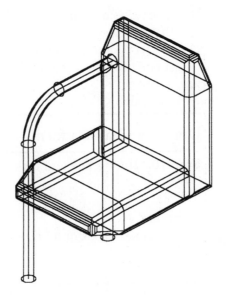

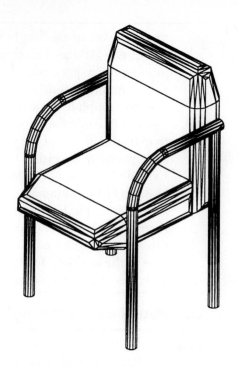

FIGURE 14–62
Copy the Leg Assembly to
the Right Side of the Chair

Prompt	Response
Specify height of extrusion or [Direction/Path/Taper angle]:	TYPE: **27<enter>** (The back leg is 27″ high.)
Command	**Union** (or TYPE: **UNION<enter>**)
Select objects:	CLICK: **the chair front leg and the back leg** (This makes the two pieces into a single piece.)
Select objects:	**<enter>**

Step 9.   **Copy the leg assembly to the right side of the chair (Figure 14–62):**

Prompt	Response
Command:	TYPE: **CP<enter>**
Select objects:	CLICK: **the chair leg assembly**
Select objects:	**<enter>**
Specify base point or [Displacement] <Displacement>:	CLICK: **any point**
Specify second point or <use first point as displacement>:	TYPE: **@20<0<enter>**
Specify second point or [Exit/Undo] <Exit>:	**<enter>**

Draw the Chair Platform

Step 10.   Draw a box and make a shell out of it:

Prompt	Response
Command:	TYPE: **BOX<enter>**

Specify corner of box or [Center]:	TYPE: **-10,-8,-6<enter>** (Notice that these are
	  absolute coordinates based on the UCS
	  located on the bottom of the front left leg.)

524

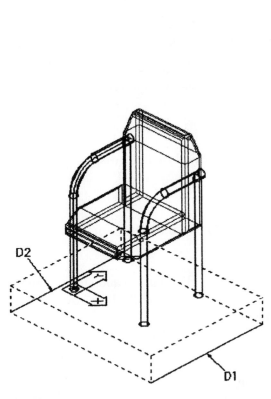

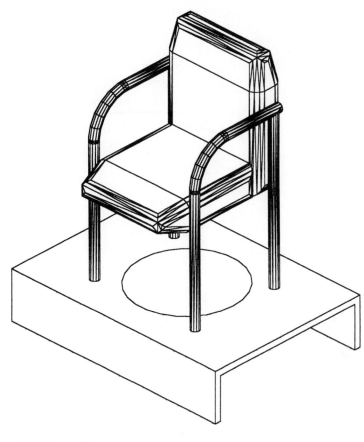

FIGURE 14–63
Draw a Box and Make a Shell of It

FIGURE 14–64
Draw a Circle and Imprint It on the Shell

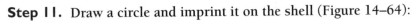

Prompt	Response
Specify corner or [Cube/Length]:	TYPE: **30,23.5,0<enter>** (absolute coordinates again)
Command:	**Solids Editing-Shell**
Select a 3D solid:	CLICK: **the box you just drew**
Remove faces or [Undo/Add/ALL]:	CLICK: **D1 and D2** (Figure 14–63)
Remove faces or [Undo/Add/ALL]:	**<enter>**
Enter the shell offset distance:	TYPE: **1<enter>**
[Imprint/seParate solids/Shell/cLean/ Check/Undo/eXit]<eXit>:	**<enter><enter>**

Step 11. Draw a circle and imprint it on the shell (Figure 14–64):

Prompt	Response
Command:	TYPE: **C<enter>**
Specify center point for circle or [3P/2P/Ttr (tan tan radius)]:	TYPE: **10,7.75<enter>**
Specify radius of circle or [Diameter]<0'−1">:	TYPE: **8<enter>**
Command:	**Solids Editing-Imprint Edges**
Select a 3D solid:	CLICK: **the shell under the chair**
Select an object to imprint:	CLICK: **the circle you just drew**
Delete the source object <N>:	TYPE: **Y<enter>**
Select an object to imprint:	**<enter>**

3D Orbit

3D Orbit allows you to obtain a 3D view in the active viewport. When 3D Orbit is active, you can right-click in the drawing area to activate the shortcut menu. This menu allows you to render the object and select parallel or perspective views while the object is being orbited. You can also access these options from the 3D Orbit toolbar.

Step 12. Use 3D Orbit to render and animate the model you have just completed:

On Your Own:

1. CLICK: The right viewport to make it active and turn the display to a single viewport.

Prompt	Response
Command:	**3D Orbit - Constrained Orbit** (or TYPE: 3DO<enter>)
Press ESC or ENTER to exit, or right-click to display shortcut-menu.	**Hold down the click button and slowly move the mouse so you get a feel for how the view changes** **RIGHT-CLICK:** to obtain the shortcut menu CLICK: **Preset Views - SW Isometric** **RIGHT-CLICK:** to obtain the shortcut menu CLICK: **Perspective** **RIGHT-CLICK:** to obtain the shortcut menu CLICK: **Visual Styles - Realistic** **RIGHT-CLICK:** to obtain the shortcut menu CLICK: **Other Navigation modes - Continuous Orbit** CLICK: **a point at the upper left edge of the display, hold down the click button, and describe a very small circle so the model rotates continuously.** Experiment with the continuous orbit display until you feel comfortable with it.

You may need to return to 3D Orbit and CLICK: **Constrained Orbit and Preset Views - SE Isometric** occasionally to return the display to a manageable view.

Prompt	Response
	CLICK: **3D Orbit and Preset View - SE Isometric with perspective projection and Realistic Visual Style to obtain a view similar to Figure 14–65.**

Step 13. On your own:

1. CLICK: **Layout 1.**
2. Use Dtext to place your name in the lower right corner in the simplex font.
3. Put the viewport boundary on a new layer and turn that layer OFF.

FIGURE 14–65
Exercise 14–3 Complete

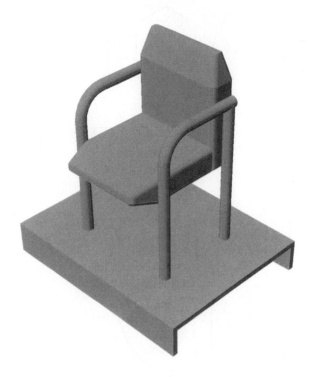

4. **Plot the drawing from the Plot dialog box. Be sure to** CLICK: **As Displayed from the Shade plot: list. Plot to fit on an 11″ × 8-1/2″ sheet.** If the shade plot option is greyed out, CLICK: **the viewport boundary** and CLICK: **Properties.** Then,CLICK: **As Displayed** from the Shade plot options.

Exercise 14–4:   Drawing Solid Models of Eight Objects

1. Draw solid models of the eight objects shown in Figure 14–66. Use the dimensions shown in the top and front views of A through H:

   Draw the top view, join it to form a continuous polyline, and extrude it to the height shown in the front view.

   Rotate the UCS 90° about the X axis, draw a rectangle at the angle shown in the front view, extrude it, move it in the Z direction so it covers the area of the extruded top view that must be removed, and subtract it from the extruded top view.

2. Arrange the objects so that they are well spaced on the page and take up most of a 9″ × 7″ area on an 11″ × 8-1/2″ sheet. Use the Hide command to remove hidden lines.

3. Your final drawing should show eight solid objects in a viewpoint similar to Exercise 14–1.

4. CLICK: **Layout1,** place your name in the lower right corner in 1/8″ letters, use Shade plot - As displayed, and plot or print the drawing on an 11″ × 8-1/2″ sheet at a scale of 1 = 1.

5. Save your drawing in two places with the name CH14-EX4.

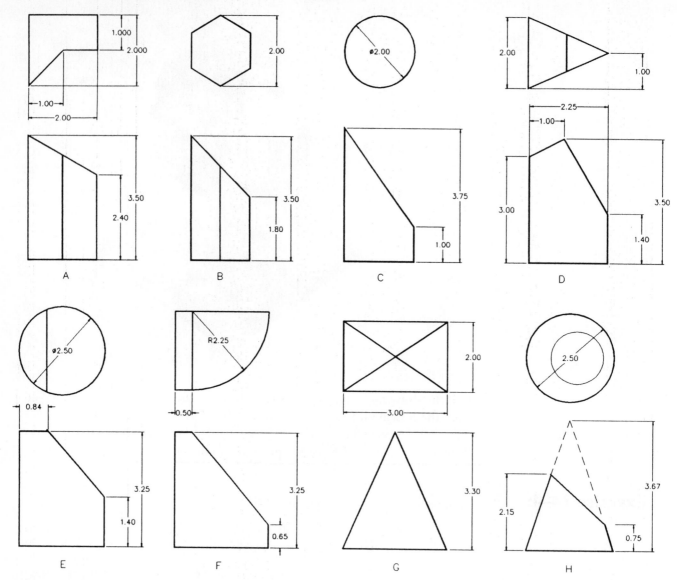

FIGURE 14–66
Exercise 14–4: Draw Solid Models of Eight Objects.

Exercise 14–5: Drawing a Solid Model of a Lamp Table

1. Draw a solid model of the lamp table shown in Figure 14–67. Scale the top and front views using a scale of 1″ = 1′-0″ to obtain the correct measurements for the model.
2. Use Revolve for the table pedestal. Use Polyline and Extrude for one table leg, and duplicate it with Polar Array. The table top can be an extruded circle or a solid cylinder.
3. Use **3D Orbit** to obtain a perspective view of your final model and CLICK: **Layout1** before you plot.
4. Place your name in the lower right corner in 1/8″ letters using simplex or an architectural font.

FIGURE 14–67
Exercise 14–5: Create a Solid
Model of a Table (Scale:
1"=11'-0)

5. Plot the drawing at a scale of 1 = 1 on an 11" × 8-1/2" sheet.
6. Return to the model tab (World UCS current) and Wblock the lamp table to a disk with the name TABLE.
7. Save your drawing with the name CH14-EX5.

Exercise 14–6: Drawing a Solid Model of a Sofa

1. Use the dimensions from Figure 14–68 to draw the sofa. Draw two rectangles measuring 27" × 6" with 3" fillets to form the bottom cushion. Extrude them both to a height of 21", and rotate one 90° about the Y axis.
2. Move one of the rectangles to intersect with the other as shown in Figure 14–69. Draw an end cap using a line and an arc with a 3" radius, join them together, and revolve them 90° as shown. Move the end cap to one corner of the cushion and copy it to the other three corners using the Mirror command. Join all parts of the cushion using the Union command.
3. Draw the back cushions in a similar manner.
4. Draw the arms, back, and base of the sofa using the Rectangle and Polyline commands, and extrude them to the dimensions shown.
5. Copy the cushions and move them to their correct locations using the Move and Rotate 3D commands.

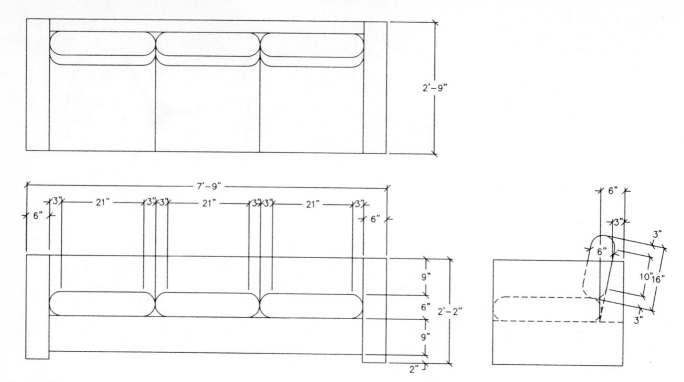

FIGURE 14–68
Exercise 14–6: Sofa Dimensions (Scale: 1/2″= 1′-0″)

FIGURE 14–69
The Parts of the Bottom Cushion

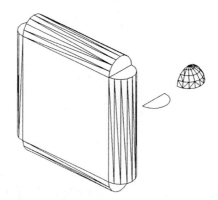

6. Use 3D Orbit to obtain a perspective view of your final model and CLICK: **Layout1** before you plot.
7. Place your name in the lower right corner in 1/8″ letters using simplex or an architectural font.
8. Plot the drawing at a scale of 1 = 1 on an 11″ × 8-1/2″ sheet.
9. Return to the model tab (World UCS current) and Wblock the sofa to a floppy disk with the name SOFA. CHECK: **Retain** so the drawing stays on the screen.
10. Save your drawing in two places with the name CH14-EX6.

Exercise 14–7: Drawing a Solid Model of a Lamp and Inserting It and the Lamp Table into the Sofa Drawing

1. Draw the lamp and the shade from the dimensions shown in Figure 14–70. Use your 1/8″ architect's scale for any dimensions not shown. Make sure the lamp is a closed polyline and the shade is a closed polyline. You will have to give the shade some thickness by offsetting its shape and closing the ends with a line. Then join all parts of the shade to form a closed polyline.

2. Revolve the two polylines to form the lamp.

3. Rotate the lamp 90° about the X axis so it is in an upright position.

4. With the World UCS current Wblock the lamp to a disk with the name LAMP. Use the center of the bottom of the lamp as the insertion point.

5. Open the drawing SOFA that you have Wblocked to the disk.

6. Insert the TABLE and LAMP models from the disk into the SOFA drawing. Place the table to the right of the sofa, and center the base of the lamp on the table top as shown in Figure 14–71.

7. Use 3D Orbit to obtain a perspective view of your final model and CLICK: **Layout1** before you plot.

8. Place your name in the lower right corner in 1/8″ letters using simplex or an architectural font.

9. Plot the drawing at a scale of 1 = 1 on an 11″ × 8-1/2″ sheet.

10. Save your drawing in two places with the name CH14- EX7.

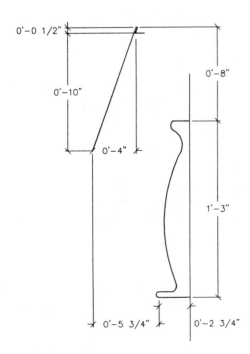

FIGURE 14–70
Exercise 14–7: Overall Dimensions of the
Lamp (Scale: 1/8″=1″)

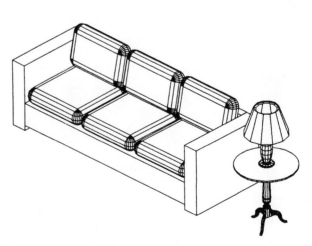

FIGURE 14–71
Exercise 14–7: Combine Solid Models

Exercise 14–8: Drawing a Solid Model of the Tenant Space Reception Seating

1. Draw the chair coffee table and corner table with a series of boxes (Figure 14–72).
2. Fillet the vertical edges of the coffee table and corner table.
3. Use the Rectangle command with 1″ fillets to draw the coffee table and corner table inlays. Extrude the rectangles 1″ and place them so they are flush with the top of the tables. Subtract the extruded rectangles from the tables and replace them with other extruded rectangles that are slightly smaller to form the inlays.
4. Use 3D Orbit to obtain a perspective view of your final model and CLICK: **Layout1** before you plot.
5. Place your name in the lower right corner in 1/8″ letters using simplex or an architectural font.
6. Plot the drawing at a scale of 1 = 1 on an 11″ × 8-1/2″ sheet.
7. Save your drawing in two places with the name CH14- EX8.

FIGURE 14–72

Exercise 14–8: Tenant Space Reception Seating Dimensions (Scale: 3/8″= 1′-0″)

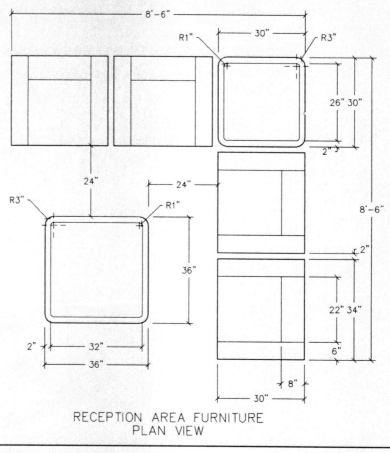

RECEPTION AREA FURNITURE
PLAN VIEW

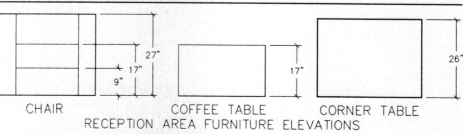

CHAIR   COFFEE TABLE   CORNER TABLE
RECEPTION AREA FURNITURE ELEVATIONS

Part III: Three-Dimensional AutoCAD

Exercise 14–9: Drawing a Solid Model of a Conference Chair

1. Use the dimensions from Figure 14–73 to draw the chair. Draw one caster with the solid Sphere command and use the Polar Array command to copy it three times.
2. The chair base can be formed with two cylinders and an extruded polyline copied three times using Polar Array.
3. Draw the bottom and back cushion with a single extruded polyline.
4. Draw the arms with a single extruded polyline.
5. Use 3D Orbit to obtain a perspective view of your final model and CLICK: **Layout1** before you plot.
6. Place your name in the lower right corner in 1/8″ letters using simplex or an architectural font.
7. Plot the drawing at a scale of 1 = 1 on an 11″ × 8-1/2″ sheet.
8. Return to model space with Tilemode ON and Wblock the conference chair to a disk with the name C-CHAIR. Use the bottom of one of the casters as the insertion point. Make sure the radio button Retain is on before you select objects.
9. Save your drawing with the name CH14- EX9.

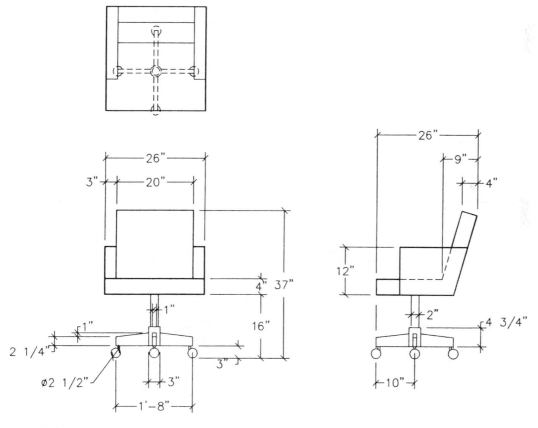

FIGURE 14–73
Exercise 14–9: Tenant Space Conference Chair Dimensions

Exercise 14–10: Drawing a Solid Model of a Conference Table and Inserting Chairs Around It

1. Use the dimensions from Figure 14–74 to draw the conference table. Draw the table bases with the Cylinder command.
2. Draw the table top with the Rectangle command using a 21″ fillet radius. The rectangle will measure 108″ × 42″.
3. Insert the C-CHAIR drawing into the conference table drawing.
4. Copy the chair seven times, and position the chairs as shown in Figure 14–75.
5. Use 3D Orbit to obtain a perspective view of your final model and CLICK: **Layout1** before you plot.
6. Place your name in the lower right corner in 1/8″ letters using simplex or an architectural font.
7. Plot the drawing at a scale of 1 = 1 on an 11″ × 8-1/2″ sheet.
8. Save your drawing in two places with the name CH14- EX10.

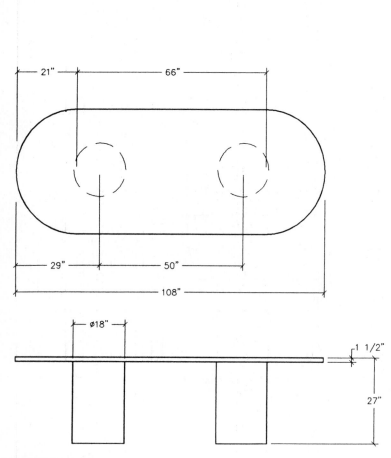

FIGURE 14–74

Exercise 14–10: Plan and Elevation Views of the Conference Table (Scale: 3/8″ = 1′–0″)

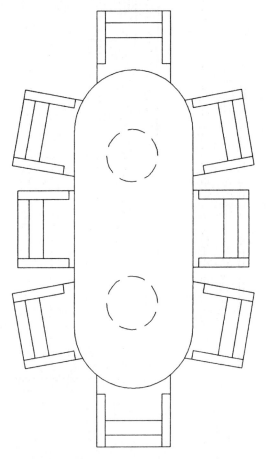

FIGURE 14–75

Exercise 14–11: Conference Table and Chair Locations

1. Which of the following is *not* a SOLID command used to draw solid primitives?
   a. Box
   b. Cylinder
   c. Rectangle
   d. Wedge
   e. Sphere

2. Which of the following is used to make rounded corners on a solid box?
   a. Chamfer
   b. Extrude
   c. Intersection
   d. Round
   e. Fillet

3. Which is the last dimension called for when the Box command is activated?
   a. Height
   b. Width
   c. Length
   d. First corner of box
   e. Other corner

4. Which is the first dimension called for when the Sphere command is activated?
   a. Segments in Y direction
   b. Segments in X direction
   c. Radius
   d. Center of sphere
   e. Diameter

5. Which of the following *cannot* be extruded with the Extrude command?
   a. Polylines
   b. Circles
   c. Regions
   d. Polygons
   e. Solids

6. Which of the following commands is used to join several lines into a single polyline?
   a. Edit Polyline
   b. Offset
   c. Union
   d. Intersection
   e. Extrude

7. Which of the following is used to make a solid by revolving a polyline about an axis?
   a. Revolve
   b. Extrude
   c. Intersection
   d. Round
   e. Fillet

8. Which of the following adjusts the smoothness of objects rendered with the Hide command?
   a. SURFTAB1
   b. MESH
   c. SEGS
   d. WIRE
   e. FACETRES

9. Which of the following allows you to rotate an object around an X,Y, or Z axis?
   a. Rotate
   b. Rotate 3D
   c. Extrude
   d. Solrot
   e. Offset

10. Which of the following sets the number of lines on rounded surfaces of solids?
    - a. FACETRES
    - b. ISOLINES
    - c. Union
    - d. Fillet
    - e. Interfere

Complete.

11. List nine Solid commands used to make solid primitives.

_____ _____ _____

_____ _____ _____

_____ _____ _____

12. List the Solid command used to extrude a polyline into a solid.

_____

13. List the Solid command used to create a new solid by cutting the existing solid into two pieces and removing or retaining either or both pieces.

_____

14. List the Solid command that allows you to join several solids into a single object.

_____

15. List the Solid command used to subtract solids from other solids.

_____

16. List the command and its option that is used to move the UCS icon so that it is displayed at the origin of the current coordinate system.

_____ _____

command option

17. List the Solid command used to create a cross-sectional area of a solid.

_____

18. List the command that creates a solid model from two or more cross-sectional areas.

_____

19. List the command that can convert a line, arc, or polyline to a wall with width and height.

_____

20. List the Solid command used to create a solid from the common volume of two intersecting solids.

_____

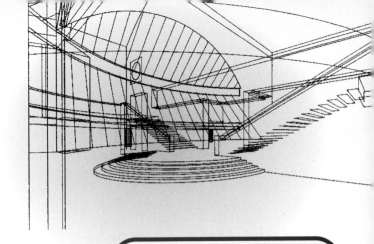

Complex Solid Models with Materials, Lighting, Rendering, and Plotting

objectives

When you have completed this chapter, you will be able to:

Correctly use the following commands and settings:

Materials Library	Background
Materials	Fog
Render	Landscape
Light	Printing of
3D Orbit	3D Models

Introduction

This chapter presents more complex models using the solids commands from Chapter 14.

This chapter also covers the Render and Animation commands, which allow you to use lights, to attach materials, and to apply backgrounds so that a photo-realistic rendering of a 3D scene can be created and an animated file produced. Although there are many means of locating lights in a 3D scene, you will use the endpoints of lines and other objects in this exercise to place lights. You will also use the existing materials in the materials library and existing backgrounds to begin using the render commands.

The first two exercises, creating a chair and a patio, will give you the complex models needed to assign materials, place lights, render, and create an animated file that can be viewed in a variety of ways.

FIGURE 15–1
Exercise 15–1: Complete

Exercise 15–1: Creating a Solid Model of Chair 2

In this exercise you will create a solid model of a chair (Figure 15–1). This chair will be inserted into the structure that you will create in Exercise 15–2. The Prompt/Response format will not be used in this exercise. The steps will be listed with suggested commands for creating this model.

Step 1. Use your workspace to make the following settings:

1. Use SaveAs... to save the drawing on the hard drive with the name CH15-EX1.
2. Set drawing Units: **Architectural**
3. Set Drawing Limits: **5',5'**
4. Set GRIDDISPLAY: **0**
5. Set Grid: **1**
6. Set Snap: **1/4**
7. Create the following Layers:

LAYER NAME	COLOR	LINETYPE
Fabric	Magenta	Continuous
Metal	Green	Continuous

8. Set **Layer Fabric** current.
9. **Use the Vports command to make two vertical viewports. Zoom-All in both viewports to start, then Zoom in closer as needed.** You will find it easier to draw in the left viewport and use the right viewport to determine if the model is proceeding as it should.
10. **Use SE Isometric from 3D Views to select a view for the right viewport.**
11. **Set FACETRES to 4; set ISOLINES to 20.**

Step 2. Draw two 32″ × 5″ cushions:

1. Draw the cushions in vertical and horizontal positions and rotate them to the positions shown using the dimensions from Figure 15–2. (Both cushions are the same size.)
2. Draw a temporary construction line to locate the bottom of the chair legs.
3. Use Rectangle to draw the bottom cushion in a horizontal position 16″ above the temporary construction line. Use the Polyline option of the Fillet command to create the 1″ fillet on all four corners at the same time.
4. Use Rotate to rotate the bottom cushion 10° as shown.
5. Use Rectangle to draw the back cushion in a vertical position, and fillet all four corners.
6. Use Rotate to rotate the back cushion 20°.

FIGURE 15–2
Dimensions for the Chair

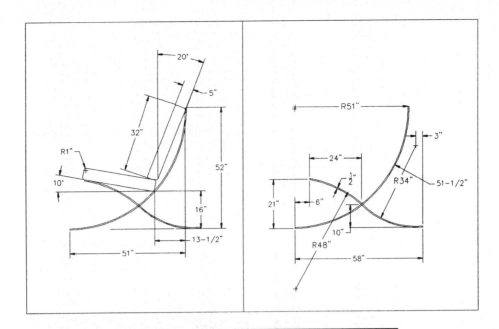

7. Use Stretch to form the bottom of the back cushion so it fits flush against the bottom cushion.

Step 3.   Draw chair legs and back support:

1. Set Layer Metal current.
2. Draw temporary construction lines as needed to locate the beginning and ending points of the three arcs.
3. Use Arc, Start-End-Radius to draw the three arcs. Be sure to use the End-point of the arc with the 48″ radius as the starting point of the arc with the 34″ radius so the two can be joined together to form a single polyline.
4. Use Edit Polyline to join the arcs with the 34″ and 48″ radii.
5. Use Offset to offset the joined arcs 1/2″ down.
6. Use Offset to offset the arc with the 51″ radius 1/2″ to the right.
7. Use the Line command to draw lines at the ends of all arcs so that the two metal legs have a thickness.
8. Use Edit Polyline to join all parts of each leg so they can be extruded.

Step 4.   Draw chair supports:

1. Draw the three supports in Figure 15–3 in the locations shown.
2. Use the Rectangle command to draw the 2″ × 1/2″ supports in either a vertical or horizontal position as needed.
3. Use the Rotate and Move commands to locate the supports in the positions shown.

FIGURE 15–3
Chair Supports Measuring
2″ × 1/2″

SUPPORTS

Step 5. Extrude cushions, legs, and supports:

1. Set Layer Fabric current so the extruded cushions will be on that layer.
2. Use the Extrude command to extrude the two cushions 36″ in the positive Z direction.
3. Set Layer Metal current.
4. Use the Extrude command to extrude the polylines forming the legs 2-1/2″ in the positive Z direction.
5. Use the Extrude command to extrude the supports 31″ in the positive Z direction.

Step 6. Move supports so they sit on top of the legs:

1. Use the Move command to move the three supports 2-1/2″ in the positive Z direction (second point of displacement will be @0,0,2-1/2).

Step 7. Join extruded legs to form a single piece.

1. Use the Union command to join the two extruded legs to form a single piece.

Step 8. Add the other set of legs:

1. Use the Copy command to copy the legs 33-1/2″ in the positive Z direction.

Step 9. Rotate chair to the upright and forward position:

1. Use the Rotate 3D command to rotate the chair 90° about the X axis. CLICK: one of the lowest points of the end of one of the chair legs as the Point on the X axis.
2. Use the Rotate 3D command to rotate the chair 90° about the Z axis. CLICK: one of the lowest points of the end of one of the chair legs as the Point on the Z axis.

Step 10. Remove hidden lines:

1. Use the Hide command to remove hidden lines so the chair appears as shown in Figure 15–1.

Step 11. Save the drawing as a Wblock:

1. Use the Wblock command to save the drawing on a disk with the name EX15-1. Use the bottom of the front of the left leg as the insertion point. CLICK: Retain to keep the drawing on the screen.
2. Save the drawing as CH15-EX1.

Step 12. Plot:

1. Plot or print the drawing at a scale of 1 = 24 from the Model tab in the center of an 8-1/2″ × 11″ sheet. CLICK: As Displayed in the Shade plot list.
2. Do not use Single Line Text to place your name on the drawing. Write your name on this drawing so you can use the drawing in Exercise 15–2.

Exercise 15–2:   Creating a Solid Model of a Patio

In this exercise you will create a solid model of an elaborate patio area and insert your chair into it (Figure 15–4). The Prompt–Response format will not be used in this exercise. The steps will be listed with suggested commands for creating this model.

Step 1.   **Use your workspace to make the following settings:**

1. **Use SaveAs... to save the drawing on the hard drive with the name CH15-EX2.**
2. Set drawing Units: **Architectural**
3. Set Drawing Limits: **50', 40'**
4. Set Grid: **2'**
5. Set GRIDDISPLAY: **0**
6. Set Snap: **6"**
7. Create the following Layers:

LAYER NAME	COLOR	LINETYPE
Border	Red	Continuous
Column	White	Continuous
Cornice	White	Continuous
Roof	White	Continuous
Pad	Red	Continuous

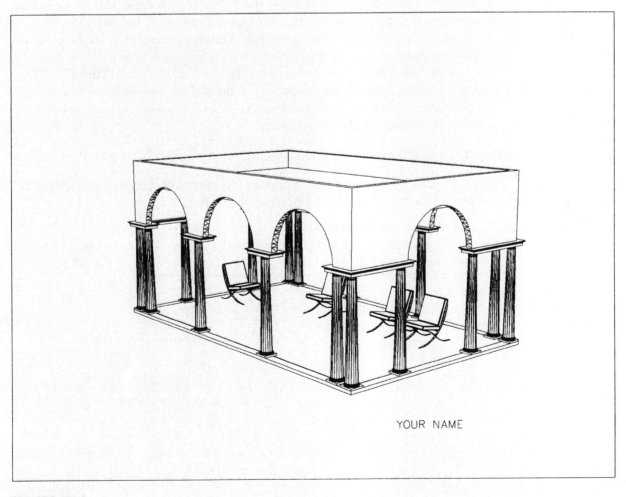

YOUR NAME

FIGURE 15–4
Exercise 15–2 Complete

8. Set **Layer Pad** current.
9. **Use the Vports command to make two vertical viewports. Zoom-All in both viewports to start, then Zoom in closer as needed.** You will find it easier to draw in the left viewport and use the right viewport to determine if the model is proceeding as it should.
10. **Use SE Isometric from 3D Views to set a viewpoint for the right viewport.**
11. **Set FACETRES to 4; set ISOLINES to 20.**

Let's begin at the bottom and work up.

Step 2. Draw the concrete pad with a border around it:

The concrete pad and the border have to be two separate objects extruded to a height of 4″. Draw the outside edge of the border and extrude it, then draw the inside edge, extrude it, and subtract it from the outside edge. Finally, draw the pad and extrude it (Figure 15–5):

1. Use the Rectangle command to draw a rectangle measuring 39′ × 24′. Start the first corner at absolute coordinates 6′,8′.
2. Use the Rectangle command to draw a rectangle measuring 37′ × 22′. Start the first corner at absolute coordinates 7′,9′ (or offset the first rectangle 1′ to the inside).
3. Use the Offset command to offset the 37′ × 22′ rectangle 1/2″ to the inside to form the concrete pad with a 1/2″ space between it and the border.
4. Use the Extrude command to extrude all three rectangles 4″ in the positive Z direction.
5. Use the Subtract command to subtract the inside of the border (the 37′ × 22′ extruded rectangle) from the outside of the border. You will have to Zoom a window so you can get close enough to pick the correct rectangle to subtract.
6. Put the border on the Border layer.

Step 3. Draw the base of the columns:

Draw the base of the columns on the lower left corner of the drawing. They will be copied after the columns are placed on them (Figure 15–6):

1. Set Layer Column current.
2. Zoom in on the lower left corner of the drawing as shown in Figure 15–6 in both viewports.

FIGURE 15–5
The Concrete Pad with a 1′ Border

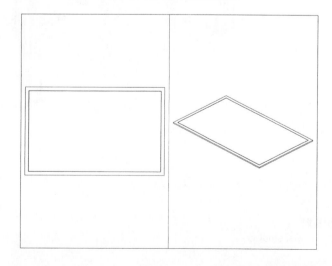

Part III: Three-Dimensional AutoCAD

FIGURE 15–6
Draw the Base of the
Column

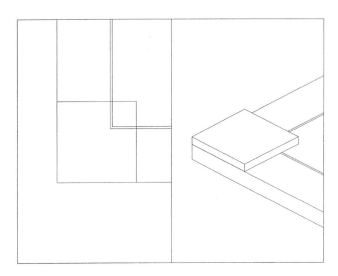

3. Use Box to draw the column base. The box measures 18″ × 18″ × 2″ height. Locate the "Corner of box" on the lower left corner of the border as shown. Use Osnap-Endpoint to click the first corner, then @18,18 to specify the other corner.

Step 4. Draw the columns:

Draw the column and rotate it so it sits on top of the base (Figures 15–7, 15–8, 15–9, 15–10, and 15–11):

1. Use the dimensions in Figure 15–7 to draw the column in an open area of your drawing. Use the Line and Arc or Circle commands to draw this figure. It may be easier to use Circle and Trim to draw the arcs on the bottom and top of the column instead of the Arc command.

 WARNING: Be sure to trim all parts of the circles so there are no double lines.

2. Use Edit Polyline to join all the parts of Figure 15–7 into a single polyline.
3. Use the Revolve command to create the solid column as shown in Figure 15–8. Select both ends of the vertical line using Osnap-Endpoint as the Axis of revolution.
4. Use the VPORTS command to split the right viewport into two horizontal viewports (three:left) and Zoom in on the bottom of the column and the box you drew as the column base, as shown in Figure 15–9 in both horizontal viewports. (You may need to adjust your view in the left viewport—TYPE: PLAN <enter>.)
5. Use the UCS command to move your UCS to the lower left corner of the top plane of the base as shown in Figure 15–9 in both right viewports.

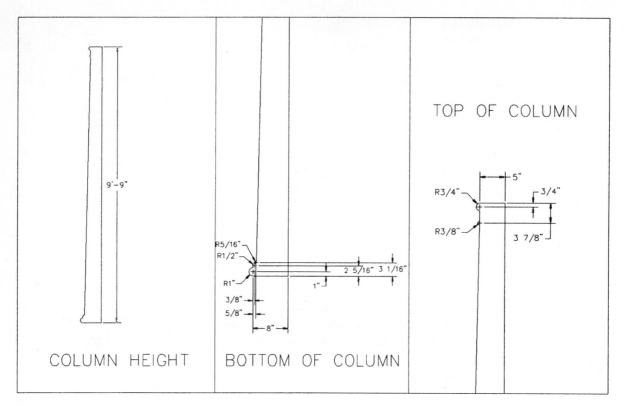

FIGURE 15–7
Dimensions for Drawing the Column

COLUMN HEIGHT   BOTTOM OF COLUMN

TOP OF COLUMN

FIGURE 15–8
The Column Revolved

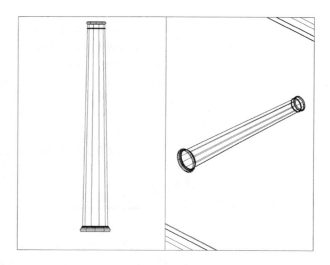

6. Use the Move command to move the column to the center of the base as shown in Figure 15–10. Use Osnap-Center as the Base point, and CLICK: the extreme bottom circular center of the column in the upper right viewport. TYPE: **9,9** as the second point of displacement to move the column to the center of the base.

7. Use the Rotate 3D command to rotate the column 90° about the X axis as shown in Figure 15–11.

8. Use the VPORTS command to return the display to two vertical viewports.

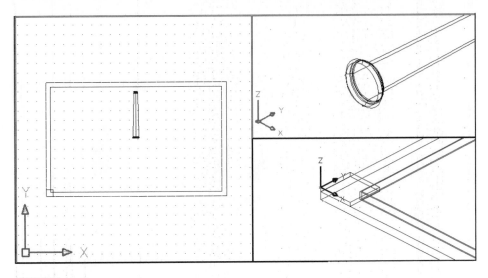

FIGURE 15–9
Move the UCS to the Top Lower Left Corner of the Base

FIGURE 15–10
Move the Column to the
Center of the Base

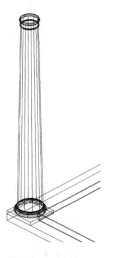

FIGURE 15–11
Rotate the Column to Its
Upright Position

Step 5. Add the cornice at the top of the column:

Insert drawing14-3 (from Exercise 14–1, Figures 14–33 through 14–38) to form the cornice at the top of the column (Figures 15–12 and 15–13):

1. Set Layer Cornice current.
2. Use the Move option of the UCS command to move the UCS to the extreme top of the column as shown in Figure 15–12. Use Osnap-Center to locate the UCS at that point.
3. Use the Insert command to insert drawing 14–3 onto the top of the column (Figure 15–13). Use the following:

 TIP: Be sure the insertion point is positive 9-1/2, negative −9-1/2.

Insertion point: TYPE: 9-1/2 in the X: box and −9-1/2 in the Y: box. (Be sure to include the minus in the Y: direction.) Leave Z: at 0. (The bottom of the cornice drawing measures 19″, as shown in Figure 14–33. Because you picked the endpoint of the lower corner as the insertion point when you Wblocked the shape, 9-1/2,−9-1/2 will place the center of the shape at the center of the column top. The shape must measure 24″ × 24″ when it is inserted. The arithmetic requires you to subtract 5″ from both measurements and divide by 2.)

After you have typed the insertion point in the X: and Y: boxes of Insertion point, TYPE: 12 in the X: Scale box and CHECK: Uniform Scale.

(The shape measures 2″ square, so an X scale factor of 12 will make the shape 24″ long.)

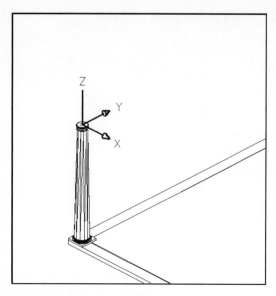

FIGURE 15–12
Move the UCS to the Center of the Top of the Column

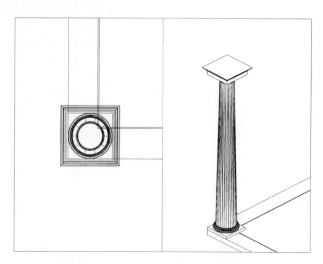

FIGURE 15–13
Inserting the Cornice

(The shape must be 24″ in the Y direction also so Uniform Scale must be checked.)

(The height of the original shape was reduced to 1/12 of the 5-1/2″ dimension shown in Figure 14–33, so a scale factor of 12 will make it 5-1/2″ in this drawing.) **Leave Rotation angle: 0.** CLICK: **OK**

4. **Use the Explode command to explode the inserted cornice so it can be joined to form longer cornices. EXPLODE IT ONLY ONCE.** If you explode it more than once, you destroy it as a solid.

5. **Go to 3D Views-Front** (on the View menu) occasionally to be sure all parts are in the correct location, then return to the previous view.

Step 6. Draw the columns and cornices at the center and one corner of the structure:

Copy the column and cornice to create supports at the center of the structure (Figures 15–14 and 15–15):

1. With Ortho ON use the Copy command and direct distance entry to copy the column, its base, and cornice three times: 2′ and 12′9″ in the positive X direction, and once 6′2″ in the positive Y direction (Figure 15–14).

2. With Ortho ON use the Copy command and direct distance entry to copy the cornice on the column that is to the far right 12″ in the positive X direction and 12″ in the negative X direction so that the cornice on this column will measure 48″ when the three are joined.

3. Use Union to join the cornice and the two copies to form a single cornice that is 48″ long (Figure 15–15).

Copy the cornice and join all the cornice shapes on the three corner columns to create the L-shaped cornice at the corner of the structure (Figure 15–16):

1. With Ortho ON use the Copy command and direct distance entry to copy the cornice on the corner column six times: 12″ and 24″ in the positive X direction and 12″, 24″, 36″, 48″, and 60″, and 72″ in the positive Y direction

Part III: Three-Dimensional AutoCAD

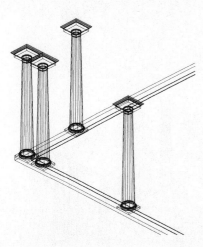

FIGURE 15–14
Copy the Base, Column, and Cornice Twice in the X Direction and Once in the Y Direction

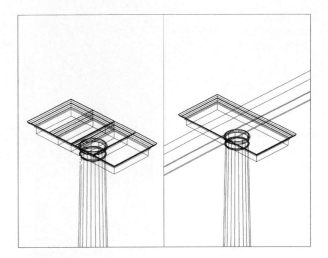

FIGURE 15–15
Copy the Cornice in the Positive X Direction and the Negative X Direction and Union of the Three Cornice Shapes

so that the cornice on the three corner columns will measure 48″ in the X direction and 96″ in the Y direction when all these shapes are joined.

2. Use Union to join all the cornice shapes on the three corner columns to form a single L-shaped cornice, Figure 15–16.

Step 7.   Draw all the remaining columns:

Mirror the existing columns twice to form the remaining columns (Figure 15–17):

1. Use the UCS command to return to the World UCS.
2. With Ortho ON use the Mirror command to form the columns on the right side of the structure. Select all existing columns, bases, and cornices. PRESS: <enter>, then using Osnap-midpoint, CLICK: D1 (Figure 15–17) as the first point of the mirror line, then CLICK: any point directly above or below D1. Do not erase source objects.
3. With Ortho ON use the Mirror command to form the columns on the back side of the structure. Select all existing columns, bases, and cornices. Press: <enter>, then using Osnap-midpoint, CLICK: D2 (Figure 15–17) as the first point of the mirror line, then CLICK: any point directly to the left or right of D2. Do not erase source objects.

Step 8.   Draw the upper part of the structure:

Draw the front and rear elevations of the upper structure (Figure 15–18):

1. Set Layer Roof current.
2. Use the UCS command to rotate the UCS 90° about the X axis.
3. Draw the upper part of the structure in an open area. You will move it to its correct location after it is completed.
4. Use the dimensions from Figure 15–18 to draw that shape with the Rectangle, Circle, and Trim commands.
5. Use Edit Polyline to join all the parts of the figure into a single polyline.
6. Use the Extrude command to extrude the polyline 8″ in the positive Z direction.

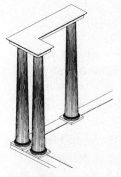

FIGURE 15–16
The L-Shaped Cornice After Using the Union and Hide Commands

FIGURE 15–17
Copying the Columns Using
the Mirror Command

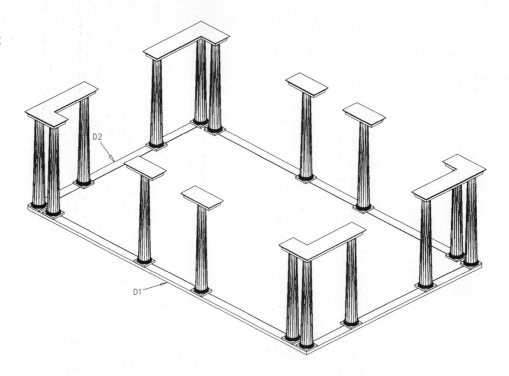

FIGURE 15–18
Dimensions for the Front
and Rear Elevations of the
Upper Structure

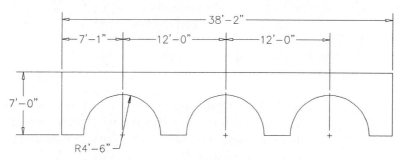

7. Use the Copy command to copy this shape 22′-6″ in the negative Z direction (Base point—CLICK: any point, Second point of displacement—@0,0, -22′6<enter>).

Draw the left and right elevations of the upper structure (Figures 15–19 and 15–20):

1. Use the UCS command to rotate the UCS 90° about the Y axis.
2. Use the dimensions from Figure 15–19 to draw that shape with the Rectangle, Circle, and Trim commands across the ends of the front and rear elevations.
3. Draw the right side of the structure on the right ends of the front and rear planes (Figure 15–20).
4. Use Edit Polyline to join all the parts of the figure into a single polyline.
5. Use the Extrude command to extrude the polyline 8″ in the negative Z direction.
6. Use the Copy command to copy this shape 37′-6″ in the negative Z direction (Base point—CLICK: any point, Second point of displacement—TYPE: @0,0,−37′6<enter> or move your mouse in the negative Z direction with ORTHO ON and TYPE: 37′6<enter>).

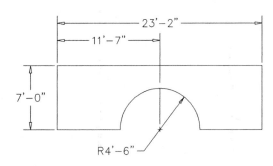

FIGURE 15–19
Dimensions for the Left and Right Elevations of the Upper Structure

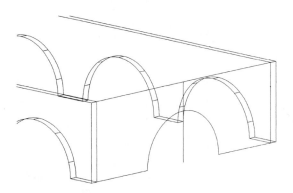

FIGURE 15–20
Draw the Right Elevation on the Right Ends of the Front and Rear Planes

---

Draw the roof and complete the upper part of the structure (Figures 15–21, 15–22, 15–23, and 15–24):

1. Make the Roof Layer current.
2. Use the UCS command to return to the World UCS.
3. Use the Rectangle command to draw a rectangle to form the flat roof inside the upper part of the structure (Figure 15–21):

   First corner—D1
   Other corner—D2

4. Use the Extrude command to extrude the rectangle 8″ in the negative Z direction.
5. Use the Move command to move the extruded rectangle 18″ in the negative Z direction (Second point of displacement—TYPE: @0,0,-18<enter>).
6. Use the Union command to join all parts of the upper structure into a single unit.
7. Use the Hide command to make sure your model is OK (Figure 15–22).
8. Use the UCS command to move the origin of the UCS to the endpoint of the lower left cornice (Figure 15–23).
9. Use the Move command to move the endpoint, D1 (Figure 15–24), of the lower right corner of the upper part of the structure to absolute coordinates **8,8,0.** Be sure you do not put the @ symbol in front of the coordinates.

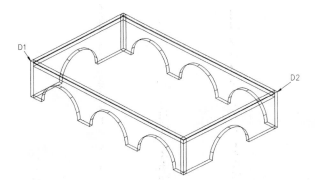

FIGURE 15–21
Draw a Rectangle to Form the Roof

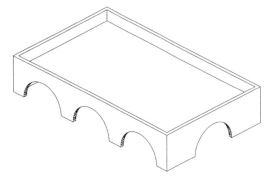

FIGURE 15–22
The Completed Upper Structure

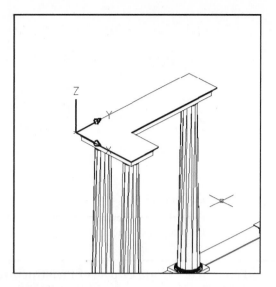

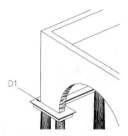

FIGURE 15–23
Move the UCS to the Top of the Cornice Corner

FIGURE 15–24
Move the Upper Structure into Position

Step 9. Insert chairs to complete the model:

Insert a chair at the correct elevation, copy it, rotate it, and complete Exercise 15–2 (Figures 15–25 and 15–26):

1. Use the UCS command to move the origin of the UCS to the top of the border surrounding the concrete pad, D1 (Figure 15–25).

FIGURE 15–25
Move the UCS to the Top of the Border Surrounding the Pad

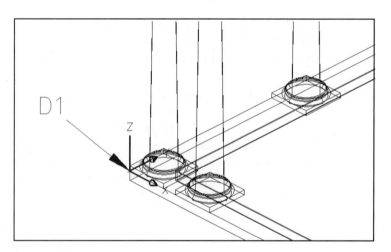

FIGURE 15–26
Locating the Chairs

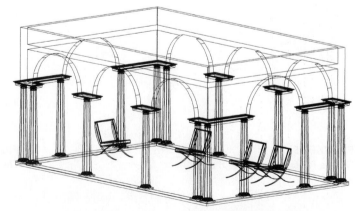

2. Use the Insert command to insert the chair drawing, EX15-1, at absolute coordinates 18′,14′,0.

3. Explode the inserted chair ONCE. If you explode it more than once you will have destroyed it as a solid.

4. With Ortho ON use the Copy command to copy the chair three times to the approximate locations shown in Figure 15–26.

5. Use the Rotate command to rotate the chair on the far left 90°.

6. Use the Viewpoint Presets dialog box to select a viewpoint of 315,10.

7. Use 3D Orbit (RIGHT-CLICK) with Perspective projection and Visual Styles - 3D Hidden to obtain a view similar to Figure 15–4.

8. With the right viewport active, use the SIngle option of the VPORTS command to return the display to a single viewport.

9. CLICK: Layout1 and place the viewport boundary on a new layer that is turned off.

10. Use the Single Line Text command (TYPE: DT<enter>) to place your name in the lower right corner 1/8″ high in the simplex font. Your final drawing should appear as shown in Figure 15–4.

11. Use the Shade plot-As Displayed option in the Plot dialog box to remove hidden lines when you plot.

Step 10. Use the SaveAs command to save your drawing in two places.

Step 11. Plot or print the drawing at a scale of 1 = 1.

Render

The Render program uses objects, lighting, and materials to obtain a realistic view of a model. A 3D graphics card is recommended for high-resolution images.

There are three degrees of rendering quality:

Render   This is the basic rendering program, which can be done relatively quickly.

Photo Real   Gives you transparent materials and shadows in addition to basic rendering of materials.

Photo Raytrace   This option gives you reflections, refraction, and precise shadows.

You have already used Render without assigning materials or locating lights. You can do this with any solid model, but for a pleasing, realistic rendering both materials and lights are necessary.

Lights

Render has four types of light that are used to light any scene. They are:

Sun   This light is present in all scenes and is used to lighten or darken all the images in the scene by the same amount. You can turn off the sunlight to simulate darkness and use only the other types of light to render the scene.

Point Lights   Point lights shine in all directions much like a common lightbulb. The intensity of a point light is controlled by selecting inverse linear, inverse square, or none for the attenuation. Inverse square has the highest intensity value; none has the lowest value.

Distant Lights   Distant lights shine as a parallel beam in one direction illuminating all objects that the light strikes. This light can be used to simulate the sun or another similar light source. You can use one or more distant lights and vary their intensity to achieve the result you want.

Spotlights   Spotlights shine in one direction in a cone shape. One of the settings for this light is the hotspot, at which the light has the greatest intensity. The other setting is the falloff, at which the light begins to decrease in intensity. Spotlights can be used in a manner similar to spotlights in a theater or to light a display.

Materials

AutoCAD has several palettes containing materials that can be attached to the surfaces of 3D objects in your drawing. You can also create new materials from scratch and modify existing materials and save them with a new name. In this exercise only existing materials will be used. If you attach a material to an object and decide you do not like its appearance, the Material dialog box allows you to detach the material from that object.

Other Commands Available to Render, Animate, and Shade 3D Models

3D Orbit   As discussed in previous chapters, the 3D Orbit command has several features that can be used to give a 3D model a photo-realistic appearance.

New View   This command allows you to add a solid, a gradient, or an image background to your model.

Render Environment   This command allows you to simulate an atmosphere that enhances the illusion of depth. The color of the fog can be changed to create different visual effects.

Motion Path Animations...   Moves a camera along a path you choose.

3D Walk   Allows you to walk through your model controlling height and speed.

Exercise 15–3:   Use Render Commands to Make a Photo-Realistic Rendering of the Solid Model in Exercise 15–2

In this exercise you will use the Material Editor and the Materials palettes to select materials to attach to your model. You will then place lights in a manner that will illuminate your model. You will then give the model perspective projection, and finally, the model will be rendered using the Render command and the Visual Styles Manager (Figure 15–27).

Step 1.   Use your workspace to make the following settings:

1. Open drawing CH15-EX2 and save it as CH15-EX3.
2. Open the Dashboard palette.
3. CLICK: the MODEL tab to return to model space
4. CLICK: in the right viewport to make it active and change the display to a single viewport if it is not already a single viewport.

Step 2.   Select materials from the palettes and place them in your drawing on the Material Editor:

Prompt	Response
Command:	**Materials... (from the View-Render menu)**
The Material Editor (Figure 15–28) appears:	**Tool Palettes**
A tool palette appears:	CLICK: **Properties in the extreme lower left corner of the palette,** then CLICK: **All Palettes** so that all tabs are available as shown in Figure 15–28

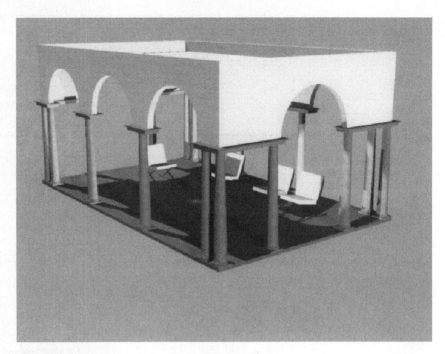

FIGURE 15–27
Exercise 15–3 Complete

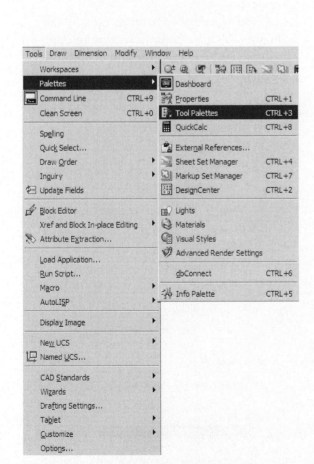

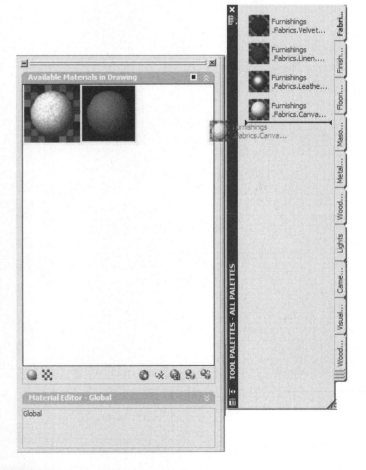

FIGURE 15–28
Load Materials onto the
Materials Editor

Prompt	Response
	CLICK: The Fabric… tab, hold your mouse over the Furnishings, Fabrics, Canvas icon and drag and drop it into the Material Editor. Use this material for the chair cushions.

You have the choice now of placing the materials in the Material Editor, checking them over, and then attaching them to the solid model shapes or placing them directly onto the shapes. In this exercise the materials are placed into the Material Editor and then dropped onto the solid shapes.

Prompt	Response
	RIGHT-CLICK: the Tabs that are not fully visible in the lower right of the Tools Palettes - All Palettes so the list of all palettes appears, Figure 15–29
	CLICK: the Metals - Materials Library name in the list so the Metals - Materials Library tab is active, and drag and drop the Ornamental metals, Aluminum, Brushed material onto the Material Editor for the chair legs and supports
	CLICK: the Masonry - Materials Library tab (Figure 15–30), scroll down through the many materials, and drag and drop the

FIGURE 15–29
Select Palettes with Materials

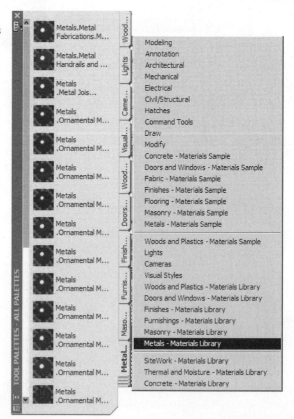

FIGURE 15–30
Scroll through Patterns on
the Palette

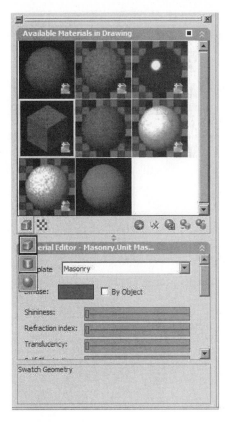

FIGURE 15–31
Available Materials with
Square Geometry Selected
for a Material

Prompt	Response
	following materials onto the Material Editor:
	Masonry, Unit Masonry, Brick, Modular, Herringbone, 1 for the patio floor pad
	Masonry, Stone, Travertine, DarkRed for the border around the patio floor pad
	Masonry, Stone, Granite, Square, Stacked, Polished, Black-White for the columns and bases
	Masonry, Stone, Marble, Square, Stacked, Polished, Pink-Black-Gray for cornices
	Masonry, Stone, Marble, Square, Stacked, Polished, White-Black-Brown for the roof
	CLICK: the Masonry, Unit Masonry, Brick, Modular, Herringbone, 1 material to make it active, and CLICK: the Swatch Geometry flyout in the lower left of the Material Editor, and CLICK: the cube icon, Figure 15–31
	Then CLICK: the Checkered Underlay icon to the right to turn it off so you can see the material a little more clearly

Prompt	Response
	Finally, CLICK: **the Toggle Display mode in the extreme upper right of the Material Editor to enlarge the display of that material, Figure 15–32**

Several features of any material in the Material Editor can be changed before or after materials are attached to the solids. In this exercise you may use the materials without editing. The five icons in the lower right of the materials display activate the following commands. From left to right they are:

Create New Material
Purge from Drawing (if the material is attached to a solid, it cannot be purged)
Indicate Materials in Use
Apply Material to Objects
Remove Material from Selected Objects

Step 3. Attach materials to the solid shapes in your drawing:

Prompt	Response
	Close the Tool Palettes
	CLICK: **the Masonry, Unit Masonry, Brick, Modular, Herringbone, 1 material** to make it active in the Material Editor
	CLICK: **Apply Material to Objects**

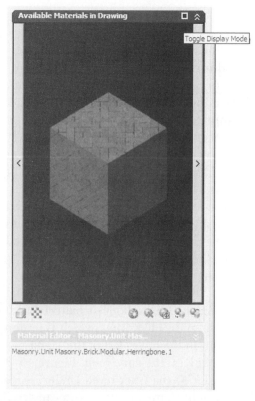

FIGURE 15–32
Toggle the Display Mode to View the Material Closely

FIGURE 15–33
Realistic Visual Style

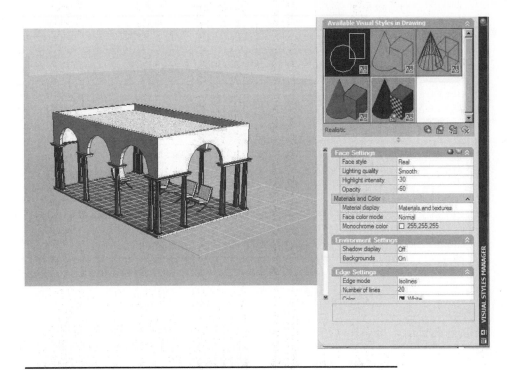

Prompt	Response
Select objects:	With the Paintbrush, CLICK: **the patio pad** (the solid forming the floor)
Select objects or [Undo]:	**<enter>**

On Your Own:

1. Use the Constrained Orbit command to rotate the model to a view similar to Figure 15–33.

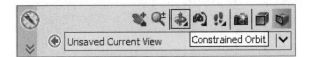

2. Attach the following materials to the remaining solids:

Material	Attach to
Furnishings, Fabrics, Canvas	chair cushions
Ornamental metals, Aluminum, Brushed	chair legs and supports
Masonry, Stone, Travertine, DarkRed	border around the patio floor pad
Masonry, Stone, Granite, Square, Stacked, Polished, Black-White	columns and bases
Masonry, Stone, Granite, Square, Stacked, Polished, Pink-Black-Gray	cornices
Masonry, Stone, Marble, Square, Stacked, Polished, White-Black-Brown	roof

Step 4. Use the Visual Style Manager, Figure 15–33, to render the model with the Realistic style.

Prompt	Response
Command:	**Visual Styles Manager** DOUBLE-CLICK: **the Realistic style icon**

The model is rendered as shown in Figure 15–33.

Now, lighting will be added, shadows turned on, the background will be selected, and the model will be rendered with the Render command to produce a realistic image.

Step 5. Add distant lights using lines to locate the lights and targets:

On Your Own:

1. With ORTHO ON use the Line command to draw 30′ lines from the midpoints of the arches on the front and right side of the patio as shown in Figure 15–34.
2. Draw a line from the midpoint of one side of the roof to the opposite side of the roof, then draw a 30′ line straight up with ORTHO ON.
3. If the Spot, Distant, and Point light command icons are not visible on the Dashboard palette, CLICK: the down arrows on the Light control panel, which becomes visible when you move your mouse in that area. Clicking the down arrows opens the Light control panel. Notice that all the panels on the Dashboard can be opened and closed as you need them.

Prompt	Response
Command:	TYPE: **LIGHT**<enter> (you can also CLICK: **Distant Light on the Dashboard and skip** **the next prompt**)

FIGURE 15–34

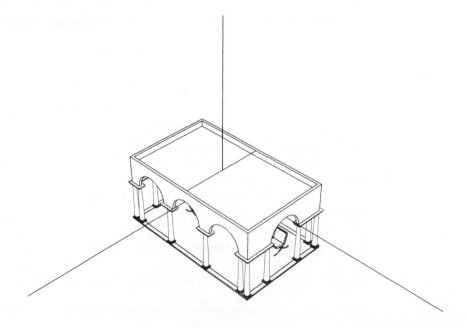

Prompt	Response
Enter light type [Point/Spot/Distant] <Distant>:	TYPE: **D\<enter\>**
Specify light direction FROM <0,0,0> or [Vector]:	**Osnap-Endpoint** CLICK: **the end farthest from the model of one of the 30' lines**
Specify light direction TO <1,1,1>:	**Osnap-Endpoint** CLICK: **the other end of the same line**
Enter an option to change [Name/Intensity/ Status/ shadoW/Color/eXit] <eXit>:	TYPE: **N\<enter\>**
Enter light name <Distantlight1>:	**\<enter\>** (to accept the name Distantlight1)
Enter an option to change [Name/Intensity/ Status/ shadoW/Color/eXit] <eXit>:	**\<enter\>**

On Your Own:

1. **Add two more distant lights at the ends of the other two 30' lines pointed toward the model.**
2. **Erase the construction lines locating the distant lights.**

Distant lights shine uniform parallel light rays in one direction only. The intensity of a distant light does not diminish over distance; it shines as brightly on each surface it strikes no matter how far away the surface is from the light. Distant lights are used to light the model uniformly. You can change the intensity of a distant light if you want all surfaces on that side to be lighter or darker.

Step 6. Add spotlights to shine on the chairs:

Prompt	Response
Command:	**Spotlight** (or TYPE: **SPOTLIGHT\<enter\>**)
Specify source location <0,0,0>:	CLICK: **an Endpoint on the L-shaped cornice on the right side of the model as shown in Figure 15–35**

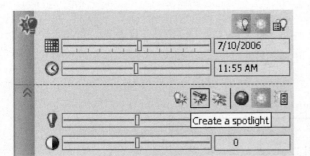

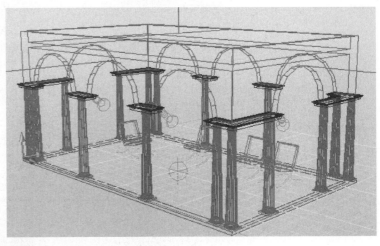

FIGURE 15–35
Locate Spotlights and Point Lights

Prompt	Response
Specify target location <0,0,-10>:	Using **Osnap-Endpoint** CLICK: **a point on the two chairs closest together**
Enter an option to change [Name/Intensity/Status/Hotspot/ Falloff/shadoW/ Attenuation/ Color/eXit] <eXit>:	TYPE: **N<enter>**
Enter light name <Spotlight1>:	**<enter>**
Enter an option to change [Name/Intensity/Status/Hotspot/ Falloff/shadoW/ Attenuation/ Color/eXit] <eXit>:	**<enter>**

On Your Own:

1. Add two more spotlights on the cornices of the two single columns on the front pointing to points on the other two chairs as shown in Figure 15–35. Name the lights Spotlight2 and Spotlight3.

A spotlight shines light in the shape of a cone. You can control the direction of the spotlight and the size of the cone. The intensity of a spotlight decreases the farther it is from the object. Spotlights are used to light specific areas of the model.

Step 7. Add a point light near the center of the patio:

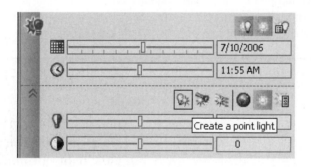

Prompt	Response
Command:	**Pointlight** (or TYPE: **POINTLIGHT<enter>**)
Specify source location <0,0,0>:	**Osnap-Endpoint** CLICK: **a point near the center of the floor of the patio.**
Enter an option to change [Name/ Intensity/Status/shadoW/ Attenuation/Color/eXit] <eXit>:	TYPE: **N<enter>**
Enter light name <Pointlight1>:	**<enter>**
Enter an option to change [Name/ Intensity/Status/shadoW/ Attenuation/Color/eXit] <eXit>:	**<enter>**

A point light shines light in all directions. The intensity of a point light fades the farther the object is from it unless attenuation is set to None. Point lights are used for general lighting.

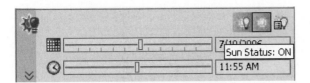

Step 8. Turn on the Sun light and adjust it to a summer month at midday:

On Your Own:

1. CLICK: Sun Status: OFF to turn it ON.
2. Adjust the sliders below the Sun Status icon to show July and 1:00 pm.

Step 9. CLICK: Perspective Projection on the 3D Navigate Control Panel on the Dashboard to change the view to a perspective view.

 TIP: Be aware that you will not be able to CLICK: points to view a window or complete many commands that require you to CLICK: a point when Perspective Projection is active.

Step 10. Make Advanced Renderer Settings:

Prompt	Response
Command:	Advanced Renderer Settings...
The Advanced Renderer Settings palette appears:	Set Destination to Window (Figure 15–36)

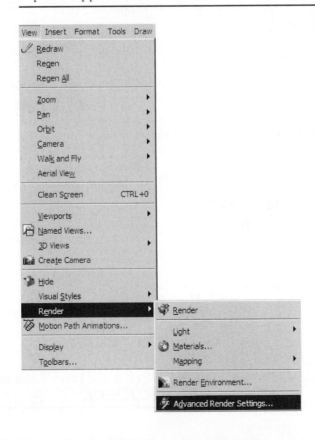

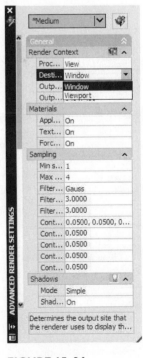

FIGURE 15–36
Render to a Window and
Turn Shadows On

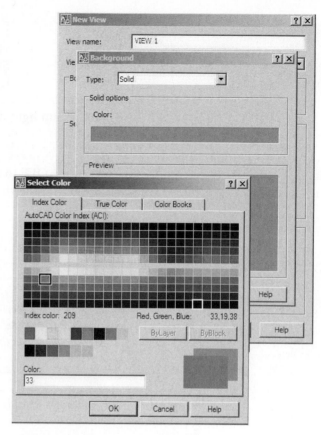

FIGURE 15–37
Set Background Color for Rendering

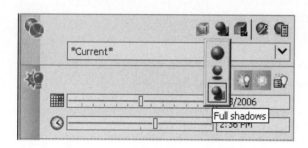

Prompt	Response
	Set Shadow Map ON (near the bottom on this figure)
	Close this palette
	CLICK: **Full shadows** on the Visual Style control panel on the Dashboard to turn shadows on

Step 11. Change the background to a color before rendering:

Prompt	Response
Command:	**Named Views...** (or TYPE: **VIEW<enter>**)
The View Manager appears:	CLICK: **New...**
The New View dialog box appears:	TYPE: **VIEW 1** in the View Name: box
	CLICK: **to put a check in Override Default Background.** (If a check is already there, you will have to CLICK: to eliminate the check, then CLICK: it again to put the check back in.)
	(You may also need to CLICK: the **ellipsis...** to the right.)
The Background dialog box appears:	CLICK: **Color:**
The Select Color dialog box, Figure 15–37, appears:	CLICK: **the Index Color tab** and CLICK: color **33**.
	CLICK: **OK**

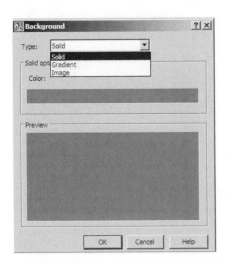

FIGURE 15–38
Background Types

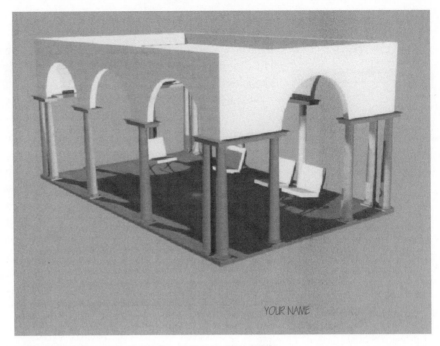

YOUR NAME

FIGURE 15–39
Exercise 15–3 Complete

Prompt	Response
The Background dialog box appears:	CLICK: **the Type: list** (Figure 15–38)

This list allows you to have a single color background or a two- or three-color gradient background or to select an image file for the background of your rendering.

Prompt	Response
	Close the list with Solid selected and CLICK: **OK**
The View Manager appears:	CLICK: **VIEW 1** in the list to the left
	CLICK: **Set Current**
	CLICK: **OK**

Step 12. Render the drawing and insert it into a paper space viewport:

Prompt	Response
Command:	**Render** (or TYPE: **RENDER<enter>**)
The rendered model appears similar to Figure 15–39.	
	CLICK: **Save** (if you like what you see—if not, add, erase, or change the intensity of lights, replace materials, and so forth)
The Render Output File dialog box appears:	TYPE: **CH15-EX3** (in the File Name: box) SELECT: **JPG** in the Files of TYPE: box **Save the file on a disk and make note of the disk and folder.**
The JPG Image Options dialog box appears:	CLICK: **OK**

Prompt	Response
	Close the Render Window
The drawing returns:	CLICK: **Layout 1**
The active model space viewport	
appears:	CLICK: **any point on the viewport border and erase the viewport**
Command:	**Insert Raster Image Reference...**
The Select Image File dialog	
box appears:	CLICK: the file **CH15-EX3** (on the disk where you saved it) (you may need to make Files of type: read **All files**)
	CLICK: **Open**
The Image dialog box appears:	With a **check in Specify on Screen for Scale**
	CLICK: **OK**
Specify scale factor <1>:	**Drag the upper right corner of the image to fill the viewport, then** CLICK:

The rendered image fills the viewport.

Step 13. TYPE: your name 3/16″ high in the City Blueprint font in the lower right corner of the drawing.

Step 14. Save the drawing in two places.

Step 15. Plot the drawing to fit on an 8-1/2″ × 11″ sheet, landscape.

Exercise 15–4: Create a Walk-Through AVI File for the Rendered 3D Patio

Step 1. Begin CH15-EX4 on the hard drive or network drive by opening existing drawing CH15-EX3 and saving it as CH15-EX4.

Step 2. Make a new layer, name it Path, color White, and make the Path layer current.

Step 3. Split the screen into two vertical viewports, and make the left viewport a plan view of the world UCS. (TYPE: UCS <enter>, then PRESS: <enter> again to accept World as the UCS, then TYPE: **PLAN**<enter>, then PRESS: <enter> again to get the plan view of the world UCS.)

Step 4. CLICK: the down arrows in the 3D Navigation Control Panel so all commands are visible.

Step 5. Use the Polyline command to draw a path similar to Figure 15–40. The exact size and angle are not important.

Step 6. Make the settings for the camera:

Prompt	Response
Command:	**Create Camera** (or TYPE: **CAMERA**<enter>)
Specify camera location:	CLICK: **Osnap-Endpoint** CLICK: **D1**, Figure 15–40

FIGURE 15–40
Draw a Path and Locate the
Camera and Target

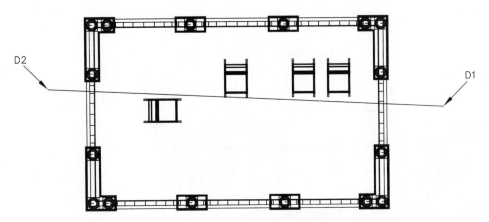

Specify target location:	CLICK: **Osnap-Endpoint** CLICK: **D2,** Figure 15–40
Enter an option [?/Name/LOcation/ Height/Target/ LEns/Clipping/ View/eXit]<eXit>:	TYPE: **N**<enter>
Enter name for new camera <Camera1>:	<enter>
Enter an option [?/Name/LOcation/ Height/Target/ LEns/Clipping/ View/eXit]<eXit>:	TYPE: **H**<enter>
Specify camera height <0">:	TYPE: **6'**<enter>
Enter an option [?/Name/LOcation/ Height/Target/ LEns/Clipping/ View/eXit]<eXit>:	TYPE: **V**<enter>
Switch to camera view? [Yes/No] <No>:	TYPE: **Y**<enter>

The camera view should be similar to Figure 15–41.

Step 7. Use the Animation Settings dialog box to make animation settings, Figure 15–42:

On Your Own:

1. Select AVI as the Format: file type.

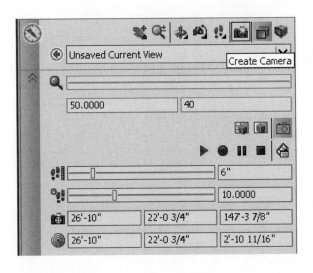

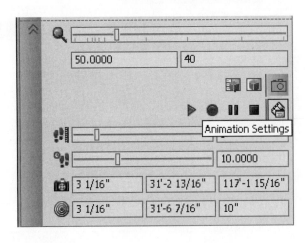

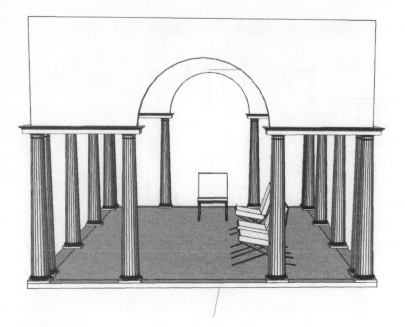

FIGURE 15–41
Camera View

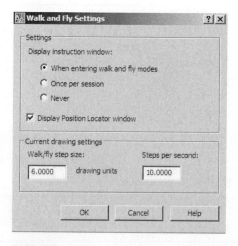

FIGURE 15–42
Animation Settings Dialog Box

2. Make all other settings as they are shown in Figure 15–42.

Step 8. Make Walk and Fly settings as shown in Figure 15–43.

Step 9. Activate the 3dwalk command and make an animation file:

Prompt	Response
Command:	**Walk** (or TYPE: **3DWALK**<enter>)

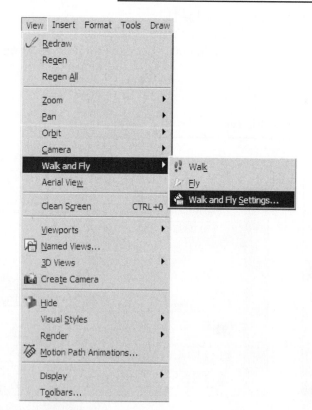

FIGURE 15–43
Walk and Fly Settings Dialog Box

Part III: Three-Dimensional AutoCAD

The Walk and Fly Navigation Mappings message Figure 15–44 appears. This message tells you that to move forward you can press and hold the up arrow or the W key. Similarly, use the left arrow or the A key to move left, down arrow or S to move back, and right arrow or D to move right. You can also hold down the CLICK: button on your mouse and move the display in the Position Locator palette as shown in Figure 15–45.

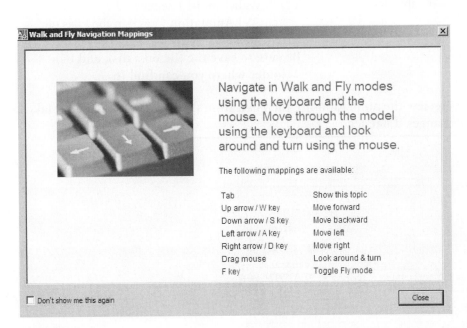

FIGURE 15–44
Instructions for Moving through the Walk

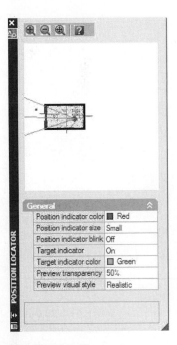

FIGURE 15–45
Use the Mouse to Move the Camera through the Walk

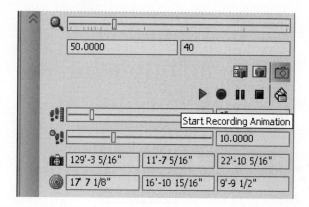

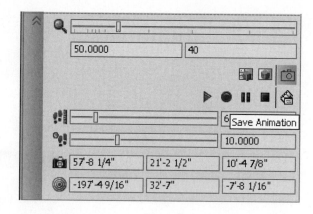

Prompt	Response
Press ESC or ENTER to exit:	**Close the Walk and Fly Navigation Mappings dialog box**
or right-click to display shortcut menu:	**Hold your mouse over the drawing and RIGHT-CLICK:**
The right-click menu appears:	**Make any necessary changes to your settings—** you probably will not have to make any
	CLICK: **any point in the drawing to get rid of the right-click menu**
	CLICK: **Start Recording Animation** on the Dashboard
	Use the up, down, left, and right arrows to move the camera along the path moving forward, back, left, and right
	When you have moved through the patio, CLICK: **Save Animation**
The Save As dialog box, Figure 15–46, appears:	TYPE: **Walk1** in the File name: box
	Select: **AVI Animation** (*.avi) in the Files of type: box
	Be sure to save the file on a disk and in a folder where you can find it.

Step 10. Preview the animation file then exit from the 3Dwalk command. Make changes if needed:

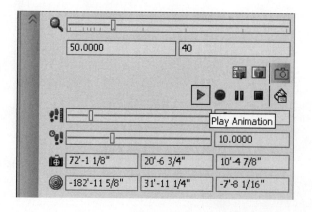

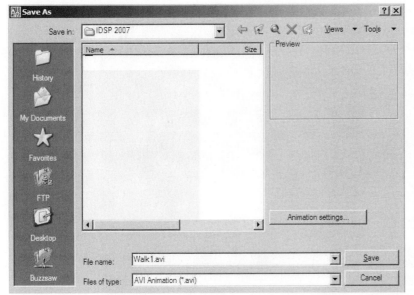

FIGURE 15–46
Save Animation File as an .avi File

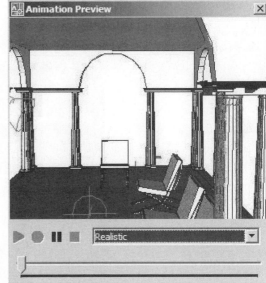

FIGURE 15–47
Play Animation Preview

Prompt	Response
Press ESC or ENTER to exit, or right-click to display shortcut menu:	CLICK: **Play Animation**
The Animation Preview program appears:	CLICK: **the Play button and view your Animation, Figure 15–47**
	Close the Animation Preview box
	PRESS: **Esc or <enter> to exit the 3Dwalk command**

If you like your animation, keep it. You can view it outside of AutoCAD by simply clicking on the .avi file using Windows Explorer. If you want to make lighting or material changes, you can do that easily and then do another 3Dwalk and save it with the same name to overwrite the original file.

Exercise 15–5: Build a Solid Model of a Living Room with Furniture, Attach Materials, Add Lights, and Render It (Figure 15–48)

Step 1. Use your workspace to make the following settings:

1. Use SaveAs… to save the drawing with the name **CH15-EX5.**
2. Set drawing Units: **Architectural**
3. Set Drawing Limits: **45′,45′**
4. **Set GRIDDISPLAY: 0**
5. **Set Grid: 12**
6. Set Snap: **3**
7. Create the following Layers:

LAYER NAME	COLOR	LINETYPE
Ceiling	White	Continuous
Chair	Green	Continuous

LAYER NAME	COLOR	LINETYPE
Coffee Table	White	Continuous
Couch	Green	Continuous
Couch cushions-back	Yellow	Continuous
Door	Cyan	Continuous
End Table	White	Continuous
Floor	White	Continuous
Glass	White	Continuous
Picture	Cyan	Continuous
Rug	Magenta	Continuous
Supports	Green	Continuous
Standing Lamp	Cyan	Continuous
SL Shade	Magenta	Continuous
Table Lamp	Red	Continuous
T Shade	Yellow	Continuous
Walls	White	Continuous
Woodwork	Yellow	Continuous

8. Set **Layer Floor** current.

Step 2. Split the screen into two vertical viewports, and make the left viewport a plan view of the world UCS. (TYPE: **UCS** <enter>, then PRESS: <enter> again to accept World as the UCS, then TYPE: **PLAN**<enter>, then PRESS: <enter> again to get the plan view of the world UCS.) **Set the right viewport to SE Isometric.**

Step 3. CLICK: the down arrows in the 3D Make control panel so all commands are visible.

Step 4. Use the rectangle and extrude commands to draw the floor:

1. The rectangle should measure 19′ × 21′.
2. Extrude the rectangle -4″ (be sure to include the minus).

Step 5. Use Rectangle, Extrude, rotate3d, Copy, and Union commands to draw the end table, Figure 15–49, Sheet 1:

1. Set Layer End Table current.
2. Draw three 1″ × 1″ rectangles.
3. Extrude one 24″, another 18″, and the last one 28″.
4. Use Rotate3d to rotate the extruded rectangles into position, Figure 15–50.
5. Copy the extruded rectangles from endpoint to endpoint to form the end table.
6. Use the Union command to make all extruded rectangles a single object.
7. Set Layer Glass current. Use the Rectangle command to draw the glass insert in the top of the end table and extrude it a negative 1/4″.

Step 6. Use Rectangle, Extrude, rotate3d, Copy, and Union commands to draw the supports for the couch and chair, Figure 15–49, Sheet 1:

1. Set Layer Support current.
2. Draw three 1″ × 1″ rectangles.
3. Extrude one 7″, another 6″, and the last one 28″.
4. Use rotate3d to rotate the extruded rectangles into position, Figure 15–51.
5. Copy extruded rectangles from endpoint to endpoint to form the support.

FIGURE 15–49
Sheet 1 of 2
Furniture Dimensions
(Courtesy of Dr. David R. Epperson, AIA)

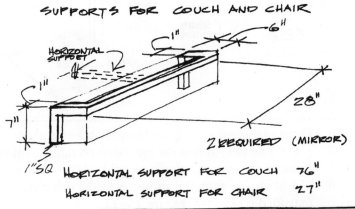

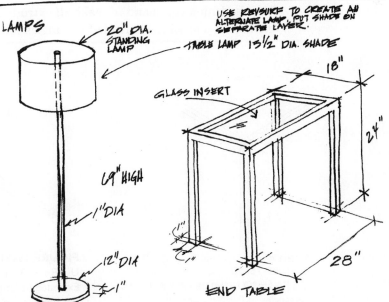

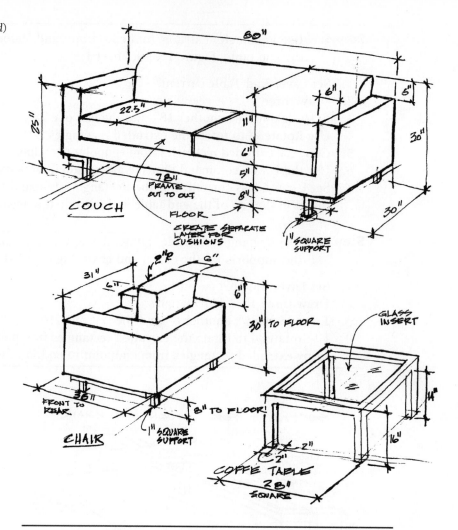

6. Draw two more 1″ × 1″ rectangles and extrude one 76″, the other 27″.
7. Use rotate3d to rotate the extruded rectangles into position, and use Move to move those rectangles from midpoint to midpoint, Figure 15–52.
8. Use Mirror to copy the supports to the other end of the 76″ and 27″ extruded rectangles, Figure 15–52.
9. Use the Union command to make all extruded rectangles for the couch a single object, and all the extruded rectangles for the chair another single object.

FIGURE 15–50
Use Rotate3D to Rotate Extruded
Rectangles to Form the End Table

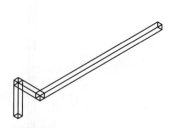

FIGURE 15–51
Use Rotate3D to Rotate
Extruded Rectangles to Form
the Support

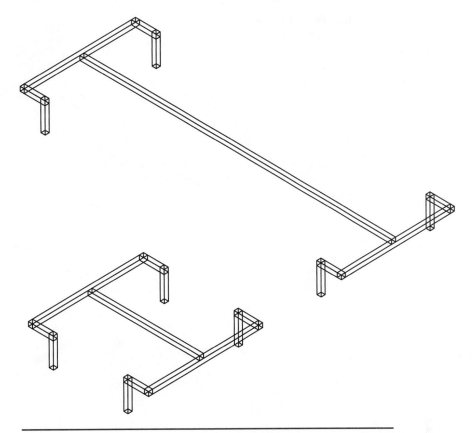

FIGURE 15–52
Rotate Horizontal Supports and Mirror Supports to the Other End

Step 7. Use the dimensions from the sketch, Figure 15–49, Sheet 2, to make the solid model of the couch and place it on the couch support:

1. Set Layer Couch current, rotate the UCS 90° about the X-axis, and draw the U shape of the couch base and arms.
2. Extrude the U shape 30″.
3. Set Layer Couch cushions-back current and draw the cushions using the Box command, or draw a rectangle and extrude it.
4. Rotate the UCS 90° about the Y axis, draw the back, and extrude it 68″. Return to the World UCS.
5. Move all parts of the couch, Figure 15–53, so they fit together to form a couch as shown in the sketch. Use Osnap-Endpoint to select base points and second points of displacement.
6. Change the 3D view to Front, then Right, Figure 15–54, and determine if the couch must be moved to the right or left to center it on the supports. Be sure ORTHO is ON when you move the couch, and do not use Osnap so you can be sure the couch is moved correctly.
7. Return the model to a SE Isometric view and use the Hide command to be sure the view is as it should be.

Step 8. Use the dimensions from the sketch, Figure 15–49, Sheet 2, to make the solid model of the chair and place it on the chair support:

1. Set Layer Chair current, rotate the UCS 90° about the X-axis, and draw the U shape of the chair base and arms.
2. Extrude the U shape 36″.
3. Draw the cushion and the back using the Box command, or draw rectangles and extrude them. Use the Union command to make one object of the back, arms, and base. Do not include the cushion in the union.

FIGURE 15–53
Pieces of the Couch

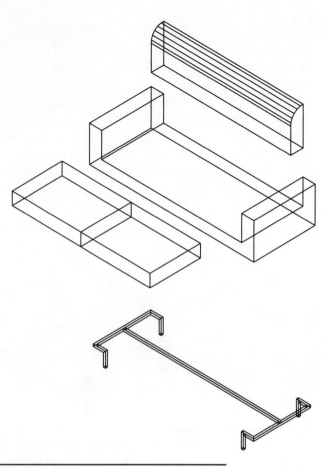

4. Rotate the UCS 90° about the Y axis, draw the back and extrude it 19″. Return to the World UCS.
5. Move all parts of the chair, Figure 15–55, so they fit together to form a chair as shown in the sketch. Use Osnap-Endpoint to select base points and second points of displacement.
6. Change the 3D view to Front, then Right, Figure 15–54, and determine if the chair must be moved to the right or left to center it on the supports. Be sure ORTHO is ON when you move the chair, and do not use Osnap so you can be sure the chair is moved correctly.
7. Return the model to a SE Isometric view and use the Hide command to be sure the view is as it should be.

Step 9. Use Rectangle, Extrude, rotate3d, Copy, and Union commands to draw the coffee table, Figure 15–49, Sheet 2:

1. Set Layer Coffee Table current.
2. Draw three 2″ × 2″ rectangles.
3. Extrude one 16″, another 28″, and the last one 28″.

FIGURE 15–54
Move Couch So It Is Centered on the Supports

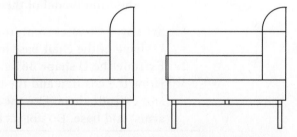

FIGURE 15–55
Pieces of the Chair

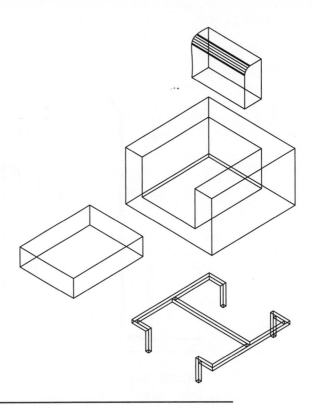

4. Use rotate3d to rotate the extruded rectangles into position as you did for the end table.
5. Copy the extruded rectangles from endpoint to endpoint to form the coffee table.
6. Use the Union command to make all extruded rectangles a single object.
7. Set Layer Glass current. Use the Rectangle command to draw the glass insert in the top of the coffee table and extrude it a negative 1/4″.

Step 10. Use Cylinder, Rectangle, and Revolve commands to draw the floor lamp, Figure 15–49, Sheet 1:

1. Set Layer Standing Lamp current.
2. Set UCS to World, then rotate the UCS 90° about the X axis in the left viewport.
3. Draw a cylinder, 6″ radius and 1″ high.
4. In the same center draw another cylinder, 1/2″ radius and 69″ high.
5. Use the Union command to make the two cylinders a single object.
6. Set Layer SL Shade current.
7. Draw a line from D1 to D2, Figure 15–56, 9-3/4″ long.
8. From D2 draw a 1/4″ × 12″ rectangle and rotate it −15°.
9. Use the Revolve command to revolve the rectangle 360° around the 1/2″ cylinder to form a lamp shade.

Step 11. Use Polyline, Rectangle, and Revolve commands to draw the table lamp, Figure 15–57:

1. Set Layer Table Lamp current.
2. Set UCS to World, then rotate the UCS 90° about the X-axis in the left viewport.
3. Use the Polyline command to draw the lamp without the shade. Draw the straight lines first and end the command, then draw short polylines to draw the curved line and end the command. Use Polyline Edit to smooth the curve and join all polylines into a single polyline.

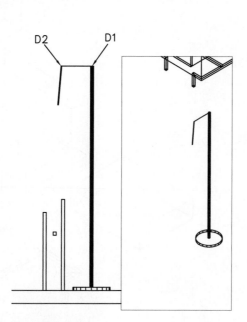

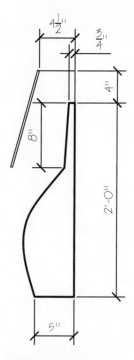

FIGURE 15–56
Draw the Lamp Shade

FIGURE 15–57
Dimensions for Table Lamps

4. Draw a 1/4″ × 12″ rectangle that is 4″ up and 4-1/2″ to the left of the lamp as shown in Figure 15–57. Then, rotate the rectangle −15°.
5. Use the Revolve command to revolve the polyline 360° to form the lamp.
6. Set Layer T Shade current.
7. Use the Revolve command to revolve the rectangle 360° to form the lamp shade.

Step 12. Copy the chairs and end tables, and place furniture in the room as shown in Figure 15–58.

FIGURE 15–58
Copy and Place Furniture

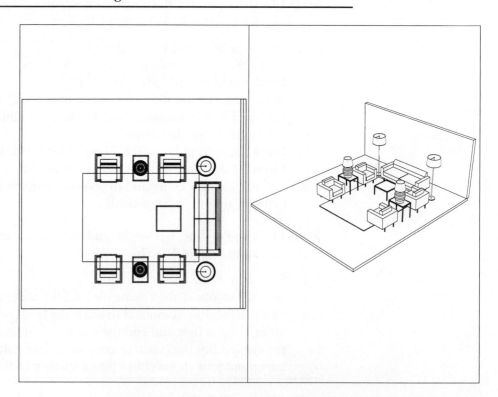

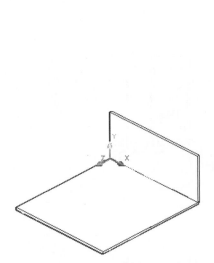

FIGURE 15-59
UCS Parallel to Back Wall

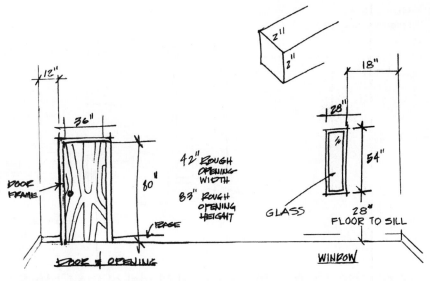

FIGURE 15-60
Window and Door Dimensions
(Courtesy of Dr. David R. Epperson, AIA)

Step 13. Set Layer Rug current. Use the Rectangle command to draw an 8'-0" × 11'-0" rug centered on the floor beneath the couch and chairs, and extrude it 1".

Step 14. On your own:

1. Use the Polysolid command (6" width, 8'4" height) to draw the back wall by selecting the endpoints of the back of the floor, then move the wall down 4".
2. Change your UCS so it is parallel to the back wall as shown in Figure 15–59, and use the dimensions from Figure 15–60 to create openings in the back wall for the window and the door.
3. Turn off all furniture layers if necessary so you can draw more easily.
4. Use the Polysolid command (6" width, 8'4" height) to draw the side walls, move them down 4", then move them to the outside of the floor (3" to the right or left so they lie on the edge of the floor).
5. Draw windows (2" × 2" sill and a rectangle for glass on the inside of the sill extruded 1/2"), doors (3" jamb and header extruded 7" and moved so they extend 1/2" from the wall), and baseboards (make the baseboards 4" × 1").
6. Draw the ceiling and extrude it 4".

Step 15. Attach appropriate materials to all objects.

Step 16. Place point, spot, and distant lights in locations to obtain a lighting pattern similar to Figure 15–48.

Step 17. Set the view to perspective projection with a view similar to Figure 15–61 and render the model.

Step 18. Save the rendering as a .jpeg file and insert it into paper space (Layout 1).

Step 19. Put your name on the drawing and plot it to fit on a 11" × 8-1/2" sheet.

Step 20. Save the drawing in two places.

FIGURE 15–61
Perspective View

Exercise 15–6: Make a Solid Model of the Chair Shown in the Sketch (Figure 15–62). Use Render Commands to Make a Photo-Realistic Rendering of the Solid Model

1. Draw a solid model of the chair shown in Figure 15–62.
2. Attach appropriate materials to the legs, back, and seat. Use one material for the legs and another for the back and seat.
3. Position distant, point, or spotlights to illuminate the chair. Adjust the sunlight so the chair shows well.
4. Use 3D Orbit to change the view to Perspective projection.
5. Use the Render command to render the scene in a single viewport.
6. Print the rendered drawing centered on an 11″ × 8-1/2″ sheet.

FIGURE 15–62
Exercise 15–6: Chair

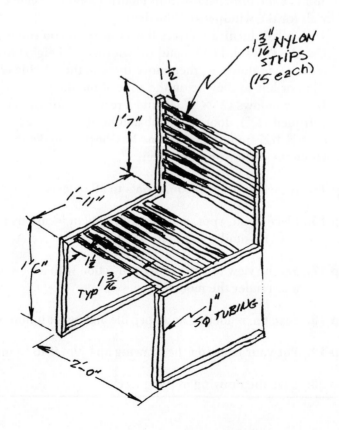

FIGURE 15–63
Exercise 15–7: Picnic Table

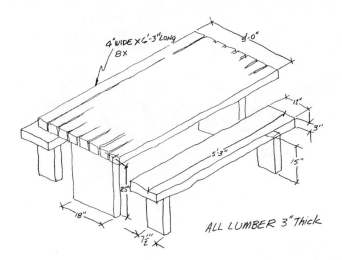

Exercise 15–7: Make a Solid Model of the Picnic Table Shown in the Sketch (Figure 15–63). Use Render Commands to Make a Photo-Realistic Rendering of the Solid Model

1. Draw a solid model of the picnic table shown in Figure 15–63.
2. Attach the same wooden-appearing material to the entire drawing.
3. Position distant, point, or spotlights to illuminate the picnic table. Adjust the sunlight so the picnic table shows well.
4. Use 3D Orbit to change the view to Perspective projection.
5. Use the Render command to render the scene in a single viewport.
6. Print the rendered drawing centered on an 11″ × 8-1/2″ sheet.

Exercise 15–8: Make a Solid Model of the Table Shown in the Sketch (Figure 15–64). Use Render Commands to Make a Photo-Realistic Rendering of the Solid Model

1. Draw a solid model of the table shown in Figure 15–64. Estimate any measurements not shown.

FIGURE 15–64
Exercise 15–8: Table

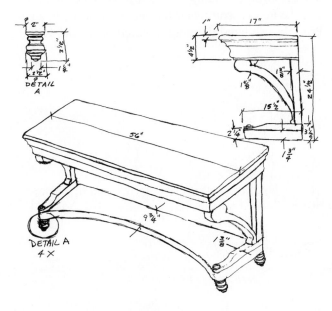

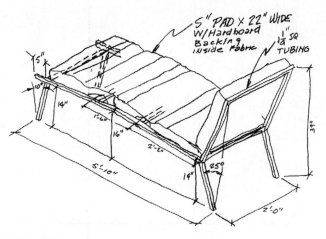

FIGURE 15–65
Exercise 15–9: Lounge

2. Attach the same wooden appearing material to the entire drawing.
3. Position distant, point, or spotlights to illuminate the table. Adjust the sunlight so the table shows well.
4. Use 3D Orbit to change the view to Perspective projection.
5. Use the Render command to render the scene in a single viewport.
6. Print the rendered drawing centered on an 11″ × 8-1/2″ sheet.

Exercise 15–9: **Make a Solid Model of the Lounge Shown in the Sketch (Figure 15–65). Use Render Commands to Make a Photo-Realistic Rendering of the Solid Model**

1. Draw a solid model of the lounge shown in Figure 15–65. Estimate any measurements not shown.
2. Attach appropriate materials to the tubing and pad. Use one material for the legs and another for the pad.
3. Position distant, point, or spotlights to illuminate the lounge. Adjust the sunlight so the lounge shows well.
4. Use 3D Orbit to change the view to Perspective projection.
5. Use the Render command to render the scene in a single viewport.
6. Print the rendered drawing centered on an 11″ × 8-1/2″ sheet.

1. Which type of light is used to lighten or darken all the images in the scene by the same amount?
   - a. Sun
   - b. Point
   - c. Distant
   - d. Spotlight
   - e. Headlight

2. Which type of light shines in one direction in a cone shape?
   - a. Sun
   - b. Point
   - c. Distant
   - d. Spotlight
   - e. Headlight

3. Which type of light shines in all directions much like a lightbulb?
   - a. Sun
   - b. Point
   - c. Distant
   - d. Spotlight
   - e. Headlight

4. Which type of light shines in a parallel direction?
   - a. Sun
   - b. Point
   - c. Distant
   - d. Spotlight
   - e. Headlight

5. Materials cannot be detached after they are attached to a model.
   - a. True
   - b. False

6. Which icon do you have to click to copy a material from the Material Editor onto a solid?
   - a. Attach
   - b. Detach
   - c. Apply Material to Objects
   - d. Preview
   - e. Scene

7. The material preview uses either a cube or a sphere so you can see what the material looks like.
   - a. True
   - b. False

8. Which of the following lights is not on the Light control panel?
   - a. Point
   - b. Blue Point
   - c. Spotlight
   - d. Distant
   - e. Sun

9. When you select a new distant lights, which of the following is the first prompt AutoCAD gives you?
   - a. Locate distant light
   - b. Click: First Point
   - c. Specify light direction TO<1,1,1>:
   - d. Specify light direction FROM<0,0,0> or [Vector]:
   - e. Specify light location<0,0,0>:

10. Which command is used to obtain a perspective projection of a solid model?
    - a. Perspective Projection
    - b. Render
    - c. SW Isometric
    - d. Viewpoint
    - e. Viewport

11. List four types of lights that can be used with the Render command.

_____   _____   _____   _____

12. List the type of light that illuminates all parts of the scene by the same amount.

_____

13. List the type of light that should be used for a lightbulb.

_____

14. List the type of light that should be used to light a display.

_____

15. List three types of backgrounds that can be used in a rendering.

_____   _____   _____

16. Describe what the Fog command is used for.

_____

17. List the two types of Projection available to you.

_____   _____

18. List six control panels on the Dashboard palette.

_____   _____   _____

_____   _____   _____

19. Which control panel on the Dashboard palette contains the Create Camera command?

_____

20. Which control panel contains the Ground shadows, Full shadows, and Shadows off settings?

_____

Index